Adapting to Evolving Consumer Experiences in Hospitality and Tourism

Maria Amélia Machado Carvalho
CEOS.PP, ISCAP, Polytechnic of Porto, Portugal

Maria Antónia Rodrigues
CEOS.PP, ISCAP, Polytechnic of Porto, Portugal

Joaquim Monteiro Pratas
CEOS.PP, ISCAP, Polytechnic of Porto, Portugal

IGI Global
Publishing Tomorrow's Research Today

Published in the United States of America by
IGI Global
701 E. Chocolate Avenue
Hershey PA, USA 17033
Tel: 717-533-8845
Fax: 717-533-8661
E-mail: cust@igi-global.com
Web site: https://www.igi-global.com

Copyright © 2025 by IGI Global. All rights reserved. No part of this publication may be reproduced, stored or distributed in any form or by any means, electronic or mechanical, including photocopying, without written permission from the publisher.
Product or company names used in this set are for identification purposes only. Inclusion of the names of the products or companies does not indicate a claim of ownership by IGI Global of the trademark or registered trademark.

Library of Congress Cataloging-in-Publication Data

Names: Carvalho, Maria Amélia Machado, 1989- editor. | Rodrigues, Maria
   Antonia, 1977- editor. | Pratas, Joaquim Monteiro, 1980- editor.
Title: Adapting to evolving consumer experiences in hospitality and tourism
   / Edited by Maria Amélia Machado Carvalho, Maria Antónia Rodrigues,
   Joaquim Monteiro Pratas.
Description: Hershey, PA : IGI Global, [2025] | Includes bibliographical
   references and index. | Summary: "In the context of the tourism and
   hospitality industry, this book aims to offer a comprehensive blend of
   theoretical insights and empirical research. It delves into sustainable
   practices, customer experiences, co-creation dynamics, technology-driven
   tourism encounters, and emerging paradigms in digital marketing. By
   fostering a deeper comprehension of the evolving market dynamics, this
   book empowers the tourism and hospitality sector to proactively embrace
   the challenges and seize the opportunities that define the present era.
   Specifically, it provides an understanding of new tourist behaviors and
   how the tourism and hospitality industry can adapt and improve their
   business strategies"-- Provided by publisher.
Identifiers: LCCN 2024042562 (print) | LCCN 2024042563 (ebook) | ISBN
   9798369370216 (hardcover) | ISBN 9798369370223 (paperback) | ISBN
   9798369370230 (ebook)
Subjects: LCSH: Tourism--Marketing. | Hospitality--Marketing. | Consumer
   satisfaction. | Consumption (Economics)--Moral and ethical aspects.
Classification: LCC G155.A1 A267 2025 (print) | LCC G155.A1 (ebook) | DDC
   910.68--dc23/eng/20240927
LC record available at https://lccn.loc.gov/2024042562
LC ebook record available at https://lccn.loc.gov/2024042563

Vice President of Editorial: Melissa Wagner
Managing Editor of Acquisitions: Mikaela Felty
Managing Editor of Book Development: Jocelynn Hessler
Production Manager: Mike Brehm
Cover Design: Phillip Shickler

British Cataloguing in Publication Data
A Cataloguing in Publication record for this book is available from the British Library.

All work contributed to this book is new, previously-unpublished material.
The views expressed in this book are those of the authors, but not necessarily of the publisher.

Table of Contents

Preface xv

Acknowledgment xxi

Chapter 1
The Impact of Global Events on Hotel Occupancy and Tourist Flows 1
    Mohammad Badruddoza Talukder, International University of Business
        Agriculture and Technology, Bangladesh
    Mushfika Hoque, Daffodil Institute of IT, Bangladesh
    Titu Miah, International University of Business Agriculture and
        Technology, Bangladesh

Chapter 2
Transforming Online Travel Agencies Using an Alert Management System:
Strategies for Airbnb Through COVID-19 31
    Anthony Hae Ryong Rhim, The University of Hong Kong, Hong Kong
    Ka Yu Chiu, The University of Hong Kong, Hong Kong
    Dickson K. W. Chiu, The University of Hong Kong, Hong Kong
    Kevin K. W. Ho, University of Tsukuba, Japan

Chapter 3
The Impact of the Aviation Hub for Tourism in Ceara, Brazil 61
    Laryssa Silva, Christus University Center, Brazil
    Zaila Oliveira, University of Maia, Portugal & CEOS.PP, Polytechnic of
        Porto, Portugal
    Sara Teixeira, CEOS.PP, Polytechnic Institute of Porto, Portugal

Chapter 4
Social Media Influencers Marketing in the Tourism Industry: Legal Insights
From Malaysia and China 87
    Junaidah Zeno, Universiti Malaysia Sabah, Malaysia
    Chunxiao Zhang, China University of Political Science and Law, China

Chapter 5
Role of Visual Image of Hospitality Industry in Promoting Tourism and
Decision-Making Process of Consumers 127
    Harsh Mehta, Pearl Academy, India

Chapter 6
The Psychology of Ethical Marketing: Navigating Ethical Consumption
Through Challenges and Opportunities 151
    Priyanshi Jindal, ABES Business School, AKTU, Ghaziabad, India
    Harshit Gouri, St. Stephen's College, Delhi, India

Chapter 7
Future of Travel: Metaverse Driven Sustainability Initiatives in Tourism and
Hospitality.. 173
    Ruchi Kakkar, Lovely Professional University, India
    Amit Kakkar, Lovely Professional University, India
    Manpreet Kaur Riyat, Lovely Professional University, India

Chapter 8
AI in Nature Reserves: Boon or Bane?.. 211
    Bassam Samir Al-Romeedy, Faculty of Tourism and Hotels, University of Sadat City, Egypt

Chapter 9
Memorable Tourism Experiences (MTEs) and Its Applications in the Indian
Hospitality Industry 233
    Oindrila Chakraborty, J.D. Birla Institute, India

Chapter 10
Technology-Driven and Personality in the Travel Experience Within a
Destination: Literature Review and Proposal for Analysis Model...................... 267
    Mourad Aarabe, Sidi Mohamed Ben Abdellah University, Morocco
    Meryem Bouizgar, National School of Business and Management of Fez, Morocco
    Nouhaila Ben Khizzou, Sidi Mohamed Ben Abdellah University, Morocco
    Lhoussaine Alla, Sidi Mohamed Ben Abdellah University, Morocco
    Ahmed Benjelloun, Sidi Mohamed Ben Abdellah University, Morocco

Chapter 11
Enhancing Guest Experience Through Smart Hotel Technologies 301
    Mohammad Badruddoza Talukder, International University of Business Agriculture and Technology, Bangladesh
    Md Zubair Rahman, International University of Business Agriculture and Technology, Bangladesh
    Musfiqur Rahoman Khan, Daffodil Institute of IT, Bangladesh

Chapter 12
Ancient Wonders, Modern Tech: AI's Role in Enhancing the Tourist
Experience at Egypt's Heritage Sites 325
    Bassam Samir Al-Romeedy, Faculty of Tourism and Hotels, University
        of Sadat City, Egypt
    Hamada Hussein, Faculty of Tourism and Hotels, University of Sadat
        City, Egypt

Chapter 13
Travel the World From the Comfort of Your Own Home: Exploring Factors
Related to Virtual Place Applications' Visitor Satisfaction 351
    Ece Özer Çizer, Yıldız Technical University, Turkey
    Şirin Gizem Köse, MEF University, Turkey
    Arzu Karaman Akgül, Yıldız Technical University, Turkey

Chapter 14
Medical Tourism in India: A Study to Identify the Growth Factors and Scope
for Medical Tourism in India 379
    Eliza Sharma, Symbiosis International University, India

Compilation of References 405

About the Contributors 475

Index 481

Detailed Table of Contents

Preface xv

Acknowledgment xxi

Chapter 1
The Impact of Global Events on Hotel Occupancy and Tourist Flows 1
    Mohammad Badruddoza Talukder, International University of Business
        Agriculture and Technology, Bangladesh
    Mushfika Hoque, Daffodil Institute of IT, Bangladesh
    Titu Miah, International University of Business Agriculture and
        Technology, Bangladesh

The hospitality and tourism industries are a critical component of the world economy. However, it is also significantly impacted by world events such as major sporting events, natural catastrophes, pandemics, and economic downturns. This study examines how big events, like the Olympics, impacted by the COVID-19 pandemic, affect tourist behavior and hotel occupancy rates. The study aims to provide valuable insights to stakeholders so they may develop strategies to enhance resilience and capitalize on opportunities by analyzing these repercussions. The three main objectives are finding new travel trends, examining how events impact travel patterns, and evaluating how economic downturns impact traveler behavior. This study offers vital guidance for academics navigating a rapidly changing environment, government decision-makers, and practitioners in the sector.

Chapter 2
Transforming Online Travel Agencies Using an Alert Management System:
Strategies for Airbnb Through COVID-19 31
    Anthony Hae Ryong Rhim, The University of Hong Kong, Hong Kong
    Ka Yu Chiu, The University of Hong Kong, Hong Kong
    Dickson K. W. Chiu, The University of Hong Kong, Hong Kong
    Kevin K. W. Ho, University of Tsukuba, Japan

The Airbnb Alert System Platform (AASP) is a framework proposed to address and administer the unprecedented downfall of Airbnb's transactions in 2020 due to the outbreak of the COVID-19 pandemic. The AASP would be a ramification reflected upon novel environmental outbreaks and observed trends, optimizing the management information system (MIS) to match changed customer needs. This chapter investigates how online travel agencies (OTAs) may improve their management information systems through an alert management system (AMS). This chapter will also provide practical design details, including user interface, Unified Modeling Language (UML) flowchart, system architecture, and specific event-condition-action (ECA) alerts.

Chapter 3
The Impact of the Aviation Hub for Tourism in Ceara, Brazil 61
    Laryssa Silva, Christus University Center, Brazil
    Zaila Oliveira, University of Maia, Portugal & CEOS.PP, Polytechnic of
        Porto, Portugal
    Sara Teixeira, CEOS.PP, Polytechnic Institute of Porto, Portugal

The tourism sector has been gaining importance for localities due to its contribution to the production chain. As a result of the growth in tourism in the state of Ceará, there has been a need to improve the city's accessibility, and the implementation of the aviation HUB plays an important role. This study aims to determine whether implementing the HUB influences tourism development in Ceará. The methodology adopted was qualitative, using semi-structured interviews with the managers of two organizations that play important roles in the tourism sector in the city of Fortaleza. The results show that the airport is essential for the growth of a destination and the HUB provides not only an increase in tourist demand with the possibility of conquering new international destinations but also contributes to an increase in tourist flows, allowing the commerce and services sector to increase demand. Due to the positive results, managers are eager to further develop Ceará as a tourist destination, in conjunction with satisfaction from the HUB.

Chapter 4
Social Media Influencers Marketing in the Tourism Industry: Legal Insights
From Malaysia and China 87
    Junaidah Zeno, Universiti Malaysia Sabah, Malaysia
    Chunxiao Zhang, China University of Political Science and Law, China

This chapter explores consumer and advertising-related laws in Malaysia and China that regulate social media influencers (SMIs) marketing in the tourism industry and aims to educate consumers in Malaysia and China on the potential risks of blindly trusting SMIs' posts while empowering them to make informed transactional decisions. It also seeks to inform key stakeholders, such as SMIs, brands, and tourism agencies, about the importance of complying with marketing and consumer laws in the tourism industry. The chapter emphasizes transparency, accuracy, and impartiality in all promotional activities. It highlights the crucial roles of enforcement authorities in monitoring compliance and enforcing laws related to SMIs marketing in the tourism industry. This chapter proposes several strategic recommendations while identifying possible challenges that may assist relevant regulatory bodies in Malaysia and China.

Chapter 5
Role of Visual Image of Hospitality Industry in Promoting Tourism and
Decision-Making Process of Consumers 127
    Harsh Mehta, Pearl Academy, India

The purpose of this study is to investigate the exploratory role of visual imagery in the hospitality sector and its influence on promoting tourism as well as the decision-making processes of consumer perceptions. By reviewing relevant literature, the authors explore the use of visual images and how these can be used presently and propose a model that explains decision-making within hospitality and tourism promotion. The findings highlight the importance of visual imagery for managing and marketing hospitality and tourism products more effectively. The study also offers a practical model that will serve as a foundation for further refinement through practitioner input. There has been limited scholarly investigation in this field, thus the study addresses a gap in research, merging image formation with practical applications for hospitality and tourism organizations.

Chapter 6
The Psychology of Ethical Marketing: Navigating Ethical Consumption Through Challenges and Opportunities 151
    Priyanshi Jindal, ABES Business School, AKTU, Ghaziabad, India
    Harshit Gouri, St. Stephen's College, Delhi, India

This research paper examines the interplay between psychology and ethical marketing, focusing on the challenges and opportunities in this field. It explores how consumers' values, emotions, and cognitive processes influence ethical purchasing decisions and the obstacles marketers face in presenting their brands authentically. The study addresses consumer trust, the pitfalls of greenwashing, and cultural impacts on ethical choices. Additionally, it highlights opportunities for businesses to meet ethical consumer demands, foster brand loyalty, and enhance social responsibility. By analyzing successful ethical marketing campaigns and psychological tactics, the paper offers practical insights for businesses to align their practices with ethics, emphasizing authenticity, transparency, and emotional engagement. It calls for further research to advance understanding in this area, promising a brighter future for both businesses and society.

Chapter 7
Future of Travel: Metaverse Driven Sustainability Initiatives in Tourism and Hospitality.. 173
    Ruchi Kakkar, Lovely Professional University, India
    Amit Kakkar, Lovely Professional University, India
    Manpreet Kaur Riyat, Lovely Professional University, India

The travel, tourism, and hospitality industries can find hope in the metaverse, which is more than just a catchphrase. It offers creative solutions for sustainability and promises to transform these sectors. This chapter examines how the metaverse reshapes tourism and hospitality industries by incorporating innovative, sustainable tourism and hospitality concepts. An understanding of sustainability and the metaverse is given in this chapter. Sustainability refers to methods that guarantee the long-term viability of resources and reduce their adverse environmental effects. There is also a discussion of the challenges of integrating the metaverse with tourism and hospitality. A team collaboration is needed to overcome the difficulties of incorporating the metaverse into travel and hospitality. Each stakeholder has a specific role to play, and their contributions are vital to the success of this transformation. This fascinating trend toward virtual tourism is more than simply a transition; it has the potential to make the sector more robust and sustainable.

Chapter 8
AI in Nature Reserves: Boon or Bane?.. 211
    Bassam Samir Al-Romeedy, Faculty of Tourism and Hotels, University
       of Sadat City, Egypt

This chapter examines the multifaceted impacts of AI adoption in natural reserves, exploring both the benefits and challenges. On the positive side, AI-powered tools can assist in real-time monitoring of wildlife populations, habitat conditions, and visitor numbers, enabling timely and data-driven decision-making for conservation. AI-based personalization of visitor experiences can also improve engagement and education. However, relying on AI algorithms raises issues related to data privacy, algorithmic bias, and the potential disruption of natural ecosystems through excessive monitoring and interventions. Through a review of academic literature, this chapter provides a balanced analysis of the advantages and disadvantages of AI integration in natural reserves. The findings aim to guide policymakers, conservation practitioners, and technology researchers in navigating the complex landscape of AI-enabled nature conservation.

Chapter 9
Memorable Tourism Experiences (MTEs) and Its Applications in the Indian
Hospitality Industry 233
    Oindrila Chakraborty, J.D. Birla Institute, India

The chapter will focus on how India's tourism industry can create lasting and enjoyable experiences through Memorable Tourism Experiences, covering areas such as hotels, restaurants, themed tourism, and guided tours. The authors through the research would aim to gather insights from both regular travellers within and outside the country, as well as hotel owners, restaurant managers, tour operators, and travel agents through two separate surveys, examining tourists' attitudes towards memorable tourism experiences(MTEs) and how businesses are implementing MTEs to enhance their sustainability and profitability.

Chapter 10
Technology-Driven and Personality in the Travel Experience Within a
Destination: Literature Review and Proposal for Analysis Model...................... 267
    Mourad Aarabe, Sidi Mohamed Ben Abdellah University, Morocco
    Meryem Bouizgar, National School of Business and Management of Fez,
        Morocco
    Nouhaila Ben Khizzou, Sidi Mohamed Ben Abdellah University,
        Morocco
    Lhoussaine Alla, Sidi Mohamed Ben Abdellah University, Morocco
    Ahmed Benjelloun, Sidi Mohamed Ben Abdellah University, Morocco

The rapid advancement of technology has had a significant and far-reaching impact on the tourism industry, affecting not only the travel experience, but also the practices and procedures associated with tourism. This study examines the relationship between personality and applied technology in the travel experience, investigating the determinants of the travel experience within a destination. This chapter presents the findings of a systematic literature review conducted in accordance with the PRISMA protocol. It offers a comprehensive conceptual and theoretical framework and provides an overview of the current research trends and implications in this field. The findings illustrate the intricate and reciprocal relationship between technological tools and travelers' personality characteristics, and their influence on the tourism experience.

Chapter 11
Enhancing Guest Experience Through Smart Hotel Technologies 301
    Mohammad Badruddoza Talukder, International University of Business
        Agriculture and Technology, Bangladesh
    Md Zubair Rahman, International University of Business Agriculture
        and Technology, Bangladesh
    Musfiqur Rahoman Khan, Daffodil Institute of IT, Bangladesh

In an era of swift technological advancement, the hotel sector is constantly looking for novel approaches to improve visitor experiences. The integration of cutting-edge hotel technologies to improve visitor satisfaction and optimize operations is examined in this abstract. A variety of solutions are included in innovative hotel technology, such as AI-powered assistants, mobile apps, IoT devices, and automated systems. These technologies provide individualized experiences, effective services, and seamless interactions. Hotels may anticipate visitor preferences and customize services accordingly by utilizing data analytics, which promotes guest loyalty and positive ratings. Intelligent technologies lower operating costs, improve resource management, and support sustainability initiatives. Nonetheless, issues like maintaining a personal touch and data security are still relevant. Notwithstanding these difficulties, implementing cutting-edge hotel technologies offer tremendous potential for revolutionizing visitor experiences and establishing new benchmarks for superior hospitality.

Chapter 12
Ancient Wonders, Modern Tech: AI's Role in Enhancing the Tourist
Experience at Egypt's Heritage Sites 325
    Bassam Samir Al-Romeedy, Faculty of Tourism and Hotels, University
        of Sadat City, Egypt
    Hamada Hussein, Faculty of Tourism and Hotels, University of Sadat
        City, Egypt

Egypt's ancient heritage sites are a major draw for global tourism, attracting millions of visitors each year. However, effectively managing and enhancing the visitor experience at these complex and historically significant locations presents ongoing challenges. This chapter explores how artificial intelligence (AI) technologies can be leveraged to improve various aspects of the tourist experience at Egypt's heritage sites. Strategic implementation of AI can significantly enhance visitor experience, satisfaction, and overall engagement at Egypt's archaeological treasures. Recommendations are provided for policymakers, tourism authorities, and industry stakeholders to effectively integrate AI capabilities while preserving the integrity of these irreplaceable cultural assets. The chapter contributes important insights into the evolving role of AI in elevating the tourist experience at the world's most iconic heritage destinations.

Chapter 13
Travel the World From the Comfort of Your Own Home: Exploring Factors
Related to Virtual Place Applications' Visitor Satisfaction.............................. 351
   Ece Özer Çizer, Yıldız Technical University, Turkey
   Şirin Gizem Köse, MEF University, Turkey
   Arzu Karaman Akgül, Yıldız Technical University, Turkey

Virtual place applications (VPA) have increased their popularity especially with the interest of innovative people. VPAs provide the opportunity to visit anywhere in the world without leaving home. In addition, the electronic world of mouth encourages people to use VPA. However, there is still a question of whether the virtual visitors will want to visit these places later, and how the price cost of the physical visit will affect this intention. In the light of these, data were collected online from the participants by questionnaire method and analyzed with structural equation model. The results of the analysis show that the relationships between entertainment, education, innovation, and e-WOM with customer satisfaction and visitor satisfaction with travel intention were significant and positive. Furthermore, the study presents the moderating role of price cost in the relationship between visitor satisfaction and travel intention.

Chapter 14
Medical Tourism in India: A Study to Identify the Growth Factors and Scope
for Medical Tourism in India 379
    Eliza Sharma, Symbiosis International University, India

The study aims to identify factors driving medical tourism in India and assess its scope from the perspective of foreign tourists. Data were collected from 150 foreign tourists seeking medical treatment in hospitals across New Delhi, Mumbai, and Bangalore using a questionnaire. The study highlighted total ten factors which attract the foreign tourists to see India as medical tourism destination. These factors are mainly healthcare infrastructure, healthcare professionals, quality of healthcare services, cost of medical services, transportation connectivity, documentation processes, Government support for medical tourism promotion, Technological innovations, medical insurance and tie ups for medical services and local or regional factors. The cost of medical services was identified as a major factor, while government support, healthcare infrastructure, and other factors need improvement. The study suggests that India's potential as a medical tourism destination can be enhanced by improving the healthcare, transportation, hospitality, infrastructure and governmental support.

Compilation of References 405

About the Contributors 475

Index 481

Preface

The tourism industry encounters a spectrum of challenges, ranging from environmental issues to the emergence of new technologies that present prospects for new products and experiences. Understanding these novel challenges and opportunities is imperative for tourism companies to adjust, innovate, and uphold competitiveness (Buhalis et al., 2019). Moreover, it enables them to foresee future market needs and enhance tourism experiences, especially after Covid pandemic.Parte superior do formulário

The overexploitation of attractions, landmarks, and destinations poses a critical challenge to global tourism. As consumers increasingly recognize social and environmental issues, there is a shift in consumer behavior towards embracing more pro-social and pro-environmental actions. Consequently, numerous emerging tourism trends aim to promote more ethical and less detrimental tourism practices. Ecotourism and indigenous tourism are prime examples of these trends, reflecting a rising concern among today's travelers for ethical and sustainable tourism options. Despite the growing interest, with some publications addressing sustainability in tourism, research remains limited (Cavalcante et al., 2021).

Moreover, several tourists look for memorable tourism experiences (MTEs) during their time at a destination (Hosany et al., 2022). Understanding the dimensions associated with MTEs is crucial for attaining a sustainable competitive advantage within the tourism industry (Wei et al., 2019). However, existing studies on MTEs are often vague and fragmented (Rather, 2020), with dimensions originally defined for MTEs being applicable primarily in a general context and not easily transferable to other contexts, such as niche tourism (Rodrigues & Carvalho, 2023). Therefore, further research on this topic is necessary (Hosany et al., 2022; Rather, 2020).

Like other sectors, the tourism and hospitality industry has experienced significant impacts from technological advancements (Grundner & Neuhofer, 2021) and the influence of social media (Tanwar et al., 2022). Over the past two decades, technology has become prevalent across all stages of a tourist's journey (Grundner & Neuhofer, 2021), adding value, streamlining services, and enriching tourist experiences. Technological innovations have facilitated the personalization of tourism experiences and the provision of technology-enhanced tourism experiences (Li & Song, 2023). For instance, artificial intelligence has broadened the application of robotics to enhance customer engagement in the tourism and hospitality industry (Doborjeh et al., 2021). Consequently, exploring the potential of technology-enhanced tourist experiences, and their advantages and disadvantages in service provision, has become a crucial focus in the hospitality and tourism industry. The previous studies identified three potential areas of disruption in service experiences: extra-sensory experiences, hyper-personalized experiences, and beyond-automation experiences (Buhalis et al., 2019). This suggests a critical need for investigation at both the macro-market and micro-firm levels to adapt to evolving consumer demands and technological shifts.

Similarly, the emergence of online booking platforms, sharing economy services, and digital marketing has revolutionized how people plan and experience travel (Brito & Pratas, 2016; Tanwar et al., 2022). Influencer marketing has steadily gained momentum over the past decade as a strategy employed by digital marketers to disseminate brand messages through social media influencers (SMIs). Numerous researchers underscore the role and significance of these SMIs in social network communication (Machado Carvalho, 2024; Rodrigues et al., 2024). Hence, delving into this domain by analyzing endorsement dynamics and strategies and scrutinizing influencer-generated content could offer valuable insights (Tanwar et al., 2022).

This book, entitled *Adapting to Evolving Consumer Experiences in Hospitality and Tourism*, provides a comprehensive analysis of the changing dynamics in the tourism and hospitality industry, exploring the impacts of global events, technological advancements, and evolving consumer behaviors. It offers valuable insights into how stakeholders can navigate challenges, capitalize on opportunities, and implement innovative strategies to enhance resilience, sustainability, and customer satisfaction in a rapidly evolving landscape.

The book provides relevant theoretical and empirical implications for the field of tourism and hospitality management, offering insights into global event impacts, technological integration, consumer behavior, and sustainable practices, while presenting practical strategies for enhancing industry resilience, innovation, and stakeholder collaboration.

ORGANIZATION OF THE BOOK

The book is organized into thirteen chapters. The book begins with the chapters that address issues relating to the impacts of global events, such as pandemics and major sporting events, on tourism behavior and hotel occupancy, as well as the adaptive responses of platforms like Airbnb during crises. The middle chapters focus on the importance of infrastructure, like aviation hubs, and legal frameworks regulating social media influencers in tourism sector. The later chapters delve into topics such as ethical marketing, memorable tourism experiences, virtual tourism, and the role of artificial intelligence and the metaverse in transforming tourism by enhancing guest experiences, improving operational efficiency, and promoting sustainability. A brief description of each of the chapters follows:

Chapter 1, entitled "The Impact of Global Events on Hotel Occupancy and Tourism Flows", was written by Mohammad Badruddoza Talukder from the College of Tourism and Hospitality Management, International University of Business Agriculture and Technology (Bangladesh), Mushfika Hoque from the Daffodil Institute of IT (Bangladesh), and Titu Miah from the International University of Business Agriculture and Technology (Bangladesh). The chapter focuses on the impact of global events, such as the Olympics and COVID-19, on visitor behavior and hotel occupancy. It examines travel trends, travel patterns, and the effects of economic downturns on the hospitality and tourism industry, aiming to offer strategies to increase industry resilience.

Chapter 2, entitled "Transforming Online Travel Agencies Using an Alert Management System: Strategies for Airbnb through COVID-19", was written by Anthony Hae Ryong Rhim, Ka Yu Chiu, and Dickson K. W. Chiu from the University of Hong Kong (Hong Kong), and Kevin K. W. Ho from the University of Tsukuba (Japan). The chapter introduces the Airbnb Alert System Platform (AASP), designed to address transaction declines during the COVID-19 pandemic. It proposes an alert management system (AMS) to improve online travel agencies' management information systems in response to environmental changes, evolving customer needs, and future crises.

Chapter 3, entitled "The Impact of the Aviation Hub for Tourism in Ceara, Brazil", was written by Laryssa Silva from the Christus University Center – UNICHRISTUS (Brazil), Zaila Oliveira from the University of Maia, Portugal; CEOS.PP, Polytechnic of Porto, ISCAP (Portugal) & Christus University Center – UNICHRISTUS (Brazil), and Sara Teixeira from the CEOS.PP, Polytechnic of Porto, ISCAP (Portugal). The chapter examines how the aviation HUB in Ceará (Brazil) influences tourism development, demonstrating how improved accessibility and international connectivity increase tourist demand and local commerce, ultimately enhancing the region's potential as a tourist destination.

Chapter 4, entitled "Social Media Influencers Marketing in the Tourism Industry: Legal Insights from Malaysia and China", was written by Junaidah Zeno from the Universiti Malaysia Sabah (Malaysia), and Chunxiao Zhang from the China University of Political Science and Law (China). The chapter explores consumer laws regulating social media influencers (SMIs) in Malaysia and China, specifically in the tourism sector. It highlights the risks of trusting SMIs blindly and emphasizes the importance of legal compliance for SMIs, brands, and tourism agencies.

Chapter 5, entitled "Role of Visual Image of Hospitality Industry in Promoting Tourism & Decision-Making Process of Consumers", was written by Harsh Mehta from the Pearl Academy (India). The chapter focuses on the role of visual imagery in the hospitality sector and its influence on tourism promotion and consumer decision-making. It reviews relevant literature to explore how visual images are currently used and the findings emphasize the importance of visual imagery for effective management and marketing in the industry.

Chapter 6, entitled "The Psychology of Ethical Marketing: Navigating Ethical Consumption through Challenges and Opportunities", was written by Priyanshi Jindal from the ABES Business School, AKTU (India), and Harshit Gouri from the St. Stephens College, University of Delhi (India). The chapter investigates the interaction between psychology and ethical marketing, focusing on how consumer values, emotions, and cognitive processes impact ethical purchasing decisions. It also addresses the challenges of presenting brands authentically in an ethical marketing context.

Chapter 7, entitled "Future of Travel-Metaverse Driven Sustainability Initiatives in Tourism and Hospitality", was written by Ruchi Kakkar, Amit Kakkar, and Manpreet Kaur Riyat from the Lovely Professional University (India). The chapter discusses how the metaverse can reshape the travel and hospitality industries by promoting sustainability and offering innovative virtual tourism experiences. It emphasizes the need for collaboration among stakeholders to overcome the challenges of integrating virtual platforms with real-world travel experiences.

Chapter 8, entitled "AI in Nature Reserves: Boon or Bane?", was written by Bassam Samir Al-Romeedy from the Faculty of Tourism and Hotels, University of Sadat City (Egypt). The chapter reviews the application of Artificial Intelligence (AI) for conservation efforts in natural reserves. The author explores the benefits and challenges of using AI in natural reserves, including improved wildlife monitoring and personalized visitor experiences. It also raises concerns about data privacy, algorithmic bias, and potential ecosystem disruptions caused by excessive monitoring.

Chapter 9, entitled "Memorable Tourism Experiences (MTEs) and its Applications in Indian Hospitality Industry", was written by Oindrila Chakraborty from the J D Birla Institute (India). The chapter focuses on Memorable Tourism Experiences (MTEs) in India's tourism industry, analyzing tourists' attitudes and how businesses implement MTEs to enhance sustainability and profitability, with insights from travelers and industry professionals.

Chapter 10, entitled "Technology-Driven and Personality in the Travel Experience within a Destination: Literature Review and Proposal for Analysis Model", was written by Mourad Aarabe from the National School of Business and Management of Fez (Morocco), Meryem Bouizgar from the National School of Business and Management of Fez (Morocco), Nouhaila Benkhizou from the National School of Business and Management of Fez (Morocco), Lhoussaine Alla from the National School of Applied Sciences o Fez (Morocco), and Ahmed Benjelloun from the National School of Business and Management of Fez (Morocco). The chapter examines the relationship between personality and applied technology in shaping travel experiences. It offers a conceptual framework and highlights research trends on how travelers' personalities influence their use of technological tools during their journeys.

Chapter 11, entitled "Enhancing Guest Experience through Smart Hotel Technologies", was written by Mohammad Badruddoza Talukder from the College of Tourism and Hospitality Management, International University of Business Agriculture and Technology (Bangladesh), Zubair Rahman from the International University of Business Agriculture and Technology (Bangladesh), and Musfiqur Rahoman Khan from the Daffodil Institute of IT (Bangladesh). The chapter analyzes how cutting-edge hotel technologies, such as AI-powered assistants and IoT devices, improve guest satisfaction and operational efficiency. It also discusses challenges related to maintaining personal connections and ensuring data security.

Chapter 12, entitled "Ancient Wonders, Modern Tech: AI's Role in Enhancing the Tourist Experience at Egypt's Heritage Sites", was written by Bassam Samir Al-Romeedy from the Faculty of Tourism and Hotels, University of Sadat City (Egypt), and Hamada Hussein from the Faculty of Tourism and Hotels, University of Sadat City (Egypt). The chapter explores how AI can improve visitor experiences at Egypt's heritage sites. It provides strategies for integrating AI to enhance tourist engagement while preserving the integrity of cultural assets, with recommendations for policymakers and stakeholders in the tourism industry.

Chapter 13, entitled "Travel the World from the Comfort of Your Own Home: Exploring Factors Related to Virtual Place Applications' Visitor Satisfaction", was written by Ece Özer Çizer from the Yıldız Technical University (Turkey), Şirin Gizem Köse from the MEF University (Turkey), and Arzu Karaman Akgül from the Yıldız Technical University (Turkey). The chapter investigates the relationship between entertainment, education, innovation, and e-WOM with customer satisfaction in virtual place applications (VPAs). It examines how price costs moderate the relationship between visitor satisfaction and travel intentions.

Chapter 14, entitled "Medical Tourism in India: A Study to Identify the Growth Factors and Scope for Medical Tourism in India", was written by Eliza Sharma from the Symbiosis International University (India). The chapter identifies key factors driving medical tourism in India, such as healthcare infrastructure, service quality, and government support. It offers suggestions to improve India's appeal as a medical tourism destination by enhancing healthcare services, transportation, and government involvement.

Maria Amélia Carvalho
CEOS.PP, ISCAP, Polytechnic Institute of Porto, Portugal

Maria Antónia Rodrigues
CEOS.PP, ISCAP, Polytechnic Institute of Porto, Portugal

Joaquim Monteiro Pratas
CEOS.PP, ISCAP, Polytechnic Institute of Porto, Portugal

Acknowledgment

The editors would like to acknowledge the IGI Global editorial team and all the researchers involved in this project for their support. Between editors, authors, and reviewers, the book had the participation and commitment of fifty-seven researchers.

Thirty-four authors from diverse countries, namely Bangladesh, Brazil, China, Egypt, Hong Kong, India, Japan, Malaysia, Morocco, Portugal, and Turkey contributed to the creation of this book. The editors would like to thank each one of the authors for their contributions.

All chapters were reviewed by two or more reviewers, whose valuable work contributed to enriching and improving the final result of the book. Therefore, we would like to thank the support of all researchers who contributed to this book in the process of reviewing each chapter, which included the collaboration of Arzu Karaman Akgül (Yıldız Technical University), Bassam Samir Al-Romeedy (Faculty of Tourism and Hotels, University of Sadat City), Dickson K.W. Chiu (The University of Hong Kong), Eliza Sharma (Symbiosis International University), Fábia Esteves (University of Porto), Giridhari Mohanta (Faculty of Management Studies, Sri Sri University), Harsh Mehta (Pearl Academy), Harshit Gouri (St. Stephen's College), José Santos (ISCAP/ Polytechnic of Porto, CEOS.PP), Junaidah Zeno (Universiti Malaysia Sabah), Lhoussaine Alla (National School of Applied Sciences of Fez), Manisha Seal (Tourism and Travel Management, Jyoti Nivas College Autonomous), Meryem Bouizgar (National School of Business and Management of Fez), Mohammad Badruddoza Talukder (International University of Business Agriculture and Technology), Monika B. Ashok (CHRIST, Deemed to be University), Mourad Aarabe (National School of Business and Management of Fez), Oindrila Chakraborty (J. D. Birla Institute), Priyanshi Jindal (ABES Business School), Sahar Hosseinikhah Choshaly (Islamic Azad University), Sara Teixeira (ISCAP/ Polytechnic of Porto, CEOS.PP), Shu-Hsiang Chen (Xi'an Jiaotong-Liverpool University), Şirin Gizem Köse (MEF University), and Zubair Rahman (International University of Business Agriculture and Technology).

The editors also appreciate IGI Global's support throughout the process.

Chapter 1
The Impact of Global Events on Hotel Occupancy and Tourist Flows

Mohammad Badruddoza Talukder
https://orcid.org/0009-0008-1662-9221
International University of Business Agriculture and Technology, Bangladesh

Mushfika Hoque
https://orcid.org/0009-0000-4645-5105
Daffodil Institute of IT, Bangladesh

Titu Miah
https://orcid.org/0009-0000-9017-6453
International University of Business Agriculture and Technology, Bangladesh

ABSTRACT

The hospitality and tourism industries are a critical component of the world economy. However, it is also significantly impacted by world events such as major sporting events, natural catastrophes, pandemics, and economic downturns. This study examines how big events, like the Olympics, impacted by the COVID-19 pandemic, affect tourist behavior and hotel occupancy rates. The study aims to provide valuable insights to stakeholders so they may develop strategies to enhance resilience and capitalize on opportunities by analyzing these repercussions. The three main objectives are finding new travel trends, examining how events impact travel pat-

DOI: 10.4018/979-8-3693-7021-6.ch001

terns, and evaluating how economic downturns impact traveler behavior. This study offers vital guidance for academics navigating a rapidly changing environment, government decision-makers, and practitioners in the sector.

INTRODUCTION

The hospitality and tourism industries are vital to the world economy as they increase GDP, employment, and intercultural exchange (Mohammad et al., 2012). However, the health of this industry is significantly impacted by world events, ranging from major international sporting events to economic crises, political upheaval, and pandemics to natural disasters and technological advancements (Deliana, 2023). These catastrophes can profoundly alter the behaviour of travellers, affect the allure of tourist destinations, and affect the operational dynamics of hotels worldwide (Hasanov, 2024).

Understanding the complex interaction between international events and tourism flows is crucial for stakeholders in the hospitality sector (Chyniak & Salyuk, 2022). Hotel occupancy rates are a critical indicator of the health of the industry and its ability to adjust to external circumstances. For instance, there was a significant decline in international travel during the 2008 financial crisis as many consumers opted for more reasonably priced domestic travel (Luo et al., 2024). Like the COVID-19 pandemic, which caused unprecedented disruptions, the company had to swiftly adapt to changing customer needs and modifications in health protocols (Chihwai, 2024). However, well-run international events like the Olympics or World Expos can increase traveller numbers, strengthen local economies and increase hotel occupancy. These events usually encourage the infrastructure of cities and increase their visibility abroad, which eventually helps the tourist industries (Borovcanin et al., 2020).

In this context, looking at how different worldwide events affect hotel occupancy and tourism flows is essential. The insights this study can provide can help scholars, industry experts, and government decision-makers develop strategies to increase resilience, take advantage of opportunities, and decrease unfavourable outcomes (Bie, 2023). A comprehensive understanding of these elements can aid the hotel industry in more effectively navigating the challenges of a rapidly evolving global landscape (Bigné et al., 2017).

The purpose of this study is to explore the evolving dynamics in the travel and tourism industry, particularly in relation to how various global events and economic conditions influence consumer behavior and hotel occupancy. By analyzing the effects of these external factors, this research aims to provide insights into the current trends shaping the industry and to help stakeholders adapt to the challenges and opportunities that arise from such changes. The specific objectives of the study are as follows:

- To determine new trends in travel preferences that are influenced by international events.
- To assess how global events, such as the Olympics and COVID-19, affect hotel occupancy and tourism patterns.
- To assess the effects of financial instability and economic downturns on domestic and international tourism patterns and hotel occupancy rates.

LITERATURE REVIEW

Global events are significant phenomena or occurrences that affect a wide range of countries and regions. Among other aspects of existence, they can influence social behaviours, political contexts, economic activities, environmental conditions, and technological advancements. Events of this nature are noteworthy because they can potentially affect large populations and have cross-border spillover effects (Talukder et al., 2024). Travel patterns abroad and hotel occupancy rates are significantly impacted by economic downturns, such as the 2008 financial crisis. Travel expenses are reduced during these periods since people have less money available (Talukder et al., 2024). Studies show that when passengers opt for shorter itineraries, more accessible places, or less expensive housing, leisure travel frequently suffers the most. The hospitality industry responds by enticing customers with bargains and promotions, but occupancy rates can drop precipitously (Chen, 2011).

The COVID-19 pandemic is a well-known illustration of how medical problems can impact travel abroad. According to Rivera-López (2023), the pandemic resulted in unprecedented travel restrictions, border closures, and a drop in demand for international travel. Many hotels had to temporarily close or repurpose their spaces due to significant drops in hotel occupancy (Liberato et al., 2024). The study demonstrates the increased importance of health and safety safeguards in passengers' decision-making and the tendency toward domestic travel. Political turmoil, such as coups, terrorism, and elections, can significantly deter tourists and result in substantial declines in hotel occupancy (Deepthi & Shariff, 2024). According to a study, terrorism hurts tourism because it gives tourists the impression that places are dangerous. In contrast, significant declines in tourist arrivals were caused by political unrest, such as the Arab Spring (Gozaly, 2017). The hotel industry usually finds attracting guests at such times challenging despite efforts to provide safety and security (Man Wai Leong et al., 2024).

Natural disasters like hurricanes, earthquakes, and tsunamis can devastate traveller infrastructure and wreck holiday preparations. The immediate effect is a sharp decline in hotel occupancy and visitor numbers (Zhang, 2023). However, studies show that the recovery period varies according to the disaster's severity and the recovery efforts' effectiveness (Collins & Hall, 2022). The tourism sector's resilience rests on its capacity to efficiently manage crises and prepare for calamities. Additionally, major international events like the Olympics and World Expos can significantly increase hotel occupancy and tourism (Jonathan C. Macabodbod, 2023). These events draw large crowds, which momentarily raises the need for lodging. Studies demonstrate how organizing such events can boost the economy by promoting awareness and encouraging steady growth in the tourism industry. However, the extent of these benefits often depends on the destination's ability to leverage the event to promote sustainable tourism growth (Tang, 2023).

A technological revolution has impacted hotel occupancy and traveller behaviour in the tourism and hospitality sectors (Yuwantiningrum, 2023). The advent of online booking platforms, virtual tours, and intelligent hotel technology has made travel planning more convenient and approachable (Liberato et al., 2024). Furthermore, hotels may be able to raise occupancy rates by using big data and analytics to optimize pricing and enhance guest experiences. Worldwide events can have wildly varied effects on traveller flows and hotel occupancy in various locations. According to Steitz and Hall (2020), regions that heavily depend on tourism, particularly emerging nations, are often more vulnerable to global shocks. However, places with diverse industries and a robust tourism infrastructure tend to be more resilient. Natural catastrophes and political unrest negatively influence hotel occupancy rates in Southeast Asia compared to other regions (Suardana et al., 2021).

Nature of Tourist Behaviour Influenced by Global Events

Tourists' dynamic conduct is greatly influenced by the nature and context of global events (Hasanov, 2024). Destination choices, health problems, risk perception, sociopolitical factors, and technological advancements significantly influence how tourists organize their trips and engage with their experiences. The tourist and hospitality sectors need to be well-versed in these behavioural trends to respond to them, adapt, and maintain resilience and growth in the face of worldwide challenges. Global events primarily affect the following aspects of tourist behaviour (Badruddoza Talukder et al., 2024).

Risk Perception and Safety Concerns

When a pandemic like COVID-19 strikes, travellers become incredibly concerned about their health and safety (Firoj & Mohammad, 2024). As a result, they tend to favour places perceived as safer and have strict health regulations. There may be a decline in tourism in areas affected by political unrest and terrorist attacks. Travellers tend to avoid destinations with a history of instability and instead favour places with a good reputation for safety (Tsypko et al., 2024).

Economic Considerations

Travelers opt for shorter, more economical trips and places as their discretionary spending declines (Hasanov, 2024). Luxury travel is declining, but demand for reasonably priced accommodations and activities is rising. Conversely, with a thriving economy, tourists are more inclined to spend money on deluxe accommodations, lengthy vacations, and luxury travel, increasing the number of people visiting well-known sites (Sgoura et al., 2024).

Flexibility and Last-Minute Bookings

Travelers are more inclined to plan last-minute visits to avoid possible interruptions when unpredictable global events happen, such as political upheaval or health problems (Yan et al., 2024). This tendency has increased the demand for flexible booking arrangements and travel insurance. Travellers may be more adaptable than other people since they choose their destinations based on current affairs and changes in the global economy (Sari, 2024; Talkuder et al., 2024).

Destination Preferences

Increases in domestic travel may be brought on by health situations and travel restrictions. Travelers choose local places that don't require travel because they believe local travel to be safer and less complicated than foreign travel. Global events can increase awareness of previously undiscovered locations (Ikonomou et al., 2024). For instance, communities that effectively manage crises may gain popularity as reliable and secure travel destinations.

Travel Purpose and Activities

Interest in outdoor activities and wellness tourism has surged since the outbreak. Travellers are drawn to locations offering outdoor activities, wellness centres, and spacious, less crowded regions (Casquero-Vera et al., 2023). Political stability and cultural events may pique the curiosity of tourists seeking illuminating and educational experiences in heritage tourism.

Technology and Digital Behavior

Travelers are booking and planning their journeys more and more through digital resources due to global events and technological advancements. When making decisions, internet reviews, virtual tours, and digital booking systems become crucial (Drohobych Ivan Franko et al., 2022). Health emergencies promote contactless services, increasing passenger convenience and safety, including smartphone payments, digital check-ins, and virtual concierges.

Sustainability and Ethical Considerations

Debates concerning climate change and international environmental events influence travellers' decisions to choose environmentally friendly travel options. Eco-tourism and accommodations with green certification are increasingly popular among ecologically conscious travellers (Lee & Park, 2021). The trend of choosing travel destinations and activities supporting local communities, preserving cultural heritage, and minimizing environmental effects is known as "responsible tourism."

Length and Frequency of Travel

Due to health concerns and budgetary constraints, shorter but more frequent travel may be required. Travellers might prefer to make multiple short excursions nearby rather than one lengthy trip far away (Subawa et al., 2024). However, the rise in remote work (exacerbated by health problems) has made longer stays possible. To combine business and pleasure, travellers select destinations that offer a combination of long-term attractions and services.

Emerging Trends in Travel Preferences Influenced by Global Events

As a result of global events that have sparked emerging trends in travel preferences, travellers are increasingly prioritizing health and safety, choosing domestic and nature-based experiences, adopting slow and sustainable travel practices, utilizing remote work opportunities, seeking cultural immersion, and embracing technology-enabled contactless travel solutions (Popşa, 2024). These changing tastes, which reflect changing consumer behaviours and beliefs in response to societal changes and international events, will influence the tourism industry.

Health and Safety Prioritization

Due to the COVID-19 pandemic, travellers are now more aware of potential health and safety risks (Mary Christine E. De Luna et al., 2024). Travellers are increasingly drawn to places with robust health systems, stringent hygienic laws, and low disease incidence. Travellers are growing more particular about flexibility when booking accommodations and activities. In response to evolving global events and travel limitations, they select suppliers who offer complimentary cancellation and modification policies (Zainordin et al., 2021).

Domestic and Regional Travel

Travel has increased due to travel restrictions and concerns about international travel security. Travellers are exploring nearby places inside their country or region to seek familiar and convenient experiences closer to home. Due to the development of regional travel corridors or bubbles provoked by international events like border closures and travel restrictions, movement between neighbouring countries with similar health rules and low infection rates has grown easier (Sir John Kotelawala Defense, 2024).

Nature-Based and Outdoor Activities

Tourists gravitate toward locations that offer outdoor activities and natural attractions, such as national parks, beaches, mountains, and rural landscapes (Amanor et al., 2024). The popularity of nature-based travel is rising due to the need for open spaces and fresh air. Global events have enticed adventure travellers who seek adrenaline activities such as hiking, camping, kayaking, and animal safaris to escape crowded tourist attractions and re-establish a connection with nature (Siti Yuliandi Ahmad & Nur Qasdina Asyura Pg Idris, 2024).

Slow and Sustainable Travel

Travelers are increasingly choosing eco-friendly accommodations, giving back to the community, and minimizing their environmental impact to prioritize sustainability and responsible travel (Xu et al., 2023). Slow travel is growing in popularity as more and more tourists choose meaningful experiences, deep cultural interactions, and relationships with local communities over hectic itinerary items. Anyone can explore and enjoy the locations you visit more fully when travelling slowly (Kukulska-Kozieł et al., 2024).

Digital Nomadism and Remote Work Travel

Individuals can now work remotely thanks to the rise of digital nomadism and remote work, which has led to an increase in the number of "workcation" tours that mix business with pleasure that individuals take. Travelers choose their locations based on lifestyle amenities, affordability, and general quality of life rather than only traditional tourist attractions (Mehdizadeh, 2024). Global events have accelerated telecommuting and transformed travel habits since more people are looking for places that support telecommuting and immersion in local culture.

Cultural and Heritage Exploration

Interest in cultural events and historical locations has increased due to travellers looking for authentic, immersive experiences that showcase local customs, arts, and cuisines (Abdunurova et al., 2022; Talkuder et al., 2023). A growing number of tourists are drawn to community-based tourism initiatives that provide opportunities for engagement with local customs, cultures, and communities, contributing to sustainable tourism and fostering cross-cultural understanding.

Technology Integration and Contactless Travel

Technological advancements are reshaping travel experiences; contactless, smartphone apps, virtual reality, and artificial intelligence are used to increase convenience, security, and customization (Sendhil et al., 2024). International events have increased the use of contactless travel solutions, such as digital payments, contactless check-ins, and touchless experiences, to decrease physical contact and improve hygiene standards.

Impact of Covid-19 on Hotel Occupancy Rates and Tourism Patterns

According to Eseroghene and Bejjani (2023), the COVID-19 pandemic altered domestic and international travel patterns and affected hotel occupancy rates. The historically low levels of international travel were temporarily alleviated by domestic travel. Hotels had to adapt to new health rules and shifting customer preferences, which had significant economic ramifications (Yuwantiningrum, 2023). Long-term rehabilitation of the tourist sector depends on its ability to address health-related issues, boost foreign travel, and develop strong backup plans in case of future emergencies (Chihwai, 2024). The COVID-19 pandemic has profoundly and extensively impacted the worldwide tourism industry, leading to notable changes in The following is a list of the pandemic's distinct effects for your understanding.

International Tourism Patterns

Travel Restrictions and Border Closures: Numerous countries imposed harsh travel restrictions and locked their borders to prevent the virus from spreading. International tourism drastically decreased due to passengers' incapacity to travel to far-off places (Y. Chen et al., 2023).

Decline in International Arrivals: According to the United Nations World Tourism Organization (UNWTO), more than 70% fewer foreign visitors in 2020 than the previous year. This exceptional reduction negatively impacted destinations that depend substantially on foreign tourists (Gani, 2022).

Shift to Regional Travel: When it was possible, there was a noticeable shift toward short- and regional-haul travel, as long-haul international travel was prohibited. The destinations that tourists picked to see were either adjacent states or regions (Asshofi & Pranata, 2021).

Increased Health and Safety Concerns: As health and safety concerns gained more attention, travellers' preferences shifted, leading to a more significant desire for safer and less crowded destinations. The significance of safety certifications and health requirements as determining travel factors has increased (Abushenkova, 2022).

Domestic Tourism Patterns

Surge in Domestic Travel: Restrictions on foreign travel led to domestic travel being a critical lifeline for the tourism industry. When constraints permitted, many people visiting neighbouring places led to a brief surge in domestic travel (Ostrowska-Tryzno & Pawlikowska-Piechotka, 2022).

Preference for Rural and Nature-Based Destinations: Places with a solid connection to the countryside and the natural world are becoming increasingly popular. Travellers sought less crowded outdoor locations following extended lockdowns to lower their infection risk and enjoy open spaces.

Changes in Booking Trends: Flexible booking practices have increased due to travellers seeking certainty in uncertain circumstances. The unpredictability of the pandemic is reflected in the rise in last-minute bookings and cancellations (Chenyambuga & Mneney, 2022).

Hotel Occupancy Rates

Initial Sharp Decline: Global hotel occupancy rates decreased as travel stopped utterly. Several hotels faced severe financial difficulty early in the epidemic, leading to layoffs and temporary closures.

Adoption of Health Protocols: Hotels must quickly adjust to new health and safety regulations to comply with local laws and reassure guests. Among these were reorganized spaces to encourage social separation, enhanced sanitary procedures, and contactless services (Bakar et al., 2022).

Shift in Accommodation Preferences: Travelers favoured smaller, independent lodging options over large corporate hotels, such as vacation rentals and boutique hotels. This shift was motivated by a desire for solitude and reduced exposure to large crowds (Isa & Mahardika, 2022).

Impact on Business Travel: The decline in business travel had a long-term effect on the revenue of many hotels. The necessity for accommodations associated with business has significantly decreased with the rise of remote work and virtual meetings.

Economic Impact

Revenue Losses: The hospitality and travel sectors suffered significant revenue losses. According to Claudio-Quiroga et al. (2024), the World Travel & Tourism Council (WTTC) estimated a $4.5 trillion loss in 2020, highlighting the grave effects on the travel and tourism business worldwide.

Job Losses: The downturn in tourism led to widespread layoffs and furloughs in the hotel sector. The sector was one of the hardest hit by the pandemic, and many employees faced dire circumstances.

Governmental Assistance Programs: Governments everywhere have implemented initiatives to support the tourism and hospitality sectors, including financial assistance, subsidies, and efforts to promote domestic travel (Yao, 2023).

Impact of the Global Event Olympics Held in 2021 in Japan on the Hotel Occupancy and Tourism Flows

Several issues, such as the COVID-19 pandemic, travel limitations, and shifts in consumer behaviour influenced the impact of the 2021 Olympics in Japan on hotel occupancy rates and tourism flows (Deliana, 2023). This study provides a comprehensive analysis of these effects, focusing on both hotel occupancy rates and overall tourism patterns.

From the Perspective of Hotel Occupancy Rates

Host Cities vs. Non-Host Cities: Due to the influx of athletes, officials, journalists, and some domestic fans, hotel occupancy rates surged during the Olympics in host cities such as Tokyo, Osaka, and Sapporo (Hasanov, 2024). However, hotels in non-host towns may not have experienced the same level of an increase in occupancy rates because most Olympic-related activities took place in the host cities (Talkuder et al., 2024).

Pre-Event Expectations vs. Reality: The hotels in the host cities anticipated a surge in bookings and occupancy in the months leading up to the Olympics. However, factors including COVID-19 bans, a drop in international travel, and last-minute cancellations may have contributed to lower occupancy rates than expected (Borovcanin et al., 2020).

Utilization of Alternative Accommodations: The occupancy rates of traditional hotels may have been impacted by adopting alternative lodging choices such as ryokans, guesthouses, and vacation rentals (Firoj & Mohammad, 2024). It is plausible that certain attendees, such as athletes' families and support staff, made various hotel choices there.

In the Perspective of Tourism Flows

International Tourism: Travel restrictions and safety concerns related to the COVID-19 epidemic significantly impacted the number of foreign visitors. Because so many countries enforced entry restrictions, quarantine laws, and aircraft cancellations, fewer international tourists travelled to Japan for the Olympics. The drop in foreign travel may have affected hotel occupancy rates, particularly in regions where foreign travel is a significant source of revenue (Matviienko & Matviienko, 2020).

Domestic Tourism: Domestic tourism made up much of the decline in foreign tourists during the Olympics. Because of travel restrictions, Japanese nationals looked at domestic destinations instead of abroad, which boosted the nation's domestic tourism sector (Piga & Melis, 2021). Hotel occupancy rates in popular tourist destinations might have increased during the Olympics since more people travelled within the country.

Long-Term Tourism Legacy: Japan gained a lot from the Olympics' extensive global publicity since it could showcase its heritage, culture, and tourist attractions to various tourists. The long-term tourism legacy of hosting the Olympics may result in increased tourism flows in the future, even though short-term factors like COVID-19 restrictions may have had an immediate impact on hotel occupancy rates (Vrondou, 2023).

Impact of Economic Downturns and Financial Instability on International and Domestic Tourism Patterns and Hotel Occupancy Rates

Financial instability and economic downturns significantly impact domestic and international travel trends and hotel occupancy rates (Lin et al., 2024). To effectively manage difficult economic circumstances, players in the tourism and hospitality sectors must thoroughly understand these repercussions (Bielan et al., 2023; Das et al., 2024). Table 1 provides an organized analysis of how financial instability and economic downturns affect travel trends and hotel occupancy rates.

Table 1. Effect on travel trends and hotel occupancy rates by financial instability and economic downturns

Aspect	Impact of Economic Downturns and Financial Instability
International Tourism Patterns	-Diminished Disposable Income: As people put critical costs ahead of recreational travel, a reduction in consumer expenditure causes a drop in foreign tourism. - Change in Preferred Destinations: Travelers may visit less costly locations or favour domestic travel over foreign travel. - Effect on Long-Haul Travel: Uncertainty in the economy may discourage long-haul travel, favouring shorter, more localized journeys or postponing long-haul travel arrangements (Illiashenko & Lytovchenko, 2023). - Reduction in Business Travel: Organizations reduce foreign business travel by cutting back on conferences, events, and corporate travel.
Domestic Tourism Patterns	- Growth in Domestic Tourism: Due to familiarity, affordability, and perceived safety, domestic travel becomes increasingly tempting. - Preference for Short Getaways: As travellers look for convenient and reasonably priced leisure options, shorter excursions and weekend getaways are becoming more and more common. - Support for Local Businesses: By bringing in business for lodging, dining, entertainment, and transportation, domestic travel boosts the regional economy. To increase demand, communities prioritize domestic marketing (LAHFIDI Abdelhaq, 2024).
Impact on Hotel Occupancy Rates	- Decreased Demand for Accommodations: As fewer people travel, hotel occupancy rates decline, leading to a decline in cancellations and fewer reservations. - Pressure on Room Rates: To draw guests, hotels may offer discounts and lower rates, which will affect Rev PAR and profitability (Deliana, 2023). - Impact on Business Travel Segment: Due to corporate travel expense reductions, hotels that host business travellers see a sharp drop in occupancy rates. - Adaptation Strategies: To be competitive, hotels cut expenses and diversify their sources of income.

Source: Author's Compilation

Conceptual Framework

Figure 1 illustrates how major world events affect hotel occupancy and tourism flows, focusing on how these events have changed travel patterns.

Figure 1. Impact of global events on the hotel occupancy and tourism flows

Global Event Impacts on Hotel Occupancy and Tourism Flows

Sets trends in travel
- High prioritization on health safety
- Increased domestic travel
- Focused on sustainable travel
- Lower frequency travel
- Contactless travel

Impact on Hotel Occupancy
- Host cities experience high occupancy rate than the non-host cities
- Gap between anticipated and real hotel occupancy due to Covid-19 restrictions and last minute cancellation
- Increase of vacation rentals affect negatively on hotel occupancy
- Enhance the number of employment to serve the guests attending global events
- Lower occupancy in which safety protocols are les practiced

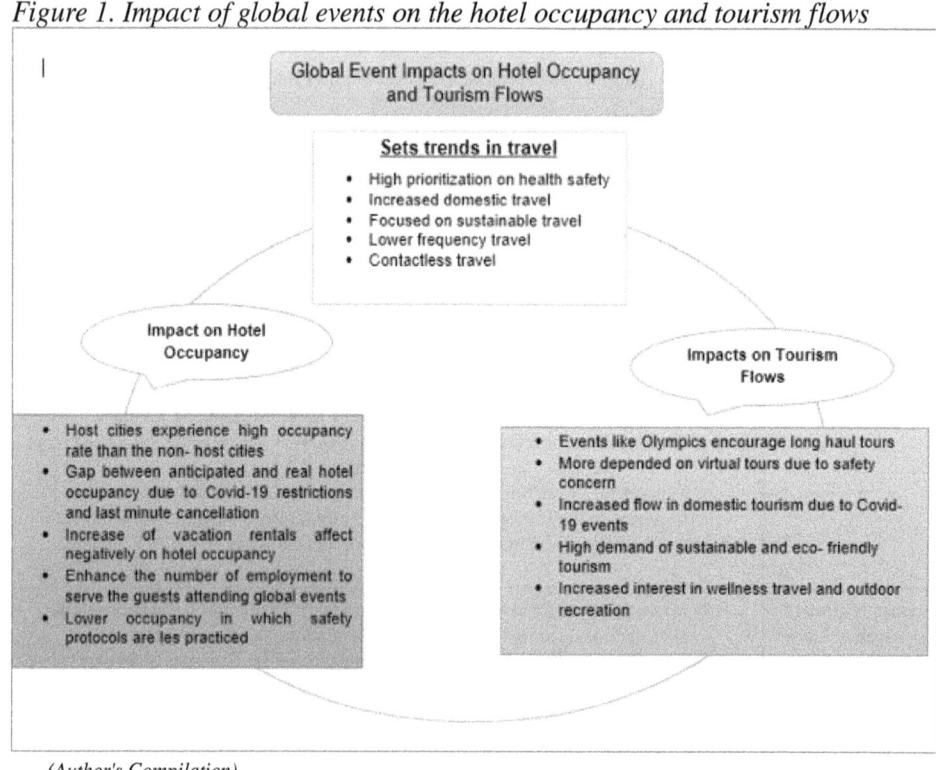

Impacts on Tourism Flows
- Events like Olympics encourage long haul tours
- More depended on virtual tours due to safety concern
- Increased flow in domestic tourism due to Covid-19 events
- High demand of sustainable and eco-friendly tourism
- Increased interest in wellness travel and outdoor recreation

(Author's Compilation)

OPPORTUNITIES OF GLOBAL EVENTS IN TOURISM AND HOSPITALITY INDUSTRY

International events give the travel and hospitality sectors much opportunity. These occasions, from international conferences and exhibitions to global sporting events and cultural festivals, can significantly increase traveller numbers, stimulate economic growth, and raise the profile of places worldwide (Akter Poli et al., 2024).

Increased Demand and Revenue

Worldwide gatherings that attract many people, such as world conferences, cultural festivals, and international athletic championships, significantly raise hotel occupancy rates. This surge in demand usually leads to higher accommodation rates in addition to filling available rooms, maximizing earnings for the hospitality sector (Hasanov, 2024). The influx of guests brings hotel money, boosting their profitability during the event season. To fully enjoy the area's attractions, customs, and cuisine, visitors frequently stay longer than the event period, helping to support the local economy further. This extended involvement fosters long-term economic growth, which sustains a thriving hospitality and tourism industry and immediately increases earnings (Kabir et al., 2024;Hsu et al., 2022).

Destination Promotion and Marketing

When a major event is held there and garners significant media coverage and an international audience, the destination's reputation is elevated internationally. Millions see the host city's scenery, culture, and infrastructure of potential tourists; this heightened visibility offers unparalleled marketing and PR opportunities (Nasiche, 2024). When a global event is well-run, the destination's reputation and brand are enhanced, and potential visitors have greater confidence in its abilities, security, and hospitality standards. Positive branding could lead to a consistent increase in tourism by projecting the region as a premier holiday destination. Long-term benefits include the capacity to attract additional conferences, events, and international get-togethers, in addition to an increase in the number of visitors (Kariru, 2023).

Infrastructure Development

Significant infrastructural improvements usually result from investments to host substantial international events that benefit current and future tourists. Travelling to the host destination is made more accessible and more efficient by improving its transportation infrastructure, such as bigger airports, improved roads, and public transportation networks (Deb et al., 2024). With managing the unexpected influx of visitors and improving everyday commutes for locals and prospective tourists, these upgrades also make the neighbourhood more aesthetically pleasing and easily accessible. The construction and renovation of hotels and event venues raise the overall bar for accommodations and facilities, increasing the location's competitiveness. Furthermore, improvements in hospitality services have raised the standard for customer care and produced more customized guest experiences due to the need to host various foreign guests. These developments benefit attendees and establish a reputation for exceptional hospitality (Mohammad et al., 2024).

Economic Growth

International events are a significant factor in the growth of the tourist and hospitality industries, providing diverse employment opportunities. These events require extensive workforce management, from employing temporary staff to filling permanent positions in newly built facilities. The increase in visitors necessitates hiring more workers for transportation, hospitality, security, crowd control, and event planning. Nearby hotels and restaurants usually recruit more staff to handle the increased demand, while newly constructed or renovated venues offer long-term career opportunities. Apart from providing temporary work, this job creation also fosters skill development and training, which will ultimately enhance the abilities of the local labour force. International events immediately boost local companies by drawing more tourists who spend more on entertainment, dining, lodging, and shopping. After the event, improved infrastructure and services attract more tourists, which boosts local governments' tax revenue and fosters long-term economic growth (Al Karim & Hassan, 2021).

Cultural Exchange and Diversity

Putting up international events offers locations a unique opportunity to showcase their rich history, traditions, and culture to a worldwide audience. These events showcase local customs, artwork, music, food, and history, drawing in and educating tourists worldwide. Cultural performances, exhibitions, and activities in the event program help promote cultural interchange and a deeper understanding of the destination's cultural identity. Long after the event, the destination's heightened global prominence raises its cultural status and attracts travellers interested in its cultural legacy (Elgahwash et al., 2023). International events can draw various travellers, expanding the destination's attractiveness and opening new markets. The influx of diverse tourists forces local businesses to grow and change, enhancing the destination's resilience and allure in the competitive international travel market.

Innovation and Technology

International event planning frequently acts as a spur for adopting new technologies designed to enhance and control the traveller experience. Destinations invest in state-of-the-art technology, including digital ticketing systems, mobile apps, and intelligent infrastructure, to improve crowd control and resource management (Dzingirai et al., 2024). These technological advancements enhance attendees' event experiences and leave a lasting legacy supporting ongoing operations and subsequent events. Long-term digital infrastructure and connectivity gains, such as broader cell networks and quicker internet, benefit present and potential visitors. A robust digital infrastructure supports a range of technologies that improve tourism offers and draws in tech-savvy tourists seeking high levels of connectivity and technological integration. Long-term benefits include a place that can adjust to the shifting demands of visitors from around the globe and is more appealing, effective, and connected (Vadym Hetman & Samoilenko, 2021).

Sustainability Initiatives

International events offer an excellent opportunity for places to showcase and introduce sustainable practices. These events usually include waste reduction initiatives, eco-friendly transportation choices, and energy-efficient technology, significantly reducing their environmental impact. The resort can gain more reputation and attractiveness by planning eco-friendly events that could lead to green certifications and accolades. These environmentally conscious features attract eco-conscious travellers and distinguish the place in a crowded market. The area's reputation as a green and sustainable travel destination promotes a more resilient and sustainable tourism sector, resulting in long-term benefits, including increasing travellers, partnerships, and investment opportunities (Ratna et al., 2024).

CHALLENGES OF GLOBAL EVENTS WHILE MANAGING HOTEL OCCUPANCY AND TOURISM FLOWS

Hotel occupancy and tourism flows during international events must be precisely handled with robust systems and flexible enough to adapt to changing conditions. These events not only offer opportunities for exposure and economic growth but also present problems that must be fixed to ensure a positive visitor experience and long-term benefits for the area (Deliana, 2023). Effective strategies include using technology, enhancing the quality of services, implementing sustainable practices, and ensuring robust security measures. By proactively addressing these issues, destinations may maximize the benefits of hosting international events while avoiding potential adverse effects. Here is a summary of some of the primary challenges.

Capacity Management

Events worldwide can result in an unprecedented surge in demand for hotel rooms. Because of the strong demand, there is a chance of overbooking when more reservations are made than rooms available. Overbooking-related customer unhappiness may compel hotels to move visitors to other rooms, often at a loss. The unanticipated rise in tourism may destabilize the area's public transportation, water and sewage systems, and other infrastructure. This can harm residents' and tourists' daily lives by resulting in gridlock in the streets, delays in public transportation, and overburdened utilities (Mohammad et al., 2012).

Price Volatility

Major international events may cause hotel rates to skyrocket due to increasing demand. Although this momentarily boosts revenue, it can deter travellers on a low budget and convey the perception that the location is costly, which could hurt tourism in the future (Uhodnikova et al., 2022). Hotel room costs and occupancy rates usually decrease sharply after the event. It could be difficult for hotels to stay solvent during off-peak seasons due to the sudden decline in revenue.

Service Quality

It becomes more challenging to deliver high-quality service when there are many guests consistently. The spike may cause staff to become overworked, leading to longer times, less personalized attention, and possibly a decline in the overall quality of the services. Hiring and training additional temporary workers can become more challenging in fulfilling the increasing demand. Ensuring that temporary personnel deliver the superior quality of service that international guests expect is imperative, however tricky, especially when there is a time constraint (Chyniak & Salyuk, 2022).

Security Concerns

As significant events are often the focus of security threats, enhanced security measures are required. This calls for increased security force deployment, intensive emergency response planning, and increased surveillance, which are costly and logistically challenging (Jonathan C. Macabodbod, 2023). Ensuring the safety of many guests in congested settings, such as hotels, is a vital responsibility. This necessitates careful planning, communication with local authorities, and sometimes stringent security standards to minimize risks and effectively manage emergencies.

Sustainability Issues

A massive event may significantly impact the environment. Careful planning and investment in sustainable practices, such as energy-efficient technologies, recycling programs, and sustainable transportation solutions, are necessary for the eco-friendly management of the expanding trash, energy, and transportation demands (Luo et al., 2024). Finding a balance between the immediate benefits of hosting an international event and the long-term sustainability of the tourism industry is crucial. An unsustainable tourism model that undergoes abrupt drops after events is generated when routine tourist development is disregarded due to an over-reliance on events of this nature.

Cultural and Social Challenges

Handling a diverse group of foreign guests requires cultural sensitivity and adaptability. Staff training, developing instructional materials, and encouraging an inclusive atmosphere are essential to ensure that regional cultures and traditions are respected while extending a warm welcome to all visitors (Borovcanin et al., 2020). Events of this magnitude can upset residents' routines and lead to tensions and sadness. Effective engagement and communication with the local community are necessary to mitigate these consequences; this includes informing residents about event schedules and potential disruptions and involving them in the planning process.

Regulatory Compliance

Different countries and regions have laws governing environmental, health, and safety requirements. Enforcing compliance with these regulations can be challenging, particularly when interacting with international participants and visitors with different requirements and expectations. Securing the necessary licenses and permissions for the event and improved hotel operations requires navigating complicated regulatory environments. This process can be costly and time-consuming, requiring careful documentation and adherence to local laws and regulations (Bie, 2023).

SOLUTIONS AND RECOMMENDATIONS

Developing thorough crisis response plans that outline the protocols for managing unanticipated events like pandemics, natural disasters, and economic downturns is advised for tourism destinations. Passengers should be able to change or cancel their reservations without incurring penalties due to flexible booking procedures implemented by the host countries. Regular simulations and training can ensure that they are ready to handle unforeseen disruptions. In turbulent times, this encourages reservations and provides passengers peace of mind.

The host countries should encourage the development of specialized travel experiences and products that cater to specific market niches, such as eco-tourism, adventure tourism, or cultural tourism. One can attract a more extensive range of guests and reduce dependence on particular events or attractions by expanding the variety of tourism services.

Tourist locations should fund destination development projects, such as infrastructure improvements, history preservation, and the development of new attractions that improve the overall visitor experience. A diversified array of offerings can attract travellers with various interests and tastes.

Tourist destinations should also use incentives like loyalty programs, advertising campaigns, and special offers to encourage domestic travel to increase spending and support local businesses. In lean economic times, highlighting the advantages of domestic travel might help boost tourism and hotel occupancy rates.

Establish partnerships with adjacent locations to create cooperative marketing campaigns and multi-destination travel packages. This tactic can help distribute visitor flows more fairly by utilizing complementary attractions.

Adopt eco-friendly tourist strategies that protect the environment, conserve cultural assets, and help the community. Initiatives promoting sustainable tourism can strengthen the resilience of a destination and draw in ethical tourists looking for genuine, responsible travel experiences.

To follow consumer behaviour, monitor tourism trends, and make well-informed judgments, tourist locations should use data analytics and market intelligence. Insights derived from data can be utilized to recognize new prospects and modify tactics instantly to enhance hotel occupancy rates and visitor traffic.

CONCLUSION

In summary, a robust association exists between the hospitality and tourism sector and global events, exerting a noteworthy influence on worldwide hotel operations, visitor behaviour, and destination allure. Understanding how certain global events, such as major international gatherings, health emergencies, and economic crises, affect hotel occupancy and tourism flows can help stakeholders better prepare for and respond to these challenges. To remain resilient and see long-term growth, the tourism and hospitality sectors must understand the dynamic nature of tourist behaviour, particularly in response to global events. Many factors significantly impact travel decisions and behaviours, including perceptions of danger, the status of the economy, health concerns, technological advancements, and shifts in societal and political norms. For instance, priorities have shifted in favour of wellness travel, domestic travel, outdoor activities, and health and safety due to the COVID-19 epidemic. During recessions, travellers typically opt for less expensive locations and shorter trips, while technological advancements drive the usage of digital tools and contactless services. Global events like the Olympics present opportunities for increased demand, enhanced destination marketing, infrastructure development, economic growth, cross-cultural exchange, technological innovation, and environmental initiatives. These events provide long-term benefits, increase tourism knowledge of the area, and attract diverse visitors. The ability of the sector to adapt to these shifting attitudes and seize the opportunities presented by global events will be crucial to its future growth and success. This study highlights the significance of investigating emerging travel trends, the unique ramifications of significant events such as the Olympics and the COVID-19 pandemic, and how unpredictable economic conditions impact traveller behaviour. The information gained can help studyers, decision-makers, and businesspeople develop strategies to boost resilience, grab opportunities, and decrease adverse effects. Ultimately, this will ensure the hospitality and tourist industry's continued existence and growth in a rapidly evolving global landscape.

FUTURE DIRECTIONS

Subsequent investigations into the effects of international events on hotel occupancy and tourism flows can provide a wealth of insights into changing patterns, new problems, and creative solutions within the tourism sector. An exciting avenue for future study is longitudinal studies to assess the long-term effects of international events, such as major sporting tournaments or the COVID-19 pandemic, on hotel occupancy rates and travel patterns. Studies can gain additional insight into destinations' resilience and recovery programs' effectiveness by tracking trends over several years. Studying how technology affects the hospitality scene during international events is also becoming more and more necessary. Subsequent study endeavours may examine the adoption of digital solutions, such as virtual reality and artificial intelligence, and their impact on visitor satisfaction, behaviour, and destination competitiveness. Sustainability is a critical topic that requires attention, and studies are prepared to look into the environmental, social, and economic facets of sustainable tourism practices to lessen the negative consequences of mass tourism. Furthermore, multidisciplinary cooperation and cross-disciplinary study hold promise for taking on challenging issues and developing thorough answers to ensure the sustainability and resilience of the tourist sector in the face of global events. By examining these areas of inquiry, future study initiatives can offer insightful data that can assist in directing industry practices, influencing regulatory choices, and promoting the growth of sustainable tourism internationally.

REFERENCES

Abdelhaq, L. (2024). Economic resilience in tourism: Forecasting financial survival in Moroccan SME hotels. *Zenodo*. https://doi.org/DOI: 10.5281/ZENODO.11110423

Abdunurova, A. A., Razakova, D. I., & Davletova, M. T. (2022). Global portrait of a modern tourist: Travel trends in marketing. *Bulletin of 'Turan'. University*, 1(1), 166–173. DOI: 10.46914/1562-2959-2022-1-1-166-173

Abushenkova, M. V. (2022). The impact of COVID-19 on the tourism and hotel business in the Kursk region. *Proceedings of the Southwest State University. Series: Economics. Sociology.Management*, 12(1), 106–114. DOI: 10.21869/2223-1552-2022-12-1-106-114

Ahmad, S. Y., & Idris, N. Q. A. P.Siti Yuliandi AhmadNur Qasdina Asyura Pg Idris. (2024). Tourist preferences, the use of social media, and travel behaviours among youth in Malaysia. *Journal of Advanced Study in Business and Management Studies*, 35(1), 44–54. DOI: 10.37934/arbms.35.1.4454

Akter Poli, T., Hasan Sawon, Md. M., Nasir Mia, Md., Ali, W., Rahman, M., Hossain, R., & Mani, L. (2024). Tourism and climate change: Mitigation and adaptation strategies in a hospitality industry in Bangladesh. *Tourism and Climate Change: Mitigation and Adaptation Strategies in a Hospitality Industry in Bangladesh*. https://doi.org/DOI: 10.53555/kuey.v30i5.3798

Al Karim, R., & Hassan, A. (2021). Investment barriers and opportunities in the tourism and hospitality industry of Bangladesh. In Hassan, A. (Ed.), *Tourism in Bangladesh: Investment and development perspectives* (pp. 417–431). Springer Nature Singapore., DOI: 10.1007/978-981-16-1858-1_25

Amanor, W. K., Adanu, E. K., Adams, C. A., & Adi, S. B. (2024). Assessing road users' preference for various travel demand management strategies for adoption in Accra, Ghana. *Preprints*. https://doi.org/DOI: 10.20944/preprints202405.1325.v1

Asshofi, I. U. A., & Pranata, P. S. J. (2021). Strategi peningkatan occupancy rate dan average room rate pada masa pandemi COVID-19 di hotel Noormans Semarang. *LITE: Jurnal Bahasa, Sastra, dan Budaya*, 16(2), 234–249. https://doi.org/DOI: 10.33633/lite.v16i2.4412

Badruddoza Talukder, M., Kumar, S., Misra, L. I., & Firoj Kabir, . (2024). Determining the role of eco-tourism service quality, tourist satisfaction, and destination loyalty: A case study of Kuakata beach. *Acta Scientiarum Polonorum. Administratio Locorum*, 23(1), 133–151. DOI: 10.31648/aspal.9275

Bakar, N. A., Rosbi, S., & Uzaki, K. (2022). Impact of coronavirus disease (COVID-19) towards hotel tourism industry. *International Journal of Advanced Engineering Study and Science*, 9(3), 043–050. https://doi.org/DOI: 10.22161/ijaers.93.6

Bie, X. (2023). Countermeasures of hotel industry for tourism crisis management under the influence of epidemic situation. *International Journal of Education and Humanities*, 11(2), 249–252. DOI: 10.54097/ijeh.v11i2.13845

Bielan, O., Humeniuk, V., Kaziuka, N., Semyrga, L., & Hryvnak, B. (2023). Financial and legal regulation of hotel and tourism business. *Economic Analysis*, 33(4), 8–16. DOI: 10.35774/econa2023.04.008

Bigné, E., Andreu, L., & Oltra, E. (2017). DMOs promote hotel occupancy in tourist destinations: An abstract. In Rossi, P. (Ed.), *Marketing at the confluence between entertainment and analytics* (pp. 999–1000). Springer International Publishing., DOI: 10.1007/978-3-319-47331-4_198

Borovcanin, D., Cuk, I., Lesjak, M., & Juvan, E. (2020). The importance of sport event on hotel performance for restarting tourism after COVID-19. *Societies (Basel, Switzerland)*, 10(4), 90. DOI: 10.3390/soc10040090

Casquero-Vera, J. A., Pérez-Ramírez, D., Lyamani, H., Rejano, F., Casans, A., Titos, G., Olmo, F. J., Dada, L., Hakala, S., Hussein, T., Lehtipalo, K., Paasonen, P., Hyvärinen, A., Pérez, N., Querol, X., Rodríguez, S., Kalivitis, N., González, Y., Alghamdi, M. A., & Alados-Arboledas, L. (2023). Impact of desert dust on new particle formation events and the cloud condensation nuclei budget in dust-influenced areas. *Atmospheric Chemistry and Physics*, 23(24), 15795–15814. DOI: 10.5194/acp-23-15795-2023

Chen, M.-H. (2011). The response of hotel performance to international tourism development and crisis events. *International Journal of Hospitality Management*, 30(1), 200–212. DOI: 10.1016/j.ijhm.2010.06.005 PMID: 32287854

Chen, Y., Qin, Z., & Yin, X. (2023). The impact of the opening policy of the COVID-19 on catering, tourism and hotel industries. *Advances in Economics. Management and Political Sciences*, 45(1), 256–262. DOI: 10.54254/2754-1169/45/20230295

Chenyambuga, D. N., & Mneney, C. E. (2022). The impact of COVID-19 pandemic on the EAC tourism and hospitality industry. *African Journal of Accounting and Social Science Studies*, 4(1), 73–92. DOI: 10.4314/ajasss.v4i1.4

Chihwai, P. (2024). COVID-19 impact and recovery on tourism in Africa: An introduction and background. In Chihwai, P. (Ed.), *COVID-19 impact on tourism performance in Africa* (pp. 3–12). Springer Nature Singapore., DOI: 10.1007/978-981-97-1931-0_1

Chyniak, V., & Salyuk, M. (2022). Trends in the functioning of the tourism sector in crisis conditions on the example of hotel enterprises of the Transcarpathian region, Ukraine. *Economics & Education*, 7(4), 20–26. DOI: 10.30525/2500-946X/2022-4-3

Claudio-Quiroga, G., De Villanueva, C. F., & Gil-Alana, L. A. (2024). Tourism and COVID-19 in three European cities: Change in persistence. *Cogent Social Sciences*, 10(1), 2358159. DOI: 10.1080/23311886.2024.2358159

Collins, C., & Hall, J. C. (2022). Presidential inauguration tourism and hotel occupancy: Evidence from the Obama and Trump inaugurals. *Tourism Economics*, 28(1), 83–88. DOI: 10.1177/1354816620956821

Das, I. R., Islam, A. S., & Talukder, M. B. (2024). Customer satisfaction in hospitality marketing from a technological perspective. In Talukder, M., Kumar, S., & Tyagi, P. (Eds.), *Impact of AI and tech-driven solutions in hospitality and tourism* (pp. 383–407). IGI Global., DOI: 10.4018/979-8-3693-6755-1.ch019

De Luna, M. C. E., Santiago, R. R. L., & Villaceran, I. N.Mary Christine E. De LunaRachelyn Ruth L. SantiagoIrvin N. Villaceran. (2024). Preferences and travel motivations of pink tourists among Filipinos. *Journal of Tourism and Hospitality Studies*, 2(1), 25–29. DOI: 10.32996/jths.2024.2.1.4

Deb, S. K., Kuri, B. C., & Nafi, S. M. (2024). Application of knowledge management in tourism and hospitality industry: A sustainable approach. In Valeri, M. (Ed.), *Knowledge management and knowledge sharing* (pp. 99–116). Springer Nature Switzerland., DOI: 10.1007/978-3-031-37868-3_7

Deepthi, S. S., & Shariff, Dr. S. J. (2024). Role of hotel industry in tourism development. *Educational Administration: Theory and Practice*. https://doi.org/DOI: 10.53555/kuey.v30i5.4347

Deliana, D. (2023). Contribution of tourism objects in Banyumas Kota Lama to the hotel occupancy. *Jurnal Manajemen Perhotelan dan Pariwisata*, 6(2), 493–504. https://doi.org/DOI: 10.23887/jmpp.v6i2.64829

Dzingirai, M., Chirodzero, T. C., & Moyo, T. (2024). Impact of COVID-19 on the tourism and hospitality industry: A case study of hotels in Mutare urban, Zimbabwe. *Journal of Hospitality, Leisure, Sport and Tourism Education*, 43, 100384. DOI: 10.1016/j.jhlste.2023.100384

Gössling, S., Hall, C. M., & Scott, D. (2021). Tourism and climate change: Impacts, adaptation, and mitigation. In Hall, C. M., & Page, S. J. (Eds.), *The Routledge handbook of tourism and sustainability* (pp. 368–381). Routledge., DOI: 10.4324/9780203072332-37

Kariru, A. N. (2023). Contemporary trends and issues in the hospitality and tourism industry. *International Journal of Study and Innovation in Social Science*, 7(4), 970–986. DOI: 10.47772/IJRISS.2023.7481

Kukulska-Kozieł, A., Noszczyk, T., Gorzelany, J., & Młocek, W. (2024). Greenery in times of crisis: Accessibility, residents' travel preferences and the impact of travel time. *Land Use Policy*, 141, 107130. DOI: 10.1016/j.landusepol.2024.107130

Lee, K.-Y., & Park, S.-H. (2021). Does face consciousness affect tourist behaviour at festival events? A Korean perspective. *Sustainability (Basel)*, 13(20), 11558. DOI: 10.3390/su132011558

Leong, M. W. A., Kocak, E., Bai, J., & Okumus, F. (2024). Macau hotel industry's response to global shocks. *Tourism Economics*, 30(7), 1914–1921. Advance online publication. DOI: 10.1177/13548166241234096

Liberato, D., Costa, E., Barradas, I., Liberato, P., & Ribeiro, J. (2024). Events' tourism and hospitality marketing. In Carvalho, J. V., Abreu, A., Liberato, D., & Rebolledo, J. A. D. (Eds.), *Advances in tourism, technology and systems* (Vol. 384, pp. 483–493). Springer Nature Singapore., DOI: 10.1007/978-981-99-9758-9_38

Lin, Y.-X., Su, C.-H., & Chen, M.-H. (2024). Undrstanding the contribution of domestic tourism to hotel industry. *Tourism Analysis*, 29(3), 367–383. Advance online publication. DOI: 10.3727/108354224X17065682130471

Luo, J., Joybari, M. M., Ma, Y., Liu, J., & Lai, K. (2024). Assessment of renewable power generation applied in homestay hotels: Energy and cost-benefit considering dynamic occupancy rates and reservation prices. *Journal of Building Engineering*, 87, 109074. DOI: 10.1016/j.jobe.2024.109074

Matviienko, N., & Matviienko, V. (2020). State and prospects of international tourism development in Japan. *Bulletin of Taras Shevchenko National University of Kyiv.Geography (Sheffield, England)*, 76–77(76-77), 64–69. DOI: 10.17721/1728-2721.2020.76-77.9

Mehdizadeh, M. (2024). The ramifications of emerging mobility modes on active travel. *Journal of Transport & Health*, 37, 101839. DOI: 10.1016/j.jth.2024.101839

Mohammad, A., Jones, E., Dawood, A. A., & Sayed, H. A. (2012). The impact of the Egyptian political events during 2011 on hotel occupancy in Cairo. *Journal of Tourism Study & Hospitality*, 1(3). Advance online publication. DOI: 10.4172/2324-8807.1000102

Mohammad, B. T., Mushfika, H., & Iva, R. D. (2024). Opportunities of tourism and hospitality education in Bangladesh: Career perspectives. *I-Manager's. Journal of Management*, 18(3), 21. DOI: 10.26634/jmgt.18.3.20385

Nasiche, N. (2024). The role of wellness tourism in the growth of the hospitality industry. *Journal of Modern Hospitality*, 3(1), 53–64. DOI: 10.47941/jmh.1954

Ostrowska-Tryzno, A., & Pawlikowska-Piechotka, A. (2022). Tourism, the hotel industry at the time of the COVID-19 pandemic. *Sport i Turystyka. Środkowoeuropejskie Czasopismo Naukowe*, 5(2), 139–152. https://doi.org/DOI: 10.16926/sit.2022.02.08

Piga, C., & Melis, G. (2021). Identifying and measuring the impact of cultural events on hotels' performance. *International Journal of Contemporary Hospitality Management*, 33(4), 1194–1209. DOI: 10.1108/IJCHM-07-2020-0749

Popşa, R. E. (2024). Exploring the Generation Z travel trends and behavior. *Studies in Business and Economics*, 19(1), 189–189. DOI: 10.2478/sbe-2024-0010

Ratna, S., Saide, S., Putri, A. M., Indrajit, R. E., & Muwardi, D. (2024). Digital transformation in tourism and hospitality industry: A literature review of blockchain, financial technology, and knowledge management. *EuroMed Journal of Business*, 19(1), 84–112. DOI: 10.1108/EMJB-04-2023-0118

Rivera-López, F. B. (2023). Analysis of the impact of the COVID-19 pandemic on hotel occupancy in the main tourist destinations in Mexico. *Revista de Desarrollo Económico*, 1–7. https://doi.org/DOI: 10.35429/JED.2023.30.10.1.7

Sari, Y. K. (2024). Gone or go on? The existence of hybrid events as urban tourism strategy. *Tourisma: Jurnal Pariwisata*, 5(2), 172. DOI: 10.22146/gamajts.v5i2.95005

Sendhil, R., C R, B., Yadav, S., G, G., Ragupathy, R., A, P., & Ramasundaram, P. (2024). Consumer perception and preference toward plant-based meat alternatives – Bibliometric trends and policy implications. *Food and Humanity*, 2, 100229. DOI: 10.1016/j.foohum.2024.100229

Sgoura, A., Kontis, A. P., & Stergiou, D. (2024). Views and motivations of members of dance groups during their participation in traditional dance tourist events. In Kavoura, A., Borges-Tiago, T., & Tiago, F. (Eds.), *Strategic Innovative Marketing and Tourism* (pp. 441–447). Springer Nature Switzerland., DOI: 10.1007/978-3-031-51038-0_48

Steitz, C., & Hall, J. (2020). The impact of conventions on hotel demand: Evidence from Indianapolis using daily hotel occupancy data. *Journal of Risk and Financial Management*, 13(10), 229. DOI: 10.3390/jrfm13100229

Suardana, W., Baharuddin, A., & Suni, M. (2021). The effect of room price on occupancy at Kenari Hotel. *Jurnal Ad'ministrare*, 8(2), 409. DOI: 10.26858/ja.v8i1.24534

Subawa, N. S., Yanti, N. K. W., Mimaki, C. A., Utami, M. S. M., & Prabarini, N. S. D. (2024). Exploring tourist behavior towards Bali wellness tourism visits. *International Journal of Innovation and Scientific Research*, 11(4), 705–730. DOI: 10.51244/IJRSI.2024.1104051

Talukder, M. B. (2020). The future of culinary tourism: An emerging dimension for the tourism industry of Bangladesh. *I-Manager's. Journal of Management*, 15(1), 27. DOI: 10.26634/jmgt.15.1.17181

Talukder, M. B. (2021). An assessment of the roles of the social network in the development of the tourism industry in Bangladesh. *International Journal of Business, Law, and Education*, 2(3), 85–93. DOI: 10.56442/ijble.v2i3.21

Talukder, M. B. (2024). Implementing artificial intelligence and virtual experiences in hospitality. In Manohar, S., Mittal, A., Raju, S., & Nair, A. J. (Eds.), *Advances in hospitality, tourism, and the services industry* (pp. 145–160). IGI Global., DOI: 10.4018/979-8-3693-2019-8.ch009

Talukder, M. B., Kumar, S., & Das, I. R. (2024). Perspectives of digital marketing for the restaurant industry. In Erol, G., & Kuyucu, M. (Eds.), (pp. 118–134). Advances in media, entertainment, and the arts. IGI Global., DOI: 10.4018/979-8-3693-0855-4.ch009

Talukder, M. B., Kumar, S., Kaiser, F., & Mia, Md. N. (2024). Pilgrimage creative tourism: A gateway to sustainable development goals in Bangladesh. In M. Hamdan, M. Anshari, N. Ahmad, & E. Ali (Eds.), *Advances in public policy and administration* (pp. 285–300). IGI Global. https://doi.org/DOI: 10.4018/979-8-3693-1742-6.ch016

Talukder, M. B., Kumar, S., Sood, K., & Grima, S. (2023). Information technology, food service quality and restaurant revisit intention. *International Journal of Sustainable Development and Planning*, 18(1), 295–303. DOI: 10.18280/ijsdp.180131

Talukder, M. B., & Muhsina, K. (2024). Prospect of smart tourism destination in Bangladesh. In Correia, R., Martins, M., & Fontes, R. (Eds.), *AI innovations for travel and tourism* (pp. 163–179). IGI Global., DOI: 10.4018/979-8-3693-2137-9.ch009

Tang, R. (2023). Can digital economy improve tourism economic resilience? Evidence from China. *Tourism Economics*. Advance online publication. DOI: 10.1177/13548166231206241

Tsypko, V., Andrusenko, S., Podpisnov, V., & Podpisnov, D. (2024). The potential of the global automotive industry as a tourist attraction. *E3S Web of Conferences, 508*, 08026. https://doi.org/DOI: 10.1051/e3sconf/202450808026

Uhodnikova, O., Sokolenko, A., Ryabev, A., Abramov, V., Pokolodna, M., Kravtsova, S., Shevchenko, V., & Miroshnichenko, Yu. (2022). Innovative approaches to the management of effective communications in tourism and the hotel and restaurant industry. *Municipal Economy of Cities*, 7(174), 9–13. DOI: 10.33042/2522-1809-2022-7-174-9-13

Vrondou, O. P. (2023). Olympic Games and mega events legacy planning as a tourism initiation strategy: Developments and implications. In Katsoni, V. (Ed.), *Tourism, travel, and hospitality in a smart and sustainable world* (pp. 265–282). Springer Nature Switzerland., DOI: 10.1007/978-3-031-29426-6_17

Xu, S., Liu, J., Li, S., Yang, S., & Li, F. (2023). Exploring and visualizing study progress and emerging trends of event prediction: A survey. *Applied Sciences (Basel, Switzerland)*, 13(24), 13346. DOI: 10.3390/app132413346

Yan, L., Alagas, E. N., Jambulingam, M., & Wang, L. (2024). Destination brand identity as a mediator between accessibility and tourist perception: Promoting Bama Yao as potential wellness tourist destination in China. *Turyzm/Tourism*, 109–120. https://doi.org/DOI: 10.18778/0867-5856.34.1.10

Yao, M. (2023). The impact of the COVID-19 on the mood of hotel employee. In X. Li, C. Yuan, & J. Kent (Eds.), *Proceedings of the 6th International Conference on Economic Management and Green Development* (pp. 1217–1224). Springer Nature Singapore. https://doi.org/DOI: 10.1007/978-981-19-7826-5_116

Yuwantiningrum, S. E. (2023). The influence of the Covid-19 pandemic and government policy on hotel room occupancy rates. *Jurnal Ilmiah Pariwisata Kesatuan*, 4(2), 61–70. DOI: 10.37641/jipkes.v4i2.2060

Zainordin, N. A. F., Syed Jaafar, S. M. R., & Md Khairi, N. D. (2021). Publication trend on travel preferences of senior tourists from 2000 to 2020. *Journal of Tourism. Hospitality and Environment Management,* 6(26), 172–185. DOI: 10.35631/JTHEM.626015

Zhang, Z. (2023). Digital operational strategies in the post-pandemic era for travel companies: A case study of Ctrip. *Highlights in Business. Economics and Management,* 23, 521–525. DOI: 10.54097/h0w3ar97

KEY TERMS AND DEFINITIONS

Crisis Management: Strategies and actions taken by the tourism and hospitality industry to mitigate the effects of global events. Effective crisis management can help reduce losses and speed recovery.

Demand Fluctuations: Variations in the demand for hotel rooms and tourism services due to external factors like global events. Understanding these fluctuations is essential for revenue management and operational planning.

Economic Impact: The financial effect that global events have on tourism and the broader economy. This includes changes in revenue for hotels, airlines, and local businesses that depend on tourism.

Global Events: Significant occurrences such as pandemics, wars, natural disasters, or major international events (e.g., the Olympics) that can influence travel behaviours, affecting both domestic and international tourism.

Hospitality Industry: The sector that provides travellers services like lodging, food, and entertainment. Global events often challenge this industry's resilience and adaptability to rapidly changing conditions.

Hotel Occupancy: The rate at which hotel rooms are occupied during a specific period. This is a key performance indicator for the hospitality industry, reflecting the health of the tourism market.

Tourist Flows: The movement patterns of tourists between destinations. Global events can disrupt or redirect these flows, impacting the demand for travel and accommodation in certain regions.

Travel Restrictions: Government-imposed limits on travel, often in response to global events such as pandemics or security threats. These restrictions can dramatically reduce tourist numbers and hotel occupancy rates.

Chapter 2
Transforming Online Travel Agencies Using an Alert Management System:
Strategies for Airbnb Through COVID-19

Anthony Hae Ryong Rhim
The University of Hong Kong, Hong Kong

Ka Yu Chiu
 https://orcid.org/0009-0005-3049-347X
The University of Hong Kong, Hong Kong

Dickson K. W. Chiu
 https://orcid.org/0000-0002-7926-9568
The University of Hong Kong, Hong Kong

Kevin K. W. Ho
University of Tsukuba, Japan

ABSTRACT

The Airbnb Alert System Platform (AASP) is a framework proposed to address and administer the unprecedented downfall of Airbnb's transactions in 2020 due to the outbreak of the COVID-19 pandemic. The AASP would be a ramification reflected upon novel environmental outbreaks and observed trends, optimizing the management information system (MIS) to match changed customer needs. This chapter

DOI: 10.4018/979-8-3693-7021-6.ch002

investigates how online travel agencies (OTAs) may improve their management information systems through an alert management system (AMS). This chapter will also provide practical design details, including user interface, Unified Modeling Language (UML) flowchart, system architecture, and specific event-condition-action (ECA) alerts.

INTRODUCTION

Online Travel Search Before and During the COVID-19 Pandemic

Traveling has never been as convenient as in contemporary times. The abundance of sophisticated technology and infrastructure with a substantial growth rate has continuously increased the travel demand (Chan & Chiu, 2022) and facilitated travelers' information needs before and during travel. Yet, overwhelming predicaments still impede the market, as observed in 2020's COVID-19 outbreak.

Figure 1. The trend for hotels and flights worldwide between 2010 and 2022 (blue: hotels; red: flights)

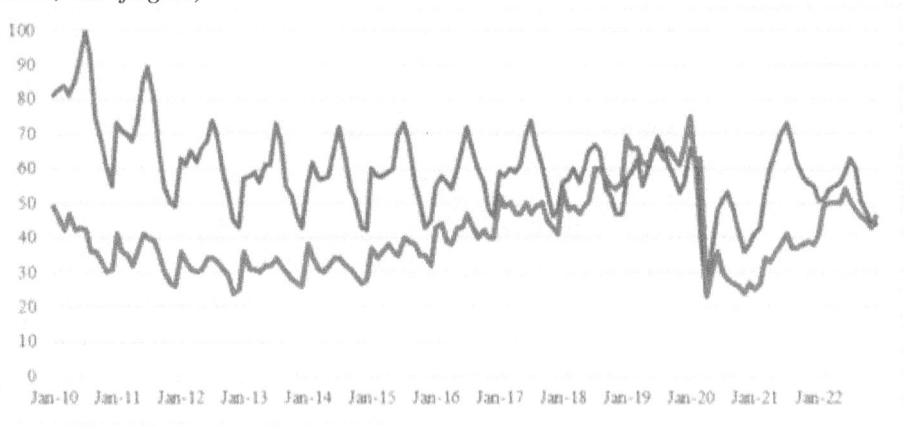

(Google Trends (http://google.com/trends))

Figure 1 shows several key characteristics of travel search trends. The yearly cyclical peaks and nadirs of the search for hotels and flights indicate a relatively higher demand for summer than winter (in the Northern Hemisphere), possibly due to year-end familial gatherings. Also, in contrast to the decline of the hotels' search, airline search has continuously increased, indicating a growing need for economic decision-making for flights. Yet, a steep drop in the search for hotels and flights from 2020 to 2022 reflects how critical COVID-19 affected the traveling industry, showing a prolonged bear market. Due to travel restrictions imposed by nearly all countries, decreased travel demand, and recommended travel reductions, health response planning has diminished the traveling industry (Chinazzi et al., 2020). Not only did the supply decrease abruptly, but the demand also serially, leaving a Keynesian effect from the supply shock toward a conceivable recession (Guerrieri et al., 2020).

Post-Pandemic Period of Shifting in Customer Behavior and Technology Adoption

In 2023, global travel and tourism spending rose 21.5% compared to previous years (2020-2022), reaching about 6 trillion US dollars but remaining below pre-pandemic periods (Statista, 2024). Following the COVID-19 pandemic, some tourists may choose more independent modes of transportation instead of public transportation because they are concerned about possible infections (Christidis et al., 2021). Besides, such actions can potentially rebalance demand for personal vehicles, walking, and micro-mobility. Therefore, tourists' behavior and preferences have significantly changed (Ni et al., 2022).

Besides, smart tourism using digital tools and platforms for booking, navigation, and personalized suggestions leverages digital technology to improve efficiency and effectiveness while enhancing tourists' overall experience (Cheng et al., 2024; Ni et al., 2022; Torabi et al., 2023). This could explain why advanced technology adoption is necessary for development after the pandemic to enhance the tourists' overall needs.

Background of Airbnb

Airbnb was established in 2007 in San Francisco, California, by Brian Chesky, Joe Gebbia, and Nathan Blecharczyk, and it was named "Air Bed and Breakfast" (Edelman & Michael Luca, 2014). The business focuses on the peer-to-peer (P2P) pluralistic economy segment, aligning with other vital industrial players such as Uber, Lift, Handy, Upwork, and Etsy, which disrupt traditional and conventional travel business models (Aloni & Erez, 2016). It also follows the distinct rule for development under the neoclassical growth theory, which requires capital, labor, and technology, allowing the entity to have more demand, such as in the case of energy efficiency, leading to additional energy consumption (Saunders & Harry D, 1992).

After its seventh funding round of US$10B valuation, Airbnb gained attention to become one of the industry giants (Rusli et al., 2014). In 2019, it became the 8th best company to work for worldwide, according to LinkedIn (Mcgauley, 2019).

Airbnb has increasingly added boutique hotels and experiences to its services but still does not target flights and high-end traditional hotels. In 2021, Airbnb had over 6 million listings worldwide (Airbnb, 2022). Compared to Expedia Group's almost 3 million lodging properties as of December 31, 2021, Airbnb had over two times more listings than Expedia (Expedia, 2022). However, revenue staggered as Expedia's 2021 annual revenue was over US$8.6B, while Airbnb's was lower at US$6B.

Two key differences lay Airbnb in a distinct market from other online travel agencies (OTAs) such as Expedia or Hotels.com: It matches individual homes as locations to stay and experiences from people willing to share their knowledge. Nonetheless, the gaps between the different OTAs are narrowing since more boutique hotels and resorts are attempting to use Airbnb as their listing platform.

The upper part of Figure 2 depicts how frequently Airbnb is searched compared to Expedia using worldwide figures. Notably, Airbnb has been superior in the past several years. The trend to search Expedia seems to be continually declining, whereas Airbnb has surged since around 2015 and surpassed Expedia's rate. However, it is evident that both search rates fell abruptly in 2020 during the pandemic and are now recovering, but search rates are recovering slower than the worldwide trend.

As successful global travel business brands, such as TripAdvisor, Trivago (Expedia group), Skyscanner, and KAYAK, have recently grown popular, the main objective of this chapter is to introduce good practices and contemporary system design of global enterprises to tourism-related businesses mentioned above through the case of Airbnb because they strategize, systematize, and manage their search engine.

Figure 2. The trend for Airbnb and Expedia worldwide between 2010 and 2022 (blue: Airbnb; red: Expedia)

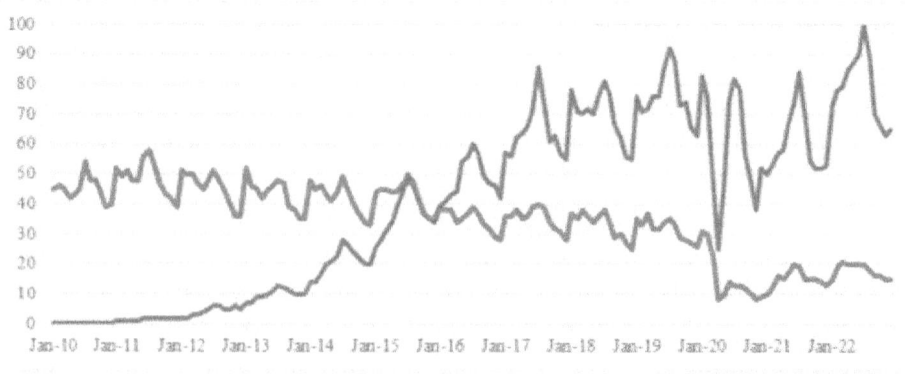

(Google Trends (http://google.com/trends))

LITERATURE REVIEW

Under the current competition from online travel agencies, Airbnb's management strategy should be supported by an enhanced management information system (MIS) under the alert management system (AMS) principles. To determine the specifics of the Airbnb Alert System Platform (AASP), OTA industry analysis, alert-based management systems, Airbnb's requirements for the system, and Airbnb-specific trends are reviewed.

Industry Analysis of OTAs

The behemoths of the conventional OTAs are Expedia Group, Priceline, and Ctrip, having a market share ranking of the same listed order. In 2015, Expedia's total reservation revenue was US$61B, whereas Priceline's and Ctrip's were US$56B and US$27B, respectively (Carey et al., 2017). Expedia has a history of acquiring Travelocity, Orbitz, Hotels.com, and more, such as the metasearch engine Trivago for vertical integration. Having a share of 9% in Ctrip, Priceline had purchased vertical functions such as the metasearch Kayak.com and horizontal ones such as OpenTable. Ctrip includes Quanr, MakeMyTrip, metasearch platform Skyscanner, and eLong towards its services. Expedia has a strong presence in the United States, whereas Priceline has a presence in Europe and Ctrip in China.

Especially in business travel, Asia is ranked first with US$1T, accounting for 38% of the business traveling segment (Dichter et al., 2016). Each area within Asia also differs in tech preference when booking, as business travelers to Singapore prefer comfort more, whereas those to India prefer various OTA offerings more. As a result, OTAs have a more substantial presence in areas encompassing economic travelers.

Over 40% of Expedia Group's Online Travel Aggregator brand transactions were reserved through mobile platforms in 2019 (Expedia Group, 2020). There was also a 40% increase from the 2018 mobile transaction rate. This trend is logical to increase emphasis on mobile user interface and process efficiency.

Usually, the OTA market is stable yearly, even though the search rate investigated in the introduction denotes a decrease in search count for Expedia worldwide. Notwithstanding, the flare-up of COVID-19 recessed the OTA economy to an all-time low where hotels and flights simultaneously are affected by global travel restriction policies. The industry is thus seeking innovative ideas such as Airbnb's Virtual Experiences or is delaying its operations to the mere hope of a slowdown of the epidemic.

Impact of COVID-19 on OTAs and the Travel Industry

Some OTAs took immediate action against COVID-19 influencing their services. For instance, one of the global leaders in online travel booking agencies, Booking.com, has responded to the epidemic by launching a "Flexible - 1 Day" program that lets users cancel reservations for free up to one day before departure. Vancia & Băltescu (2022) also explained that along with prioritizing health and cleanliness practices, Booking.com observes the trends toward early vacation planning and exploring neighboring locations. Another example is the Chinese OTA, Ctrip: longer stays at places are becoming more preferred by tourists, and both domestic and environmentally friendly travel has grown in popularity (Hospitalitynet, 2021). Additionally, Middle East OTA Almosafer discovered through its research on their Middle East travel and lodging business that, during the pandemic, travelers choose last-minute reservations, shorter travel dates, and places close to their homes (De Brito, 2021).

Alert Management System

The origin of an Alert Management System (AMS) is an automated patient management system in the medical sector, as proposed by Kafeza et al. (2004). In automated patient management for healthcare, data on entities are collected, set with administrator-defined symptom alerts, and sent to the server for alert-driven process execution. The system architecture comprises three main components: patient data sources, patient data collecting devices, and the server. Medics input pre-determined symptoms from these devices to re-examine the patients for further data collection. Next, the device delivers the gathered information to the server for additional analysis. Then, the decisions are ultimately alerted to humans for further decisions or actions after storing user data in the database.

Another example of such systems is online m-services providing user-friendly interfaces integrating multiple backend service provider platforms, contributing to a multi-agent mobile workforce management framework. Upon the AMS, supplementary methods of the knowledge basket are to implement intelligent adaptations by maintaining a constantly updated backend database (Chiu, Lee, Leung, Au, & Wong, 2003). User data fed from the front-end server to iterate ubiquitous optimization would also contribute to AMS (Hong et al., 2007).

Requirements for AMS in MIS

The requirements for AMS in MIS include the following:

Agents: They automate the information delivery process by delegating tasks. For instance, software agents support travelers' decision-making by producing packages of travel itineraries based on the user's profile (Schiaffino et al., 2009). In AMS, specific agents (some can reside on travelers' mobile devices) help alert signal management or machine learning analysis based on their locations and roles in the system architecture.

Multi-agent information systems (MAIS): Multi-agent clusters are designed to handle specific tasks (Chiu et al., 2005), allowing the system to be relatively decentralized but simultaneously achieve optimal performance (Nedic et al., 2009). Global optimization is achieved through MAIS with minimal delay rates.

Semantic web technologies and ontology: Ontology is the bag of concepts provided to the semantic web procedures to build a semantic experience (Vesin et al., 2012). Personalization is the key feature of semantic analysis through this technology, which combines natural language processing (NLP) and artificial intelligence to profile each user.

Knowledge basket approach: The knowledge basket centers on a database to store filtered knowledge from pre-computation or human-directed strategies (Chiu et al., 2005). In contrast to brute-force caching or total pre-computation, the knowledge basket allows algorithms to reduce the time complexity and errors.

Ubiquitous Tourist Assistant System (UTAS): Using ubiquitous agents to extract contextual user data, UTAS supports users with a more personalized experience (Hong et al., 2007), aligning with semantic web technologies and ontology.

Data warehouse: This term refers to data integration where subject-oriented, nonvolatile, and time-variable data are collected for online analytical processing systems (OLAP) (Sen et al., 2011; Thusoo et al., 2010). Methods of warehousing ranged from infrastructure-based to vendor-based and modeling-based. Airbnb should aim for enterprise resource planning (ERP) to provide business intelligence utilizing agile software development methodologies.

The Connection Between AASP and Reality

The tourist and hospitality industries are paying more attention to algorithmic management, which creates new avenues for corporate strategy and expansion through data aggregation and analysis (Cheng & Foley, 2019). The link between AASP and reality could be closed together and positively impact customer satisfaction, trust, and engagement. By adapting to changing consumer preferences and market trends, AASP can stay relevant and competitive, ultimately shaping how tourists experience and interact with hospitality services.

Factors Affecting Airbnb

There are also several factors affecting the operation of Airbnb.

Environmental Issues Affect Airbnb Critically: Future mass-scale viral diseases would affect Airbnb's demand. Despite efforts like virtually transforming "experiences," revenue drops are already predicted. Also, regulations for Airbnb have been strengthened, such as home registration requirements in Paris, which have otherwise been fined EUR12.5M, and two-thirds of listings in New York have been illegalized (Investopedia, 2019).

Fastest-Growing Hosts Are Seniors: The fastest-growing supplier segment is the age group over 60, with 400,000 seniors as hosts in 2018 (Airbnb Newsroom, 2018) and a 66% increase in senior travelers in 2018 from 2017.

Average San Francisco Airbnb Guest Spends 5.5 days and up to US$1,045: As a benchmark from Airbnb's headquarters location, their average San Francisco travelers spend approximately six days and US$1,000 for each travel, which is segmented closer to short-term rentals.

Increased Professionalism in Host Inventory Management: Professional hosting tools are provided to hosts from the information system to compete with Booking.com and Expedia's HomeAway. In cases where Expedia acquired Airbnb's landlord support services, Pillow and ApartmentJet, in 2018, constantly compete for host aid services (Expedia Group, 2018). There are also incidents where co-hosts are hired to manage the listings. Along with the trend to serve a whole end-to-end traveling experience, investment in user travel aid is also forecastable.

METHODOLOGY

This study mainly applies heuristic qualitative case analyses on Airbnb with applications of the AMS to its MIS. An in-depth dive into Airbnb's SWOT and its derived strategies would present the system blueprint for the Airbnb Alert System Platform (AASP). Supplementary quantitative research to the blueprint was conducted to excavate covert rules from the online hotel booking demand. The Key Performance Indicators (KPIs) related to AAPS are illustrated to find the matching Event Condition Action (ECA) for triggering management attention and actions.

After designing the KPIs and ECA, this chapter presents the architectural structure frame of AASP by setting the conceptual alert class architecture. Business process dynamics are analyzed per the embedded AMS. Then, the UML use case diagram, conceptual main entities and relationships, flow chart of AASP, three-tier architecture system, and the UML class diagram provide further design details of the AASP framework.

SWOT and TOWS Analysis of Airbnb

We first conduct a SWOT analysis of Airbnb, as summarized in Table 1, by classifying the SWOT for AASP, strategic planning, and the relative standpoint of Airbnb in the industry (Helms et al., 2010).

Table 1. SWOT analysis for Airbnb

Strengths	Weaknesses
• Open API for a better ecosystem • The dominant leader in the P2P home lending economy • Efficient communication platform between travelers and host • Low fee for the lender (3~5%) • It has "Experiences" as services • It has a performance dashboard	• Pricing for travelers (6~12%) and experience providers (20%) is high • Lack of business travelers as users • The internal risk prediction function (algorithm) needs improvement • No insight analysis for travelers
Opportunities	Threats
• Increasing demand for boutique hotels to be listed on Airbnb • Large partnerships such as with Fannie Mae to support lenders • Partnerships with Seville City Hall, Swiss government (for tax), Pan America Health Organization, etc.	• State regulations for home listings are high and are trending to remain high • Fragile environmental factors restricting traveling • Competitor OTA presence is still higher worldwide.

Source: Authors own creation

The TOWS matrix is derived by selecting one from each of the rows and columns of SWOT, allowing S-O, W-O, S-T, and W-T strategies to be formed by combining the two specifications (Weihrich, 1982). Table 2 shows our analysis with one external factor collaborated with an internal factor to produce a different strategy.

Table 2. TOWS matrix of Airbnb

S-O Strategies	W-O Strategies
• Promote "Experiences" with municipal organizations to develop the market • Creative open API application initiatives for boutique hotel interfaces	• More incentives for travelers and experience providers by partnership sponsors • Contracts with boutique hotels to provide exclusive services for business travelers
S-T Strategies	W-T Strategies
• May collaborate with other relatively non-overlapping key players such as Expedia.com to overcome the recessing market	• Enhancement of internal and external risk prediction and alerts • Additional traveler guide/support services development that is differentiated from competitor OTAs

Source: Authors own creation

OTA Booking Trends from Association Rule Mining

From Kaggle.com (a subsidiary of Google), an open refined dataset of hotel booking based on Antonio, Almeida, and Nunes's article was used to perform association rule mining with W-Apriori and FP-Growth algorithms to capture additional market demand trends (Antonio et al., 2019). This study utilizes RapidMiner, a data mining and text-mining software, for the algorithm structuring and process design, with results illustrated in Figures 3 to 6. The results revealed specific key demand trends having the highest statistical support and confidence levels, such as booking cancellation (less than 69.5 days) resulting in higher cancellations, specific cohorts of customers continually booking the same hotel brands, and non-refundable hotels booked over 69.5 days in advance canceled.

Figure 3. FP-growth algorithm

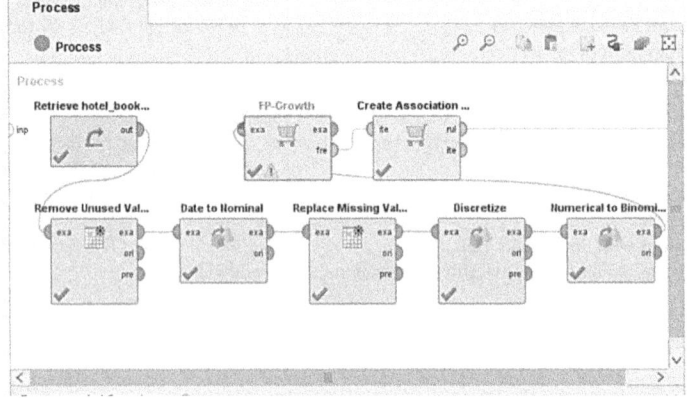

(Authors own creation)

Figure 4. FP-growth algorithm results

Size	Support	Item 1	Item 2	Item 3
1	0.500	adr		
1	0.498	lead_time		
1	0.479	arrival_date_day_of_month		
1	0.477	arrival_date_week_number		
1	0.411	total_of_special_requests		
1	0.400	stays_in_week_nights		
1	0.370	is_canceled		
1	0.341	arrival_date_year		
1	0.335	hotel		
1	0.308	stays_in_weekend_nights		
1	0.151	booking_changes		
2	0.255	adr	lead_time	
2	0.240	adr	arrival_date_day_of_month	
2	0.250	adr	arrival_date_week_number	
2	0.245	adr	total_of_special_requests	
2	0.215	adr	stays_in_week_nights	
2	0.195	adr	is_canceled	
2	0.210	adr	arrival_date_year	

(Authors own creation)

Figure 5. W-Apriori algorithm

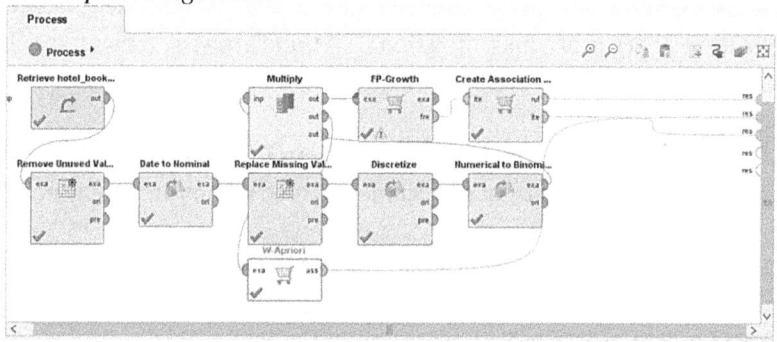

(Authors own creation)

Figure 6. W-Apriori algorithm results

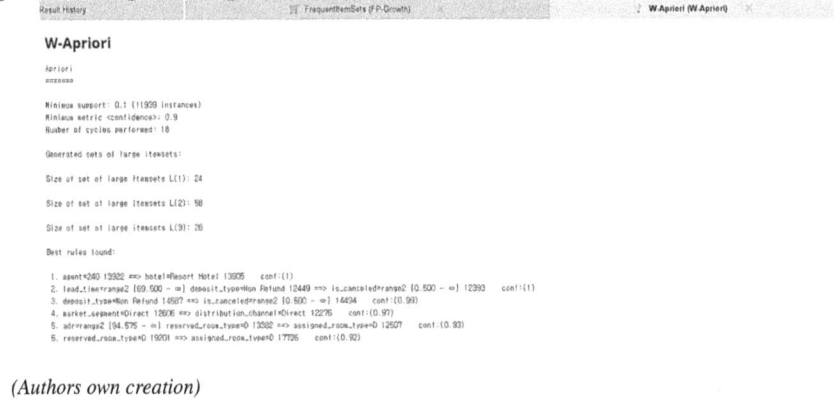

(Authors own creation)

Segmented KPIs and ECAs of AASP

Next, we apply the results from the SWOT analysis, TOWS strategies, and booking trend association rule mining to determine the KPIs of the AASP, targeting risk minimalization (RM), profit maximization (PM), and growth momentum (GM). We identify 21 aggregated KPIs affiliated with these three main categories.

KPI_1. Environmental risk minimalization (RM): Previously high-impacted factors such as epidemics or governmental restrictions are monitored through this KPI.

KPI_2. Internal risk minimalization (RM): Risks such as host scams are identified through this KPI, which may be addressed by integrating social media into personal verification to minimize anonymity.

KPI_3. Alternative risk recognition (RM): Through machine learning agent operations, the AAMS monitors significant numerical changes from economy indexes, ranging from S&P500 to specific travel market indexes.

KPI_4. Abnormal canceling detection (RM): Measures whether abnormal rates of users or hosts denying their matches are prevalent.

KPI_5. Negativity detection in reviews (RM): Amidst the norm of positive reviews on Airbnb, negativity may impact the credibility of listings more than expected (Bridges et al., 2016).

KPI_6. Competitor activity detection (RM): The AAMS continually monitors the activities of other OTA competitors to keep up with the trend efficiently.

KPI_7. Effective alert system to renters and bookers (PM): Software agents alert the renters and bookers on travel management and property management (e.g., Expedia launched Trip Assistance in 2019 and Airbnb's Performance Dashboard in 2019) and any phenomenal incidences affecting itineraries.

KPI_8. Expansion of "Experiences" (PM): This is to expand the count of experiences listed in "Experiences" and the count of people who booked them.

KPI_9. General P/L ratio growth (PM): This aims to increase the fundamental profit of the Airbnb businesses, divided into homes booking P/L and "Experiences" booking P/L.

KPI_10. Abnormal booking detection (PM): Unlike anomaly canceling alerts, which focus on abrupt canceling, anomaly booking alerts are raised upon slowdown or acceleration of bookings by determining the derivative of the booking change rate. Also, excessive pre-booking above monthly averages is marked by this KPI.

KPI_11. Abnormal availability detection (PM): This tracks the slowdown or acceleration of availability by statistically calculating the change rates.

KPI_12. Change in host segment detection (PM): The fastest-growing host segment is over 60 years old.

KPI_13. Change in customer segment detection (PM): Similar to KPI_12, the fastest-increasing segment is the customers over 60.

KPI_14. Alternative bookings growth (GM): Unconventional housing growth (e.g., treehouses or aluminum pods) is estimated. Airbnb has prior experience in early 2020, opening a competition for the most creative housing, funding US$1M for ten ideas. This initiative was paused due to COVID-19 and will be resumed after the pandemic.

KPI_15. End-to-end travel platform establishment (GM): Airbnb aims to construct a traveling experience from beginning to end with only its services.

KPI_16. Open API usage growth (GM): This promotes more 3rd party developers to utilize Airbnb's framework in their applications, fostering a higher impact in society.

KPI_17. Larger city bookings growth rate (GM): The best revenue stream for Airbnb is through large city booking commission fees. More offerings should be listed from metropolitan cities.

KPI_18. Prominent effects from social funding and investment (GM): This accounts for the returns from investments and social initiatives (e.g., Expedia Group's "Inspired Expedia" television campaign).

KPI_19. Increase of long-term rentals (GM): The newly developed area of long-term rentals would bring new revenue streams to Airbnb.

KPI_20. Increase of market share (GM): The increase in market share would not necessarily mean an increase in profits but would direct a stronger influence in the market, such as being an oligarch. The market includes not only ordinary homes but also experiences, boutique hotels, and alternative housing.
KPI_21. Partnerships growth (GM): This includes municipal, corporate, or non-profit partnerships. The characteristics differ from each type, but generally, the stated order is of standard importance for growth indication.

The ECA rules corresponding to each KPI according to the number attached would further be implemented in the machine learning agents of AMS and the relational database of AAPS. The bold and italic formatted ECAs represent alerts corresponding to entities other than Airbnb management.

ECA_1.1. Epidemic alert when movement detected (by machine learning (ML))
ECA_1.2. Government regulation/restriction alert when movement is detected (by ML)
ECA_2.1. Data breach alert when movement detected (by ML)
ECA_2.2. Scam host alert when movement detected (by ML)
ECA_3.1. Alternative economic risk alert upon movement detected (by ML)
ECA_4.1. Abnormal acceleration or slowdown of cancellation alert weekly upon $-2\sigma < \Delta x < 2\sigma$.
ECA_5.1. Negative host feedback alert upon x < 20% satisfaction (20% due to lower commission)
ECA_5.2. Negative guest feedback alert upon x < 10% satisfaction (10% due to higher commission)
ECA_6.1. Competitor new activity alert when movement detected (by ML)
***ECA_7.1.** State-wide phenomenon affecting travel alert*
***ECA_7.2.** Traveler alert for due dates and itinerates (by BDI agents)*
***ECA_7.3.** Lender alert for guest management and property management (by BDI agents)*
ECA_8.1. "Experiences" low listing rate alert upon listing x < 70% of last week
ECA_8.2. "Experiences" low booking rate alert upon booking x < 70% of last week
ECA_9.1. Home bookings low-profit alert upon profit x < 60% of last week
ECA_9.2. "Experiences" bookings low-profit alert upon profit x < 60% of last week
ECA_10.1. Excessive advanced booking alert upon x > 69.5 days
ECA_10.2. Abnormal acceleration or slowdown of booking alert upon weekly $-2\sigma < \Delta x < 2\sigma$

ECA_11.1. Abnormal acceleration or slowdown of availability alert upon weekly $-2\sigma < \Delta x < 2\sigma$
ECA_12.1. Host segment changes trend alert (by ML)
ECA_13.1. Customer segment changes trend alert (by ML)
ECA_14.1. Alternative housing listing low growth alert upon listing count x < 70% of last month
ECA_15.1. Competitor acquisition, new business alert (by ML)
ECA_16.1. Open API used application low growth alert upon application count x < 50% of last month
ECA_17.1. Large city listing low growth alert upon listing count x < 70% of last month
ECA_18.1. Investment low return alert upon listing growth x < 7% for each week after investment
ECA_19.1. Long-term rental low growth alert upon listing growth x < 3% of last month
ECA_20.1. Market share low growth alert upon growth x < 5% of last month
ECA_21.1. Partnership low growth alert upon growth x < 4% of last month

Design and Implementation of System

We design the fundamental bedrock of AASP that extends a three-tier architecture of users, service processes, and a database warehouse for data to be collected (Chiu et al., 2003), as shown in Table 3. The AASP is a Multi-Agent Information System (MAIS) that interfaces users to the services provided by Believe-Desire-Intention (BDI) agents. The BDI agents monitor and execute the business processes required by Airbnb, facilitated by events, exceptions, risks, process software modules, and data collected. ECA and KPIs should be customized for the BDI agents, which manage the alert system intelligently with optimization algorithms (Chiu et al. 2005). The software mentioned above is implemented with an industry-standard 3-tier approach comprising DBMS-based, service-based, and user-based components, which can work with website and application data collected from internal databases and external business partners for internal and cross-organization system integration (e.g., hotels and payment platforms).

Table 3. Proposed AASP infrastructure

Airbnb Alert System Platform 1.0 User Interface	
Multi-Agent Information System (MAIS)	
Believe-Desire-Intention (BDI) Agents	
Events, exceptions, and environmental risks	Requirements for data and processes

DBMS-based, service-based, user-based 3-tier implementation
Website- and application-based alert data collection
Source: Adapted from Chiu, Cheung, & Leung (2005infr)

Next, we present our redesign for Airbnb's business processes based on the new AASP with three parties: the user, the supplier, and the Airbnb mid- and senior-level managers. As shown in Figure 7, the users start the booking process by accessing their accounts and logging on to Airbnb. New users may access Airbnb through Google Ads for the first time. Afterward, itinerary searches are done either through the web or mobile apps. The booking procedure begins with the supplier level as an end-to-begin trigger upon purchase completion. The user continues using the home or experience they booked and finalizes their journey with a review. Incentives such as gamified user experience (user levels) are suggested for higher user retention rates (Hew et al., 2016).

Figure 7. Business processes and AMS redesign for Airbnb based on AASP

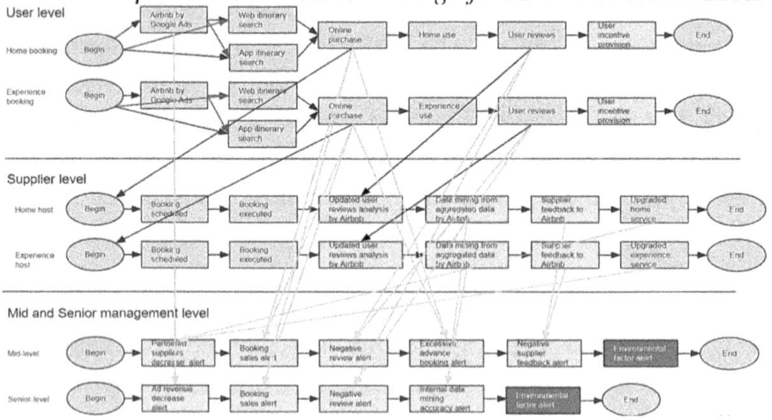

(Authors own creation)

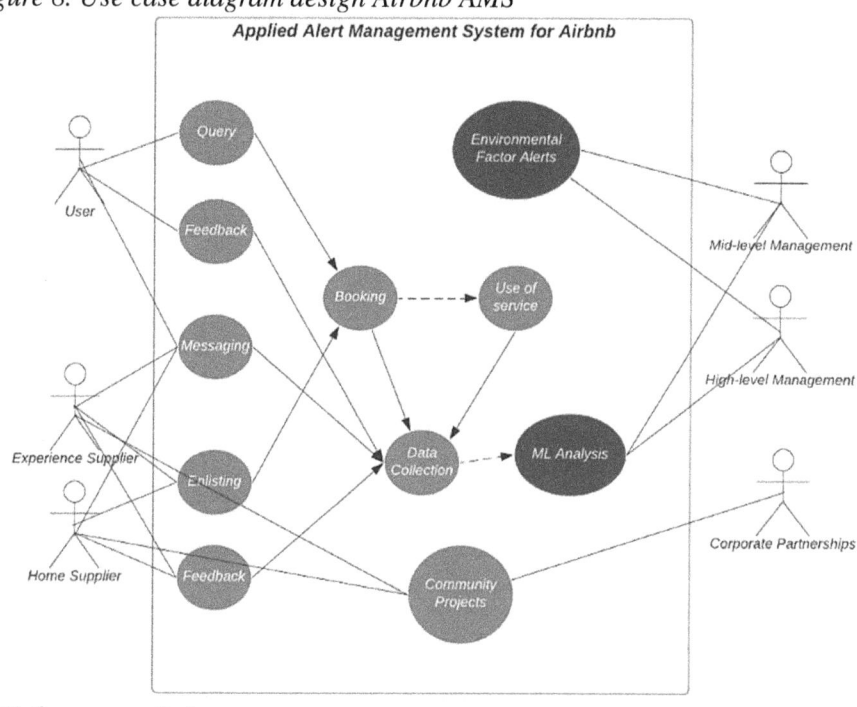

Figure 8. Use case diagram design Airbnb AMS

(Authors own creation)

For the supplier, the process of preparing the booking begins after the user purchases the booking. After the booking is exhausted, hosts receive an insight analysis from AASP based on the aggregated reviews of the users. Then, the hosts are requested to leave feedback on the whole hosting experience to the corporate managers.

The mid-level and senior-level managers then apply the alerts to each modifying operation and improvement strategy. The environmental factor alert process of AASP is crucial to fast notification to the managers.

Then, we develop the use case diagram for the AASP (see Figure 8). First, the six stakeholders that utilize the system include users (travelers), experienced suppliers, home suppliers, mid-level management, high-level management, and partnerships. These parties form an ecosystem for AMS that is observable through the use case diagram.

Figure 9 shows our entity and relationship design, illustrating the interactions among the entities regarding their data transmission traces. The entities with the most connections are hubs for data collection, e.g., "Product" with four connections.

For the flowchart, our design includes five different urgency levels to identify severity according to the alert model of Kafeza et al. (2004) embedded into the BDI agent for alert processing, as shown in Figure 10.

Figure 9. Main entities and relationships conceptual design for the AASP

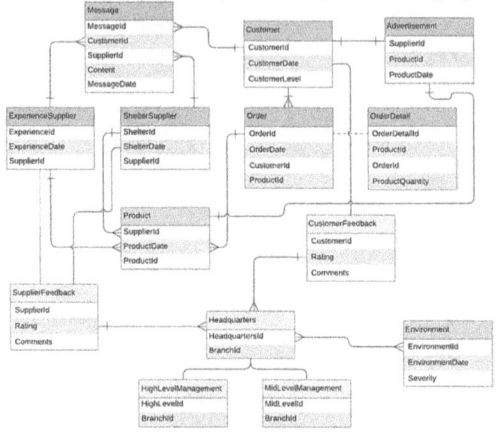

(Authors own creation)

Figure 10. Flowchart of AASP

(Authors own creation)

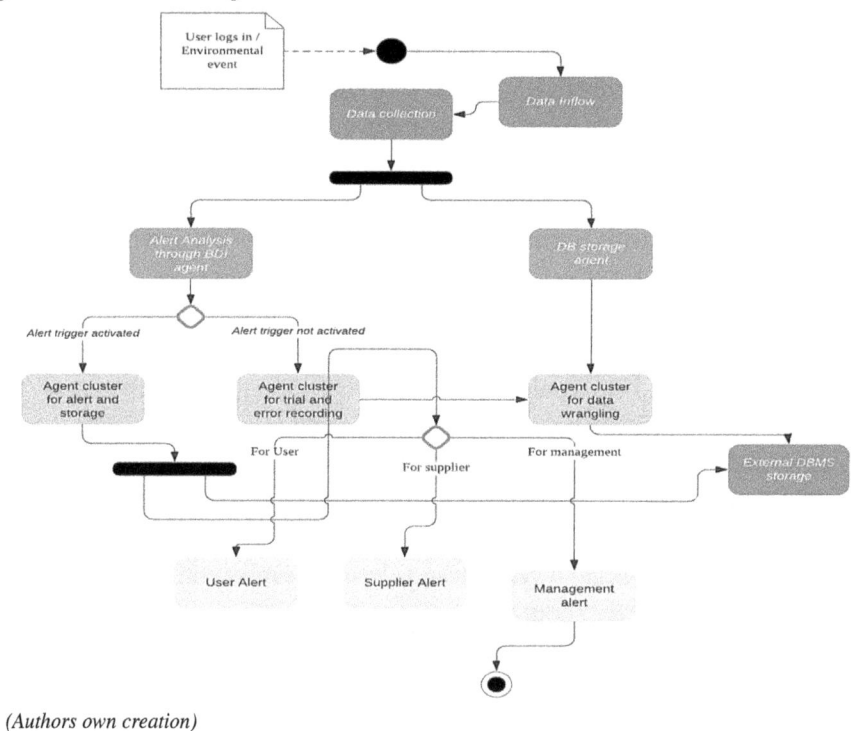

Figure 11. Three-tier system architecture redesign based on the AASP

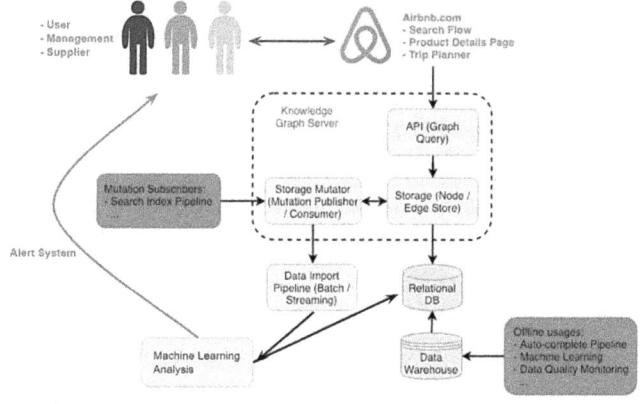

(Authors own creation)

Finally, Figure 11 shows our new design with the Knowledge Graph Server comprising a multi-modal cluster of agents, Data Import agents, and Machine Learning Analysis agents (Chiu et al., 2005.). User data collected through the AASP's user interface are then transferred to BDI agents (machine learning analysis) to discover whether raising alerts is necessary (Hong et al., 2007).

Due to the large amount of data storage, an external cloud data warehouse is necessary, for example, from Amazon Web Services (AWS) or Google Cloud Platform (GCP). The database is constantly updated with new data, where additional statistical models test for potential alerts. Business analytics are also conducted through the global distribution system gateway (GDS).

Within the AMS, an upgraded Ubiquitous Tourist Assistant System (UTAS) can provide a semantic and smart allocation of alerts by deciphering the users' feedback (Hong et al., 2007). Natural language processing (NLP) with UTAS can stem comments, remove stop-words, and lemmatize them to update user-specific trends constantly. Alerts are raised based on the relative negativity and criticalness of events.

The e-monitoring system with multiple monitoring agents helps the interoperability between front-end and backend systems and alerts the preset entities (Cheong et al., 2007). The backend server should concentrate on statistics and machine learning algorithms to determine whether information collected from the front-end system triggers alerts.

The user interface of AASP should be accessible for users and hosts by adding a social network account login method to track IP verification. After logging in, the user can select their preferred alert modules, and relevant alerts can pop up on the screen in an ergonomic-friendly manner.

DISCUSSION

Applicability of the System

Along with the TOWS matrix strategies, the recommended direction of AASP implementation should embrace all the ECAs to perform effectively. Nonetheless, certain areas require additional caution.

In information authentication, KPI_2 (internal risk minimalization) and KPI_11 (abnormal availability detection) are heavily affected by whether host activities are transparent and moral, which requires additional measures beyond the AMS to be applied and solved effectively. The two methods of handling this are social media profiling and remaining reviews and conserving them per person.

For social media integration, Airbnb's user registration should be combined with social networking features, such as attaching at least one verified account of a different platform. This approach can prevent hoax accounts or host scams and increase Airbnb's credibility.

Concerning data maintenance for individuals, deregistered users should maintain their unique ID on Airbnb to store their past negative reviews or scam occurrences. Notably, the policies on user data retention differ among countries, which may require significant efforts to comply with.

Further, open data is a trend in global terms, especially in data handling economies, which is on par with Airbnb's promoted open API policy of AAPS's KPI_16. Data openness aids society as a free donation and enhances economic risk predictability when other competitors share their collected data. IT magnates like Microsoft promote open data access, encouraging second-hand research and enhanced knowledge provision (Financial Times, 2020). The main problems for actual implementation lie in two categories: international data policies and data breach threats.

As governmental policies often fall behind IT trends concerning international data policies, technological innovations usually emerge in the economy before new economic regulations. Open data follow similar trends, where data privacy is first considered before data openness. There are movements to provide open datasets worldwide, but more social recognition to mandate an open culture is required for practical open API usage.

Also, data breach threats are often observed. Threats such as data breaches, leaks, and fraud are more frequent in open API environments than in private. Despite premier firewalls, modern architectural systems using the cloud as an external database are prone to mass data leakage (Zuo et al., 2019).

Key Success Factors of AASP

This case analysis has covered several Key Success Factors (KSF) of the solution, including (i) efficient and effective machine learning modeling (which needs the constant update of the model after trial and error), (ii) inputs for environmental factors are determined correctly, (iii) minimized error rate, (iv) maximized collection of data, (v) effective firewall against data leakage, which needs to align with user data privacy protection, and (vi) execution after alerting.

Application in Tourism Businesses and Markets

The COVID-19 pandemic has changed the tourism business in both domestic and international markets. Although the pandemic has hit the tourism industry hard, governments have developed policies and campaigns to sustain the industry and help it survive (Handler & Tan, 2022; Sakawa et al., 2022). Furthermore, the tourism industry is generally expected to revive after the pandemic (Yagasaki, 2021). Bhatia et al. (2022) suggested tourism stakeholders rethink, revive, and reset their market position. This chapter uses our analysis of the Airbnb alert system platform development as an example to explore the development of a suitable MIS with contemporary technologies to help OTAs better manage their businesses. Many OTAs in the market, such as international corporations like TripAdvisor, Trivago (Expedia group), Skyscanner, and KAYAK, and other local operations, such as Rakuten, Jalan, and Ikyu (in Japan), can develop or acquire similar systems to strengthen their operations and management.

The Airbnb example developed based on the international dataset would help cater to a system that can address the needs of international tourists and partners to provide better services to international visitors. Besides, we recommend that OTA companies consider developing similar systems with contemporary technologies to enhance their competitiveness in the global market. Besides, we encourage system developers and scholars to collect local data to improve the systems and cater to local needs.

The Challenge of OTAs Faced in the Pandemic

One of the challenges OTAs faced during the pandemic was providing comprehensive services to tourists that were different before the pandemic. For example, Stay Japan, a specialized OTA in special interest tourism, now offers information on local attractions and transportation booking in addition to arranging accommodations (Ohe, 2022). As a result, it would attract an increasing number of tourists because of the all-around services and well-prepared arrangements in tourism.

Another challenge OTAs struggled with during the pandemic was the impact on travel types and distance. Travelers have been discouraged by China's travel restrictions, pandemic control measures, and frequent nuclear acid tests, which have affected both internal travel patterns and sorts of travel (Jiang, 2022). Thus, the pandemic affects the mode of traveling and arrangements habits of worldwide and local tourists.

CONCLUSION

During the COVID-19 pandemic, the tourism and travel industries have been severely affected. Tourism demand has decreased significantly worldwide, and governments have had to provide domestic travel subsidies to encourage people to take local trips to support the industry. Citizens have generally experienced significant

REFERENCES

Airbnb. (2018). Ageless travel: The growing popularity of Airbnb for the over 60s. Airbnb Newsroom. https://news.airbnb.com/ageless-travel-the-growing-popularity-of-airbnb-for-the-over-60s/

Airbnb. (2022). Shareholder letter Q4 2021. Airbnb. https://s26.q4cdn.com/656283129/files/doc_financials/2021/q4/Airbnb_Q4-2021-Shareholder-Letter_Final.pdf

Aloni, E. (2016). Pluralizing the "sharing" economy. *Washington Law Review (Seattle, Wash.)*, 91(4), 1397–1459. https://digitalcommons.law.uw.edu/wlr/vol91/iss4/2/

Antonio, N., Almeida, A. D., & Nunes, L. (2019). Hotel booking demand datasets. *Data in Brief*, 22, 41–49. DOI: 10.1016/j.dib.2018.11.126 PMID: 30581903

Bhatia, A., Roy, B., & Kumar, A. (2022). A review of tourism sustainability in the era of COVID-19. *Journal of Statistics and Management Systems*, 22(8), 1871–1888. DOI: 10.1080/09720510.2021.1995196

Bridges, J., & Vásquez, C. (2016). If nearly all Airbnb reviews are positive, does that make them meaningless? *Current Issues in Tourism*, 21(18), 2065–2083. DOI: 10.1080/13683500.2016.1267113

Carey, R., Ross, D., & Seitzman, N. (2017). The (ongoing) trouble with travel distribution: Customer experience. McKinsey & Company. https://www.mckinsey.com/industries/travel-transport-and-logistics/our-insights/the-ongoing-trouble-with-travel-distribution-customer-experience

Chan, M. M. Wa, Dickson, & Chiu. (2022). Alert-driven customer relationship management in online travel agencies: Event-condition-actions rules and key performance indicators. In *Building a brand image through electronic customer relationship management* (pp. 286–303). IGI Global.

Cheng, M., & Foley, C. (2019). Algorithmic management: The case of Airbnb. *International Journal of Hospitality Management*, 83, 33–36. DOI: 10.1016/j.ijhm.2019.04.009

Cheng, W., Tian, R., & Chiu, D. K. W. (2024). Travel vlogs influencing tourist decisions: Information preferences and gender differences. *Aslib Journal of Information Management*, 76(1), 86–103. DOI: 10.1108/AJIM-05-2022-0261

Cheong, F. K. W., Dickson, K. W., Chiu, S. C., & Cheung, P. C. K., & Hung. (2007). Developing a distributed e-monitoring system for enterprise website and web services: An experience report with free libraries and tools. *IEEE International Conference on Web Services (ICWS 2007)*. https://doi.org/DOI: 10.1109/ICWS.2007.77

Chinazzi, M., Davis, J. T., Ajelli, M., Gioannini, C., Litvinova, M., Merler, S., & Piontti, A. P. Y. (2020). The effect of travel restrictions on the spread of the 2019 novel coronavirus (COVID-19) outbreak. *Science*, 368(6489), 395–400. DOI: 10.1126/science.aba9757 PMID: 32144116

Chiu, D. K. W., Cheung, S. C., Kafeza, E., & Leung, H.-F. (2003). A three-tier view-based methodology for m-services adaptation. *IEEE Transactions on Systems, Man, and Cybernetics. Part A, Systems and Humans*, 33(6), 725–741. DOI: 10.1109/TSMCA.2003.819489

Chiu, D. K. W., Cheung, S. C., & Leung, H.-F. (2005). A multi-agent infrastructure for mobile workforce management in a service-oriented enterprise. *Proceedings of the 38th Annual Hawaii International Conference on System Sciences*. https://doi.org/DOI: 10.1109/HICSS.2005.28

Chiu, D. K. W., Kok, D., Lee, A. K. C., & Cheung, S. C. (2005). Integrating legacy sites into web services with WebXcript. *International Journal of Cooperative Information Systems*, 14(01), 25–44. DOI: 10.1142/S0218843005001006

Chiu, D. K. W., Lee, O. K. F., Leung, E. W. K., Au, M. C. W., & Wong, H.-F. (2005). A multi-modal agent-based mobile route advisory system for public transport network. *Proceedings of the 38th Annual Hawaii International Conference on System Sciences*. https://doi.org/DOI: 10.1109/HICSS.2005.30

Christidis, P., Christodoulou, A., Navajas-Cawood, E., & Ciuffo, B. (2021). The post-pandemic recovery of transport activity: Emerging mobility patterns and repercussions on future evolution. *Sustainability (Basel)*, 13(11), 6359. DOI: 10.3390/su13116359

Clarke, P., & Newcomer, E. (2020). Airbnb's future depends on a post-pandemic travel boom. *The Irish Times*. https://www.irishtimes.com/life-and-style/travel/airbnb-s-future-depends-on-a-post-pandemic-travel-boom-1.4238881

De Brito, C. (2021). Almosafer study reveals Saudi's top post-pandemic travel trends. https://connectingtravel.com/news/almosafer-study-reveals-saudis-top-post-pandemic-travel-trends

Dichter, A., Cheryl, S. H., Lim, D.-Y., & Lin. (2016). Cracking the world's biggest business-travel market. *McKinsey & Company.* https://www.mckinsey.com/industries/travel-transport-and-logistics/our-insights/cracking-the-worlds-biggest-business-travel-market

Edelman, B. G., & Luca, M. (2014). Digital discrimination: The case of Airbnb. SSRN *Electronic Journal.* https://doi.org/DOI: 10.2139/ssrn.2377353

Expedia. (2022). 2021 Annual Report. *Expedia.* https://s27.q4cdn.com/708721433/files/doc_financials/2021/ar/Expedia-Group-2021-Annual-Report.pdf

Expedia Group. (2018). Expedia group acquires Pillow and ApartmentJet to enhance its alternative accommodations marketplace for residents, owners and managers in urban markets. *Expedia Group.* https://www.prnewswire.com/news-releases/expedia-group-acquires-pillow-and-apartmentjet-to-enhance-its-alternative-accommodations-marketplace-for-residents-owners-and-managers-in-urban-markets-300737677.html

Expedia Group. (2020). Expedia group reports fourth quarter and full year 2019 results. https://www.sec.gov/Archives/edgar/data/1324424/000132442420000006/earningsrelease-q42019.htm

Financial Times. (2020). Microsoft throws weight behind open data movement. *Financial Times.* https://www.ft.com/content/661b16ff-f86c-4dad-a557-2e231501bf58

Guerrieri, V., Lorenzoni, G., Straub, L., & Werning, I. (2020). Macroeconomic implications of COVID-19: Can negative supply shocks cause demand shortages? *National Bureau of Economic Research.* https://www.nber.org/papers/w26918

Handler, I., & Tan, C. S. L. (2022). Impact of Japanese travelers' psychographics on domestic travel intention during the COVID-19 pandemic. *Journal of Vacation Marketing.* Advance online publication. DOI: 10.1177/13567667221122108

Helms, M. M., & Nixon, J. (2010). Exploring SWOT analysis - Where are we now? *Journal of Strategy and Management,* 3(3), 215–251. DOI: 10.1108/17554251011064837

Hew, K., Foon, B., Huang, K. W. S., Chu, D., & Chiu, D. K. W. (2016). Engaging Asian students through game mechanics: Findings from two experiment studies. *Computers & Education,* 92, 221–236. DOI: 10.1016/j.compedu.2015.10.010

Hong, D., Chiu, D. K. W., Shen, V. Y., Cheung, S. C., & Kafeza, E. (2007). Ubiquitous enterprise service adaptations based on contextual user behavior. *Information Systems Frontiers,* 9(4), 343–358. DOI: 10.1007/s10796-007-9039-2

Hospitalitynet. (2021). Trip.com group and WTTC publish 'Trending in Travel' report uncovering current and upcoming consumer trends. *Hospitalitynet*. https://www.hospitalitynet.org/news/4107747.html

Jiang, Y. (2022). OTA platforms online travel in the post-epidemic era: Case study of Trip.com group. *Highlights in Business, Economics and Management*, 2, 322-326. https://drpress.org/ojs/index.php/HBEM/article/view/2381

Kafeza, E., Chiu, D. K. W., Cheung, S. C., & Kafeza, M. (2004). Alerts in mobile healthcare applications: Requirements and pilot study. *IEEE Transactions on Information Technology in Biomedicine*, 8(2), 173–181. DOI: 10.1109/TITB.2004.828888 PMID: 15217262

Matsuura, T., & Saito, H. (2022). The COVID-19 pandemic and domestic travel subsidies. *Annals of Tourism Research*, 92, 103326. DOI: 10.1016/j.annals.2021.103326 PMID: 34815608

McGauley, J. (2019). These are the top companies to work for right now, according to LinkedIn. *Thrillist*. https://www.thrillist.com/news/nation/top-companies-to-work-for-2019-linkedin-ranking

Miyawaki, A., Tabuchi, T., Tomata, Y., & Tsugawa, Y. (2021). Association between participation in the government subsidy programme for domestic travel and symptoms indicative of COVID-19 infection in Japan: Cross-sectional study. *BMJ Open*, 11(4), 49069. DOI: 10.1136/bmjopen-2021-049069 PMID: 33849861

Nedic, A., & Ozdaglar, A. (2009). Distributed subgradient methods for multi-agent optimization. *IEEE Transactions on Automatic Control*, 54(1), 48–61. DOI: 10.1109/TAC.2008.2009515

Ni, J., Chiu, D. K. W., & Ho, K. K. W. (2022). Information search behavior among Chinese self-drive tourists in the smartphone era. *Information Discovery and Delivery*, 50(3), 285–296. DOI: 10.1108/IDD-05-2020-0054

Ohe, Y. (2022). Rural tourism under the new normal: New potentials from a Japanese perspective. *WIT Transactions on Ecology and the Environment*, 256, 51–62. DOI: 10.2495/ST220051

Rusli, M., Spector, D., Macmillan, E. M., & Rusli, A. (2014). TPG-led group closes $450 million investment in Airbnb. *The Wall Street Journal*.

Sakawa, H., & Watanabel, N. (2022). Impact of the COVID-19 outbreak on stock market returns: Evidence from Japanese-listed tourism firms. *Applied Economics*, 54(46), 5373–5377. DOI: 10.1080/00036846.2022.2044996

Saunders, H. D. (1992). The Khazzoom-Brookes postulate and neoclassical growth. *The Energy Journal (Cambridge, Mass.)*, 13(4), 131–179. DOI: 10.5547/ISSN0195-6574-EJ-Vol13-No4-7

Schiaffino, S., & Amandi, A. (2009). Building an expert travel agent as a software agent. *Expert Systems with Applications*, 36(2), 1291–1299. DOI: 10.1016/j.eswa.2007.11.032

Sen, A., & Sinha, A. P. (2011). IT alignment strategies for customer relationship management. *Decision Support Systems*, 51(3), 609–619. DOI: 10.1016/j.dss.2010.12.014

Statista. (2024). Total travel and tourism spending worldwide from 2019 to 2023, by type. https://www.statista.com/statistics/298060/contribution-of-travel-and-tourism-to-the-global-economy-by-type-of-spending/

Thusoo, A., Shao, Z., Anthony, S., Borthakur, D., Jain, N., Sarma, J. S., & Liu, H. (2010). Data warehousing and analytics infrastructure at Facebook. *Proceedings of the 2010 ACM SIGMOD International Conference on Management of Data.* https://doi.org/DOI: 10.1145/1807167.1807278

Top cities where Airbnb is legal or illegal. (2019). *Investopedia.* https://www.investopedia.com/articles/investing/083115/top-cities-where-airbnb-legal-or-illegal.asp

Torabi, Z.-A., Rezvani, M. R., Hall, C. M., & Allam, Z. (2023). On the post-pandemic travel boom: How capacity building and smart tourism technologies in rural areas can help - Evidence from Iran. *Technological Forecasting and Social Change*, 193, 122633. DOI: 10.1016/j.techfore.2023.122633 PMID: 37223653

Vancia, A. P. P., & Băltescu, C. A. (2022). Travel trends during the COVID-19 pandemic: A view of online travel agencies. *Proceedings of the International Conference on Business Excellence, 16*(1), 906-917. https://doi.org/DOI: 10.2478/picbe-2022-0085

Vesin, B., Ivanović, M., Klašnja-Milićević, A., & Budimac, Z. (2012). Protus 2.0: Ontology-based semantic recommendation in programming tutoring system. *Expert Systems with Applications*, 39(15), 12229–12246. DOI: 10.1016/j.eswa.2012.04.052

Weihrich, H. (1982). The TOWS matrix: A tool for situational analysis. *Long Range Planning*, 15(2), 54–66. DOI: 10.1016/0024-6301(82)90120-0

Yagasaki, N. (2021). Impact of COVID-19 on the Japanese travel market and the travel market of overseas visitors to Japan, and subsequent recovery. *IATSS Research*, 45(4), 451–458. DOI: 10.1016/j.iatssr.2021.11.008

Zuo, C., Lin, Z., & Zhang, Y. (2019). Why does your data leak? Uncovering the data leakage in cloud from mobile apps. *2019 IEEE Symposium on Security and Privacy (SP)*. https://doi.org/DOI: 10.1109/SP.2019.00009

KEY TERMS AND DEFINITIONS

Alert Management System: A procedure that enables businesses to receive, evaluate, rank, act upon, and keep track of security warnings produced by security solutions.

Event-Condition-Action: A shortened term for the active rule framework shown in active database systems and event-driven architecture.

Management Information System: An information system that helps an organization coordinate, regulate, analyze, and visualize information in addition to being utilized for decision-making.

Multi-Agent Information Systems: A computerized system comprising numerous intelligent entities that communicate with one another.

Natural Language Processing: A subfield of artificial intelligence that allows machines to understand, produce, and work with human language.

Online Travel Agencies: A site that acts as a search engine to reserve travel connects providers across the travel industries to assist travelers easily in planning their trip.

Peer-To-Peer: A distributed application design that divides work or responsibilities among peers.

Ubiquitous Tourist Assistant System: It aligns with ontology and semantic web technologies by providing users with a more personalized experience by extracting contextual user data by ubiquitous agents.

Unified Modeling Language: A standardized modeling language made up of interconnected diagrams created to assist system and software developers in business modeling and other non-software systems and in defining, visualizing, building, and documenting the artifacts of software systems.

APPENDIX I

Table 4. Table of abbreviations

Abbreviation	Full Form
AASP	Airbnb Alert System Platform
MMIS	Management Information System
OTAs	Online Travel Agencies
AMS	Alert Management System
UML	Unified Modeling Language
ECA	Event-Condition-Action
P2P	Peer-To-Peer
MAIS	Multi-Agent Information Systems
NLP	Natural Language Processing
UTAS	Ubiquitous Tourist Assistant System
OLAP	Online Analytical Processing Systems
ERP	Enterprise Resource Planning
KPIs	Key Performance Indicators
RM	Risk Minimalization
PM	Profit Maximization
GM	Growth Momentum
BDI	Believe-Desire-Intention
AWS	Amazon Web Services
GCP	Google Cloud Platform
GDS	Global Distribution System Gateway
UTAS	Ubiquitous Tourist Assistant System
KSF	Key Success Factors

Source: Authors own creation

Chapter 3
The Impact of the Aviation Hub for Tourism in Ceara, Brazil

Laryssa Silva
Christus University Center, Brazil

Zaila Oliveira
 https://orcid.org/0000-0002-7002-7626
University of Maia, Portugal & CEOS.PP, Polytechnic of Porto, Portugal

Sara Teixeira
 https://orcid.org/0000-0002-3768-0420
CEOS.PP, Polytechnic Institute of Porto, Portugal

ABSTRACT

The tourism sector has been gaining importance for localities due to its contribution to the production chain. As a result of the growth in tourism in the state of Ceará, there has been a need to improve the city's accessibility, and the implementation of the aviation HUB plays an important role. This study aims to determine whether implementing the HUB influences tourism development in Ceará. The methodology adopted was qualitative, using semi-structured interviews with the managers of two organizations that play important roles in the tourism sector in the city of Fortaleza. The results show that the airport is essential for the growth of a destination and the HUB provides not only an increase in tourist demand with the possibility of conquering new international destinations but also contributes to an increase in tourist flows, allowing the commerce and services sector to increase demand. Due to the positive results, managers are eager to further develop Ceará as a tourist destination, in conjunction with satisfaction from the HUB.

DOI: 10.4018/979-8-3693-7021-6.ch003

INTRODUCTION

With a great diversity of climates, reliefs, landscapes, paradisiacal locations, and diverse cultures, Brazil represents a strong potential for the tourism business. Data revealed by Ministério do Turismo (2018) confirm that demand for national destinations has been intense in recent years. The scenario shows that the tourism segment presents a variety of business options, such as travel agencies, tour guides, transportation for tourists, travel souvenirs and food focused on typical Brazilian foods to attract the attention of tourists who want to know more about local gastronomy. The business that comes from tourism directly and indirectly covers other sectors. The interrelationship of the various activities forms a complex business network. Latest data from Ministério do Turismo (2020) point out that the number of non-resident tourists entering Brazil was close to 6.35 million, with the majority coming from South America (56.6%), Europe (24.1%), and North America (11.8%). Air travel is the most frequent way of getting to the country (67.5%). Most visitors to Brazil come for leisure (54.3%), followed by visits to relatives and friends (25.1%), and then for business (15.4%).

However, the tourism production chain is a crucial component of the global economy, exerting an effect on economic activities such as transportation, car rental, hotels, food, entertainment, interpretation of tourist information, tour guides, foreign exchange, and the consumption of products and services. There are countless activities involved in the growth of the tourism sector (Rios et al., 2021; SETUR, 2017). The domestic tourism market in Brazil plays a crucial role and is the basis of the market. However, there are opportunities to increase the flow of foreign tourists influenced by factors such as income, prices, and exchange rates (Rabahy, 2020).

In this context, Brazil has been growing stronger as a tourist destination, and the state of Ceará has seen an evolution in the tourism sector in recent years, especially in international tourism. Tourism in Brazil has increased economic activity through jobs and revenue in various sectors. Data from the Department of Tourism indicates that the demand for Ceará's destinations via Fortaleza increased by 20.56% between 2010 and 2016, with the capital concentrating the largest tourist flow (Santos & Costa, 2022; SETUR, 2017). According to Governo do Estado do Ceará (2017), three million tourists visit Ceará every year. One of the criteria that favor visits is nature tourism. This considerable increase in recent years has favored job creation and the population's income level. In 2016, the tourist flow grew by 4.5% per year, and the share of revenue generated by tourism in the GDP (Gross Domestic Product) increased from 9.4% to 11.7% (SETUR, 2017). The tourism industry is central to Ceará. In Fortaleza, tourist activities are spread across the coastal zone and appropriate space and economic resources, and the city's competitiveness is strengthened by its strong infrastructure, accessibility, and local economy (Dias & Coriolano, 2022; Martinz et al., 2022).

To support this increase in tourist activities in Ceará, there was a need to expand the city's international airport and establish a KLM/Air France/GOL HUB to boost tourism, a crucial economic activity for Fortaleza (Gonçalves et al., 2021).

Considering the current reality of tourism in Ceará, the aim was to understand the link between the current tourist flow and the implementation of the aviation HUB formed by the partnership between the airlines Air France/KLM/GOL in Fortaleza. The analysis of the implementation of the aviation HUB focuses on the following question that guides this research: How has implementing the aviation HUB in Fortaleza influenced tourism development in Ceará? The general objective of the study is to determine whether the implementation of the HUB influences the development of tourism in Ceará, causing changes in tourist demand for the destination.

This study is justified by the contribution that the tourism sector makes to the market and other services. Research now has a more strategic focus, to direct companies toward planning their customers. It is understood that with this new scenario of implementing the aviation HUB, it is important for the market to be aware of the changes that will be necessary for innovation in tourism in Ceará.

THEORETICAL FRAMEWORK

Tourist Destination

The environment in which the relationship between the consumer-tourist and the tourist product takes place can be called a tourist destination. In recent years, Brazilian tourist destinations have been changing in line with market changes with the help of the national tourist trade and institutions that qualify and develop the sector, where image is one of the main factors in the sales of tourist destinations in Brazil (Ministério do Turismo, 2015).

However, a tourist destination should be understood as a complex socio-geographic system with established boundaries, encompassing a specific territory or region that attracts visitors, which requires interpretation, planning, and management that considers individual elements and their interactions (Dudnyk et al., 2023; Kh et al., 2021; Timón, 2023). These include attractions, infrastructure, and services that form the basis of tourist activities (Dudnyk et al., 2023; Esipova & Gokova, 2020; Page & Connell, 2020). In this approach it is possible to treat the tourist site as an organization that aims to meet the needs of customers (tourists), the destination is also considered a specific type of tourism product because it has an accumulation of tourism products that are negotiated in a particular place (Dias & Cassar, 2004).

The image of a tourist destination plays a key role in attracting visitors and influencing their behavior before, during, and after their visit (Castro et al., 2019). Therefore, image is of paramount importance for a person's behavior about tourism products and destinations, where the impulse in the face of this image can cause different opinions. The tourist destination connects demand, transportation, supply, and tourism marketing in an appropriate and fundamental structure for the system since the image and the destination excite tourists. The destination is the location of the tourist flow, as it is exactly where the services to serve tourists are located (Cooper et al., 2007). Thus, understanding and managing image is an element in differentiating offers in a competitive market. In other words, it makes it possible to solve problems in the management of tourist destinations and maintain a competitive advantage (Castro et al., 2019; Chagas, 2009).

Therefore, understanding that tourism is an activity with a fragmented structure and therefore requires the involvement of various factors, a tourist destination's competitive advantages may depend on its ability to operationalize an integrated and complex product in a way that provides satisfactory tourist experiences for its consumers (Figure 1).

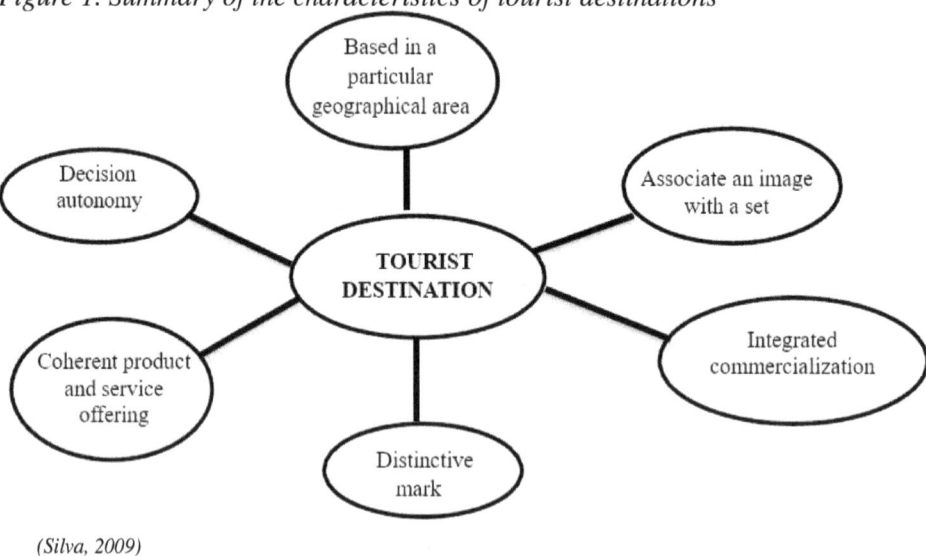

Figure 1. Summary of the characteristics of tourist destinations

(Silva, 2009)

A destination's image is seen by the tourism market and its consumers (tourists) because of its various internal and external factors, so the image can be perceived by tourists in different ways and in different situations. The image of tourist destinations plays a major role in analyzing the quality of services and products during the trip.

Studies on the image of destinations are increasingly in trend, whether in terms of their concepts, measurement, or formation and especially the process of image formation, given that it is one of the stimuli for tourists to travel (Chagas et al., 2016).

Since a destination's competitive advantages depend heavily on the tourist experience and the final product, the ability to please consumers and partnerships between public and private organizations, even if directly or indirectly related to the sector's service provision, take on a decisive position (Silva, 2009). The main elements of competitiveness include the natural environment, tourism policy, quality of service and prices (Tleuberdinova et al., 2022). Successful destination competitiveness requires cooperation between governments, the private sector, local communities, and tourists (Dyikanov & Maksüdünov, 2024).

Destinations in different parts of the world are competing hard to attract tourists and this increases the need to know the process of forming an image that suits their target audience. The construction of a destination's image is the key to tourism development. When a destination monitors the formation of its image, it becomes more attractive and gains a competitive edge in the global market (Chagas, 2008). By analyzing the topic of tourist flows in Ceará, it is possible to see through data and tables the evolution of the state as a tourist destination.

Tourist Flows in Ceará

Tourist flows refer to the movement of people for tourism purposes, both internationally and nationally (Raun et al., 2020). Understanding flows is important for tourism development and provides insights into the economic impact of tourism (Belgibayeva et al., 2020). Tourist flows are closely linked to transportation infrastructure, especially air travel (Gonçalves et al., 2021).

Located in the northeastern region of Brazil, the state of Ceará has three macroecosystems characterized by the coast, the mountains and the hinterland, guaranteeing diversity and differentiation for tourism products. With a strategic geographical location, "six and a half hours by flight from the main destinations in the northern hemisphere and an average of five hours from the main capitals of South America, Ceará is the gateway to the Northeast for international tourism" (SETUR, 2017). But it wasn't just the physical and geographical characteristics that influenced the vision of opening Ceará to tourism.

Tourism in Ceará has led to significant territorial transformations and economic development, resulting in numerous physical and territorial changes, requiring proper planning and management (Dias & Coriolano, 2022; Diógenes et al., 2020). The capital of the state of Ceará, Fortaleza, has become touristified and spectacularized, with tourist activities spreading along the coastal zone, being crucial for economic activity, undergoing significant investment in infrastructure and air transport (Dias

& Coriolano, 2022; Gonçalves et al., 2021). Ceará's coastal areas have undergone socio-spatial transformations, with planning focused on modern maritime practices such as tourism and second-home ownership (Castro & Pereira, 2019).

The increase in the number of people traveling has meant that tourist flows and revenues have grown more and more, making the tourism sector of paramount importance for the state's strategies. Ceará is an important national and international tourist destination. According to the Governo do Estado do Ceará (2024), this was the state in the North and Northeast regions that attracted the most international tourists in May 2024. By May, the international flow had increased by 60.34% compared to the same period last year.

Tourism plays a significant role in Ceará's economy, especially in the coastal regions, where the state's main tourist destinations are Fortaleza, Aracati, Jijoca de Jericoacoara and Nova Olinda (Fernandes et al., 2020). The city of Fortaleza is the main entry point for tourists visiting the state and ranks 4th in overall tourism competitiveness among Brazilian destinations, with strengths in access, tourist infrastructure and the local economy (Diógenes et al., 2020; Martinz et al., 2022).

Data from Ministério do Turismo (2018) says that the increase in the number of towns on Ceará's tourism map has grown by 25% compared to the previous map and reinforces the desire of managers to work with tourism to provide jobs and income. According to the ministry, 32 municipalities are in categories A, B, and C, which are those that concentrate the flow of domestic and international tourists. For example, Caucaia, Fortaleza, Jijoca de Jericoacoara and Sobral. The other 42 municipalities fall into categories D and E. These destinations have a national and international tourist flow and some play an important role in the regional tourist flow and need support to create jobs and accommodation establishments.

Characterization of an Airport as a HUB

Many people see the relationship between transportation and tourism, after all, anyone who has ever gone on vacation or business realizes that to get to their destination they must use a means of transport: car, plane, bus, ship, train, and others. Thus, in the tourism supply chain, transportation is identified as a key component, in addition to accommodation, food and beverage services, travel agencies, and tourist attractions (Rios et al., 2021). In this case, based on the facts, tourism does not exist without transportation. As a way of defining the activity of transport in the case of tourism, it can be analyzed as the activity that connects the origin of a tourist trip to a particular destination (Palhares, 2002).

Tourism and transportation have an extremely important relationship, as they are responsible for transporting people to their destinations. The efficiency of transportation systems helps tourist destinations advance in their development.

HUBs, central nodes in various transportation and innovation networks, can be seen as a demonstration of this relationship, as they facilitate the movement of people (Csizmadia, 2020; Silva et al., 2015). A transport hub system denotes a network of Transport Interchange Hubs (TIHs) designed to improve urban mobility and efficiency by facilitating the optimization of passenger flow, minimizing travel times, and increasing service quality. These hubs can be strategically located using mathematical models to determine optimal placements based on passenger traffic and route efficiency (Moskvichev & Leonova, 2021). Governo of Brasil (2024) mentions that tourists are traveling more and more by plane, with a greater flow of passengers at airports, making air transport increasingly significant for Brazilian tourism. In May 2024 alone, 8.2 million passengers passed through Brazil's five main airports.

In the same way that tourism and transport are related, air transport and airports are related, because air transport needs airports. To Silva et al. (2015, p. 305), "The airport is the place where people embark, disembark or connect for the most varied reasons and interests, whether for business, tourism or any other reason, which is fundamental to the economic development of regions and vice versa."

With the growth of air transport, the concept of the airport has expanded, becoming more than just a means of moving cargo and people, but also a commercial center for industrial and distribution facilities, with offices, leisure areas, and parking lots. Airports are increasingly becoming the new frontiers of globalization in the world, and it is through them that people from different places, immigrants, and tourists arrive (Vidrago, 2015).

The new change in the air transport market has brought new performance to the sector. Before the release of air transport, airlines used the Point-to-Point system model (direct flight system where flights operate directly between specific destinations without the need for intermediate stops) and after the release, airlines created new strategies due to the increased competitiveness between airlines, this system is called HUB-AND-SPOKE which is a strategic network in the aviation industry that involves centralizing air traffic through a main hub airport, connecting several spokes to efficiently manage flight schedules and passenger traffic. This system allows for a diversified market by increasing the number of routes on offer and the quantities of flights, giving people travel advantages by connecting flights through central hubs before reaching their final destination. (Palhares, 2002; Kowalska-Napora, 2018; Sun et al., 2021; Zgodavová et al., 2018).

Unlike other modes of transportation, air travel uses natural routes, the air, with more flexible routes and despite the existence of airways, flexibility is often restricted or encouraged due to regulations in the sector. A good example of this situation was the deregulation of North American air transport, which began in 1978. North American airlines began to operate domestic routes whenever they wanted and necessary and without the need for prior authorization from the granting authority, so their operations began to concentrate on one or a few strategic airports, and the number of locations served was expanded by the HUB-AND-SPOKE system in Figure 2 (Palhares, 2002).

Figure 2. Types of transport networks: linear, HUB-AND-SPOKE and grid

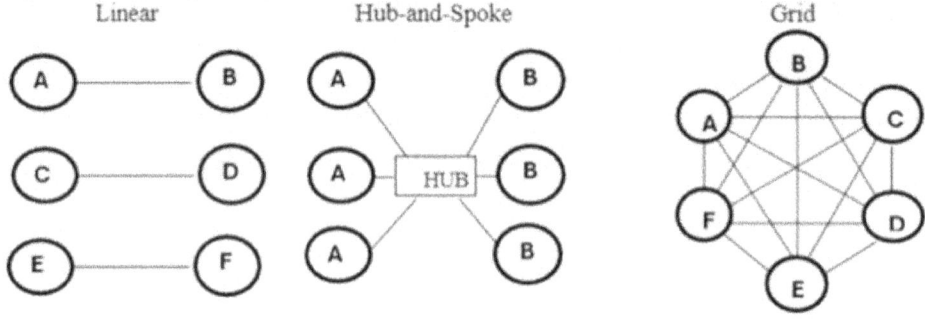

(Palhares, 2002)

Figure 2 shows six locations served by linear, HUB-AND-SPOKE and grid networks. For these locations to be interconnected, 15 routes would be needed, as shown in Figure 2 for the grid network. In the HUB-AND-SPOKE system, the 15 links can be interconnected in just six routes, since they are concentrated in a single airport that acts as a HUB, but it is possible to find errors in this type of centralized network, such as an increase in the duration of the total journey, delays due to the large movement of aircraft at the HUB airport. However, there is a gain for the airlines in terms of operating costs from such a system, and it is more advantageous for the passenger to be able to pay lower fares (Palhares, 2002).

The concept of airport hubs is crucial for airlines, offering benefits in passenger movement, requiring careful consideration of demand, geographical location and available infrastructure (Moura et al., 2021). This type of system allows for more economical routes, generating value and creating competitive advantages (Lima et al., 2019). Airports that serve as hubs play an important role in the air transport industry, connecting passengers, cargo and airlines globally (Jiang & Hao, 2024). The expansion of airport infrastructure, particularly in the aviation sector, is closely linked to the growth of tourism (Gonçalves et al., 2021).

There are a few examples of airports that use HUBs to handle passengers: Atlanta (USA) HUB of the alliance between Delta Airlines and Air France, which serves the east coast of the United States with connections to Europe, Latin America and Asia. Chicago (USA) HUB of United Airlines and American Airlines in alliance with Lufthansa, O'Hare airport serving the Midwestern (USA) market with connections to Asia and Europe. In 2000 "it handled 72,144,244 passengers (id.), making it the second busiest airport in the world in this respect and, in 2001, the first in terms of landings and take-offs". And the Amsterdam (Netherlands) KLM HUB in alliance with Northwest can reach all of Europe, Africa, Asia, the Middle East and North America. Schiphol Airport in 2000 had "a volume of 39,606,925 pax (id.), making it the tenth busiest airport in the world" (Palhaes, 2002, p. 36).

Table 1 shows some definitions of the Hub-and-Spoke system by different authors (Soutelino, 2006) which show that an airport with this system can connect most of its flights to it, and airlines can offer combinations with greater destination options and frequencies, as well as being able to reduce prices.

Table 1. Hub-and-spoke system definitions

Author	Definition
Bania, Bauer & Zlatoper (1998, p.53)	"... the hub-and-spoke system has most flights going to a hub airport from a rim, thus concentrating an airline's activities in a few places. Traveling between two hub airports, the first flight is always to the hub and then from there to the destination."
Berry, Carnall & Spiller (1996, p.1)	In the hub-and-spoke system, passengers change planes at the hub airport on the way to their destination.
Bootsma (1997, p.4)	In the hub-and-spoke system, the network is designed in such a way that routes are concentrated in a few facilities at the connections, called hubs. Destinations up to the hub are called hubs. To maximize possible connections, the airline operating the hub usually draws up timetables within a certain time frame.
Goetz & Sutton (1997)	An airline's largest hub.
Burghouwt & Hakfoort, (2001, p. 311)	The hub-and-spoke system is a combination of point-to-point connections with traffic transfer at a central hub.
Button (1998, p.20)	In the hub-and-spoke system, (...) airlines generally use one or two major airports (...). Flights are planned at banks which allow passengers to continue their journey via connections to more destinations.
Rietveld & Brons (2001)	The hub-and-spoke system enables airlines to supply transportation services with many combinations of origins and destinations with a high number of frequencies and low prices.

Source: Soutelido (2006)

So, the hub-and-spoke system concentrates flights at a few central airports (hubs), where passengers make connections, allowing airlines to offer various combinations of origin and destination with high frequency and lower cost.

Advantages of the HUB System

Airlines that operate with the HUB system have numerous advantages over airlines that use the point-to-point system. They can gain greater bargaining power over their competitors by having services and facilities in the same terminal. They also facilitate efficient passenger handling and economic route operations (Lima et al., 2019). In addition to making passengers disembark and embark on the same aircraft only with a different flight number and if there is competition in the HUB, passengers have lower prices (Siqueira, 2008).

With the HUB, the airline can offer lower prices, making up for those seats that are available to users of the miles program. The dynamics of prices depend on competition and demand. Prices decrease when there is competition in the HUB and increase when there isn't, thus generating more profitability. The airline's bargaining power ends up discouraging competitors from entering the airport where it operates the HUB system (Soutelino, 2006).

According to Soutelino (2006), in addition to the bargaining power compared to other companies that don't operate with the HUB system, there are other advantages it provides, such as a greater number of direct flights, ease of transferring flights, shorter connection times for short-haul flights, the possibility of maximizing the routes with the greatest demand, structuring connecting traffic, a lower rate of lost or damaged baggage and providing the local market with greater options for flights and routes.

In the economy, the advantage of the HUB system is characterized by the creation of new workplaces that require a greater demand for services such as banks, stores, supermarkets, and restrooms. The "hub-and-spoke" system is seen as the right and mature way out of the airline crisis: by concentrating flights in a HUB, the company can offer more flight frequencies to destinations than low-cost airlines. The main reason for concentrating flights at a particular airport is to reduce labor costs, equipment and other additional costs (Soutelino, 2006).

Disadvantages of the HUB System

Despite the advantages, the HUB system also has disadvantages for both parties, which the author Siqueira (2008), says that the airlines face the following problems: Delays in the chain; congestion in the airport infrastructure; extra costs with "handling" (an English name that encompasses all the services that provide support for aircraft, passengers, baggage, cargo and mail) and fuel.

The movement of several aircraft together puts a strain on airport infrastructure and its processes for handling passengers, cargo, baggage and aircraft services. Delayed slots or waves can lead to a loss of connection in the HUB-and-Spoke system or at other Spoke airports (Siqueira, 2008).

In large hubs, such as Chicago: Atlanta, London: Los Angeles, and Frankfurt, there is a high risk of collisions between aircraft in their transit area (aircraft parking area) due to the heavy movement of aircraft and support vehicles. The movement of numerous aircraft together causes delays in unloading baggage, aircraft landing in areas far from the "fingers" (boarding bridges), and congestion in customs, air traffic, and immigration areas (Soutelino, 2006).

The disadvantages for passengers are the length of the trip and the lack of comfort it brings. When choosing a HUB and Spoke system, the passenger has a longer trip than a point-to-point system, because there is a wait at the HUB airport for the flight to depart to the destination. In addition to the delay in reaching the passenger's destination, the passenger runs the risk of missing the connection at the HUB if the flight to the HUB is delayed (Soutelino, 2006).

METHODOLOGY

To achieve the objectives of this research, a qualitative approach was conducted involving strategic market players. Semi-structured interviews were conducted with two managers who play important roles in the tourism sector of the city of Fortaleza. The main criterion for choosing them was the characterization of the reality under study, that is, the aviation hub/tourism sector binomial, which will be composed of the Ceará Tourism Department (SETUR) and a hotel chain in Fortaleza. Initially, the intention was to apply the research to a group of entities in the tourism sector of the city of Fortaleza. However, since some of the chosen entities were not available, the research was only applied to two entities.

This study presents methodological limitations that may affect the generalizability of its findings. A primary limitation is the small sample size, comprising only two tourism sector managers from Fortaleza. While these managers play crucial roles, the limited sample diminishes data representativeness and may not reflect the diverse experiences of other sector stakeholders. Bryman (2016) argues that small qualitative samples can undermine external validity by failing to capture the complexity of social dynamics. Furthermore, selection bias is a concern, as interviewee selection was based on availability rather than systematic criteria that would provide a comprehensive sector overview. As noted by Patton (2014) and Creswell and Creswell (2017) a limited interviewee pool can introduce biases, particularly when participants have vested interests in the study's subject. In the case of public managers or large corporations, there is a possibility that their responses could be shaped by institutional interests aimed at fostering a favorable perception of the aviation hub's influence on tourism.

The questionnaire was formulated comprehensively to allow the interviewee to express and verbalize their opinions and reflections on the subject. Regarding the number of questions, the aim was to adapt the length to obtain the information necessary to conduct the study and at the same time not to become tiresome for the interviewees.

Given the research problem, the first five questions were the same for all participants, with the remaining questions being asked according to the interviewee's area of expertise. The interviews, which lasted approximately 1 hour/1 hour and 30 minutes, were audio-recorded, with prior authorization, and transcribed in full. To develop the reading of the responses and work on the meaning of the statements, a purposeful analysis of the content of the interviews was carried out (Bardin, 2016).

RESULTS

In this chapter, the results were analyzed considering three subthemes: "Impact of the HUB on tourist demand", "Impact on the local economy" and "Impact of the HUB on the attraction of the tourist destination". The interview, composed of eight general and specific questions, was applied to the managers of two entities that represent relevant roles in the city's tourism sector, namely, the Ceará State Tourism Secretariat (SETUR), here referred to as interviewee 1 (E1), and a hotel chain in Fortaleza, referred to as interviewee 2 (E2).

Impact of the HUB on Tourist Demand

In line with existing literature that indicates that transportation is identified as a key component in the development of a tourist destination (Rios et al., 2021), the interviewees' discourse reveals that the airport is seen as a factor of great relevance for the evolution of a tourist destination, since its absence would impede the development of tourism-related activities. The interviewees mention that the accessibility provided by the airport is very important for a destination. For example, interviewee 2 said that:

> *"Well, an airport is essential for the growth of a destination due to ease of access, especially when it comes to a capital city, where we expect many tourists from abroad, the airport is of fundamental importance."*

Interviewee 2 also confirms the importance of the airport with statements such as: *"Our biggest demand for tourists in Ceará today has already surpassed that, now in 2018, we have reached 3.6 million tourists, of which 342 thousand are international tourists, right? So, all of this is thanks to our Fortaleza Airport... So, the airport, a destination without airports, it doesn't work... Fraport is even in the process of expanding, right? When you go to the airport, you can clearly see the renovation that is taking place. We are going from 6 million to 9 million and there is a third phase of expansion that will go up to 12 million passengers per year, right? So, all of this contributes to a consolidated tourist destination."*

When asked about the influence of the implementation of the HUB at Fortaleza airport on the growth in tourist demand for the Ceará destination, the speech was positive, since the interviewees mentioned the qualities of the HUB system and how this system has a significant increase in the state's tourist demand due to the connectivity that the HUB impacts on the airport, with a greater number of direct flights, ease of flight transfers, shorter connection times for short-distance flights and others (Soutelino, 2006). Interviewee 2 mentions *"For Fortaleza airport...the HUB is a turning point; we will have a number before and after the arrival of the HUB in Fortaleza"*. Both mention that they believe there will be great growth in business tourism, as well as leisure tourism, both national and international. For example, when they mention that:

"According to our data here, in the first year of... it was just in May, right, of the implementation of the HUB, we grew... only in international flow, 102.83%, that is, while Brazil is growing 3.4% per year, world tourism is growing 3% per year and Ceará is growing 102.83% per year, this is very significant, this is thanks to the HUB, right, because we went from four international destinations to twelve international destinations today, so all of this influences, in addition to the international issue, we have the national issue, we grew 16.68%" (E1).

"The airport is already a great opportunity for the development of the state, to have greater development and with the arrival of the HUB we open doors to practically the entire world, right, there is the ease of direct flights, including... Also, of connecting flights" (E2).

The hotel chain (E2) was asked about hotel occupancy, and whether it was possible to verify any relationship between the volume of passengers at the HUB in Fortaleza and other tourist cities. Interviewee 2 mentioned that there had not yet been a major impact on its occupancy, because "regarding hotel occupancy, we have not yet had a major impact. With the HUB our occupancy is still the same as before the HUB, but we know that without the HUB it would certainly be lower". According to the interviewee, "the information we receive is that the number of passengers arriving in Fortaleza is higher than in the past, before the HUB".

Impact on the Local Economy

The interviewees believe in the relevance of the strategic product HUB for the tourism sector, since tourism contributes to the development of other sectors of the economy and involves the entire production chain of the state. The phenomena caused in this sector interfere with other sectors of the economy and represent an essential milestone for the economy of countries, since it involves several services to its consumers (tourists), thus forming the production chain of tourism, that is, everything that must be presented to serve tourists in a pleasant manner (Borges, 2009). The interviewees mention that:

"The HUB... it works as if it were a, let's suppose, for example, a spoke on a bicycle, right, you have the central axis where the airport would be and the spokes are the connections, right, so it connects, it connects, Ceará to Brazil and to the world, right" (E1).

"When this tourist arrives here, this demand that grew in the first year there is already... 20%, almost 21%, so we can already see that what happened? With this, there is a demand in the hotel industry, because these tourists need to stay... lodged in the hotel sector, there is also a growing demand in the food sector, restaurants, beach huts, fast food, etc... right, travel agencies, because at the travel agency, they can buy tourist packages... tours, in addition, the hotel itself, they can book through the agencies, so there is also a great demand, this expansion of travel agencies, the tourist guide, everyone wins, an entire production chain that benefits from this increase in this tourist demand, right, this tourist demand in the first year, we calculated, generated R$702.00 million within the state's economy, that is, it is quite representative, right, and only in the first year" (E1).

"The HUB logically increases and fosters tourism, both for leisure and business, and tourism has a direct impact on all sectors of our production chain. If you think that a tourist arriving here will use a means of transportation, let's say a taxi driver, stay at a hotel, try our cuisine, and visit our stores, then just in these four areas that I mentioned, it is already reaching many our production chain" (E2).

In the analysis of the sectors that would benefit most from the implementation of the HUB at Fortaleza airport, the managers' speech mentioned which sectors they believed would have the greatest impact from this new system. However, Soutelino (2006), in the economy, the advantage of the HUB system is characterized as the creation of new work points that require a greater demand for services such as banks, stores, supermarkets and restrooms. The HUB system is indicated as the right and mature way to overcome the crisis in airlines. Interviewee 2 mentions that:

"Practically the entire economy is impacted, right? Because from the moment that, let's say, a tourist takes a taxi, then that taxi driver, if he earns more, he will spend more in his neighborhood, he will consume more, he will buy more

clothes, he will have more leisure time with his family, so what that taxi driver earned from the tourist is impacted in his neighborhood".

Furthermore, both interviewees mention that:

"It will be the service sector. Tourism is part of the state's service sector. Today, the state of Ceará really focuses on service, right? An average of 70%, 72% of our GDP, which is all the wealth that the state produces, comes from the service sector. So, the service sector will be one of the sectors that will benefit the most from this, from the HUB. In addition to service, of course, there will be commerce, right? commerce and service, because when tourists arrive, they... make purchases, they go to the mall, they buy crafts, they buy souvenirs, they want to take a souvenir home for their family. So, these are the sectors that will really benefit the most: it will be this tourism chain, right? As I said, between accommodation, food, tours, entertainment, car rentals, travel agencies, these factors that are more on the front line are the ones that will be impacted the most... immediately, right?" (E1).

"Tourists affect the entire production chain of a city, right? So, I think the impact is general. Obviously, there are those who are most impacted. A survey was conducted last year... As president of the ABIH partnership with UNIFOR and FECOMÉRCIO, we showed the impact, in this case, it was on business tourism, right? This impact is greater, in the case of business tourists, it is greater on the hotel industry, so 38% of what they leave in the city goes to the hotel industry, 17% goes to commerce, 17% goes to bars and restaurants, and the rest is diluted in other sectors of the city" (E2).

Regarding the role of the state's development attributed to the implementation of the HUB, the managers clearly stated that this implementation has a positive impact on the sectors and that everyone benefits, especially the state, since its development is a consequence of the evolution of its sectors with the arrival of more tourists. The interviewees revealed that:

"Hotels, agencies, tour guides, right, these people on the front line, right, car rental companies and, in addition, the commercial sectors, because the tourist goes to the mall, he's going to buy handicrafts, he's going to buy souvenirs, so all of this, right, all of this he ends up... leaving his expenses here and everyone benefits from this, definitely" (E1).

"Of course... I'm sure that the arrival of the HUB will impact all sectors of our economy, as I said, tourists have an impact and what the HUB will do is bring more tourists, so logically the impact will be general for all sectors of the economy, not just commerce, but also services, right? As I said, let's say 38% of what tourists leave in the city goes to the hotel industry, 34% goes to commerce, bars and restaurants, so if you add the 38 to 34, it's already a very big impact" (E2).

However, for the hotel chain manager (E2), "The HUB is still in a maturation period, let's say that the trend is to grow every day. In my opinion, there is no single reason why the HUB does not bring growth to our city, to our occupancy, to our hotel industry, to our tourism and to our economy in general". The responses reveal that the HUB's contribution is a relevant factor for the growth in demand for the tourist destination when it mentions that:

"We haven't seen this impact on the hotel industry yet, firstly because we know that there is a huge demand for beach hotels, this bigger impact, the HUB started in May, so we have already seen a huge growth in international tourism in the second half of the year, this international tourism is largely due to our winds, due to kite flying, so certainly the hotel occupancy in the inns and hotels on the beaches where the wind is better, where there is already a history like Cumbuco, Flexeiras, Jericoacoara and the Guajirú Islands where there is a huge demand for kite flying, I am absolutely certain that the increase in demand was much greater. There is also the HUB, which also brings many connecting passengers, so there is a very large movement of disembarkations at the airport also coming from people who are going to make a connection, so, in my opinion as a hotelier and not as ABIH, if there were no HUB, we would have had a much lower occupancy rate during this period of the year, from February onwards, than we have had, which unfortunately is a little lower than last year, but if it were not for the HUB it would be worse, that is my opinion."

Impact of the HUB on the Attraction of the Tourist Destination

Regarding the question about what needs to be done so that Fortaleza is not just a connection point and can attract international and national visitors, even in a competitive reality like today's, the manager of the Tourism Department (E1) stated that the State of Ceará has been consolidating itself as a tourist destination when he said that "Today the state of Ceará can be said to be consolidated in terms of tourism, why? Because in 2007 we planned to structure the city. Interviewee 1 also states that:

"Not only Fortaleza, but the entire state, so that we could receive these tourists, because in 2007 we were already receiving around 2.3 million tourists, but we realized that the state was not prepared, so we needed to build infrastructure precisely for this issue of competitiveness, so that we could keep the tourists within our state and move away from that niche of sun and beach.
We wanted to move away from that issue, tourists come to Ceará looking only for sun and beach, right, tourists come only to visit relatives and friends, are they good tourists? It's great, excellent, spectacular, but to be a destination today, there's a lot of talk about the issue of innovation and... tourism is... the issue of

intelligence, right, so, that's what, precisely this technological issue, so, we need to be an intelligent destination and for that we invested a lot in technological tools, for example, today we have the DISCOVER CEARÁ app, where the tourist arrives and wants, for example, I want to know where to buy handicrafts, he goes there on this app. Today, young people are very aware of... smartphones, technology, the internet, so we also had to adapt. Today, you either innovate or you'll be left behind. Furthermore, the issue of Ceará's marketing campaign is present at all national and international tourism fairs, right? And precisely to promote. In addition, we have promotions broadcast on radio, television, billboards, etc. We have campaigns carried out in shopping malls, in cinemas, in-flight magazines, whatever you want. Thousands of people travel on one of those flights there, on one of those planes, every day, every week, every month. So, all of this makes Ceará position itself as a tourist destination, it's seen, it's... it's put in the spotlight and, logically, people will certainly have a desire or a desire to come and visit us, and certainly, in addition to getting to know Ceará, they will leave satisfied.

We are also very concerned about this issue of qualification, right? The people of Ceará are already hospitable, entrepreneurial people, but they also need to have a bit of that tact to know how to welcome people well, you know? This is a big concern, we spend a lot on this issue too, we invest a lot in this issue of professional qualification, both for the entrepreneur and for the front-line professional, who is his employee."

Ministério do Turismo (2015) stated that he has been adapting Brazilian tourist destinations to market changes with the help of the national tourism trade and institutions that qualify and develop the sector. Image is one of the main factors for sales of tourist destinations in Brazil, and this is what is happening with Ceará. It has been adapting to changes and creating plans.

When asked about the measures taken to promote Ceará as a tourist destination by the Secretary of Tourism (E1), interviewee 1 mentioned the advances and plans that have been made in the state to gain more power as a tourist destination because "We work very hard on this issue of fairs, because these are the fairs where all the states of Brazil are concentrated." He also revealed that:

"We have this space here, which is the Ceará events center, where today an average of 24% of our tourist flow comes to Ceará motivated by business and event tourism, right? It was another facility concerned with diversifying these tourist segments, not just focusing on sun and beach. It was developed precisely for that, to attract large events, large national and international fairs, and today we have a facility that is considered, in terms of modernity, it is number

1 in South America and in terms of size it is the second largest facility in South America too, right? We only lose to Anhembi in São Paulo.

Promotions, as I said, include radio, television, cinema, billboards, and shopping malls. We also have this issue of participating in fairs, this direct contact with operators and agencies. We develop itineraries. We now have the Cliffs itinerary, which is a very rich itinerary. It is already on the shelves and being sold by several operators. There is also the coffee itinerary in the Guaramiranga region. We also have the Pindoretama itinerary. In addition, we have a great vocation for religious tourism. We have five major destinations in Ceará. Juazeiro do Norte, Padre Cícero, which has an average of 2.5 million visitors per year. Canindé, São Francisco, has an average of 2.0 million visitors per year in that region. All of this is very strong. Quixadá, São Benedito, Barbalha, the festival of Saint Anthony, is very popular throughout Brazil. All of these are potentials and vocations that the state explores and invests in so that we can attract these tourists. This segmentation of sports and adventure tourism is very strong, so we also have a geopark there in the Cariri region, in addition to religious tourism, the geopark is a spectacle, which is worth visiting for tourists, especially international tourists, who really like this thing of sports and adventure tourism, especially nature tourism, so it is very strong, so we have a wealth that needs to be explored, Ceará is already explored, but there are even more opportunities for us to explore, even more".

DISCUSSION AND CONCLUSION

This research work started from the question of whether implementing the aviation hub in Fortaleza represents a factor of influence in the development of tourism in Ceará. To obtain answers to this research, interviews were conducted with entities located in the city of Fortaleza, namely the Ceará State Tourism Secretariat (SETUR) and the Sonata Hotel.

Based on the reflection on the data obtained and presented in the analysis of the results, it was possible to understand the vision of these entities regarding the implementation of the HUB system at the Fortaleza-CE Airport and the impact it is having on their sectors in its first year of implementation and its importance for tourism.

The general objective of the study was to analyze whether the implementation of the HUB has an influence on the development of tourism and whether it has caused changes in the tourist demand for the destination. The specific objectives were: i) To identify the role of the airport in the context of the tourist destination; ii) To understand the relationship between the implementation of the HUB and the tourist flows in Ceará; iii) To verify whether there has been an increase in the demand for the services of other actors in the tourism sector. The results were collected through an interview, which made it possible to identify the perception of these agents regarding the HUB at Fortaleza Airport, since they are present in the tourism sector daily, they were able to mention the dimension of this new factor more clearly. The interviews were separated and analyzed one by one, identifying the two points of view of the general and specific questions.

Starting with the first question of the interview in which the entities SETUR and Hotel Sonata were asked about the contribution of airports in the development of a tourist destination, we can analyze the first specific objective of the research. The results show that the airport has an essential contribution to the development of a destination due to its accessibility and one of the greatest demands of tourists is through it, a destination with an airport has greater competitive advantages due to the ease with which people can get there.

The second question of the interview in which the entities answered about the influence of the HUB at Fortaleza Airport on the growth of tourist demand for the destination Ceará, is understood as the second objective of the research. The results were clear, showing growth. For example, in its first year alone, tourist flow grew 102% per year, and with the HUB, more international destinations were conquered. Before the HUB, there were four destinations, and today there are twelve destinations. Data from INFRAERO states that many large airports were negative, while Fortaleza had national and international growth of 20.34%. So, these data and these results show that the HUB is indeed a unique factor for the airport and also for the state, making Ceará connected to the world. The third and fourth questions of the interview allow us to verify whether there was an increase in demand for services from other players in the tourism sector, which refers to the third objective of the research. With the results of these questions in the interview script, it was possible to see that the points of view are very similar regarding the connection that the tourism sector has with the entire production chain of a state, knowing that tourists need all sectors to arrive and move around a destination. Data from a survey reported in the interview mentions that 38% of what a business tourist leaves in the city goes to the hotel industry, 17% to bars, restaurants, and shops, and the rest to other sectors. And the IBGE states that 52 sectors will be positively impacted, with gains in employment and income. So, with the arrival of more tourists, all sectors are impacted, large companies, and small companies, all of them benefit from the increase in tourist flow. However, it was possible to identify, with the responses of the entities, that trade and services have a greater impact on the evolution of tourism.

With the results of the interviews with SETUR and HOTEL SONATA, it was possible to analyze and confirm that the implementation of the HUB in its first year of implementation has already shown excellent results, which indicate great advances and promising development for the sectors of the economy. And consequently, with the advances in the sectors, the state can have continuous evolution.

The results also showed that the state of Ceará has plans and concerns to ensure that the state is not only seen as a place for sun and beach but also as a smart destination rich in technology. The state is concerned with its promotion, technological advances, and qualifications.

It was concluded that an airport with a HUB system gives the destination a way to connect with other countries, giving the state easier access. And the first year is nothing compared to what an airport with a HUB system can bring to a tourist destination.

More broadly, the implications of the findings of this research contribute to other regions considering the implementation of a HUB system as a strategy for tourism development of the destination as well as for economic development. As can be seen from the results, the impacts of the HUB system extend to other sectors beyond tourism, since the increase in the number of people visiting the destination will imply an increase in spending on services and products, which will contribute to boosting the economy of the region.

REFERENCES

Bardin, L. (2016). *Análise de conteúdo*. Edições.

Belgibayeva, Z. Z., Nadyrov, S. M., Zhanguttina, G. O., Belgibayev, A. K., & Belgibayev, A. A. (2020). Tourist flows of kazakhstan: Statistics, geography, trends. *Научный Журнал. Вестник НАН РК*, (6), 232–239.

Borges, C. (2009). *Globalização e turismo: Análise de seus impactos no Estado do Ceará na década 1992/2002*. Gráfica e Editora Nacional.

Bryman, A. (2016). *Social Research Methods*. Oxford University Press.

Castro, J., Pérez, J., & Alomoto, L. (2019). Imagen del destino desde la perspectiva del turista. *Turismo e Sociedade*, 26, 45–66. DOI: 10.18601/01207555.n26.02

Chagas, M. M. das. (2008). IMAGEM DE DESTINOS TURÍSTICOS: Uma discussão teórica da literatura especializada. *Turismo: Visão e Ação*, 10(3), 3. Advance online publication. DOI: 10.14210/rtva.v10n3.p435-455

Chagas, M. M. das. (2009). Formação da Imagem de Destinos Turísticos: Uma discussão dos principais modelos internacionais. *Caderno Virtual de Turismo, 9*(1), Article 1. https://www.ivt.coppe.ufrj.br/caderno/article/view/333

Chagas, M. M. D., Marques Júnior, S., & Silva, V. H. D. (2016). *Imagens de destinos turísticos: Conceitos, modelos e casos*. https://memoria.ifrn.edu.br/handle/1044/961

Cooper, C., Fletche, J., Fyall, A., Gilbert, D., & Wanhill, S. (2007). *Turismo: Principios e prática* (3rd ed.). Bookman.

Creswell, J. W., & Creswell, J. D. (2017). *Research Design: Qualitative, Quantitative, and Mixed Methods Approaches*. SAGE Publications.

Csizmadia, N. (2020). Hubs in the Network: Hub Cities. *World Scientific Book Chapters*, 301–307.

da Silva, E. A. M., Sobrinho, F. L. A., & Fortes, J. A. A. S. (2015). A importância geoestratégica do Aeroporto Internacional de Brasília no desenvolvimento do turismo regional. *Caderno Virtual de Turismo*, 15(3), 3. https://www.ivt.coppe.ufrj.br/caderno/article/view/1220

da Silva Castro, T., & Pereira, A. Q. (2019). Produção dos territórios turísticos no Ceará. *Ateliê Geográfico*, 13(2), 51–72. DOI: 10.5216/ag.v13i2.58288 de Moura, I. R., dos Santos Silva, F. J., Costa, L. H. G., Neto, E. D., & Viana, H. R. G. (2021). Airport pavement evaluation systems for maintenance strategies development: A systematic literature review. *International Journal of Pavement Research and Technology*, 14(6), 676–687. DOI: 10.1007/s42947-020-0255-1

Dias, D., & Coriolano, L. N. (2022). A Metrópole Fortaleza-Ce Turistificada. *Caderno de Geografia*, 32(69), 575. DOI: 10.5752/P.2318-2962.2022v32n69p575

Dias, R., & Cassar, M. (2004). *Fundamentos do marketing turístico*. Pearson Universidades.

Diógenes, L. G. G., do Nascimento, A. P., de Oliveira, R. M. A., de Oliveira, G., & da Silva, F. J. A. (2020). *Achados recentes sobre a qualidade da água do rio cocó em um trecho urbano da cidade de Fortaleza–Ceará*. https://repositorio.ufc.br/handle/riufc/59213

Dudnyk, I., Borysiuk, O., & Saichuk, V. (2023). GEOGRAPHICAL INTERPRETATION OF THE TOURIST PROCESS. *Ekonomichna Ta Sotsialna Geografiya*, 42–52. DOI: 10.17721/2413-7154/2023.89.42-52

Dyikanov, K., & Maksüdünov, A. (2024). Bibliometric Exploration of Tourism Destination Competitiveness Studies: A Comprehensive Overview. [JAVStudies]. *Journal of Academic Value Studies*, 10(1), 1. Advance online publication. DOI: 10.29228/javs.73403

Esipova, S. A., & Gokova, O. V. (2020). Marketing tools as a way to promote tourism destination. *International Conference on Economics, Management and Technologies 2020 (ICEMT 2020)*, 602–605. https://www.atlantis-press.com/proceedings/icemt-20/125940056

Fernandes, L. M. M., Soares, J. R. R., & Coriolano, L. N. M. T. (2020). Governança na política de regionalização do turismo no Estado do Ceará/Brasil. *RPER*, 55(55), 95–108. DOI: 10.59072/rper.vi55.15

Gonçalves, T. E., Lima, F. E. S., & de Araújo, E. F. (2021). Turismo e transporte aéreo: O HUB KLM/AIRFRANCE no aeroporto internacional de Fortaleza. *Geografia Ensino & Pesquisa*, •••, e06–e06. DOI: 10.5902/2236499445343

Governo do Brasil. (2024). *Mais de 8 milhões de passageiros movimentaram os principais aeroportos em maio*. Secretaria de Comunicação Social. https://www.gov.br/secom/pt-br/assuntos/noticias/2024/07/mais-de-8-milhoes-de-passageiros-movimentaram-os-principais-aeroportos-em-maio

Governo do Estado do Ceará. (2017). *Turismo*. Governo do Estado do Ceará. https://www.ceara.gov.br/turismo

Governo do Estado do Ceará. (2024, June 25). *Pelo segundo mês seguido, Ceará foi o estado que mais recebeu turistas internacionais das regiões Norte e Nordeste.* Governo do Estado do Ceará. https://www.ceara.gov.br/2024/06/25/pelo-segundo-mes-seguido-ceara-foi-o-estado-que-mais-recebeu-turistas-internacionais-das-regioes-norte-e-nordeste/

Jiang, X., & Hao, P. (2024). Hub Airport End-Around Taxiway Construction Planning Development: A Review. *Applied Sciences (Basel, Switzerland)*, 14(8), 8. Advance online publication. DOI: 10.3390/app14083500

Kh, N., Komilova, N., Usmonov, M., Safarova, N., Matchanova, A., & Murtazaeva, G. (2021). *Tourist Destination as an Object of Research of Social and Economic Geography.* 2058–2067.

Kowalska-Napora, E. (2018). The hub- and- spoke: Central Airport Project. *AUTOBUSY – Technika, Eksploatacja. Systemy Transportowe*, 19(12), 12. Advance online publication. DOI: 10.24136/atest.2018.557

Lima, L., Iamanaka, L., & Okano, M. (2019). A proposta de valor de um Hub aeroportuário: Uma análise sob a lente teórica dos modelos de negócios. *Research. Social Development*, 9(3), e13932314. Advance online publication. DOI: 10.33448/rsd-v9i3.2314

Martinz, J., Anjos, S., & Sohn, A. (2022). Determinantes da competitividade em destinos turísticos: Um estudo sobre a cidade de Fortaleza. *Revista de Turismo Contemporâneo*, 10(2). Advance online publication. DOI: 10.21680/2357-8211.2022v10n2ID23926

Ministério do Turismo. (2015). *Plano Nacional de Turismo.* https://www.gov.br/turismo/pt-br/assuntos/assuntos-categoria/plano-nacional-de-turismo

Ministério do Turismo. (2018). *Ceará vive novo boom na economia do turismo.* https://www.gov.br/turismo/pt-br/assuntos/noticias/ceara-vive-novo-boom-na-economia-do-turismo

Ministério do Turismo. (2020). *Estudo da Demanda Turística Internacional—Brasil 2019.* Ministério do Turismo. https://www.gov.br/turismo/pt-br/acesso-a-informacao/acoes-e-programas/observatorio/demanda-turistica/demanda-turistica-internacional-1/demanda-turistica-internacional

Page, S. J., & Connell, J. (2020). Tourism and entrepreneurship. In *Tourism* (pp. 262–279). Routledge., https://www.taylorfrancis.com/chapters/edit/10.4324/9781003005520-15/tourism-entrepreneurship-stephen-page-joanne-connell DOI: 10.4324/9781003005520-15

Palhares, G. L. (2002). *Transportes Turísticos*.

Patton, M. Q. (2014). *Qualitative research & evaluation methods: Integrating theory and practice*. Sage publications. https://www.google.com/books?hl=pt-PT&lr=&id=ovAkBQAAQBAJ&oi=fnd&pg=PP1&dq=Patton,+M.+Q.+(2015).+Qualitative+Research+%26+Evaluation+Methods.+SAGE+Publications.&ots=ZSY-6svBH2&sig=DMS3wgSBqe4wAF2g2J2m-lcIoSU

Rabahy, W. A. (2020). Análise e perspectivas do turismo no Brasil. *Revista Brasileira de Pesquisa em Turismo*, 14(1), 1–13. Advance online publication. DOI: 10.7784/rbtur.v14i1.1903

Raun, J., Shoval, N., & Tiru, M. (2020). Gateways for intra-national tourism flows: Measured using two types of tracking technologies. *International Journal of Tourism Cities*, 6(2), 261–278. DOI: 10.1108/IJTC-08-2019-0123

Rios, M. V., Levino, N. de A., & Finger, A. B. (2021). Atividades características da cadeia do turismo: Uma revisão sistemática da literatura. *Revista Turismo em Análise*, 32(2), 2. Advance online publication. DOI: 10.11606/issn.1984-4867.v32i2p344-366

Santos, C., & Costa, D. (2022). Turismo no Brasil: Estratégias e contribuições para economia brasileira. *E-Acadêmica*, 3(3), e5433350. DOI: 10.52076/eacad-v3i3.350

SETUR. (2017). *Evolução recente do turismo no Ceará 2006/16*. https://www.setur.ce.gov.br/wp-content/uploads/sites/59/2016/11/evolucao-turismo-2006-2016-artigo.pdf

Silva, J. S. de S. e. (2009). *A visão holística do turismo e a sua modelação* [doctoralThesis, Universidade de Aveiro]. https://ria.ua.pt/handle/10773/1853

Siqueira, M. C. (2008). *Critérios para preparação de aeroportos para operar como hub*. DOI: 10.26512/2008.06.TCC.1606

Soutelido, A. L. D. (2006). *Desmistificando o sistema Hub-and-Spoke*. https://docplayer.com.br/5502890-Desmistificando-sistema-hub-and-spoke.html

Sun, M., Tian, Y., Zhang, Y., Nadeem, M., & Xu, C. (2021). Environmental Impact and External Costs Associated with Hub-and-Spoke Network in Air Transport. *Sustainability (Basel)*, 13(2), 2. Advance online publication. DOI: 10.3390/su13020465

Timón, D. (2023). El Concepto de destino turístico: Una aproximación geográfico-territorial. *Revista de Estudios Turísticos*, 45–68. DOI: 10.61520/et.1602004.936

Tleuberdinova, A., Kulik, X., Pratt, S., & Kulik, V. B. (2022). Exploring the Resource Potential for the Development of Ecological Tourism in Rural Areas: The Case of Kazakhstan. *Tourism Review International*, 26(4), 321–336. Advance online publication. DOI: 10.3727/154427222X16716277765989

Vidrago, B. (2015). *Aeroportos*. Seminário Aeroespacial II -Técnico Lisboa. https://id .tecnico.ulisboa.pt/cas/login?service=https:%2F%2Ffenix.tecnico.ulisboa.pt%2Fapi %2Fcas-client%2Flogin%2FaHR0cHM6Ly9mZW5peC50ZWNuaWNvLnVs aXNib2EucHQvZG93bmxvYWRGaWxlLzU2MzU2ODQyODcyNzk2MC 9HcnVwbyUyMDA0LnBkZg==

Zgodavová, Z., Rozenberg, R., & Szabo, S. (2018). Analysis of Point-to-Point versus Hub-and-Spoke airline networks. *2018 XIII International Scientific Conference - New Trends in Aviation Development (NTAD)*, 158–163. DOI: 10.1109/NTAD.2018.8551733

ADDITIONAL READING

Albayrak, M. B. K., Özcan, İ. Ç., Can, R., & Dobruszkes, F. (2020). The determinants of air passenger traffic at Turkish airports. *Journal of Air Transport Management*, 86, 101818. DOI: 10.1016/j.jairtraman.2020.101818

Castro, M. I., & Fontoura, M. P. (2021). *Improving the air connectivity of hub airports: an instrument to boost the economic performance of EU countries?* (No. 2021/0200). ISEG-Lisbon School of Economics and Management, REM, Universidade de Lisboa.

Chen, X., Xuan, C., & Qiu, R. (2021). Understanding spatial spillover effects of airports on economic development: New evidence from China's hub airports. *Transportation Research Part A, Policy and Practice*, 143, 48–60. DOI: 10.1016/j.tra.2020.11.013

Chiappa, G., Loriga, S., & Meleddu, M. (2020). Determinants of travellers' expenditures at airports. *European Journal of Tourism Research*, 26, 2605–2605. DOI: 10.54055/ejtr.v26i.1936

Gao, Y. (2021). What is the busiest time at an airport? Clustering US hub airports based on passenger movements. *Journal of Transport Geography*, 90, 102931. DOI: 10.1016/j.jtrangeo.2020.102931

Janko, K., Bloch, J. H., & Lassen, C. (2020). The making of hub airports. In *Mobilising Place Management* (pp. 184–207). Routledge. DOI: 10.4324/9780429199042-11

Papatheodorou, A. (2021). A review of research into air transport and tourism: Launching the Annals of Tourism Research Curated Collection on Air Transport and Tourism. *Annals of Tourism Research*, 87, 103151. DOI: 10.1016/j.annals.2021.103151

Sendo, K. (2021). Increasing Air Traffic Effect on Developing Regional and Megahub Airports in Asia-Pacific Region. *American Journal of Theoretical and Applied Business*, 7(3), 65–71. DOI: 10.11648/j.ajtab.20210703.12

KEY TERMS AND DEFINITIONS

Airport: Location that allows aircraft to arrive and depart to various points around the world.

Ceará: Consists of one of the twenty-six states of Brazil, located in the northeastern part of the country.

Flow Tourism: Movement of tourists between different locations.

Hub-and-Spoke: System where flights are organized so that all journeys of passengers, cargo, or both are channeled through a central airport.

Point-to-Point: Operating system where flights are made directly between airports without needing to go through a hub or connection center.

Tourism Destination: Geographic location (e.g. city, country) that attracts tourists to its offerings (e.g. attractions, services, and experiences).

Tourism: Activity of moving people to other places for e.g. leisure, business.

Chapter 4
Social Media Influencers Marketing in the Tourism Industry:
Legal Insights From Malaysia and China

Junaidah Zeno
https://orcid.org/0000-0003-3923-3162
Universiti Malaysia Sabah, Malaysia

Chunxiao Zhang
https://orcid.org/0009-0005-9483-0156
China University of Political Science and Law, China

ABSTRACT

This chapter explores consumer and advertising-related laws in Malaysia and China that regulate social media influencers (SMIs) marketing in the tourism industry and aims to educate consumers in Malaysia and China on the potential risks of blindly trusting SMIs' posts while empowering them to make informed transactional decisions. It also seeks to inform key stakeholders, such as SMIs, brands, and tourism agencies, about the importance of complying with marketing and consumer laws in the tourism industry. The chapter emphasizes transparency, accuracy, and impartiality in all promotional activities. It highlights the crucial roles of enforcement authorities in monitoring compliance and enforcing laws related to SMIs marketing in the tourism industry. This chapter proposes several strategic recommendations while identifying possible challenges that may assist relevant regulatory bodies in Malaysia and China.

DOI: 10.4018/979-8-3693-7021-6.ch004

INTRODUCTION

Consumers have consistently been swayed by the views and endorsements of others, whether salespersons promoting a product, personal recommendations from friends, or celebrity endorsements in advertisements. Nowadays, much of this influence is derived from SMIs, encompassing celebrities and regular individuals with significant followers on social media platforms (SMPs) (Burns, 2021). The notion of digital influencers began to emerge with the rise of social networking sites in the mid-2000s. Blogs, YouTube, and subsequently, Facebook and Twitter were among the first platforms that enabled ordinary people to connect with vast audiences. The launch of Instagram in the 2010s further amplified this trend, offering followers insights into the influencers' lifestyles while also serving as a convenient source for product recommendations (Hayes, 2019). Nowadays, platforms like TikTok are further advancing the influencer phenomenon. Initially, 'ordinary' individuals started sharing content that swiftly garnered attention, leading to the growth of their follower base (Schouten et al., 2021). The SMPs subsequently turned this informal activity into a profitable full-time profession, signifying a shift from hobbyist to paid professional content creator (Joshi et al., 2023). Influencers are categorized based on their follower count. Celebrities or public figures with extensive reach, usually those with over 1 million followers, are called mega-influencers. Macro-influencers have between 100,000 and 1 million followers, while micro-influencers have between 1000 and 100,000 people (Rachmad, 2024, p. 10). Other scholars divided influencers into four categories. Mega-influencers can reach 150 million people, whereas macro-influencers have a potential audience of 15 to 150 million. Influencers with 1.5 million to 15 million people are referred to as medium influencers, while mini-influencers have up to 1.5 million followers. Regardless of classification, influencers have emerged as a powerful marketing tool, prompting brands to adjust their marketing strategies and expenditures to harness the potential of this new digital force (Sicilia & López, 2023, pp. 1,9).

SMIs are well-recognized figures in today's digital landscape, with scholars defining them in various contexts. While SMIs need no introduction, it remains essential to identify their roles for the sake of this chapter. Influencers are those who exert influence, inspire or guide the actions of others. Specifically, an influencer can generate interest in consumer products by posting about them on social media (Meriam-Webster Online Dictionary). In the realm of digital platforms, SMIs provide cost-effective alternatives to conventional marketing strategies. Brands often utilize SMIs to promote their products, services, or ideas while efficiently conveying messages to a broader audience. SMIs have established credibility and substantial followers, positioning them as integral to efficiently disseminating messages to wide and targeted audiences in a more engaging and relatable way. They can effectively convey product information, influence the opinions or beliefs of others, and enhance online engagement (Goanta & Ranchordás, 2020a, p. 4). As their fame grew, SMIs became key avenues for advertising (Archer et al., 2021, p. 108). Furthermore, brands are acutely aware of the prominence and impact of SMIs on their followers, which explains why they approach SMIs to endorse products in exchange for monetary incentives or complimentary materials (De Veirman et al., 2020, p. 127).

SMIs are pivotal in bridging the gap between brands and their audiences, i.e., consumers, by delivering engaging and valuable content. SMIs marketing offers an affordable means for small and medium businesses to enhance brand awareness and target niche markets. It also provides global companies with a scalable way to reach diverse audiences and adapt to distinct contexts (Ilieva et al., 2024, pp. 28,29). Influencer marketing has gained widespread prominence. Since 2019, the global influencer marketing market has more than tripled, with projections for 2024 estimating a market value of $24 billion (Dencheva, 2024). This growth highlights the increasing importance of influencers as a key intermediary in engaging and reaching audiences. As influencer marketing expands, more social media users aspire to become influencers themselves (Joshi et al., 2023). This increasing aspiration signifies the growing appeal of SMIs marketing, which is crucial in driving its expansion and development. Research on SMIs marketing is exceptionally significant in the realm of tourism. The appealing nature of SMIs lies not just in their ability to showcase places but also in their capacity to redefine travel trends. Previously obscure destinations are now brought into the limelight, while conventional attractions are seen through a novel lens. The ripple effect of this phenomenon impacts relevant industries, necessitating businesses, hospitality sectors, and local economies to adjust in response to the evolving preferences shaped by SMIs (Pettersen-Sobczyk, 2023, pp. 585,590).

The tourism industry has seen a paradigm shift in recent years owing to the significant role of SMIs marketing (Stoldt et al., 2019, p. 3). SMIs are pivotal in promoting tourism-related products and activities, including travel destinations, accommodations, transportation, souvenirs or local products, attractions, dining experiences, festivals, cultural immersion and tour activities that enhance the overall appeal of a particular place. Certain SMIs have played a role in reviving the tourism industry amidst the global crisis caused by the COVID-19 outbreak (Fedeli & Cheng, 2023, p. 324). For instance, they highlighted destinations that adhere to health protocol, thus restoring followers' confidence in travelling. When international travel was still in the recovery phase, many SMIs shifted their focus to domestic tourism and promoted local destinations to audiences, which not only benefitted the local economy but also met the increasing demand for safer and closer-to-home travel choices (Travel Mindset). In a broader sense, SMIs have been increasingly influential in shaping travel destinations due to their personalized advertising, engaging postings, ability to reach vast and targeted audiences and provide high-quality, focused content. Traditional marketing often lacks these traits. For starters, SMIs use customized marketing to share their trip experiences, encompassing challenges and pleasures. Such authenticity renders their posts believable and relatable. Second, SMIs often initiate engagements with their audience via their postings. Followers can ask questions and give comments, followed by responses from the SMIs. This interaction fosters a communal ambience and nurtures a connection between the SMIs, their followers and the destinations reviewed. Third, SMIs can reach specific audiences. This focused outreach enables key stakeholders such as tourism authorities and businesses to connect more effectively with niche audiences, e.g., adventure travel, luxury vacations, eco-tourism and local destination cuisine. Finally, SMIs often produce exceptional content that captures the essence of a destination, which tourism businesses can utilize for marketing purposes, saving them time and resources.

THEORETICAL PERSPECTIVES OF SMIS MARKETING IN THE TOURISM INDUSTRY

Influencers have emerged as opinion leaders (OLs) by leveraging their large, devoted fan bases and their perceived authenticity and expertise in specific niches. Unlike traditional celebrities, SMIs often create more personal and relatable content, thus fostering trust with their audience. Social psychology research suggests that individuals are more likely to follow advice from those they trust or see as experts, a notion known as social proof. Positioned as trendsetters, SMIs shape consumer preferences and behaviors via their posts, reviews, and endorsements. Studies indicate that SMIs marketing campaigns generate higher engagement and conversion rates, as followers perceive their opinions to be more genuine than corporate advertising. This makes influencers key OLs in today's digital landscape (Solomon, 2020, p. 443). An OL is an individual who holds the power and ability to influence the consumption decisions of others via informal means (Iyengar et al., 2011; Katz & Lazarsfeld, 2006). This influence stems from the OLs' credibility and experience in a particular field, which allows them to effectively guide the decisions and perspectives of their followers (Iyengar et al., 2011). Nevertheless, deploying OLs alone does not guarantee enhanced sales. The strategic framing of the message tone and the type of products also helps to improve sales. Positive messages are more effective in stimulating purchases, while negative messages increase the likelihood of consumers avoiding a product. Negative comments from OLs can spread rapidly and severely deter purchases (Tobon & García-Madariaga, 2021, p. 759). From the standpoint of the tourism sector, these theories suggest that the structure of messages from OLs can significantly influence consumer behavior. Positive messages strongly influence purchase decisions, motivating consumers to book tourism-related products and activities. While negative messages, on the other hand, may generate a higher level of virality, they are less likely to lead to purchases. The structure of the endorsements, therefore, is equally crucial in influencer marketing within the tourism sector as they must align with consumers' expectations and foster a positive brand image.

Rachmad (2024, pp. 5,6,7) proposes several theories centered on how influence is created, enhanced, and expanded via digital technologies, social interactions and direct engagement. The Digital Influence Theory (DIT) employs followers, engagement rates and online presence to reach and influence behavior. Such influence is amplified by the Network Influence Theory (NIT), which focuses on how information circulates within social networks, emphasizing the structure and strength of connections in helping influencers disseminate their content more effectively. Trust is a cornerstone of influencer marketing. As the Trust-Based Marketing Theory (TBMT) explains, the trust developed between influencers and their audience enhances marketing efficacy, loyalty and purchasing decisions. The Authenticity and Credibility Theory (ACT) reinforces this idea, highlighting that trust often stems from influencers' perceived authenticity and credibility, making these elements essential to fostering long-lasting trust and influence. Additionally, the Engagement Influencer Theory (EIT) suggests that active interactions such as likes, comments, and shares help boost the visibility and impact of influencer content. This engagement is further enhanced through the Interactive Marketing Theory (IMT), which advocates two-way interactions between influencers and their audience to boost engagement. The Social Media Influence Theory (SMIT) complements the theories mentioned by exploring how influencers establish and expand their influence across SMPs. The Personalized Influence Theory (PIT) enhances their influence by tailoring messages to individual preferences, boosting engagement and satisfaction. Together, all these theories form a cohesive framework that explains the intricate dynamics of SMIs marketing, where influence is built on digital presence, trust, active engagement, and personalized interactions across vast social media networks.

In the context of SMIs marketing in the tourism industry, the theories proposed by Rachmad (2024, pp. 5,6,7) can be applied to explore the significance of SMIs in shaping consumer purchasing behavior and promoting tourism-related products and activities. Metrics such as follower count and engagement rates are proxies for SMIs reach and effectiveness. Thus, SMIs with a solid digital presence can affect travel decisions by recommending less-known destinations and using their influence to stimulate interest in that particular destination (DIT). The reach of SMIs is magnified through their ability to disseminate content across multiple SMPs and through their followers. Their well-connected networks, e.g., collaborations with other influencers, rapidly spread information about tourism-related products and activities (NIT). Followers are likelier to rely on recommendations from trusted sources when making travel decisions. SMIs demonstrate credibility and establish this trust by sharing authentic experiences personal narratives, and actively engaging with their followers in real-time (e.g., live broadcast) (TBMT). Authenticity is crucial in the tourism industry as tourists often seek real and genuine experiences. Influencers who portray destinations, for instance, with sincerity using unfiltered stories or candid moments can significantly foster deeper trust with audiences as they are seen as more trustworthy (ACT). Engaging actively with audiences, such as responding to comments, can heighten tourism-related posts' visibility. The interaction draws more attention and potentially influences the audience's travel preferences and decisions (EIT). Two-way communication between SMIs and their followers can create a sense of involvement and strengthen their bond. This can take the form of answering questions during live sessions via SMPs, including giving travel tips or inviting followers to vote on their next travel destination (IMT and SMIT). Personalization is also essential for addressing specific travel preferences. SMIs may tailor their travel recommendations to niche audiences such as adventure explorers or environmentally conscious tourists. By offering personalized travel content, SMIs can effectively resonate with their audience's interests, increasing the likelihood of engagement, brand loyalty, and conversion (such as booking a trip to the recommended destination) (PIT).

Significance of the Discussion

Exploring the legal framework surrounding SMIs marketing in the tourism industries of Malaysia and China is crucial, considering the substantial exchange of tourists between these regions. For instance, Malaysian tourism officials predict a significant rise in tourists from China as airlines launch new connecting routes and increase the weekly frequency of flights between the two nations (The Star, 2024b). Similarly, China has emerged as the preferred destination for Malaysians at the recent exhibition organized by the Malaysian Association of Tour and Travel Agents in March 2024, owing mainly to influencers' short videos or viral posts on social media. Additionally, China relaxed its visa requirements in December 2023, attracting Malaysian tourists to choose the country as their destination (Ramli, 2024).

Presently, Malaysia and China have not implemented a sufficient regulatory framework for SMIs marketing in the tourism sphere, which explains why the legal liabilities of SMIs for promoting tourism-related products and activities in these two jurisdictions remain unsettled. Unquestionably, research on SMIs marketing has been widely explored within the academic community. Examples include an overview of the past, present and future trends in influencer marketing within the tourism and hospitality sectors (Polat et al., 2024), the role of Instagram travel influencers in the selection of tourism locations, with a focus on sustainable destinations (Kilipiri et al., 2023), the underlying motivations why consumers follow SMIs on Instagram within the hospitality and tourism sectors (Bastrygina et al., 2024) and how attachment to SMIs mediates the relationship between authenticity, pleasure and travel intention when viewing SMIs videos (Zhu et al., 2023). However, while studies on SMIs marketing have been conducted, there is still a scarcity of research dedicated to SMIs marketing within the tourism industry (Fedeli & Cheng, 2023, p. 324; Ingrassia et al., 2022, p. 2). The limitation is particularly evident in the regulatory framework that governs the marketing of tourism-related products and activities via SMIs. Several legal studies have explored SMIs practices, focusing primarily on general advertising laws and consumer protection (e.g., Antoniou (2024) and contributions in the book edited by Goanta and Ranchordás (2020b)) without delving deeply into the unique challenges and ethical concerns in the tourism industry. This gap highlights the need for more tailored regulations to effectively address issues related to SMIs marketing in the tourism sector.

With SMIs wielding significant influence over consumer behavior, comprehensive research on the intersection of SMIs marketing, advertising law and consumer law is imperative. Some countries are beginning to establish policies and guidelines for SMIs. For example, in the United States, the Federal Trade Commission has introduced 'Disclosures 101 for Social Media Influencers', which mandates influencers to transparently disclose material connections (e.g., payments, free products) with brands in their social media posts to ensure that consumers can accurately evaluate the credibility of endorsements (Federal Trade Commission, 2019). Similarly, in the United Kingdom (UK), the Advertising Standards Authority and the Competition and Markets Authority compel SMIs to clearly reveal paid partnerships and gifts received so that consumers may appropriately assess the authenticity of the postings (Goodship, 2019).

The tourism industry as a whole, however, has yet to develop similar standards (Fedeli & Cheng, 2023, p. 325). Malaysia and China arguably experience comparable situations. As both countries have distinct regulatory environments, the legal analysis of SMIs marketing may facilitate cross-border understanding, allowing each region's relevant stakeholders (e.g., SMIs and businesses) to learn the other's regulatory requirements. These stakeholders can develop tailored marketing strategies that comply with local regulations, ensuring effective and legally sound campaigns. In summary, understanding how consumer and advertising-related laws apply to endorsements by SMIs is essential for maintaining high compliance and minimizing the risks of deceptive marketing while fostering ethical advertising activities in the tourism business. Ultimately, the chapter offers valuable insights to policymakers in both regions on potential areas needing updates in laws and regulations. Strengthened regulations will enhance consumer trust, benefit the tourism industry, and further promote economic growth in both countries.

LEGAL ISSUES RELATED TO SMIS MARKETING IN THE TOURISM INDUSTRY

The legal issues associated with SMIs marketing include false and misleading claims, the need for transparency and disclosures and the practice of barter collaboration or in-kind sponsorship. Complying with the laws that govern these aspects is vital in maintaining consumer trust and confidence while also upholding the integrity of the tourism industry.

False and Misleading Claims

SMIs may make false and misleading claims about tourism products and related activities to their followers, driven by a desire for financial gain or increased visibility. These practices can take many forms, such as giving inaccurate testimonials, exaggerating the benefits of a specific tourism activity, or fabricating stories about experiences in the places visited. The advent of photo-editing technologies (e.g., Adobe Photoshop and mobile editing apps) has further exacerbated the issue, increasing concerns about the authenticity of the images shared by SMIs. Over-edited photos can place unrealistic expectations on consumers, leading them to purchase fallacy. For example, SMIs edited a photo to create the illusion of a luxurious room with more appealing amenities and services than it actually has. Tourists may face unexpected costs and disappointment if they reserve the same room only to discover that it significantly differs from what the SMIs portray. It may be smaller, or the view may vary from what was stated by the SMIs. Other instances that can lead to frustrations among tourists include exaggerated scenic views and overrated local cuisine. In a worst-case scenario, if SMIs inaccurately depict a place as safer than it truly is, it can compromise the safety of unprepared tourists.

The prevalence of extensively edited images has prompted the introduction of laws aimed at ensuring transparency and honesty in advertising. These regulations seek to safeguard consumers from falling prey to manipulated content that distorts reality and to uphold the integrity of marketing practices. Worldwide initiatives have started to address these issues. For instance, the UK's Advertising Standards Authority has enforced rules against using filters that amplify the effect of products. The use of filters in advertisements is acceptable as long as they do not overstate the product's effectiveness to a misleading extent. In such cases, the advertiser must prove that the filter does not mislead consumers. Even if a filter accurately represents the product's efficacy, the advertiser must provide evidence to support any visual claims and ensure they are not misleading (ASA, 2021a; ASA, 2021b). Similarly, France implemented a law mandating that influencers disclose whenever they digitally alter their appearance. This legislation requires influencers and content creators to inform their online audiences whenever they use an augmented reality (AR) filter or digitally modify their face or body in images they post. Additionally, the law stipulates that they must clearly indicate when a post is a paid promotion. Non-compliance with these regulations can lead to penalties of up to six months in prison or a fine of €300,000 (Duboust, 2023; Kemp, 2023). Ultimately, by prohibiting digitally altered photos, the law ensures that the advertised experiences and destinations reflect reality, thereby protecting consumers from being misled by exaggerated or unrealistic representations. For audiences engaging with tourism-related products and activities, the legislation ensures that potential tourists receive accurate portrayals of destinations, accommodations, and experiences, helping them make more informed decisions and reducing the likelihood of disappointment upon arrival.

Transparency and Disclosures

Collaboration with SMIs has become a prevalent practice in the tourism industry. This strategic partnership leverages the influencers' broad reach to enhance visibility and attract potential tourists. For example, tourism agencies partnered with airline companies to offer free destination packages to SMIs with significant followers in exchange for favorable reviews. To illustrate further, Tourism Malaysia has collaborated with AirAsia Airlines to bring Taiwanese influencers and bloggers to promote Malaysia as a preferred tourist destination (Tourism Malaysia, 2023). In addition, Malacca (one of the states in Malaysia) has appointed Fan Bingbing, a prominent actress and influencer from China, as its ambassador for the 'Visit Malacca 2024' campaign. Fan Bingbing has a massive social media following; thus, the state aims to leverage her presence and influence in promoting Malacca internationally and attract more tourists from China and Asia (The Star, 2024a).

Collaboration with SMIs is a legitimate and effective marketing strategy when conducted ethically and in compliance with applicable laws. Despite being widely practiced, such collaboration raises concerns about the authenticity and credibility of shared experiences as they are often rooted in financial incentives. In other words, while SMIs marketing itself is not inherently illegal, issues can arise if SMIs do not adequately disclose commercial ties and maintain transparency in their posts. When SMIs endorse a brand or product without clearly revealing that it's a paid promotion, it can mislead their audience, potentially influencing their purchasing decisions. The blurred lines between personal and commercial content on social media make it easy for sponsored posts to blend into the regular stream of updates, which can deceive consumers if the commercial intent is not transparently disclosed (Ducato, 2020, p. 233). In the tourism industry, tourists may not suspect bias in the SMIs' recommendations unless they are aware that the trip or experiences were sponsored. Thus, SMIs must disclose when their content is sponsored or part of a paid partnership to empower tourists to comprehend the nature of the endorsements and make informed travel decisions.

Research indicates that trust in SMIs positively influences consumer decision-making. Most consumers are more inclined to seek information from SMIs and have visited a place based on their recommendations. Similarly, consumers are likely to make the final decision to schedule a vacation or purchase tourist products based on SMIs' recommendations (Pop et al., 2022). While trust plays a crucial role in consumer decisions, it may diminish once consumers become aware that the endorsements are financially motivated, prompting them to question its authenticity. Therefore, requiring SMIs to disclose the nature of their endorsements clearly can help maintain a balance, enabling consumers to make more informed decisions. The infamous Frye Festival event is significant in understanding the importance of transparency. McFarland, the co-founder and principal organizer, was imprisoned for engaging in multiple fraudulent schemes. The event's failure drew attention to the role and ethical liability of SMIs, who play a major part in promoting the festival. Several high-profile SMIs failed to reveal their financial ties to the event, which led many attendees to buy tickets without realizing the highly praised endorsements were paid promotions (Higgins, 2019). In essence, transparency and disclosure are crucial for empowering consumers to make well-informed transactional decisions. These core aspects must take precedence over the goal of attracting potential tourists to the country regardless of whether the collaboration involves government agencies or private sectors. Otherwise, if the enforcement is selective, it defeats the very purpose of having consumer and advertising-related laws in the first place.

Barter Collaboration or In-Kind Sponsorship

Some SMIs approach businesses requesting gratuitous items such as complimentary meals, accommodations, and vacations or asking for discounted rates in exchange for positive reviews and promotional endorsements. This is a barter collaboration or in-kind sponsorship founded on reciprocal advantage. The arrangement is mutually advantageous, with the business gaining visibility and the SMIs getting complimentary items. However, such practices present both ethical and legal concerns. There is a potential that the SMIs postings lack impartiality. SMIs may exaggerate too much in promoting a business to meet their obligations, creating a false perception of the quality or value of tourism-related products and activities.

In this regard, consumers are disadvantaged, as they are more likely to base their decision on biased information.

Fortunately, not all hotels are receptive to such requests, valuing unbiased guest feedback. For instance, the White Moose Café has sarcastically rejected an influencer requesting complimentary stays in exchange for promotional content on her social media platforms (The White Moose Café). In another similar incident, the White Banana Beach Club in Siargao, Philippines, made headlines in 2019 when it publicly declined a request from an influencer who sought a free stay at the resort in exchange for promotional posts (Mezzofiore, 2019). Both examples highlight that while a barter collaboration serves as an effective marketing strategy, it is essential to oversee them with explicit legal standards and transparency to maintain the integrity of the parties involved while safeguarding the interests of prospective tourists.

UNDERSTANDING THE LEGAL LANDSCAPE OF INFLUENCER MARKETING IN THE TOURISM INDUSTRY

Malaysia

Numerous statutes have been enacted to regulate the tourism industry in Malaysia. Some notable Acts include the Tourism Industry Act 1992, the Malaysian Tourism Promotion Board Act 1992, and the Innkeepers Act 1952. There are also regulations designed specifically to regulate tourism-related businesses, such as the Tourism Industry (Tour Operating Business and Travel Agency Business) Regulations 1992 and Tourism Industry (Licensing and Control of Tourist Guides) Regulations 1992. While these statutes and regulations provide a robust legal framework for the tourism industry, they do not specifically address SMIs' marketing or involvement in promoting Malaysia's tourism-related products and activities. This presents a notable gap in the regulatory landscape of the tourism sector in Malaysia. Nevertheless, while not directly related to the tourism sector, some Acts may be applicable to regulate SMIs marketing to safeguard consumers. These include the Consumer Protection Act 1999 (CPA), the Trade Descriptions Act 2011 (TDA) and the Communications and Multimedia Act 1998 (CMA). These Acts address false, misleading, and deceptive conduct and representations, ensuring that consumers have access to accurate information while overseeing online content to ensure it adheres to ethical standards.

The CPA

The CPA applies to all goods and services supplied to consumers in offline and online transactions (Section 2). Goods are primarily purchased, used or consumed for personal, domestic or household purposes. On the other hand, services include any rights, benefits, privileges, or facilities that are provided or to be provided under any contract (Section 3). Arguably, tourism-related products and activities can be classified as goods and services. For instance, local crafts, souvenirs, and merchandise that are meant to attract tourists are goods under the CPA if purchased for personal use. Offering accommodations (e.g., hotels, resorts, budget hostels) with various facilities may also be considered services. SMIs may be held responsible for their posts meant to promote these items on their social platforms. Under the CPA, 'advertisement' encompasses all forms of advertising, including spoken, written or sounds. This may also include notices, catalogues, price lists, circulars, labels, cards, films or pictures and advertisements via radio, television, telecommunications, or other similar means (Section 3). In this context, social media may fall under the interpretation of 'similar means'.

Sections 8, 9 and 10 regulate false, misleading, and deceptive representation and conduct that lead a consumer into error about the goods and services. Persons accountable for making the advertisement are those who directly or indirectly claim to supply the products and on whose behalf the advertisement is made (Section 18). Unfortunately, the CPA does not expressly define the person who can be held responsible for making advertisements. Therefore, only time will tell whether SMIs are accountable for any 'indirect claims' made with regard to tourism-related products and activities through their endorsement. In essence, SMIs must ensure that their endorsement reflects the genuine features, benefits, and limitations of the tourism-related products or services that they endorse. Failure to comply with these provisions may expose SMIs to risks of false, misleading, and deceptive representation and conduct, which thus lead to legal consequences such as fines, imprisonment or both, as specified under Section 25.

The TDA

The TDA applies to goods and services (Preamble), i.e., all kinds of moveable property and services of any description, whether industrial, trade or professional (Section 2). 'Trade' was defined as '[t]he business of buying and selling or bartering goods or services' (Garner, 2024, p. 1803). The scopes seem to align with tourism-related products and activities, which is akin to the CPA. Trade description of goods is an indication, whether direct or indirect, by any means of, among others, the nature or design, quantity, quality, size, methods of production and manufacture, performance, physical or technological characteristics, expiry date, testing and approval by any person and other history (e.g., previous ownership) (Section 6). When a trade description is materially inaccurate or misleading, it is considered a false trade description (Section 7). Furthermore, anything that is not explicitly listed under Section 6 may nevertheless be construed as a false trade description if it is false to a material degree (Section 7(3)). SMIs are likely to fall under the category of persons who risk committing false trade descriptions. Section 5 emphasizes that any person who applies false trade descriptions to any goods or exposes for supply any goods with false trade descriptions commits an offence. On conviction, the SMIs will be liable to a fine of up to RM100,000.00, imprisonment with a maximum duration of three years or both. The punishments are more severe for the second and subsequent offence (Section 5).

In addition, the TDA also makes it an offence for those making misstatements other than false trade descriptions. As such, SMIs may be liable under the Act if their statement and conduct can lead any person into error (Section 13). For example, by knowingly or recklessly making false and misleading statements about services, accommodation, or facilities. This includes, but is not limited to, the nature, location, amenities, and rates of such services (Section 17). The TDA explicitly prohibit false and misleading statements in an advertisement. The onus of proving otherwise rests on the accused (Section 18). The TDA defines 'advertisement' as all forms of advertising, including spoken, written, or sound. This may also include notices, catalogues, price lists, circulars, labels, cards or other documents, films or pictures and advertisements via radio, television, or any other way, including electronically (Section 2). The TDA also holds responsible the person who directly or indirectly offers to supply the products and the person on whose behalf the advertisement is created (Section 19). Endorsements made by SMIs via their social media channels may qualify as 'advertisement' under the TDA because it was made through 'electronic means'. However, to be legally responsible, SMIs shall fall within the first limb of Section 19; namely, they must be seen as the person who indirectly offers to supply the products they promote. Presently, the TDA is silent on the inclusion of SMIs. Therefore, further clarification is essential to facilitate legal compliance and ensure that SMIs remain within the bounds of the law despite having significant followings on their social channels.

The CMA

The CMA was enacted to regulate the rapidly converging communications and multimedia industries. It aims to ensure a fair and competitive market while protecting the interests of consumers. The CMA empowers the Malaysian Communications and Multimedia Commission (the Commission) to formulate a voluntary industry code that will only be effective upon registration (Sections 95 and 96). While compliance with the Code is voluntary (Section 98), the Commission may direct a person or a class of persons to comply with the registered voluntary industry code (Section 99). Otherwise, non-compliance with the Commission's directions will result in a fine not exceeding RM200,000.00, which can also be recoverable as a civil debt (Section 100).

The Commission has introduced the Malaysian Communications and Multimedia Content Code 2022 (the Code), reflecting its continued dedication to fostering a responsible and ethical digital content environment. Pursuant to Section 95, the Code was registered and became effective on 30 May 2022. The Code was initially established in 2004 before being revamped to ensure it remains aligned with global practices. The notable development was the explicit inclusion of SMIs within the regulatory ambit of the Code. The Code viewed 'influencers' as "person(s) or group(s) who either on a personal capacity share their own independent opinions or are engaged and paid by Advertisers (either in cash or other consideration) to advertise products or services on their own social media channels because of their social media influence on Consumers". In this context, a consumer is defined as any individual who receives, acquires, uses, or subscribes to communication and multimedia content within the meaning of the CMA. (Part 1: Definitions and Interpretations).

The Code dictates that advertising be designed in a way that maintains consumer trust while avoiding exploiting their inexperience or lack of knowledge. It should be clear, accurate, and free from misleading content, with no information omitted or presented ambiguously in a way that could deceive consumers. Essential details that consumers need to make informed decisions must be provided transparently. Advertisements must not include statements, images, or claims that could mislead consumers regarding the product, its nature, origin, or the advertiser. Additionally, testimonials and endorsements used in ads must be authentic and reflect the genuine experience of the individual over a reasonable period. In particular, SMIs must transparently declare any paid partnerships or sponsorships that are easily understood and in the same language as the endorsement. Disclosures should be prominently displayed alongside the endorsement content, and upfront labels should be used that are immediately noticeable and easily comprehensible (e.g., 'Advertisement', 'Ad', 'sponsored'). It is important to avoid vague or confusing terms (e.g., 'sp', 'spon', or 'collab') or any abbreviations or shorthand that may confuse the public or consumers. If the endorsement was via a video, the disclosure should be included in the video itself rather than only in the description accompanying it. Likewise, in the case of a live stream, the information must be repeated on a regular basis to keep viewers who only see part of the broadcast informed (Part 3: Advertisement (Marketing Communications)).

The Code serves as a framework for industry self-regulation by establishing guidelines for content provisions. Complaints related to the Code should initially be resolved between the involved parties; if unresolved, they can be escalated to the Complaints Bureau. The public may also submit written complaints detailing the specific code violation and supporting evidence. The Complaints Bureau has the authority to impose penalties, such as written reprimands, fines up to RM50,000, or mandates to remove or cease the offending content. In cases of significant breaches, the Bureau may refer the matter to the Commission for further action. The decisions made by the Bureau on the interpretation of the Code are final (Part 8: Code Administration).

Legislative Challenges in the Regulations of SMIs in Malaysia

Governing SMIs in tourism marketing in Malaysia presents several legislative challenges, particularly in ensuring compliance with existing consumer protection and advertising laws. The CPA and TDA were designed to safeguard the interests of consumers and regulate the accuracy of information provided in marketing and advertising. Both Acts mandate that any description, statement or other representation in advertising must not be false or misleading. In the context of SMIs marketing, the challenge lies in determining whether SMIs fall within the purview of the statutes. Currently, no provisions in either Act explicitly define an 'influencer' or refer to SMIs. If SMIs do not fall within the ambit of these legislations, businesses in the tourism industry can use them to attract prospective customers or tourists without concern about violating the laws themselves. Section 18 of the CPA and Section 19 of the TDA hold two types of persons liable for the advertisement, i.e., (i) the person who directly or indirectly claims to supply the products and (ii) the person on whose behalf the advertisement is made. It is argued that SMIs do not neatly align with these provisions. SMIs often do not profess to supply products; instead, they serve as intermediaries sharing personal experiences or views on a product or service. Their role is more about shaping perceptions than engaging in the actual supply of goods or services. Although they may be compensated for their endorsements, SMIs may not act on behalf of the businesses in a legal sense. They operate as independent content creators who choose to endorse certain products or services, often with a degree of personal discretion. Their endorsements, while impactful, are not made 'on behalf' of a brand in the same way that a traditional advertisement is. As such, it may be argued that SMIs do not fit the existing descriptions specified in Sections 18 and 19, which present challenges to holding them accountable under the CPA and TDA.

Additionally, the lines between personal opinion and advertisement have become increasingly blurred, especially with SMIs significantly shaping consumers' transactional decisions. The amalgamation of personal opinions and advertisements challenges consumers and regulators. Consumers may lack awareness that the content they are engaging with is promotional in nature, potentially leading to misguided decisions based on what they perceive as genuine recommendations. Simultaneously, the absence of clear regulatory guidelines leaves SMIs in a grey area where the boundaries of legal responsibility are not well established. This is also the challenge under the CMA. While SMIs fall within the purview of the CMA via the Content Code 2022, there may be issues in balancing freedom of expression with the need to protect consumers from misleading content. SMIs, as content creators, operate simultaneously in personal and commercial spaces, raising issues of accountability and transparency. The decentralized nature of social media platforms makes it difficult for regulatory bodies to monitor and enforce compliance effectively, especially when content is created by SMIs who may not be fully aware of the legal implications of their actions.

Propose Reforms: Blending Legislative and Non-Legislative Approaches

The CPA and TDA safeguard consumer rights and ensure fair trade practices. However, both Acts were enacted when SMIs marketing was not prevalent. Thus, the statutes do not entirely address these practices. SMIs operate in a legal grey area that the CPA and TDA do not adequately address. Both Acts fail to consider the complexities of modern marketing, creating a gap between the current legal framework and the way products and services are marketed today. Such lacuna thus highlights the urgent need for legislative review. Specifically, the CPA and TDA need to acknowledge the explicit role of SMIs marketing in its continued quest to protect consumers. Establishing a legal standard is essential to mitigate the potential for SMIs to manipulate consumers, given their substantial capacity to exert influence. Therefore, the CPA and TDA should clearly define to what extent they apply to SMIs marketing, including clarifying the liabilities of the brands behind the posts. Marketing via influencers is rapidly growing. Thus, it is important that influencers and brands are both held accountable for their respective roles (Davis, 2023, p. 71). Revising these statutes will provide clearer guidance to SMIs and brands. Additionally, it fosters a more transparent and trustworthy environment while preserving consumers' rights in the digital age. Most importantly, revising the CPA and TDA is not only a legal necessity but also a response to the evolving nature of marketing.

This ensures that the laws in Malaysia remain relevant and efficient in protecting consumer interests, not just in the tourism industry but also in the broader context of the e-commerce landscape.

Setting precise benchmarks that specify the standards SMIs must adhere to when sharing material information is also crucial. This includes disclosing sponsorships or commercial ties with the relevant brands. Once consumers are fully aware of the true nature of the endorsements, they will be able to make well-informed buying decisions. The CPA, TDA and CMA (and, to some extent, the Code established under the CMA) may utilize the ACCURATE information framework as a yardstick. By adhering to this framework, SMIs can be guided to produce content that aligns with legal standards and fosters trust with their audience. Among others, the ACCURATE information framework requires that the information shared is easily accessible and comprehensible to average consumers, enabling them to make informed decisions. Additionally, the information should be understandable, clear, sufficient, trustworthy, unbiased, transparent, and easily obtainable without incurring unnecessary costs for consumers to find and process (Zeno, 2022, p. 246). Adhering to the ACCURATE principles may help consumers better grasp the genuine intent behind SMIs postings or reviews, thus empowering them to make decisions that reflect their true preferences. The fundamental tenets of the ACCURATE framework are interrelated. Thus, SMIs marketing may be considered to have met the established standards if it exhibits most, if not all, of the ACCURATE information aspects.

In addition, enforcement authorities also play a significant role in ensuring legal compliance and maintaining the integrity of marketing practices as outlined in the CPA, TDA and CMA. Regulatory bodies must monitor SMIs marketing for potential misrepresentation and proactively educate them about their legal obligations to ensure truthfulness and transparency. They can establish enforcement units and dedicated personnel for real-time monitoring who are experts in leveraging technology to track trends, identify violations, and respond swiftly to consumer complaints. However, enforcement bodies may face challenges monitoring compliance and enforcing related laws due to financial limitations and the rapidly evolving nature of digital marketing strategies. Despite these constraints, enforcement authorities have a pivotal role in balancing the creative development of digital marketing and the need to protect consumers. Failing to do so risks undermining the industry's reputation, losing consumers' trust and negatively affecting Malaysia's tourism sector.

Relying solely on the legislation and authorities for protection against misleading and deceptive practices is insufficient. Consumers must also take responsibility by being informed and prudent in their decisions. They must learn to evaluate the information posted by SMIs for potential biases. A profound understanding of how SMIs marketing operates enables them to make informed choices, thereby reducing the risk of falling prey to false claims or exaggerated promotions. This proactive approach not only empowers consumers but also complements the efforts of regulatory authorities, creating a more balanced and effective consumer protection system in Malaysia.

China

The regulation of SMIs marketing is a complicated issue in China. A special law regulating SMIs in the tourism industry does not exist. The Consumer Protection Law, the E-Commerce Law, the Anti-unfair Competition Law, the Tourism Law, the Advertising Law, and subordinated regulations can all protect consumers. These legislations and regulations adopt different regulatory approaches to setting obligations for business operators, e-business operators, tourism service operators, advertising parties and platforms.

The regulatory frameworks in these laws can be categorized into two approaches. The first approach is consumer protection. As listed in Table 1 (summary of the key provisions of applicable laws and regulations), although the overall legislative purposes are specific and different, the relevant provisions in the Consumer Protection Law, the E-Commerce Law, the Anti-unfair Competition Law, and the Tourism Law set up similar rights and obligations, and even adopt highly similar expressions. On the one hand, the Consumer Protection Law and the E-Commerce Law explicitly provide consumers with the right to know true and accurate information about goods and services. On the other hand, these four sectoral legislations impose similar information-disclosing obligations for the counterparties, i.e., requiring business operators, e-business operators and tourism services operators to disclose accurate, authentic, comprehensive and timely information about the goods and services. These goods and services providers are prohibited from false or misleading commercial promotion.

The second approach is advertising regulation. In accordance with their role in the promotion, the Advertising Law categorizes advertising parties into four types: advertisers, advertising agents, advertisement publishers, and endorsers. An advertiser refers to the party that designs, produces or publishes advertisements on its own or authorizes a third party to promote the sale of goods and services. Advertising agents provide advertising services under the authorization of others. Advertisement publishers publish advertisements for advertisers and advertising agents. Endorsers can be natural persons, legal persons or other forms of organizations that make recommendations or certifications of goods and services in their own names or images in advertisements (Article 2).

On the basis of such categorization, the Advertising Law sets up a three-layered liability framework. As Table 1 shows, firstly, the advertiser bears the most stringent liability. Advertisers are fully responsible for the truthfulness of the advertisement and the compensation liabilities when consumer harm occurs. The other three types of advertising parties will be held jointly and severally liable with the advertiser if they knew or should have known the false nature of the advertisement but still designed, produced, published, recommended or certified the goods and services. Secondly, advertising agents and advertisement publishers will be held liable when they fail to provide effective contact information of advertisers. In the case of goods and services concerning the life and health of consumers, they shall be held jointly and severally liable with the advertisers. Thirdly, endorsers are prohibited from recommending or certifying goods or services that they have not used. Otherwise they will be held liable only in the certain specific circumstances mentioned above. Apart from the compensation perspective, the Advertising Law sets different administrative penalties for these four types of advertising parties. Considering both the civil liabilities and administrative penalties, the endorsers bear comparatively fewer legal liabilities than advertisers, advertising agents and advertisement publishers.

In 2016, the State Administration for Market Regulation (SAMR) issued an 'Interim Measures for the Administration of Internet Advertising' (No.87 [2016] of SAMR Order), which was revised and replaced by the 'Measures for the Administration of Internet Advertising' (No.72 [2023] of SAMR Order) in 2023. SMIs can be regarded as advertisers, advertising agents and, advertisement publishers, or endorsers, depending on the role played by SMIs in specific circumstances. An improvement in this 2023 regulation for online advertisements is the clarification of information disclosing obligations when the promotion is presented in the forms such as 'experience sharing' and 'consumption evaluation': such forms of promotion need to be made clearly identifiable as advertisements.

The first issue in regulating SMIs in the Chinese context is whether the content published by SMIs constitutes the commercial advertisement regulated by the Advertising Law, which is defined as the 'direct or indirect introduction of the goods and services via certain media and format' (Article 2). Normally, however, the promotion by SMIs is not done via media. The SMIs might have contractual relationships with the Multi-Channel Networks (MCNs) or broker companies, but these companies cannot be regarded as typical forms of media, either. It has been argued that SMIs are similar to the salespersons in traditional offline shops. Rather than advertising conducts, their promotion activities are sales in the online context (Ma, 2021, p. 38). Following the logic of this argument will exclude the applicability of the Advertising Law, providing more space for the free development of the emerging business model at the cost of insufficient consumer protection. This argument, however, has not gained much appeal. Traditional offline salespersons do not have a comparable influence on consumers and do not need to certify the quality of goods and services (Wang, 2021, p. 87). Despite the lack of media in the process of information flows, SMIs perform the same functions as advertising parties (Ma, 2021, p. 37). It has been generally accepted that the various forms of promotion made by SMIs constitute advertising conducts; the content published by them should be regarded as advertisement (Liu & Li, 2021; Ma, 2021; Zhang, 2020).

The second issue is the legal status of the SMIs. The SMIs can serve as tourism operators, goods and services providers, and (e-)business operators when they promote their own goods and services. However, under the second approach, there were controversies over the legal status of SMIs due to their unique nature. Apart from the interactive characteristics of SMIs, these influencers often bargain with the goods and services providers on behalf of consumers to help them get discounts. Scholars, therefore queried whether SMIs in such circumstances should be regarded as endorsers who make recommendations and certifications under the authorization of advertisers (Liu, 2020). There is no widely agreed-upon consensus about the legal status of SMIs under the second approach (Ma, 2021, p. 39; Song, 2020, p. 14). Different legal status means the applicability of different layers of liabilities.

In the context of SMIs in the tourism sector, SMIs can be goods and services providers themselves. For example, a tourist resort operator can create a social media account in his or her own name and attract many followers to become a SMI. The operator can then post photos and videos to exhibit the scenery, the goods and services of the resort for promotion. When the operator is an organization, its employees who have many followers can also post photos and videos, share experiences and make comments (consumption evaluation) to attract consumers. Such promotion activities constitute professional conducts; and the operator bears the liabilities (Qiu, 2020). In such scenarios, the resort operators constitute tourism operators under the Tourism Law, goods and services providers under the Consumer Protection Law, e-business operators under the E-Commerce Law, and business operators under the Anti-Unfair Competition Law. The operators then have to comply with the rules and fulfil the obligations set in these sectoral laws and regulations. Consumers can seek compensation from the operators for the damage caused by the goods or services.

However, the issue of the legal status of SMIs remains controversial under the second approach. The Advertising Law and the 2023 Regulation do not provide a one-size-fits-all answer to this question. Scholars hold different views. Song (2020) argues that SMIs should be regarded essentially as endorsers; they may also constitute other types of advertising parties, depending on the concrete circumstances (Song, 2020, p. 14). Ma (2021) considers that the third layer of liability - the endorser regulatory framework - cannot provide sufficient protection for consumers and suggests the escalation of regulatory stringency to the second layer. It is suggested that SMIs shall bear the responsibilities of advertising agents and advertisement publishers in principle. If the SMIs can prove that the MCNs and platforms have played a leading role in the production and publication of the adverting information and they have only performed the role of mouthpiece, they can bear the responsibilities of endorsers (Ma, 2021, p. 39). Ma (2021) further suggests extending the scope of information-disclosing obligations to advertisers. If the advertisers have material connections such as personal or financial relationships with the SMIs, they should bear the responsibility to remind and supervise the SMIs to fulfill the information disclosing obligations and make the content identifiable as 'advertisements'. The SMIs can claim for exemptions of liabilities if they can prove the failure of advertisers to fulfill the supervisory obligation (Ma, 2021, p. 39). The argument of Ma (2021) suits the current social context better.

In the scenarios illustrated above, the tourist resort operators should be held liable as advertisers, i.e., to bear the first layer of liability. If the contexts slightly change, i.e. the SMIs do not have employment relationships with the resort operators and are purely external parties, the liability layer of SMIs will stay at the second or/and third layer. For example, the same subject can carry out advertising activities including the production, publication, recommendation, and certification. This is actually the commonly seen scenarios. Many SMIs on Xiaohongshu ('Little Red Book') and Weibo play active roles in designing the content of the advertisements, posting them on their social media, and making recommendations in their own names. In such circumstances, the same subjects play the triple functions of advertising agents, advertisement publishers and endorsers (Liu & Li, 2021, p. 77; Ma, 2021, p. 36). The SMIs and the tourism operators (also goods and service providers and (e-)business operators) co-create the advertisements. If the SMIs make recommendations and certifications in their own names independent of the operators and attract consumers by endorsing their own credibility, they constitute purely endorsers (Liu & Li, 2021, p. 77) and thus bear the third layer obligations.

Table 1. Summary of the key provisions of applicable laws and regulations in China

NO	STATUTE & ADMINISTRATIVE REGULATION	ESSENTIAL PROVISIONS AND EXPLANATIONS
1	Consumer Protection Law (2013 amended version)	**Purpose:** protecting consumers and guaranteeing fair transactions between consumers and various business operators. ● **Rights of Consumers:** the right to know the true information of the goods and services (**Article 8**); the right to fair trading (**Article 10**). ● **Obligations of Business Operators:** the obligation to provide true and complete information about the goods and services provided (i.e., prohibition of false and misleading promotion, **Article 20**); the obligation to guarantee the quality of goods and services to be consistent with that indicated in advertisements or promotion (**Article 23**). ● **Liabilities of advertising agents and advertisement publishers:** advertising agents and publishers shall be held liable when they fail to provide effective contact information of business operators (**Article 45**); in contexts where the goods and services concern the life and health of consumers, organizations or natural persons shall be held jointly and severally liable with the providers if they make recommendations where false advertising or promotion is involved (**Article 45**). ■ **Possible penalties for false and misleading promotion** (**Article 56**): depending on the seriousness of the false and misleading promotion, penalties 1), 2), 3) and 4) can be imposed in combination. 1) warning; 2) or confiscation of illegal gains; 3) or imposing a fine of not less than one but not more than ten times of the illegal gains; 4) or imposing a fine of not more than 500,000 CNY in circumstances without illegal gains; 5) or shut down for rectification; 6) or revocation of business license.
2	E-Commerce Law	**Purpose:** protecting consumers and guaranteeing fair transactions between consumers and various business operators in E-commerce contexts. ● **Rights of consumers:** the right to know and the right of choice (**Article 17**). ● **Obligations of e-business operators:** the obligations to disclose information relating to the goods and services in a fully, authentically, accurately and timely manner (i.e. prohibition of false and misleading commercial promotion, **Article 17**).
3	Anti-Unfair Competition Law	**Purpose:** protecting consumers and the fair market order. ● **Obligations of business operators:** prohibition of false and misleading information about the provided commodities and services (**Article 8**). ● Possible penalties for false and misleading promotion (Article 20): ■ imposing a fine of not less than 200,000 CNY and not more than 1000,000 CNY; ■ or imposing a fine of not less than 1000,000 CNY and not more than 2000,000 CNY (in serious circumstances); ■ or revocation of business license.

continued on following page

Table 1. Continued

NO	STATUTE & ADMINISTRATIVE REGULATION	ESSENTIAL PROVISIONS AND EXPLANATIONS
4	Tourism Law (2018 amended version)	**Purpose:** protecting the rights and interests of both tourists and tourism operators, guaranteeing the order of tourism market, and promoting the sustainable development of the tourism industry. ● **Information disclosing obligations of the travel agencies:** the obligation to provide authentic and accurate information; the prohibition of false or misleading promotion (**Article 32**). ● Possible penalties of false or misleading promotion (**Article 97**): ■ rectification, confiscating illegal gains and imposing a fine of not less than 5,000 CNY but not more than 50,000 CNY; ■ or imposing a fine of not less than one time but not more than five times of the illegal gains (when the illegal gains are more than 50,000 CNY); ■ or shut down for rectification; ■ or revocation of business license; ■ and imposing a fine of not less than 2,000 CNY but not more than 20,000 CNY on the directly responsible person in charge and other directly liable persons.

continued on following page

Table 1. Continued

NO	STATUTE & ADMINISTRATIVE REGULATION	ESSENTIAL PROVISIONS AND EXPLANATIONS
5	Advertising Law	**Purpose:** protecting consumers. ● prohibition of false and misleading promotion: **Article 4** and **Article 28**. ● **Information disclosing obligations**: the obligations of the advertising parties (including advertisers, advertising agents, advertisement publishers and endorsers) to provide true and accurate information (**Article 8**); the obligations to make the advertisements to be identifiable to consumers (**Article 14**). ● Allocation of liabilities: ■ Advertisers: full responsibility (**Article 4, Article 56(1)**). The advertising agent, advertisement publisher and the endorser shall be held jointly and severally liable with the advertiser if they knew or should have known the false nature of the advertisement but still designed, produced, published, recommended or certified the goods and services (**Article 56(3)**). ■ Advertising agents and advertisement publishers: liable when they fail to provide effective contact information of advertisers (**Article 56(1)**). In the case of goods and services concerning the life and health of consumers, the advertising agents, publishers and endorsers shall be held jointly and severally liable with the advertisers (**Article 56(2)**). ■ Endorsers: a special obligation to disclose true information. Endorsers are prohibited from recommending or certifying the goods or services that they have not used (**Article 38**). ● **Possible penalties for misleading and false promotion** (Article 55) applicable to advertisers, advertising agencies and advertisement publishers: ■ stop advertising; ■ imposing a fine of not less than three times but not more than five times of the advertising costs; or imposing a fine of not less than 200,000 CNY and not more than 1000,000 CNY if the advertising costs cannot be calculated; ■ if the advertising parties committed such illegal advertising for more than three times within two years or have other serious circumstances, the fine imposed should be of not less than five times but not more than ten times of the advertising costs; or imposing a fine of not less than 1000,000 CNY and not more than 2000,000 CNY if the advertising costs cannot be calculated; ■ or revocation of business license. ● Possible penalties for endorsers (Article 61): ■ confiscating of illegal gains and imposing a fine of not less than one time but not more than two times of the illegal gains.
6	Measures for the Administration of Internet Advertising (2023, Administrative Regulation)	● Information disclosing obligations: ● Obligations to disclose true information (**Article 13**). ● Obligation to make advertisement identifiable (**Article 9**). Article 9(3) makes explicit rules for influencer marketing: when the promotion of goods and services is in the form of knowledge imparting, experience sharing, or consumption evaluation or other means, accompanied by a shopping link or any other purchase method, the advertisement publisher shall clearly indicate 'advertisement'.
7	Interim Provisions on the Administration of Online Tourism Business Services (2020, Administrative Regulation)	● **Information disclosing obligations:** online tourism services operators have the obligations to provide authentic and accurate information about the tourism services (**Article 12**). ● Prohibition from false promotion (**Article 12**).

Source: Authors own creation

A COMPARATIVE REFLECTION AND STRATEGIC RECOMMENDATIONS

Malaysia and China have general consumer protection and advertising laws that may be applicable to SMIs marketing, thereby ensuring that they operate within legal boundaries. For instance, both countries prohibit misleading marketing practices in which SMIs must present accurate and truthful information to their audience, especially when promoting tourism-related products and activities. Despite the development of existing regulatory frameworks, significant gaps remain in addressing the role of SMIs within the tourism industry. Currently, no specific legislation governs SMIs in promoting tourism-related products and activities. In Malaysia, while the Code established under the CMA offers some guidance for regulating influencers, concerns about its effectiveness persist. Furthermore, SMIs enjoy the right to freedom of expression as guaranteed by the Federal Constitution, the supreme law in Malaysia (Articles 10 and 4). Balancing the constitutional right and the responsibility to shield consumers from misleading content, therefore, presents a notable challenge. SMIs may argue that their posts represent personal opinions, leaving it to consumers to interpret the content when making informed decisions. Meanwhile, in China, although the platform liability clauses are not directly applicable to SMIs, they form a more comprehensive understanding of the regulatory landscape. The legislation and regulations in China impose a series of gatekeeper liabilities on platforms, requiring them to guarantee the truthfulness of the advertisements, either provided by traditional advertising organizations or by SMIs. For example, the 2023 Regulation mandates platforms to verify the authenticity of the quality standard grades, credit ratings and other information of the operators. China's regulatory framework, while stricter, is similar to Malaysia's. It is still evolving and faces difficulties with cross-border collaborations, making it challenging to hold international influencers accountable. The lack of comprehensive and enforceable regulations in Malaysia and China thus fosters an environment conducive to deceptive marketing practices. Insufficient disclosure requirements and penalties for non-compliance further encourage SMIs to not transparently reveal paid partnerships or commercial ties in their social media postings. The absence of definitive cross-border enforcement mechanisms further exacerbates these risks. As tourism marketing becomes more globalized, with SMIs in Malaysia promoting tourism destinations in China and vice versa, the lack of clear legal frameworks governing such cross-border collaborations amplifies the risk of regulatory inconsistencies and undermines consumer protection standards. Consequently, it heightens the potential for misinformation, leaving consumers vulnerable and exposed to unethical marketing practices.

The legal gaps present significant, multifaceted consequences for various stakeholders. From a consumer perspective, the lack of robust regulations mandating transparency in promotional content may lead to uninformed travel decisions. This issue is especially pronounced in the tourism industry, as consumers rely heavily on peer recommendations and experiential content to guide their choices for intangible materials associated with tourism-related products and activities. Such regulatory flaws may harm tourism businesses' reputations while diminishing the efficacy of SMIs endorsements as consumer trust erodes. Moreover, without defined legal frameworks, consumers may face challenges in obtaining compensation or redress for misleading or deceptive promotions. From a business standpoint, the lack of legal recourse may affect the long-term viability of influencer marketing. Companies risk facing reputational harm when collaborating with influencers who fail to adhere to transparent advertising standards. Furthermore, the lack of a well-defined legislative framework may lead to inconsistent agreements between brands and SMIs, leading to legal conflicts over content ownership, payment arrangements, and intellectual property rights. With respect to SMIs, the ambiguity of existing guidelines regulating their activities generates uncertainty regarding compliance, potentially leading to penalties or reputational harm if violations are later discovered. The absence of comprehensive regulation encourages irresponsible behavior among influencers, as the threat of legal consequences remains minimal. This situation creates a cyclical issue in which ethical SMIs are disadvantaged by those who engage in deceptive practices, ultimately undermining trust within the influencer marketing landscape. Malaysia and China have consumer and advertising-related laws. However, when it comes to regulating SMIs marketing, the scope of the existing legal framework remains limited, with relatively weaker enforcement and fewer penalties for non-compliance. This highlights the need for both jurisdictions to review and revise existing legislation to better align with the evolving digital marketing landscape, fostering competitiveness and consumer trust. The regulatory approaches implemented in the UK can serve as a model for Malaysia and China to adopt, thereby enhancing its legal structures to address the challenges posed by SMIs more effectively.

Several regulatory bodies in the UK oversee the regulation of SMIs marketing. Key institutions include the Advertising Standards Authority (ASA), the Committee of Advertising Practice (CAP), the Competition and Markets Authority (CMA), the Office of Communications (Ofcom) and Trading Standard Services (TSS). The ASA ensures that advertisements across various media comply with established advertising standards, while the CAP is responsible for drafting the Advertising Codes. The CAP has revised its guidance, the 'Influencers' Guide to Making Clear that Ads are Ads,' (the Influencers' Guide) to ensure influencers clearly state when their content is advertising. The Influencers' Guide is a best practice guide setting out the rules of influencer marketing, including advice regarding affiliate marketing, how to make clear when ads are ads, and what happens if the content is not disclosed. Failure to disclose a commercial relationship leaves brands and influencers at risk of action from the ASA (CAP, 2023). The ASA also regulates influencer marketing in the UK through the UK Code of Non-broadcast Advertising and Direct & Promotional Marketing (the CAP Code). The Consumer Protection from Unfair Trading Regulations 2008 (the CPUTRs) also contains rules prohibiting influencers from engaging in hidden advertising. Unlike the CAP code, the CPUTRs do not require that the brand exercise control over the content. The CPUTRs are enforced by the CMA and through local government agencies known as the TSS. The CMA ensures healthy market competition by preventing and mitigating anti-competitive practices. When the CMA identifies potential consumer harm in a particular market or business practice, it has the authority to investigate and initiate legal actions to rectify the issue. The ASA, CMA, TSS, and Ofcom have regulatory responsibilities to ensure paid-for endorsements are appropriately labelled on SMPs. The rules they enforce apply to content creators, intermediaries (e.g., marketing and talent agencies), brands and SMPs (ASA; Competition & Markets Authority, 2022; Gov.UK; Ofcom, 2021).

To enhance awareness and ensure compliance, the ASA has publicly disclosed its rulings on hidden advertising by content creators (ASA, 2024b). As part of its enforcement measures, the ASA has also listed influencers who have repeatedly breached the CAP Code by engaging in hidden advertising on their social media channels (ASA, 2022). Publicly naming influencers who consistently violate advertising regulations serves as a deterrent in terms of reputation and legal accountability. This practice undermines the credibility of the individuals involved and sends a clear message to other content creators about the importance of adhering to regulatory standards. By highlighting such breaches, the ASA promotes ethical practices and fosters transparency, enhancing consumer trust in online advertising. Furthermore, repeated violations can discourage businesses from partnering with these influencers, as their reputational damage risks brand integrity and consumer confidence. However, not all online advertisements will fall within the remit of the ASA. Some websites, apps, SMPs and retail platforms often cater to advertisers and consumers across multiple countries, complicating regulatory oversight. To address these complexities, the ASA has established guidelines clarifying when online advertisements come within its purview. Key factors include whether the brands have a registered company address in the UK, if the website's top-level domain ends with '.uk', and whether the ads specifically target UK consumers. These measures protect UK consumers from falling prey to potentially misleading and deceptive content while fostering a more transparent and fair advertising landscape (ASA, 2024a).

Apart from emulating similar approaches in the UK, implementing blockchain technology is another potential strategy for consideration. Blockchain is a decentralized technology where data (e.g., advertising and marketing) is stored in linked blocks that form a chain. Each block contains a unique code from the previous block, a timestamp, and transaction data. The blockchain is a database shared across a network of computers (called a distributed network), allowing any network participant to verify transactions. Cryptography secures these interactions, making them permanent and tamper-proof. Key features include immutability, where data cannot be erased once added; pseudonymity, where participants use cryptographic addresses instead of real identities; and programmability, enabling automated transactions through smart contracts. These aspects create a secure and transparent system with wide-ranging applications beyond cryptocurrencies (Manda et al., 2024, p. 90). Blockchain enhances transparency and trust in marketing by securely recording every transaction in a way that cannot be altered. These records are stored across multiple computers, making them accessible and auditable by all stakeholders. Marketers can track and share each step of a product's journey, from manufacturing to retail, offering insights into its origin, labor practices, and environmental impact. This allows consumers to verify the information and make informed decisions, ultimately building more vital trust and loyalty towards the brand (Manda et al., 2024, p. 93). Blockchain technology can transform social media marketing by enhancing transparency, security, and content authenticity. It allows influencers to take full ownership of their content, making each post unique and easily traceable, which reduces content theft. By implementing blockchain, SMPs can ensure that every account is tied to a real person or entity, minimising the presence of spam and fake bots. Additionally, data on the blockchain is stored permanently, safeguarding content even if a platform resets (Prelipcean et al., 2023, pp. 51,52). In the tourism industry, integrating blockchain can be particularly valuable. Blockchain technology fosters trust between influencers, tourists, and tourism brands by ensuring content creation and partnership transparency. It verifies influencers' reviews via a blockchain-based online review system that acts as a verification tool. Moreover, the enhanced security and data permanence can reassure tourists that the recommendations they follow are genuine, hence mitigating misleading information while increasing engagement and consumer satisfaction in the tourism sector.

While adopting approaches from the UK, which has more experience regulating SMIs, may present cost-effective benefits, implementing them in Malaysia and China could bring distinct challenges. One of the primary concerns is the financial issue associated with developing regulations and ensuring compliance. Governments must allocate sufficient resources to hire experts to analyze data and identify appropriate legal measures to govern SMIs in a dynamic digital landscape. If adhering to the law is costly, market participants, particularly small business enterprises, may resist if they perceive these costs as detrimental to profitability and market competitiveness. Additionally, adopting technologies such as blockchain involves significant costs, given the need for research, development, and continuous monitoring. Adequate funding is therefore vital for recruiting skilled resources and developing technological infrastructure. Lack of support from intelligence personnel can result in a risk of a mismatch between regulatory goals and regulatory instruments, leading to ineffective regulation. Lawmakers are also prone to cognitive biases when drafting information policies, often displaying overconfidence or over-optimism in determining the level of regulatory intervention. This can lead to significant errors, such as underestimating implementation costs (Choi & Pritchard, 2003, p. 28). These biases can be further compounded by the lack of comprehensive data related to emerging technology. Integrating blockchain into the online marketplace, for instance, requires collaboration between authorities, technological experts, and industry stakeholders to ensure seamless implementation and mitigate potential legal issues. If the regulatory framework for blockchain-based marketing is underdeveloped, it may lead to accountability issues in cases of misleading advertisements or fraudulent activities. There will be a challenge in balancing the duty to protect consumers and promote innovation in the digital market. In this regard, input from expert intelligence is crucial as it provides legislators with the necessary insights to accurately interpret existing information and gather new data for informed policymaking. A legal framework is ineffective without proper enforcement mechanisms, particularly in a rapidly evolving digital marketplace. Therefore, establishing a dedicated enforcement agency to monitor SMIs' activities is crucial to ensure legal compliance while evaluating the relevance of existing laws. Furthermore, if lawmakers decide to incorporate emerging technology, such as blockchain, into existing regulatory frameworks, they must ensure it is consistently updated to remain effective and efficiently serve its intended purpose.

CONCLUSION

SMIs emerged as key mediators in tourism marketing due to their ability to convey personal, authentic travel experiences that resonate with consumers. Their shared experiences are significant nowadays, especially in intangible products like travel services; first-hand reviews and recommendations are highly valued. Adherence to legal frameworks, maintaining transparency, and building consumer trust are vital factors for the long-term viability of these SMIs. Malaysia and China have consumer and advertising-related laws prohibiting misleading and deceptive advertising practices. However, there is no specific legislation that directly governs SMIs marketing within the tourism industry. Some relevant regulations on SMIs are embedded within broader parent Acts rather than being part of a dedicated statute. Both regions have acknowledged the roles of influencers and the need to govern them via the implementation of the Malaysian Communications and Multimedia Content Code 2022 and the Measures for the Administration of Internet Advertising' (No.72 [2023] of SAMR Order (China). Nonetheless, it remains crucial for both jurisdictions to precisely define the legal status of SMIs in existing legislation to determine the extent of their legal accountability for their postings. This regulatory gap leaves room for exploitation and ambiguity, highlighting the need for more tailored, modernized legal provisions in a quest to provide robust consumer protection. While SMIs can develop strong ties with their audiences, their credibility can be compromised when promotional content is not acknowledged transparently. This poses risks not only to consumers but also to brands that rely on influencer endorsements. Cross-border interaction between brands and influencers presents both opportunities and legal challenges. Thus, differences in consumer protection and advertising regulations between Malaysia and China may complicate the governance of international influencer campaigns, hence the need for more harmonized legal frameworks to address these issues. Given the substantial tourist exchange between Malaysia and China, it is vital to examine the legitimacy of SMIs marketing in the tourism sectors of both countries and implement strategic planning. Strengthened legal compliance and coordinated efforts by all key stakeholders can boost consumers' confidence, thus increasing repeat visitation rates and promoting both countries as desirable tourist destinations. In this regard, policymakers play a critical role in developing a comprehensive legal framework that addresses the unique challenges of SMIs marketing. Once the proper regulations are in place, businesses and SMIs must strictly comply with these laws. Meanwhile, consumers must stay informed about their rights and the nature of SMIs marketing to make better travel decisions. Complementary measures, such as public awareness campaigns and industry self-regulation initiatives, may reinforce these efforts.

There are several actionable recommendations, each tailored to the distinct but interrelated obligations of policymakers, businesses, SMIs and consumers. These recommendations highlight the collaborative efforts required from these stakeholders to address the challenges in the influencer marketing landscape effectively. First, policymakers in Malaysia and China need to ensure that current consumer and advertising regulatory frameworks effectively address the specific challenges of SMIs marketing. Otherwise, new regulations should be developed to address existing gaps whilst clear policy guidelines should be formulated to ensure legal clarity for stakeholders. Enhancing monitoring and enforcement mechanisms is essential to ensure adherence to the laws. Furthermore, lawmakers must address the complexities of cross-border influencer collaborations, including jurisdictional issues and inconsistent disclosure standards (if any). Relevant ministries could initiate discussions aimed at formulating actionable strategies. Integrating blockchain technology could be a viable solution to enhance government control of businesses in the digital marketplace, especially in challenging-to-supervise cyberspace. Blockchain's immutable ledger system records every transaction or activity, ensuring that data cannot be altered or deleted. This feature would improve the verification of advertisements and review authenticity while facilitating the tracking of an advertisement's lifecycle, hence mitigating risks such as click fraud. Furthermore, blockchain technology benefits brands and SMIs by enabling smart contracts to autonomously manage payments when predefined conditions, such as view targets, are met. Additionally, blockchain technology can assist authorities in monitoring cross-border marketing collaborations, helping to navigate jurisdictional challenges more effectively. Imposing stricter regulations on brands enhances the likelihood of SMIs complying with legal requirements due to their business affiliations. By holding brands accountable for any legal violations by SMIs, the responsibility is shared, motivating both parties to adhere to the law. The government may incentivize businesses that fully comply with the law or respond to their recommendations, such as integrating blockchain technology into business operations. This approach not only enhances the reputation of businesses among potential tourists but also fosters trust with international consumers. Additionally, the government could partner with consumer advocacy groups to initiate public awareness campaigns that educate stakeholders about the legal requirements and the nature of influencer marketing. These efforts would ensure a more informed and compliant ecosystem.

For businesses, partnering with SMIs has become a progressively feasible strategy for reaching wider audiences, particularly when traditional advertising methods diminish efficacy. However, the prevalence of SMIs marketing brings forth regulatory challenges that businesses must address meticulously. Adherence to legal frameworks, ensuring transparency, and building consumer trust are all essential considerations for business viability. Therefore, businesses can actively participate in discussions to formulate industry standards which can assist policymakers in comprehending their needs more effectively. This would enable the development of regulatory measures that balance consumers' interests with the pursuit of business profitability. Businesses can show their support for government initiatives by integrating blockchain technologies, such as smart contracts, into their operations. These contracts may address payment-related matters, how endorsement should be legally presented, and contain explicit reminders of the regulations that must be observed when fulfilling contractual obligations. Businesses must ensure that the SMIs they engage comply with regulatory requirements, as non-compliance may result in legal liability being imposed on the business. Key legal provisions can be included in their smart contracts to mitigate this risk, such as the requirement to disclose all paid partnerships transparently. Businesses may assist in evaluating the effectiveness and gaps in using blockchain for further improvement. They may also establish their internal policies to supplement governmental regulations for SMIs. These internal policies can be embedded within the smart contracts, incorporating clear terms and conditions to ensure compliance. Most importantly, the internal policies and smart contracts should align with consumer protection and advertising laws, primarily when collaborating with international influencers.

The primary duty of SMIs is to ensure their endorsements are genuine to secure consumers' trust. At the same time, they must comply with consumer and advertising laws, such as avoiding misleading and deceptive content and being transparent when sharing experiences in their postings. To meet their legal obligations to brands who engage them, SMIs may use available tools on social media platforms, such as paid partnership tags, to transparently disclose sponsored content to their viewers. Consumers, on the other hand, can contribute to creating a fair and safe digital marketplace by proactively educating themselves about their legal rights. Without this awareness, they may fail to recognize instances where SMIs do not transparently disclose their commercial affiliations, resulting in consumer deception and undermining the purpose of consumer and advertising legislation. Additionally, consumers can assist in mitigating the prevalence of fake reviews, which can distort purchasing decisions. Policymakers would benefit from consumer aid in this regard. Where available, consumers should leverage advanced technologies like blockchain-based review verification systems to ensure their travel decisions are founded on accurate, verified reviews. These proactive measures enhance individual travel experiences and support the broader travel community by fostering transparency and trust in tourism-related products and services.

Advancing Knowledge: Key Areas for Future Research

As explored in this chapter, the increasing prominence of SMIs marketing poses various challenges to consumer protection and advertising law in Malaysia and China. With SMIs marketing poised for continued growth, several key trends warrant further analysis. First, this chapter focuses on SMIs in tourism-related products and activities in general. Future studies may explore each category more precisely, e.g., hotels, the food and restaurant industry, airlines, and the leisure industry. Second, this chapter is centered on SMIs who create and share content within the tourism industry rather than on the digital platforms they utilize. Future research could delve into the roles of SMPs as intermediaries and gatekeepers for SMIs. Such exploration would offer valuable insights into the intricate legal dynamics governing SMIs marketing, the liabilities of digital platforms and the protection of tourists' interests in the tourism industry. Third, future research may analyze the need to differentiate between professional and non-professional influencers (ordinary individuals) for liability purposes. The fourth concern for prospective studies is to examine the legal aspect of 'de-influencing', i.e., SMIs who review certain products negatively. Fifth, legal research in this area may continue exploring the rise of virtual influencers. While virtual influencers act similarly to human influencers, they also introduce unique legal and ethical considerations, e.g., who will be liable for law infringements. Finally, as the tourism industry grows worldwide, further research may focus on cross-border collaborations between influencers and brands. Influencers in Malaysia may promote tourist destinations in China and vice versa, targeting both local and international tourists. However, this raises complex legal questions regarding jurisdiction and compliance with advertising regulations across multiple countries. Upcoming research should examine how influencers and tourism brands navigate the legal landscapes of different jurisdictions when engaging in cross-border campaigns, exploring how these legal frameworks either facilitate or hinder international influencer marketing efforts.

REFERENCES

Advertising Standards Authority [ASA]. (2024). *Advertising codes: The UK advertising codes lay down rules for advertisers, agencies and media owners to follow*. ASA. Retrieved September 20, 2024, from https://www.asa.org.uk/codes-and-rulings/advertising-codes.html

Antoniou, A. (2024). When likes go rogue: Advertising standards and the malpractice of unruly social media influencers. *Journal of Media Law*, 1-44.

Archer, C., Wolf, K., & Nalloor, J. (2021). Capitalising on chaos: Exploring the impact and future of social media influencer engagement during the early stages of a global pandemic. *Media International Australia, Incorporating Culture & Policy*, 178(1), 106–113. DOI: 10.1177/1329878X20958157

ASA. (2021a, February 3). Beauty and cosmetics: The use of production techniques. Retrieved July 15, 2024, from https://www.asa.org.uk/advice-online/cosmetics-the-use-of-production-techniques.html

ASA. (2021b, February 11). The (mis)use of social media beauty filters when advertising cosmetic products. Retrieved July 15, 2024, from https://www.asa.org.uk/news/the-mis-use-of-social-media-beauty-filters-when-advertising-cosmetic-products.html

ASA. (2022). Non-compliant social media influencers. Retrieved September 20, 2024, from https://www.asa.org.uk/codes-and-rulings/non-compliant-social-media-influencers.html

ASA. (2024a, July 29). Remit: Country of origin. Retrieved September 20, 2024, from https://www.asa.org.uk/advice-online/remit-country-of-origin.html

ASA. (2024b). Rulings. Retrieved September 20, 2024, from https://www.asa.org.uk/codes-and-rulings/rulings.html?topic=4DF9FA97-F0A0-4B57-A8E73F8D695F073E,E5C6E825-2A0C-43EF-92C89820C76B6726&issue=B62E671E-81D6-42FD-8BDA1611D194B1D3,9EDD13C6-91FE-4698-A7517E0C28EB1729,&media_channel=2FED54B5-5B19-40BC-B75BD73F29665855&date_period=past_year

Bastrygina, T., Lim, W. M., Jopp, R., & Weissmann, M. A. (2024). Unraveling the power of social media influencers: Qualitative insights into the role of Instagram influencers in the hospitality and tourism industry. *Journal of Hospitality and Tourism Management*, 58, 214–243. DOI: 10.1016/j.jhtm.2024.01.007

Burns, K. S. (2021). The history of social media influencers. In *Research perspectives on social media influencers and brand communication* (pp. 1–22). IGI Global.

Choi, S. J., & Pritchard, A. C. (2003). Behavioral economics and the SEC. *Stanford Law Review*, 56(1), 1–73. DOI: 10.2307/1229705

Committee of Advertising Practice [CAP]. (2023). Updated guidance for influencer marketing. ASA. Retrieved September 20, 2024, from https://www.asa.org.uk/news/updated-guidance-for-influencer-marketing.html

Competition & Markets Authority [CMA]. (2022, November 3). Guidance: Hidden ads: Being clear with your audience. Gov.UK. Retrieved September 20, 2024, from https://www.gov.uk/government/publications/social-media-endorsements-guide-for-influencers/social-media-endorsements-being-transparent-with-your-followers

Davis, O. (2023). The new normal: Navigating legal challenges in the world of influencer marketing & how ADR can help. *Pepperdine Dispute Resolution Law Journal*, 23, 70.

De Veirman, M., De Jans, S., Van den Abeele, E., & Hudders, L. (2020). Unraveling the power of social media influencers: A qualitative study on teenage influencers as commercial content creators on social media. In *The regulation of social media influencers* (pp. 126–166). Edward Elgar Publishing. DOI: 10.4337/9781788978286.00015

Dencheva, V. (2024, February 6). Influencer marketing market size worldwide from 2016 to 2024. *Statista*. Retrieved September 20, 2024, from https://www.statista.com/statistics/1092819/global-influencer-market-size/

Duboust, O. (2023, June 5). France has approved a law that targets influencers. What does it mean for social media stars? *Euronews*. Retrieved July 15, 2024, from https://www.euronews.com/next/2023/06/05/france-has-approved-a-law-that-targets-influencers-what-does-it-mean-for-social-media-star

Ducato, R. (2020). One hashtag to rule them all? Mandated disclosures and design duties in influencer marketing practices. In *The regulation of social media influencers* (pp. 232–273). Edward Elgar Publishing. DOI: 10.4337/9781788978286.00020

Fedeli, G., & Cheng, M. (2023). Influencer marketing and tourism: Another threat to integrity for the industry? *Tourism Analysis*, 28(2), 323–328. DOI: 10.3727/108354222X16510114086370

Federal Trade Commission. (2019). Disclosures 101 for social media influencers. Retrieved July 15, 2024, from https://www.ftc.gov/business-guidance/resources/disclosures-101-social-media-influencers

Garner, B. A. (2024). *Black's law dictionary* (12th ed.).

Goanta, C., & Ranchordás, S. (Eds.). (2020a). *The regulation of social media influencers.* Edward Elgar Publishing. DOI: 10.4337/9781788978286

Goanta, C., & Ranchordás, S. (2020b). *The regulation of social media influencers.* Edward Elgar Publishing. DOI: 10.4337/9781788978286

Goodship, P. (2019). Influencer marketing: What you need to know. Competition and Markets Authority. Retrieved July 15, 2024, from https://competitionandmarkets.blog.gov.uk/2019/04/30/influencer-marketing-what-you-need-to-know/

Gov.UK. (2022). Regulatory roles in tackling hidden advertising. Retrieved September 20, 2024, from https://assets.publishing.service.gov.uk/media/63626ba6d3bf7f04f3a5479c/221020_CMA_ASA_Ofcom_-_Regulatory_Landscape.pdf

Hayes, A. (2019, October 18). The age of the influencer - How it all began! *LinkedIn*. Retrieved September 20, 2024, from https://www.linkedin.com/pulse/age-influencer-how-all-began-amelia-neate

Higgins, M. (2019, March 25). Frye festival aftermath: New rules for influencers? *UC Law Review*. Retrieved July 15, 2024, from https://uclawreview.org/2019/03/25/fyre-festival-aftermath-new-rules-for-influencers/

Ilieva, G., Yankova, T., Ruseva, M., Dzhabarova, Y., Klisarova-Belcheva, S., & Bratkov, M. (2024). Social media influencers: Customer attitudes and impact on purchase behaviour. *Information (Basel)*, 15(6), 359. DOI: 10.3390/info15060359

Ingrassia, M., Bellia, C., Giurdanella, C., Columba, P., & Chironi, S. (2022). Digital influencers, food and tourism: A new model of open innovation for businesses in the Ho. Re. Ca. sector. *Journal of Open Innovation*, 8(1), 50. DOI: 10.3390/joitmc8010050

Iyengar, R., Van den Bulte, C., & Valente, T. W. (2011). Opinion leadership and social contagion in new product diffusion. *Marketing Science*, 30(2), 195–212. DOI: 10.1287/mksc.1100.0566

Joshi, Y., Lim, W. M., Jagani, K., & Kumar, S. (2023). Social media influencer marketing: Foundations, trends, and ways forward. *Electronic Commerce Research*, •••, 1–55. DOI: 10.1007/s10660-023-09719-z

Katz, E., & Lazarsfeld, P. F. (2006). *Personal influence: The part played by people in the flow of mass communications* (1st ed.).

Kemp, A. (2023, April 9). 'We applaud this movement of transparency': Marketers react to French influencer law. *The Drum*. Retrieved July 15, 2024, from https://www.thedrum.com/news/2023/06/05/we-applaud-movement-transparency-marketers-react-french-influencer-law

Kilipiri, E., Papaioannou, E., & Kotzaivazoglou, I. (2023). Social media and influencer marketing for promoting sustainable tourism destinations: The Instagram case. *Sustainability (Basel)*, 15(8), 6374. DOI: 10.3390/su15086374

Liu, S. (2020). Thinking about the legal attribute of live broadcast for goods promotion. *Research on China Market Regulation*, 5, 21–23.

Liu, Y., & Li, N. (2021). The legal regulation of the false promotion of the live broadcast e-commerce. *Intellectual Property*, 5, 68–82.

Ma, H. (2021). Research on the advertising regulation of influencer marketing in the era of social networks. [Philosophy and Social Science]. *Journal of Southwest University (Natural Science Edition)*, 23(1), 32–40.

Malaysia, T. (2023, March 17). Tourism Malaysia - Air Asia collaboration brings Taiwanese influencers and bloggers to promote Malaysia. *Tourism Malaysia*. Retrieved October 1, 2023, from https://www.tourism.gov.my/media/view/tourism-malaysia-air-asia-collaboration-brings-taiwanese-influencers-and-bloggers-to-promote-malaysia

Manda, V. K., Sagi, S., & Yadav, A. (2024). Blockchain in advertising and marketing: Revolutionizing the industry through transparency and trust. In *New trends in marketing and consumer science* (pp. 89–112). IGI Global., DOI: 10.4018/979-8-3693-2754-8.ch005

Merriam-Webster Online Dictionary. (n.d.). Influencer. In https://www.merriam-webster.com/dictionary/influencer

Mezzofiore, G. (2019, May 4). Beach club owner rips into freeloading Instagram 'influencers'. *CNN Travel*. Retrieved July 15, 2024, from https://edition.cnn.com/travel/article/instagram-influencers-beach-club-philippines-intl-scli/index.html

Mindset, T. (2024). Hot tips from Webinar 2: Influencer marketing during and post. *COVID*, 19, •••. Retrieved July 15, 2024, from https://www.travelmindset.com/hot-tips-from-webinar-2-influencer-marketing-during-and-post-covid-19/

Ofcom. (2021, July 12). Video-sharing platform guidance: Guidance for providers on advertising harms and measures. Retrieved September 20, 2024, from https://www.ofcom.org.uk/siteassets/resources/documents/consultations/category-1-10-weeks/219750-proposals-for-the-regulation-of-advertising-on-video-sharing-platforms-/associated-documents/vsp-guidance-harms-and-measures.pdf?v=327263

Pettersen-Sobczyk, M. (2023). Social media influencer marketing in the promotion of tourist destinations. *Tourism Management*, 42, 31–45.

Polat, E., Çelik, F., Ibrahim, B., & Gursoy, D. (2024). Past, present, and future scene of influencer marketing in hospitality and tourism management. *Journal of Travel & Tourism Marketing*, 41(3), 322–343. DOI: 10.1080/10548408.2024.2317741

Pop, R.-A., Săplăcan, Z., Dabija, D.-C., & Alt, M.-A. (2022). The impact of social media influencers on travel decisions: The role of trust in consumer decision journey. *Current Issues in Tourism*, 25(5), 823–843. DOI: 10.1080/13683500.2021.1895729

Prelipcean, M., Acatrinei, C., Gradinescu, I., & Cânda, A. (2023). The impact of blockchain technology on marketing through social media. *Journal of Emerging Trends in Marketing and Management*, 1, 46–54.

Qiu, B. (2020). The legal liabilities in advertising endorsements and influencer marketing. *Research on China Market Regulation*, 5, 26–29.

Rachmad, Y. E. (2024). *The future of influencer marketing: Evolution of consumer behavior in the digital world. PT.* Sonpedia Publishing Indonesia.

Ramli, A. (2024). China shines as Malaysians' top holiday destination. *Travel Weekly Asia*. Retrieved May 31, 2024, from https://www.travelweekly-asia.com/Travel-News/Trade-Shows-and-Events/China-shines-as-Malaysians-top-holiday-destination

Schouten, A. P., Janssen, L., & Verspaget, M. (2021). Celebrity vs. influencer endorsements in advertising: The role of identification, credibility, and product-endorser fit. In Geuens, M., De Pelsmacker, P., & Van den Bergh, K. (Eds.), *Leveraged marketing communications* (pp. 208–231). Routledge. DOI: 10.4324/9781003155249-12

Sicilia, M., & López, M. (2023). What do we know about influencers on social media? Toward a new conceptualization and classification of influencers. In *The Palgrave handbook of interactive marketing* (pp. 593–622). Springer., DOI: 10.1007/978-3-031-14961-0_26

Solomon, M. R. (2020). *Consumer behaviour: Buying, having and being* (13th ed.). Pearson.

Song, Y. (2020). Business model and legal regulation of live broadcast for goods promotion. *Research on China Market Regulation*, 8, 9–16.

Stoldt, R., Wellman, M., Ekdale, B., & Tully, M. (2019). Professionalizing and profiting: The rise of intermediaries in the social media influencer industry. *Social Media + Society*, 5(1), 2056305119832587. Advance online publication. DOI: 10.1177/2056305119832587

The Star. (2024a, June 8). Fan Bingbing's appointment as tourism ambassador to draw international tourists, says Melaka CM. Retrieved July 15, 2024, from https://www.thestar.com.my/news/nation/2024/06/08/fan-bingbing039s-appointment-as-tourism-ambassador-to-draw-international-tourists-says-melaka-cm

The Star. (2024b, April 2). Tourism Malaysia eyes five million Chinese tourists. Retrieved May 31, 2024, from https://www.thestar.com.my/news/nation/2024/04/02/tourism-malaysia-eyes-five-million-chinese-tourists

The White Moose Café. (2018, January 16). *Facebook post*. https://www.facebook.com/WhiteMooseCafe/

Tobon, S., & García-Madariaga, J. (2021). The influence of opinion leaders' eWOM on online consumer decisions: A study on social influence. *Journal of Theoretical and Applied Electronic Commerce Research*, 16(4), 748–767. DOI: 10.3390/jtaer16040043

Wang, T. (2021). The definition of legal status and responsibilities of influencers in live broadcast for goods promotion. *Foreign Economic Relations and Trade*, 7, 86–88.

Zeno, J. (2022). Information in consumer contracts: Reforming consumer protection law in Malaysia. *Asian Journal of Comparative Law*, 17(2), 242–267. DOI: 10.1017/asjcl.2022.18

Zhang, T. (2020). Analysis of the multiple legal status of digital influencers in goods promotion. *Research on China Market Regulation*, 5, 12–15.

Zhu, C., Fong, L. H. N., Liu, C. Y. N., & Song, H. (2023). When social media meets destination marketing: The mediating role of attachment to social media influencer. *Journal of Hospitality and Tourism Technology*, 14(4), 643–657. DOI: 10.1108/JHTT-04-2022-0119

KEY TERMS AND DEFINITIONS

Communications and Multimedia Act 1998 (CMA): Legal framework in Malaysia that regulates the communications and multimedia sectors, including broadcasting, telecommunications, and internet services.

Consumer Protection Act 1999 (CPA): Malaysian law designed to safeguard consumer rights by regulating unfair trade practices, product safety, and service standards. It provides legal recourse for consumers in cases of fraud, deceptive advertising, and defective products or services.

Opinion Leaders (OLs): Individuals who have significant influence within a specific community or industry, often due to their expertise, credibility, or social standing.

State Administration for Market Regulation (SAMR): China's central regulatory authority responsible for market supervision, product quality, anti-monopoly enforcement, and ensuring fair competition. It also oversees advertising standards and consumer protection.

Social Media Influencers (SMIs): Individuals who have built a large and engaged following on social media platforms. They shape consumer behavior and public opinion by sharing content, product endorsements, and personal opinions, often collaborating with brands for promotional purposes.

Social Media Platforms (SMPs): Digital platforms that facilitate social networking and content sharing among users. These platforms enable users to interact, share media, and engage with content creators, including influencers.

Trade Descriptions Act 2011 (TDA): Malaysian law that prevents false or misleading descriptions of goods and services. It aims to ensure accuracy in product labeling, advertising, and marketing, protecting consumers from deceptive or fraudulent business practices.

Malaysian Communications and Multimedia Content Code 2022 (The Code): Set of guidelines governing content creation and distribution across all media in Malaysia. It ensures that content is ethical, responsible, and aligns with cultural and social standards, covering areas such as advertising, online content, and broadcasting.

Chapter 5
Role of Visual Image of Hospitality Industry in Promoting Tourism and Decision-Making Process of Consumers

Harsh Mehta
https://orcid.org/0000-0002-6983-704X
Pearl Academy, India

ABSTRACT

The purpose of this study is to investigate the exploratory role of visual imagery in the hospitality sector and its influence on promoting tourism as well as the decision-making processes of consumer perceptions. By reviewing relevant literature, the authors explore the use of visual images and how these can be used presently and propose a model that explains decision-making within hospitality and tourism promotion. The findings highlight the importance of visual imagery for managing and marketing hospitality and tourism products more effectively. The study also offers a practical model that will serve as a foundation for further refinement through practitioner input. There has been limited scholarly investigation in this field, thus the study addresses a gap in research, merging image formation with practical applications for hospitality and tourism organizations.

DOI: 10.4018/979-8-3693-7021-6.ch005

INTRODUCTION

The hospitality industry plays an indispensable role in the promotion and growth of global tourism, serving as a vital contributor to the economic and cultural exchange that tourism fosters. Central to the marketing strategies employed by hospitality and tourism businesses is the use of visual imagery, which has emerged as an essential tool for shaping travelers' perceptions, building brand identity, and influencing decision-making processes. The strategic deployment of visual representations—such as photographs, videos, and digital media—has become one of the most effective means of communicating the unique attractions, services, and cultural significance of tourist destinations. Through these representations, tourism promoters can create compelling narratives that not only attract potential visitors but also enhance the competitive advantage of the destinations they seek to promote.

Visual imagery's role in tourism marketing is extensively documented, highlighting its profound impact on destination branding, consumer behavior, and the overall success of tourism enterprises. Early scholars, such as Font (1997), emphasized the significance of visual imagery in shaping the image of tourist destinations. This perspective has been supported and expanded by contemporary researchers, including Araújo (2018) and Malik (2020), who argue that visual representations convey critical elements of a destination's identity, such as its culture, heritage, and unique attributes. Moreover, the increasing reliance on digital platforms for information dissemination has further elevated the importance of visual content, making it a central component of tourism marketing strategies in the modern era (Govers et al., 2007).

THE ROLE OF VISUAL IMAGERY IN DESTINATION BRANDING

Destination branding has become a cornerstone of tourism marketing, as it helps establish a recognizable and distinct identity that differentiates one destination from another. In an increasingly competitive global tourism market, destinations must not only highlight their physical and cultural attractions but also create a cohesive brand that resonates with potential visitors. Visual imagery is fundamental to this process, as it allows destinations to project their unique selling propositions in ways that are engaging, memorable, and emotionally compelling.

According to Font (1997), the image of a tourist destination is one of the most powerful tools available for creating and sustaining its appeal. Destination branding relies heavily on visual elements to construct a narrative that aligns with the aspirations and desires of target audiences. Photographs, videos, and other forms of visual content enable destinations to showcase their landscapes, architecture, cultural heritage, and lifestyle offerings, presenting them in an idealized yet enticing manner. As Araújo (2018) argues, effective visual imagery can significantly enhance a destination's appeal by providing potential visitors with a tangible sense of the experiences that await them. In this way, visual imagery not only informs but also inspires, allowing consumers to envision themselves within the destination and motivating them to travel.

In constructing a destination's brand identity, visual representations must also reflect the cultural and historical significance of the place. Malik (2020) contends that the use of visual imagery to highlight a destination's cultural heritage and unique attributes is a key factor in shaping tourists' perceptions. Images that convey the authenticity of a destination's traditions, festivals, architecture, and local way of life can create a sense of connection and allure that is difficult to achieve through textual descriptions alone. In this regard, visual imagery serves not only as a tool for attraction but also as a medium through which the identity of a place is constructed and communicated to a global audience.

Visual Imagery in the Digital Age: A New Paradigm for Tourism Marketing

The rise of digital platforms and social media has revolutionized the way in which visual imagery is used in tourism marketing. With the proliferation of online travel agents (OTAs), review websites, and social media platforms, visual content has become more accessible and influential than ever before. Today's travelers increasingly rely on visual stimuli to inform their travel decisions, making the strategic use of photographs, videos, and virtual tours an essential aspect of tourism promotion (Govers et al., 2007).

One of the key advantages of visual imagery in the digital age is its ability to reach a wide and diverse audience. Social media platforms such as Instagram, Facebook, and Pinterest are dominated by visual content, providing destinations and hospitality businesses with unparalleled opportunities to showcase their offerings to potential travelers around the world. User-generated content—travel photos, videos, and reviews shared by tourists—has further enhanced the visibility and attractiveness of destinations, creating a cycle of visual influence that perpetuates tourism growth. As Munar and Jacobsen (2014) note, the role of social media in tourism promotion has fundamentally shifted the balance of power from traditional marketers to travelers themselves, who now act as co-creators of the visual narratives that shape destination branding.

The effectiveness of visual imagery in digital tourism marketing lies in its ability to evoke emotions, memories, and associations that can influence travelers' perceptions and decisions. Sullivan (2013) points out that the human brain processes images 60,000 times faster than text, making visual content an ideal medium for capturing attention and conveying messages quickly and efficiently. This efficiency in communication is particularly important in a digital environment where consumers are constantly bombarded with information from multiple sources. High-quality visual content, therefore, serves as a critical differentiator, allowing destinations and hospitality businesses to stand out in an increasingly crowded marketplace.

Moreover, digital platforms have facilitated the integration of innovative visual tools, such as virtual reality (VR) and augmented reality (AR), into tourism marketing strategies. These technologies allow potential travelers to engage with destinations in immersive and interactive ways, offering virtual tours of hotels, attractions, and landmarks. By providing a more vivid and realistic sense of the experiences that await them, these tools can enhance consumer engagement and drive higher conversion rates. As tourism marketers continue to explore new ways to leverage visual technology, the importance of visual imagery in tourism promotion is only expected to grow.

THE SHIFT TO DIGITAL PLATFORMS: EXPANDING REACH AND ACCESSIBILITY

One of the most significant changes brought about by the digital age is the expansion of reach and accessibility through online platforms. In the past, tourism marketing relied heavily on traditional media channels such as brochures, television advertisements, and travel magazines, all of which had limited distribution and were costly to produce. The advent of the internet revolutionized this model by providing tourism marketers with a global platform to showcase destinations and services at a fraction of the cost. Websites, social media, and digital advertisements have replaced traditional marketing materials, enabling destinations to present visually engaging content to a worldwide audience with minimal barriers.

This digital expansion is particularly evident in the rise of Online Travel Agents (OTAs) such as Expedia, Booking.com, and Airbnb. These platforms not only provide booking services but also offer a rich array of visual content that helps consumers make informed decisions. High-quality images, videos, and 360-degree virtual tours have become standard features on these platforms, allowing potential tourists to virtually experience hotels, attractions, and restaurants before making a booking decision. This ease of access to visual content significantly reduces the uncertainty that accompanies travel planning, as consumers can see exactly what they are purchasing, thus increasing confidence, and reducing perceived risk.

The role of search engines like Google cannot be overlooked either. Visual search tools, such as Google Images, allow users to explore travel destinations through visual cues. According to a study by Choi, Lehto, and Morrison (2007), travelers often start their search for travel options by viewing images of destinations, which serve as the first point of interaction and inspiration. The democratization of access to visual content through digital platforms means that consumers are no longer solely reliant on curated content produced by tourism boards or hotel chains. Instead, they have an entire ecosystem of visual resources at their fingertips, ranging from professional photos to user-generated content, all of which contribute to shaping their perceptions and travel decisions.

Social Media as a Dominant Platform for Visual Tourism Marketing

Perhaps the most transformative force in visual tourism marketing is the rise of social media. Platforms such as Instagram, Facebook, YouTube, Pinterest, and TikTok have fundamentally changed how travelers discover, share, and engage with destinations. Unlike traditional marketing campaigns that rely on passive consumption, social media platforms facilitate active participation from users, turning tourists into content creators who share their experiences through images and videos.

Instagram has become one of the most influential platforms in visual tourism marketing due to its image-centric nature. According to a 2021 study by Skift, 70% of travelers post photos of their vacations on Instagram, and 48% use the platform to find new travel destinations. The hashtag culture on Instagram enables users to search for destinations through keywords like #travel, #vacation, and specific location tags. Destinations that successfully leverage these platforms can benefit from organic marketing, as travelers voluntarily share aesthetically appealing images and videos, essentially acting as ambassadors for those locations.

The importance of social media in visual tourism marketing is further supported by the concept of "social proof." As posited by Cialdini (2001), people tend to conform to the actions of others, especially when making decisions under uncertainty. In tourism, social proof manifests through user-generated visual content, which can be seen in the form of travel photos, vlogs, and reviews. When prospective travelers see images of others enjoying a destination, it creates a sense of validation and credibility that is more persuasive than traditional advertisements. A study by Gretzel, Yuan, and Fesenmaier (2000) found that peer-shared content, particularly visuals, holds more influence over travel decisions than professionally produced materials because it is perceived as more authentic and relatable.

Moreover, visual storytelling on platforms like YouTube has become an effective tool for destination marketing. Video blogs (vlogs) created by travel influencers offer immersive and authentic narratives of travel experiences, providing potential tourists with in-depth insights into destinations. These vlogs, often shared on multiple social media platforms, combine entertainment with information, making them powerful tools for influencing travel choices. Research by Chung and Buhalis (2008) found that video content not only enhances engagement but also significantly boosts brand recall, making it an effective medium for destination branding in the digital age.

USER-GENERATED CONTENT (UGC): THE NEW POWER OF VISUAL INFLUENCE

User-generated content (UGC) has emerged as one of the most potent forces in shaping visual tourism marketing. Unlike traditional marketing campaigns where the destination or service provider controls the narrative, UGC allows travelers to share their own experiences, providing an authentic and often unfiltered view of the destination. Platforms like TripAdvisor, Yelp, and Google Reviews are flooded with user-uploaded images, many of which offer a more realistic representation of tourist experiences than professional marketing photos. These images are often candid, less polished, and provide insights into the everyday experiences that travelers can expect when visiting a destination.

The influence of UGC in tourism marketing is supported by the notion of authenticity, which has become increasingly important to modern travelers. As stated by MacCannell (1999), modern tourists seek "authentic" experiences that reflect the true culture and essence of a destination, rather than the staged or superficial representations often shown in marketing materials. UGC is perceived as more credible because it comes from real travelers who have no vested interest in promoting a particular destination. A study by Xiang and Gretzel (2010) found that over 70% of travelers trust peer reviews and user-uploaded images more than content produced by tourism organizations. This trust in UGC underscores its importance in influencing travel decisions, as consumers are more likely to book a destination that has positive visual endorsements from fellow travelers.

Furthermore, UGC also contributes to destination visibility through the phenomenon of "viral marketing." When a particular destination gains popularity through social media shares, it can quickly become a trending travel spot. This phenomenon was observed with destinations such as Bali, Santorini, and Iceland, where viral images on Instagram and travel vlogs propelled these locations into the spotlight, driving a surge in tourism. A study by Sigala (2016) highlights that viral marketing, driven by user-generated visual content, has the potential to exponentially increase the exposure of a destination, making it one of the most cost-effective marketing strategies available in the digital age.

Virtual Reality (VR) and Augmented Reality (AR): The Future of Visual Tourism Marketing

As technology continues to evolve, new forms of visual content, such as virtual reality (VR) and augmented reality (AR), are being integrated into tourism marketing strategies. VR and AR provide immersive experiences that allow potential travelers to explore destinations virtually before making a decision to visit. For instance, VR tours of hotels, resorts, and attractions offer an unprecedented level of detail and engagement, allowing users to experience the ambiance and layout of a place as if they were physically present. AR, on the other hand, enhances real-world environments by overlaying digital content onto them, offering interactive experiences such as virtual guides or enhanced views of landmarks.

These technologies are particularly valuable in the pre-booking phase of the travel decision-making process, where they help reduce uncertainty and build consumer confidence. Research by Tussyadiah, Wang, and Jia (2017) found that travelers who engage with VR content are more likely to book a destination due to the heightened sense of familiarity and reduced perceived risk. This aligns with the broader trend of consumers seeking more informed and immersive travel planning experiences. As VR and AR technologies continue to advance, they are expected to become integral components of visual tourism marketing, providing destinations with new ways to engage and attract travelers.

Additionally, VR and AR technologies offer the potential for more personalized marketing experiences. For instance, destinations can tailor VR experiences to specific consumer segments, such as adventure travelers, luxury tourists, or family vacationers, providing them with virtual experiences that align with their preferences. This level of personalization, combined with the immersive nature of VR and AR, enhances emotional engagement and can significantly influence travel decisions.

CHALLENGES AND ETHICAL CONSIDERATIONS IN THE DIGITAL USE OF VISUAL IMAGERY

While the digital age has undoubtedly expanded the scope and impact of visual imagery in tourism marketing, it also presents several challenges and ethical considerations. One of the primary challenges is the potential for over-saturation and visual fatigue. With the sheer volume of visual content available on social media and travel platforms, consumers are often overwhelmed by the abundance of options, making it difficult for destinations to stand out. Research by Nadkarni and Hofmann (2012) suggests that the constant exposure to travel-related visuals on platforms like Instagram and Pinterest can lead to diminishing returns, as consumers become desensitized to the images they see. To counteract this, destinations must continually innovate their visual marketing strategies, using creativity, storytelling, and emerging technologies to capture and maintain the attention of potential travelers.

Another challenge is the risk of misrepresentation and the ethical concerns surrounding the use of idealized imagery. In an effort to attract tourists, some destinations and hospitality businesses may use heavily edited or misleading images that do not accurately reflect the reality of the experience. This can lead to disappointment and negative reviews, which can ultimately harm a destination's reputation. Ethical tourism marketing calls for transparency and honesty in the use of visual content, ensuring that the images presented to consumers are truthful representations of what they can expect.

Finally, the rise of UGC also poses challenges for destination marketers, as they have less control over the narrative being presented. While UGC can provide valuable authenticity, it can also include negative or damaging content that may detract from a destination's appeal. Managing this dynamic requires a careful balance between encouraging UGC and curating content that aligns with the destination's brand image.

The Rise of Visual Literacy and its Impact on Tourism Marketing

One of the underlying reasons for the growing importance of visual imagery in tourism marketing is the rise of visual literacy—the ability to interpret, negotiate, and make meaning from information presented in the form of images. As society becomes increasingly visually oriented, the capacity to understand and create visual content has emerged as a critical skill in navigating the complex visual culture of the 21st century (Felten, 2008). This shift towards visual literacy has profound implications for the way in which tourism marketers approach the creation and dissemination of visual content.

Visual literacy is particularly important in the context of tourism because of the highly experiential nature of travel. Potential tourists are not only seeking information about destinations; they are also looking to envision the emotional and sensory experiences that travel will provide. Visual content, therefore, must do more than merely depict a destination's physical attributes—it must also convey the intangible qualities of adventure, relaxation, cultural immersion, and personal fulfillment that motivate people to travel. In this sense, the rise of visual literacy has transformed visual imagery from a supplementary element of tourism marketing to a central component that shapes consumer behavior at every stage of the decision-making process.

The Role of Visual Imagery in the Consumer Decision-Making Process

The consumer decision-making process in tourism and hospitality is complex and multifaceted, involving several key stages: the recognition of a need or desire to travel, the search for information, the evaluation of alternatives, the decision to book, and post-purchase behavior. Throughout these stages, visual imagery serves as a vital source of information, inspiration, and validation, shaping perceptions and guiding choices.

At the initial stage, visual imagery plays a crucial role in sparking interest and desire. According to Baloglu and McCleary, destination images formed largely through visual content significantly influence tourists' perceptions and decision-making processes. High-quality, captivating images of landscapes, accommodations, and activities can trigger the desire to travel by presenting destinations in an aspirational light. In this regard, platforms like Instagram, Pinterest, and travel blogs serve as powerful tools for introducing potential travelers to new destinations.

Once a traveler's interest is piqued, they enter the information search and evaluation stages, where they compare various destinations and hospitality offerings. Visual content is instrumental in this process, as it allows consumers to visualize their potential experiences and assess the attractiveness of different options. Research shows that detailed, vivid images can enhance mental simulations of a destination, increasing emotional engagement and reducing perceived risk (MacInnis & Price). This is particularly important in the tourism industry, where the decision to travel often involves significant financial and emotional investment.

During the decision-making phase, visual imagery serves as a form of validation. For example, a series of beautiful images on a hotel's website can reassure a potential guest that they are making the right decision, increasing the likelihood of booking. Virtual tours and 360-degree images, which provide a comprehensive understanding of a property's layout and amenities, are also effective in reducing uncertainty and enhancing consumer confidence.

Even after the purchase decision has been made, visual imagery continues to play a role in shaping post-purchase behavior. Travelers frequently share their own travel experiences through photos and videos on social media platforms, contributing to the promotion of the destination and influencing future tourists. This user-generated content serves as a form of digital word-of-mouth marketing, further enhancing the visibility and appeal of the destination (Gretzel, 2018). In this way, visual imagery remains a critical factor in the entire consumer decision-making cycle, from initial awareness to post-travel engagement.

Visual Imagery, Identity, and Authenticity in Tourism Promotion

The identity of a tourist destination is closely tied to its visual representation. Destinations use visual imagery to construct and communicate their brand identity, distinguishing themselves from competitors and creating a distinct image in the minds of potential tourists. This branding process involves highlighting unique features, such as cultural heritage, natural beauty, or architectural marvels, to create an identity that is both recognizable and appealing.

However, this practice raises important questions about authenticity and the potential for misrepresentation. As destinations strive to present an idealized image, there is a risk of oversimplifying or even distorting the reality of the place. Mac-Cannell argues that tourism often involves a form of staged authenticity, where the visual representation of a destination is crafted to meet tourist expectations rather than reflect the true nature of the place. This phenomenon is particularly prevalent in destinations that rely heavily on mass tourism, where visual trends and popular aesthetics may lead to the homogenization of tourist experiences.

Nevertheless, the balance between authenticity and idealization in visual imagery is a delicate one. While staged authenticity may detract from the genuine cultural experience of a place, it can also be argued that tourism marketing necessarily involves a degree of curation and narrative construction. As Jenkins (2003) points out, the very act of selecting which images to present and how to frame them is inherently subjective, and every representation is, to some extent, a simplification of the complex realities of a destination. The key challenge for tourism marketers, therefore, is to strike a balance between promoting an aspirational image and maintaining a sense of authenticity that resonates with culturally sensitive and experience-seeking travelers.

Visual imagery plays a critical role in the hospitality and tourism industries, shaping the way destinations are perceived, experienced, and remembered by travelers. As a powerful tool for destination branding, visual representations help create a distinct and memorable identity for tourist locations, influencing consumer behavior throughout the decision-making process. The rise of digital platforms and social media has further amplified the importance of visual content, providing destinations with new opportunities to reach and engage global audiences.

At the same time, the increasing prominence of visual literacy in contemporary culture has elevated the expectations of consumers, who now demand not only informative but also emotionally compelling visual experiences. This shift underscores the need for tourism marketers to adopt sophisticated visual strategies that balance aesthetic appeal with authenticity, ensuring that the images they present accurately reflect the cultural and experiential richness of the destinations they promote.

Ultimately, the continued evolution of visual technology—such as virtual reality and augmented reality—promises to further enhance the role of visual imagery in tourism marketing, offering travelers more immersive and interactive ways to engage with destinations. As the tourism industry continues to grow and diversify, visual imagery will remain a central and indispensable component of its marketing strategies, shaping the future of travel experiences and consumer engagement.

Visual Imagery in Hospitality Industry: Impact on Consumer Perception, Decision-Making, and Destination Promotion

In the dynamic landscape of the hospitality industry, visual imagery plays a pivotal role in shaping consumer perceptions and driving tourism. As the sector becomes increasingly competitive, the importance of visual elements in marketing and branding strategies has grown. This literature review explores the impact of visual imagery on promoting tourism and influencing consumer decision-making, highlighting key studies and theoretical frameworks that elucidate the relationship between visual representation and consumer behavior.

To understand the role of visual images in the hospitality industry, it is crucial to consider several theoretical perspectives. The Visual Influence Theory posits that visual stimuli significantly affect consumer attitudes and behaviors (Petty & Cacioppo, 1986). In the context of hospitality, visual images serve as a powerful tool for creating first impressions and shaping expectations. Additionally, the Aesthetic Experience Theory (Berlyne, 1971) suggests that aesthetically pleasing images can enhance consumer satisfaction and influence their perceptions of quality and value.

Understanding how consumers perceive and interpret visual information is essential. According to Gestalt psychology, humans tend to perceive visual elements as wholes rather than just a collection of parts (Köhler, 1947). This holistic perception plays a significant role in how consumers evaluate travel destinations and hospitality services. Moreover, the Elaboration Likelihood Model (Petty & Cacioppo, 1986) suggests that visual stimuli can influence attitudes and decision-making either through a central route (careful and thoughtful consideration) or a peripheral route (emotional and superficial processing).

Visual imagery is a cornerstone of brand identity in the hospitality industry. According to a study by Govers and Go (2009), the visual representation of a destination or hospitality service contributes significantly to brand perception. High-quality images that showcase desirable attributes, such as luxury accommodations or scenic views, can create a positive brand image and differentiate a service from its competitors. These images often evoke emotional responses that align with the desired brand positioning, thereby influencing consumer preferences.

Furthermore, research by Kim, Lee, and Lee (2016) demonstrates that visual consistency across various marketing channels—such as websites, social media, and brochures—reinforces brand identity and trust. Consumers are more likely to engage with and choose services that present a cohesive and appealing visual narrative. This consistency helps build brand credibility and fosters consumer loyalty.

Visual imagery plays a crucial role in destination marketing by influencing tourists' choices. According to a study by Choi, Lehto, and O'Leary (2007), promotional images of destinations significantly affect tourists' perceptions and intentions to visit. Images that highlight unique attractions, cultural experiences, and natural beauty can attract potential visitors and create a sense of urgency or desire to explore.

Moreover, the Role of Imagery in Tourism Choice Model (Beerli & Martin, 2004) suggests that tourists use visual images to form expectations about a destination. Positive imagery can enhance perceived value and desirability, leading to higher likelihoods of travel. Conversely, negative or unappealing images can deter potential visitors and impact overall destination attractiveness.

Image appeal in consumer photography refers to a picture's ability to pique the interest of third-party viewers (Savakis, Stephen, & Loui, 2000). In tourism, visual image appeal refers to a picture's ability to pique the curiosity of potential visitors and motivate them to visit the place, whether as first-time or repeat visitors. Researchers believe that compelling visual information in advertisements influences how people perceive their travel experiences (Olson, McAlexander, & Roberts,1986; Scarles, 2004). Depending on their expectations, tourists may find different visuals appealing. A study examines the components of a destination picture from a promotion segmentation standpoint, Identified four components of destination image. Visitors' personal expectations may influence how they perceive a destination's image Ahmed (1996). Visual images of destinations can inspire consumers to imagine their experiences, leading to increased purchasing intentions and action. Researchers from psychology and advertising coined the phrase "mental simulation" and "consumption visions" Consumers create mental models of future consumption scenarios. Mental simulation often contains self-reflection, allowing consumers to relate to events with relevant features (Phillips, Olson, & Baumgartner, 1995). Consumers are more likely to envision detailed and self-enacting experiences.

Destination marketers should understand how tourists view and define visitation expectations based on their own perspectives. Research suggests that tourists are more likely to visit a destination if their view of it aligns with their own self-concept (Westwood, Morgan, Pritchard, & Ineson, 1999). To promote a destination, DMOs should create appealing imagery that highlights its essential traits, whether genuine or imagined (Jenkins, 1999; Tasci, Gartner, & Tamer Cavusgil, 2007). According to Cornelissen (2005), DMOs play a crucial role in presenting place signifiers to tourists through their marketing materials, including graphics and photography. To connect with travelers, DMOs must give appealing and intimate photographs that evoke happy memories and recollections.

Understanding travelers and matching their experience profiles is crucial for DMOs to make effective marketing decisions. The study aims to examine the impact of visual images on tourists' experience expectations.

This study attempts to identify potential visitors' perceptions and expectations of destination experiences, as well as their perceptions of enticing visual image and its effect on consumer decision making. DMOs can create visually appealing promotional materials for various experiential target markets by aligning picture content with their perceptions and expectations. Philadelphia was chosen as a context because to its unique blend of history and modernity, offering a diverse range of experiences for potential travelers.

Visual imagery often evokes emotional responses, which can significantly influence consumer behavior. The Affective Response Theory (Mehrabian & Russell, 1974) posits that visual stimuli can evoke pleasure, arousal, and dominance—all of which affect consumer attitudes and behaviors. Cognitive responses, such as perceived quality and value, are also shaped by visual information. Brand Image and Identity: Visual elements, including logos, color schemes, and imagery, are crucial in establishing a hotel's brand identity. Successful branding ensures that potential customers can easily recognize and differentiate one establishment from its competitors (Kapferer, 2012). Visual consistency across marketing materials enhances brand recall and loyalty.

Website and Social Media Presence: Online presence, particularly through websites and social media, is indispensable in the modern hospitality industry. High-quality images of rooms, amenities, dining options, and local attractions enable consumers to visualize their potential experiences (Tussyadiah & Fesenmaier, 2009). Social media platforms, with their emphasis on visual content, further amplify this effect, as user-generated content (UGC) often serves as social proof influencing others' decisions. Destinations use iconic images and videos to appeal to target audiences. For instance, tropical beaches, historical landmarks, and vibrant cityscapes are commonly used to attract tourists (Gunn, 1972). These visuals not only highlight the unique selling propositions (USPs) of a destination but also stimulate interest and desire in potential travelers (Jenkins, 2003). Collaborating with influencers who produce visually appealing content can draw their followers to destinations or establishments. Influencers create relatable and aspirational content that resonates with their audience, effectively turning their personal experiences into persuasive visual marketing tools (Gretzel, 2018).

In the digital age, user-generated content (UGC) has become a significant factor in shaping visual imagery and influencing consumer decisions. Social media platforms and review sites allow consumers to share their experiences through images and videos, which can impact the perceptions of potential travelers. Research by Buhalis and Law (2008) indicates that UGC can serve as a form of social proof, where positive visual content from other travelers reinforces the attractiveness of a destination or hospitality service.

However, the quality and authenticity of UGC can vary, and businesses must navigate the challenges of managing and leveraging such content effectively. Studies by Tuzunkan and İslamoğlu (2020) suggest that while UGC can enhance credibility, it can also pose risks if negative or misleading content is not addressed. Therefore, a balanced approach to integrating UGC with professional visual content is essential for maintaining a positive brand image and influencing consumer perceptions.

The consumer decision-making process involves several stages: problem recognition, information search, evaluation of alternatives, purchase decision, and post-purchase behavior (Kotler & Keller, 2016). Visual imagery plays a crucial role at each stage by providing information, facilitating comparisons, and reinforcing the decision post-purchase. During the evaluation of alternatives, consumers rely heavily on visual information available through brochures, websites, and reviews. Visual representations of hotel rooms, facilities, and guest experiences help potential customers assess the quality and suitability of options available to them (Vermeulen & Seegers, 2009).

One critical challenge is ensuring that visual images are authentic representations of the actual experience. Misleading images that fail to match reality can lead to dissatisfaction, negative reviews, and a damaged reputation (Choi & Mattila, 2004). Therefore, it is essential for hospitality marketers to balance attractiveness with authenticity.

Advancements in technology, such as virtual reality (VR) and augmented reality (AR), are providing new ways for the hospitality industry to utilize visual imagery. VR tours of hotel properties or AR-enhanced travel guides offer immersive and interactive experiences, potentially transforming how consumers make travel decisions (Tussyadiah, Wang, & Jia, 2017).

Visual imagery plays a critical role in the hospitality industry by shaping brand perceptions, influencing destination choices, and impacting consumer decision-making. Theoretical frameworks and empirical research highlight the significance of high-quality, consistent, and engaging visual content in promoting tourism and enhancing consumer experiences. As technology advances, the integration of innovative visual tools, such as VR and AI-driven personalization, will continue to reshape the landscape of hospitality marketing. Understanding and leveraging the power of visual imagery is essential for businesses aiming to attract and retain customers in an increasingly competitive market.

RESEARCH METHODOLOGY

The primary aim of this research is to explore the role of visual imagery in the hospitality industry in enhancing tourism promotion and influencing the decision-making process of consumers. The specific objectives of the study are as follows:

- to examine the impact of visual imagery on consumer perceptions and expectations in the hospitality industry;
- to analyze the effectiveness of visual marketing strategies in promoting tourism destinations and services;
- to investigate the influence of visual images on consumer decision-making processes and booking behaviors;
- to identify best practices and innovative approaches in the use of visual imagery for marketing in the hospitality and tourism sectors; and
- to assess the relationship between visual image quality and consumer satisfaction and loyalty in the hospitality industry.

The present research used a mixed-methods approach, incorporating both qualitative and quantitative techniques, to thoroughly examine the function of visual images in the hospitality sector and their influence on tourism promotion and consumer decision-making. This method collects both statistical data and in-depth insights, enabling a more nuanced view of the phenomenon. The research is structured around a conceptual framework that links visual image attributes (e.g., aesthetics, authenticity, emotional appeal) with consumer responses (e.g., perception, preference, decision-making). The framework hypothesizes that well-crafted visual images positively influence consumers' tourism choices and perceptions of hospitality services. Therefore, the following hypotheses are formulated:

H1: Visual images significantly influence consumers' perceptions of hospitality services.
H2: Aesthetic quality of visual images positively affects consumer preferences for tourism destinations.
H3: Authentic and culturally relevant images enhance consumer trust and likelihood of booking.
H4: Emotional appeal of visual images increases consumer engagement and intention to visit.

To ensure comprehensive and consistent data collection, several instruments were employed.

- **Interview and Focus Group Guides:** These were carefully developed to maintain consistency and depth across qualitative data collection, enabling a thorough exploration of participant perspectives.
- **Survey Questionnaire:** A structured questionnaire was designed using validated scales and items aimed at measuring key variables such as perception, preference, and decision-making processes.
    The collected data was analyzed using a combination of qualitative and quantitative techniques.
- **Qualitative Data Analysis:** Thematic and content analysis were utilized to identify key themes and extract meaningful insights from the qualitative data.
- **Quantitative Data Analysis:** Various statistical methods were applied, including descriptive statistics, correlation analysis, regression analysis, and hypotheses testing, to interpret the quantitative data.

Ethical standards were rigorously upheld throughout the study:

- **Informed Consent:** All participants were fully informed about the purpose of the study, their rights, and the confidentiality of their data before providing consent.
- **Confidentiality:** Participant data was anonymized to protect their identities and securely stored to ensure privacy.
- **Ethical Approval:** The study received approval from the relevant institutional review board to ensure compliance with ethical guidelines.

FINDINGS AND DISCUSSIONS

Qualitative Phase: In-Depth Interviews

Participants in the study identified several key themes regarding the role of visual imagery in attracting tourists and enhancing hospitality services.

- **Importance of Visual Images:** Participants emphasized that visual images are crucial in attracting potential tourists and conveying the essence of hospitality services.
- **Aesthetic Appeal:** High-quality, aesthetically pleasing images were highlighted as influential in creating a positive first impression.

- **Authenticity and Cultural Relevance:** Authentic images reflecting local culture and experiences were seen as enhancing trust and interest among consumers.
- **Emotional Connection:** Images that evoke emotions were found to increase consumer engagement and the likelihood of booking.

Illustrative quotes from participants reinforced these themes, with one stating:
"Visuals are the first thing that catches the eye; they create that initial desire to explore further."
Another participant added:
"People want to see the real experience, not just a polished version. Authenticity is key."
Focus groups provided additional insights into consumer behavior, which can be summarized into the following key points:

- **Decision-Making Process**: Consumers reported that visual images play a significant role in their decision-making process, often serving as a deciding factor between similar options.
- **Trust and Credibility**: Images that appear authentic and reflect real customer experiences enhance trust and credibility.
- **Emotional Appeal**: Images that evoke positive emotions and create a sense of anticipation are more likely to influence travel decisions.

Participant feedback further illustrated these points, with one noting:

- "When I see beautiful pictures of a place, it makes me want to go there immediately."

Conversely, another participant remarked:

- "If the pictures look staged, I tend to look for reviews to see if the reality matches."

Quantitative Phase: Survey Results

Most participants are male (53.3%), younger adults, particularly in the 25-34 age range (40%) and well-educated, with half holding a bachelor's degree and nearly 27% having a master's degree (Table 1).

Table 1. Demographics of respondents

Demographic	Frequency	Percentage
Gender		
Male	160	53.3%
Female	140	46.7%
Age		
18-24	60	20%
25-34	120	40%
35-44	80	26.7%
45-54	30	10%
55 and above	10	3.3%
Education Level		
High School	50	16.7%
Bachelor's Degree	150	50%
Master's Degree	80	26.7%
Doctorate	20	6.7%

Source: Author own creation

The survey results regarding the impact of visual images on decision-making highlight the significant influence these images have on consumer behavior. The mean scores for statements assessing the influence of visual images show a strong agreement among respondents (Table 2).

Table 2. Impact of visual images on decision-making

Statement	Mean	Standard Deviation	Percentage Agreement (Strongly Agree + Agree)
Visual images influence my choice of destination	4.2	0.85	84%
Aesthetic quality of images affects my preference	4.0	0.90	80%
Authentic images increase my trust	4.3	0.75	86%
Emotional appeal of images affects my decision	4.1	0.82	82%

Source: Author own creation

H1: Visual Images Significantly Influence Consumers' Perceptions of Hospitality Services

The regression analysis results support this hypothesis, with a coefficient of 0.75 for the visual image score and a significant p-value of <0.001 (Table 3). This indicates a strong positive relationship between visual imagery and consumer perceptions, reinforcing the notion that effective visual representation can enhance consumers' views of hospitality services.

Table 3. Regression analysis results: hypothesis 1

Variable	Coefficient	Standard Error	t-Value	p-Value
Constant	1.5	0.25	6.00	<0.001
Visual Image Score	0.75	0.10	7.50	<0.001

Source: Author own creation

H2: Aesthetic Quality of Visual Images Positively Affects Consumer Preferences for Tourism Destinations

The correlation analysis shows a strong positive correlation coefficient of 0.68 with a p-value of <0.001 (Table 4), providing robust evidence that aesthetic quality significantly influences consumer preferences. This highlights the necessity for high-quality visual content in marketing strategies.

Table 4. Correlation analysis: hypothesis 2

Variable	Correlation Coefficient	p-Value
Aesthetic Quality	0.68	<0.001

Source: Author own creation

H3: Authentic and Culturally Relevant Images Enhance Consumer Trust and Likelihood of Booking

Regression analysis also supports this hypothesis, with an authenticity score coefficient of 0.85 and a significant p-value of <0.001 (Table 5). The results suggest that authentic imagery not only builds consumer trust but also increases the likelihood of bookings, emphasizing the importance of representing local culture and genuine experiences in marketing efforts.

Table 5. Regression analysis: hypothesis 3

Variable	Coefficient	Standard Error	t-Value	p-Value
Constant	1.2	0.30	4.00	<0.001
Authenticity Score	0.85	0.12	7.08	<0.001

Source: Author own creation

H4: Emotional Appeal of Visual Images Increases Consumer Engagement and Intention to Visit

The correlation analysis shows a strong positive correlation coefficient of 0.72 with a p-value of <0.001 (Table 6), indicating that images that evoke emotional responses significantly enhance consumer engagement and their intention to visit. This underscores the importance of emotionally resonant imagery in marketing strategies for the hospitality sector.

Table 6. Correlation analysis: hypothesis 4

Variable	Correlation Coefficient	p-Value
Emotional Appeal	0.72	<0.001

Source: Author own creation

Summary of Findings

The qualitative findings indicate that visual images play a critical role in shaping perceptions, building trust, and influencing consumer decisions in the hospitality and tourism industry. The quantitative results corroborate these findings, demonstrating that visual image attributes such as aesthetic quality, authenticity, and emotional appeal significantly impact consumer preferences and decision-making. This study underscores the importance for hospitality and tourism organizations to strategically utilize high-quality, authentic, and emotionally engaging visual content to attract and retain consumers.

CONCLUSION

This study delves into the critical role of visual imagery in shaping traveler decision-making and driving tourism promotion within the hospitality sector. By employing a mixed-methods approach, the research provides a comprehensive understanding of how visual representations influence consumer perceptions and behaviors.

Our findings unequivocally demonstrate that visual imagery serves as a powerful tool for attracting potential tourists. High-quality, aesthetically pleasing visuals create a positive first impression, captivating consumers and fostering interest in a destination or hospitality offering. The study's qualitative data revealed that both industry stakeholders and consumers underscored the importance of visually appealing content in conveying the essence of hospitality services.

Beyond aesthetics, authenticity emerged as a key factor in building trust and credibility with consumers. Authentic images that reflect local culture and real experiences were perceived as more trustworthy and likely to enhance consumer engagement. Regression analysis further confirmed this, revealing a significant positive relationship between authenticity and trust, ultimately influencing booking likelihood.

The study's quantitative analysis provides compelling evidence that visual imagery significantly influences consumer decision-making. A substantial majority of respondents (84%) acknowledged the impact of visuals on their destination choices. Moreover, regression analysis demonstrated a strong positive correlation between visual image scores and consumer perceptions. These findings highlight the pivotal role of visual content in shaping consumer preferences and driving bookings.

Practical Implications for the Hospitality Industry

The insights gleaned from this research offer valuable practical implications for stakeholders within the hospitality industry. To effectively attract and retain consumers, organizations should prioritize the integration of high-quality, authentic, and emotionally resonant visual content in their marketing strategies.

The following suggestions outline tailored approaches for Destination Marketing Organizations (DMOs), hotel marketers, and Online Travel Agencies (OTAs) to optimize their use of visual imagery, ensuring it resonates with modern consumers and drives success in an increasingly competitive market.

- **Destination Marketing Organizations (DMOs):** Develop and curate visually appealing content that showcases the unique cultural heritage, natural beauty, and experiences offered by the destination. Collaborate with local photographers and videographers to ensure authenticity and high-quality production.
- **Hotel Marketers:** Utilize visually compelling imagery in all marketing materials, including websites, social media, and promotional campaigns. Focus on capturing the ambiance, amenities, and unique selling points of the property.

- **Online Travel Agencies (OTAs):** Provide users with high-resolution, authentic images of accommodations and destinations. Offer features that allow users to explore properties through virtual tours or immersive visual experiences.

Future Research Directions

While this study provides valuable insights, further research is needed to explore emerging trends and technologies within the field of visual imagery and hospitality. Potential areas of investigation include:

- the impact of new technologies (AR, VR) on visual imagery and consumer engagement.
- how visual content influences different market segments (e.g., luxury travelers, budget-conscious travelers, families).
- the role of user-generated content (UGC) in shaping consumer perceptions and driving tourism promotion.
- the effectiveness of visual storytelling techniques in conveying the emotional experience of hospitality services.

REFERENCES

An, S., Suh, J., & Eck, T. (2019). Examining structural relationships among service quality, perceived value, satisfaction and revisit intention for Airbnb guests. *International Journal of Tourism Sciences*, 19(3), 145–165. DOI: 10.1080/15980634.2019.1663980

Camprubí, R., Guia, J., & Comas, J. (2013). The new role of tourists in destination image formation. *Current Issues in Tourism*, 16(2), 203–209. DOI: 10.1080/13683500.2012.733358

Font, X. (1997). Managing the tourist destination's image. *Journal of Vacation Marketing*, 3(2), 123–131. DOI: 10.1177/135676679700300203

Gartner, W. C. (1994). Image formation process. *Journal of Travel & Tourism Marketing*, 2(2-3), 191–216. DOI: 10.1300/J073v02n02_12

Gretzel, U. (2017). Influencer marketing in travel and tourism. In Sigala, M., & Gretzel, U. (Eds.), *Advances in social media for travel, tourism and hospitality* (pp. 147–156). Routledge. DOI: 10.4324/9781315565736-13

Gupta, V. (2019). The influencing role of social media in the consumer's hotel decision-making process. *Worldwide Hospitality and Tourism Themes*, 11(4), 378–391. DOI: 10.1108/WHATT-04-2019-0019

Han, H., Hsu, L. T. J., & Lee, J. S. (2009). Empirical investigation of the roles of attitudes toward green behaviors, overall image, gender, and age in hotel customers' eco-friendly decision-making process. *International Journal of Hospitality Management*, 28(4), 519–528. DOI: 10.1016/j.ijhm.2009.02.004

Ingram, H., & Grieve, D. (2013). Exploring the nature and effects of perception and image in hospitality and tourism. *Worldwide Hospitality and Tourism Themes*, 5(1), 7–13. DOI: 10.1108/17554211311292402

Jenkins, O. (2003). Photography and travel brochures: The circle of representation. *Tourism Geographies*, 5(3), 305–328. DOI: 10.1080/14616680309715

Köhler, W. (2015). *The task of Gestalt psychology*. Princeton University Press. DOI: 10.1515/9781400868964

Kotler, P., Keller, K. L., Brady, M., Goodman, M., & Hansen, T. (2016). *Marketing management* (3rd ed.). Pearson Higher Ed.

Liu, X., Nicolau, J. L., Law, R., & Li, C. (2023). Applying image recognition techniques to visual information mining in hospitality and tourism. *International Journal of Contemporary Hospitality Management*, 35(6), 2005–2016. DOI: 10.1108/IJCHM-03-2022-0362

Rahimizhian, S., Ozturen, A., & Ilkan, M. (2020). Emerging realm of 360-degree technology to promote tourism destination. *Technology in Society*, 63, 101411. DOI: 10.1016/j.techsoc.2020.101411

Vermeulen, I. E., & Seegers, D. (2009). Tried and tested: The impact of online hotel reviews on consumer consideration. *Tourism Management*, 30(1), 123–127. DOI: 10.1016/j.tourman.2008.04.008

KEY TERMS AND DEFINITIONS

Consumption Visions: Consumption visions are mental representations of future consumption experiences, often involving the visualization of oneself interacting with a product or service. These visions are influenced by factors such as advertising, personal desires, and cultural norms.

Decision-Making: Using mental simulations to evaluate different options and choose the most desirable course of action.

Emotional Connection: Associating positive emotions (e.g., happiness, satisfaction) with the consumption experience.

Imagination: The ability to create mental representations of events that haven't yet occurred.

Mental Simulation: Mental simulation is the cognitive process of imagining a future event or scenario, often involving the visualization of actions, outcomes, and emotions. It allows individuals to mentally rehearse situations, predict consequences, and make informed decisions.

Prediction: Anticipating potential outcomes or consequences based on past experiences and knowledge.

Purchase Behavior: Influencing consumer decisions by making products or services more desirable and appealing.

Visualization: Creating mental images of oneself using or benefiting from a product or service.

Chapter 6
The Psychology of Ethical Marketing:
Navigating Ethical Consumption Through Challenges and Opportunities

Priyanshi Jindal
https://orcid.org/0009-0001-8116-8192
ABES Business School, AKTU, Ghaziabad, India

Harshit Gouri
https://orcid.org/0009-0006-4507-8989
St. Stephen's College, Delhi, India

ABSTRACT

This research paper examines the interplay between psychology and ethical marketing, focusing on the challenges and opportunities in this field. It explores how consumers' values, emotions, and cognitive processes influence ethical purchasing decisions and the obstacles marketers face in presenting their brands authentically. The study addresses consumer trust, the pitfalls of greenwashing, and cultural impacts on ethical choices. Additionally, it highlights opportunities for businesses to meet ethical consumer demands, foster brand loyalty, and enhance social responsibility. By analyzing successful ethical marketing campaigns and psychological tactics, the paper offers practical insights for businesses to align their practices with ethics, emphasizing authenticity, transparency, and emotional engagement. It calls for further research to advance understanding in this area, promising a brighter future for both businesses and society.

DOI: 10.4018/979-8-3693-7021-6.ch006

INTRODUCTION

In recent years, the landscape of consumer behavior has been notably shaped by an unprecedented surge in the significance of ethical consumption. This shift reflects a growing consciousness among consumers about the impact of their purchasing decisions on societal and environmental welfare. As a result, the domain of marketing has undergone a substantial transformation, wherein the authenticity and ethical portrayal of brands have become integral for consumer trust and loyalty (Tanveer et al., 2021a).

Understanding the psychology that underpins ethical marketing has emerged as a critical factor in deciphering this paradigm shift in consumer behavior. It is not merely about showcasing ethical credentials but comprehending the intricate interplay between consumer values, emotions, and cognitive processes that drive ethical choices. This understanding is pivotal for businesses aiming to connect with an increasingly conscientious consumer base (Hemker et al., 2021a).

The purpose of this paper is to delve deeply into this dynamic relationship between psychology and ethical marketing, addressing the challenges and opportunities it presents. By exploring the psychology behind ethical consumption, the study aims to provide a comprehensive framework for businesses and marketers. The objective is not only to decode the evolving landscape of consumer ethics but also to delineate the strategies necessary to navigate this terrain effectively.

This paper's structure encompasses a systematic exploration, examining various dimensions of the psychology of ethical marketing. It includes sections dedicated to delineating the theoretical framework, highlighting the challenges faced by marketers, outlining the opportunities present in ethical marketing, dissecting effective strategies, discussing practical implications, and finally, concluding with a call for further research in this domain. The methodology involves an in-depth review of existing literature, case studies, and psychological insights to construct a robust understanding of the subject matter.

THEORETICAL FRAMEWORK

Introduction to Ethical Marketing and Its Evolution

Ethical marketing has come a long way in recent years. It's no longer just a marketing strategy; it's now a fundamental part of how businesses operate. It's all about promoting products and services while keeping in mind their impact on the environment, society, and ethical standards (Coffin & Egan–Wyer, 2022; Nill, 2022).

This change has been driven by a shift in how society sees the world (Painter et al., 2019). There is a growing concern about ethical and sustainable practices, and an expectation for businesses to do the same. The shift in values has pushed businesses to change the way they operate.

As ethical marketing has grown, it has become closely connected to how people think and make choices. Businesses have realized that understanding why people buy things is essential to showing that they care about ethical values. This connection between ethical marketing and the way people thinks and make decisions is crucial in today's world. It helps businesses navigate the complicated world of what people want and why they buy things (Demjanovičová & Varmus, 2021; Triana, 2022).

This journey of ethical marketing, from its early days to now, shows how business is changing. It's a sign that companies need to think about more than just making money; they need to think about their impact on the world (Rovolis & Habibipour, 2024). This paper explores the history of ethical marketing and how it relates to the way people think and make choices, giving a better understanding of the challenges and opportunities that come with it.

The Psychology of Consumer Decision-Making

Consumer decision-making is a multifaceted process that delves into the intricate world of how individuals choose products and services in the marketplace. This decision-making process is significantly influenced by psychological factors. In this section, we unravel the key elements that drive consumer choices:

1. **Cognitive Processes**: Cognitive processes encompass the rational, logical, and information-processing aspects of decision-making. Consumers engage in cognitive evaluation when assessing products or services (de Ruyter et al., 2022). This includes a detailed analysis of product attributes, features, specifications, and how well they align with their needs and desires. Cognitive processes also involve the consideration of practical factors, such as price, quality, and functionality (Adwan & Altrjman, 2024). Understanding these cognitive aspects is crucial in comprehending the initial stages of consumer decision-making.

2. **Emotional Processes:** Emotions play a pivotal role in consumer behavior and decision-making. Consumers often make choices based on emotional responses to products or brands. Emotions can range from positive feelings like happiness, trust, and excitement, to negative emotions such as fear, anger, or anxiety (Carpenter & Niedenthal, 2018).These emotional responses are frequently triggered by various factors, including personal preferences, brand loyalty, advertising, and the overall experience associated with a product or service. This section explores how emotions can override cognitive factors, leading consumers to make decisions that align with their emotional states or values.
3. **Social and Cultural Influences**: Consumer decision-making is not isolated from societal and cultural influences. These external factors can significantly shape the choices individuals make (Bault & Rusconi, 2020). Cultural norms, family values, peer pressure, and broader societal trends all contribute to consumer behavior. Understanding how these influences affect decision-making is essential for marketers seeking to connect with diverse audiences (Antunes, 2021).
4. **Motivation and Needs**: Consumers are often driven by specific motivations and needs when making decisions. These can include basic needs like food and shelter, but also higher-level needs like social belonging, esteem, and self-fulfilment, as proposed by Maslow's Hierarchy of Needs (Delgado Quintana, 2022). Recognizing the hierarchy of needs and the motivations behind consumer decisions is key to tailoring marketing messages and products to address these needs effectively (Kapferer & Valette-Florence, 2021).
5. **Decision-Making Heuristics and Biases:** Human beings often rely on mental shortcuts or heuristics when making decisions (Johnson et al., 2021). Additionally, cognitive biases can distort the decision-making process. Marketers should be aware of these heuristics and biases to craft effective strategies that align with how consumers naturally make choices.

Understanding of these psychological elements is central to comprehending consumer decision-making. By gaining insights into the cognitive and emotional processes, social and cultural influences, motivations, and decision-making biases, businesses can develop more effective marketing strategies that resonate with their target audience and drive consumer choices.

Link Between Ethical Marketing and Consumer Behavior

The relationship between ethical marketing and consumer behavior is complex and interconnected. Consumers' actions and choices are profoundly affected by the marketing messages they are exposed to, which can either reaffirm their ethical values or provoke a reassessment of those beliefs. In this section, we delve into the various dimensions of this intricate relationship:

1. **Shaping Consumer Attitudes:** Ethical marketing initiatives can significantly influence consumer attitudes. When consumers encounter marketing campaigns that emphasize ethical considerations, they may become more inclined to consider ethical factors when making purchasing decisions (Ahmad et al., 2023; Batlles-de la Fuente & Abad-Segura, 2023). These campaigns often convey a brand's commitment to social and environmental responsibility, encouraging consumers to develop positive attitudes towards the brand and its products.
2. **Impact on Purchase Intention:** Ethical marketing can directly impact consumers' purchase intentions (Alam et al., 2023). When consumers perceive a brand as genuinely committed to ethical values, they are more likely to express an intention to purchase its products or services (Sianturi et al., 2022). Ethical marketing campaigns can serve as a catalyst, translating positive attitudes into concrete buying decisions.
3. **Fostering Brand Loyalty:** Ethical marketing plays a pivotal role in building and sustaining brand loyalty. Consumers who align with a brand's ethical principles are more likely to develop long-lasting relationships with that brand (Tanveer et al., 2021b). Ethical branding reinforces the bond between the brand and its customers, promoting repeat purchases and brand advocacy.
4. **Word-of-Mouth Advocacy:** Satisfied consumers who resonate with a brand's ethical message often become advocates who share their positive experiences with others. Ethical marketing can trigger word-of-mouth recommendations and endorsements, which carry significant weight in influencing the purchasing decisions of potential customers.
5. **Consumer Behavior Change:** Ethical marketing has the potential to induce shifts in consumer behavior. It can encourage individuals to make ethical choices that they might not have considered otherwise (Sweeney et al., 2020). This change in behavior can (Fritzsche, 1987) extend beyond purchasing decisions to encompass lifestyle changes and social causes that align with the brand's ethical values.
6. **Ethical Dissonance:** On the flip side, if a brand's marketing claims are perceived as insincere or "greenwashing" (misleading consumers by falsely presenting a product as environmentally friendly), this can lead to ethical dissonance (Djafarova & Foots, 2022). Consumers may become disillusioned and disenchanted with the brand, leading to negative consequences for the brand's reputation and consumer trust.

The dynamic interplay between ethical marketing and consumer behaviour is essential for businesses seeking to navigate the evolving landscape of conscious consumerism. By aligning their marketing strategies with genuine ethical principles and effectively conveying their commitment to ethical values, businesses can foster positive attitudes, encourage ethical choices, and build lasting relationships with consumers who value ethics in their purchasing decisions.

CHALLENGES IN ETHICAL MARKETING

Ethical marketing, while crucial for fostering consumer trust and brand loyalty, is fraught with challenges that demand careful navigation. This section outlines key challenges, illuminating the hurdles businesses face in authentically portraying their brands as ethical.

1. **Greenwashing and its Impact**: Greenwashing is a misleading practice that involves making false or exaggerated claims about the environmental benefits of a product. It can undermine consumer confidence and loyalty, as well as harm the reputation of the company (Somany, 2023). Greenwashing also has a negative impact on the environment, as it can divert attention and resources from genuine solutions and create confusion among consumers. Therefore, it is important to avoid greenwashing and to communicate authentically and transparently about the environmental aspects of a product.
2. **Consumer Skepticism and Cynicism:** Consumers face a barrage of information and have become more distrustful than ever. Negative attitudes towards marketing messages, especially those that claim ethical practices, can reduce the impact of ethical marketing efforts (Hemker et al., 2021b). Creating and sustaining trust requires openness and consistent ethical practices to overcome consumer distrust.
3. **The Influence of Cultural and Social Factors:** Cultural and social factors have a significant impact on ethical standards. Different cultures may have different views on what is ethical or not in marketing. Therefore, marketers need to be aware of the cultural and social contexts of their target markets, and tailor their messages accordingly (Albarq, 2024). By doing so, they can avoid offending or alienating potential customers, and instead create positive and respectful relationships with them.
4. **Regulatory and Legal Challenges:** Ethical marketing often intersects with regulatory landscapes and legal frameworks (Crispin P. Noguerra, 2023). Navigating the complex web of regulations, ensuring compliance, and avoiding legal pitfalls can be challenging. Businesses must stay abreast of evolving eth-

ical standards and legal requirements to align marketing practices with ethical principles without risking legal repercussions.

Addressing these challenges demands a holistic approach. Businesses must prioritize authenticity, transparency, and cultural sensitivity in their marketing endeavors. By understanding and mitigating these obstacles, brands can foster genuine connections with consumers, reinforcing their commitment to ethical practices and navigating the intricate landscape of ethical marketing successfully.Top of Form

OPPORTUNITIES IN ETHICAL MARKETING

While ethical marketing presents challenges, it also offers significant opportunities for businesses to align with consumer values and contribute positively to society. Key opportunities that can be harnessed to build brand success and consumer trust.

1. **Building Trust and Credibility**: Authentic ethical practices are foundational in establishing and maintaining trust with consumers (Ladwein & Sánchez Romero, 2021). Demonstrating a genuine commitment to ethical values builds credibility, fostering long-term relationships with consumers who prioritize transparency and integrity in the brands they support.
2. **Fostering Brand Loyalty and Positive Consumer Attitudes**: Ethical marketing creates an emotional connection with consumers who share similar values. By consistently communicating ethical principles, businesses can foster brand loyalty and positive attitudes (Tanveer et al., 2021c). Consumers are more likely to choose and remain loyal to brands that align with their ethical beliefs.
3. **Creating a Competitive Advantage**: In an increasingly conscientious marketplace, ethical practices differentiate brands and confer a competitive advantage. Consumers are inclined to support businesses that go beyond profit motives, preferring those that actively contribute to social and environmental well-being (Krivokuća, 2020). Ethical marketing positions a brand as a responsible and socially conscious choice.
4. **Contributing to Social and Environmental Causes**: Ethical marketing provides a platform for businesses to contribute meaningfully to social and environmental causes (Pittman et al., 2022). Aligning marketing efforts with impactful initiatives not only addresses societal challenges but also resonates positively with consumers who seek to support businesses engaged in positive social and environmental endeavors.

5. **Leveraging Social Media and Technology for Ethical Marketing:** The digital age offers unprecedented opportunities to amplify ethical marketing messages (Mpinganjira & Maduku, 2019). Social media platforms provide a direct and immediate channel for businesses to engage with consumers, share their ethical initiatives, and create a community around shared value. Leveraging technology enables businesses to communicate transparently, fostering a sense of authenticity in their ethical practices.

Embracing opportunities requires a commitment to genuine ethical practices, effective communication, and a strategic approach to aligning business objectives with societal and environmental needs. By capitalizing on these opportunities, businesses can not only thrive in an ethical marketplace but also contribute positively to the well-being of consumers and the broader community.

THE PSYCHOLOGY OF EFFECTIVE ETHICAL MARKETING

How ethical marketing works involves looking at real examples where companies have successfully integrated ethical principles into their marketing. By studying these cases, we can uncover the psychological aspects that connect with consumers, build trust, and encourage positive actions. These real-life examples help us see the underlying reasons why ethical marketing is effective, showing how it goes beyond just selling products and actually influences people's attitudes and behaviors for the better.

For example, Dove's "Real Beauty" campaign represents a paradigm shift in the beauty industry, challenging long-standing norms and fostering a more inclusive narrative. This case study explores the psychological underpinnings of this campaign, shedding light on its effectiveness and offering insights for future ethical marketing endeavors (Feng et al., 2019). Dove's "Real Beauty" campaign stood out by championing authenticity and diversity (Danthinne et al., 2022). The brand opted for a more realistic portrayal of women, showcasing individuals of various body shapes, sizes, and ethnicities. The campaign aimed to redefine beauty by challenging societal norms and promoting a positive body image. The campaign had a profound psychological impact on consumers. By portraying relatable images of beauty, Dove fostered a sense of connection and empowerment among its audience (de Lenne et al., 2021). Studies have shown that exposure to diverse representations of beauty can positively influence self-esteem and body image, challenging the harmful effects of unrealistic beauty standards perpetuated by traditional marketing.

Other example, Chipotle's "Food with Integrity" campaign is a pioneering initiative in the fast-food industry, emphasizing a commitment to sourcing high-quality ingredients produced sustainably and responsibly. Launched in 2001, the campaign aimed to promote transparency in the food supply chain, connecting consumers with the sources of their meals (Wang et al., 2020). Chipotle pledged to use naturally raised meats, organic produce, and locally sourced ingredients, aligning the brand with values like environmental sustainability and animal welfare. The core of Chipotle's ethical marketing lies in transparency, a value often overlooked in the fast-food sector. The company openly shares information about its suppliers, farming practices, and ingredient sources. This transparency establishes trust and credibility, as consumers feel more connected to the origins of their food (Assenza & Lewis, 2019). Chipotle also capitalizes on storytelling, using narratives to convey its commitment to ethical sourcing and responsible business practices. Chipotle's ethical marketing approach has a profound psychological impact on consumers. By aligning with values such as sustainability and animal welfare, the brand taps into consumers' desire to make ethical choices (Ragas & Roberts, 2009). This creates a positive association between the brand and the consumer's self-image, as individuals feel good about supporting a socially responsible company. Moreover, the transparency fosters a sense of empowerment, allowing consumers to make informed choices about their food consumption.

Crucial Findings

Positive Consumer Perception: The "Real Beauty" campaign contributed to a positive shift in consumer perception, associating Dove with authenticity and inclusivity.
Emotional Engagement: Dove's emphasis on real stories and personal experiences resonated emotionally with consumers, fostering a stronger brand-consumer relationship.
Market Share Growth: The campaign's success translated into increased market share for Dove, indicating that ethical marketing can be not only morally commendable but also financially rewarding.
Consumer Trust: The campaign significantly boosts consumer trust by offering transparent information about sourcing and production practices.
Positive Association: Ethical marketing creates a positive brand image, making consumers more likely to choose Chipotle over competitors with less transparent practices.
Empowerment: Consumers appreciate being informed, feeling empowered to make ethical choices and supporting a brand that aligns with their values.

Recommendations for Future Ethical Marketing Endeavors

Authenticity is Key: Brands should prioritize authenticity in their messaging, steering away from exaggerated or misleading portrayals.

Inclusivity Matters: Embrace diversity in all its forms to ensure that marketing efforts reflect the rich tapestry of the consumer base.

Engage Emotionally: Develop campaigns that resonate emotionally with consumers, as emotional engagement tends to create lasting connections and positive brand associations.

Educational Initiatives: Incorporate educational elements in campaigns to raise awareness about societal issues and promote positive change to embrace their natural beauty. By celebrating diversity and authenticity, Dove not only connected with consumers on a personal level but also sparked conversations about beauty standards and self-esteem.

Enhanced Communication: Brands should prioritize clear and accessible communication about ethical practices, ensuring consumers can easily access information about sourcing and production.

Storytelling Strategies: Incorporate compelling narratives to convey the brand's commitment to ethical practices, fostering an emotional connection with consumers.

Collaborations and Partnerships: Collaborate with ethical organizations and partners to strengthen the brand's credibility and commitment to ethical values.

Continuous Improvement: Regularly update and improve ethical practices, demonstrating a long-term commitment to sustainability and responsible business.

Psychological Tactics for Enhancing Ethical Marketing Effectiveness

Effectively navigating the landscape of ethical marketing involves a nuanced understanding of psychological tactics (Table 1) that resonate with consumers, foster trust, and inspire positive behavioral responses. In this section, we explore a range of strategic approaches that leverage human psychology to enhance the impact of ethical marketing (Islam, 2020). From the emotional resonance created by compelling storytelling to the persuasive influence of social proof and the motivation instilled by rewards, each tactic is a carefully crafted tool designed to connect with consumers on a deeper level (Schwepker, 2019). This exploration aims to shed light on how businesses can employ these psychological strategies to not only communicate their ethical commitments but also inspire meaningful and lasting connections with a conscious consumer audience.

Table 1. Psychological tactics

Psychological Tactics	Description
Emotional Appeal	Connect with consumers on an emotional level, leveraging emotions like empathy, joy, or purpose.
Storytelling	Craft compelling narratives that highlight ethical practices, fostering a deeper connection with the audience.
Social Proof	Provide evidence of positive actions, endorsements, or testimonials to influence others toward ethical consumption.
Cognitive Consistency	Align ethical messaging with consumers' existing beliefs and values to maintain cognitive consistency.
Behavioral Nudging	Encourage small, manageable steps towards ethical choices, making them more appealing and accessible to consumers.
Visual Impact	Utilize visually compelling content such as images, infographics, or videos to convey ethical messages memorably.
Scarcity and Urgency	Incorporate elements of scarcity or urgency to drive ethical decision-making, emphasizing limited-time offers or urgency.
Value Alignment	Emphasize shared values between the brand and the consumer to build a sense of kinship and loyalty.
Reward Systems	Introduce rewards or incentives for ethical choices, creating a positive reinforcement loop for consumers.
Educational Initiatives	Provide information and educational content about ethical practices and their impact to foster awareness and understanding.

Source: Authors own creation

Strategies for Conveying Authenticity and Transparency

In the dynamic landscape of ethical marketing, conveying authenticity and transparency is paramount for fostering trust and building lasting connections with conscious consumers. This section explores a range of strategic approaches (Table 2) that businesses can employ to communicate their ethical commitments genuinely (Mathews & Nair, 2020). From fostering open communication channels and detailing ethical practices to utilizing certifications and sharing behind-the-scenes content, each strategy contributes to creating an atmosphere of transparency (Hagenbuch & Mgrdichian, 2020). By embracing these practices, brands not only reinforce their dedication to ethical principles but also empower consumers with the information they need to make conscientious choices (Ospital et al., 2023; Steils et al., 2022). This exploration aims to illuminate how weaving authenticity and transparency into ethical marketing strategies goes beyond mere communication—it forms the bedrock of meaningful relationships between businesses and ethically minded consumers.

Table 2. Strategies for conveying authenticity and transparency

Strategies for Conveying Authenticity and Transparency	Description
Open Communication Channels	Establish clear and open lines of communication with consumers. Encourage feedback and address concerns openly.
Detailed Ethical Practices Disclosure	Clearly articulate and disclose specifics of ethical practices, such as sustainable sourcing or fair labor conditions.
Use of Certifications and Labels	Incorporate recognized ethical certifications and labels into product packaging, providing tangible proof of commitment.
Behind-the-Scenes Content	Offer glimpses behind the scenes, showcasing production processes, introducing team members, and providing ethical insights.
Storytelling with Impact	Share impactful stories about the brand's journey toward ethical practices, creating emotional connections with consumers.
Realistic Goal Setting	Set and communicate realistic ethical goals, acknowledging challenges transparently to showcase genuine commitment.
Stakeholder Engagement	Engage with various stakeholders transparently, communicating ethical objectives and involving them in the decision-making.
Ethical Supply Chain Mapping	Provide a clear map of the supply chain, detailing the origins of raw materials and manufacturing processes for transparency.
Interactive Sustainability Reports	Develop interactive reports allowing consumers to explore the impact of ethical initiatives, enhancing transparency.
Admitting Mistakes and Taking Responsibility	Admit mistakes openly, take responsibility, and outline corrective actions when ethical lapses occur.

Source: Authors own creation

Impact of Consumer Emotions and Moral Engagement

The interplay between consumer emotions and moral engagement is pivotal in unraveling the tapestry of ethical marketing (Xie et al., 2019). This section delves into the profound impact that emotions and moral connection (Table 3) wield in shaping consumer behavior and perceptions. From forging emotional resonance that transcends mere transactions to fostering moral engagement that aligns consumers with a brand's ethical values, these elements are not merely facets of marketing but keystones of enduring relationships. Exploring the nuances of this emotional and ethical dynamic unveils how businesses can authentically connect with consumers, inspire trust, and cultivate a shared commitment to ethical choices (Malti et al., 2020). As we navigate through the impact of consumer emotions and moral engagement, it becomes evident that ethical marketing transcends the transactional and, instead, cultivates a realm where values, emotions, and conscious choices converge to shape a sustainable and meaningful brand-consumer relationship.

Table 3. Impact of consumer emotions and moral engagement

Impact of Consumer Emotions and Moral Engagement	Description
Emotional Resonance	Connect with consumers emotionally, leveraging emotions like empathy, joy, or a sense of purpose to create a lasting impact.
Enhanced Brand Loyalty	Foster brand loyalty by appealing to consumers' emotions. Positive emotional experiences contribute to long-term customer commitment.
Positive Word-of-Mouth	Emotional connections drive positive word-of-mouth marketing as satisfied and emotionally engaged customers are likely to share their experiences.
Heightened Consumer Satisfaction	Ethical marketing that taps into positive emotions contributes to heightened consumer satisfaction, enhancing overall brand perception.
Increased Consumer Trust	Establish trust by addressing consumers' emotional needs and engaging them morally. Trust is a critical factor in ethical brand relationships.
Greater Moral Engagement	Encourage consumers to engage morally with the brand's ethical initiatives, fostering a sense of shared values and a commitment to ethical choices.
Deeper Connection with the Brand	Emotional resonance and moral engagement create a deeper connection between consumers and the brand, influencing purchase decisions.
Positive Impact on Purchase Decisions	Emotional and morally engaging marketing influences consumers positively, contributing to informed and ethically aligned purchase decisions.
Contribution to Brand Advocacy	Engaged and emotionally connected consumers are more likely to become brand advocates, actively promoting the brand's ethical initiatives.
Long-Term Positive Impact	Ethical marketing that elicits positive emotions and moral engagement contributes to a long-term positive impact on brand perception and consumer behavior.

Source: Authors own creation

Practical Implications in Ethical Marketing

In navigating the complex landscape of ethical marketing, practical implications serve as a compass for businesses and marketers seeking to authentically integrate ethical principles into their practices. This section unfolds a comprehensive guide, offering indispensable insights into guidelines, strategies, and the pivotal role of education and awareness in ethical consumption (Vidgen et al., 2020). From fostering authenticity and continuous ethical evaluation to aligning marketing efforts with genuine ethical practices, businesses are presented with a roadmap for building trust and meeting the evolving expectations of conscientious consumers. As we explore the practical dimensions of ethical marketing, the emphasis is not merely on meeting a trend but on cultivating a sustainable commitment to ethical values, ensuring businesses play an active role in fostering positive change within industries and societies at large.

Guidelines for Businesses and Marketers

Businesses and marketers navigating the realm of ethical marketing should prioritize authenticity as a foundational principle. This involves transparent communication about ethical practices, avoiding greenwashing, and fostering genuine trust with consumers. A commitment to continuous ethical evaluation ensures that business practices align with evolving ethical standards. Stakeholder engagement, including employees, suppliers, and local communities, is vital for a holistic approach to ethical decision-making (Trentesaux & Caillaud, 2020). Clear and consistent communication of ethical commitments, along with seeking third-party verification, enhances credibility and provides external validation.

Strategies to Align Marketing Efforts with Genuine Ethical Practices

Integrating ethical values into the core identity of a brand is essential for genuine alignment with marketing efforts. Crafting compelling narratives that highlight the brand's ethical journey through storytelling creates emotional connections with consumers. Collaborating with influencers and advocates who share ethical values amplifies the impact of ethical marketing. Actively involving consumers in ethical initiatives through participatory campaigns or feedback mechanisms fosters a sense of shared responsibility (Hemker et al., 2021a; Martinho et al., 2021). Implementing measurable impact metrics and transparently sharing progress reports demonstrate accountability and a commitment to continuous improvement.

The Role of Education and Awareness in Ethical Consumption

Education and awareness play a pivotal role in fostering ethical consumption. Developing consumer education programs that provide resources for informed decision-making is crucial. Collaborating with non-governmental organisations (NGOs) and educators to create educational content ensures the dissemination of information about ethical practices. Promoting ethical literacy by integrating ethical considerations into mainstream education curricula equips the younger generation with the knowledge needed for ethical decision-making (Hemker et al., 2021a; Singh et al., 2012). Launching public awareness campaigns through various media channels contributes to creating a culture where ethical considerations are integral to purchasing decisions. Ensuring the accessibility of information through digital platforms and product labeling empowers consumers to make ethical choices effortlessly.

These practical implications underscore the multifaceted approach required for businesses to authentically embrace ethical marketing, align marketing efforts with genuine ethical practices, and actively contribute to education and awareness for ethical consumption.

CONCLUSION

In unraveling the intricate interplay between consumer psychology and ethical marketing, several key findings emerge. The resonance of emotional connections, the impact of moral engagement, and the strategies for conveying authenticity highlight the dynamic and evolving nature of ethical marketing. Businesses that authentically align with ethical practices can build trust, foster brand loyalty, and positively impact consumer behavior.

Understanding the psychology of ethical marketing emerges as a cornerstone in the contemporary business landscape. As consumers increasingly prioritize ethical considerations, businesses equipped with insights into the cognitive and emotional aspects of decision-making can make informed and resonant ethical marketing decisions. This understanding is not just a tool for meeting consumer demands but a strategic imperative for building enduring relationships and contributing positively to societal values.

The future of ethical marketing holds profound implications for both businesses and society at large. Ethical considerations will likely continue to influence consumer preferences and shape market dynamics. For businesses, embracing ethical marketing is not just a means of staying relevant; it is an opportunity to lead with purpose, contribute to social and environmental causes, and create a positive impact on a global scale. As ethical marketing becomes more integral to brand identity, businesses that prioritize authenticity and transparency stand to gain not only in consumer trust but also in long-term sustainability.

In closing, the exploration of ethical marketing underscores its transformative potential. Yet, as the landscape evolves, the need for continued research becomes evident. The call for ongoing exploration extends to the realms of consumer behavior, the evolving role of technology, and the impact of ethical marketing on broader societal paradigms. As businesses and researchers collaborate, the potential to shape a future where ethical considerations are not just a market trend. but an intrinsic part of commerce and culture becomes a shared responsibility. This call to action invites continued investigation and innovation in the realm of ethical marketing, inspiring a future where businesses and consumers coalesce in a sustainable and ethical marketplace.

REFERENCES

Adwan, A. A., & Altrjman, G. (2024). The role of social media marketing and marketing management in promoting and developing brand sustainability strategy. *International Journal of Data and Network Science*, 8(1), 439–452. DOI: 10.5267/j.ijdns.2023.9.011

Ahmad, N., Ahmad, A., & Siddique, I. (2023). Responsible tourism and hospitality: The intersection of altruistic values, human emotions, and corporate social responsibility. *Administrative Sciences*, 13(4), 105. DOI: 10.3390/admsci13040105

Alam, M. N., Ogiemwonyi, O., Hago, I. E., Azizan, N. A., Hashim, F., & Hossain, M. S. (2023). Understanding consumer environmental ethics and the willingness to use green products. *SAGE Open*, 13(1), 215824402211497. DOI: 10.1177/21582440221149727

Albarq, A. N. (2024). Mobile services sector in Saudi Arabia: A systematic literature review of the effective strategies for enhancing customer satisfaction. *International Journal of Data and Network Science*, 8(1), 585–596. DOI: 10.5267/j.ijdns.2023.8.026

Antunes, A. C. (2021). The role of social media influencers on the consumer decision-making process. In Antunes, A. C. (Ed.), *Handbook of research on promoting brands with social media influencers* (pp. 138–154)., DOI: 10.4018/978-1-7998-4718-2.ch008

Assenza, P., & Lewis, M. S. (2019). Can Chipotle compete by delivering "food with integrity"? *The CASE Journal*, 15(4), 233–252. DOI: 10.1108/TCJ-08-2018-0092

Batlles-de la Fuente, A., & Abad-Segura, E. (2023). Exploring research on the management of business ethics. *Cuadernos de Gestión*, 23(1), 11–21. DOI: 10.5295/cdg.221694ea

Bault, N., & Rusconi, E. (2020). The art of influencing consumer choices: A reflection on recent advances in decision neuroscience. *Frontiers in Psychology*, 10, 3009. Advance online publication. DOI: 10.3389/fpsyg.2019.03009 PMID: 32038387

Carpenter, S. M., & Niedenthal, P. M. (2018). Emotional processes in risky and multiattribute health decisions. *Psychology & Health*, 33(1), 58–76. DOI: 10.1080/08870446.2017.1314478 PMID: 28452564

Coffin, J., & Egan-Wyer, C. (2022). The ethical consumption cap and mean market morality. *Marketing Theory*, 22(1), 105–123. DOI: 10.1177/14705931211058772

Danthinne, E. S., Giorgianni, F. E., Ando, K., & Rodgers, R. F. (2022). Real beauty: Effects of a body-positive video on body image and capacity to mitigate exposure to social media images. *British Journal of Health Psychology*, 27(2), 320–337. DOI: 10.1111/bjhp.12547 PMID: 34278653

de Lenne, O., Vandenbosch, L., Smits, T., & Eggermont, S. (2021). Framing real beauty: A framing approach to the effects of beauty advertisements on body image and advertising effectiveness. *Body Image*, 37, 255–268. DOI: 10.1016/j.bodyim.2021.03.003 PMID: 33773395

de Ruyter, K., Keeling, D. I., Plangger, K., Montecchi, M., Scott, M. L., & Dahl, D. W. (2022). Reimagining marketing strategy: Driving the debate on grand challenges. *Journal of the Academy of Marketing Science*, 50(1), 13–21. DOI: 10.1007/s11747-021-00806-x PMID: 34426711

Delgado Quintana, E. M. (2022). Role of motivational theories in the study of consumer behavior. *Revista Científica Sinapsis*, 2(21). Advance online publication. DOI: 10.37117/s.v2i21.662

Demjanovičová, M., & Varmus, M. (2021). Changing the perception of business values in the perspective of environmental sustainability. *Sustainability (Basel)*, 13(9), 5226. DOI: 10.3390/su13095226

Djafarova, E., & Foots, S. (2022). Exploring ethical consumption of generation Z: Theory of planned behaviour. *Young Consumers*, 23(3), 413–431. DOI: 10.1108/YC-10-2021-1405

Feng, Y., Chen, H., & He, L. (2019). Consumer responses to femvertising: A data-mining case of Dove's "Campaign for Real Beauty" on YouTube. *Journal of Advertising*, 48(3), 292–301. DOI: 10.1080/00913367.2019.1602858

Fritzsche, D. J. (1987). Marketing/business ethics. *Business & Professional Ethics Journal*, 6(4), 65–79. DOI: 10.5840/bpej19876432

Hagenbuch, D. J., & Mgrdichian, L. M. (2020). Mindful marketing: A strategy-based, branded approach for encouraging ethical marketing. *Marketing Education Review*, 30(1), 15–28. DOI: 10.1080/10528008.2019.1686993

Hemker, S., Herrando, C., & Constantinides, E. (2021a). The transformation of data marketing: How an ethical lens on consumer data collection shapes the future of marketing. *Sustainability (Basel)*, 13(20), 11208. DOI: 10.3390/su132011208

Islam, G. (2020). Psychology and business ethics: A multi-level research agenda. *Journal of Business Ethics*, 165(1), 1–13. DOI: 10.1007/s10551-019-04107-w

Johnson, C. K., Gutzwiller, R. S., Gervais, J., & Ferguson-Walter, K. J. (2021). Decision-making biases and cyber attackers. In *2021 36th IEEE/ACM International Conference on Automated Software Engineering Workshops (ASEW)* (pp. 140–144). https://doi.org/DOI: 10.1109/ASEW52652.2021.00038

Kapferer, J.-N., & Valette-Florence, P. (2021). Which consumers believe luxury must be expensive and why? A cross-cultural comparison of motivations. *Journal of Business Research*, 132, 301–313. DOI: 10.1016/j.jbusres.2021.04.003

Krivokuća, M. (2020). Social responsibility in the application of integrated marketing communication. *Serbian Journal of Engineering Management*, 5(2), 33–41. DOI: 10.5937/SJEM2002033K

Ladwein, R., & Sánchez Romero, A. M. (2021). The role of trust in the relationship between consumers, producers and retailers of organic food: A sector-based approach. *Journal of Retailing and Consumer Services*, 60, 102508. Advance online publication. DOI: 10.1016/j.jretconser.2021.102508

Malti, T., Peplak, J., & Acland, E. (2020). Emotional experiences in moral contexts. In Jensen, L. A. (Ed.), *The Oxford handbook of moral development* (pp. 243–263). Oxford University Press., DOI: 10.1093/oxfordhb/9780190676049.013.14

Martinho, A., Herber, N., Kroesen, M., & Chorus, C. (2021). Ethical issues in focus by the autonomous vehicles industry. *Transport Reviews*, 41(5), 556–577. DOI: 10.1080/01441647.2020.1862355

Mathews, S., & Nair, S. R. (2020). Ethical consumerism and effectiveness from a cause-related marketing (CRM) perspective. In Mathews, S., & Nair, S. R. (Eds.), *Handbook of research on marketing and promoting brands with cause-related marketing* (pp. 186–210)., DOI: 10.4018/978-1-5225-8270-0.ch008

Mathews, S., & Nair, S. R. (2020). Ethical consumerism and effectiveness from a cause-related marketing (CRM) perspective (pp. 134–153). In *Ethical and sustainable business practices for a global economy* (1st ed.). IGI Global. https://doi.org/ DOI: 10.4018/978-1-5225-8270-0.ch008

Mpinganjira, M., & Maduku, D. K. (2019). Ethics of mobile behavioral advertising: Antecedents and outcomes of perceived ethical value of advertised brands. *Journal of Business Research*, 95, 464–478. DOI: 10.1016/j.jbusres.2018.07.037

Nill, A. (2022). Socially responsible marketing: A moving target in need of a normative-ethical doctrine. *Journal of Macromarketing*, 42(4), 583–589. DOI: 10.1177/02761467221099815

Noguerra, C. P.Jr. (2023). Ethical and legal challenges in information system development and implementation. *International Journal of Advanced Research in Science. Tongxin Jishu*, •••, 852–858. DOI: 10.48175/IJARSCT-12383

Ospital, P., Masson, D., Beler, C., & Legardeur, J. (2023). Toward product transparency: Communicating traceability information to consumers. *International Journal of Fashion Design, Technology and Education*, 16(2), 186–197. DOI: 10.1080/17543266.2022.2142677

Painter, M., Hibbert, S., & Cooper, T. (2019). The development of responsible and sustainable business practice: Value, mind-sets, business models. *Journal of Business Ethics*, 157(4), 885–891. DOI: 10.1007/s10551-018-3958-3

Pittman, M., Oeldorf-Hirsch, A., & Brannan, A. (2022). Green advertising on social media: Brand authenticity mediates the effect of different appeals on purchase intent and digital engagement. *Journal of Current Issues and Research in Advertising*, 43(1), 106–121. DOI: 10.1080/10641734.2021.1964655

Ragas, M. W., & Roberts, M. S. (2009). Communicating corporate social responsibility and brand sincerity: A case study of Chipotle Mexican Grill's "Food with Integrity" program. *International Journal of Strategic Communication*, 3(4), 264–280. DOI: 10.1080/15531180903218697

Rovolis, G., & Habibipour, A. (2024). When participatory design meets data-driven decision making: A literature review and the way forward. *Management Science Letters*, 14(2), 107–126. DOI: 10.5267/j.msl.2023.9.002

Schwepker, C. H.Jr. (2019). Strengthening customer value development and ethical intent in the salesforce: The influence of ethical values person–organization fit and trust in manager. *Journal of Business Ethics*, 159(3), 913–925. DOI: 10.1007/s10551-018-3851-0

Sianturi, C. M., Pasaribu, V. A. R., Pasaribu, R. M., & Simanjuntak, J. (2022). The impact of social media marketing on purchase intention. *SULTANIST: Jurnal Manajemen dan Keuangan, 10(1)*, 60–68. https://doi.org/DOI: 10.37403/sultanist.v10i1.425

Singh, J. J., Iglesias, O., & Batista-Foguet, J. M. (2012). Does having an ethical brand matter? The influence of consumer perceived ethicality on trust, affect, and loyalty. *Journal of Business Ethics*, 111(4), 541–549. DOI: 10.1007/s10551-012-1216-7

Somany, N. (2023). Greenwashing in business: Examining the impact of deceptive environmental claims on consumer behavior and corporate accountability. *International Journal of Social Science and Economic Research*, 08(04), 908–920. DOI: 10.46609/IJSSER.2023.v08i04.024

Steils, N., Martin, A., & Toti, J.-F. (2022). Managing the transparency paradox of social-media influencer disclosures. *Journal of Advertising Research*, 62(2), 148–166. DOI: 10.2501/JAR-2022-008

Sweeney, J., Payne, A., Frow, P., & Liu, D. (2020). Customer advocacy: A distinctive form of word of mouth. *Journal of Service Research*, 23(2), 139–155. DOI: 10.1177/1094670519900541

Tanveer, M., Ahmad, A.-R., Mahmood, H., & Haq, I. U. (2021a). Role of ethical marketing in driving consumer brand relationships and brand loyalty: A sustainable marketing approach. *Sustainability (Basel)*, 13(12), 6839. DOI: 10.3390/su13126839

Tanveer, M., Ahmad, A.-R., Mahmood, H., & Haq, I. U. (2021b). Role of ethical marketing in driving consumer brand relationships and brand loyalty: A sustainable marketing approach. *Sustainability (Basel)*, 13(12), 6839. DOI: 10.3390/su13126839

Tanveer, M., Ahmad, A.-R., Mahmood, H., & Haq, I. U. (2021c). Role of ethical marketing in driving consumer brand relationships and brand loyalty: A sustainable marketing approach. *Sustainability (Basel)*, 13(12), 6839. DOI: 10.3390/su13126839

Trentesaux, D., & Caillaud, E. (2020). Ethical stakes of Industry 4.0. *IFAC-PapersOnLine*, 53(2), 17002–17007. DOI: 10.1016/j.ifacol.2020.12.1486

Triana, N. (2022). The need for sustainability and CSR in undergraduate business education. *Journal of Undergraduate Research (Gainesville, Fla.)*, 24. Advance online publication. DOI: 10.32473/ufjur.24.130792

Vidgen, R., Hindle, G., & Randolph, I. (2020). Exploring the ethical implications of business analytics with a business ethics canvas. *European Journal of Operational Research*, 281(3), 491–501. DOI: 10.1016/j.ejor.2019.04.036

Wang, J., Tao, J., & Chu, M. (2020). Behind the label: Chinese consumers' trust in food certification and the effect of perceived quality on purchase intention. *Food Control*, 108, 106825. DOI: 10.1016/j.foodcont.2019.106825

Xie, C., Bagozzi, R. P., & Grønhaug, K. (2019). The impact of corporate social responsibility on consumer brand advocacy: The role of moral emotions, attitudes, and individual differences. *Journal of Business Research*, 95, 514–530. DOI: 10.1016/j.jbusres.2018.07.043

KEY TERMS AND DEFINITIONS

Consumer Skepticism: Tendency of consumers to doubt or question the truthfulness, motives, or credibility of marketing claims, especially those related to product quality, ethics, or sustainability.

Emotional Resonance: The ability of a message, experience, or piece of content to evoke strong, meaningful emotions in an audience, creating a deep, personal connection.

Ethical Consumption: The practice of purchasing goods and services that are produced in a way that minimizes harm to people, animals, and the environment.

Ethical Marketing: The practice of promoting products or services in a way that is honest, transparent, and socially responsible.

Greenwashing: Deceptive practice where a company falsely markets its products or practices as environmentally friendly to appear more sustainable or eco-conscious than they actually are.

Chapter 7
Future of Travel:
Metaverse Driven Sustainability Initiatives in Tourism and Hospitality

Ruchi Kakkar
Lovely Professional University, India

Amit Kakkar
Lovely Professional University, India

Manpreet Kaur Riyat
https://orcid.org/0000-0002-1190-0819
Lovely Professional University, India

ABSTRACT

The travel, tourism, and hospitality industries can find hope in the metaverse, which is more than just a catchphrase. It offers creative solutions for sustainability and promises to transform these sectors. This chapter examines how the metaverse reshapes tourism and hospitality industries by incorporating innovative, sustainable tourism and hospitality concepts. An understanding of sustainability and the metaverse is given in this chapter. Sustainability refers to methods that guarantee the long-term viability of resources and reduce their adverse environmental effects. There is also a discussion of the challenges of integrating the metaverse with tourism and hospitality. A team collaboration is needed to overcome the difficulties of incorporating the metaverse into travel and hospitality. Each stakeholder has a specific role to play, and their contributions are vital to the success of this transformation. This fascinating trend toward virtual tourism is more than simply a transition; it has the potential to make the sector more robust and sustainable.

DOI: 10.4018/979-8-3693-7021-6.ch007

INTRODUCTION TO TOURISM AND HOSPITALITY INDUSTRY

The hospitality and tourism industry is a vast sector that includes all the economic activities that directly or indirectly contribute to travel and tourism. It encompasses a range of businesses, including restaurants, hotels, cruise lines, airlines, and tour companies. This industry, driven by people's desire to travel to new locations, experience different cultures, and engage in leisure activities, has shown remarkable resilience in the face of challenges. Despite the setbacks of the COVID-19 pandemic, the industry is rebounding with an emphasis on security, cleanliness, and sustainability. It significantly contributes to intercultural communication, job development, and economic growth. The global tourism and hospitality market was valued at US$ 8207 million in 2023 and is expected to grow at a compound annual growth rate (CAGR) of 3% between 2024 and 2029 when it is expected to reach a valuation of US$ 9800 million. With 10% of the global GDP contributed by the tourism and hospitality sector, it is the largest industry in the world. As a leisure activity with convenient travel options, the tourism and hospitality market has expanded into a multibillion-dollar industry (Market Data Forecast Study, 2024). Many developing nations, including the Maldives, Nepal, Thailand, and the United Arab Emirates, depend heavily on this industry for their economies. This confidence was reflected in the success of the Indian hotel industry in 2023, as key performance metrics, including occupancy rate, average rate (ARR), and revenue per available room (RevPAR), saw notable increases. In the dynamic world of hotel operations, the average room rate stands as a crucial metric in determining the profitability and success of a hotel's revenue management strategy. The average room rate reflects the average price paid per occupied room, considering the various room rates charged across different room types and booking channels. The average room rate is computed over a range of time periods, providing a snapshot of the hotel's performance and the prevailing market conditions. As room occupancy fluctuates throughout the year, the average room rate continues to evolve, reflecting the hotel's ability to adapt to changing demand patterns and its responsiveness to market dynamics. ARR helps in devising pricing strategies for the Hotels. It also helps benchmark the room rents as per the industry norms. Based on the high occupancy rate, the hotels can adjust their room rents to increase their ARR during the peak seasons. Similarly, Revenue per Available Room is a crucial metric used in the hotel industry to measure the financial performance of a hotel. This metric calculates occupancy and average room rates to provide a comprehensive understanding of a hotel's revenue generation capabilities (Gultek & Héroux, 2019). The importance of RevPAR lies in its ability to capture the efficiency with which a hotel utilises its available room inventory. It is obtained by dividing the total room revenue by the total number of available rooms (Lee et al., 2019). This metric is particularly useful in the hotel industry because it allows for easy comparisons between different hotels, different time periods, and different markets (Sainaghi et al., 2021). The industry's national occupancy rate at the end of 2023 was between 63 and 65%, up 3-5 percentage points (pp) from the year before and almost back to the pre-pandemic level of 65–67% in 2019 (Lamba et al., 2023). The outstanding INR 7,400–7,600 ARR for 2023 beat the statistics from 2022 by 21-23% and 2019 by 24-26%, demonstrating the sector's capacity to push rates in response to the strong demand. RevPAR increased by 29-31% from 2022 and 19-21% from 2019 to INR 4,662-4,940 in 2023 thanks to a spike in average rates. With 9.2 million international visitor arrivals in 2023—a stunning 49% year-over-year gain and just over 15% short of record levels last seen in 2019—inbound tourism showed an encouraging revival (Lamba et al., 2023). The data highlights a strong recovery in the hotel and tourism industry, signalling a return to pre-pandemic performance. Increased occupancy rates and higher room revenues show the sector's ability to respond to growing demand. The surge in international visitor arrivals further underscores renewed interest in travel, reinforcing the industry's rebound. These trends suggest that hotels are successfully adapting pricing strategies and benefiting from increased tourism, signalling a solid recovery and future growth potential.

The rise in per capita income and steady economic expansion are the main drivers of the worldwide tourism and hospitality business. Notably, governmental organisations and agencies of emerging economies play a significant role in the market, more so than developed economies. Their efforts to encourage travel and draw in a variety of international visitors fuel the expansion of the global travel and hospitality industry.

As a result, annual spending on business and leisure travel has increased. Travel has allowed more people to stay in hotels, which has expanded the hospitality markets. Other industries benefit from expanding the global tourism market, including aviation, transportation, lodging, food and beverage, retail, entertainment and events, travel services, construction, and arts and crafts.

Figure 1. Components of tourism and hospitality industry

(Authors own creation)

People's freedom of movement is the foundation of the worldwide tourism industry. Still, the COVID-19 epidemic has directly halted people's freedom of movement, negatively impacting tourism (Guridno & Guridno, 2020). The COVID-19 pandemic has directly impacted the travel and hospitality industries. The global hospitality and tourism sector grew more slowly as a result of restrictions on travel. It closed borders, caused a lack of trust among consumers, caused health concerns, economic uncertainty, labour shortages, supply chain disruptions, job cuts, shutdowns of businesses, economic hardships, and constrained domestic and international travel due to fear. Travelers' views of travel and the hazards involved have been impacted by terrorism, which has had a detrimental impact on the worldwide tourism and hospitality sectors (World Travel & Tourism Council, 2023). Travellers to undeveloped and impoverished nations face significant security threats, a massive obstacle for the worldwide international tourism industry.

Following the pandemic, the travel and hotel industries are rebounding, showcasing their adaptability and resilience. Many factors are contributing to this rebound. After COVID-19, the hospitality and tourism sectors have emphasised security and cleanliness, adapting to the new normal. The industry was quick to adopt sanitisation techniques and strict hygiene guidelines to foster the trust of pandemic-worried tourists. Hotels and restaurants have started using technology for electronic payments, smartphone menus, and contactless check-in, demonstrating their readiness to embrace technological advancements. The industry is expanding because of changes in the tastes of tourists. More individuals want to take shorter, more local excursions and frequent trips, and the industry is ready to cater to these changing preferences. Many people take "staycations" at lodgings in their hometowns to unwind, and the industry is offering them the comfort and safety they seek. The travel industry is also emphasizing sustainability by offering tourists eco-friendly accommodations and activities, showing its commitment to a greener future.

Artificial intelligence chatbots for visitor services and virtual reality have become part of this industry for location previewing. The sector extensively uses targeted web marketing, providing experiences and virtual tours to entice passengers and help them regain trust. The government should be the main force behind the industry's rebirth (Dube et al., 2021). Governments in numerous nations, including Canada, Vietnam, the United States, Germany, France, and others, have established the Tourism and Hospitality Recovery Program to assist hospitality businesses in surviving and rebuilding. This program includes business aid, rental and wage subsidies, tax deferrals, monetary assistance, guaranteed loans, and financial compensation to tourists. India's Ministry of Tourism introduced the Dekho Apna Desh Initiative and strongly emphasised promoting domestic travel. To boost the tourism industry during the pandemic, the Ministry has issued several fiscal relief measures, including tax breaks and financial aid, which have helped many businesses stay afloat (India's Hospitality Sector Revitalizing article, 2022).

Issues Plaguing Tourism and Hospitality Industry

The tourism and hospitality industries certainly face numerous challenges like other industries. Financial crises and geopolitical upheaval primarily reduce travel demand, reducing revenue. Natural and cultural resources are the other contributors that are threatened by two environmental issues: global warming and over-tourism. The inclinations and actions of travellers are changing due to various variables like digital change, health concerns, and sustainability. Authenticity and customised experiences are in high demand. Technology unquestionably gives opportunities for increased productivity and better visitor experiences but also raises issues with the privacy of information, cybersecurity, and the digital divide.

In addition, the industry is confronted with challenges like low salaries in some areas and seasonality, which increase labour shortages, skills gaps, and high turnover rates (Dube et al., 2021). The quality of visitor experiences, including lodging, transportation, and connectivity, can be adversely affected by political unrest, terrorism, economic downturns, currency fluctuations, and adherence to various and constantly changing regulations (such as safety standards, immigration laws, and general data protection regulation (GDPR)) in multiple jurisdictions (Gautam, 2021). These factors can also significantly impact tourist flows and business operations in particular regions (Ahlfeldt et al., 2015; Cheer, 2020; Kuo et al., 2012; UNICEF, 2016).

Pandemics have left the hospitality and tourist industry with never-before-seen obstacles, such as restricting the supply side (closure of lodging and recreational facilities) and the demand side (freedom of movement, fear of infection, etc.). Many business setups in the tourism and hospitality sector have experienced financial difficulty in the Covid scenario due to lower revenues during lockdowns and ongoing operational issues (Sun et al., 2022). Closures, layoffs, and trouble obtaining funding have resulted from this. Even after COVID-19, this industry continued to encounter other challenges, such as travel limitations and reluctance on the part of travellers to make reservations, particularly for foreign travel. Travelers' top worries were health and safety, even in the face of vaccination campaigns. Strictly adhering to health rules increased the complexity of operations and business costs. They are more comfortable staying closer to home, boosting domestic tourism but impacting international destinations. Cleanliness and sanitation protocols became a top priority for many travellers. Hotels and airlines raised prices to offset increased expenses, which could deter some customers. The balance between offering competitive prices and covering costs became very difficult.

The sector also had to deal with a labour deficit made worse by limitations on immigration, lower worker participation because of health issues, and a skills gap. Reduced staff implies fewer hours available for maintenance, cleaning, and one-on-one care. Operations may be further strained by overworked staff members who experience burnout and a revolving door of workers (Gautam, 2021). Hiring and keeping competent employees got more complicated. Disruptions to the global supply chain impact the price and availability of commodities and services necessary for the operations of the tourism and hospitality industries, such as food, drink, and facilities. Businesses that operate abroad have increased complexity and operational hurdles due to adjusting to changing health standards, travel limitations, and border control procedures across different countries.

Metaverse Ecosystem

The Metaverse concept is prevalent in modern technology, providing an imaginary networked future of virtual worlds. It helps to imagine social networks in three dimensions (3D) where people interact, collaborate, and have fun as avatars and imagine travelling in virtual reality or seeing shows with friends worldwide (Lee et al., 2021). This immersive internet has the potential to transform how we interact, shop, and learn thoroughly. Even while the Metaverse is still in its early stages, it has the potential to blur the lines between the actual world and virtual realities. The network of virtual and augmented reality (VR/AR) environments, platforms, and services is connected and comprises the Metaverse ecosystem. It includes various tools, programs, and digital resources to build dynamic and engaging virtual environments (Yang et al., 2024). The Metaverse is a multiuser, eternal, post-reality environment that combines digital virtuality and physical reality. Its foundation combines technologies like virtual reality (VR) and augmented reality (AR) that allow multidimensional interactions with digital objects, real and virtual people called avatars and virtual surroundings. Virtual reality is an environment that is virtual in nature and is built with the help of technologies that provide a unique experience to individuals. Through computer technologies, virtual reality (VR) provides three-dimensional experiences in a virtual environment. Similarly, Augmented reality is an amalgamation of the virtual and natural environments (Morales et al., 2023). Both realities provide a unique immersive experience to the users. To achieve an immersive experience, one has to use glasses, gloves, or other controllers, enabling users to feel and see virtual/augmented reality.

Figure 2. Elements of metaverse

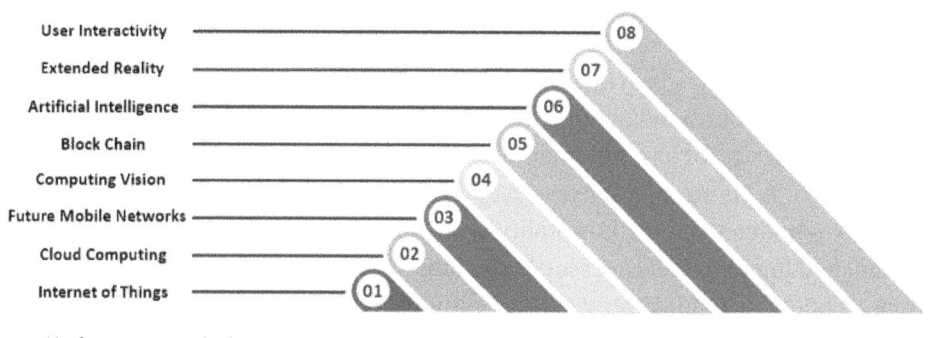

- User Interactivity — 08
- Extended Reality — 07
- Artificial Intelligence — 06
- Block Chain — 05
- Computing Vision — 04
- Future Mobile Networks — 03
- Cloud Computing — 02
- Internet of Things — 01

(Authors own creation)

It offers a range of products and services to provide users with a virtual world experience. Virtual environments that users may create, interact with, and explore on platforms such as Roblox, Second Life, and Decentraland. Inevitable augmented reality (AR) services allow for the overlaying of digital content onto the actual environment, such as Snapchat and Facebook's AR Studio. Possessing Digital Assets that users can purchase, sell, and exchange within the Metaverse, such as virtual products, avatars, apparel, and real estate, is another benefit of the Metaverse (Schöbe & Leimeister, 2023). Additionally, it offers tokens and cryptocurrencies that can be used in decentralised virtual worlds for ownership, governance, and commerce. Through Social VR Platforms, Metaverse facilitates communication and collaboration with others in virtual settings, making it an excellent social media platform. Metaverse tours have been organised by the museum websites using 3-D graphics, 360-degree videos and augmented reality technologies to provide an immersive experience to the visitors without actually visiting the museum (Hoffman, 2020).

Events such as conferences, concerts, seminars, and other gatherings can now be held in virtual settings thanks to Metaverse. It functions via various interactive experiences, animations, and 3D models. Training environments, simulations, and virtual classrooms leverage the Metaverse for education and training. It has also demonstrated its worth as an entertainment tool by providing immersive gaming, virtual performances and concerts, and immersive storytelling experiences. The metaverse ecosystem could completely change how we work, play, and live (Li et al., 2024). It might open up fresh doors for communication with others, business ventures, and artistic expression.

The potential adoption of the Metaverse in the Tourism and Hospitality industry is not just a change but a revolution waiting to happen. This innovative technology offers a range of benefits, from enhancing guest-host engagement to providing real-time services, thereby improving the overall guest experience. The future is indeed promising and full of exciting possibilities.

For many years, technological advancement and tourism have coexisted (Buhalis, 2020). While certain technologies bring about minor and everyday enhancements, others completely transform the industry by causing massive upheavals (Buhalis et al., 2023b). The fourth industrial revolution (Industry 4.0) theory, which translates to the convergence of the physical, digital, and biological worlds (Lukanova & Ilieva, 2019), is giving rise to a new paradigm that is gradually changing the competitive environment of the hospitality and tourism sectors (Buhalis et al., 2019). To remain competitive, businesses in the tourist and hospitality industries need to adopt technological advancements that promote real-time services and maximise guest-host engagement (Buhalis & Sinarta, 2019). At present, it is much more difficult in dynamic, intelligent environments in which it is expected that the influence of robotics, AI, the Metaverse, and service automation will only grow on the standard and experience of services provided (Jabeen et al., 2022). In the 'Industry 4.0' age, the demands and expectations of consumers are rapidly evolving. They are increasingly seeking unique experiences and demonstrating a growing reliance on mobile devices. This 'new consumer' dynamic is compelling businesses in the service delivery sector to closely monitor and adapt to technological trends to thrive in the competitive travel industry (World Travel & Tourism Council, 2023).

The fourth industrial revolution, known as 'Industry 4.0,' is characterised by the pervasive integration of digital technologies into most industrial processes and procedures. Within the travel and hospitality sectors, this period is often referred to as 'Hotel 4.0.' "Hotel 4.0" is the term used to describe the application of Industry 4.0

concepts to the hospitality sector, emphasising utilising cutting-edge technology to optimise service delivery, boost visitor experiences, and improve hotel operations. This concept emphasises the importance of businesses' ability to inform clients about their goods and services and how much they know about them, which will determine their success in the future (Khaled & Alena, 2021). The sector constantly evolves to rethink optimal operational practices and capitalise on technology paradigm shifts. These changes are often disruptive but necessary for businesses to thrive in the competitive travel industry.

Figure 3. Metaverse in tourism and hospitality industry

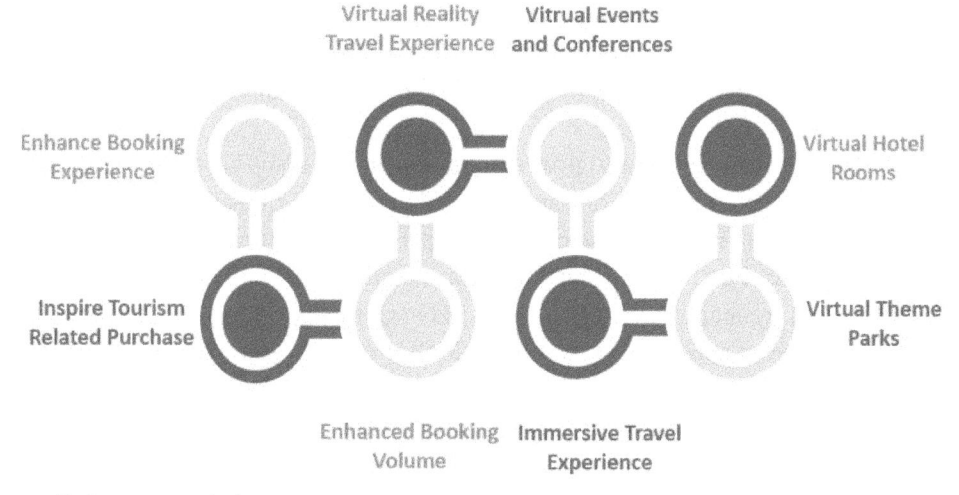

(Authors own creation)

With the convergence of advanced technologies like artificial intelligence (AI), virtual reality (VR), augmented reality (AR), and others, the tourism and hospitality sectors within the Metaverse are transforming (Buhalis et al., 2023b). The Metaverse is a virtual shared environment that offers immersive and captivating experiences that transcend physical boundaries. At the forefront of this change is virtual tourism, which enables users to utilise VR headsets to experience sites globally from the comfort of their homes. State-of-the-art virtual reality (VR) technology lets users digitally explore historic locations, stroll along gorgeous beaches, or visit bustling city centres. It does this by offering convincing recreations of actual places.

The tourism industry needs augmented reality (AR) to enhance in-person vacation experiences. With AR applications, travellers can explore real-world environments with interactive features, historical context, and real-time support (Guttentag et al.,

2018). The hospitality industry is witnessing a transformation in customer service and guest experiences thanks to the Metaverse. Virtual concierges driven by AI chatbots offer 24/7 assistance, handle bookings, suggest local attractions, and even simulate virtual room visits before a reservation. Employing data analytics and machine learning to anticipate needs and preferences increases convenience while personalising the visitor experience. Blockchain technology significantly enhances the privacy and accountability of transactions in the Metaverse. Furthermore, the Metaverse fosters collaboration and community-building between tourism experts and enthusiasts through virtual conferences, trade shows, and networking events; these online gatherings transcend national boundaries, enabling participation and knowledge sharing globally.

The Metaverse has numerous applications in the tourism and hospitality industry. For instance, virtual tourism can provide immersive experiences of global destinations, virtual reality (VR) and augmented reality (AR) can be used for marketing and customer engagement, and virtual conferences can enhance global networking opportunities.

The Metaverse has the potential to revolutionise the travel and hospitality industries by changing people's perceptions and interactions with various places worldwide. The Metaverse can revolutionise consumers' perception of travel, lodging options, and destinations. Facilitating virtual meetings, conferences, and events reduces the necessity for physical travel and broadens networking opportunities globally. This not only enhances accessibility and inclusion for participants worldwide but also reduces costs and environmental impact. The future of the tourism and hospitality sectors is bright, with the Metaverse offering new and exciting ways for travellers to enjoy virtual travel experiences with virtual destinations.

Virtual Tourism

Virtual tourism takes holiday planning to a new dimension. Visitors can explore realistic 3D environments, gaining precise insights into local cultures, accommodations, and attractions. This dynamic and entertaining approach significantly enhances the holiday planning process.

Guest Experiences

Lodging facilities can use the Metaverse to give potential guests an immersive preview of their rooms, amenities, and eating options by enabling them to offer virtual tours. With customised previews, virtual reality (VR) and augmented reality (AR) can mimic real-world experiences like dining or spa treatments, making them effective marketing tools that raise consumer satisfaction.

Travel Planning

Travellers can experience virtual versions of those locations before choosing a vacation. This makes it possible to create immersive experiences that highlight nearby hotels, restaurants, and cultural landmarks. Whenever someone makes travel arrangements, applications for augmented reality can superimpose instructions, travel information, and points of interest on the actual world, improving navigation and trip planning. Travellers are uneasy about the boarding and hotel facilities before they go anywhere. Virtual tours are valid for hotels, resorts, and tourist destinations since they allow prospective customers to explore rooms, services, and facilities virtually. Resorts and hotels can provide virtual concierge services, allowing visitors to schedule appointments, make reservations, and get tailored suggestions by interacting with virtual assistants. Virtual reality (VR) can produce individualised experiences based on visitor preferences, such as unique food options, activities, and accommodation settings. To practice customer service situations, safety protocols, and operational activities within virtual hotel environments, hospitality workers can participate in virtual training simulations.

Travel Marketing and Booking Experiences

Virtual worlds are useful for destinations and hospitality providers to showcase their offerings and draw potential guests through tailored advertising efforts. The Metaverse provides access to new sources of income. In hotels, it can offer exceptional experiences, sell virtual goods, and make money from virtual tours through ticket sales and sponsorships.

Travel companies and platforms might offer immersive booking experiences that let customers plan and reserve lodging, activities, and travel inside virtual settings. Through virtual simulations, travel agents and tour guides can become more knowledgeable about places and provide better services.

Travel Experiences

To improve their trip, tourists might utilise virtual surroundings to become more fluent in the languages and customs of the places they intend to visit. Travelers can learn about history and culture at a distance by visiting virtual museums and historical sites, encouraging cross-cultural dialogue and education. By providing virtual tours and experiences tailored to individual requirements, the Metaverse can increase accessibility for tourists with disabilities and promote diversity in the travel industry. Hotels and coworking spaces can provide digital nomads and remote workers with virtual office locations where they can interact, hold meetings, and use business services from a distance. Virtual conferences and events can also be held at hotels and conference centres, including keynote speeches, virtual trade exhibits, and immersive networking possibilities. Potential consumers can be drawn in by interactive virtual experiences that let them engage with brand ambassadors, participate in virtual events, and post about their experiences on social media.

Digital Replicas of Hotel Properties

Hotels can build digital replicas of their locations on Rendezverse, a metaverse platform where visitors can communicate and participate in virtual activities. To highlight its properties and improve client interaction, the Hilton hotel brand is investigating metaverse experiences. Although the Metaverse is still relatively new to the tourist and hospitality industries, these applications show how immersive technologies can improve visitor experiences, expedite processes, and change how people explore and engage with destinations worldwide.Top of Form The tourism and hospitality sectors stand to benefit significantly from the Metaverse, which will present fascinating new avenues for traveller interaction and hotel experiences.

Social Media Marketing

Social media marketing plays a more significant role in the hospitality and tourism business regarding client interaction (Leung et al., 2015; Ma et al., 2023). Hotels increasingly need social media sites like Facebook, Instagram, and Twitter as marketing tools to reach prospective customers and advertise their services (Chakraborty et al., 2023). A recent Statista analysis projects that by 2027, there will be an astounding 6 billion social media users globally, demonstrating a sharp increase in the acceptance and popularity of social media platforms globally (Statista, 2021). The report shows that as of 2021, there were more than 4.26 billion active social media users worldwide. This demonstrates how hotels have many opportunities to interact with a large audience through social media. It is possible to think of the interaction between social media and the Metaverse as symbiotic (Dwivedi et al., 2022). Social media's ability to spread knowledge, spark curiosity, and encourage user participation makes it crucial in propelling metaverse technology uptake (Buhalis et al., 2022). As per Benrimoh et al. (2022), the tourism and hospitality sectors are just two areas that the rapid progress of metaverse technology has significantly impacted. Within this framework, social media platforms have become essential agents for influencing user attitudes and encouraging the generalisation of metaverse technology.

Sustainability in the Tourism and Hospitality Industry

Due to the massive traffic of humans in the hospitality and tourism sector, the need for sustainability is the utmost desire. One must know what sustainability is before understanding the need for sustainability in this industry. Our world has limited resources such as clean water, fertile land, and fossil fuels. Overconsumption and pollution are examples of unsustainable practices that are rapidly depleting these resources. Climate change results from greenhouse gas emissions from human activity, especially the combustion of fossil fuels (Gahlawat & Lakra, 2020). This results in an imbalance in weather patterns, raises sea levels, and jeopardises ecosystems. Plant and animal species rapidly decline due to unsustainable activities, including habitat loss and deforestation; ecosystems are becoming upset; the natural world's ability to combat climate change is weakened, and biodiversity loss threatens food security. We can protect these resources for current and future generations by practising sustainability.

In this case, sustainable practices that support conservation and responsible land management are critical to protecting biodiversity and helping mitigate climate change by promoting renewable energy and reducing pollution (Chen et al., 2023). People can use more resources because of the growth in population and income sources. This causes issues such as resource scarcity, pollution, and environmental degradation. Waterborne infections, respiratory disorders, and other health concerns can result from pollution caused by unsustainable activities. Sustainability supports a healthy environment, clean air, and pure water—all essential to human well-being. Extreme weather, a shortage of resources, and societal unrest can all result from unsustainable activities (Rockstrom et al.,2009).

Figure 4. Sustainability in the tourism and hospitality industry

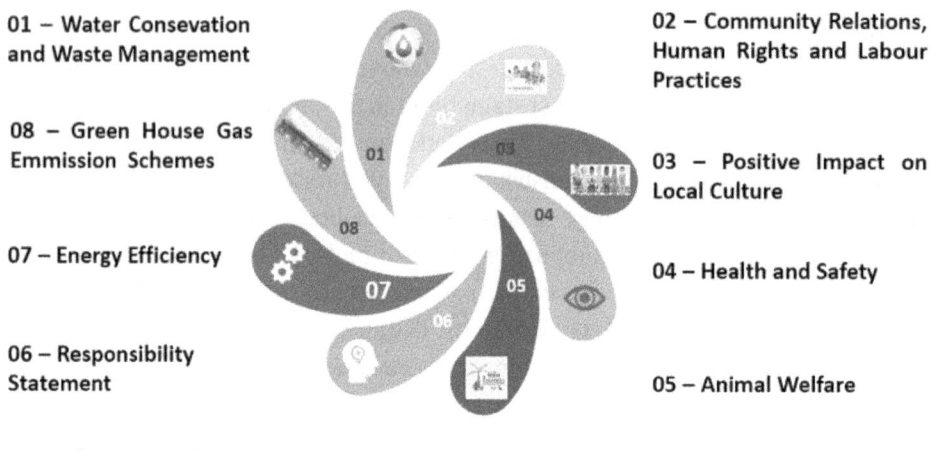

01 – Water Consevation and Waste Management

08 – Green House Gas Emmission Schemes

07 – Energy Efficiency

06 – Responsibility Statement

02 – Community Relations, Human Rights and Labour Practices

03 – Positive Impact on Local Culture

04 – Health and Safety

05 – Animal Welfare

(Authors own creation)

Livelihoods and economies are affected by this. Sustainability promotes long-term economic growth by guaranteeing a healthy environment and conscientious resource management (Arslan et al., 2022). Marginalised populations are frequently disproportionately affected by the effects of environmental deterioration and unequal access to resources. To guarantee that everyone has access to clean water, sanitary conditions, and a healthy environment, sustainability supports resource management. Humans can ensure the following by implementing sustainable activities.

- A healthier and cleaner world with pure water, fresh air, and robust ecosystems.
- A more stable climate through lessening pollutants and climate change.
- Preserving the environment's resources for the next generations.
- Financial advantages in green technologies, sustainable practices, and renewable energy.
- Societies that are more equal regarding resource distribution and environmental health.

It becomes unclear who is in charge of implementing sustainability. Sustainability is a global issue that calls for a multifaceted strategy; it is not simply about individual acts. First, everyone must live a sustainable lifestyle by minimising waste, using less energy, selecting eco-friendly items, and patronising ethical companies. Governments can implement policies that support ethical manufacturing methods, resource conservation, and renewable energy. Promoting responsible behaviour requires educating people and communities about sustainability problems and solutions. Technological developments in sustainable agriculture, green technologies, and renewable energy are essential for a sustainable future.

Protecting Resources and Natural Beauty

Our planet's resources and natural beauty are vital to the tourist and hospitality sectors. Resources are wasted more when there are more individuals in one area. However, the things that draw travellers may significantly suffer from conventional tourism practices. Here is where sustainability becomes essential (Blanco-Cerradelo et al., 2022). Physical resource consumption is decreased by having virtual experiences in the metaverse, such as meetings, events, and tours conducted virtually (e.g., paper, plastic, transportation fuels). As a result, waste production is reduced, and the environmental impact of hospitality activities is decreased.

Water Consumption and Waste Management

Tourism and Hospitality industry uses between 3.5% to 5.8% of the global available fresh water, and freshwater usage is less than many other industries like power and agriculture. However, this industry depends heavily on the availability of fresh water. Tourism and hospitality cannot do much to stall water wastage in other industries, but they can take steps to stop water wastage and manage it within their own industries. Unsustainable tourism can result in pollution, environmental deterioration, and the depletion of natural resources in popular tourist destinations. In such cases, eco-friendly measures like prudent trash disposal, water conservation, and energy-saving aid in safeguarding these tourist spots for coming generations (Obersteiner et al., 2021). There is less need for actual travel because of the metaverse's ability to facilitate virtual tourism experiences. By providing tourists with immersive virtual destinations, traditional tourism's adverse environmental effects are reduced as fewer people fly, drive, or use physical resources to experience the world. Digital twins or simulation models of hotels, resorts, and other tourism-related facilities can be made in the metaverse. Before implementing water and waste management systems in the real world, operators can simulate and optimise them using these virtual counterparts. They can experiment with various water-saving devices, recycling schemes, or trash minimisation methods to determine the options with the best practical application. In order to visualise real-time data on water usage, hotels and resorts can incorporate smart water management systems into their metaverse models, including sections where water-saving devices (such as faucets with low flows and showers) can be installed, leak monitoring, and virtual dashboards that display consumption patterns. Managers can reduce water consumption by using a virtual environment to monitor this data and make informed decisions.

Green House Gas Emission Schemes

The tourism sector's travel, lodging, and activities all majorly impact greenhouse gas emissions. The industry's environmental impact can be reduced by adopting sustainable practices that encourage environmentally friendly transportation options, energy-efficient structures, and responsible trash disposal (Zhang, 2021). Sustainable practices can lead to cost savings for businesses, such as reduced energy and water consumption, responsible waste management, and attracting environmentally conscious employees.

Biodiversity Preservation

Tourism can potentially threaten species and strain delicate ecosystems. To preserve biodiversity in tourist places, sustainable measures are crucial. These include encouraging responsible wildlife interaction, reducing habitat disruption, and supporting conservation programs. Sustainable practices can contribute to the long-term sustainability of tourism destinations by preserving the natural beauty and resources that draw visitors.

Local Economy

Local economies that depend on tourism stand to gain significantly from sustainable practices. As more and more travellers seek environmentally friendly vacation choices, companies that embrace sustainability have the potential to gain a competitive edge and attract eco-aware tourists. This positive shift can bring hope for the economic prosperity of local communities.

Positive Impact on Local Culture

Sustainable tourism encourages conscientious engagement with nearby communities. It promotes the limitation of detrimental societal effects, the honouring of cultural customs, and the patronising of neighbourhood businesses. This emphasis on local culture fosters a sense of respect and appreciation among tourists.

Community Relations, Human Rights and Labor Practices

Sustainable tourism promotes fair treatment of workers in the sector by guaranteeing respectable pay, secure working conditions, and chances for local employment. Travelling sustainably fosters an appreciation for regional customs and cultures, which in turn promotes a more fulfilling tourist experience and aids in preserving cultural assets for future generations. This emphasis on human rights and labour practices evokes a sense of empathy and support among the audience.

Health and Safety

In the hospitality and tourism sector, integrating health and safety with sustainability practices is crucial for creating a responsible and enjoyable experience for visitors and local communities (Moreno-Luna et al., 2021). Sustainable practices reduce pollution and waste, emphasise food safety, ensure that staff work in safe, cleanliness and hygiene in accommodations and facilities to protect guest health, plan for emergencies and support local communities by promoting health-conscious practices and respecting local cultures and traditions.

With these many benefits and impacts of sustainability on the hospitality and tourism industry, restoring sustainability has become the top priority for hotels worldwide. To maintain growth, the industry must pay attention to the following measures:

- Reduction of waste and conservation of water, energy, and materials through ethical sourcing.
- Encourage tourists to use electric vehicles, bicycles, walking, and public transportation.
- Provides excursions and events that reduce their adverse effects on the environment and aid in conservation efforts.
- Encourage local eateries and farmers to provide travellers with fresh, in-season, and sustainable food options.
- Work with regional groups to ensure tourism enhances their quality of life while preserving their environment and culture.

The tourism and hospitality sectors have the potential to be positive forces if they adopt a sustainable approach. It may enhance local communities, save the environment, and make travel for everyone more enjoyable and responsible.

METAVERSE WITH OTHER EMERGING TECHNOLOGIES

Artificial Intelligence has the potential to significantly improve user experiences, automate tasks, and customise interactions in the metaverse. In the metaverse, chatbots or virtual assistants driven by artificial intelligence (AI) can converse with users in real-time, offering personalised experiences, responding to questions, and assisting them in exploring virtual worlds or hotel settings. Artificial Intelligence has the capability to examine user behaviour and preferences within the metaverse and provide tailored suggestions for travel destinations, accommodations, and entertainment. Additionally, it can forecast consumer behaviour and trends, allowing companies to better tailor their offerings. Artificial intelligence (AI)-powered real-time language translation systems can make it easier for people from different nations to communicate in various languages within the metaverse, increasing the inclusivity of international travel and hospitality services. By establishing a connection between actual objects and the Internet, the Internet of Things (IoT) can facilitate real-time data exchange between the physical and metaverse, thereby augmenting the realism and interactivity of virtual worlds. IoT-enabled devices in the travel and hospitality industries can be controlled and replicated via the metaverse. From anywhere in the globe, users may virtually adjust smart room settings, including lighting, temperature, and water use. Real-time data can be fed into the metaverse via IoT sensors in physical locations like hotels or tourist attractions. Real-time monitoring of water and waste management by IoT can be optimised and visualised in the metaverse. Through haptic feedback, IoT could facilitate the development of sensor-enabled avatars that interact with actual settings, enhancing the sense of tangibility in metaverse experiences. Blockchain provides decentralised, transparent, and safe solutions for a variety of metaverse tasks, such as ownership verification and transaction processing. Secure, decentralized transactions in the metaverse, such as hotel reservations, virtual tour payments, and in-person purchases, can be facilitated using blockchain technology. Transactions can be automated with smart contracts, guaranteeing transparency and security without the need for middlemen. Blockchain guarantees traceability and verification of digital ownership across the metaverse. This can assist travel agencies in securely managing data access and preserving intellectual property rights over digital material, such as virtual tours and AI-generated experiences.

Metaverse, Sustainability and Tourism and Hospitality Industry

The metaverse-driven sustainable tourism (MDST) is a cutting-edge travel and exploration strategy that places a premium on social inclusion, environmental responsibility, and economic resilience. The MDST concept, which has its roots in sustainability, redefines and improves the tourist experience by utilising the potential of the metaverse, a virtual, networked space. MDST can benefit from enabling devices (e.g., MR/VR apps and devices), empowering platforms (e.g., graphic processing units or graphic designing skills), networking infrastructure (e.g., 5G mobile networks), and technologically literate users (e.g., information and communications technologies [ICTs] and digital literacy). The foundation of metaverse-driven sustainable tourism is the four-layer architecture of metaverse tourism, which emphasises the use of technology, user-generated content, and artificial intelligence to merge real and virtual worlds.

The UN's adoption of the Sustainable Development Goals (SDGs) signifies a worldwide consensus to tackle sustainability issues. By developing digital platforms supporting community involvement, economic opportunity, and cross-cultural exchange, MDST may support global collaboration and align with the SDGs. The UNWTO has embraced the Global Code of Ethics for Tourism (UNWTO, 2020) and acknowledged sustainable tourism as a vehicle for community development and empowerment in partnership with the international tourist community. MDST aligns with several SDGs, including those related to education, health, and industry innovation, thereby demonstrating its potential to contribute to global sustainability.

MDST meets travellers' changing requirements and expectations in a post-pandemic world. It shows promise as a revolutionary solution to pandemic-related problems. MDST supports a more integrated and conscientious future for the industry by integrating AI, personalisation, and immersive experiences, aligning with broad sustainability objectives. An MDST platform uses AI algorithms to examine user feedback, past interactions, and preferences, thereby providing a safe and personalised travel experience in the post-pandemic world.

The advent of MDST offers a ground-breaking chance to synchronise the travel and tourism sector with SDGs, promoting a responsible and transformative travel approach (Taran, 2024). In light of the SDGs, several essential findings highlight MDST's potential as a sustainable tourism revolution:

- Preserving culture and promoting global awareness support SDG 4 (high-quality education) and SDG 11 (sustainable cities and communities).
- Community empowerment and inclusivity support SDGs 17 (partnerships for the goals) and 9 (industry, innovation, and infrastructure).
- Technology innovation for sustainable development contributes to SDG 9 (Industry, Innovation, and Infrastructure) and responsible consumption (SDG 12).
- Education and information sharing align with SDG 4 (Quality Education).
- Health considerations and pandemic resilience align with SDG 3 (Good Health and Well-Being).

MDST is a method that policymakers can utilise to accomplish SDGs about global partnerships, responsible consumption, sustainable land use, and climate action. Defining criteria for developing MDST initiatives can result from cooperative efforts with international partners. By incorporating MDST into CSR programs, this sector may demonstrate its dedication to environmental sustainability. Encouraging virtual ecotourism projects and participating in cooperative platforms show corporate social responsibility and improve brand reputation. Agile approaches are tools that developers can use to handle uncertainty and adjust to changing consumer preferences. Quick prototyping, ongoing user feedback, and quick revisions guarantee that MDST projects stay updated with emerging technologies and user demands.

The travel and hospitality sectors require more visitors, which equates to more incredible resource waste. For the growth of this sector, more tourists mean more resource wastage. Growth and sustainability can be maintained with AI and Metaverse in this industry. In other words, this industry can expand while remaining sustainable with the aid of Metaverse.

Metaverse tourism may not require physical travel, enabling virtual location discovery (Kouroupi & Metaxas, 2023). This reduces carbon emissions and the environmental impact of travel by flying, cruising, and driving less. One effective tool for teaching about the environment is the Metaverse. Consider immersive exhibitions that highlight vulnerable ecosystems, endangered animals, or the consequences of climate change. This may increase consciousness and motivate sensible travel practices.

Virtual ecotourism experiences can be made more accessible by the Metaverse (Yasintha et al., 2022). Consider exploring a virtual canopy or participating in a virtual reef cleanup. In addition to raising money for conservation initiatives, this can teach tourists about ethical tourism. Through the Metaverse, this industry can demonstrate its dedication to sustainability. Eco-friendly activities, conservation programs, and chances for responsible travel can all be highlighted through virtual tours. Experiences in the Metaverse can aid in controlling overtourism in well-known locations (Kouroupi & Metaxas, 2023). The impact of tourists on delicate ecosystems and cultural places can be reduced by permitting virtual exploration.

The Metaverse allows travel businesses and lodging establishments to advertise eco-friendly travel options and experiences. This may inspire travellers to organise their physical travels in an environmentally responsible manner.

Envision travelling through a virtual version of the National Park, discovering more about its distinct ecology, and even participating in virtual conservation efforts is possible through Metaverse. Hotels may showcase their eco-friendly initiatives in the Metaverse with the Sustainable Accommodation Showcase. Virtual tours can highlight waste reduction programs, locally produced food, and eco-friendly hotels with energy-saving features (Olorunsola, 2020).

Metaverse Adoption Challenges in Tourism and Hospitality

Despite the Metaverse's potential benefits, the travel and hospitality sectors encounter several significant challenges in its adoption. These obstacles include:

Figure 5. Barriers to augment metaverse in tourism and hospitality industry

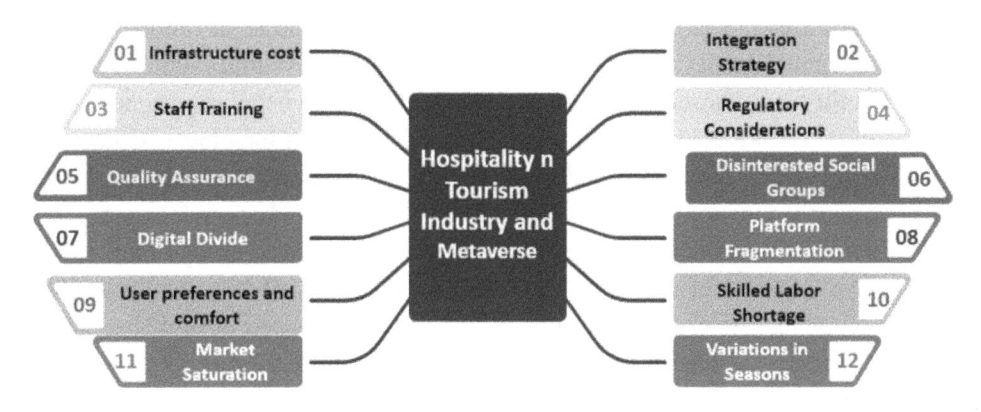

[Diagram showing Hospitality in Tourism Industry and Metaverse at center with 12 barriers: 01 Infrastructure cost, 02 Integration Strategy, 03 Staff Training, 04 Regulatory Considerations, 05 Quality Assurance, 06 Disinterested Social Groups, 07 Digital Divide, 08 Platform Fragmentation, 09 User preferences and comfort, 10 Skilled Labor Shortage, 11 Market Saturation, 12 Variations in Seasons]

(Authors own creation)

- **Infrastructure Cost**: Strong technical infrastructure, such as fast internet, VR/AR gear, and suitable software, is needed to implement the Metaverse. The initial investment and continuing maintenance expenditures of such infrastructure may challenge numerous enterprises in the tourism and hospitality sector (Khan et al., 2020). Creating and sustaining Metaverse platforms might have high initial expenses. Companies must carefully assess the possible return on investment, weighing the advantages of virtual interaction against the implementation's financial viability (Pöhler et al., 2023). Specific knowledge and resources are needed to create captivating and immersive material for the Metaverse, which requires a considerable investment. Hotels, tour companies, and other travel locations must invest in 3D modelling, interactive narrative, and virtual environment design to create engaging virtual experiences.
- **Integration Strategy:** Planning and coordination are essential for integrating Metaverse experiences into current business processes. Hotels and tourism enterprises must effectively incorporate virtual services with their physical offerings to uphold brand integrity and enhance customer satisfaction (Santos & Freitas, 2022)
- **Staff Training:** Employee training is necessary for Metaverse platform management and operation to be done correctly (Yilmaz et al., 2023). Workers must be proficient in navigating virtual environments, assisting clients digitally, and resolving any technical difficulties that may come up when interacting virtually.

- **Regulatory Considerations:** The regulatory structures that oversee virtual settings may grow increasingly intricate as the Metaverse develops. Businesses in the hospitality industry must know the legal ramifications of intellectual property rights, online transactions, and virtual event organising.
- **Quality Assurance:** Upholding good standards in virtual experiences is essential for preserving brand reputation and consumer happiness. Companies want systems to collect feedback, quickly fix technological issues, and continuously enhance virtual products.
- **Disinterested social groups:** Certain social or cultural groups may oppose or be sceptical of adopting Metaverse technologies. Businesses in the hospitality industry must carefully manage these views to ensure that virtual experiences adhere to various cultural conventions and values.
- **Digital Divide:** Not everyone can access basic computers or high-speed internet. This could prevent a sizable segment of the populace from taking advantage of the metaverse experiences provided by travel and hospitality companies.
- **Platform Fragmentation:** The Metaverse does not have a single, cohesive platform, which means it is still in the early stages of development (Ng, 2022). This implies that user experiences could be fragmented due to incompatibilities between various platforms and devices.
- **User Preferences and Comfort:** Not everyone will find metaverse experiences appealing. Some people prefer using traditional travel techniques or find virtual excursions less fulfilling than the real thing (Baker et al.,2023). Some people find technology uncomfortable, particularly virtual reality headsets (Angelov et al., 2020). Some users need to get used to a learning curve, and others might get motion sickness. Not every customer can access or knows the VR/AR technologies needed to access the Metaverse. There is a chance of leaving out market segments who would find it difficult to interact with virtual experiences, such as older people or those with impairments. Virtual environments gather significant user data, raising concerns about security and privacy. Hospitality organisations must adhere to strict data protection laws to safeguard client information online (O'Connor, 2020). Given the dynamic nature of tourism, customer preferences for metaverse experiences may also evolve. Companies must be adaptable and responsive to these changes to remain competitive.
- **Skilled Labour Shortage**: Creating and overseeing metaverse experiences requires new abilities (Lee et al., 2021). Companies might have to spend money on educating current staff members or recruiting fresh applicants with knowledge of metaverse technologies.

- **Market Saturation**: The market is highly saturated due to the growth of internet booking portals, OTAs (internet Travel Agencies), and alternative housing options like Airbnb. Customers' expectations and the competitive landscape are shifting due to new technologies like virtual reality tours, AI-driven suggestions, and intelligent hotel features. Travellers today demand tailored experiences, flawless online transactions, and distinctive products.
- **Variations in Seasons**: Demand might fluctuate significantly due to local events, holidays, and seasonal changes (Cannas, 2012). Using efficient revenue management techniques is essential to maximising profitability and optimising pricing all year round. Due to seasonal fluctuations in travel trends, targeted marketing initiatives are necessary to draw tourists during off-peak times.

Despite these obstacles, the travel and hospitality sectors have many intriguing opportunities in the Metaverse. As technology advances and becomes more accessible, these difficulties might not be as pressing as they seem. Businesses can begin investigating the Metaverse in the interim by developing experiences that require fewer resources, such as virtual tours or pre-trip briefings.

Mitigating Metaverse and Sustainability Challenges in Tourism

To tackle these obstacles, one must adopt a calculated strategy, work with technological partners, and continuously adjust to changing customer tastes and market trends. Although the Metaverse has the potential to revolutionise the travel and hospitality sector, these obstacles must be removed for it to be successfully implemented and widely embraced. The industry should implement the following recommended strategies to lessen the difficulties.

Figure 6. Integrating metaverse and sustainability in the tourism and hospitality industry

(Authors own creation)

- **Sustainable Metaverse Practices**: Reducing travel-related emissions and energy consumption are the first steps in this approach. The industry must promote energy-efficient gear and data centres for Metaverse infrastructure. To balance energy use, a significant investment is needed in carbon offset programs or renewable energy sources (Crespi et al., 2021). Virtual tourist experiences should be encouraged in addition to traditional travel to reduce travel emissions.
- **Hardware Solutions and Standards**: Cloud-based solutions or partnering with hardware makers to offer packaged offerings to lessen dependency on pricey personal hardware (Zhang & Yue, 2020). Adoption of industry-wide standards is necessary to guarantee seamless user experiences and cross-platform interoperability.
- **High-speed Internet and Inclusion**: To eliminate digital exclusion, the industry must prioritise broadband accessibility and digital inclusion. This includes providing inexpensive VR/AR devices to various populations and equitable access to high-speed internet (Vagadia, 2020). To make this campaign successful, training courses will be available to users to acquaint them with Metaverse platforms and technologies.

- **Data Security and Privacy**: Data security and privacy are crucial issues in today's digital age. Strong and unambiguous data security and privacy regulations in the Metaverse are recommended. Robust authentication and encryption procedures must be provided to safeguard user information (Huang, 2014). Emphasis must be placed on obtaining express user consent for data collection and usage and on transparent policies.
- **Cultural Collaboration with AI:** According to trends, people nowadays also like learning about and experiencing other cultures (Zhang et al., 2021). Accurate portrayal of cultural assets requires collaboration with local populations. To encourage cultural preservation and understanding, local stakeholders must create and administrate virtual tourism initiatives and educational programs within the Metaverse.
- **Workforce Training**: The unskilled labour force is the most significant obstacle to adopting the Metaverse in tourism and hospitality. Investing in training programs to equip workers for new positions in the digital economy is imperative.
- **AI and Security:** Using AI raises questions about the project's legitimacy. Training AI algorithms must be implemented to reduce biases in virtual encounters (Schwartz et al., 2022). A reliable system will be in place to shield users from identity theft and unauthorised usage of virtual identities. Government regulations and standards about employing AI and virtual identities in the Metaverse must be adequately enforced.
- **Blended Experiences:** Mixing complementary metaverse elements, such as pre-visualization tours or immersive cultural events, with real-world travel will attract more customers and help reduce costs (Mcdougall, 2020).
- **Accessible Introductory Experiences:** For beginners, offer low-barrier entry points such as interactive virtual exhibitions or 360-degree videos. Work along with regional or global museums to produce 360-degree videos of well-known tourist locations, hotels, airlines, or cruise ships; virtual walkthroughs of hotels or restaurants; and simulations that resemble games and allow users to experience virtual hotels. Tourist sites with AR-enabled maps that offer more details and background.
- **Inclusive Metaverse Design:** To facilitate different types of disabilities and create inclusive and accessible metaverse experiences. Change the mouse sensitivity, voice commands, keyboard shortcuts, and other control parameters. Include speech-to-text (STT) for users who are deaf or hard of seeing, text-to-speech (TTS) for users who are blind or hard of seeing, audio descriptions of virtual worlds, make avatars that symbolise a variety of physical prowess; include stories can also help to include disabled persons in this industry.

BREAKING BARRIERS: STAKEHOLDER ROLE IN METAVERSE ADOPTION IN TOURISM

"Breaking Barriers: Stakeholder Role in Metaverse Adoption in Tourism" delves into how essential stakeholders, from tech developers to business executives, tackle the challenges impeding the adoption of Metaverse technologies. This analysis focuses on cooperative endeavours and tactical measures intended to improve uptake, stimulate creativity, and eventually revolutionise the travel experience in the digital era. Table 1 highlights the barriers and the roles various stakeholders can play in removing these barriers in adopting.

Table 1. Barriers and the role of stakeholders

Barriers to Adopting Metaverse Technology	Stakeholders that can solve the Problem
Up-front costs: High initial investment in VR/AR equipment, software development, and infrastructure	**Investors:** Funding support **Technology providers:** Cost-effective solutions and scalable technologies **Government Agencies:** Grants or subsidies to support technology innovation in tourism
Metafusion: Integrating metaverse technology with existing systems and ensuring technical compatibility	**IT Consultants:** Offer expertise in technology integration and systems compatibility. **Technology Providers:** Develop user-friendly and interoperable platforms. **Businesses:** Invest in training and development for staff to manage new technologies.
Technoskepticism: Difficulty gaining user acceptance and guest encouragement with metaverse experiences, especially for technology-unfamiliar individuals.	**Marketing Teams:** Create awareness campaigns to educate potential users about the benefits and uses of metaverse technology. **Customer Experience Experts:** Design engaging and intuitive metaverse experiences to enhance user appeal. **Technology Providers:** Ensure user-friendly interfaces and support for onboarding new users.

continued on following page

Table 1. Continued

Barriers to Adopting Metaverse Technology	Stakeholders that can solve the Problem
Metasecure: Protecting user data and ensuring privacy within the metaverse.	**Cybersecurity Experts:** Implement robust security measures and protocols to protect user data. **Legal Advisors:** Guide data privacy regulations and compliance. **Technology Providers:** Incorporate robust security features in their platforms.
Contentcrafting: Developing high-quality, immersive content that provides value to users requires significant resources and expertise.	**Content Creators:** Develop engaging and high-quality virtual content for the metaverse. **Technology Providers:** Offer tools and support for content creation. **Businesses:** Invest in creative talent and resources for content development.

Source: Authors own creation

Technology Providers

Technology companies are essential in facilitating metaverse integration in the travel and hospitality sectors by providing scalable and reasonably priced solutions. These suppliers are responsible for creating systems that can accommodate expansive virtual worlds while being flexible enough to meet the sector's changing demands. To guarantee broad adoption, they must develop user-friendly and interoperable platforms that enable smooth communication between various metaverse ecosystems.

User-friendly interfaces are crucial when onboarding new users, especially those who may not be familiar with the intricacies of virtual environments. Technology vendors prioritise providing users with an intuitive interface that makes it simple to interact with the metaverse. This covers the platform's overall usability and aesthetics, ensuring a wide range of users can utilise it.

Another vital issue that technology suppliers need to handle is security. Safeguarding user data and ensuring transactions are conducted securely are critical as the metaverse becomes increasingly integrated with travel and hospitality. To protect against potential attacks, providers must include strong security measures like multi-factor authentication and encryption.

Moreover, a fundamental aspect of the metaverse experience is content creation. Technology companies should give consumers and companies the resources and assistance they need to produce engaging, high-calibre content. This permits flexibility and creativity inside the platform and provides user-friendly development kits, templates, and client support. The tourism and hospitality sectors can effectively integrate the metaverse by prioritising technology suppliers who prioritise cost-effectiveness, scalability, user-friendliness, security, and content production.

Businesses (Metaverse Service Providers)

Technology providers must prioritise investing in human capital and creative resources to integrate the metaverse successfully. Training and development are crucial to equipping employees to oversee and run new technology in the metaverse. Continuous learning will guarantee that teams stay knowledgeable about the newest technologies, platforms, and best practices as the digital world changes, encouraging creativity and operational effectiveness.

At the same time, spending money on creative talent is essential to creating immersive, captivating content that appeals to users. A captivating metaverse experience starts with high-quality material, which calls for a combination of technological know-how and artistic vision. Companies may create engaging content and differentiate themselves in a crowded market by investing money in hiring and developing creative personnel. When combined, these expenditures will enable tech companies to promote the adoption of the metaverse, improve user experiences, and keep a competitive edge in this quickly expanding digital space.

Marketing (Market Experts)

To inform prospective users about the advantages and uses of the metaverse, awareness campaigns must be developed. The immersive experiences that the metaverse provides—like virtual travel, interactive events, and personalised services—should be the main emphasis of marketing campaigns. These efforts can demystify the technology and make it more approachable and appealing to a broader audience by presenting success stories and concrete benefits. Furthermore, utilising influencer relationships, social media, and tailored content can increase interaction and create a vibrant community around adopting the metaverse.

Customer Experience (Customer Service Experts)

Enhancing user appeal requires designing metaverse experiences that are both intuitive and interesting. A smooth and user-friendly interface guarantees that users can easily interact and explore the virtual environment. Customised avatars and content are two examples of personalised experiences that can significantly increase customer pleasure and loyalty. Additionally, adding interactive aspects and gamification components can enhance user engagement and enjoyment in the metaverse and entice users to explore the platform more. Iterative design upgrades and ongoing user feedback are essential for fine-tuning the experience to match changing user expectations.

Cybersecurity (Cyber Experts)

Strong security rules and procedures must be implemented as the metaverse gains traction to safeguard user information. This includes personal data encryption, safe authentication procedures, and frequent security audits to spot and stop possible attacks. Maintaining data security and privacy will increase user trust, which is necessary for broad adoption. Further enhancing security can be done by teaching users about safe habits in the metaverse, like identifying phishing efforts and safeguarding their accounts.

Investors

Investors are critical in supplying the capital required to establish and grow metaverse projects. By providing financial backing, investors allow businesses to investigate cutting-edge technology, construct infrastructure, and design captivating virtual worlds. Startups and established enterprises need support to compete in a quickly changing digital market and bring creative ideas to reality.

Government Agencies

Government organisations help promote technological innovation in tourism by providing grants, subsidies, or tax breaks. These financial incentives have the potential to significantly reduce entrance barriers for small and medium-sized businesses, enabling them to test and use metaverse technology. The government also assists in establishing public-private partnerships that encourage innovation and guarantee the industry's widespread adoption of sustainable practices.

Legal Support

Legal counsel is essential for helping businesses navigate the complicated world of data privacy laws and compliance. Because the metaverse entails gathering and handling enormous volumes of user data, legal counsel ensures that companies comply with pertinent laws and regulations, such as GDPR, to safeguard user privacy and prevent financial penalties. Their knowledge aids businesses in resolving legal issues and upholding customer confidence.

Content Creators

The metaverse experience revolves around content creators who are in charge of producing engaging, superior virtual material. Their technical expertise and inventiveness give virtual worlds life, attracting and engrossing users. Content creators are critical to the success of metaverse tourism projects because they create experiences that connect with audiences and drive user engagement and happiness.

For this sector's growth and sustainability, all stakeholders must gather on a common platform to mitigate various issues. Collaborations must be encouraged between governments, tourism providers, technology developers, and environmental organisations. Maintaining an open line of communication with stakeholders to handle new issues and opportunities is vital. The tourism and hospitality sectors may experience further growth due to creative projects and research examining the convergence of metaverse technology and sustainable tourist practices (Allam et al., 2022).

RECOMMENDATIONS FOR THE INDUSTRY

The tourism and hospitality industry shall incorporate the 4I taxonomy of Metaverse, which involves imitation, intensification, interaction, and integration. The industry shall adopt the metaverse ecosystem to reduce the need for actual travel by providing engaging virtual experiences, hence reducing carbon footprints. The industry shall utilise the metaverse to imitate environmentally friendly travel, enabling visitors to see places, engage in cultural pursuits, and go to events without endangering the environment. Digital twins can be created in the metaverse related to lodging facilities, resorts, and tourist destinations. Virtual models shall be developed to simulate and evaluate sustainable methods like waste reduction, water conservation, and energy-efficient systems before practising in the real world. The water and waste conservation activities shall be more entertaining and rewarding by giving guests incentives for practising eco-friendly behaviour, including turning to recycling or conserving water when staying in virtual hotels. Employees can participate in immersive, remote virtual training sessions in the metaverse to learn about sustainable operations, waste management, and energy saving. This strategy reduces travel-related emissions while providing opportunities for ongoing learning. IoT sensors can be used with metaverse models to track energy, water, and trash production. Businesses can make data-driven decisions and dynamic adjustments to their sustainability strategy with AI-powered metaverse insights. Blockchain technology can be deployed to make transactions in the metaverse safe and environmentally responsible. Use smart contracts to implement reward systems that encourage visitors to participate in environmentally friendly activities, such as packages for responsible travel or virtual carbon offset programs.

Future Research Agenda

Since there is no model development or data collecting involved, the current effort is mainly theoretical in nature. Researchers can work on the metaverse in the tourist sector by implementing models and gathering information from people who visit virtual locations within the metaverse. The researchers can examine people's inclinations, driving forces, and degrees of involvement inside the metaverse. Research on cross-national comparisons of user motives and metaverse involvement levels is also possible.

REFERENCES

Angelov, V., Petkov, E., Shipkovenski, G., & Kalushkov, T. (2020, June). Modern virtual reality headsets. In *2020 International Congress on Human-Computer Interaction, Optimization and Robotic Applications (HORA)* (pp. 1-5). IEEE.

Arslan, H. M., Khan, I., Latif, M. I., Komal, B., & Chen, S. (2022). Understanding the dynamics of natural resources rents, environmental sustainability, and sustainable economic growth: New insights from China. *Environmental Science and Pollution Research International*, 29(39), 58746–58761. DOI: 10.1007/s11356-022-19952-y PMID: 35368236

Baker, J., Nam, K., & Dutt, C. S. (2023). A user experience perspective on heritage tourism in the metaverse: Empirical evidence and design dilemmas for VR. *Information Technology & Tourism*, 25(3), 265–306. DOI: 10.1007/s40558-023-00256-x

Benrimoh, D., Chheda, F. D., & Margolese, H. C. (2022). The best predictor of the future—The metaverse, mental health, and lessons learned from current technologies. *JMIR Mental Health*, 9(10), e40410. DOI: 10.2196/40410 PMID: 36306155

Blanco-Cerradelo, L., Diéguez-Castrillón, M. I., Fraiz-Brea, J. A., & Gueimonde-Canto, A. (2022). Protected areas and tourism resources: Toward sustainable management. *Land (Basel)*, 11(11), 2059. DOI: 10.3390/land11112059

Buhalis, D. (2020). Technology in tourism—from information communication technologies to eTourism and smart tourism towards ambient intelligence tourism: A perspective article. *Tourism Review*, 75(1), 267–272. DOI: 10.1108/TR-06-2019-0258

Buhalis, D., Harwood, T., Bogicevic, V., Viglia, G., Beldona, S., & Hofacker, C. (2019). Technological disruptions in services: Lessons from tourism and hospitality. *Journal of Service Management*, 30(4), 484–506. DOI: 10.1108/JOSM-12-2018-0398

Cannas, R. (2012). An overview of tourism seasonality: Key concepts and policy. *AlmaTourism*, 3(5), 40–58.

Chen, X. H., Tee, K., Elnahass, M., & Ahmed, R. (2023). Assessing the environmental impacts of renewable energy sources: A case study on air pollution and carbon emissions in China. *Journal of Environmental Management*, 345, 118525. DOI: 10.1016/j.jenvman.2023.118525 PMID: 37421726

Christofi, M., Vrontis, D., Shams, R., Belyaeva, Z., & Czinkota, M. R. (2022). Sustained competitive advantage for sustainable hospitality and tourism development: A stakeholder causal scope analysis. *Journal of Hospitality & Tourism Research (Washington, D.C.)*, 46(5), 823–825. DOI: 10.1177/10963480221091976

Dube, K., Nhamo, G., & Chikodzi, D. (2021). COVID-19 cripples global restaurant and hospitality industry. *Current Issues in Tourism*, 24(11), 1487–1490. DOI: 10.1080/13683500.2020.1773416

Dwivedi, Y. K., Hughes, L., Wang, Y., Alalwan, A. A., Ahn, S. J. G., Balakrishnan, J., & Wirtz, J. (2023).

Efthymiou, L. (2018). Worker body-art in upper-market hotels: Neither accepted, nor prohibited. *International Journal of Hospitality Management*, 74, 99–108. DOI: 10.1016/j.ijhm.2018.02.012

G, S., Chakraborty, D., Polisetty, A., Khorana, S., & Buhalis, D. (2023). Use of metaverse in socializing: Application of the big five personality traits framework. *Psychology & Marketing, 40*(10), 2132–2150. https://doi.org/DOI: 10.1002/mar.21863

Gahlawat, I. N., & Lakra, P. (2020). Global climate change and its effects. *Integrated Journal of Social Sciences*, 7(1), 14–23.

Gautam, P. (2021). The effects and challenges of COVID-19 in the hospitality and tourism sector in India. *Journal of Tourism and Hospitality Education*, 11, 43–63. DOI: 10.3126/jthe.v11i0.38242

Go, H., & Kang, M. (2023). Metaverse tourism for sustainable tourism development: Tourism agenda 2030. *Tourism Review*, 78(2), 381–394. DOI: 10.1108/TR-02-2022-0102

Gultek, M., & Heroux, L. (2019). Marketing strategies of alternative revenue sources for full-service hotels in the United States and Canada: A comparative revenue management approach. *Journal of Tourism and Hospitality Management*, 7(2), 1–9. DOI: 10.15640/jthm.v7n2a1

Guridno, E., & Guridno, A. (2020). COVID-19 impact: Indonesia tourism in new normal era. [IJMH]. *International Journal of Management and Humanities*, 4(11), 31–34. DOI: 10.35940/ijmh.K1049.0741120

Guttentag, D., Griffin, T., & Lee, S. H. (2018). The future is now: How virtual reality and augmented reality are transforming tourism. In *The Sage Handbook of Tourism Management* (pp. 443–462). Sage. DOI: 10.4135/9781526461490.n30

Hoffman, S. K. (2020). Online exhibitions during the COVID-19 pandemic. *Museum Worlds*, 8(1), 210–215. DOI: 10.3167/armw.2020.080115

Huang, X., Xiang, Y., Bertino, E., Zhou, J., & Xu, L. (2014). Robust multi-factor authentication for fragile communications. *IEEE Transactions on Dependable and Secure Computing*, 11(6), 568–581. DOI: 10.1109/TDSC.2013.2297110

India's hospitality sector reviving article (2022). Retrieved from https://www.aninews.in/news/national/general-news/indias-hospitality-sector-reviving-steadily-post-covid-1920221018102232/

Ivanov, S., & Webster, C. (Eds.). (2020). *Robots, Artificial Intelligence, and Service Automation in Travel, Tourism, and Hospitality*. Emerald Publishing.

Jabeen, F., Al Zaidi, S., & Al Dhaheri, M. H. (2022). Automation and artificial intelligence in hospitality and tourism. *Tourism Review*, 77(4), 1043–1061. DOI: 10.1108/TR-09-2019-0360

Kazandzhieva, V., & Filipova, H. (2019). Customer attitudes toward robots in travel, tourism, and hospitality: A conceptual framework. In S. Ivanov & C. Webster (Eds.), *Robots, Artificial Intelligence, and Service Automation in Travel, Tourism and Hospitality* (pp. 79-92). Emerald Publishing. DOI: 10.1108/978-1-78756-687-320191004

Khaled, G., & Alena, F. (2021). Industry 4.0 and human resource management in the hotel business. *Human Progress*, 7(2), 1–10.

Khan, N., Hassan, A. U., Fahad, S., & Naushad, M. (2020). Factors affecting the tourism industry and its impacts on the global economy. *SSRN*. DOI: 10.2139/ssrn.3559353

Kouroupi, N., & Metaxas, T. (2023). Can the Metaverse and its associated digital tools and technologies provide an opportunity for destinations to address the vulnerability of overtourism? *Tourism and Hospitality*, 4(2), 355–373. DOI: 10.3390/tourhosp4020022

Lamba., ….. (2023). HVS India hospitality industry overview 2023. Retrieved from https://www.hvs.com/article/9918-hvs-india-hospitality-industry-overview-2023#:~:text=Inbound%20tourism%20displayed%20promising%20signs,highs%20last%20experienced%20in%202019

Lee, L. H., Braud, T., Zhou, P., Wang, L., Xu, D., Lin, Z., . . . Hui, P. (2021). All one needs to know about the metaverse: A complete survey on technological singularity, virtual ecosystem, and research agenda. *arXiv preprint arXiv:2110.05352*.

Lee, S., Pan, B., & Park, S. (2019). RevPAR vs. GOPPAR: Property-and firm-level analysis. *Annals of Tourism Research*, 76, 180–190. DOI: 10.1016/j.annals.2019.04.006

Leung, X. Y., Bai, B., & Stahura, K. A. (2015). The marketing effectiveness of social media in the hotel industry: A comparison of Facebook and Twitter. *Journal of Hospitality & Tourism Research (Washington, D.C.)*, 39(2), 147–169. DOI: 10.1177/1096348012471381

Li, X., Kim, J. S., & Lee, T. J. (2021). Collaboration for community-based cultural sustainability in island tourism development: A case in Korea. *Sustainability (Basel)*, 13(13), 7306. DOI: 10.3390/su13137306

Li, Y., Gunasekeran, D. V., RaviChandran, N., Tan, T. F., Ong, J. C. L., Thirunavukarasu, A. J., Polascik, B. W., Habash, R., Khaderi, K., & Ting, D. S. W. (2024). The next generation of the healthcare ecosystem in the metaverse. *Biomedical Journal*, 47(3), 100679. DOI: 10.1016/j.bj.2023.100679 PMID: 38048990

Lukanova, G., & Ilieva, G. (2019). Robots, artificial intelligence and service automation in hotels. In *Travel, Tourism, and Hospitality* (pp. 157-183). Emerald Publishing. DOI: 10.1108/978-1-78756-687-320191009

Ma, J., Scott, N., & Wu, Y. (2023). Tourism destination advertising: Effect of storytelling and sensory stimuli on arousal and memorability. *Tourism Review*, ahead-of-print. https://doi.org/DOI: 10.1108/TR-07-2022-0319

Market data forecast report. (n.d.). Retrieved from https://www.marketdataforecast.com/market-reports/big-data-market

Mcdougall, P. B. R. (2020). Digital tools. *Psychology and Marketing*, 40(4), 750–776. DOI: 10.1002/mar.21767

Morales, J., Cornide-Reyes, H., Rossel, P. O., Sáez, P., & Silva-Aravena, F. (2023, July). Virtual reality, augmented reality, and the metaverse: Customer experience approach and user experience evaluation methods. In *International Conference on Human-Computer Interaction* (pp. 554-566). Cham: Springer Nature. DOI: 10.1007/978-3-031-35915-6_40

Ng, D. T. K. (2022). What is the metaverse? Definitions, technologies, and the community of inquiry. *Australasian Journal of Educational Technology*, 38(4), 190–205. DOI: 10.14742/ajet.7945

O'Connor, P. (2020). Data privacy and the travel sector. In *Handbook of e-Tourism* (pp. 1-14).

Obersteiner, G., Gollnow, S., & Eriksson, M. (2021). Carbon footprint reduction potential of waste management strategies in tourism. *Environmental Development*, 39, 100617. DOI: 10.1016/j.envdev.2021.100617 PMID: 34513580

Olorunsola, V. O. (2020). *Green practices: The experiences of guests in eco-centric hotels in the UK* (Master's thesis, Eastern Mediterranean University).

Pillai, R., & Sivathanu, B. (2020). Adoption of AI-based chatbots for hospitality and tourism. *International Journal of Contemporary Hospitality Management*, 32(10), 3199–3226. DOI: 10.1108/IJCHM-04-2020-0259

Pöhler, L., & Teuteberg, F. (2023). Suitability-and utilization-based cost–benefit analysis: A techno-economic feasibility study of virtual reality for workplace and process design. *Information Systems and e-Business Management*, •••, 1–41. DOI: 10.1007/s10257-023-00622-0

Rockström, J., Steffen, W., Noone, K., Persson, A., Chapin, F. S.III, Lambin, E. F., Lenton, T. M., Scheffer, M., Folke, C., Schellnhuber, H. J., Nykvist, B., de Wit, C. A., Hughes, T., van der Leeuw, S., Rodhe, H., Sörlin, S., Snyder, P. K., Costanza, R., Svedin, U., & Foley, J. A. (2009). A safe operating space for humanity. *Nature*, 461(7263), 472–475. DOI: 10.1038/461472a PMID: 19779433

Sainaghi, R., Abrate, G., & Mauri, A. (2021). Price and RevPAR determinants of Airbnb listings: Convergent and divergent evidence. *International Journal of Hospitality Management*, 92, 102709. DOI: 10.1016/j.ijhm.2020.102709

Santos, J., & Freitas, A. (2022). The impact of the metaverse on tourism and hospitality: A new era of digital experiences. *Journal of Tourism and Hospitality Management*, 10(2), 45–56. DOI: 10.20868/jthm.2022.10.2.45

Schöbel, S. M., & Leimeister, J. M. (2023). Metaverse platform ecosystems. *Electronic Markets*, 33(1), 12–25. DOI: 10.1007/s12525-023-00623-w

Statista. (2021). Social media & user-generated content. Retrieved from https://www.statista.com/statistics/278414/number-of-worldwide-social-network-users/

Sun, J., Sarfraz, M., Khawaja, K. F., Ozturk, I., & Raza, M. A. (2022). The perils of the pandemic for the tourism and hospitality industries: Envisaging the combined effect of COVID-19 fear and job insecurity on employees' job performance in Pakistan. *Psychology Research and Behavior Management*, 15, 1325–1346. DOI: 10.2147/PRBM.S365972 PMID: 35642192

Tran, L. T. T. (2024). Metaverse-driven sustainable tourism: A horizon 2050 paper. *Tourism Review*, ahead-of-print. https://doi.org/DOI: 10.1108/TR-12-2023-0857

Tung, V., & Au, N. (2018). Exploring customer experiences with robotics in hospitality. *International Journal of Contemporary Hospitality Management*, 30(7), 2680–2697. DOI: 10.1108/IJCHM-06-2017-0322

United Nations World Tourism Organization. (2020). *Global code of ethics for tourism*. Retrieved from https://www.unwto.org/global-code-of-ethics-for-tourism

World Travel & Tourism Council. (2023). The impact of terrorism on global tourism. Retrieved from https://www.wttc.org/research/policy-research/impact-of-terrorism-on-tourism

Yang, L., Ni, S. T., Wang, Y., Yu, A., Lee, J. A., & Hui, P. (2024). Interoperability of the metaverse: A digital ecosystem perspective review. *arXiv preprint arXiv:2403.05205*. DOI: 10.2139/ssrn.4929167

Yasintha, P. N., Ginting, R. T., & Wirantari, I. D. A. P. (2022). The potential of virtual methods as a means of ecotourism education in the era of Society 5.0. In M. A. S. Megafury Apriandhini (Chair), *Proceedings of the 4th OSC* (p. 304).

Yilmaz, M., O'Farrell, E., & Clarke, P. (2023). Examining the training and education potential of the metaverse: Results from an empirical study of next generation SAFe training. *Journal of Software (Malden, MA)*, 35(9), e2531. DOI: 10.1002/smr.2531

Zhang, J. (2021). Impacts of the emissions policies on tourism: An important but neglected aspect of sustainable tourism. *Journal of Hospitality and Tourism Management*, 47, 453–461. DOI: 10.1016/j.jhtm.2021.02.006

Zhang, X., & Yue, W. T. (2020). Integration of on-premises and cloud-based software: The product bundling perspective. *Journal of the Association for Information Systems*, 21, 1507–1551. Advance online publication. DOI: 10.17705/1jais.00645

Zhang, Y., Zong, R., Kou, Z., Shang, L., & Wang, D. (2021). Collablearn: An uncertainty-aware crowd-AI collaboration system for cultural heritage damage assessment. *IEEE Transactions on Computational Social Systems*, 9(5), 1515–1529. DOI: 10.1109/TCSS.2021.3109143

KEY TERMS AND DEFINITIONS

Content Crafting: Content crafting is the process of carefully generating, enhancing, and improving textual, graphic, or multimedia content to successfully convey a message, engage a viewer, or achieve a specific goal.

Eco-Tourism: Eco-tourism is a type of environmentally conscious travel that emphasises visiting habitats in a way that respects the local way of life, the environment, and local communities.

Extended Reality (XR): Extended Reality (XR) is an umbrella term that encompasses all immersive technologies that blend the physical and digital worlds, such as augmented reality (AR), virtual reality (CR) and mixed reality (MR).

Immersive Experience: An immersive experience is characterised by an environment or situation in which a person becomes completely engaged and involved, often getting the feeling that they are a part of the experience itself.

Stakeholders: Stakeholders are people, organisations, or groups having vested interests in a project, business, or institution's performance, decisions, or outcome. They can be impacted by their activities and decisions.

Sustainability: Sustainability refers to the practice of solving present-day problems without compromising the ability of future generations to meet their own needs. Its foundation is preserving the equilibrium between social advancement, environmental preservation, and economic expansion.

Sustainable Development Goals (SDGs): SDGs are the 17 interrelated global goals adopted by The United Nations in 2015 to address the sustainable development agenda set for 2030. They provide a shared blueprint for peace and prosperity for people and the planet, aiming to address global challenges and promote sustainable development in various social, economic, and environmental dimensions.

Chapter 8
AI in Nature Reserves:
Boon or Bane?

Bassam Samir Al-Romeedy
Faculty of Tourism and Hotels, University of Sadat City, Egypt

ABSTRACT

This chapter examines the multifaceted impacts of AI adoption in natural reserves, exploring both the benefits and challenges. On the positive side, AI-powered tools can assist in real-time monitoring of wildlife populations, habitat conditions, and visitor numbers, enabling timely and data-driven decision-making for conservation. AI-based personalization of visitor experiences can also improve engagement and education. However, relying on AI algorithms raises issues related to data privacy, algorithmic bias, and the potential disruption of natural ecosystems through excessive monitoring and interventions. Through a review of academic literature, this chapter provides a balanced analysis of the advantages and disadvantages of AI integration in natural reserves. The findings aim to guide policymakers, conservation practitioners, and technology researchers in navigating the complex landscape of AI-enabled nature conservation.

INTRODUCTION

AI technologies have become vital in the tourism and hospitality sector, significantly improving customer experiences through personalized services. By analyzing extensive datasets, AI systems provide real-time, tailored recommendations and communications, enhancing customer satisfaction and loyalty. Additionally, AI streamlines operations, with chatbots managing routine inquiries and revenue

DOI: 10.4018/979-8-3693-7021-6.ch008

Copyright © 2025, IGI Global. Copying or distributing in print or electronic forms without written permission of IGI Global is prohibited.

management systems optimizing pricing and inventory based on demand forecasts, helping businesses maximize profitability (Limna, 2023; Bharadiya, 2023).

As the tourism and hospitality sectors continue to evolve, strategically incorporating AI technologies will be essential for businesses to remain competitive, improve efficiency, and provide exceptional customer experiences. The integration of AI is increasingly critical in promoting sustainable practices within the tourism industry. AI-driven analytics can help tourism operators and policymakers understand the complex interactions between tourist behaviors, environmental impacts, and local community needs. By analyzing extensive datasets on factors such as energy consumption, waste production, and visitor patterns, AI systems can identify opportunities to improve resource efficiency, reduce ecological footprints, and balance the interests of all stakeholders. This data-driven approach enables the implementation of more informed strategies, ensuring the long-term sustainability and resilience of tourism destinations (Al-Romeedy, 2024a; Farahat, 2023; Al-Romeedy, 2024b).

Nature reserves face various challenges that make the use of AI essential for effective conservation and management. Issues like poaching, illegal logging, and resource overexploitation are difficult to monitor continuously due to the vast and remote nature of these areas. Traditional wildlife tracking and illegal activity detection methods are often inefficient and costly. Moreover, predicting environmental changes and species behavior is complicated by the intricate dynamics of ecosystems. AI offers a solution by enabling real-time monitoring with drones, sensors, and cameras, which can detect patterns in poaching, deforestation, and track endangered species while modeling environmental shifts. This facilitates faster, data-driven decision-making, enhancing biodiversity protection and sustainable resource management (Katswera, 2023; Al-Romeedy, 2024c, d). The integration of AI technologies within nature reserves holds transformative potential for conservation efforts, offering numerous advantages that can greatly enhance the management and protection of these vital ecosystems. However, this integration also introduces several challenges and potential drawbacks that warrant careful consideration (Chisom et al., 2024; Gupta et al., 2024). This duality raises the fundamental question: does the integration of AI in nature reserves ultimately bring more benefits than drawbacks?

AI has become an invaluable asset in enhancing the monitoring and management of natural reserves. One of its most significant benefits is its ability to improve wildlife tracking and environmental monitoring. AI-powered drones and camera traps can collect extensive data on animal movements, behaviors, and population dynamics with unprecedented accuracy. This real-time data collection enables conservationists to make well-informed decisions and quickly address potential threats (Dauvergne, 2020). Predictive analytics, another application of AI, is transforming our understanding and response to environmental changes (Soori et al., 2023). AI models can forecast the impacts of climate change on natural reserves, aiding in the development of strategies to mitigate these effects (Kaack et al., 2022). For instance, AI can predict shifts in species distributions or changes in vegetation cover, enabling proactive conservation measures. Furthermore, AI can predict natural disasters such as wildfires or floods, providing crucial lead time to protect these areas (Chisom et al., 2024; SP et al., 2024). AI also improves resource management within natural reserves by analyzing patterns of illegal activities like poaching or logging, suggesting optimized patrol routes for rangers to enhance anti-poaching efforts. Additionally, AI can help manage visitor access, balancing the need for tourism revenue with conservation goals by forecasting and controlling visitor flows to minimize environmental impact (Guan et al., 2021; Khan et al., 2024).

Despite its numerous advantages, integrating AI into nature reserves presents significant challenges. A major concern is data privacy and security; if AI systems and data are not properly safeguarded, poachers could misuse this information to target wildlife, thus undermining conservation efforts. Another critical issue is the high cost of implementing AI technologies. Deploying AI systems in natural reserves can be expensive, and limited funding may impede the adoption of these technologies, especially in developing countries (Nishant et al., 2021; Shaw et al., 2019; Farahat, 2023). Moreover, there may be a shortage of specialized technical expertise needed to operate and maintain AI systems, requiring significant investment in training and capacity building. While AI can greatly enhance conservation efforts, there is a risk of over-reliance. It should complement rather than replace traditional conservation practices and knowledge. Ethical considerations are also paramount when deploying AI in nature reserves, particularly concerning privacy, especially in areas inhabited by indigenous communities. Ensuring the ethical use of AI and respecting the rights and privacy of all stakeholders is crucial (Alasadi & Baiz, 2023; Al-Romeedy, 2024a; Kochupillai et al., 2022).

Using AI in nature reserves holds significant promise for bolstering conservation endeavors, presenting a potent tool for safeguarding these essential ecosystems. Nonetheless, it's imperative to tackle the accompanying challenges to ensure the ethical and efficient deployment of AI. Striking a careful balance between its advantages and disadvantages, AI can be seamlessly incorporated into conservation tactics, safeguarding natural reserves for posterity and turning potential pitfalls into definite advantages. This study conducts an exhaustive examination of the diverse ramifications of AI in nature reserves, drawing insights from an in-depth review of existing literature. The research investigates the diverse avenues through which AI could bolster conservation endeavors, ranging from enhanced surveillance and monitoring to predictive modeling of environmental risks and efficient resource management. Additionally, the study delves into legitimate apprehensions regarding AI's potential drawbacks in natural settings, encompassing concerns like ecological disruption, data security risks, and the pitfalls associated with algorithmic biases and inaccuracies. By comprehensively examining the intricate relationship between AI and conservation, the study seeks to offer insights for policymakers, conservationists, and technology experts striving to leverage AI's potential for the betterment of our environment.

AI AND SUSTAINABLE TOURISM

AI is transforming the tourism sector by fostering sustainability through novel technologies aimed at boosting resource efficiency, mitigating environmental footprint, and enhancing visitor satisfaction. Through AI integration, tourism entities can foster more eco-friendly practices that positively impact the environment, local residents, and the overall industry. An essential use of AI in sustainable tourism lies in optimizing resource utilization. AI algorithms can scrutinize data concerning energy consumption, water usage, and waste production to pinpoint inefficiencies and propose enhancements (Khan et al., 2024; Dauvergne, 2020). As an illustration, AI-driven systems have the capability to modify heating, ventilation, and air conditioning configurations in hotels according to occupancy trends, thereby lowering energy usage. Likewise, AI can enhance water management within establishments and offer guidance on waste disposal methods to diminish contributions to landfills. These AI-driven analyses assist tourism providers in curbing their environmental impact while simultaneously saving expenses (Tien, 2023).

AI also assumes a pivotal function in bolstering the conservation endeavors of both natural reserves and cultural landmarks. Through predictive analytics, AI can anticipate shifts in the environment and gauge human influence on these sites, allowing preemptive actions to mitigate potential harm. For instance, AI can track visitor behaviors and forecast instances of overcrowding, which might otherwise degrade fragile ecosystems. By regulating visitor numbers and enforcing capacity restrictions, heritage sites can safeguard their authenticity while continuing to offer fulfilling experiences for visitors. Furthermore, AI can contribute to habitat restoration initiatives by analyzing data related to species populations and environmental conditions, ensuring the effectiveness and sustainability of conservation endeavors (Fei et al., 2023; Chisom et al., 2024). Moreover, AI-driven personalization enhances the visitor experience while advancing sustainable tourism. By assessing individual preferences and behaviors, AI can suggest eco-friendly travel options, including sustainable accommodations, low-impact activities, and locally sourced, organic dining choices. This tailored approach not only meets the increasing demand for sustainable travel but also educates tourists about the significance of supporting environmentally conscious practices. Additionally, AI can facilitate virtual tourism experiences, reducing the necessity for physical travel and thereby lowering carbon emissions linked to transportation (Khan et al., 2024; Hu et al., 2021; Kim et al., 2024).

AI further promotes sustainable tourism through enhanced supply chain management. With AI, tourism operators can identify and engage with sustainable suppliers, ensuring that their practices adhere to environmental and social responsibility standards (Sifolo & Henama, 2024; Horng et al., 2018). For instance, AI can assist in identifying suppliers committed to renewable energy, fair labor practices, and sustainable materials. By incorporating sustainability criteria into procurement procedures, tourism enterprises play a pivotal role in fostering a more sustainable industry (Dauvergne, 2020). Furthermore, AI improves the capacity to monitor and assess the effects of tourism endeavors. Sophisticated analytics can monitor various metrics like carbon emissions, waste production, and biodiversity impacts, offering valuable data for assessment and enhancement. This transparency empowers tourism operators to establish and attain sustainability objectives, adhere to regulations, and showcase their dedication to responsible approaches. Additionally, AI-generated insights can guide policymaking, assisting governments and entities in formulating strategies that harmonize tourism expansion with environmental conservation (Baratta et al., 2023; Sacco et al., 2023).

The Positive Effects of AI Adoption in Nature Reserves

The use of artificial intelligence (AI) in nature reserves has transformed conservation efforts, offering significant benefits for biodiversity management and protection. AI technologies have enhanced monitoring and surveillance by analyzing large datasets from camera traps, drones, and sensors in real time, enabling swift detection of illegal activities such as poaching and habitat destruction. This automation facilitates proactive responses to threats and environmental disruptions. Additionally, AI-powered predictive models help identify risks like wildfires, invasive species, and climate impacts, allowing for preventive measures. AI also improves resource allocation, reducing costs and manpower while maximizing coverage. Overall, AI enhances decision-making and conservation efficiency, promoting the long-term sustainability of protected areas.

Enhanced Monitoring and Surveillance

The integration of AI in nature reserves revolutionizes monitoring and surveillance, offering enhanced capabilities to manage wildlife populations, habitat health, and environmental conditions. AI-powered systems process vast datasets from diverse sources in real-time, enabling continuous monitoring and rapid response to potential threats (Zhanget al., 2024; Chisom et al., 2024). These systems automate data analysis, identifying patterns and anomalies indicative of environmental disturbances or illegal activities, such as poaching or habitat destruction. Additionally, AI-driven predictive modeling forecasts risks like wildfires or invasive species encroachment, empowering managers to implement proactive mitigation measures (Şengönül et al., 2023; Li, 2019). Furthermore, AI optimizes resource allocation for monitoring activities, maximizing coverage while minimizing costs and manpower requirements (Khan et al., 2023; Fang & Savkin, 2024).

Improved Resource Management

The integration of AI in nature reserves revolutionizes resource management, enhancing sustainability and conservation efforts. AI-driven analysis of environmental data enables informed decision-making and optimized allocation of resources (Wang et al., 2023; Dauvergne, 2020). By integrating data from diverse sources, including sensor networks and satellite imagery, AI provides insights for effective distribution of water, energy, and personnel (Neethirajan, 2024; İşler et al., 2024). Additionally, AI aids in visitor management by predicting visitation patterns, regulating access, and improving the visitor experience, leading to reduced environmental impact (Khan et al., 2024; Farahat, 2023). AI supports adaptive decision-making by identifying trends, detecting environmental changes, and simulating management strategies' impacts (Sarker, 2024; Platz, 2022). Moreover, AI optimizes resource-intensive tasks like habitat restoration, freeing up human resources for other conservation priorities (Sarker, 2024; Platz, 2022).

Enhanced Visitor Experience

Integrating AI in nature reserves significantly enhances the visitor experience and promotes the sustainability of these protected areas. AI optimizes visitor flow and distribution by leveraging data from sensors, cameras, and mobile devices to monitor patterns, track crowd densities, and predict peak visitation periods. This real-time information allows reserve managers to implement dynamic access control, redirect visitors to less-crowded areas, and provide tailored guidance (Farahat, 2023). Additionally, AI facilitates personalized and immersive experiences by analyzing visitor preferences, interests, and behaviors. AI algorithms can curate personalized itineraries, recommend educational content, and provide contextual information, fostering a deeper connection between visitors and the natural environment and promoting greater appreciation for biodiversity and conservation efforts (Hughes-Noehrer, 2023). AI-powered interpretive tools, such as interactive digital guides and augmented reality applications, enhance the visitor experience by integrating digital information with the physical environment. These technologies bring the reserve's stories to life, enrich educational opportunities, and foster a sense of discovery, improving visitor satisfaction and encouraging engagement with the conservation mission (Pisoni et al., 2021; Gaafar, 2020). Additionally, AI assists in managing visitor amenities and infrastructure by monitoring facility usage, predicting demand, and optimizing service allocation. This ensures efficient resource utilization, maintaining high guest satisfaction while minimizing environmental impact (Seraj et al., 2023; Khan et al., 2024).

Efficient Maintenance and Operations

Integrating AI technologies into nature reserve operations enhances efficiency, sustainability, and cost-effectiveness. AI optimizes resource management by monitoring infrastructure condition in real-time, enabling proactive maintenance and minimizing disruptions to visitor experiences. Additionally, AI aids in scheduling and deploying maintenance crews based on predictive analytics, leading to cost savings and more effective operations. By analyzing historical data and environmental factors, AI helps predict maintenance needs, optimize work schedules, and coordinate personnel and equipment deployment. This contributes to overall improved management and maintenance of nature reserves (Gaafar, 2020; Ukato et al., 2024; Javaid et al., 2022). AI can optimize natural resource utilization in nature reserves by monitoring environmental data and aiding in decision-making regarding resource allocation and conservation strategies (Wang et al., 2023; Adanma & Ogunbiyi, 2024; Thangamani et al., 2024). Additionally, AI contributes to energy consumption optimization and renewable energy integration, leading to cost savings and reduced carbon footprint (Boza & Evgeniou, 2021; Belghachi, 2023; Dauvergne, 2022).

Advanced Research and Conservation Efforts

The integration of AI technology in nature reserves offers significant advantages for research and conservation efforts. AI processes vast amounts of data from diverse sources, providing insights into ecosystems and wildlife populations (Dauvergne, 2020; Himeur et al., 2022; Sharma & Barua, 2023). This data-driven approach informs conservation strategies, such as identifying wildlife corridors and predicting climate change impacts. AI also facilitates scientific research by automating data collection and analysis, enabling long-term monitoring and innovative conservation approaches (Farahat, 2023). AI technology, such as camera traps and acoustic monitoring devices, offers continuous wildlife observation, providing insights into behavior and population dynamics. Machine learning applied to this data enhances understanding of food webs, human impacts, and environmental changes (Gómez, 2022). Additionally, AI aids predictive modeling and scenario planning, allowing reserve managers to explore environmental impacts and develop adaptive management strategies for long-term resilience (Gaafar, 2020).

Intelligent Habitat Monitoring and Modeling

The integration of AI in nature reserves revolutionizes habitat monitoring and modeling, providing real-time insights into ecosystem dynamics. AI processes diverse ecological data to detect patterns and anomalies, aiding in habitat modeling and identifying critical conservation areas (Chisom et al., 2024; Mandal & Ghosh, 2024). AI-driven models predict habitat suitability and guide conservation actions, such as habitat restoration and species management, to enhance ecosystem resilience (Bibri et al., 2024; Duflot et al., 2018). Additionally, AI-enabled sensor networks enable timely detection of environmental changes and human impacts, facilitating proactive conservation efforts (Khan et al., 2024; Roy, 2024).

Wildlife Population Dynamics and Behavior Analysis

The integration of AI in nature reserves enhances wildlife population analysis, leveraging data from various sources like camera traps and GPS trackers. AI processes this data, identifying patterns and correlations to understand wildlife behavior and responses to environmental changes (Gonzalez et al., 2016; Nandutu et al., 2022). This insight aids in developing targeted conservation strategies, addressing challenges like habitat fragmentation and human-wildlife conflict (Mandal & Ghosh, 2023; Guo et al., 2023). For instance, AI analysis of tracking data informs habitat management, while acoustic monitoring reveals animal communication and social behaviors (Rajest et al., 2023; Brickson et al., 2023).

Several national parks and nature reserves worldwide have successfully adopted AI systems to combat poaching and enhance wildlife monitoring. In Zambia's Kafue National Park, AI tools like EarthRanger and SMART enable real-time tracking of wildlife and quick responses to poaching threats. Kruger National Park in South Africa uses AI-integrated systems, such as Postcode Meerkat, to detect human movements and prevent rhino poaching. Similarly, Tanzania's Serengeti National Park employs AI-powered camera traps to monitor wildlife and detect illegal activities. In Mongolia, AI assists in identifying snow leopards through unique markings, aiding conservation efforts. Nepal's Chitwan National Park utilizes SMART monitoring tools to predict poaching hotspots, leading to a significant reduction in illegal activities. These cases highlight AI's pivotal role in improving wildlife protection and conservation across the globe.

Harmful Effects of Using AI In Nature Reserves

While AI brings many advantages to nature reserves, its use also introduces risks that could hinder conservation efforts if not carefully managed. A key concern is the potential for unintended ecological impacts, where AI tools like sensors and cameras may disrupt wildlife behavior, causing stress or altering natural processes such as migration and breeding. Additionally, AI's reliance on data can lead to biased decision-making, as incomplete or flawed datasets might result in ineffective conservation measures, especially when rare species are overlooked. Technological malfunctions and overdependence on AI pose further risks, as system failures could leave wildlife vulnerable and reduce human vigilance. The adoption of AI also risks widening the digital divide, favoring wealthier reserves with more resources while disadvantaging underfunded areas. Ethical issues around autonomous decision-making and the opacity of AI systems raise concerns about accountability and trust. Moreover, AI's scalability and sustainability present challenges, as its energy demands, resource consumption, and frequent upgrades may counteract its environmental benefits, leading to greater electronic waste. These challenges underscore the importance of a thoughtful, balanced approach to AI implementation in conservation.

Unintended Ecological Consequences

A primary concern regarding the use of AI in nature reserves is the potential for unintended ecological consequences. While AI can offer benefits like enhanced monitoring and optimization, it also poses risks that must be recognized (Nishant et al., 2020). AI-powered systems can disrupt the natural balance of ecosystems within nature reserves. For example, the use of AI-enabled sensors and cameras to track animal movements and behaviors could inadvertently cause distress or alter the natural patterns of wildlife, leading to negative impacts on their health, breeding, and social dynamics (Akter, 2024; Coghlan & Parker, 2023). Additionally, the algorithms used in AI systems may perpetuate or amplify existing biases in data collection and analysis. If the training data is incomplete, skewed, or lacks diversity, the resulting algorithms may make flawed or biased decisions that undermine the effectiveness of conservation efforts. For instance, an AI-powered species identification system trained on limited data may fail to accurately recognize certain rare or endangered species, leading to missed opportunities for targeted interventions and potentially exacerbating their decline (Schwartz et al., 2022; Coeckelbergh, 2020).

Technological Failures and Overreliance

The implementation of AI in nature reserves raises concerns about potential technological failures and overreliance on AI-driven systems. Despite its promise in conservation, AI remains vulnerable to technical issues and errors. Malfunctions in AI surveillance or decision-making systems could undermine conservation efforts, risking wildlife populations (Farahat, 2023). Furthermore, excessive dependence on AI might lead to complacency among conservationists, eroding their ability to adapt to environmental changes (Kalyani, 2023). Additionally, the complexity of AI algorithms poses transparency challenges, potentially fostering skepticism or resistance to AI adoption in conservation (Busuioc, 2021).

Exacerbating Digital Divides

The adoption of AI in nature reserves raises concerns about deepening digital disparities, potentially hindering equitable and inclusive reserve management (Akindele, 2024). This disparity may arise from limited access to AI technologies, primarily benefiting well-funded reserves, while leaving resource-constrained ones at a disadvantage (Al-Romeedy, 2024a; Farahat, 2023). Additionally, the development and deployment of AI systems might prioritize the perspectives of larger organizations, neglecting the specific needs of local communities and indigenous groups (Raji et al., 2022; Gaafar, 2020).

Ethical Concerns in Autonomous Decision-Making

The incorporation of AI into nature reserves brings forth ethical dilemmas, particularly surrounding autonomous decision-making. AI technologies, such as predictive models and automated systems, can operate without direct human supervision, prompting concerns about accountability and transparency. A key worry is the potential reinforcement of biases within conservation decisions, as AI learns from historical data that may contain systemic biases (Rodgers et al., 2023). Furthermore, the complexity of AI algorithms makes them opaque, hindering stakeholders' ability to understand decisions and assess their accuracy. This opacity undermines trust in AI and raises concerns about its impact on wildlife and communities (Bleher & Braun, 2022). Delegating decision-making to AI may also diffuse accountability, shifting responsibility away from humans (Busuioc, 2021).

Limitations in Scalability and Generalizability

The application of AI in nature reserves raises concerns about scalability and generalizability, impacting their effectiveness and sustainability (Ray, 2023; John et al., 2022). Natural ecosystems' complexity and heterogeneity pose challenges, as solutions tailored to one reserve may not apply to others due to unique conditions and management needs. This lack of generalizability leads to higher costs and necessitates specialized expertise for each reserve (Farahat, 2023; Gaafar, 2020). Additionally, the dynamic nature of environments presents scalability challenges, as AI systems may become outdated or ineffective with changing conditions (Bibri et al., 2024; Branke, 2012).

Increased Energy and Resource Consumption

The implementation of AI in nature reserves can result in heightened energy and resource usage, potentially counteracting conservation objectives (Xiang et al., 2021). Furthermore, integrating AI technologies typically involves installing specialized hardware like sensors, cameras, and communication networks, which increases resource consumption and greenhouse gas emissions due to manufacturing, transportation, and maintenance activities. Additionally, reliance on cloud-based platforms and remote data processing centers for some AI applications may worsen energy and resource consumption. These centralized hubs, often powered by fossil fuels or energy-intensive data centers, can indirectly impact the environment (Wan et al., 2020; Al-Azab & Zaki, 2023).

Unsustainable Long-Term Maintenance

Relying on AI technologies within nature reserves can also present challenges regarding their ongoing maintenance and sustainability (Galaz et al., 2021). One notable concern is the possibility for these AI-driven systems to become outdated or necessitate frequent upgrades, leading to a continual need for replacement and the accumulation of electronic waste. Given the relatively short lifespan of AI-powered hardware and software, reserve managers may face a perpetual cycle of equipment upgrades and disposal, which can be both resource-intensive and financially burdensome (Farahat, 2023). Additionally, the specialized skills and expertise needed to maintain and service these AI-enabled systems may not be readily available within the local communities neighboring the nature reserves. This reliance on external technical support might not be easily accessible or sustainable in the long term, particularly in remote or resource-constrained areas (Al-Romeedy, 2024a).

In this vein, the integration of AI in nature reserves offers both advantages and challenges, largely based on its application and management. On the positive side, AI improves wildlife protection and ecosystem management by enhancing monitoring, surveillance, and real-time data analysis, which supports informed decision-making. It helps allocate resources efficiently, predicts environmental risks, and enriches visitor experiences, all while reducing human effort and cost. However, it also presents potential downsides, such as disrupting animal behavior through constant monitoring or perpetuating data biases. Overdependence on AI or technological failures could hinder conservation efforts, while its energy demands and maintenance costs may offset environmental gains. Additionally, ethical issues related to transparency, autonomous decision-making, and increasing digital inequality further complicate AI's use. Thus, while AI can significantly benefit nature reserves, its success hinges on careful, responsible, and sustainable implementation.

CONCLUSION AND RECOMMENDATIONS

This study aims to inform policymakers, conservation practitioners, and technology researchers about the complex interplay between AI and nature conservation. By integrating AI technologies within nature reserves, the research highlights significant implications for utilizing these advanced tools to benefit protected natural areas.

Policymakers wield significant influence in shaping the integration of AI in nature reserves. To leverage AI's potential effectively, they must develop comprehensive regulatory frameworks ensuring ethical and sustainable AI usage. These policies should prioritize establishing standards for data collection, storage, and utilization to safeguard wildlife and human privacy. Moreover, policymakers should incentivize the adoption of renewable energy sources and environmentally friendly practices in AI operations to mitigate ecological impacts. Supporting capacity-building initiatives is crucial to equip conservationists worldwide with the necessary skills and resources for implementing and maintaining AI systems. Policymakers should also actively involve local and indigenous communities, integrating their knowledge to ensure AI-driven conservation strategies respect and benefit these populations. By fostering collaboration and offering clear guidelines, policymakers can create an environment conducive to the ethical and efficient utilization of AI in nature reserves.

At the forefront of integrating AI technologies in nature reserves are conservation practitioners. To fully harness the benefits of AI, they must prioritize enhancing technical expertise within their teams and continuously updating their skills to keep pace with technological advancements. Collaboration with local communities is vital to incorporate traditional ecological knowledge into AI-driven conservation strategies effectively. Conservation practitioners should ensure that AI tools complement, rather than replace, traditional conservation methods, fostering a balanced approach that capitalizes on the strengths of both approaches. Regular monitoring and evaluation of AI systems are essential to detect potential biases and ethical concerns, maintaining fairness and effectiveness in conservation efforts. Furthermore, conservation practitioners should advocate for sustainable practices in AI usage, including minimizing electronic waste and adopting energy-efficient technologies. By embracing a comprehensive approach that integrates technology, community engagement, and sustainable practices, conservation practitioners can enhance the efficacy and sustainability of their conservation endeavors.

Technology researchers also play a crucial role in crafting AI solutions tailored to the distinctive challenges of conservation. Their efforts should concentrate on crafting AI systems that are resilient, flexible, and attuned to the ecological and societal nuances of nature reserves. Prioritizing the creation of algorithms that mitigate biases and uphold fairness in conservation endeavors is essential. Collaborating closely with conservation practitioners and local communities is paramount to grasp the specific requirements and obstacles of various ecosystems, ensuring that AI tools effectively address these concerns. Researchers should also emphasize the development of energy-efficient and environmentally sustainable AI systems, thereby reducing the ecological footprint of technology. Moreover, they should contribute to capacity-building initiatives by devising user-friendly tools and furnishing training resources to assist conservationists in leveraging AI technologies proficiently. By aligning their research with the principles of sustainability, inclusivity, and pragmatism, technology researchers can significantly augment the positive impact of AI in nature reserves.

Importantly, the effective incorporation of AI into nature reserves hinges on a collaborative effort among policymakers, conservation practitioners, and technology researchers. Policymakers are tasked with furnishing the regulatory and financial backing necessary for the adoption and longevity of AI technologies. Conservation practitioners bear the responsibility of guaranteeing the ethical and proficient utilization of these technologies, integrating them harmoniously with conventional methods and community insights. Technology researchers are called upon to persist in their innovation, crafting AI solutions that are versatile, eco-friendly, and user-friendly. Through collective action, these stakeholders can cultivate a synergistic milieu wherein AI augments conservation endeavors, safeguards biodiversity, and promotes the sustainable management of nature reserves. Moving forward, it is imperative to prioritize the establishment of inclusive platforms for data exchange and cooperation, nurturing international networks comprising conservationists and researchers. Such initiatives will facilitate the sharing of best practices, real-world examples, and technological breakthroughs, thereby stimulating ongoing enhancements in conservation strategies driven by AI. Through collaborative endeavors, policymakers, conservation practitioners, and technology researchers can fully leverage AI's capabilities to advance nature reserves and play a pivotal role in the global endeavor to preserve biodiversity on our planet.

REFERENCES

Adanma, U. M., & Ogunbiyi, E. O.Uwaga Monica AdanmaEmmanuel Olurotimi Ogunbiyi. (2024). Artificial intelligence in environmental conservation: Evaluating cyber risks and opportunities for sustainable practices. *Computer Science & IT Research Journal*, 5(5), 1178–1209. DOI: 10.51594/csitrj.v5i5.1156

Akter, M. S. (2024). Harnessing technology for environmental sustainability: Utilizing AI to tackle global ecological challenges. [JAIGS]. *Journal of Artificial Intelligence General Science*, 2(1), 61–70.

Al-Azab, M. R., & Zaki, H. S. (2023). Towards sustainable development: Antecedents of green entrepreneurship intention among tourism and hospitality students in Egypt. *Journal of Hospitality and Tourism Insights*. https://doi.org/DOI: 10.1108/JHTI-03-2023-0146

Al-Romeedy, B. (2024a). Breaking chains, building futures - Blockchain's impact on sustainable tourism. In *Promoting responsible tourism with digital platforms*. IGI Global. DOI: 10.4018/979-8-3693-3286-3.ch006

Al-Romeedy, B. (2024b). AI and HRM in tourism and hospitality in Egypt: Inevitability, impact, and future. In *HRM, artificial intelligence, and the future of work: Critical insights from the Global South*. Palgrave Macmillan. DOI: 10.1007/978-3-031-62369-1_13

Al-Romeedy, B. (2024c). Sky high sustainability – Shaping the future of green aviation through innovation. In *Sustainability in travel and tourism* (pp. 44–53). Bharti Publications.

Al-Romeedy, B. (2024d). Sustainable tourism innovations - A green entrepreneurship perspective. In *Sustainability in travel and tourism* (pp. 54–63). Bharti Publications.

Alasadi, E. A., & Baiz, C. R. (2023). Generative AI in education and research: Opportunities, concerns, and solutions. *Journal of Chemical Education*, 100(8), 2965–2971. DOI: 10.1021/acs.jchemed.3c00323

Aloisi, A., & De Stefano, V. (2022). *Your boss is an algorithm: Artificial intelligence, platform work, and labour*. Bloomsbury Publishing. DOI: 10.5040/9781509953219

Baratta, A., Cimino, A., Longo, F., Solina, V., & Verteramo, S. (2023). The impact of ESG practices in industry with a focus on carbon emissions: Insights and future perspectives. *Sustainability (Basel)*, 15(8), 6685. DOI: 10.3390/su15086685

Belghachi, M. (2023). A review on explainable artificial intelligence methods, applications, and challenges. [IJEEI]. *Indonesian Journal of Electrical Engineering and Informatics*, 11(4), 1007–1024. DOI: 10.52549/ijeei.v11i4.5151

Bharadiya, J. P. (2023). Machine learning and AI in business intelligence: Trends and opportunities. [IJC]. *International Journal of Computer*, 48(1), 123–134.

Bibri, S. E., Krogstie, J., Kaboli, A., & Alahi, A. (2024). Smarter eco-cities and their leading-edge artificial intelligence of things solutions for environmental sustainability: A comprehensive systematic review. *Environmental Science and Ecotechnology*, 19, 100330. DOI: 10.1016/j.ese.2023.100330 PMID: 38021367

Bleher, H., & Braun, M. (2022). Diffused responsibility: Attributions of responsibility in the use of AI-driven clinical decision support systems. *AI and Ethics*, 2(4), 747–761. DOI: 10.1007/s43681-022-00135-x PMID: 35098247

Boza, P., & Evgeniou, T. (2021). Artificial intelligence to support the integration of variable renewable energy sources to the power system. *Applied Energy*, 290, 116754. DOI: 10.1016/j.apenergy.2021.116754

Branke, J. (2012). *Evolutionary optimization in dynamic environments*. Springer.

Brickson, L., Zhang, L., Vollrath, F., Douglas-Hamilton, I., & Titus, A. J. (2023). Elephants and algorithms: A review of the current and future role of AI in elephant monitoring. *Journal of the Royal Society, Interface*, 20(208), 20230367. DOI: 10.1098/rsif.2023.0367 PMID: 37963556

Busuioc, M. (2021). Accountable artificial intelligence: Holding algorithms to account. *Public Administration Review*, 81(5), 825–836. DOI: 10.1111/puar.13293 PMID: 34690372

Chisom, O. N., Biu, P. W., Umoh, A. A., Obaedo, B. O., Adegbite, A. O., & Abatan, A. (2024). Reviewing the role of AI in environmental monitoring and conservation: A data-driven revolution for our planet. *World Journal of Advanced Research and Reviews*, 21(1), 161–171. DOI: 10.30574/wjarr.2024.21.1.2720

Coeckelbergh, M. (2020). *AI ethics*. MIT Press. DOI: 10.7551/mitpress/12549.001.0001

Coghlan, S., & Parker, C. (2023). Harm to nonhuman animals from AI: A systematic account and framework. *Philosophy & Technology*, 36(2), 25. Advance online publication. DOI: 10.1007/s13347-023-00627-6

Dauvergne, P. (2020). *AI in the wild: Sustainability in the age of artificial intelligence*. MIT Press. DOI: 10.7551/mitpress/12350.001.0001

Dauvergne, P. (2022). Is artificial intelligence greening global supply chains? Exposing the political economy of environmental costs. *Review of International Political Economy*, 29(3), 696–718. DOI: 10.1080/09692290.2020.1814381

Duflot, R., Avon, C., Roche, P., & Bergès, L. (2018). Combining habitat suitability models and spatial graphs for more effective landscape conservation planning: An applied methodological framework and a species case study. *Journal for Nature Conservation*, 46, 38–47. DOI: 10.1016/j.jnc.2018.08.005

Fang, Z., & Savkin, A. V. (2024). Strategies for optimized UAV surveillance in various tasks and scenarios: A review. *Drones (Basel)*, 8(5), 193. DOI: 10.3390/drones8050193

Farahat, E. (2023). Applications of artificial intelligence as a marketing tool and their impact on the competitiveness of the Egyptian tourist destination (Doctoral dissertation, Minia University).

Fei, G., Xiong, K., Fei, G., Zhang, H., & Zhang, S. (2023). The conservation and tourism development of World Natural Heritage sites: The current situation and future prospects of research. *Journal for Nature Conservation*, 72, 126347. DOI: 10.1016/j.jnc.2023.126347

Gaafar, H. (2020). Artificial intelligence in Egyptian tourism companies: Implementation and perception. *Journal of Association of Arab Universities for Tourism and Hospitality*, 18(1), 66–78. DOI: 10.21608/jaauth.2020.31704.1028

Galaz, V., Centeno, M. A., Callahan, P. W., Causevic, A., Patterson, T., Brass, I., & Levy, K. (2021). Artificial intelligence, systemic risks, and sustainability. *Technology in Society*, 67, 101741. DOI: 10.1016/j.techsoc.2021.101741

Gómez, J. V. (2022). Enhancing mammal conservation in multi-functional landscapes using artificial intelligence, joint species distribution modeling, and ecological experimentation (Doctoral dissertation, University of Minnesota).

Gonzalez, L. F., Montes, G. A., Puig, E., Johnson, S., Mengersen, K., & Gaston, K. J. (2016). Unmanned aerial vehicles (UAVs) and artificial intelligence revolutionizing wildlife monitoring and conservation. *Sensors (Basel)*, 16(1), 97. DOI: 10.3390/s16010097 PMID: 26784196

Guan, W., Zhang, H., & Leung, V. C. (2021). Customized slicing for 6G: Enforcing artificial intelligence on resource management. *IEEE Network*, 35(5), 264–271. DOI: 10.1109/MNET.011.2000644

Guo, W., Lv, C., Guo, M., Zhao, Q., Yin, X., & Zhang, L. (2023). Innovative applications of artificial intelligence in zoonotic disease management. *Science in One Health*, 2, 100045. DOI: 10.1016/j.soh.2023.100045 PMID: 39077042

Gupta, R., Nair, K., Mishra, M., Ibrahim, B., & Bhardwaj, S. (2024). Adoption and impacts of generative artificial intelligence: Theoretical underpinnings and research agenda. *International Journal of Information Management Data Insights*, 4(1), 100232. DOI: 10.1016/j.jjimei.2024.100232

Heilig, T., & Scheer, I. (2023). *Decision intelligence: Transform your team and organization with AI-driven decision-making*. John Wiley & Sons.

Himeur, Y., Rimal, B., Tiwary, A., & Amira, A. (2022). Using artificial intelligence and data fusion for environmental monitoring: A review and future perspectives. *Information Fusion*, 86, 44–75. DOI: 10.1016/j.inffus.2022.06.003

Horng, J. S., Hsu, H., & Tsai, C. Y. (2018). An assessment model of corporate social responsibility practice in the tourism industry. *Journal of Sustainable Tourism*, 26(7), 1085–1104. DOI: 10.1080/09669582.2017.1388384

Hu, J., Xiong, L., Lv, X., & Pu, B. (2021). Sustainable rural tourism: Linking residents' environmentally responsible behavior to tourists' green consumption. *Asia Pacific Journal of Tourism Research*, 26(8), 879–893. DOI: 10.1080/10941665.2021.1925316

Hughes-Noehrer, L. (2023). Artificial intelligence, museum environments, and their constituents: A cross-disciplinary study using recommender systems to explore digital collections (Doctoral dissertation, New York University).

Kahane, S. (2022). The impact of artificial intelligence on job displacement: Evidence from recent developments. *Economics of Innovation and New Technology*, 31(1), 76–93.

Kashiwagi, K., Yokoyama, H., & Furukawa, Y. (2023). Machine learning and decision support for wildlife conservation. *Conservation Biology*, 37(2). Advance online publication. DOI: 10.1111/cobi.13870

Kinsella, E. (2022). *Artificial intelligence and environmental governance: An interdisciplinary approach*. Routledge.

Krauss, J., Tonn, A., & Peters, M. (2023). Ethical implications of artificial intelligence in wildlife conservation: Balancing benefits and harms. *Journal of Environmental Ethics*, 30(3), 195–212.

Kumar, A., Tripathi, S., Bansal, A., Tiwari, V., & Kumar, A. (2023). Artificial intelligence in smart tourism: A systematic review and future research agenda. *Tourism Management Perspectives*, 45, 270–290.

Lau, L. C., Wong, Y. Y., & Tham, S. Y. (2023). AI-enabled wildlife conservation: A systematic review of applications, challenges, and future directions. *Conservation Biology*, 37(1). Advance online publication. DOI: 10.1111/cobi.13824

Li, H., Chen, Y., Sun, L., & Wu, G. (2022). AI for environmental management: Current status and future prospects. *Environmental Science & Technology*, 56(10), 6345–6365.

Li, H., Wang, D., Jiang, W., & Yang, C. (2024). The impact of AI on eco-friendly practices in tourism: Evidence from China. *Sustainability*, 16(1), 289.

Li, W., & Leung, R. (2023). Data-driven conservation: How artificial intelligence can transform wildlife monitoring. *The Journal of Wildlife Management*, 87(2), 129–139.

Liu, S., Chen, L., Yu, H., Zhang, Y., & Yu, Y. (2022). The use of AI technology for wildlife conservation: A review. *Environmental Research Letters*, 17(8), 083010.

Mali, S. (2022). Artificial intelligence for biodiversity conservation: Opportunities and challenges. *Journal of Environmental Management*, 312, 114840.

Mansouri, R., Amari, M., & El-Haibi, A. (2023). Integrating AI with sustainable practices in tourism: A systematic literature review. *Journal of Tourism Management*, 89, 104387.

Manzoor, A., & Khan, M. A. (2023). AI-powered tourism management: An examination of applications and implications. *Tourism Management Perspectives*, 45, 1030–1041.

Mehta, P. (2022). Artificial intelligence and wildlife conservation: A review of techniques and applications. *Ecological Informatics*, 68, 101686.

Mohammed, A. A. (2023). The role of AI in promoting sustainable tourism in Egypt. *Journal of Sustainable Tourism*, 31(1), 19–36.

Naumov, M., & Naumova, E. (2023). AI technologies and their potential in wildlife management. *Ecology and Evolution*, 13(6), e9935.

Ntem, E., & Cheng, C. (2022). The impact of AI on wildlife conservation: A systematic review. *Biodiversity and Conservation*, 31(5), 1333–1351.

O'Neil, C. (2016). *Weapons of math destruction: How big data increases inequality and threatens democracy*. Crown Publishing.

Oropeza, S. A., Chinchilla, E. R., & Ordoñez, L. M. (2022). Artificial intelligence and sustainable urban development: A systematic literature review. *Sustainable Cities and Society*, 83, 103886.

Peters, G., Rauschenbach, T., & Rojas, R. (2022). AI-based approaches to biodiversity monitoring: Recent advances and future directions. *Frontiers in Ecology and the Environment*, 20(8), 490–499.

Reyes, F. A., Ahrens, D., & Amiri, A. (2023). The role of AI in sustainable tourism practices: A global perspective. *Tourism Management*, 98, 104572.

Schuman, S. J., & Rojas, R. (2023). Machine learning and big data for wildlife conservation: Current trends and future directions. *The Journal of Wildlife Management*, 87(5), 847–860.

Seyfang, G., & Haxeltine, A. (2022). *Green growth and sustainable prosperity: Disentangling the contradictions*. Cambridge University Press.

Shin, K., Lee, Y., & Lee, H. (2024). AI for wildlife protection: A survey of current applications and future trends. *Wildlife Biology*, 2024(1), 1–13.

Tchamyou, V. S., & Niyonzima, M. (2023). Artificial intelligence and environmental sustainability in Africa: Opportunities and challenges. *African Journal of Science, Technology, Innovation and Development*, 15(3), 255–268.

Valverde, M. D., & Echeverri, D. (2024). The role of AI in achieving the UN sustainable development goals: A systematic review. *Sustainability Science*, 19, 51–67.

Vasan, P., & Khemka, K. (2024). Artificial intelligence for sustainable tourism: Opportunities and challenges. *Sustainable Tourism*, 32(2), 277–290.

Wang, S. Y., Lin, J. F., & Huang, Y. C. (2023). Examining the impact of AI on sustainability practices in tourism: An integrated framework. *Tourism Management Perspectives*, 47, 195–207.

Wang, T., Li, H., & Zhang, J. (2024). Artificial intelligence and biodiversity: How AI can contribute to species conservation. *Journal of Environmental Management*, 310, 114948.

Wang, Z., & Zhan, H. (2022). AI in wildlife conservation: An overview of applications and challenges. *Biodiversity and Conservation*, 31(8), 2139–2160.

Zhang, L., Liu, Q., & Wei, Y. (2023). AI-driven environmental monitoring: Innovations and applications. *Sensors (Basel)*, 23(5), 2845. PMID: 36905051

Zhu, X., & Zhang, Q. (2023). Understanding the role of AI in promoting green technology: A framework for research. *Technology Analysis and Strategic Management*, 35(2), 233–247.

KEY TERMS AND DEFINITIONS

AI-Enabled Nature Conservation: The application of artificial intelligence tools to safeguard, monitor, and rehabilitate natural environments and biodiversity.

Artificial Intelligence: The creation of machines that mimic human cognitive functions, allowing them to perform tasks such as problem-solving, learning, and decision-making.

Ecological Footprints: An indicator of the environmental impact of human activities, measuring the amount of natural resources used and the waste produced relative to Earth's capacity to regenerate those resources.

Ecosystems: Networks of organisms and their environments, functioning together in a balanced and interdependent way.

Nature Reverse: An initiative focused on rehabilitating ecosystems to their pre-disturbance condition by mitigating environmental damage.

Sustainability: The approach of utilizing resources in a way that fulfills current demands without jeopardizing the ability of future generations to meet their needs.

Sustainable Tourism: A tourism approach that reduces environmental harm, benefits local communities, and preserves natural resources for future travelers.

Chapter 9

Memorable Tourism Experiences (MTEs) and Its Applications in the Indian Hospitality Industry

Oindrila Chakraborty
J.D. Birla Institute, India

ABSTRACT

The chapter will focus on how India's tourism industry can create lasting and enjoyable experiences through Memorable Tourism Experiences, covering areas such as hotels, restaurants, themed tourism, and guided tours. The authors through the research would aim to gather insights from both regular travellers within and outside the country, as well as hotel owners, restaurant managers, tour operators, and travel agents through two separate surveys, examining tourists' attitudes towards memorable tourism experiences(MTEs) and how businesses are implementing MTEs to enhance their sustainability and profitability.

INTRODUCTION

The world economy beckons with the tourism industry. The tourism industry, often known as the travel industry, fuels the desire of people to explore new horizons across the borders. It encompasses the movement of people for various purposes, from leisure and relaxation on pristine beaches to cultural immersion across the cities. This vast sector thrives on providing experiences that cater to a wide range

DOI: 10.4018/979-8-3693-7021-6.ch009

of interests, from adrenaline-pumping adventure tours to serene wellness retreats. One of the most significant and vital sectors of the global economy is tourism, controlling the GNP of many countries (Sagayama et al., 2018). Thus, the creation of tourist' interests, benefits, advantages, values and associated services are involving all closely allied individuals, businesses, organisations for the sake of a common goal. The common goal is to earn the maximum revenues and contribute hugely in the sector (Aho, 2001). Simply expressed, the tourism sector is a varied, distinctive group made up of all active tourist establishments on the market with the purpose of earning revenues and in return being valued by the travellers. In the light of this, the tourist sector is the home to several national and international organisations in different countries as a close-knit family to benefit the tourists. The tourism sector is decided on the services and infrastructure needed to manage the flow of tourists and cater to their requirements from arrival to departure (Croes, 2021). Just like nutrition- the basic need for human survival (Kabus, 2015), tourism industry is also gradually shifting towards a basic and quintessential need with some micro-segmentation such as recreational, architectural, and cultural needs, breaking it into some pockets of micro-economic markets. There are, of course, several forms of tourism, including agritourism, rural tourism, gourmet tourism, enotourism or oenotourism, wine tourism, or vinitourism and tourism focused on local cuisines (Seddighi, 2002) to attract tourists. Numerous studies have also suggested that a destination's brand is a competitive factor and it is known as 'Territorial Branding' (Ritchie & Crouch, 2000). Thus, it is becoming almost imperative to work more and more on inimitable territorial brands to build more revenues through creating fond memories that can persuade repeat visits, leading to the concept of memorable tourism experiences (MTEs).

Memorable Tourism Experiences (MTEs) or Unforgettable Travel Experiences (UTEs) are those that leave an everlasting impression on a traveller's mind. Defined as experiences that leave a lasting positive impression on tourists and can be fondly recalled through story telling (Kim & Chen 2020), MTEs can influence future travel decisions, generate positive recommendations, and foster a sense of attachment to a place (Hapsari, 2018; Kim et al., 2012). They are the experiences those people fondly reminisce about and are eager to revisit as a destination. MTEs/UTEs can be anything from sampling a new cuisine to immersing in a cultural celebration and strengthening a positive association with the customers.

THE CONCEPT AND BACKGROUND OF MEMORABLE TOURISM EXPERIENCES (MTES)

Background

The concept of Memorable Tourism Experiences (MTEs) is a relatively recent phenomenon within tourism research, although the desire to create positive travel experiences has likely existed for centuries. The first sign of change started surfacing in the early 20th century, followed by latter part of the century.

Early Stages (Pre-20th Century)

The early days of tourism lacked a formal focus on creating memorable experiences and precisely was focused on practicalities. Travel was primarily for the wealthy, and the emphasis was on tangible deliverables like pricing, transportation, accommodation, and basic sightseeing itineraries.

Shift in the Mid-20th Century: Rise of Tourist Satisfaction

Following the rise of mass tourism in the mid-20th century, research began to explore tourist satisfaction more than tangible part of the journey. This was further elaborated with the measurement of the probable factors affecting tourists' satisfaction like impeccable augmentation of services, service quality, value for money, and meeting basic needs.

Late 20th Century: The Turning Point

In the latter half of the 20th century, a significant shift occurred from customer satisfaction towards customer experience. Researchers began acknowledging that tourism is more than just visiting a place. It's about the total experience, encompassing emotions, memories, and personal growth (Hapsari, 2018; Kim et al., 2012).

Early 2000s: Pioneering MTE Research and Experiential Marketing

The early 2000s saw pioneering studies applying the concept of 'Experiential Marketing' to tourism (Kim & Chen 2020) to gain the heart share and mindshare of the tourists, making the experience as a part of their permanent fond memories. This emphasized creating unique and engaging experiences that cater to emotions and personal connections. Around the same time, research delved into the psychological aspects of travel memories. Studies explored how emotions and the significance attached to experiences contribute to lasting impressions (Kim, 2012).

21st Century: The MTE Boom and Identification of Factors

Since the early 2000s, MTE research has flourished in the best possible way. Scholars have identified various factors that contribute to memorable experiences, including: 1. Uniqueness and Novelty (Kim, 2012), 2. Emotional Connection (Tung & Ritchie, 2011), 3. Personal Growth (Sthapit & Coudounaris, 2017), 4. Social interaction (Kim, 2012; Tung & Ritchie, 2011), 5. Destination and Service Quality (Sthapit & Coudounaris, 2017). Later on, these factors were extended further to create a new set of factors to build up the horizon called, memorable tourism experiences (MTEs). Figure 1 diagrammatically shows the transition from customer deliverables based on practicalities or tangibilities to intangibilities like Memorable Tourism Experiences.

Figure 1. Showing the transition of concept from customer deliverables to memorable tourism experiences

Practicalities ⇒ Satisfaction ⇒ Memorable Tourism Experience

(Author own creation)

FACTORS INFLUENCING MEMORABLE TOURISM EXPERIENCE

Tourist spots which are repeatedly visited by the same set of travellers and loved by them, are often identified by a set of factors associated with their memories. Nine of such factors which are identified as significantly contributing to an unforgettable travel experience or MTEs are given below:

1) Uniqueness and Novelty

Engaging in new and different activities is a great way to create enduring memories. This could involve sampling a new dish, exploring a historical landmark, or participating in an exhilarating adventure. As per literature review, encountering new and unfamiliar activities can enhance memorability (Hapsari, 2018; Kim et al., 2012). Tourists who are highly involved in an experience, feeling immersed and engaged, are more likely to create lasting memories (Kim et al., 2012).

2) Authenticity & Local Culture

Immersing oneself in the local culture, including food, traditions, and interactions with residents, is a powerful driver of MTEs (Hapsari, 2018; Kim et al., 2012). These experiences can foster a sense of connection and understanding. Taking a plunge in local home stay, learning to cook traditional dishes, or taking part in a community festival could be some of the examples of experiencing authentic local culture.

3) Personalization based on Personal Significance and Shared Experiences

Experiences that hold personal meaning or are shared with loved ones tend to be more memorable (Kim et al., 2012) and that is why experiences that cater to a traveller's interests are more likely to be etched in their memory. This highlights the importance of catering to individual interests and creating opportunities for connection. This could involve a personalized tour, enrolling in a workshop, or embarking on a hike suited to the traveller's fitness level.

4) Emotional Connection

Building relationships with locals can also make a trip more memorable. This could involve striking up conversations with vendors at a market, embarking on a guided tour with a local expert, or getting involved in community volunteering (Hapsari, 2018).

5) Positive Emotions, Serendipity, and Emotional Engagement

Positive emotions associated with the experience, such as joy, excitement, or surprise, contribute to memorability (Kim et al., 2012). Unplanned, delightful experiences (serendipity) can also leave a lasting impact (Hapsari, 2018). Kim et al. (2012) further emphasizes the role of perceived value in creating MTEs. Experiences that evoke strong emotions are more likely to be cherished. Tourists who feel they received a good return on their investment, both financially and experientially, are more likely to have positive memories (Kim et al., 2012). This could involve witnessing a breath-taking sunset, visiting a poignant historical site, or taking part in an exhilarating adventure.

6) Increased Satisfaction

Memorable experiences enhance overall satisfaction with a destination (Kim et al.,2012).

7) Repeat Visitation and Attachment

Tourists who have MTEs are more likely to return to a destination in the future, because they feel attachment to the destination due to fond memories (Kim & Chen, 2020). If not personally coming back to the same destination, they may inspire others to visit the place.

8) Positive Recommendations and Storytelling

Tourists are more likely to recommend destinations and experiences to others, that they found memorable. They generally express their fondness to the place through storytelling related to their unique experiences associated with the place. (Kim & Chen, 2020).

9) Destination and Service Quality

The service quality of various service centres (hotels, restaurants, grooming and wellness centres etc.) at the tourist spot becomes one of the many reasons for remarkable experiences and fond memories at a location and could be a reason for repeat visit to the place. During the storytelling part, it could be a major part of discussion and can be a significant reason to attract travellers to the destination time and again.

SOME NOTEWORTHY INITIATIVES OF TERRITORIAL BRANDING TO CREATE MEMORABLE TOURISM EXPERIENCES

Some nations have relied heavily on destination branding or territorial branding to create meaningful memories. The list includes Australia, Brazil, Colombia, and Spain along with many other countries. Since 1983, Spain has been a representation of Joan Miró's artwork (a sun, a star, and trembling red, yellow, and black letters). Later, it relaunches a marketing initiative under the name "*Smile! You Are in Spain.*" The year 2009 revealed that 14 of Spain's 17 regions had their own distinct brand identities. Colombia began promoting itself in 2004 under the slogan "*Colombia *is passion*!" This led to an increase in tourism in 2006. The European of National Tourism Organization (NTO) has been doing an excellent job regarding territorial branding.

As already mentioned, territorial branding is the process of creating a distinctive identity and image for a particular place, such as a city, region, or country to build memorable tourism experiences (MTEs). It involves developing a set of values, attributes, and symbols through authentic taste of local cultures, festivals, cuisines etc. that reflect the unique characteristics and strengths of the place and that can be used to promote it to visitors, investors, and residents. Some unique examples of global destination branding to create MTEs are given below:

- **'I Love NY'** – This is a well-known branding campaign that was launched by the state of New York in 1977. The campaign used a heart symbol and the slogan "I Love NY" to promote tourism in the state. The campaign was very successful and is still in use today.
- **'Visit California'** – This is a branding campaign that was launched by the state of California to promote tourism in the state. The campaign uses the tagline "Dream Big" and features images of the state's beaches, mountains, and cities.
- **'Incredible India'** – This is a branding campaign that was launched by the government of India to promote tourism in the country. The campaign uses the tagline 'Incredible India' and features images of the country's rich cultural heritage, natural beauty, and diverse landscapes.
- **'Cool Britannia'** – This was a branding campaign that was launched by the UK government in the late 1990s to promote British culture and creativity. The campaign was aimed at a young, urban audience and used images of musicians, artists, and fashion designers to promote a new, modern image of Britain.
- **'I Amsterdam'** – This is a branding campaign that was launched by the city of Amsterdam to promote tourism in the city. The campaign uses the tagline "I Amsterdam" and features images of the city's canals, museums, and nightlife.
- **'Singapore: Passion Made Possible'** – This is a branding campaign launched by the Singapore Tourism Board to promote tourism and business opportunities in Singapore. The campaign focuses on the idea that Singapore is a place where people can pursue their passions and achieve their dreams.
- **'Sydney, Australia: Feel the Heartbeat'** – This is a branding campaign launched by the City of Sydney to promote tourism in the city. The campaign focuses on Sydney's vibrant culture, diverse communities, and world-class attractions.

- **'Think New Mexico'** – This is a branding campaign launched by the state of New Mexico to promote economic development and attract businesses to the state. The campaign focuses on New Mexico's natural beauty, rich culture, and entrepreneurial spirit.
- **'Cape Town: Live it. Love it'** – This is a branding campaign launched by the City of Cape Town to promote tourism in the city. The campaign focuses on Cape Town's natural beauty, cultural heritage, and diverse attractions.
- **'Swiss Made'** – This is a branding campaign used by the Swiss government and Swiss companies to promote Swiss products and services. The campaign emphasizes Switzerland's reputation for quality, precision, and innovation.
- **'Dubai: A City of Dreams'** – This is a branding campaign launched by the Dubai Department of Tourism and Commerce Marketing to promote tourism in the city. The campaign emphasizes Dubai's luxury and modernity, as well as its cultural heritage and natural beauty.
- **'Sweden: The Spirit of Innovation'** – This is a branding campaign launched by the Swedish government to promote the country as a hub of innovation and entrepreneurship. The campaign focuses on Sweden's reputation for creativity, sustainability, and technological excellence.
- **'Hello BC'** – This is a branding campaign launched by the British Columbia tourism board to promote tourism in the Canadian province. The campaign emphasizes the natural beauty of British Columbia, as well as its diverse attractions and experiences.
- **'Tokyo: Endless Discovery'** – This is a branding campaign launched by the Tokyo Metropolitan Government to promote tourism in the city. The campaign highlights Tokyo's unique blend of tradition and modernity, as well as its food, shopping, and nightlife.
- **'Scotland: A Spirit of its Own'** – This is a branding campaign launched by VisitScotland to promote tourism in Scotland. The campaign emphasizes Scotland's natural beauty, cultural heritage, and hospitality, as well as its reputation for innovation and creativity.
- **'Berlin: The Place to Be'** – This is a branding campaign launched by the Berlin tourism board to promote tourism in the city. The campaign highlights Berlin's vibrant culture, creative scene, and diverse neighbourhoods.
- **'Taste of Tasmania'** – This is a branding campaign launched by the Tasmanian government to promote the island state's food and beverage industry. The campaign focuses on Tasmania's fresh, high-quality produce, as well as its scenic beauty and outdoor experiences.
- **'Incredible Ice Land'** – This is a branding campaign launched by the Icelandic tourism board to promote tourism in Iceland. The campaign em-

phasizes Iceland's natural wonders, including its glaciers, waterfalls, and hot springs.
- **'Bavaria: Traditions and Innovations'** – This is a branding campaign launched by the Bavarian government to promote tourism and economic development in the German state. The campaign highlights Bavaria's rich cultural heritage, as well as its reputation for technological innovation and entrepreneurship.
- **'Explore Minnesota'** – This is a branding campaign launched by the Minnesota tourism board to promote tourism in the US state. The campaign emphasizes Minnesota's natural beauty, outdoor recreation, and cultural attractions.

This is just the tip of the iceberg! There are ample such examples, where enormous efforts have been put forth to highlight the uniqueness and novelty of the place through territorial branding, creating MTEs.

PROBABLE USAGE OF MEMORABLE TOURISM EXPERIENCES IN INDIA

India, a land of vibrant culture, breath-taking landscapes, and ancient traditions, has immense potential to create unforgettable experiences for tourists and can offer a plethora of opportunities for creating MTEs. Tourists can engage in novel activities like attending a vibrant Holi festival (Hapsari, 2018) or embarking on a tiger safari (Kim et al., 2012). Immersing oneself in the rich tapestry of Indian culture, from experiencing the warmth of local hospitality to exploring ancient temples, can leave a lasting impression (Hapsari, 2018). Sharing these experiences with loved ones or having unexpected encounters can further enhance their memorability (Hapsari, 2018). There are Five areas, by focusing on which, India can transform tourism from mere sightseeing into a transformative journey that fosters emotional connections, personal growth, and a deeper understanding of the country's melting pot of diversity and can leverage its unique strengths to craft truly memorable journeys:

1. Hyper-Personalization

Tailored Itineraries

It is all about moving beyond the generic tours and catering to specific interests like yoga retreats in the Himalayas or workshop in Ashrams for wellness seekers, culinary tours exploring regional cuisines for food enthusiasts, or wildlife safaris for nature lovers. Also, there can be micro segmentation within each of the domains. Like within the culinary tours there can be arrangement of regional foods from hilly region like Garhwali or North Indian foods for spicy food lovers, Bengali or Gujrati foods for dessert lovers etc.

Local Immersion

The trip organizers can facilitate homestay experiences in villages, allowing tourists to experience daily life and connect with communities. There can be additional arrangement for organizing interactions with artisans or participating in local festivals or learning traditional crafts. This can enrich the experience of the travellers with the local taste of the culture creating unique memories which can translate into stories to be told to the other people.

Skill-Based Workshops

To create remarkable memories, it is always great to offer opportunities to learn a new skill like cooking a regional dish, mastering basic Hindi phrases, or playing a traditional instrument or learning regional song or dance. This fosters a deeper connection with the culture.

2. Emotional Connection

Storytelling and Mythology

Weaving narratives around historical sites and monuments, bringing them to life is another part of creating fond memories. The local guides could be employed and trained as storytellers to create virtually live experiences of the past or there can be heritage walks conducted with a focus on folklore and mythology.

Spiritual Experiences

It is always an excellent idea to facilitate visits to ashrams, meditation centres, or pilgrimage sites to create memories. There can be packages to offer yoga and mindfulness sessions, allowing tourists to connect with India's spiritual essence.

Festival Participation

Integrating tourists into vibrant festivals like Holi or Diwali as already mentioned could be a way to generate emotional connections with the destination. The set of tourists can witness the preparations, participate in rituals (if respectful), and experience the joy and first-hand energy for uniqueness of the festivities.

3. Uniqueness and Novelty

Off-the-Beaten-Path Destinations

Promoting the lesser-known yet stunning locations like the serene backwaters of Kerala, the majestic Northeast with its diverse tribes, or the historical gems of Rajasthan beyond the usual forts could be a grand idea to create MTEs.

Adventure Activities

Offering opportunities for trekking in the Himalayas or white-water rafting on the Ganges or exploring wildlife sanctuaries in unique ways like the elephant safaris or the camel rides in the Thar Desert or the birdwatching tours could be part of memories.

Culinary Explorations

It is always advisable to go beyond restaurant meals and to organize visits to local markets, cooking demonstrations with home cooks, or street food tours, allowing tourists to savour authentic flavours and regional specialties.

4. Seamless Integration of Technology

Mobile Applications

Developing location-based apps offering historical information, cultural insights, and augmented reality experiences at tourist destinations could be useful to create MTEs.

E-Ticketing and Hassle-Free Travel

Implementing go-to online booking systems for transportation and attractions and streamlining the travel experience could render a smooth service 24/7.

Virtual Reality Experiences

Showcasing the destinations and activities through virtual reality experiences could allow tourists to virtually explore India before their trip and could enhance the attraction of the place manifold.

5. Sustainability and Responsible Tourism

Eco-Tourism Initiatives

Promoting responsible travel practices like supporting homestays run by local communities, minimizing waste generation, and opting for eco-friendly transportation can introduce sustainability and the quality of the service.

Wildlife Conservation Awareness

Integrating wildlife safaris with interesting facts sharing and educational talks on conservation efforts, fostering respect for the environment could help in sustainability goal and balance of the ecosystem.

Cultural Sensitivity

Educating the tourists on local customs and traditions and ensuring respectful interactions with communities can elevate the experiences.

MAIN FOCUS OF THE CHAPTER

The chapter would delve into the application of memorable tourism experience in India across various tourism sectors like hotels, restaurants, theme-based tourism and walks etc. The study would take initiatives to capture the perspective of the people, who engage in frequent touring in and outside the country as well as the perspective of the hoteliers, restaurants, trip managers/ tour organisers, travel agents etc. through two different surveys, exploring the customers' behaviour towards MTEs and organizational point of view to apply the concept of MTEs in their business to increase the sustainability and revenue for a robust business model.

RESEARCH DESIGN

The chapter aims to gain insights from regular travellers inside and outside the country, as well as hoteliers, restaurant managers, tour operators and travel agents through two separate surveys, examining tourists' attitudes towards memorable tourism experiences (MTEs) and how companies implement memorable tourism experiences to enhance their sustainability and profitability. The chapter reviews the literature related to the topic of the chapter. In all the cases, a prior approval has been taken before recording the responses. The respondents contacted through a referral technique. Both the surveys have been qualitative in nature and the questions have been subjected to generate a common theme through the process of category coding or pattern coding for the investigating the purposes. Pattern coding or category coding is a process of generating themes or categories based on the points of communality of the responses. In other words, it is a process of finding a common pattern of responses to categorise the attitude into different micro-segments to draw an inference. In all the cases, anonymity has been maintained to allow respondents for freedom of expression and to avoid any apprehensions or prejudices. The responses have been recorded through structured questionnaire via online survey forms, WhatsApp messages, video calls and face to face interviews with insightful discussion on the open-ended questions. The research design has been depicted through Figure 2 and sample profile have been provided below via Table 1, Figure 3, Table 2, and Figure 4. The following research questions have been explored through the study:

1. What is the awareness level of the tourists visiting different places in India about memorable tourism experiences?
2. What is the awareness level of the organizations involved in the tourism industry about memorable tourism experiences?
3. Are the factors of memorable tourism experiences really important to affect the choices of destination for the tourists?
4. What are the challenges and issues affecting the memorable tourism experiences of the tourists?
5. What are the current trends to affect tourists' attraction to crate MTEs?

Figure 2. Showing the design of the chapter

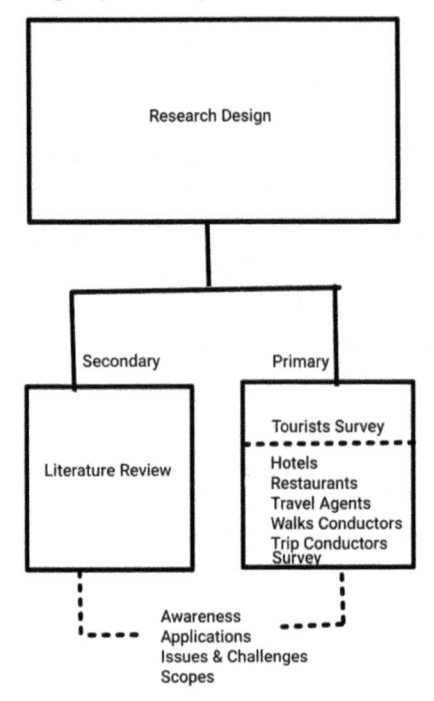

```
                    ┌─────────────────────┐
                    │   Research Design   │
                    └──────────┬──────────┘
                    ┌──────────┴──────────┐
                Secondary              Primary
                    │                      │
            ┌───────────────┐    ┌──────────────────┐
            │               │    │ Tourists Survey  │
            │  Literature   │    │------------------│
            │    Review     │    │ Hotels           │
            │               │    │ Restaurants      │
            │               │    │ Travel Agents    │
            │               │    │ Walks Conductors │
            └───────┬───────┘    │ Trip Conductors  │
                    │            │ Survey           │
                    │            └────────┬─────────┘
                    └──── Awareness ──────┘
                         Applications
                         Issues & Challenges
                         Scopes
```

(Author own creation)

Table 1. Showing the sample profile of tourists

Sr. No.	Category	Number of Respondents	Percentage
1	Outsider Tourists	109	62
2	Indian Tourists	67	38
Total		176	100

Source: Author own creation

Figure 3. Showing the sample profile of tourists through graphical expression

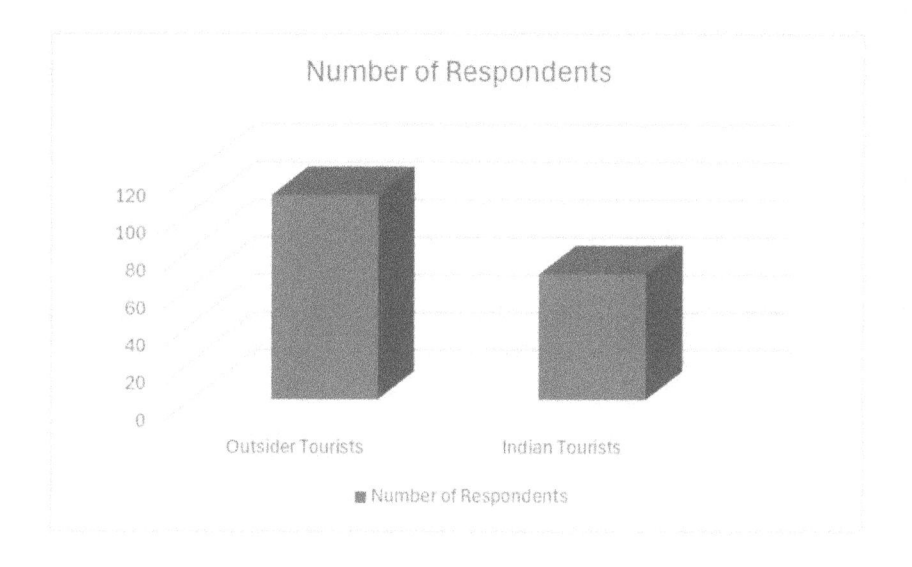

(Author own creation)

Table 2. Showing the sample profile of organizational survey

Sr. No.	Category	Number of Respondents	Percentage
1	Hotels	18	20
2	Restaurants	43	49
3	Trip Organizers	14	16
4	Home Stay	5	6
5	Walk Organizers	8	9
Total		88	

Source: Author own creation

Figure 4. Showing the sample profile of organizational survey

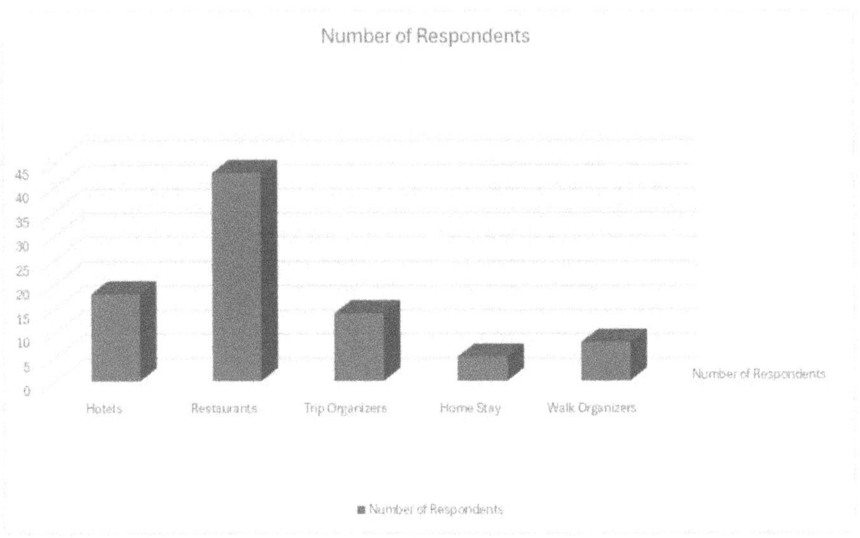

(Author own creation)

TRENDS OF USING MEMORABLE TOURISM EXPERIENCES (MTES) IN INDIA

The tourism industry is constantly evolving, and the way the tourism industry has been creating continuous promising experiences, MTEs has never been unexpected exception. By understanding the trends, tourism businesses could cater to the evolving needs of travellers and create new avenues to MTEs those are not only enjoyable but also leave an ever-lasting impact. Below is a glimpse into some of the key trends shaping the future of MTEs, some of these have been identified during the in-depth discussion with the respondents and insightful information revealed by them:

1. Hyper-Personalization and Customization

Focus on Individual Needs

Tourists are increasingly seeking experiences tailored to their specific interests, preferences, and travel styles. Gone are the days of one-size-fits-all itineraries. A mass segmentation may have a confused positioning for creating everlasting memories and to bring back all customers irrespective of democratic variabilities to the destination. Hence, most of the travel planners are developing multiple options keeping in mind the specific need of the microsegments.

Customization Options

Most of the travel companies come up with a plethora of choices to create a wholesome basket to choose from while going for a rise in platforms. Travel companies offering highly customizable need-based experiences and packages, especially for high end customers, are done to avoid generalization of mass market. Tourists can choose destinations, activities, accommodation, and pace, based on their desires and convenience and thus reaching a higher level of satisfaction and elation.

Technology Integration

Mobile applications and AI-powered recommendations play a vital role in suggesting personalized experiences and facilitating on-the-go adjustments. Many a times trip organizers are developing bespoke packages befitting the need based on AI recommendations and data analytics.

2. Authenticity and Local Immersion

Beyond Tourist Traps

Tourists are craving genuine connections with local cultures and communities. They want to go beyond popular tourist destinations and experience the essence of a place. Because of this tendency many of the trip organizers are planning to take the tourists to the off-beat or unconventional places, which are less explored and close to nature with intact authenticity and local culture.

Community-Based Tourism

Travelers are opting for homestays, local food tours, and workshops led by community members, seeking a deeper understanding of local life.

Experiential Learning

MTEs will increasingly incorporate opportunities for hands-on learning - cooking classes, traditional craft workshops, or volunteering experiences that contribute to the local community. These are basically parts of emotional connection and engagement of the tourists which later on they include in the storytelling as the proud moment of their lives.

3. Sustainability and Wellness

Eco-Conscious Travel

Tourists are becoming more environmentally conscious, seeking sustainable travel options with minimal impact on the environment.

Ecotourism and Conservation

Travel experiences focused on wildlife conservation, responsible waste management, and supporting local communities are in high demand.

Wellness Integration

MTEs will increasingly incorporate wellness aspects - yoga retreats, meditation sessions, or nature walks - catering to the growing desire for holistic travel experiences.

4. Technology as a Tool, Not a Replacement

Technology Plays a Supportive Role

While technology like VR can provide a taste of a destination, MTEs are leveraging it to enhance experiences, not replace real-world interaction. It is giving a prior promise of experiences which await the tourists.

Augmented Reality (AR)

AR applications can add an interactive layer to sightseeing, providing historical information or cultural insights at tourist destinations.

Seamless Digital Experiences

Technology is streamlining the travel experience - online booking, mobile ticketing, and real-time communication with tour operators.

5. Storytelling and Emotional Connection

The Power of Narrative

MTEs would be built around compelling narratives that connect tourists to the place on an emotional level. This could involve local folklore, historical events, or personal stories of the people.

Sensory Experiences

Creating experiences that engage multiple senses - sight, sound, smell, taste, and touch - could leave a lasting impression on tourists. Because of this, most of the tourist spots have light and sound programmes to elevate the experiences.

Transformative Travel

The focus would shift from simply visiting a place to experiencing a personal transformation through the MTE through attending workshops and sessions etc.

TRENDS IN MEMORABLE TOURISM EXPERIENCES (MTES) IN INDIA

India's tourism landscape is embracing the global MTE trend with its own unique twists. By embracing these trends, India is gradually solidifying its position as a leading MTE destination, offering unforgettable experiences that cater to the evolving needs of global travellers while showcasing the country's unique culture, heritage, and natural beauty.

1. Experiential Luxury

Moving Beyond Opulence

Luxury travel in India is shifting from just opulent hotels to immersive experiences. Tourists seek unique stays like heritage palaces, luxury eco-camps, or houseboats on tranquil backwaters.

Customization for Discerning Travellers

High-end experiences are tailored to specific interests - private wildlife safaris, culinary tours exploring regional delicacies with renowned chefs, or personalized wellness retreats with Ayurvedic treatments.

2. Focus on Rural and Off-the-Beaten-Path Destinations

Beyond the Golden Triangle

Tourists are venturing beyond established tourist circuits like the Golden Triangle (Delhi, Agra, Jaipur) to explore hidden gems – the serene Northeast with its tribal cultures, the majestic Himalayas offering adventure activities, or the untouched beauty of the Andaman and Nicobar Islands.

Community-Based Tourism in Rural Areas

Homestays in villages, interaction with local artisans, and participation in traditional festivals are becoming popular ways to experience rural life and support local communities.

3. Sustainable and Responsible Tourism

Eco-Conscious Travel Practices

Tourists are increasingly opting for eco-friendly tours that minimize environmental impact. This includes responsible waste management, supporting wildlife conservation initiatives, and choosing accommodations with sustainable practices.

Responsible Volunteering

MTEs are incorporating volunteer opportunities with local NGOs, allowing tourists to contribute to social causes while experiencing the country.

4. Digital Storytelling and Tech-Enhanced Experiences

Virtual Reality (VR) and Augmented Reality (AR)

VR experiences might showcase historical sites or iconic landmarks before the visit, while AR apps can provide interactive information about monuments or cultural practices during sightseeing.

Social Media Integration

Engaging social media campaigns showcasing unique MTEs and promoting responsible tourism practices are a growing trend.

5. Focus on Wellness and Holistic Experiences

Yoga and Ayurveda Integration

India's rich heritage of wellness practices is finding its way into MTEs. Yoga retreats, Ayurvedic spa experiences, and meditation sessions are becoming popular inclusions for holistic well-being.

Nature-Based Experiences

MTEs are increasingly incorporating activities that connect tourists with nature – trekking in the Himalayas, wildlife safaris, or spending time in serene natural settings like Kerala's backwaters.

6. Focus on Uniqueness

Focus on Skill-based Learning

Workshops on traditional crafts like pottery or textile weaving might be offered as part of MTEs, allowing tourists to learn a new skill while engaging with local culture.

Culinary Delights

Food tours exploring regional cuisines or cooking classes with local chefs are becoming a popular way to experience India's diverse culinary traditions.

According to the survey carried out among trip and walk organizers, hotels, and restaurants, the majority of tourists prefer customized or personalized services chosen from multiple options suiting their preferences (Table 3). Also, the set of tourists like to enjoy a pre-trip immersive experience through virtual reality and augmented reality integrated and accessed through social media and other virtual platforms. It is noteworthy that people nowadays seek out unique destinations that offer personal growth opportunities through activities like grooming sessions and workshops and authentic local culture.

Table 3. Showing the trends of creating MTEs as per travel related organizations

Sr. No.	Trends in creating MTEs	Number of Respondents	Percentage
1	Personalized service	85	97
2	Multiple options for customised need	86	98
3	Technological integration/ website/use of VR & AR/social media Integration	83	94
4	Personal engagement	84	95
5	Immersive experience	74	84
6	Unconventional experience	85	97
7	Authentic local experience	86	98
8	Unique workshop and sessions	73	83

Source: Author own creation

ISSUES AND CHALLENGES OF USING MEMORABLE TOURISM

While Memorable Tourism Experiences act as a bundle of powerful tools to be the harbourage for the tourism industry, it has its own baggages or challenges, especially with the applicability part.

Meeting Diverse Expectations

Since, tourists come from varied backgrounds with different interests and desires, crafting a one-size-fits-all MTE is difficult. Subsequently the positioning statement of the MTEs becomes confusing to serve the mixed segments. The actual challenge becomes to cater to individual preferences while maintaining logistical feasibility and economic viability. The solution is to offer customizable itineraries or modular experiences to a group of combined tourists based on their common interests.

Balancing Authenticity and Tourist Comfort

It becomes a huge burden to preserve the cultural essence of destinations while ensuring tourist safety and comfort. For instance, some traditional practices might be unfamiliar or uncomfortable for visitors and also it becomes a problem, in case, a torrent of sudden tourism emerge in a place to infiltrate impurities in pristine local culture. The solution could be to provide options for immersive experiences through VR with clear explanations and respecting cultural boundaries.

Standardization vs. Personalization

The challenge is to find the balance between offering some level of standardization (e.g., safety protocols) while allowing for personalization to create a unique experience. The solution could be establishing core experiences with opportunities for customization, such as local guide interaction or optional activities.

Measuring and Evaluating MTEs

The Challenge of measuring and evaluating MTEs is that it is subjective and can alter as per the need of each of the individuals. Traditional tourist satisfaction surveys might not capture the essence of a memorable experience, but a survey to find out the uniqueness and personalized emotional association of a place with a group of tourists may unravel the essence of memorable tourism experiences. Additionally the solution may incorporate techniques to develop methods that go beyond basic satisfaction ratings, incorporating storytelling, emotional response analysis, or social media sentiment analysis.

Sustainability and Responsible Tourism

The challenge is maintaining the Balance between the creation of MTEs and responsible tourism practices. Over-tourism may result in environmental degradation and can subsequently threaten the very experiences of MTEs. The solution is to set boundaries and to promote eco-friendly practices, to support local communities managing the visitors flow to popular destinations to the extent so that the sustainability of the ecosystem is not destroyed.

Technological Integration

The challenge of Technological Integration is that while technology can enhance experiences, over-reliance on it can create a disconnect with the destination and its culture failing to create a bond between the tourists and the culture. The solution again lies in the balance, using technology thoughtfully, such as for educational purposes or facilitating communication, but ensuring the balance with real-world interactions.

Managing Tourist Expectations

Creating over expectation in social media and idealised over promise in the portrayals can create unrealistic expectations about destinations and experiences. Tourists might be disappointed if reality does not match with their virtual perception. The solution lies in the setting of realistic expectations through transparent marketing and communication, showcasing the true essence of the destination alongside its potential challenges. This will reduce the chance of performance gap and communication gap in the service quality delivery.

ISSUES AND CHALLENGES OF MTES IN INDIA

While India has immense potential for creating memorable tourism experiences (MTEs), there are specific challenges like Infrastructure and Service Quality issues, Skilled Workforce and Training related issues, Bureaucracy and Regulations related issues, sustainability concerns, cultural sensitivity, safety and security challenges etc. which the torrent sector often faces in implementing the approach.

Infrastructure and Service Quality Related Issues

India's vastness presents disparities in uneven infrastructure. While major cities boast modern facilities, rural areas might lack proper transportation, sanitation, or accommodation options. The challenge lies in ensuring a consistent level of service quality across the country to meet tourist expectations. The simple solution is a substantial investment in infrastructure development in tourist destinations, particularly in rural India. Partnering with local communities to create homestays with basic amenities can enhance the authenticity while improving service quality.

Skilled Workforce and Training Related Issues

This challenge in Indian tourism industry might lack a sufficient workforce trained to deliver personalized and engaging experiences. Tour guides with in-depth knowledge of local culture and storytelling skills are crucial for MTEs, while there is no universal training programme available for the guide fraternity. The solution could be developing training programmes focused on cultural sensitivity, storytelling techniques, and customer service for tourism professionals to render a live experiences of the historical tours.

Bureaucracy and Regulations Related Issues

The navigating complex bureaucratic procedures can be time-consuming in India and discourage potential entrepreneurs from creating unique MTE offerings. The solution lies in streamlining permitting processes and regulations for tourism businesses. Providing clear guidelines and online portals can ease the bureaucratic regulatory framework.

Sustainability Concerns

Over-tourism and Resource Management is becoming a serious concern for India. India's growing popularity can lead to over-tourism in certain destinations, putting a strain on natural resources and local communities. The challenge lies in balancing tourism growth with the preservation of cultural heritage and natural ecosystems. While the solution is promoting sustainable tourism practices, such as responsible waste management, encouraging off-season travel, and supporting eco-friendly tour operators.

Cultural Sensitivity Related Issues

Respecting traditions is the base to maintain cultural sensitivity. India's diverse cultures and traditions require sensitivity from the tourists, especially the ones visiting from outside India. Inappropriate behaviour at religious sites or lack of understanding of local customs can create friction. The main challenge is to educate tourists on cultural etiquette and fostering respect for local traditions. The solution could be providing pre-trip information on cultural norms, offering orientation sessions, and encouraging interaction with local guides who can bridge the cultural gap.

Safety and Security Concerns

There is perception vs. reality dilemma hovering in India. The country might have been perceived as unsafe, particularly for solo travellers. The challenge is to ensure the safety and security of tourists while addressing any genuine concerns effectively. The solution is implementing robust security measures in tourist destinations, promoting responsible tourism practices amongst tourists, and leveraging technology (close circuit camera, drone vigilance etc.) for real-time information and emergency assistance.

Marketing and Targeting the Right Audience

The challenge is to effectively communicate the diverse MTE possibilities. The principal challenge is to pitch the right audience without confusing the segregation, marketing, and positioning of each of the destination, while communicating one of the solutions could be developing targeted marketing campaigns highlighting unique MTE offerings based on tourist interests (adventure, wellness, heritage, culture etc.) and utilizing digital platforms for wider reach.

According to the survey of the tourists, the main worry among the travelling public is the state of infrastructure and safety measures. Other secondary concerns include the quality of services, preservation of local culture, and availability of engaging activities. However, the primary focus remains on infrastructure and safety concerns, often leading to a sense of fear among tourists. The concerns of the tourists are all depicted through Table 4.

As per the survey conducted with trip organizers, hotels, and restaurants (Table 5), the key problem is achieving standardization of rules and tour itineraries while preserving a personal touch of the tourists. Due to this the campaigning become arduous with confused segmentation, marketing and positioning. Another challenge is the red tapism with lengthy paperwork to delay the tours as it hampers the smooth

continued on following page

Table 5. Continued

running of the show compromising the quality of expectation of the tourists. The survey highlighted the difficulty of engaging tourists in cultural programmes and rituals without compromising their authenticity or the cultural atmosphere. Sometimes it becomes a hindrance to engage the tourists in cultural programmes and rituals without disturbing the ambience of the same. It becomes also troublesome sometimes to maintain the sustainability goal, especially for heritage centres and green ecosystem. Striking a balance between tourism and sustainability, particularly for heritage sites and green ecosystems, is another challenge identified. The survey raised a question about the possibility of achieving personal comfort for tourists while adhering to local cultural norms. Finding solutions that bridge this gap is essential to ensure a positive experience for tourists while upholding cultural respect. It is also another concern to find well skilled guides to engage the tourists with lively storytelling and engrossing them with the uniqueness of the culture. By addressing these challenges, India can move towards creating a robust MTE for diverse ecosystems that cater to various tourist needs and demands while ensuring responsible and sustainable tourism practices.

Table 4. Showing the challenges faced the tourists in India

Sr. No.	Challenges faced by the Tourists	Number of Respondents	Percentage
1	Infrastructure (Stay & Transportation)	73	41
2	Safety Concerns	102	58
3	Service Quality	47	27
4	Authentic Local Guides	32	18
5	Engaging and Interesting Programmes	21	12
6	Local Taste	54	31

Source: Author own creation

Table 5. Showing the challenges faced the organisations involved in Tourism

Sr. No.	Challenges faced by the Organizations	Number of Respondents	Percentage
1	Standardization protocol	48	55
2	Bureaucracy/Delay in processing	39	44
3	Difficult segmentation and Positioning/ difficult to design campaign/ difficult advertising content creation	73	83
4	Difficulty in balancing culture of sensitivity and engagement of the tourists	76	86

Sr. No.	Challenges faced by the Organizations	Number of Respondents	Percentage
5	Difficulty in managing expectation of the tourists	75	85
6	Difficulty in finding trained and skilled workforce	23	26
7	Difficulty in maintaining sustainability goals	21	24
8	Difficulty in providing personal comfort in authentic local environment	69	78
9	Difficulty in convincing tourists about responsible behaviour	77	88

Source: Author own creation

DISCUSSION

Although there is lack of awareness of the term- memorable tourism experiences (MTEs) among the tourists and the organisers, both parties agreed on the acceptance of the components. The majority of the tourists mostly value components like uniqueness and novelty, authentic local culture, emotional engagement and service quality & customer satisfaction. However, the emotional connection and personalisation are not as significant to them as per survey. Table 6 shows the awareness level of tourists, while Table 7 shows the awareness level of the organisers. Table 8 depicts the significance of the components of memorable tourism experience for the tourists, while Table 9 depicts the importance of the components for the organisers. Table 10 portrays the inclination of the public to spread positive word of mouth through reminiscing and storytelling of the fond memories of the place that they visited. Many times, emotional connection helps in repeat visit to the same place. The storytelling part also encourages other visitors to visit the place and thus enriching the revenue model of the destination.

Table 6. Showing the awareness level of the term of MTEs for the tourists visiting India

Sr. No.	Aware of the term Memorable Tourism Experiences	Number of Respondents	Percentage
1	Yes	9	5
2	No	167	95

Source: Author own creation

Table 7. Showing the awareness level of the term of MTEs for the trip organizers and other involved organization in India

Sr. No.	Aware of the term Memorable Tourism Experiences	Number of Respondents	Percentage
1	Yes	21	24
2	No	67	76

Source: Author own creation

Table 8. Showing the importance of contributing factors to create MTEs as per tourists

Sr. No.	Factors Affecting MTEs	Extremely Important	Percentage	Important	Percentage	Neutral	Percentage	Unimportant	Percentage	Extremely Unimportant	Percentage	Total
1	Uniqueness and Novelty	158	90	10	6	4	2	4	2	0	0	176
2	Authenticity & Local Culture	138	78	19	11	7	4	12	7	0	0	176
3	Personalization	86	49	79	45	7	4	4	2	0	0	176
4	Emotional Connection	45	26	28	16	11	6	78	44	14	8	176
5	Positive Emotions, Serendipity and Emotional Engagement	105	60	57	32	14	8	0	0	0	0	176
6	Increased Service Quality and Satisfaction	148	84	24	14	4	2	0	0	0	0	176

Source: Author own creation

Table 9. Showing the importance of contributing factors to create MTEs as per organizations

Sr. No.	Factors Affecting MTEs	Extremely important	Percentage	Important	Percentage	Neutral	Percentage	Unimportant	Percentage	Extremely Unimportant	Percentage	Total
1	Uniqueness and Novelty	85	97	3	3	0	0	0	0	0	0	88
2	Authenticity & Local Culture	82	93	4	5	2	2	0	0	0	0	88
3	Personalization	74	84	12	14	2	2	0	0	0	0	88
4	Emotional Connection	56	64	17	19	8	9	4	5	3	3	88
5	Positive Emotions, Serendipity and Emotional Engagement	80	91	6	7	1	1	1	1	0	0	88
6	Increased Service Quality and Satisfaction	84	95	2	2	2	2	0	0	0	0	88

Source: Author own creation

Table 10. Showing the inclination of the tourists towards storytelling about the fond memories of the destinations

Sr. No.	Inclination towards Storytelling of Fond Memories about Destinations	Number of Respondents	Percentage
1	Yes	142	81
2	No	9	5
3	May be	25	14

Source: Author own creation

FUTURE RESEARCH DIRECTIONS

This study is completely based on qualitative data analysis and no statistical analysis has been conducted to draw definitive inference based on hypothesis testing. Hence it is a bare necessity to conduct further statistical analysis to conclude the explored content.

CONCLUSION

Memorable tourism experience (MTEs) is a trending key concept prevailing in tourism industry which helps in crafting tourism experiences. The tourism Industry thrives on creating experiences that stay with travellers long after they return home from the destination. These memorable moments are not just about ticking off landmarks; they are about fostering connections, sparking emotions, and offering a deeper understanding of a place and its culture, embedded in their mind and heart-share through etching permanent memories. There are plenty of researches, suggesting the impact of personalization, novelty, and emotional engagement as the key ingredients in crafting unforgettable experiences and leading to MTEs. Tourists crave authenticity and a chance to immerse themselves in the local way of life, while still maintaining a level of comfort and respect for cultural norms. The challenge lies in striking a balance between standardization – ensuring a smooth experience through fixed rules, regulations and procedures – and customization – catering to individual preferences. Furthermore, navigating bureaucratic hurdles and ensuring sustainable practices are crucial aspects that should not detract from the enjoyment of the destination. By focusing on these elements, tourism providers can create experiences that resonate with travellers, fostering positive memories and encouraging them to return for more visits. Ultimately, these memorable experiences not only

REFERENCES

Aho, S. K. (2001). Towards a general theory of touristic experiences: Modelling experience process in tourism. *Tourism Review*, 56(1), 33–37. DOI: 10.1108/eb058368

Croes, R., Ridderstaat, J., Bak, M., & Zientara, P. (2021). Tourism specialization, economic growth, human development and transition economies: The case of Poland. *Tourism Management*, 82, 104181. DOI: 10.1016/j.tourman.2020.104181

Hapsari, R. A. (2018). Psychological factors affecting memorable tourism experiences. *Request PDF – ResearchGate*.https://www.researchgate.net/publication/332807375_Psychological_factors_affecting_memorable_tourism_experiences

Kabus, J. (2015). Marketing in tourism. *AD ALTA International Interdisciplinary Research Journal*, 5, 34–37.

Kim, S. H., & Chen, J. S. (2020). Pengaruh memorable tourist experience terhadap storytelling behavior (The influence of memorable tourist experiences on storytelling behaviour). *E-Journal UNDIP*, 24(2), 1–10.

Kim, Y., Ritchie, B. W., & McCormick, J. (2012). A review of memorable experiences and their implications for tourism experiences in management and marketing science. *Tourism Management*, 33(6), 1443–1456. DOI: 10.1016/j.tourman.2012.02.007

Kim, Y., Yeon, S., & Kim, J. (2012). A review of memorable experiences and their implications for tourism experiences. *Management and Marketing Science*.https://journals.openedition.org/tourisme/5053

Oh, H., Kim, Y., & Morrison, A. M. (2007). The roles of emotions in current consumption experiences and future consumption intentions. *Journal of Business Research*, 60(9), 462–469. DOI: 10.1016/j.jbusres.2007.01.014

Ritchie, J. R. B., & Crouch, G. I. (2000). The competitive destination: A sustainable perspective. *Tourism Management*, 21(1), 1–7. DOI: 10.1016/S0261-5177(99)00080-1

Sagayama, H., Shizuma, K., Toguchi, M., Mizuhara, H., Machida, Y., Yamada, Y., Ebine, N., Higaki, Y., & Tanaka, H. (2018). Effect of the health tourism weight loss programme on body composition and health outcomes in healthy and excess-weight adults. *British Journal of Nutrition*, 119(10), 1133–1141. DOI: 10.1017/S0007114518000582 PMID: 29759101

Seddighi, H. R., & Theocharous, A. L. (2002). A model of tourism destination choice: A theoretical and empirical analysis. *Tourism Management*, 23(5), 475–487. DOI: 10.1016/S0261-5177(02)00012-2

Sthapit, S., & Coudounaris, C. (2017). Memorable tourism experiences and critical outcomes among nature-based visitors: A fuzzy-set qualitative comparative analysis approach. *Journal of Sustainable Tourism*, 25(11), 1729–1748. DOI: 10.1080/09669582.2016.1251986

Tung, P. C., & Ritchie, B. W. (2011). Measuring memorable tourism experiences. *Journal of Travel Research*, 50(3), 300–312. DOI: 10.1177/0047287510385460

KEY TERMS AND DEFINITIONS

Memorable Tourism Experiences: memorable tourism experience is a travel encounter that leaves a lasting positive impression on a tourist. It goes beyond the typical sightseeing experience and engages the traveller on a deeper level, fostering emotional connections, a sense of novelty, and a newfound understanding of a place and its culture. This type of experience is often personalized, catering to the individual's interests and preferences, while also ensuring respect and immersion in the local way of life.

Tourist Destination: A tourist destination is a place, typically a city, town, region, or even an entire country, that attracts visitors for leisure, recreational, or cultural purposes.

Tourist: A tourist is a person who travels to a place outside their usual environment for leisure, recreational, or cultural purposes.

APPENDIX I: TOURISTS' SURVEY

This survey is completely meant for academic purposes and has no connection with any commercial usage. The information will be kept confidential without any publication of name or any other details.

Age:
Gender:
Educational Qualification:

1. Are you aware of the term memorable tourism experiences? Yes/ no
2. Do you believe in creating fond memories while you visit any destination? Yes/ no/ maybe
3. How important is it to you have uniqueness and novelty in a travelling destination? Extremely important/ important/ neutral/ unimportant/ extremely unimportant
4. How important is it to you have emotional engagement in a travelling destination? Extremely important/ important/ neutral/ unimportant/ extremely unimportant
5. How important is it for you have emotional connection with a tourist destination? Extremely important/ important/ neutral/ unimportant/ extremely unimportant
6. How important is it for you to have some personalised grooming sessions meant for you? Extremely important/ important/ neutral/ unimportant/ extremely unimportant
7. How important is it for you to have very high customer satisfaction at the tourist spot? Extremely important/ important/ neutral/ unimportant/ extremely unimportant
8. How important is it for you to have best service quality at the tourist spot? Extremely important/ important/ neutral/ unimportant/ extremely unimportant
9. How important is it for you to have exposure to authentic local culture of the tourist spot? Extremely important/ important/ neutral/ unimportant/ extremely unimportant
10. When you select any tourist spot to visit what are the criteria that you look forward to?......
11. Do you like to visit a tourist spot, which gives you uniqueness and novelty, emotional connect, self-grooming sessions, exposure to local culture? Yes/ no /maybe
12. What are the challenges you have faced while visiting different tourist spots in India?......
13. Did you find any current trends or initiatives to attract tourist in India?......
14. If you like any tourist destination, do you like to share the stories about the fond memories of that place? Yes/ no/ maybe

APPENDIX II: ORGANISATIONAL SURVEY

The purpose of the survey is completely academic and there is no chance of commercial usage. The opinion will be completely confidential and the personal details will never be exposed in the public forum.

Name of the organisation(optional):

Nature of the organisation: hotel/ restaurant/ trip organising agency/ walk organising agency/ travel agent/ home stay/other (please specify)

1. Are you ever heard of the term memorable tourism experience? Yes/ no/ maybe
2. What are the general demands of the tourist to visit different places in India?...
3. Please read the following statements from the point of view of tourist who like to visit different places in India and rate each statement on the scale of 5 while 1 is extremely unimportant and 5 is extremely important:

A. The place has to be unique and full of novelty.
B. The place should have some thing to evoke emotional connection.
C. It should serve the local taste of the destination like cultural programme, local cuisine, local art exhibition (Mela, Haat, Bazar etc.), local festivities, local rituals.
D. It should have some personal and Wellness sessions to engage the tourist.
E. It is quintessential to have eco system related goals or sustainability goes to attract tourists in India.

4. What are the challenges that you often face from the tourists while visiting India?.....
5. What are the current trends to attract tourist in India?....
6. How important is it to you have uniqueness and novelty in a travelling destination? Extremely important/ important/ neutral/ unimportant/ extremely unimportant
7. How important is it to you have emotional engagement in a travelling destination? Extremely important/ important/ neutral/ unimportant/ extremely unimportant
8. How important is it for you have emotional connection with a tourist destination? Extremely important/ important/ neutral/ unimportant/ extremely unimportant
9. How important is it for you to have some personalised grooming sessions meant for you? Extremely important/ important/ neutral/ unimportant/ extremely unimportant
10. How important is it for you to have very high customer satisfaction at the tourist spot? Extremely important/ important/ neutral/ unimportant/ extremely unimportant
11. How important is it for you to have best service quality at the tourist spot? Extremely important/ important/ neutral/ unimportant/ extremely unimportant.

Chapter 10
Technology-Driven and Personality in the Travel Experience Within a Destination:
Literature Review and Proposal for Analysis Model

Mourad Aarabe
https://orcid.org/0009-0003-9772-6683
Sidi Mohamed Ben Abdellah University, Morocco

Meryem Bouizgar
https://orcid.org/0009-0009-0943-2057
National School of Business and Management of Fez, Morocco

Nouhaila Ben Khizzou
Sidi Mohamed Ben Abdellah University, Morocco

Lhoussaine Alla
https://orcid.org/0000-0002-7238-1792
Sidi Mohamed Ben Abdellah University, Morocco

Ahmed Benjelloun
https://orcid.org/0009-0004-9673-2747
Sidi Mohamed Ben Abdellah University, Morocco

DOI: 10.4018/979-8-3693-7021-6.ch010

Copyright © 2025, IGI Global. Copying or distributing in print or electronic forms without written permission of IGI Global is prohibited.

ABSTRACT

The rapid advancement of technology has had a significant and far-reaching impact on the tourism industry, affecting not only the travel experience, but also the practices and procedures associated with tourism. This study examines the relationship between personality and applied technology in the travel experience, investigating the determinants of the travel experience within a destination. This chapter presents the findings of a systematic literature review conducted in accordance with the PRISMA protocol. It offers a comprehensive conceptual and theoretical framework and provides an overview of the current research trends and implications in this field. The findings illustrate the intricate and reciprocal relationship between technological tools and travelers' personality characteristics, and their influence on the tourism experience.

INTRODUCTION

The advent of new technologies has had a profound impact on the tourism industry, including significant changes to the travel experience and the way in which the industry operates in general. The implementation of smart tourism applications has enabled more efficient resource management and enhanced the competitiveness and sustainability of the tourism experience (Aarabe et al., 2024b; Erdem & Şeker, 2022). The advent of virtual reality, augmented reality, and artificial intelligence has profoundly impacted the personalization of the travel experience and consumer behavior (Cuomo et al., 2021; Topsakal et al., 2022). The use of online booking platforms, the integration of virtual and augmented reality, and the adoption of the Internet of Things in tourist destinations has been shown to contribute positively to the provision of immersive and memorable travel experiences that are co-created by stakeholders (Aarabe et al., 2024a; Buhalis, 2019).

Despite the efforts of numerous scholars to elucidate the nexus between technology, tourist personality, and the travel experience within a destination (Anaya & Lehto, 2020; Neuhofer et al., 2014; Wang et al., 2016)., It is evident that there are several research gaps that require further investigation. Theoretically, these concepts have been studied in isolation, with few works attempting to examine their interactions within a unified conceptual framework (Kim et al., 2019; Sertkan et al., 2018). Examining this interaction within an integer conceptual framework is essential to capture the dynamic interaction between the tourist's personality and travel behavior. Methodologically, the majority of current research employs quantitative approaches, such as questionnaire surveys (Jovanović et al., 2019). While this approach provides precious insights, there needs to be a more contextualized understanding of the technological travel experience. To fill this gap, qualitative and mixed approaches will be relevant to understanding how tourists interact with technology in a real context. Empirically, there is a problem of generalizing results due to the focus of current research on specific destinations (Wang et al., 2016). Comparative studies of different destinations incorporating different technologies are needed to understand how technologies can shape the travel experience. Such studies will enable researchers to draw robust conclusions about the moderating role of destination specificities on the travel experience. Furthermore, few studies have examined how travel personality interacts with emerging technologies in the tourism context (Quesnel & Riecke, 2018). Understanding how different personality types enhance engagement and immersion with technological innovations is essential to designing personalized travel experiences. Finding the answers to these research gaps is crucial to offering important theoretical and practical implications for tourism.

This study aims to address the aforementioned gap in the literature by examining the interplay between technology and travelers' personality traits on the tourism experience. The fundamental question guiding this study is: How does the interaction between technology and personality traits shape perception, behavior, and the travel experience?

The response to this problem is based on three specific objectives:
- examine the impact of technology on the travel experience.
- analyze how personality traits influence tourists' perceptions and behaviors.
- study the interaction between technology and personality traits and their impact on the travel experience.

To address the research objective, this chapter is structured into four sections. The first section will establish a theoretical and conceptual framework of key terms, particularly those related to technologies in the tourism field. It will also explore theories and models concerning the travel experience and the personality traits of travelers and tourist destinations. The second section will detail the methodological approach used in this research, primarily a systematic literature review following the PRISMA protocol. The third section will present a descriptive and qualitative analysis to identify trends and implications in the relationship between technology and personality. The fourth section will discuss the results and the main directions for future research, with a focus on how technology and personality traits interact with the tourism industry. Finally, the chapter will conclude with a summary of the key points, contributions, limitations, and future research directions.

THEORETICAL AND CONCEPTUAL FRAMEWORK

Travel Experience in a Tourist Destination

Tourist Destination

A tourist destination can be defined as a geographical area that attracts visitors for a variety of reasons, including its natural or cultural attractions, its tourism infrastructure, and its overall image (Hultman et al., 2015). It represents more than just a physical place; it is a complex set of tangible and intangible elements that create a unique experience for visitors. These destinations are not merely random places that attract visitors; rather, they possess distinct qualities that make them attractive to tourists.

Destinations such as Portugal, Barcelona, and Thrissur exemplify how a strong commitment to accessible tourism initiatives can increase inclusion and visitor satisfaction by addressing travelers' diverse physical, sensory, and cognitive needs (García-Milon et al., 2020). This focus on accessibility underscores the growing recognition of the importance of creating inclusive environments, as recognized by Leiras & Eusébio, (2024) in their efforts to promote accessible tourism destinations.

In contrast, vacation resorts are locations constructed or modified with the express purpose of providing accommodation for tourists during their leisure periods. Such establishments may include seaside resorts, ski resorts, or historic towns, offering a range of services and activities designed to satisfy vacationers' needs and desires (Jovanović et al., 2019). This specialization gives rise to distinctive challenges in relation to space management, environmental impact, and interaction with local communities.

The study of destinations is of central importance within the field of tourism. From an economic perspective, understanding the dynamics of regional development is of paramount importance. Tourist destinations are frequently economic engines, generating employment and revenue (Alla et al., 2023; EL JAOUHARI & Lhoussaine, 2022; Hmioui et al., 2017). Consequently, a more comprehensive grasp of their operational dynamics is vital to guarantee sustainable tourism development (Wang et al., 2017). Conversely, destination research offers a more profound insight into marketing and branding (Boudri et al., 2024). The distinctive character of a destination, encompassing its defining attributes, exerts a pivotal influence on visitor attraction (Kim & Stepchenkova, 2017).

The undertaking of research to determine the most appropriate destination for visitors serves to enhance the overall experience of the latter. By analyzing the various components of a given location, researchers can better comprehend how these elements impact tourist satisfaction and the likelihood of a return visit (Hultman et al., 2015). It provides a more nuanced understanding of tourist motivations, preferences, and behaviors, thus informing the development and marketing strategies that are most likely to be effective (Jani, 2014). Furthermore, destination research facilitates the harmonization of visitors, local residents, and environmental needs, thereby contributing to the development of more sustainable tourism (Calisto & Sarkar, 2024). Ultimately, destination research facilitates a more nuanced comprehension of consumer behavior and enables the integration of novel technologies into the tourism experience. For instance, virtual reality has the potential to transform the way destinations are perceived and experienced by visitors (Quesnel & Riecke, 2018).

Travel Experience

The travel experience concept has become a key area of focus within tourism research, particularly emphasizing understanding travelers' perceptions, emotions, and interactions during their journey (Scott et al., 2017). It is a multifaceted construct comprising tangible and intangible elements (Z. Chen & Fu, 2023). Volo, (2013) puts forth the proposition of incorporating spatial and temporal dimensions into the concept, with a particular focus on the significance of tourists' spontaneous annotations. Tussyadiah, (2013) proposes a theoretical framework for the design of human-centered tourism experiences, which is based on an iterative design process and a holistic approach to the experience. The concept of the tourism experience is presented as both a meta-concept, representing the value propositions of a destination, and an operational concept, through which the design elements can be orchestrated (Tussyadiah, 2013). A comprehensive understanding of and approach to the design of tourism experiences is paramount for effective marketing and management of destinations (Dagustani et al., 2018).

The tourism experience is a complex and multidimensional phenomenon, the influence of which is shaped by many factors. The cultural tourism experience is shaped by a multitude of aspects, including social interactions, the authenticity of local experiences, the quality of service, the cultural heritage of the destination, and the personal challenges encountered by the visitor (Cetin & Bilgihan, 2016). The demographic characteristics and previous experiences of travelers have been shown to influence their perception and interpretation of experiences (Pasaco-González et al., 2023). It has been demonstrated that the quality of the tourism experience positively affects tourist satisfaction and loyalty to a destination (da Costa Mendes et al., 2010).

Technological advancement is pivotal in enhancing the satisfaction levels associated with travel experiences. As evidenced by research conducted by Y. Chen et al., (2024), identified a multitude of factors, including novelty, trust in technology, aesthetics, education, and authenticity, as key determinants of satisfaction in this context. The integration of augmented reality (AR) and virtual reality (VR), in conjunction with personalized recommendations via geolocation services and real-time information offered by mobile applications, has been identified as a key factor in improving the travel experience (Hien & Trang, 2024). Moreover, smart tourism technologies are proving invaluable in managing travel planning and transactional risks while simultaneously offering tourists the opportunity to explore novel experiences (Goo et al., 2022). These technologies are acknowledged for their capacity to augment tourists' overall experience and elevate their level of satisfaction (Goo et al., 2022). The availability of information, accessibility, interactivity, personalization, and security are all significant factors influencing tourist perceptions and satisfaction (Pai et al., 2020). By facilitating access to information and fostering engagement with the activities offered by the destination, these technologies enable travelers to enjoy a seamless travel experience. Furthermore, the integration of these technologies into travel planning allows travelers to access pertinent information, receive personalized recommendations, and ensure their safety throughout their journey. In this way, they assist in alleviating travelers' uncertainties and concerns while also enhancing their overall satisfaction with the travel experience (C. D. Huang et al., 2017).

In the contemporary tourism sector, the integration of technology is a prerequisite for providing personalized experiences, which are now a fundamental aspect of the industry. As observed by Sustacha et al., (2023), the concept of smart tourism experience is centered on using sophisticated digital technologies to elevate the quality and personalization of travel experiences. This entails modifying tourism services to align with each traveler's particular preferences and requirements, leveraging real-time data to facilitate well-informed decision-making, and fostering engagement with the tourism environment through mobile devices and other digital platforms (Nouhaila et al., 2024).

The evidence presented here demonstrates that personalized, technology-enabled experiences significantly transform tourist perceptions and behaviors. By leveraging these technologies, destinations can establish a more engaging and tailored travel environment, attracting repeat business and enhancing their reputation in the global tourism market (Benbba et al., 2022). The adoption of technology in the tourism sector not only optimizes the traveler experience; it also enhances satisfaction metrics, promoting customer loyalty and retention (Palumbo, 2015).

Personality Traits in a Tourism Experience

The examination of personality traits is of central importance in the comprehension of the behaviors and experiences of travelers. A substantial body of research has been conducted to examine the relationship between tourists' personality characteristics and various aspects of their travel experiences, including their motivations, preferences, and behaviors. The Big Five model, a foundational construct in the field of personality psychology, is emerging as a pivotal instrument for elucidating the motivations and behaviors of travelers (Alves et al., 2022). This factorial approach identifies five fundamental personality dimensions that exert a significant influence on tourism experiences.

The first is openness to experience, defined as a personality trait characterized by curiosity, creativity, and receptivity to novel ideas and experiences. In the context of tourism, Jani, (2014) discovered a positive correlation between openness to experience and using the Internet as a source of information before travel. This suggests that individuals with a high score in this dimension are more inclined to plan and explore various travel options. The second dimension pertains to conscientiousness. This trait is associated with organization, reliability, and self-discipline. Jani et al., (2014) found that individuals who exhibited high conscientiousness sought more information about their destinations and planned their trips with greater thoroughness.

Concerning the third dimension, namely extraversion, individuals exhibiting this trait are sociable, energetic, and assertive. Kim & Stepchenkova, (2017) observed that highly extroverted individuals perceive destinations more positively and seek social experiences when traveling. The fourth dimension pertains to agreeableness, which is defined by traits such as kindness, cooperation, and empathy. Although less studied in the context of tourism, this trait can influence travelers' interactions with locals and their overall satisfaction (Schwartz, 2012). The final dimension relates to neuroticism (or emotional stability). Individuals with high neuroticism scores tend to exhibit greater anxiety and emotional instability (Tešin et al., 2023). This trait has been found to influence memorable tourist experiences negatively.

Figure 1. Big five factors

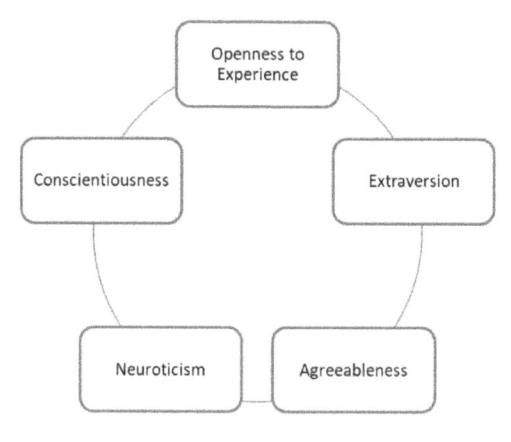

Based on (Alves et al., 2023; Jani, 2014; & Jani et al., 2014)

In addition to the Big Five model, other personality traits have been the subject of investigation within the context of tourism. For instance, sensation-seeking propels some travelers to pursue intense and unconventional experiences. As demonstrated by (Cavusoglu & Avcikurt, 2021), individuals with elevated scores in this domain are more prone to partake in adventurous or risky tourism activities. The allocentric-psychocentric continuum, based on Plog's theory, describes travelers' preferences for familiar or exotic destinations. Those who are allocentric are attracted to adventure and discovering new cultures, whereas those who are psychocentric prefer familiar, comfortable environments. (Bouhtati et al., 2024; Kim et al., 2019) have investigated the influence of these traits on destination choice and travel behavior.

The concept of destination personality, as proposed by Ekinci & Hosany, (2006), is a valuable lens through which to understand how travelers perceive and interact with the places they visit (Hultman et al., 2015) demonstrated that a congruence between the traveler's personality and that of the destination can influence satisfaction and return intentions. A destination may be perceived as adventurous, relaxing, or culturally significant, which can influence the experience.

Understanding travelers' personality traits has significant implications for the tourism industry. This allows marketing professionals to segment their target audience, personalize their offerings, and enhance the overall visitor experience (Buhalis & Law, 2008). Furthermore, the advent of technologies such as virtual reality in the tourism industry has demonstrated that travelers' personalities can influence their adoption and appreciation of these innovations. Quesnel & Riecke, (2018) have investigated the extent to which personality traits can predict experiences of wonder in virtual reality environments. Their findings highlight the importance of considering individual differences when designing technologically enhanced tourism experiences.

The findings of Jani et al., (2014) indicate that personality traits can influence how tourists conduct online research. The study revealed a correlation between the Big Five personality factors and travel curiosity, indicating that certain traits can drive individuals to seek out new information and experiences when planning their trips. Furthermore, the study by Otoo et al., (2021) classified older tourists according to their personality traits, emphasizing the necessity of recognizing the potential for age-related differences in behavior among travelers. In another study, Jeon et al., (2018) investigated the enhancement of visitor flow experiences on destination marketing organization websites through the lens of Plog's personality model. This research underscores the influence of a destination's personality on visitors' overall perceptions and intentions, emphasizing the necessity of aligning marketing strategies with travelers' characteristics.

Technology Driven and Tourism

Tourism Technologies-Driven

The tourism technology-driven has resulted in significant changes, with technological advances being used to enhance customer experiences and streamline operational processes. The advent of artificial intelligence (AI), the Internet of Things (IoT), virtual reality, and mobile applications has precipitated a profound transformation in the manner by which organizations interact with customers and manage destinations (Mazilescu, 2019; Roy & Pagaldiviti, 2023). These technologies facilitate the personalization of services, real-time data analysis, and improved decision-making in the field of tourism (Aliyah et al., 2023). he Internet of Things (IoT) plays a pivotal role in the development of smart tourism destinations (STDs), facilitating the efficient management of experiences (Ordóñez et al., 2022). While AI and IoT present unparalleled opportunities for personalizing recommendations and data collection, several challenges remain, including data security and confidentiality (Aliyah et al., 2023). The incorporation of these technologies enhances the competitiveness of destinations and businesses, which has resulted in the advancement of smart destinations to the benefit of tourists and local residents alike (Ordóñez et al., 2022).

The advent of advanced technologies is effecting a profound transformation of the contemporary travel industry, altering how individuals engage in tourism. Technological solutions in this field encompass a range of digital platforms, software, and hardware, all of which are dedicated to facilitating global travel (Anaya & Lehto, 2020). Such innovations include the advent of online booking engines, travel apps, and virtual reality tools designed to enhance efficiency and convenience for businesses and travelers. In order to enhance the personalization of services, streamline operational procedures, and facilitate a seamless experience for travelers at each stage of their journey, companies are leveraging technology (Ayutthaya & Koomsap, 2018). Advances such as artificial intelligence (AI) and virtual reality (VR) enable travelers to benefit from tailored recommendations and immersive experiences before they depart (Hoang & Trang, 2023). Smart tourism technologies (STT) are transforming visitors' interactions with destinations via IoT devices and augmented reality features (Hien & Trang, 2024). These innovations improve connectivity, boost efficiency, and encourage sustainable practices within the tourism industry.

The smart tourism field is transforming with the integration of IoT devices, as evidenced by a growing body of research (G. Chen, 2022; Pai et al., 2020; Sustacha et al., 2023). The advent of the Internet of Things (IoT) and other intelligent technologies has fundamentally altered how tourists interact with their destinations, facilitating the integration of physical objects and technology (Aliyah et al., 2023).

This has facilitated a more personalized and seamless travel experience for visitors. One of the principal advantages of IoT devices in the context of tourism is the convenience they afford travelers (Almobaideen et al., 2016). These wearable devices, from smartphones to smart wearables, facilitate tourists' access to real-time information about their destinations. They enable them to make reservations, assist in itinerary planning, and facilitate seamless connections with other travelers or tourism professionals (Pai et al., 2020). This real-time access to information and services has significantly transformed how tourists navigate unfamiliar locales, ultimately enhancing their overall experience. Moreover, IoT devices have empowered tourists to engage in interactive experiences across various destinations (Ding & Xu, 2021).

Previous research on technologies in the tourism context has drawn upon several different models and theories. The Technology Acceptance Model (TAM) by Davis, (1989) has been a prominent framework in research on intelligent tourism. It posits that the acceptance of new technologies is contingent on five factors: perceived usefulness, ease of use, trust, attitude, and social implications (Bano & Siddiqui, 2024; El Archi & BENBBA, 2023). TAM has been applied in the context of various technologies, including mobile applications and augmented reality (Hung & Hang, 2020). It has also been used to provide professionals with practical insights to inform the development of strategies for fostering smart tourism technologies (Hien & Trang, 2024). Additionally, other models are employed, including the TPB (Bano & Siddiqui, 2024) and the UTAUT (Y.-C. Huang, 2023) models.

Tourism Destination Technologies-Driven

The use of technology in tourism has been driven by the need to enhance competitiveness, manage experiences, and promote sustainability in the tourism sector (Benbba et al., 2022). The application of intelligent support systems, which utilize big data and the Internet of Things, has facilitated more informed decision-making in the field of destination management (Bouhtati et al., 2023; Mrsic et al., 2020). The implementation of technology-based strategies to enhance the tourism experience through investment in smart cities and digital platforms (Roopchund, 2020). Information and communication technologies (ICTs) are particularly important for urban development, offering opportunities to organize and promote global tourism (Calza et al., 2022). In conclusion, the strategic adoption of technologies in tourism destinations mitigates negative impacts and offers a competitive advantage in an increasingly globalized market (Sustacha et al., 2023).

Smart tourism destinations are influenced by technology in order to enhance the visitor experience and facilitate destination management (Femenia-Serra et al., 2019). The impact of smart technologies on tourism experiences can be observed in two key areas: informativeness and interactivity. To address challenges such as over-tourism, data-driven destination management systems can be implemented using big data and the Internet of Things (IoT) to improve decision-making (Mrsic et al., 2020). In this way, smart technologies have reinvented the post-pandemic tourism sector through destination marketing (Junqueiro et al., 2022). However, further investigation is required to ascertain the effectiveness of smart destination efforts in managerial transformation, marketing, and tourism experiences (Femenia-Serra et al., 2019).

METHODOLOGY

The systematic literature review has become a well-established methodology in the fields of management and the social sciences. It is used to synthesize existing research and identify research (Amjad et al., 2023). The PRISMA (Preferred Reporting Items for Systematic Reviews and Meta-Analyses) protocol is a set of guidelines designed to enhance the transparency and replicability of systematic literature reviews. It involves a structured process for identifying, selecting, and including studies based on pre-established eligibility criteria (Mateo, 2020; Moher et al., 2009; Page et al., 2021). Adherence to this protocol ensures the exhaustive nature of the reviews, thereby minimizing bias and facilitating the replication or extension of the findings by other researchers.

An initial search of titles, keywords, and abstracts in reputable databases, including Scopus, Web of Science, ScienceDirect, Dimensions, and MDPI, was conducted using a search equation that encompassed all relevant keywords related to the topic. This phase yielded a total of 71 references. The corpus was reduced to 53 articles following the established inclusion and exclusion criteria. In particular, the exclusion of duplicates and other types of search, as well as the inclusion of articles available in full text and falling within the domain of commerce, management, tourism, and services, were applied (Peer-reviewed articles undergo critical evaluation by experts in the field, which adds credibility to the findings). A review of the titles, abstracts, and keywords allowed us to identify 25 articles that were deemed relevant for inclusion in this study. In order to maximize the yield of the systematic literature review, we employed the snowball effect, whereby an additional nine references cited by the articles under review were included, resulting in a final corpus of 34 articles (Wohlin, 2014).

Figure 2. Summary of SLR methodology

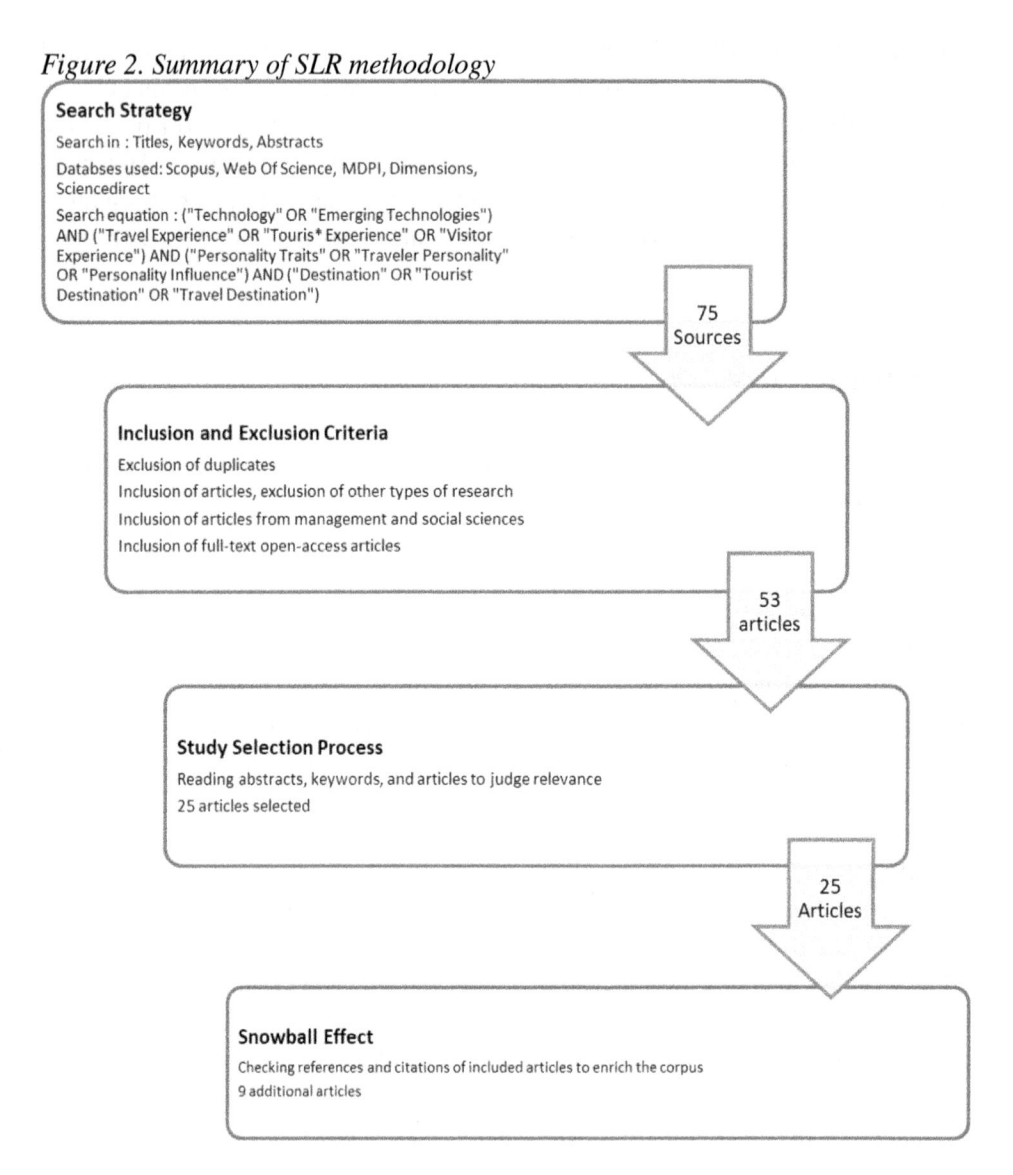

Search Strategy

Search in : Titles, Keywords, Abstracts

Databses used: Scopus, Web Of Science, MDPI, Dimensions, Sciencedirect

Search equation : ("Technology" OR "Emerging Technologies") AND ("Travel Experience" OR "Touris* Experience" OR "Visitor Experience") AND ("Personality Traits" OR "Traveler Personality" OR "Personality Influence") AND ("Destination" OR "Tourist Destination" OR "Travel Destination")

⬇ 75 Sources

Inclusion and Exclusion Criteria

Exclusion of duplicates

Inclusion of articles, exclusion of other types of research

Inclusion of articles from management and social sciences

Inclusion of full-text open-access articles

⬇ 53 articles

Study Selection Process

Reading abstracts, keywords, and articles to judge relevance

25 articles selected

⬇ 25 Articles

Snowball Effect

Checking references and citations of included articles to enrich the corpus

9 additional articles

(Author's own creation)

RESULTS

Descriptive Analysis

This section presents a descriptive analysis of our corpus to identify insights and research trends on the relationship between personality and technology and their impact on the travel experience in a tourist destination. This analysis encompasses the distribution of articles included in our literature review according to year of publication, source, database, and methodological approach. The objective is to gain a comprehensive understanding of the extent and depth of research in this field and to examine various perspectives.

As illustrated in Figure 3, the distribution of references by year of publication reveals a growing interest in the subject over recent years. Four articles were published in 2024, while two, three, and four articles were published in 2023, 2022, and 2020, respectively. Additionally, there are three references for 2015, 2019, and 2021. Subsequently, there are two references each for 2014, 2017, and 2018. The remaining three contributions are distributed across the years 2003, 2012, and 2013.

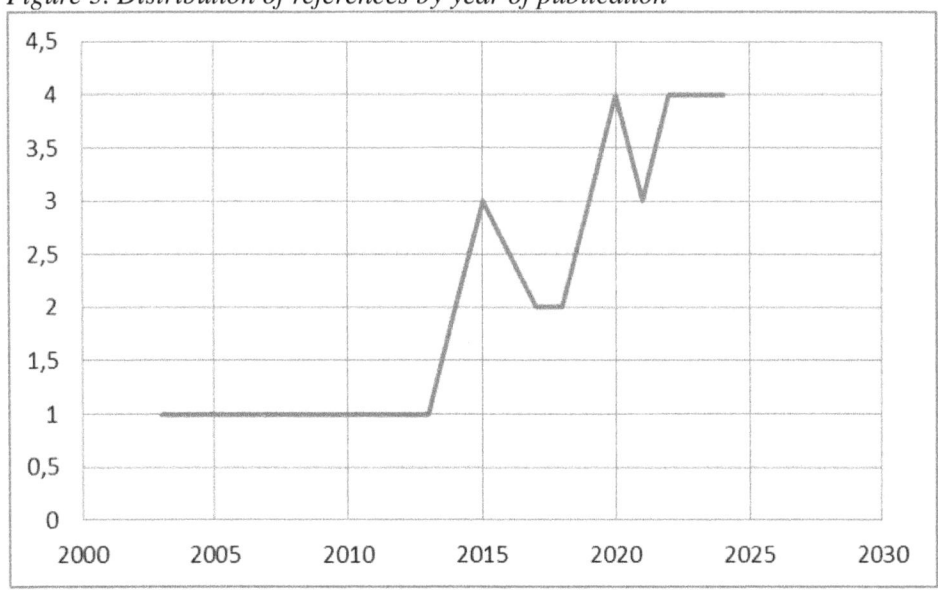

Figure 3. Distribution of references by year of publication

(Author's own creation)

The 34 articles are distributed across 23 sources, with the majority of sources specializing in tourism and management. The "International Journal of Economics and Management" is the most frequently cited source, with four publications. The "Journal of Business Research" is the second most frequently cited source, with three references. The remaining sources are listed in the following table.

Table 1. Distribution by sources

Publication Title	Number of corresponding resources
International Journal of Economics and Management	4
Journal of Business Research	3
Asia Pacific Journal of Tourism Research	2
Computers in Human Behavior	2
Journal of Hospitality and Tourism Management	2
Journal of Travel & Tourism Marketing	2
Journal of Travel Research	2
Journal of Vacation Marketing	2
Anatolia	1
Cogent Business & Management	1
Contemporary economics	1
Current Issues in Tourism	1
Expert Systems with Applications	1
FRONTIERS IN PSYCHOLOGY	1
Information Technology & Tourism	1
Journal for Nature Conservation	1
Journal of Destination Marketing & Management	1
Leisure/Loisir	1
Social and Management Research Journal (SMRJ)	1
Sustainability	1
Tourism Management	1
Tourism Management Perspectives	1
User Modeling and User-Adapted Interaction	1
Total	34

Source: Author's own creation

The majority of quality references are indexed in reputable databases. Our corpus includes 20 articles from Scopus, 11 from Sciencedirect, 2 from Web Of Science, and a single publication from MDPI (Figure 4).

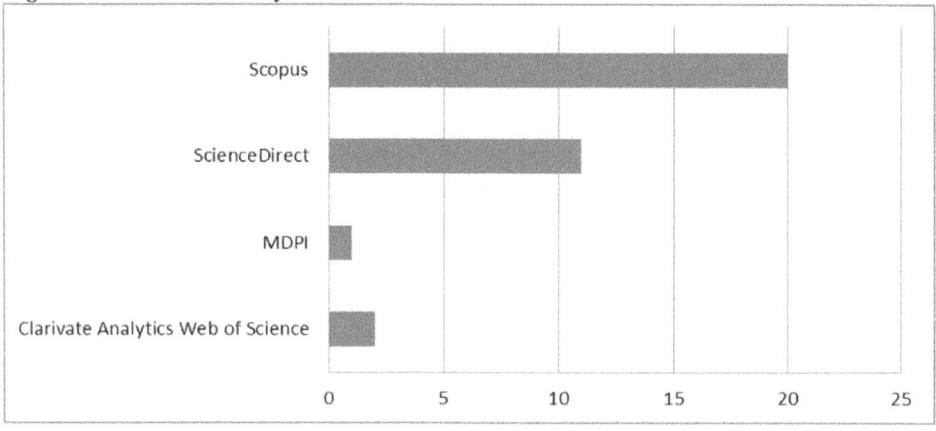

Figure 4. Distribution by database

(Author's own creation)

The corpus includes a variety of methodological approaches, comprising 12 qualitative studies, 13 quantitative studies, and 9 studies employing a mixed-method approach. This variety helps illustrate the multifaceted nature of research into the travel experience as it relates to personality and technology.

Figure 5. Distribution by methodological approach

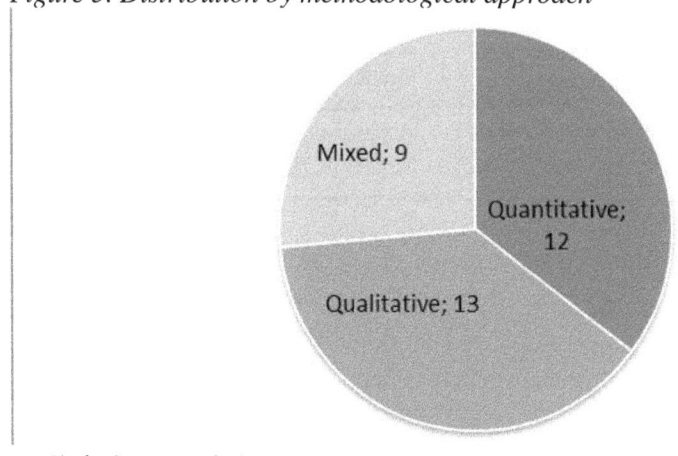

(Author's own creation)

The data set comprises a comprehensive and diverse array of documents spanning multiple years, and a range of methodological approaches are employed to enhance the depth and breadth of research perspectives in this field.

Qualitative Analysis

This section presents a qualitative analysis of the impact of personality and technology on the travel experience in a tourist destination. The analysis begins by examining the relationship between technology and the travel experience (Table 2), followed by investigating the impact of personality traits on the travel experience (Table 3), and finally, the analysis investigates the relationship between technology and personality (Table 4).

Table 2. Technology on travel experience

Authors	Objective	Main results
Wang et al. (2016)	A Conceptual framework for the technological preparation of travelers in the context of tourist satisfaction.	• Travelers' perceived quality of technology-based services positively impacts their satisfaction and future behavioral intentions.
Oncioiu & Priescu (2022), and YiFei & Othman (2024)	Identify the role of virtual reality (VR) in the selection of a tourist destination.	• VR offers an immersive experience in a digital environment as an alternative to physical travel, particularly in the context of pandemics. This enriches the tourist experience by increasing the perception of tourist destinations. • VR is influencing communication needs, modes, and contexts as an essential tool for tourism professionals, offering memorable experiences. • Immersive content influences emotional engagement and tourist response.
Mohamad et al. (2022)	Examining the influence of experiences shared on social networks and subjective norms on tourists' decision to choose a destination through the adoption of TPBs	• Sharing experiences on social networks significantly influences tourists' behavioral intention to visit a destination. • Subjective standards influence tourists' attitudes, behavior, and decisions.

Source: Author's own creation

Table 3. Impact of personality traits on travel experience

Authors	Objective	Key findings
Wang et al. (2016)	Evaluation of the link between eWOM and the 5 personality traits with the intention of choosing a tourist destination using the Information Adoption Model (IAM)	• The credibility and quality of information influence the perception of its usefulness, which impacts the adoption of information and the intention to choose a tourist destination. • eWOM has a significant influence on the choice of travel destination. • Extroverted, agreeable, and imaginative people use eWOM to make decisions, while conscious and nervous people do not.
Tan & Tang (2013)	examine the influence of personality traits on tourist information-seeking behavior and post-trip feedback channels	• Individuals with openness to experience prefer personal experiences, WOM, and other sources of tourist information • Conscientious individuals prefer on-site sources, especially site visitors. • Agreeable individuals are positively influenced by information sources and feedback channels. • Extraversion and Neuroticism are negatively influenced by the perception of others as a source of anticipation. • Traditional (face-to-face) WOM is perceived as more useful than eWOM and other sources of tourist information. However, online WOM is preferred for post-trip feedback due to its wider reach, which is a dynamic worth noting.
Tan (2020)	Examine how temporal distance and personality traits influence the perception of travel constraints	• Conscientious, safety-conscious individuals perceive safety-related constraints and lack of interest more strongly. • Agreeable individuals who value trust and compliance perceive safety constraints more strongly. • Open-minded individuals are less constrained by a lack of interest, time, and money.
Otoo et al. (2021)	Classification of personality traits of seniors according to their motivations, preferences, and travel characteristics	• American seniors can be divided into three main tourist typologies: psychocentric, midcentric, and allocentric. • Unlike Americans, Chinese seniors are mainly psychocentric and midcentric, which indicates they are less open to long, adventurous journeys and cultural exchanges. • Senior women are predominantly associated with psychocentric traits, suggesting risk aversion.

Source: Author's own creation

Table 4. Interaction between technology and personality traits

Auteurs	Objective	Key findings
Wang et al. (2016)	Proposal for a conceptual framework on the technological preparation of travelers in the context of tourist satisfaction	• Personal orientation toward technology does not influence how travelers evaluate the quality of TES. • Bad experiences due to technical failures result in low satisfaction, whatever the traveler's attitude. • Technology-based services minimize anxiety, optimize utility, and reduce security • Differences were observed between traveler behavior • Optimism and innovation positively influence the relationship between satisfaction with technology-based services, satisfaction in general, and satisfaction and behavior.
Oliveira et al. (2020)	Examine the motivations and disincentives that influence travelers to share their experiences on social networks.	• The main reasons travelers share their experiences on social networks are perceived pleasure and self-fulfillment. • Lurker's behavior is influenced by security and privacy concerns.
Alves et al. (2023)	Establish a link between tourists' personalities and travel preferences by proposing solutions to improve recommendation systems in the tourism sector.	• Recommendation systems that incorporate personality dimensions, such as the Big Five, can better respond to the varied preferences of group members.

Source: Author's own creation

DISCUSSION AND FUTURE RESEARCH DIRECTIONS

Discussion

The findings of this literature review indicate that technology and personality traits have a significant influence on the traveler experience. Technological advances, including virtual reality, social media, and recommendation systems, have the potential to positively impact tourist perception and behavior. Importantly, travelers' personality traits play a key role in shaping their unique perceptions and travel preferences. The interaction between technology and personality traits underscores the need for a personalized tourism marketing and services approach.

The results indicate that the perception of the quality of technology-based services exerts a considerable influence on tourist satisfaction and their future behavioral intention toward tourist destinations. This is mainly the case when the focus is on the need to invest in advanced technology solutions to enhance the travel experience (Wang et al., 2016). Virtual reality has emerged as a powerful tool in the field of tourism, particularly during the global pandemic caused by the covid 19 (Oncioiu & Priescu, 2022; YiFei & Othman, 2024). Several studies have demonstrated that virtual reality (VR) experiences can benefit tourist relationship management processes and the intention to visit a tourist destination (Leung et al., 2023). Virtual reality (VR) provides an immersive digital experience as an alternative to physical travel experiences during health crises (Godovykh et al., 2022). Virtual reality (VR) is an indispensable tool for tourism professionals, enabling them to enhance the customer experience, influence emotional engagement, and shape perceptions of destinations (Oncioiu & Priescu, 2022). Several studies have demonstrated the considerable influence of social networks on tourist behavioral intention and destination choice (Mohamad et al., 2022). Social media platforms allow travelers to search for information, select destinations, and share experiences (Kasim et al., 2019). User-generated content, peer recommendations, and updates on social networks facilitate informed decision-making and diverse travel experiences (Javed et al., 2020).

The role of electronic word-of-mouth (eWOM) in travel destination choice and purchase intention has been highlighted by numerous researchers (Nechoud et al., 2021; Tapanainen et al., 2021; Wang et al., 2016). The credibility and quality of eWOM affect the adoption of information and the intention to visit a destination (González-Rodríguez et al., 2022). Personality traits have been identified as playing an essential role in the use of eWOM and the perception of travel constraints (Otoo et al., 2021; Tan, 2020; Tan & Tang, 2013; Wang et al., 2016). Individuals who are extroverted, agreeable, and imaginative are more likely to adopt eWOM information in order to make decisions (Wang et al., 2016). The information adoption model has been validated to predict behavioral intention for tourist destinations (Tapanainen et al., 2021). Motivations, preferences, and decisions are inextricably linked to personality traits, which are further influenced by demographic particularities such as the personalities of seniors and women and ethnicities (Otoo et al., 2021). These findings underscore the significance of eWOM in tourism marketing strategies and consumer decision-making processes.

A review of the literature on the use of technology-based services in the tourism industry reveals a complex and multifaceted relationship between technology readiness, innovation, optimism, perceived service quality, and consumer satisfaction (Wang et al., 2016). In the context of tourism, technology-based services serve to mitigate anxiety, enhance utility, and mitigate safety concerns (Pradhan et al., 2018). Travelers disseminate their experiences on social networks for perceived pleasure, altruistic motivations, personal satisfaction, and self-actualization (Oliveira et al., 2020). Additionally, expected performance, hedonic motivations, and habits have been identified as significant predictors of users' intentions to share their travel experiences on social networks (Crespo et al., 2017). Nevertheless, concerns about privacy and time constraints act as disincentives to engaging and sharing travel experiences online, particularly among those who observe but do not actively participate (Oliveira et al., 2020). The following figure presents a conceptual model that examines the impact of technology and personality traits on the travel experience.

Figure 6. Illustrative analysis model

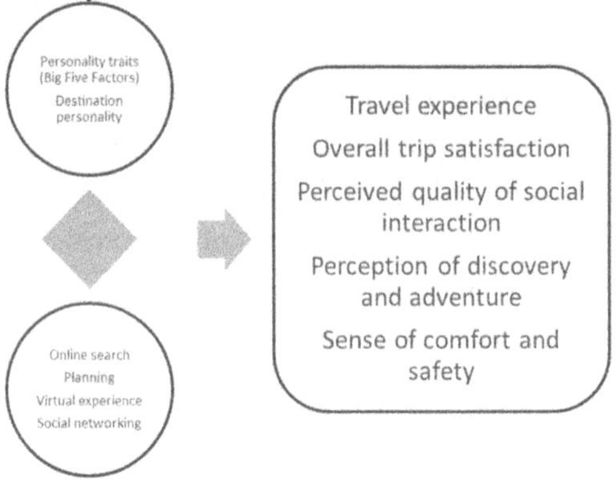

(Author's own creation)

Future Research Directions

Following a comprehensive examination of the interrelationship between driven technology and personality traits, on the one hand, and the travel experience, on the other, it is evident that a concentrated effort is required to identify and prioritize future research avenues and directions. This will ensure that future research is focused on addressing the most pressing issues and expanding the boundaries of our topic. It is crucial to acknowledge the significance of technology in the co-creation of tourism experiences. This can be achieved by conducting comprehensive empirical tests that consider the distinctive characteristics of destination personality and travelers' personality traits. Table 5 provides a summary of the principal avenues for future research on the enhancement of travel experiences through the integration of technology-driven and destination personality.

Table 5. Mains future research directions

Authors	Mains Future Research Directions
Neuhofer et al. (2014)	• Empirically exploring the impact of technology on the tourism experience • Creating tourism experiences based on co-creation and the intensity of technological implementation
Hultman et al. (2015)	• Analyze the relationships between destination personality, tourist satisfaction, and tourist identification with the destination • Examining the impact of electronic word-of-mouth (eWOM) on tourists' future intentions to revisit a destination
Mariani et al. (2023)	• Analysis of AI-powered chatbots and virtual assistants in the tourism sector
Jani et al. (2014)	• Examination of personality traits (Big Five Factor theory) and the use of information on Internet search behavior for travel planning

Source: Author's own creation

CONCLUSION

This literature review elucidates the intricate interrelationship between nascent technologies, personality traits, and the travel experience in a destination context. It demonstrates the potential of technologies such as virtual reality to alter the tourism experience markedly. Nevertheless, it is of the utmost importance to take into account travelers' distinctive personality traits when developing and implementing these technologies. Indeed, personality traits exert a profound influence on the perception and utilization of technologies, as well as on satisfaction and the travel experience.

The findings from this study carry significant practical implications for professionals in the tourism industry. With a comprehensive understanding of how travelers' personality traits interact with technology, tourism organizations can customize their offerings to better align with customer expectations and preferences. For instance, travelers who are open to new experiences may be more open to augmented reality and virtual reality tools for trip planning. Moreover, the adoption of technologies enables the creation of personalized experiences to cater to the specific needs of different customer segments, thereby boosting customer satisfaction and loyalty.

As with all research, this review is subject to certain limitations. Firstly, many studies have examined personality trait factors in tourism, with notable methodological and contextual variability. This limits the generalizability of the findings. Most research is focused on specific technologies, such as virtual reality, and there is a need for greater attention to be paid to other technologies. Ultimately, most studies have focused on immediate effects, and there is a clear need for longitudinal approaches to study the long-term impact of intensive technology use on the travel experience.

Future research directions can be pursued along multiple avenues. The potential for advanced technologies such as AR, VR, and AI to interact with different personality traits to enhance the visitor experience should be explored. A longitudinal study is needed to assess the long-term impact of intensive use on the authenticity of the travel experience. Furthermore, it would be beneficial to investigate the ability of technologies to facilitate the creation and personalization of experiences based on the specific characteristics of a given destination. Lastly, a theoretical model should be developed that integrates travelers' personality traits, destination characteristics, and the benefits of technologies to predict and enhance the travel experience.

In conclusion, this literature review provides an overview of the current state of research into the interaction between technology, traveler personality, and experience within destinations and suggests promising avenues for future research. By integrating these perspectives, future research can benefit from a deeper understanding of the possibilities for improving the travel experience in the context of emerging technologies.

REFERENCES

Aarabe, M., Khizzou, N. B., Alla, L., & Benjelloun, A. (2024a). Marketing Applications of Emerging Technologies : A Systematic Literature Review. In *AI and Data Engineering Solutions for Effective Marketing* (p. 23-47). IGI Global. DOI: 10.4018/979-8-3693-3172-9.ch002

Aarabe, M., Khizzou, N. B., Alla, L., & Benjelloun, A. (2024b). Smart Tourism Experience and Responsible Travelers' Behavior : A Systematic Literature Review. In *Promoting Responsible Tourism With Digital Platforms* (p. 128-147). IGI Global. DOI: 10.4018/979-8-3693-3286-3.ch008

Aliyah, L., Lukita, C., Pangilinan, G., Chakim, M., & Saputra, D. (2023). Examining the impact of artificial intelligence and internet of things on smart tourism destinations : A comprehensive study. *Aptisi Transactions on Technopreneurship*, 5(2sp), 135–145. DOI: 10.34306/att.v5i2sp.332

Alla, L., Bentalha, B., & Elyoussfi, A. (2023). Intelligence territoriale et positionnement stratégique des regions au Maroc : Le cas de la région de Fès Meknes en perspective. *Le concept de l'intéligence en sciences juridiques, économiques et sociales*, 215-237.

Almobaideen, W., Allan, M., & Saadeh, M. (2016). Smart archaeological tourism : Contention, convenience and accessibility in the context of cloud-centric IoT. *Mediterranean Archaeology & Archaeometry. International Journal*, 16(1), 227–227.

Alves, P., Martins, H., Saraiva, P., Carneiro, J., Novais, P., & Marreiros, G. (2022). Group Recommender Systems for Tourism : How does Personality predicts Preferences for Attractions, Travel Motivations, Preferences and Concerns? DOI: 10.21203/rs.3.rs-1762820/v1

Alves, P., Martins, H., Saraiva, P., Carneiro, J., Novais, P., & Marreiros, G. (2023). Group recommender systems for tourism : How does personality predict preferences for attractions, travel motivations, preferences and concerns? *User Modeling and User-Adapted Interaction*, 33(5), 1141–1210. DOI: 10.1007/s11257-023-09361-2 PMID: 37359944

Amjad, A., Kordel, P., & Fernandes, G. (2023). The systematic review in the field of management sciences. *Zeszyty Naukowe. Organizacja i Zarządzanie/Politechnika Śląska*. https://yadda.icm.edu.pl/baztech/element/bwmeta1.element.baztech-12a05f97-6339-4215-a0a7-cb6e0963c108

Anaya, G. J., & Lehto, X. (2020). Traveler-facing technology in the tourism experience : A historical perspective. *Journal of Travel & Tourism Marketing*, 37(3), 317–331. DOI: 10.1080/10548408.2020.1757561

Ayutthaya, D. H. N., & Koomsap, P. (2018). Embedding Memorable Experience to Customer Journey. In Moon, I., Lee, G. M., Park, J., Kiritsis, D., & VonCieminski, G. (Eds.), *Advances in Production Management Systems: Production Management for Data-driven, Intelligent, Collaborative, and Sustainable Manufacturing, APMS 2018* (Vol. 535, pp. 222–229). Springer-Verlag Berlin., DOI: 10.1007/978-3-319-99704-9_27

Bano, N., & Siddiqui, S. (2024). Consumers' intention towards the use of smart technologies in tourism and hospitality (T&H) industry : A deeper insight into the integration of TAM, TPB and trust. *Journal of Hospitality and Tourism Insights*, 7(3), 1412–1434. DOI: 10.1108/JHTI-06-2022-0267

Benbba, B., Ismaili, F. E. A., & Archi, Y. E. (2022). Smart tourism destination et développement durable : Quels apports à l'expérience touristique? *Alternatives Managériales Economiques,* 4(0), Article 0. DOI: 10.48374/IMIST.PRSM/ame-v1i0.36926

Boudri, R., Bentalha, B., & Benjelloun, O. (2024). Phygital Marketing and the Pain of Paying : An Amazon Go Netnographic Case Study. In *AI and Data Engineering Solutions for Effective Marketing* (p. 348-363). IGI Global. https://www.igi-global.com/chapter/phygital-marketing-and-the-pain-of-paying/350762

Bouhtati, N., Alla, L., & Bentalha, B. (2023). Marketing Big Data Analytics and Customer Relationship Management : A Fuzzy Approach. In *Integrating Intelligence and Sustainability in Supply Chains* (p. 75-86). IGI Global. https://www.igi-global.com/chapter/marketing-big-data-analytics-and-customer-relationship-management/331980

Bouhtati, N., Alla, L., & Ed-Daakouri, I. (2024). Smart Data Analysis and Prediction of Responsible Customer Behaviour in Tourism : An Exploratory Review of the Literature. *Promoting Responsible Tourism With Digital Platforms*, 189-212.

Buhalis, D. (2019). Technology in tourism-from information communication technologies to eTourism and smart tourism towards ambient intelligence tourism : A perspective article. *Tourism Review*, 75(1), 267–272. DOI: 10.1108/TR-06-2019-0258

Buhalis, D., & Law, R. (2008). Progress in information technology and tourism management : 20 years on and 10 years after the Internet—The state of eTourism research. *Tourism Management*, 29(4), 609–623. DOI: 10.1016/j.tourman.2008.01.005

Calisto, M. de L., & Sarkar, S. (2024). A systematic review of virtual reality in tourism and hospitality : The known and the paths to follow. *International Journal of Hospitality Management*, 116, 103623. DOI: 10.1016/j.ijhm.2023.103623

Calza, F., Trunfio, M., Pasquinelli, C., Sorrentino, A., Campana, S., & Rossi, S. (2022). *Technology-driven innovation. Exploiting ICTs tools for digital engagement, smart experiences, and sustainability in tourism destinations*. SLIOB. Enzo Albano Edizioni Naples. https://www.disaq.uniparthenope.it/wp-content/uploads/2022/02/Technology-driven-innovation-Exploiting-ICTs-tools-for-digital-engagement-smart-experiences-and-sustainability-in-tourism-destinations.pdf

Cavusoglu, F., & Avcikurt, C. (2021). *The Relationship between Personal Traits, Travel Motivation, Perceived Value and Behavioural Intention of Tourists Participating in Adventure Activities.* DOI: 10.5281/ZENODO.5831677

Cetin, G., & Bilgihan, A. (2016). Components of cultural tourists' experiences in destinations. *Current Issues in Tourism*, 19(2), 137–154. DOI: 10.1080/13683500.2014.994595

Chen, G. (2022). Tourism Management Strategies under the Intelligent Tourism IoT Service Platform. *Computational Intelligence and Neuroscience*, 7750098, 1–11. Advance online publication. DOI: 10.1155/2022/7750098 PMID: 35463292

Chen, Y., Wang, X., Le, B., & Wang, L. (2024). Why people use augmented reality in heritage museums : A socio-technical perspective. *Heritage Science*, 12(1), 108. DOI: 10.1186/s40494-024-01217-1

Chen, Z., & Fu, S. (2023). Research on the Evaluation of the Effect of Tourism Revitalization of Intangible Cultural Heritage in China in the Context of New Media. *Applied Mathematics and Nonlinear Sciences*, 9(1), 20230518. DOI: 10.2478/amns.2023.2.00518

Cuomo, M. T., Tortora, D., Foroudi, P., Giordano, A., Festa, G., & Metallo, G. (2021). Digital transformation and tourist experience co-design : Big social data for planning cultural tourism. *Technological Forecasting and Social Change*, 162, 120345. DOI: 10.1016/j.techfore.2020.120345

da Costa Mendes, J., Oom do Valle, P., Guerreiro, M. M., & Silva, J. A. (2010). The tourist experience : Exploring the relationship between tourist satisfaction and destination loyalty. *Tourism: An International Interdisciplinary Journal*, 58(2), 111–126.

Dagustani, D., Kartini, D., Oesman, Y. M., & Kaltum, U. (2018). Destination Image of Tourist : Effect of Travel Motivation and Memorable Tourism Experience. *ETIKONOMI*, 17(2), 307–318. DOI: 10.15408/etk.v17i2.7211

Davis, F. D. (1989). Technology acceptance model : TAM. *Al-Suqri, MN, Al-Aufi, AS. Information Seeking Behavior and Technology Adoption*, 205, 219.

Ding, M., & Xu, Y. (2021). Real-Time Wireless Sensor Network-Assisted Smart Tourism Environment Suitability Assessment for Tourism IoT. *Journal of Sensors*, 2021(1), 8123014. DOI: 10.1155/2021/8123014

Ekinci, Y., & Hosany, S. (2006). Destination Personality : An Application of Brand Personality to Tourism Destinations. *Journal of Travel Research*, 45(2), 127–139. DOI: 10.1177/0047287506291603

El Archi, Y., & Benbba, B. (2023). The Applications of Technology Acceptance Models in Tourism and Hospitality Research : A Systematic Literature Review. *Journal of Environmental Management and Tourism*, 14(2), 379. DOI: 10.14505/jemt.v14.2(66).08

EL JAOUHARI, S., & Lhoussaine, A. (2022). L'approche territoriale et la gestion de l'impact de la pandémie de Covid-19 : Cas des collectivités territoriales. *Alternatives Managériales Economiques*, 4(1), 245–265.

Erdem, A., & Şeker, F. (2022). Tourist experience and digital transformation. In *Handbook of research on digital communications, Internet of Things, and the future of cultural tourism* (pp. 103–120). IGI Global., https://www.igi-global.com/chapter/tourist-experience-and-digital-transformation/295499 DOI: 10.4018/978-1-7998-8528-3.ch006

Femenia-Serra, F., Perles-Ribes, J. F., & Ivars-Baidal, J. A. (2019). Smart destinations and tech-savvy millennial tourists : Hype versus reality. *Tourism Review*, 74(1), 63–81. DOI: 10.1108/TR-02-2018-0018

García-Milon, A., Juaneda-Ayensa, E., Olarte-Pascual, C., & Pelegrín-Borondo, J. (2020). Towards the smart tourism destination : Key factors in information source use on the tourist shopping journey. *Tourism Management Perspectives*, 36, 100730. DOI: 10.1016/j.tmp.2020.100730 PMID: 32834961

Godovykh, M., Baker, C., & Fyall, A. (2022). VR in tourism : A new call for virtual tourism experience amid and after the COVID-19 pandemic. *Tourism and Hospitality*, 3(1), 265–275. DOI: 10.3390/tourhosp3010018

González-Rodríguez, M. R., Díaz-Fernández, M. C., Bilgihan, A., Okumus, F., & Shi, F. (2022). The impact of eWOM source credibility on destination visit intention and online involvement : A case of Chinese tourists. *Journal of Hospitality and Tourism Technology*, 13(5), 855–874. DOI: 10.1108/JHTT-11-2021-0321

Goo, J., Huang, C. D., Yoo, C. W., & Koo, C. (2022). Smart Tourism Technologies' Ambidexterity : Balancing Tourist's Worries and Novelty Seeking for Travel Satisfaction. *Information Systems Frontiers*, 24(6), 2139–2158. DOI: 10.1007/s10796-021-10233-6 PMID: 35103046

Herrero Crespo, A., San Martín Gutiérrez, H., & García de los Salmones, M. del M. (2017). *Explaining the adoption of social networks sites for sharing user-generated content : A revision of the UTAUT2*. https://repositorio.unican.es/xmlui/handle/10902/12845

Hien, H. N., & Trang, P. H. (2024). Decoding smart tech's influence on tourist experience quality. *Asian Journal of Business Research Volume, 14*(1). https://ajbr.co.nz/ajbr/ajbr240167.pdf

Hmioui, A., Alla, L., & Bentalha, B. (2017). *Piloting territorial tourism in Morocco Proposal for a tourism index for the destination Fez [Pilotage de la touristicité territoriale au Maroc Proposition d'un indice de touriscticité pour la destination Fès]*. https://ideas.repec.org/p/hal/journl/hal-02334913.html

Hoang, H., & Trang, P. H. (2023). Navigating the Rise of Smart Tourism : Implications of Technology and Data for Sustainable Industry Growth. *Brawijaya Journal of Social Science*, 3(1), 1. Advance online publication. DOI: 10.21776/ub.bjss.2023.003.01.1

Huang, C. D., Goo, J., Nam, K., & Yoo, C. W. (2017). Smart tourism technologies in travel planning : The role of exploration and exploitation. *Information & Management*, 54(6), 757–770. DOI: 10.1016/j.im.2016.11.010

Huang, Y.-C. (2023). Integrated concepts of the UTAUT and TPB in virtual reality behavioral intention. *Journal of Retailing and Consumer Services*, 70, 103127. DOI: 10.1016/j.jretconser.2022.103127

Hultman, M., Skarmeas, D., Oghazi, P., & Beheshti, H. M. (2015). Achieving tourist loyalty through destination personality, satisfaction, and identification. *Journal of Business Research*, 68(11), 2227–2231. DOI: 10.1016/j.jbusres.2015.06.002

Hung, N. T., & Hang, V. T. T. (2020). A studying on factors affecting decision to use smart tourism applications using extended TAM. *WSEAS Transactions on Business and Economics*, 17, 288–299. DOI: 10.37394/23207.2020.17.30

Jani, D. (2014). Big five personality factors and travel curiosity : Are they related? *Anatolia*, 25(3), 444–456. DOI: 10.1080/13032917.2014.909366

Jani, D., Jang, J.-H., & Hwang, Y.-H. (2014). Big Five Factors of Personality and Tourists' Internet Search Behavior. *Asia Pacific Journal of Tourism Research*, 19(5), 600–615. DOI: 10.1080/10941665.2013.773922

Javed, M., Tučková, Z., & Jibril, A. B. (2020). The role of social media on tourists' behavior : An empirical analysis of millennials from the Czech Republic. *Sustainability (Basel)*, 12(18), 7735. DOI: 10.3390/su12187735

Jeon, H., Ok, C. M., & Choi, J. (2018). Destination marketing organization website visitors' flow experience : An application of Plog's model of personality. *Journal of Travel & Tourism Marketing*, 35(4), 397–409. DOI: 10.1080/10548408.2017.1358234

Jovanović, T., Božić, S., Bodroža, B., & Stankov, U. (2019). Influence of users' psychosocial traits on Facebook travel–related behavior patterns. *Journal of Vacation Marketing*, 25(2), 252–263. DOI: 10.1177/1356766718771420

Junqueiro, Â., Correia, R., Carvalho, A., & Cunha, C. R. (2022). Smart Technologies in Tourist Destination Marketing : A Literature Review. In T. Guarda, F. Portela, & M. F. Augusto (Éds.), *Advanced Research in Technologies, Information, Innovation and Sustainability* (Vol. 1676, p. 283-293). Springer Nature Switzerland. DOI: 10.1007/978-3-031-20316-9_22

Kasim, H., Abdurachman, E., Furinto, A., & Kosasih, W. (2019). Social network for the choice of tourist destination : Attitude and behavioral intention. *Management Science Letters*, 9(13), 2415–2420. DOI: 10.5267/j.msl.2019.7.014

Kim, H., & Stepchenkova, S. (2017). Understanding destination personality through visitors' experience : A cross-cultural perspective. *Journal of Destination Marketing & Management*, 6(4), 416–425. DOI: 10.1016/j.jdmm.2016.06.010

Kim, H., Yilmaz, S., & Choe, Y. (2019). Traveling to your match? Assessing the predictive potential of Plog's travel personality in destination marketing. *Journal of Travel & Tourism Marketing*, 36(9), 1025–1036. DOI: 10.1080/10548408.2019.1683485

Leiras, A., & Eusébio, C. (2024). Perceived image of accessible tourism destinations : A data mining analysis of Google Maps reviews. *Current Issues in Tourism*, 27(16), 2584–2602. DOI: 10.1080/13683500.2023.2230338

Leung, W. K., Chang, M. K., Cheung, M. L., & Shi, S. (2023). VR tourism experiences and tourist behavior intention in COVID-19 : An experience economy and mood management perspective. *Information Technology & People*, 36(3), 1095–1125. DOI: 10.1108/ITP-06-2021-0423

Mariani, M. M., Hashemi, N., & Wirtz, J. (2023). Artificial intelligence empowered conversational agents : A systematic literature review and research agenda. *Journal of Business Research*, 161, 113838. DOI: 10.1016/j.jbusres.2023.113838

Mateo, S. (2020). Procédure pour conduire avec succès une revue de littérature selon la méthode PRISMA. *Kinésithérapie, la Revue*, 20(226), 29–37. DOI: 10.1016/j.kine.2020.05.019

Mazilescu, V. (2019). Tourism and travel can effectively benefit from technologies associated with Industry 4.0. *XXth International Conference "Risk in Contemporary Economy*. https://scholar.archive.org/work/7yqickbjhrchvp7jygzgy4kxai/access/wayback/http://www.rce.feaa.ugal.ro/images/stories/RCE2019/Mazilescu.pdf

Mohamad, N., Tan, V., & Tan, P. P. (2022). Travel experience on social media : The impact towards tourist destination choice. [SMRJ]. *Social and Management Research Journal*, 19(2), 21–52. DOI: 10.24191/smrj.v19i2.19253

Moher, D., Liberati, A., Tetzlaff, J., & Altman, D. G.The PRISMA Group. (2009). Preferred Reporting Items for Systematic Reviews and Meta-Analyses : The PRISMA Statement. *PLoS Medicine*, 6(7), e1000097. DOI: 10.1371/journal.pmed.1000097 PMID: 19621072

Mrsic, L., Surla, G., & Balkovic, M. (2020). Technology-Driven Smart Support System for Tourist Destination Management Organizations. In A. Khanna, D. Gupta, S. Bhattacharyya, V. Snasel, J. Platos, & A. E. Hassanien (Éds.), *International Conference on Innovative Computing and Communications* (Vol. 1087, p. 65-76). Springer Singapore. DOI: 10.1007/978-981-15-1286-5_7

Nechoud, L., Ghidouche, F., & Seraphin, H. (2021). The influence of eWOM credibility on visit intention : An integrative moderated mediation model. *Journal of Tourism* [JTHSM]. *Heritage & Services Marketing*, 7(1), 54–63.

Neuhofer, B., Buhalis, D., & Ladkin, A. (2014). A Typology of Technology-Enhanced Tourism Experiences. *International Journal of Tourism Research*, 16(4), 340–350. DOI: 10.1002/jtr.1958

Nouhaila, B. K., Aarabe, M., & Alla, L. (2024). The Impact of Digitalisation on the Customer Experience in Medical Tourism : A Systematic Review. In *Impact of AI and Tech-Driven Solutions in Hospitality and Tourism* (pp. 408–428). IGI Global., DOI: 10.4018/979-8-3693-6755-1.ch020

Oliveira, T., Araujo, B., & Tam, C. (2020). Why do people share their travel experiences on social media? *Tourism Management*, 78, 104041. DOI: 10.1016/j.tourman.2019.104041 PMID: 32322615

Oncioiu, I., & Priescu, I. (2022). The Use of Virtual Reality in Tourism Destinations as a Tool to Develop Tourist Behavior Perspective. *Sustainability (Basel)*, 14(7), 4191. DOI: 10.3390/su14074191

Ordóñez, M. D., Gómez, A., Ruiz, M., Ortells, J. M., Niemi-Hugaerts, H., Juiz, C., Jara, A., & Butler, T. A. (2022). IoT technologies and applications in tourism and travel industries. In *Internet of Things–The call of the edge* (pp. 341–360). River publishers., https://www.taylorfrancis.com/chapters/oa-edit/10.1201/9781003338611-8/iot-technologies-applications-tourism-travel-industries-dolores-ord%C3%B3%C3%B1ez-andrea-g%C3%B3mez-maurici-ruiz-juan-manuel-ortells-hanna-niemi-hugaerts-carlos-juiz-antonio-jara-tayrne-alexandra-butler DOI: 10.1201/9781003338611-8

Otoo, F. E., Kim, S., Agrusa, J., & Lema, J. (2021). Classification of senior tourists according to personality traits. *Asia Pacific Journal of Tourism Research*, 26(5), 539–556. DOI: 10.1080/10941665.2021.1876118

Page, M. J., McKenzie, J. E., Bossuyt, P. M., Boutron, I., Hoffmann, T. C., Mulrow, C. D., Shamseer, L., Tetzlaff, J. M., Akl, E. A., & Brennan, S. E. (2021). The PRISMA 2020 statement : An updated guideline for reporting systematic reviews. *BMJ (Clinical Research Ed.)*, 372, •••. https://www.bmj.com/content/372/bmj.n71.short PMID: 33782057

Pai, C.-K., Liu, Y., Kang, S., & Dai, A. (2020). The Role of Perceived Smart Tourism Technology Experience for Tourist Satisfaction, Happiness and Revisit Intention. *Sustainability (Basel)*, 12(16), 16. Advance online publication. DOI: 10.3390/su12166592

Palumbo, F. (2015). Developing a new service for the digital traveler satisfaction : The Smart Tourist App. *The International Journal of Digital Accounting Research*, 15, •••. https://core.ac.uk/download/pdf/60666233.pdf. DOI: 10.4192/1577-8517-15_2

Pasaco-González, B. S., Campón-Cerro, A. M., Moreno-Lobato, A., & Sánchez-Vargas, E. (2023). The Role of Demographics and Previous Experience in Tourists' Experiential Perceptions. *Sustainability (Basel)*, 15(4), 3768. DOI: 10.3390/su15043768

Pradhan, M. K., Oh, J., & Lee, H. (2018). Understanding travelers' behavior for sustainable smart tourism : A technology readiness perspective. *Sustainability (Basel)*, 10(11), 4259. DOI: 10.3390/su10114259

Quesnel, D., & Riecke, B. E. (2018). Are You Awed Yet? How Virtual Reality Gives Us Awe and Goose Bumps. *Frontiers in Psychology*, 9, 2158. DOI: 10.3389/fpsyg.2018.02158 PMID: 30473673

Roopchund, R. (2020). Mauritius as a Smart Tourism Destination : Technology for Enhancing Tourism Experience. In Pati, B., Panigrahi, C. R., Buyya, R., & Li, K.-C. (Eds.), *Advanced Computing and Intelligent Engineering* (Vol. 1089, pp. 519–535). Springer Singapore., DOI: 10.1007/978-981-15-1483-8_44

Roy, B. K., & Pagaldiviti, S. R. (2023). Advancements in arena technology : Enhancing customer experience and employee adaptation in the tourism and hospitality industry. *Smart Tourism*, 4(1), 2330. DOI: 10.54517/st.v4i2.2330

Schwartz, S. H. (2012). An Overview of the Schwartz Theory of Basic Values. *Online Readings in Psychology and Culture*, 2(1). Advance online publication. DOI: 10.9707/2307-0919.1116

Scott, N., & Jun, G. G. J., & Ma JianYu, M. J. (Éds.). (2017). *Visitor experience design*. CABI. DOI: 10.1079/9781786391896.0000

Sertkan, M., Neidhardt, J., & Werthner, H. (2018). What is the "Personality" of a tourism destination? *Information Technology & Tourism*, 21(1), 105–133. DOI: 10.1007/s40558-018-0135-6

Sustacha, I., Baños-Pino, J. F., & Del Valle, E. (2023). The role of technology in enhancing the tourism experience in smart destinations : A meta-analysis. *Journal of Destination Marketing & Management*, 30, 100817. DOI: 10.1016/j.jdmm.2023.100817

Tan, W.-K. (2020). Destination selection : Influence of tourists' personality on perceived travel constraints. *Journal of Vacation Marketing*, 26(4), 442–456. DOI: 10.1177/1356766720942556

Tan, W.-K., & Tang, C.-Y. (2013). Does personality predict tourism information search and feedback behaviour? *Current Issues in Tourism*, 16(4), 388–406. DOI: 10.1080/13683500.2013.766155

Tapanainen, T., Dao, T. K., & Nguyen, T. T. H. (2021). Impacts of online word-of-mouth and personalities on intention to choose a destination. *Computers in Human Behavior*, 116, 106656. DOI: 10.1016/j.chb.2020.106656

Tešin, A., Kovačić, S., & Obradović, S. (2023). The experience I will remember : The role of tourist personality, motivation, and destination personality. *Journal of Vacation Marketing*, 13567667231164768. Advance online publication. DOI: 10.1177/13567667231164768

Topsakal, Y., Icoz, O., & Icoz, O. (2022). *Digital Transformation and Tourist Experiences*., DOI: 10.4018/978-1-7998-8528-3.ch002

Tussyadiah, I. (2013). Expectation of Travel Experiences with Wearable Computing Devices. In Xiang, Z., & Tussyadiah, I. (Eds.), *Information and Communication Technologies in Tourism 2014* (pp. 539–552). Springer International Publishing., DOI: 10.1007/978-3-319-03973-2_39

Volo, S. (2013). Conceptualizing experience : A tourist based approach. In *Marketing of tourism experiences* (pp. 19–34). Routledge., https://www.taylorfrancis.com/chapters/edit/10.4324/9781315875293-6/conceptualizing-experience-tourist-based-approach-serena-volo

Wang, Y., So, K. K. F., & Sparks, B. A. (2016). Technology Readiness and Customer Satisfaction with Travel Technologies : A Cross-Country Investigation. *Journal of Travel Research*, 56(5), 563–577. DOI: 10.1177/0047287516657891

Wang, Y., So, K. K. F., & Sparks, B. A. (2017). Technology Readiness and Customer Satisfaction with Travel Technologies : A Cross-Country Investigation. *Journal of Travel Research*, 56(5), 563–577. DOI: 10.1177/0047287516657891

Wohlin, C. (2014). Guidelines for snowballing in systematic literature studies and a replication in software engineering. *Proceedings of the 18th International Conference on Evaluation and Assessment in Software Engineering*, 1-10. DOI: 10.1145/2601248.2601268

YiFei, L., & Othman, M. K. YiFei. (2024). Investigating the behavioural intentions of museum visitors towards VR : A systematic literature review. *Computers in Human Behavior*, 155, 108167. DOI: 10.1016/j.chb.2024.108167

KEY TERMS AND DEFINITIONS

Artificial Intelligence: the imitation of human intelligence by machines, mainly through data collection, processing, and analysis algorithms, chatbots, robotics, and virtual assistants.

Augmented Reality: a technology for superimposing digital information (images, text, etc.) on an environment in real-time.

Internet of Things: a system of interconnected computing devices and digital appliances based on network adaptation and data exchange.

Personality Traits: a description of personality traits regarding openness, nervousness, etc.

Personalization: adapting services, products, or experiences to people's preferences and needs.

Smart Tourism: using smart technologies in the tourism industry to enhance tourism services' efficiency, sustainability, and personalization.

Tourist Experience: the subjective and emotional perception of the traveler during interactions with a destination or tourism organization.

Virtual Reality: a 3D environment enabling people to interact in a virtual world through physical movements of computer-generated body parts.

Chapter 11
Enhancing Guest Experience Through Smart Hotel Technologies

Mohammad Badruddoza Talukder
 https://orcid.org/0009-0008-1662-9221
International University of Business Agriculture and Technology, Bangladesh

Md Zubair Rahman
 https://orcid.org/0000-0001-5601-4581
International University of Business Agriculture and Technology, Bangladesh

Musfiqur Rahoman Khan
 https://orcid.org/0009-0005-7416-2533
Daffodil Institute of IT, Bangladesh

ABSTRACT

In an era of swift technological advancement, the hotel sector is constantly looking for novel approaches to improve visitor experiences. The integration of cutting-edge hotel technologies to improve visitor satisfaction and optimize operations is examined in this abstract. A variety of solutions are included in innovative hotel technology, such as AI-powered assistants, mobile apps, IoT devices, and automated systems. These technologies provide individualized experiences, effective services, and seamless interactions. Hotels may anticipate visitor preferences and customize services accordingly by utilizing data analytics, which promotes guest loyalty and positive ratings. Intelligent technologies lower operating costs, improve resource management, and support sustainability initiatives. Nonetheless, issues like maintaining a personal touch and data security are still relevant. Notwithstanding these difficulties, implementing cutting-edge hotel technologies offer tremendous

DOI: 10.4018/979-8-3693-7021-6.ch011

Copyright © 2025, IGI Global. Copying or distributing in print or electronic forms without written permission of IGI Global is prohibited.

potential for revolutionizing visitor experiences and establishing new benchmarks for superior hospitality.

INTRODUCTION

In the ever-changing hospitality business, hotels must provide outstanding experiences for their guests to separate themselves from competitors and develop loyalty in a market that is becoming increasingly competitive (Verma et al., 2021). Incorporating intelligent technologies into hotel operations is crucial to revolutionizing the experiences they provide to their guests (Talukder, 2024). Internet of Things (IoT) gadgets and artificial intelligence (AI) powered systems are innovative technologies transforming how hotels connect with their clients and administer their services.

This introduction investigates how novel hotel technologies improve the enjoyment of hotel guests, optimize operational efficiency, and attempt to promote sustainability. Using data analytics and automation, hotels can personalize their services to cater to the tastes of each unique client, identify their needs, and deliver individualized experiences that leave an indelible impression. However, as hotels embrace these developments, they must also grapple with problems such as guaranteeing data security, balancing technology-driven efficiencies, and preserving a human touch in their interactions with guests. This essay tries to clarify the transformational potential of intelligent hotel technologies in altering the landscape of the guest experience. This will be accomplished by comprehensively assessing these trends and their repercussions.

Figure 1. Enhancing guest experience from security to smart technologies integration

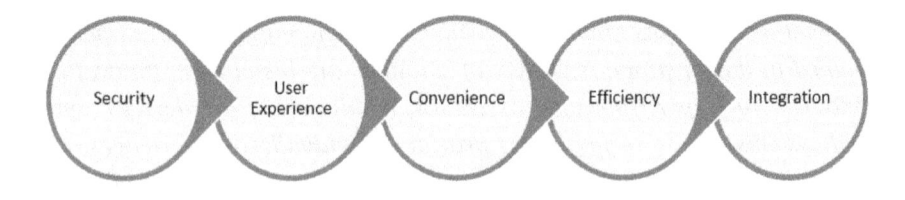

(Author Compilation)

According to Das et al. (2024), the hospitality industry has recently undergone a paradigm shift because of the rapid integration of intelligent technology to improve guests' experience. According to Pelet et al. (2023), a comprehensive examination of the study being conducted now reveals a growing body of data demonstrating how innovative hotel technologies are transforming the sector's landscape.

According to studies, personal experiences are essential in determining guests' level of pleasure and loyalty. The Internet of Things (IoT) devices and AI-powered systems are examples of intelligent technologies that enable hotels to collect and analyze data from guests to personalize services to the interests of individual guests. Intelligent room controls, for example, allow visitors to personalize their surroundings, including the lighting and temperature settings, resulting in a more comfortable stay tailored to their specific preferences.

Kumar et al. (2021) state that implementing mobile applications and digital platforms has streamlined the guest journey. This has enabled the implementation of seamless booking procedures, mobile check-ins, and concierge services. The hotel staff's operating efficiency is optimized, and the guests' convenience is increased thanks to this technology. According to Talukder (2024), intelligent technologies are crucial to improve hotel security and safety standards. These technologies also contribute to the creation of personalized experiences. Using surveillance systems, access control mechanisms, and biometric authentication methods helps secure the safety of guests and their goods, which in turn helps to create trust and confidence in the guests.

Additionally, intelligent hotel technologies contribute to sustainability by reducing energy consumption and boosting resource utilization. Kumar et al. (2024) state that Internet of Things sensors monitor energy usage, water consumption, and waste management systems. This enables hotels to discover areas that could be improved and apply more environmentally friendly methods.

Even while there are many advantages to using intelligent hotel technologies, there are still some challenges to overcome, notably about the privacy and security of data. To successfully deploy these technologies, hotels must consider protecting guest data and maintaining compliance with regulatory norms.

In general, the research that has been conducted on the topic highlights the revolutionary potential of intelligent hotel technology in terms of boosting the visitor experience, improving operational efficiency, and driving sustainability initiatives (Talukder et al., 2023). However, additional research is required to investigate the long-term effects of these technologies on the level of happiness and loyalty experienced by guests, as well as the overall competitiveness of the hospitality industry.

INTERNET OF THINGS DEVICES IN GUEST ROOMS

The article "IoT Devices in Guest Rooms" investigates how smart devices such as thermostats, lights, and voice assistants are becoming a part of hotel rooms. The purpose of these devices is to make the stays of hotel guests more comfortable and hassle-free (Pelet et al., 2021). According to Medagedara and Liyanage (2024), these devices are like small assistants because they enable visitors to personalize the settings of their rooms, save energy, and even order room service with a simple voice command. However, like any other great technology, some obstacles must be overcome. The primary concerns that require more analysis are the issues regarding the protection of visitor data, the guarantee that all the gadgets can work together without any problems, and the guarantee that guests will find them easy to use (Iqbal & Wajid, 2024). These devices aren't just about making hotel stays more luxurious; they also can make visitors happier and increase the likelihood that they will return. Therefore, it is not only about giving visitors the impression that they are staying in the future but also about providing hotels with an advantage in a highly competitive sector, where even the most minor details can have a significant impact (Simon et al., 2024).

Mobile Applications for a Seamless Interaction With Guests

Mobile applications make visitors feel they are carrying a magic wand, as they will completely alter how they interact with hotels. Imagine this: you pull out your phone, and with just a few taps, you have already reserved your room, checked in, and even placed an order for room service—all without ever having to wait in line or for assistance (Ng, 2016).

Not only does it make your life easier, but it also has the potential to transform the hotel industry completely. According to Casebourne (2024), these applications are comparable to a hidden weapon because they streamline everything behind the scenes to ensure the stay is as smooth as silk. Connectivity is their driving force; ease is not the only objective. It is now possible for hotels to get to know their guests better than ever before, allowing them to personalize their services to cater to their preferences and make them feel like royalty (Ossai & Wickramasinghe, 2022).

There are challenges to overcome, such as safeguarding the user data and ensuring the application's simplicity and feasibility. However, the advantages are more significant in number. Using mobile applications, hotels can transform an average stay into an unforgettable one, providing you with memories that will last a lifetime. According to Zhang and Jun (2023), the future of the hospitality industry lies in hands.

AI-Powered Personalization

"AI-powered personalization" is comparable to having your genie in use within the hospitality business. Hotels use artificial intelligence (AI) to make guests feel incredibly privileged with personalized experiences (Mustafa Ayobami Raji et al., 2024). This is similar to how Aladdin had his genie grant his desires. Imagine this: as soon as a guest enters the hotel room, the lights adapt to the level of brightness that he prefers, the temperature is adjusted to the perfect level, and his preferred music begins playing—all without his having to raise a finger (Ashok Choppadandi, 2023). In other words, that is the beauty of personalization powered by AI.

Using clever algorithms to learn about the visitors' tastes and then using that information to make their stay as pleasant and joyful as possible is the key to success, according to Taneja and Tripathi's research from 2020. But it is not just about the conveniences of everyday life. Artificial intelligence can also assist hotels in anticipating the guest's needs before they are even aware of it. According to Sodiq Odetunde Babatunde et al. (2024), artificial intelligence is about making the stay unforgettable. This includes generating personalized recommendations for activities and amenities and ensuring visitors find preferred snacks in their rooms or designated areas. There are, without a doubt, obstacles to conquer, such as protecting privacy and ensuring that artificial intelligence is correct every time. If it does work, however, it is similar to a guest having a personal concierge, guaranteeing every single moment of the stay is a magical experience. The term "Smart Check-In and Keyless Entry Systems" is comparable to having a VIP pass for the hotel stay. These systems allow one to check in and out without using one's keys. Imagine strolling right to one's room and unlocking the door with just a tap of one's phone, rather than waiting in line to check in and fumble about for the room key (Raghunandan, 2022).

Keyless Access Systems and Clever Check-in Systems

Hotels make a guest's arrival a more accessible experience by providing keyless access systems and clever check-in systems. Through this system, one can move quickly through the lobby and head straight to his room; he will no longer be required to wait at the front desk. It is like a celebrity, with everything. On the other hand, it is not only about convenience but also about having peace of mind. Keyless access eliminates the possibility of the room key being misplaced or stolen (Putrada et al., 2023). The phone becomes the key; as long as a guest has that, he can go without problems. Undoubtedly, obstacles must be conquered, such as ensuring that technology is dependable and available to everyone (Gade et al., 2022). However, when it functions correctly, it is as if the guests have a unique red carpet spread for them every time, they enter the hotel. This is the future of hospitality management, where everything can be found at one's fingertip.

Virtual Concierge Services

Virtual Concierge Services are like having a friendly helper ready to assist the guests with everything they need while staying in a hotel room. That's precisely what "Virtual Concierge Services" are all about. Instead of searching for a concierge desk or waiting on hold to speak to someone, a visitor can send a quick message or ask a question through his smartphone or tablet (Liu & Jia, 2021). These virtual concierges are like super-smart assistants powered by fancy technology, such as AI chatbots or virtual assistants. They are like one's genie, ready to grant wishes—from recommending the perfect dinner spot to helping a guest book tickets for that show he has been dying to see (De Bruyne, 2023). They're available 24/7, no matter where one is in the hotel. Whether the guest lounges in the room or soaking up the sun by the pool, they are always there to lend a helping hand. Sometimes, they might not get the request precisely right, or their response might be slightly delayed. But overall, virtual concierge services are like having a knowledgeable friend by one's side throughout his stay, ensuring everything goes smoothly and the guests have the best experience possible (Murphy & Schegg, 2006).

Data Analytics for Guest Insights

"Data Analytics for Guest Insights" is like having a secret sauce recipe for perfecting a hotel stay. Imagine this: behind the scenes, the hotel collects all sorts of information about the guests—like their preferences, habits, and favorite snacks. Then, they use fancy data analytics tools to analyze all that data and figure out how to make their stay as impressive as possible (Said, 2023). For example, they might notice that one specific guest always orders extra pillows or that he loves trying new restaurants. Equipped with this understanding, they can customize their services to the visitor's preferences, like making sure plenty of pillows are waiting for him in your room or recommending the hottest new dining spots in town. But it's not just about making the stay more comfortable—it's about making it unforgettable. By crunching all that data, hotels can uncover hidden patterns and insights they would never have noticed otherwise (Anubala & Chandigarh, 2024). Maybe they'll discover that guests who order room service on their first night are more likely to extend their stay or that guests who attend the hotel's yoga classes are happier overall. Armed with this information, they can fine-tune their offerings to create experiences that guests will remember long after checking out. Of course, there are challenges along the way, like ensuring that all that data stays safe and secure and that guests feel comfortable with how their information is used. But when it's done right, data analytics for guest insights can turn an ordinary hotel stay into an extraordinary one, leaving guests feeling like they've been taken care of (Milton, 2024).

Enhancing Safety and Security With Smart Technologies

Enhancing Safety and Security with Smart Technologies is like having the protection of a superhero during a hotel stay. Imagine this: behind the scenes, the hotel uses all sorts of clever gadgets and gizmos to keep its guests safe and secure (Abhijeet & Deni Noul, 2024). For example, they might have intelligent surveillance cameras to spot trouble before it happens or access control systems that ensure only authorized people can enter certain areas. They might even have emergency response systems that automatically alert the right people if something goes wrong. But it's not just about preventing problems—it's also about enhancing the peaceful experience of the guests. With intelligent technologies keeping an eye on things, guests can unwind and stay without worrying about anything (Johnson et al., 2024). It's like having a bodyguard watching over a person to ensure nothing wrong happens. There are challenges to overcome, like ensuring all those fancy gadgets work together seamlessly and ensuring that the privacy of the hotel dwellers is always protected. But when it's done right, enhancing safety and security with innovative technologies can make their hotel stay feel like a fortress of comfort and protection, where they can rest easy knowing they are in good hands (Jaime et al., 2023).

Sustainability Initiatives Through Smart Technologies

Besides smart sensors and water systems, hotels use innovative technologies to tackle sustainability challenges in other areas. One exciting initiative involves the implementation of intelligent waste management systems. These devices use sensors to track the amount of waste in the bins (Chinonye et al., 2024). Waste collection schedules are optimized throughout the hotel, and the quantity of waste dumped in landfills is reduced. By separating and recycling materials more efficiently, hotels can lessen their environmental effect and help a circular economy.

Furthermore, hotels are exploring using renewable energy sources to power their operations. Solar panels, wind turbines, and other renewable energy source devices are being integrated into hotel facilities to generate clean, renewable energy onsite (Umar, 2023). Intelligent energy management systems are essential to maximizing renewable energy sources, ensuring that the hotel maximizes its use of sustainable energy while minimizing its reliance on fossil fuels. Another area of focus is sustainable transportation options for guests. Hotels are partnering with ride-sharing services, offering electric vehicle charging stations, and promoting alternate modes of mobility like biking and public transportation to lessen carbon emissions associated with the guest's travel. Hotels can encourage guests to make sustainable choices by providing convenient and eco-friendly transportation options. Moreover, hotels incorporate sustainable building materials and designs to minimize environmental impact during construction and operation. Green construction techniques, like reusing resources, optimizing natural lighting, and implementing energy-efficient HVAC systems, help reduce energy and resource consumption while enhancing indoor air quality and guest comfort (Manfreda & Mijač, 2024).

Overall, sustainability initiatives through intelligent technologies are transforming the hospitality industry, enabling hotels to operate more sustainably while enhancing the guest experience. By embracing these innovative solutions, hotels can demonstrate their commitment to environmental stewardship and inspire guests to make sustainable choices during their stay and beyond.

Challenges and Considerations in Implementing Smart Hotel Technologies

It comes with challenges and considerations, like picking up a new dish or riding a bike. Sure, it is exciting to think about all the cool gadgets and gizmos that can make one's hotel stay even better, but there are a few bumps in the road that hoteliers need to navigate (Çeltek, 2023). One big challenge is ensuring all these intelligent systems work together smoothly. It's like trying to get friends to agree on what movie to watch—it can be tricky! Different technologies might use various protocols or systems, making their coordination challenging. But with some patience and tech-savvy know-how, hotels can overcome these interoperability issues and create a seamless experience for guests. Another consideration is ensuring that guests find these innovative technologies easy to use. After all, there's no point in having a fancy app or high-tech room controls if nobody knows how to use them!

Hotels must invest time and resources into training their staff and providing clear instructions to visitors to ensure everyone feels comfortable and confident using these new technologies (Sarker & Khan, 2024). There are also concerns about privacy and security. With all the data being collected and shared by these intelligent systems, ensuring that guests' personal information is protected and that the hotel follows all the necessary regulations and guidelines is essential. By implementing robust security measures and being transparent about how guest data is used, hotels can help guests feel safe and secure while still enjoying the benefits of innovative technology (Akel & Noyan, 2024). Cost-effectiveness is also paramount. Implementing innovative hotel technologies can be a significant investment, and hotels must carefully weigh the upfront costs against the potential long-term benefits. But when done right, these technologies can enhance the guest experience, improve operational efficiency, and drive revenue growth.

So, while there may be some challenges and considerations to remember, the potential rewards of implementing innovative hotel technologies are worth it (Katuk et al., 2023). With creativity, perseverance, and a willingness to embrace the future, hotels can create a magical experience for their guests while keeping up with the ever-changing hospitality industry.

FUTURE TRENDS AND INNOVATIONS

While gazing into the crystal ball of hospitality, a future filled with innovative and fascinating trends that could revolutionize the hotel experience can be envisioned through minimal imagination. From futuristic technologies to eco-friendly practices, the future of hospitality is ripe with possibilities. One trend that will shape the future of hotels is the rise of artificial intelligence (AI) and machine learning. The guests can now imagine a hotel where every part of their stay is personalized to their preferences, from the room's temperature to the recommendations for local attractions. Guests of the future will begin to expect hoteliers to anticipate their guest's needs and deliver tailored experiences from the moment of checking in that will make them feel pampered and valued.

Augmented reality (AR), virtual reality combined, and (VR) are another fascinating concept—experiences in the hotel environment (Das et al., 2024). Guests may soon be able to take virtual tours of hotel facilities, previewing rooms and amenities before they even arrive. AR could also enhance onsite experiences, providing interactive guides to local attractions or overlaying historical information onto architectural landmarks. Combining augmented and virtual reality (AR/VR) is an additional intriguing idea. Hotels in the future emphasize eco-friendly practices and green technologies. Hotels may adopt renewable energy sources, such as solar panels and wind turbines, to reduce their emissions impact while implementing water-saving measures and recycling programs to minimize waste. Guests can expect to see more eco-friendly amenities and programs meant to lessen the effects of their stay. The future of hotel design is also likely to be influenced by trends in wellness and well-being. Hotels may incorporate biophilic design elements, bringing nature indoors to create a calming and rejuvenating environment (Talukder et al., 2021). Facilities for well-being like yoga classes, meditation areas, etc, and spa facilities may become standard offerings, enabling visitors to unwind and rejuvenate while visiting.

Technology will continue to be a key component in shaping the future of hotels, with innovations such as intelligent rooms and Internet of Things (IoT) devices becoming increasingly common. Guests may soon be able to control every aspect of their room with their smartphone, from setting the thermostat and lighting to placing an order with room service and maintaining the entertainment system. IoT devices can also provide valuable data insights that hotels can use to improve operational efficiency and enhance the guest experience. As the world becomes increasingly connected, hotels must change to accommodate the requirements of tech-savvy travelers (Talukder et al., 2024). High-speed Wi-Fi and seamless connectivity will be essential, allowing guests to stay connected and productive while on the go. Hotels may also offer innovative tech amenities such as robot butlers and drone delivery services, providing guests with unique and memorable experiences that set them apart. The future of hospitality is bright and full of exciting possibilities. From AI-powered personalization to AR-enhanced experiences, hotels are poised to embrace new technologies and trends that guarantee a rise in the bar for the visitor experience. By anticipating trends and embracing innovation, Hotels have the power to produce lifelong memories that entice visitors to return (Kumar et al., 2024).

Voice-Controlled Room Automation

Voice-controlled room automation is sure to provide the experience of having a personal assistant ready to fulfill every command with only the sound of one's voice. A visitor can enter a room after a long day of travel and say, "Hey, room, turn on the lights and set the temperature to a cozy 700 degrees," this will be good enough for your room to recognize your needs and respond instantly, creating the perfect ambiance for relaxation (Rane et al., 2023). With this innovative technology, hotels are revolutionizing the guest experience, making controlling room amenities easier and more convenient. Whether any guests want to adjust the lighting, change the temperature, or even order room service, all one must do is speak up, and your wishes are granted. But it is not just about convenience; voice-controlled room automation also enhances accessibility for guests of all abilities (Lvov & Komppula, 2023). For people with various limitations or limited mobility, controlling room features with voice commands can make a difference, allowing them to enjoy a comfortable and independent stay.

There are factors to consider when implementing voice-controlled room automation. Privacy and security are top priorities, and hotels must ensure that guest privacy is protected and that voice data is securely handled (Bagriya et al., 2024). Additionally, it is essential to provide guests with clear instructions on using the technology and offer alternative control methods for those who may prefer them. Overall, voice-controlled room automation is a game-changer for the hospitality industry, offering guests a seamless and personalized experience that enhances their comfort and convenience (Maharana & Mahapatra, 2022). With just a few simple words, guests can transform their hotel room into a home away from home, making their stay unforgettable.

Robotic Assistance in Hospitality

Robotic assistance in hospitality is like having a helpful friend or staff who never gets tired or takes a break. Picture: a friendly robot greets the guests as they walk into the hotel lobby, ready to assist them with everything from checking in to carrying their luggage to their room (Koerten & Abbink, 2023). These robotic helpers can handle various tasks, from delivering room service orders to providing information about hotel amenities and local attractions. One of the main advantages of robotic support in hospitality is its ability to improve efficiency and streamline operations. By automating routine tasks, hotels can free up employees to concentrate on offering individualized service and attending to guests' unique needs.

Additionally, robotic assistance can enhance the guest experience by providing prompt and reliable service around the clock (Saravanan, 2023). However, careful thought is still necessary while implementing robotic assistance in hospitality. It's essential to balance automation and human interaction, ensuring guests feel valued and cared for (Uribe Rivera et al., 2024). Additionally, hotels must invest in proper training and upkeep to guarantee that the robots can function safely and adequately. Overall, robotic assistance has the potential to revolutionize the hospitality industry, offering hotels a cost-effective way to enhance service and improve guest satisfaction. With the help of these friendly robots, hotels can produce lasting impressions that entice visitors to return time and time (Ye et al., 2022).

Personalized Marketing Through Data Analytics

Personalized marketing through data analytics provides a shopper who knows the visitors' preferences and can tailor the message accordingly. Guests will feel cared for when they receive an email from their favorite hotel chain with special offers for their dream destination, including the activities they love based on their previous bookings and interests (Carneiro et al., 2023).

This creative marketing strategy uses the strength of data analytics to analyze customer behavior, preferences, and demographics. By understanding each guest's unique preferences and purchasing history, hotels can create targeted marketing campaigns that resonate with individual guests on a personal level. But personalized marketing goes beyond just sending targeted emails. Hotels can also use data analytics to personalize website content, social media ads, and even in-room experiences. For example, a guest who has previously booked spa treatments might receive promotions for discounted massages upon their next visit, while a family traveling with children might receive recommendations for nearby family-friendly attractions. Among the main advantages of customized marketing is its ability to enhance the guest experience and foster loyalty. By delivering relevant and timely offers, hotels can show guests that they understand and value their preferences, increasing satisfaction and repeat business.

However, hotels need to strike the right balance between personalization and privacy. Guests want to feel understood and valued, but they also want to know that their personal information is handled responsibly (Mota et al., 2024). Hotels must be transparent about collecting and using guest data and ensure they have appropriate safeguards to protect guests, create meaningful connections, and drive business results (Siahaan & Brina, 2024). By harnessing the power of data, hotels can deliver personalized experiences that delight guests and keep them coming back for more.

Augmented Reality Experiences for Guests

Augmented Reality (AR) experiences provide guests a new dimension of fun and discovery during their hotel stay. This can be described with the following imaginary situation: a guest is putting on a pair of AR glasses or opening an app on their smartphone, and suddenly, the world around him transforms into a magical wonderland filled with interactive surprises and adventures (Aburub, 2023).

With AR technology, hotels can offer guests unique and engaging encounters that surpass conventional entertainment formats. From virtual tours of local attractions to interactive games and storytelling experiences, AR allows guests to explore and enjoy. One of the most exciting aspects of AR experiences is their ability to bring destinations and historical landmarks to life in a whole new way. Imagine walking through a hotel lobby and using AR to see virtual guides pop up, offering fascinating insights into the hotel's history and architecture (Lim et al., 2024). Or perhaps a person could use AR to explore virtual reconstructions of famous landmarks or watch historical events unfold right before his eyes. AR experiences could also completely change how people and guests interact with hotel amenities and services. Instead of flipping through a traditional guest directory, he could use AR to access virtual maps and guides that help him navigate the hotel. Or maybe one could use AR to scan a menu at the hotel restaurant and see virtual images of each dish before selecting it. Implementing AR experiences in hotels comes with its own set of challenges. Making sure the technology is accessible and easy to use for guests of all ages and tech-savviness levels is crucial, as is providing adequate training and support to hotel staff (Liu & Jia, 2021).

Additionally, hotels must consider privacy concerns and ensure that guest data is handled responsibly and securely. AR experiences can potentially transform the hotel's guest experience, offering guests exciting and unforgettable encounters that make an impact. By embracing AR technology, hotels can create a truly immersive and memorable stay for their guests, setting themselves apart from the competition and redefining the future of hospitality (Shaikh Mohammed Shaukat, 2023).

Blockchain for Secure Transactions and Guest Identity Management

Blockchain for secure transactions and guest identity management is like having a digital vault that keeps the guests' personal information and transactions secure during their hotel stay. Imagine entering the hotel room knowing that one's credit card information and identity are protected by an unbreakable digital seal, ensuring that only authorized parties can access the data (Byeon et al., 2023). Blockchain technology is an unchangeable, decentralized ledger that keeps track of transactions across multiple computers securely and transparently. Each transaction is encrypted and connected to the preceding one, forming a chain of blocks that is nearly hard to tamper with (Ong et al., 2024). Because of this, blockchain is the perfect way to guarantee the security and integrity of guest transactions and identity management in the hospitality industry.

The main advantage of utilizing blockchain technology for secure transactions is its ability to eliminate the need for intermediaries like banks and payment processors, thereby reducing the risk of fraud and unauthorized access to guest data (Domazet et al., 2023). By securely storing transaction records on a distributed ledger, hotels can ensure that guest payments are processed quickly and securely without third-party verification. Blockchain also offers a unique solution for guest identity management, allowing hotels to securely store and verify guest identities without compromising privacy or security. Rather than depending on centralized databases that can be hacked and data breaches, blockchain enables hotels to securely store guest identities on a decentralized network, ensuring the privacy and security of sensitive information (Liang et al., 2023). Implementing blockchain technology in the hospitality industry comes with its own set of challenges. Hotels must invest in robust security measures to help safeguard against online dangers and guarantee adherence to data protection regulations.

Additionally, educating staff and guests about blockchain technology and its benefits is essential to ensure widespread adoption and acceptance. Blockchain for secure transactions and guest identity management holds great promise for the future of the hospitality industry (Hassanien et al., 2021). By leveraging blockchain technology, hotels can provide guests with peace of mind, knowing that the highest standards of security and integrity protect their transactions and personal information.

Figure 2. Conceptual framework

(Author Compilation)

SOLUTIONS AND RECOMMENDTIONS

Enhancing the guest experience through innovative hotel technologies is more than just a passing trend; it is a crucial strategy for hotels aiming to remain competitive and cater to the needs of today's travelers (Talukder et al., 2024). Here are some recommendations on how hotels can harness intelligent technologies to elevate the guest experience:

1. **Seamless Connectivity**: In today's digital age, a reliable Wi-Fi connection is non-negotiable for guests. Investing in robust Wi-Fi infrastructure ensures that guests can stay connected effortlessly throughout their stay, whether catching up on work emails or streaming their favorite shows.
2. **Personalized Comfort**: Implementing bright room controls like IoT devices allows guests to customize their room environment according to their preferences. Everything from lighting to changing the temperature, giving guests control over their surroundings enhances their comfort and satisfaction.
3. **Efficient Check-in Process**: Mobile check-in and keyless entry systems offer guests a hassle-free arrival experience (Das et al., 2024). By allowing guests to check in and access their rooms using smartphones, hotels streamline the check-in process and minimize contact points, enhancing convenience and safety.

4. **Tailored Experiences**: Leveraging data analytics enables hotels to customize visitor experiences according to their tastes and past behavior. From recommending local attractions to suggesting personalized amenities, offering tailored experiences makes guests feel valued and understood.
5. **24/7 Assistance**: Integrating virtual concierge services powered by AI chatbots ensures guests can access assistance and recommendations around the clock. Whether guests need dining recommendations or help with room service, virtual concierges provide prompt and efficient support.
6. **Safety and Security**: Implementing innovative technologies like surveillance systems and access control solutions enhances guest safety and security (Talukder, 2024). Features such as facial recognition and real-time monitoring ensure guests feel secure throughout their stay.
7. **Environmental Responsibility**: Embracing sustainability initiatives through innovative technologies demonstrates a commitment to environmental responsibility. Implementing energy-efficient solutions and waste management systems reduces the hotel's ecological footprint and appeals to eco-conscious travelers.
8. **Tech Amenities**: Offering tech amenities such as wireless charging stations and in-room tablets enhances the guest experience. Access to streaming services and digital content guarantees that entertainment alternatives are available for guests (Talukder, 2024). And they are tailored to their preferences.
9. **Staff Training and Support**: Investing in staff Training guarantees that staff members are adept at using intelligent technologies and providing exceptional service. Giving staff members the required instruments and materials enables them to leverage technology effectively to meet guest needs.
10. **Continuous Improvement**: Regularly seeking guest feedback and adapting strategies based on their suggestions is essential for enhancing the guest experience. By actively listening to guest feedback and implementing changes accordingly, hotels are committed to continuous improvement and guest satisfaction.

CONCLUSION

In today's rapidly evolving hospitality landscape, embracing innovative hotel technologies isn't just about staying trendy but prioritizing guest satisfaction above all else. For instance, hotels can create a memorable stay that exceeds expectations by seamlessly integrating technologies like intelligent mirrors, voice-activated assistants, and personalized mobile apps into the guest experience. Comprehensive Wi-Fi ensures guests can stay connected effortlessly, while intelligent room controls empower them to customize their environment for ultimate comfort. Mobile check-in and keyless entry streamline the arrival process, enhancing both convenience and safety. Personalized experiences, driven by data analytics, cater to individual preferences in ways that were previously unimaginable. For example, hotels can offer tailored dining, entertainment, and even room temperature recommendations by analyzing guests' past preferences and behaviors. Virtual concierge services provide instant assistance and recommendations at guests' fingertips. Intelligent technologies bolster safety and security, giving travelers peace of mind. Sustainability initiatives appeal to environmentally conscious visitors and are dedicated to responsible practices. Tech amenities such as wireless charging and in-room tablets add modern conveniences to the guest experience. However, it is crucial to recognize the pivotal role of staff training and support. Well-trained staff provide exceptional service and assist guests in navigating the technology seamlessly, enhancing their overall experience. Lastly, maintaining a constant guest feedback loop allows hotels to refine their services continually, ensuring they consistently exceed expectations. By leveraging technology to enhance convenience, personalization, safety, and sustainability, hotels can craft an unforgettable experience that keeps guests returning for more. However, the journey doesn't end there. Success in the hospitality industry hinges on understanding and adjusting to the changing requirements of contemporary tourists, ensuring that each stay is not just a temporary accommodation but a cherished memory. This is why maintaining a constant guest feedback loop is crucial, as it allows hotels to continually refine their services, ensuring they consistently exceed expectations and foster growth.

Further Study Directions

More research should be done on how to improve the experience of hotel guests by implementing modern technology, and it should include a variety of essential areas. Specifically, researchers should concentrate on performing impact assessment studies to measure the impacts of particular technologies on guests' happiness and the efficiency of operations. Additionally, they should investigate successful implementations to find best practices and eliminate hurdles to adoption. Deeper insights into establishing linked smart environments may be gained via advanced data analytics techniques for personalising visitor experiences and integrating future technologies like the Internet of Things and artificial intelligence. To guarantee confidence and compliance with legislation, it is essential to investigate concerns regarding data security and privacy of guests. In addition, highlighting the environmental benefits of innovative technology may be accomplished by examining how these technologies help sustainability and reduce energy use. Cross-cultural comparisons might be helpful for a better grasp of the various tastes of guests throughout the world. At the same time, economic assessments such as cost-benefit and return on investment studies may be used to establish whether these technologies are financially viable.

Examining future trends and developments, such as augmented reality (AR), virtual reality (VR), and predictive analytics, will help hotels anticipate the demands of their guests and drive further improvements in the hospitality sector. This will ensure that hotels continue to be competitive and improve the experiences they provide for their guests.

Related Readings

Enhancing guest experience through innovative hotel technologies involves leveraging advanced digital solutions to improve comfort, convenience, and satisfaction. Automated check-in and check-out processes through mobile apps and self-service kiosks reduce wait times and streamline the arrival and departure experience. Smart room controls, including voice assistants, smart thermostats, and adaptive lighting systems, allow guests to personalize their environment easily. Data analytics enable hotels to remember guest preferences and offer customized dining, entertainment, and activity recommendations. Enhanced connectivity, with robust high-speed Wi-Fi and smart TVs, ensures guests can stay connected and entertained throughout their stay. Comprehensive resources on this topic include books like "The Smart Hotel: Using Technology to Revolutionize the Hotel Experience" by Adam McIntosh, which explores various smart technologies and their applications; articles such as "Smart Hotels: The Future of the Hospitality Industry" by Emily Collins, which provides an in-depth look at current and future trends; and industry reports like Deloitte's "The Future of Smart Hotels: 2024 and Beyond," which analyzes the impacts of these technologies. Research papers, such as "The Impact of Smart Room Technologies on Guest Satisfaction" by Liu, Zhang, and Wang, offer empirical evidence of the benefits of these innovations. At the same time, websites like Hospitality Net and Skift provide ongoing insights into the latest developments in hotel technology.

REFERENCES

Abhijeet, D., & Noul, D. (2024). Safety at the core: IoT, knowledge management, and sustainable development. https://doi.org/DOI: 10.13140/RG.2.2.33544.64007

Aburub, F. (2023). Applying augmented reality in tourism: Analyzing relevance as it concerns consumer satisfaction and purchase intention. In Shishkov, B. (Ed.), *Business modeling and software design* (Vol. 483, pp. 278–288). Springer Nature Switzerland., DOI: 10.1007/978-3-031-36757-1_19

Akel, G., & Noyan, E. (2024). Exploring the criteria for a green and smart hotel: Insights from hotel managers' perspectives. *Journal of Hospitality and Tourism Insights.* https://doi.org/DOI: 10.1108/JHTI-08-2023-0555

Ashok, C. (2023). Enhancing customer experience in e-commerce through AI-powered personalization: A case study. *Tuijin Jishu/Journal of Propulsion Technology, 43*(4), 516–524. https://doi.org/DOI: 10.52783/tjjpt.v43.i4.6018

Bagriya, S., Khandewal, S., Mohammd, S., Sharma, S., & Mahala, V. (2024). Microcontroller based voice control home automation system. *International Journal for Research in Applied Science and Engineering Technology*, 12(4), 2918–2923. DOI: 10.22214/ijraset.2024.60163

Byeon, H., Kumar, P., Manu, M., Maaliw, R. R., Singh, P. P., & Maranan, R. (2023). Editable blockchain for secure IoT transactions. In *2023 Second International Conference on Smart Technologies for Smart Nation (SmartTechCon)* (pp. 255–263). https://doi.org/DOI: 10.1109/SmartTechCon57526.2023.10391293

Carneiro, T., Picoto, W. N., & Pinto, I. (2023). Big data analytics and firm performance in the hotel sector. *Tourism and Hospitality*, 4(2), 244–256. DOI: 10.3390/tourhosp4020015

Casebourne, I. (2024). Left to their own devices: An exploration of context in seamless work-related mobile learning. *British Journal of Educational Technology*, 55(4), 1772–1789. Advance online publication. DOI: 10.1111/bjet.13410

Çeltek, E. (2023). Analysis of smart technologies used in smart hotels. *Journal of Business Research - Turk, 15.* https://doi.org/DOI: 10.20491/isarder.2023.1754

Chinonye, E. U., Ofodile, O. C., Okoye, C. C., & Akinrinola, O. (2024). Sustainable smart cities: The role of fintech in promoting environmental sustainability. *Engineering Science & Technology Journal*, 5(3), 821–835. DOI: 10.51594/estj.v5i3.906

Das, I. R., Talukder, M. B., & Kumar, S. (2024). Implication of artificial intelligence in hospitality marketing. In Kumar, S., Talukder, M. B., & Pego, A. (Eds.), *Advances in hospitality, tourism, and the services industry* (pp. 291–310). IGI Global., DOI: 10.4018/979-8-3693-1978-9.ch014

De Bruyne, N. (2023). Building a caring network of formal and informal help (offline and online) in a super-diverse neighbourhood. *International Journal of Integrated Care*, 23(S1), 542. DOI: 10.5334/ijic.ICIC23200

Domazet, E., Rahmani, D., & Mechkaroska, D. (2023). Blockchain empowering Web 3.0: Decentralized trust and secure transactions for the future Internet. In *2023 31st Telecommunications Forum (TELFOR)* (pp. 1–4). https://doi.org/DOI: 10.1109/TELFOR59449.2023.10372778

Gade, S., Chatterjee, U., & Mukhopadhyay, D. (2022). PAKAMAC: A PUF-based keyless automotive entry system with mutual authentication. *Journal of Hardware and Systems Security*, 6(3–4), 67–78. DOI: 10.1007/s41635-022-00126-8

Hassanien, A. E., Torky, M., Goda, E., Snasel, V., & Gaber, T. (2021). Proof of space transactions: A novel blockchain protocol for secure authentication of satellite transactions. https://doi.org/DOI: 10.21203/rs.3.rs-820584/v1

Iqbal, Z., & Wajid, S. (2024). Guardians of the IoT realm: A comparative analysis of cryptographic security solutions for bolstering IoT device networks. *Lahore Garrison University Research Journal of Computer Science and Information Technology*, 8(1). Advance online publication. DOI: 10.54692/lgurjcsit.2024.081484

Jaime, F. J., Muñoz, A., Rodríguez-Gómez, F., & Jerez-Calero, A. (2023). Strengthening privacy and data security in biomedical microelectromechanical systems by IoT communication security and protection in smart healthcare. *Sensors (Basel)*, 23(21), 8944. DOI: 10.3390/s23218944 PMID: 37960646

Katuk, N., Wan Abdullah, W. A. N., Sugiharto, T., & Ahmad, I. (2023). Smart technology: Ecosystem, impacts, challenges, and the path forward. *Information System and Smart City*, 1(1). Advance online publication. DOI: 10.59400/issc.v1i1.63

Koerten, K., & Abbink, D. (2023). Selecting robots to take over tasks in hospitality settings: Joining two research fields. In Marques, J., & Marques, R. P. (Eds.), *Digital transformation of the hotel industry* (pp. 65–86). Springer International Publishing., DOI: 10.1007/978-3-031-31682-1_4

Kumar, S., Talukder, M. B., & Kaiser, F. (2024). Artificial intelligence in business: Negative social impacts. In Dadwal, S., Goyal, S., Kumar, P., & Verma, R. (Eds.), (pp. 81–97). Advances in human resources management and organizational development. IGI Global., DOI: 10.4018/979-8-3693-0724-3.ch005

Kumar, S., Talukder, M. B., & Pego, A. (Eds.). (2024). *Utilizing smart technology and AI in hybrid tourism and hospitality*. IGI Global., DOI: 10.4018/979-8-3693-1978-9

Liang, H.-W., Chu, Y.-C., & Han, T.-H. (2023). Fortifying health care intellectual property transactions with blockchain. *Journal of Medical Internet Research*, 25, e44578. DOI: 10.2196/44578 PMID: 37594787

Lim, W. M., Mohamed Jasim, K., & Das, M. (2024). Augmented and virtual reality in hotels: Impact on tourist satisfaction and intention to stay and return. *International Journal of Hospitality Management*, 116, 103631. DOI: 10.1016/j.ijhm.2023.103631

Liu, J., & Jia, F. (2021). Construction of a nonlinear model of tourism economy forecast based on wireless sensor network from the perspective of digital economy. *Wireless Communications and Mobile Computing*, 2021(1), 1–14. DOI: 10.1155/2021/8576534

Lvov, A., & Komppula, R. (2023). The essence of the hotel room in the hotel business – The hotel managers' perspective. *European Journal of Tourism Research*, 36, 3609. DOI: 10.54055/ejtr.v36i.3158

Maharana, P., & Mahesh, M. (2024). Digital transformation in hospitality: Current trends and future prospects. In P. Jena & B. Singh (Eds.), *Trends in hospitality management: The role of AI and robotics* (pp. 1–20). Springer International Publishing. https://doi.org/DOI: 10.1007/978-3-031-12940-1_1

Mehra, A. (2024). A comparative analysis of smart and traditional hotels: The impact on guest experiences. *Tourism Review*. Advance online publication. DOI: 10.1108/TR-05-2023-0238

Milton, T.Dr.T. Milton. (2024). Artificial intelligence transforming hotel gastronomy: An in-depth review of AI-driven innovations in menu design, food preparation, and customer interaction, with a focus on sustainability and future trends in the hospitality industry. *International Journal for Multidimensional Research Perspectives*, 2(3), 47–61. DOI: 10.61877/ijmrp.v2i3.126

Mishra, V., & Das, R. (2023). Blockchain-based smart contracts for tourism industry: A secure and transparent approach. *Tourism Review*, 78(4), 1013–1026. DOI: 10.1108/TR-07-2022-0269

Moges, Y. E., Lajoie, J., & Giebelhausen, M. D. (2023). Effect of digital payment on customer satisfaction in hotel industry: A study in Ethiopia. *Journal of Tourism and Services*, 14(26), 117–136. DOI: 10.29036/jots.v14i26.1771

Mordor Intelligence. (2023). *Artificial Intelligence in hospitality market - growth, trends, COVID-19 impact, and forecasts (2024-2029)*. https://www.mordorintelligence.com/industry-reports/artificial-intelligence-in-hospitality-market

Murray, K., Chen, C., Kuo, T. C., Chen, Y., & Hu, C. (2023). Blockchain and tourism: A systematic literature review and future research agenda. *Tourism Management Perspectives*, 52, 107–121. DOI: 10.1016/j.tmp.2022.06.013

Nabi, S., Khan, M., & Khan, S. (2023). Security and privacy in smart home environments: A review of contemporary trends and future directions. *Journal of Network and Computer Applications*, 239, 103723. DOI: 10.1016/j.jnca.2023.103723

Nightingale, E. (2023). The future of the hotel industry: Smart technologies and their implications. *Journal of Hospitality and Tourism Management*, 49, 50–60. DOI: 10.1016/j.jhtm.2023.09.002

Oliha, J. S., Biu, P. W., & Obi, O. C. Johnson Sunday OlihaPreye Winston BiuOgagua Chimezie Obi. (2024). Securing the smart city: A review of cybersecurity challenges and strategies. *Engineering Science & Technology Journal*, 5(2), 496–506. DOI: 10.51594/estj.v5i2.827

Om, S. (2023). The role of artificial intelligence in the hospitality industry. In P. Jena & B. Singh (Eds.), *Artificial Intelligence and the Future of Tourism and Hospitality* (pp. 37–57). Springer International Publishing. https://doi.org/DOI: 10.1007/978-3-031-37614-3_3

Pawlik, L., Wroblewska, A., Kaczmarek, A., & Kaczmarek, P. (2024). Digital transformation and consumer behavior in the hospitality industry: Implications for managers. *Journal of Business Research*, 171, 353–362. DOI: 10.1016/j.jbusres.2023.12.045

Pugh, M., & Robinson, R. (2024). The impact of mobile payment systems on hotel guest experiences: Evidence from the UK hospitality sector. *Tourism Management Perspectives*, 51, 145–153. DOI: 10.1016/j.tmp.2024.03.004

Santos, J. R., Gonçalves, R. F., & Gonçalves, M. C. (2023). Consumer perceptions of sustainability in hotels: A study in Portugal. *Sustainability*, 15(2), 928. DOI: 10.3390/su15020928

Scelza, R. (2023). Smart cities: A technological approach to urban challenges. *Technological Forecasting and Social Change*, 189, 123284. DOI: 10.1016/j.techfore.2023.123284

Tiwari, P., & Sharma, A. (2024). Examining the influence of smart technologies on consumer decision-making in the hospitality sector. *Journal of Retailing and Consumer Services*, 72, 102143. DOI: 10.1016/j.jretconser.2023.102143

Vallespin, G., & Zubeldia, J. M. (2023). Impact of COVID-19 on the perception of security in hotels: A perspective from customers. *International Journal of Hospitality Management*, 106, 102257. DOI: 10.1016/j.ijhm.2022.102257

Zhang, H. (2024). The evolving role of technology in hospitality: A critical review. *International Journal of Hospitality Management*, 112, 102262. DOI: 10.1016/j.ijhm.2022.102262

KEY TERMS AND DEFINITIONS

Automated Systems: Automated systems are technology-driven processes that perform tasks without human intervention. In hotels, automated systems can include self-service kiosks for check-in/check-out, automated room controls, and systems for managing bookings and guest requests. These systems improve efficiency, reduce human error, and enhance the overall guest experience by providing quick and seamless service.

Data Analytics: Data analytics involves examining large sets of data to uncover patterns, correlations, and insights that can inform decision-making. In the context of the hospitality industry, data analytics can be used to personalize guest experiences, optimize pricing strategies, improve operational efficiency, and enhance marketing efforts by understanding guest behavior and preferences.

Data Security: Data security involves protecting digital information from unauthorized access, corruption, or theft throughout its lifecycle. In the hospitality industry, ensuring data security is critical for safeguarding guest information, such as personal details, payment information, and preferences. Robust data security measures help prevent breaches, maintain trust, and comply with privacy regulations.

Guest Experience: Guest experience encompasses all interactions and impressions a guest has with a hotel, from booking and check-in to their stay and check-out. It includes the quality of service, comfort, convenience, and overall satisfaction with the amenities and services provided. Enhancing guest experience is crucial for fostering loyalty, positive reviews, and repeat business.

Hospitality Industry: The hospitality industry is a broad category of fields within the service sector that includes lodging, food and beverage service, event planning, theme parks, travel, and tourism. It focuses on providing services and experiences to guests, often emphasizing customer satisfaction and quality of service.

Smart Hotel Technologies: Smart hotel technologies refer to advanced digital and automated systems integrated into hotel operations to enhance guest experiences and streamline management processes. These technologies include Internet of Things (IoT) devices, voice assistants, smart thermostats, automated check-in/check-out systems, and mobile apps that allow guests to control various aspects of their stay, such as room lighting and temperature, from their smartphones.

Sustainability: Sustainability in the hospitality industry refers to adopting practices that reduce environmental impact and promote ecological balance. This includes energy conservation, waste reduction, using renewable resources, and implementing eco-friendly technologies and practices. Sustainable hotels aim to minimize their carbon footprint and contribute positively to the environment and community.

Chapter 12
Ancient Wonders, Modern Tech:
AI's Role in Enhancing the Tourist Experience at Egypt's Heritage Sites

Bassam Samir Al-Romeedy
Faculty of Tourism and Hotels, University of Sadat City, Egypt

Hamada Hussein
Faculty of Tourism and Hotels, University of Sadat City, Egypt

ABSTRACT

Egypt's ancient heritage sites are a major draw for global tourism, attracting millions of visitors each year. However, effectively managing and enhancing the visitor experience at these complex and historically significant locations presents ongoing challenges. This chapter explores how artificial intelligence (AI) technologies can be leveraged to improve various aspects of the tourist experience at Egypt's heritage sites. Strategic implementation of AI can significantly enhance visitor experience, satisfaction, and overall engagement at Egypt's archaeological treasures. Recommendations are provided for policymakers, tourism authorities, and industry stakeholders to effectively integrate AI capabilities while preserving the integrity of these irreplaceable cultural assets. The chapter contributes important insights into the evolving role of AI in elevating the tourist experience at the world's most iconic heritage destinations.

DOI: 10.4018/979-8-3693-7021-6.ch012

INTRODUCTION

Egypt is home to an extraordinary array of cultural heritage sites, each possessing unique historical significance and captivating allure. These sites provide tangible connections to the country's ancient civilizations, offering insights into the ingenuity, beliefs, and achievements of past eras. Among the most iconic of these heritage sites is the Giza Pyramid Complex, which includes the legendary Pyramids of Giza and the enigmatic Sphinx. Another renowned heritage site is the Valley of the Kings, situated near Luxor. This expansive necropolis served as the final resting place for numerous pharaohs and their families, with tombs that house exquisite artwork, hieroglyphics, and artifacts, offering invaluable insights into ancient Egyptian royal culture (Fritze, 2021; Mustafa, 2021; Schoch & McNally, 2005).

Preserving and protecting these heritage sites is critically important, not only for their intrinsic cultural value but also for their role in fostering sustainable tourism and economic development. Ongoing conservation efforts, improved security measures, and strategic management plans are essential to ensure that these ancient wonders continue to inspire and educate visitors for generations to come (Chhabra, 2010).

Artificial Intelligence (AI) has emerged as a transformative technology in the realm of heritage site management and preservation. The integration of AI systems has significantly enhanced various aspects of heritage site stewardship, from monitoring and maintenance to visitor engagement. AI-powered technologies facilitate precise, real-time monitoring of the structural health and environmental conditions of heritage sites (Chashyn et al., 2024; Cameron, 2021). Advanced data analysis capabilities inherent in AI algorithms empower decision-makers to predict future challenges and take timely, effective measures to safeguard the physical integrity of these invaluable cultural assets (Bibri et al., 2024). Moreover, AI-driven tools, such as 3D modeling and digital reconstruction, have revolutionized the way heritage sites are documented, studied, and presented to the public, contributing to the holistic preservation and celebration of humanity's shared heritage (Farahat et al., 2022). Beyond the physical preservation of heritage sites, AI-enabled solutions have also transformed the visitor experience, personalizing tour itineraries, providing real-time information, and facilitating multilingual interpretation, fostering deeper engagement and a more enriching encounter for tourists (Farahat, 2023).

The transformative impact of AI extends beyond the realm of conservation and preservation at heritage sites. AI has revolutionized the way visitors engage with and experience these cultural treasures, opening up new avenues for accessibility, education, and immersive exploration. AI-driven virtual tours, augmented reality (AR) experiences, and interactive digital exhibits have empowered heritage sites to reach global audiences in unprecedented ways. These technologies allow visitors, both on-site and remote, to delve into the rich history and architectural marvels of heritage sites, seamlessly blending the physical and digital realms. By bringing the past to life through captivating, multimedia-driven narratives, AI-enabled experiences have the potential to foster deeper understanding, appreciation, and personal connection with cultural heritage (Chisom et al., 2024; Hutson & Hutson, 2024).

However, the integration of AI within heritage site management and visitor engagement is not without its challenges. Concerns surrounding data privacy, ethical considerations in the representation and interpretation of cultural heritage, and the substantial investment required in technology and expertise must be carefully addressed. Balancing these complexities with the substantial benefits that AI offers is crucial for the sustainable and responsible integration of this transformative technology (Mohamed et al., 2022). As heritage authorities and stakeholders navigate this dynamic landscape, it is imperative to develop robust governance frameworks, prioritize user privacy, and ensure that the cultural significance of heritage sites is authentically and respectfully conveyed. By striking this delicate balance, the integration of AI can unlock new avenues for the preservation, presentation, and appreciation of the world's cultural treasures, ensuring that these invaluable legacies are protected and celebrated for generations to come (Al-Romeedy, 2024b).

The integration of AI at heritage sites has significantly enhanced the tourist experience by providing more interactive, personalized, and informative visits. AI-driven technologies such as virtual tours and augmented reality (AR) applications enable tourists to explore heritage sites in innovative ways. For example, visitors can use AR to view reconstructions of historical events or architectural features that no longer exist, offering a deeper understanding and connection to the site's history. AI chatbots and virtual guides provide real-time information and answers to visitor queries, creating a more engaging and educational experience. These technologies make heritage sites accessible to a wider audience, including those who may not be able to visit in person, thereby democratizing cultural heritage (Farahat, 2023; Al-Romeedy, 2024c).

AI significantly enhances the visitor experience at heritage sites by personalizing interactions based on individual preferences and behaviors. AI algorithms analyze visitor data to recommend tailored tour routes, highlight specific exhibits of interest, and provide content in multiple languages, catering to international tourists (Farahat et al., 2022). This customization ensures each visitor enjoys a unique and enriching experience. Additionally, AI helps manage crowd control by predicting visitor flow and suggesting optimal visiting times, improving overall comfort and satisfaction. Despite these benefits, challenges such as ensuring data privacy, maintaining the authenticity of the heritage experience, and investing in necessary infrastructure and training must be addressed. Balancing these considerations is crucial for successfully leveraging AI to enhance the tourist experience at heritage sites (Centorrino et al., 2021; Khan et al., 2024).

This study examines the potential of AI technologies to elevate the tourist experience at Egypt's heritage sites. Through a comprehensive review of scholarly literature, the research delves into the multifaceted ways in which AI can be leveraged to improve various aspects of the visitor journey. As well, the study explores how AI-powered applications can enhance pre-visit planning and trip personalization, providing tourists with customized itineraries, real-time availability updates, and personalized recommendations based on their interests and preferences. During the on-site experience, the research investigates how AI-driven audio guides, translation services, and immersive storytelling can foster deeper engagement and understanding of the sites' historical and cultural significance. Furthermore, the study analyzes the role of AI in optimizing crowd management, improving accessibility, and enhancing the overall safety and security of heritage sites. By illuminating the transformative potential of AI in the context of Egypt's heritage tourism, this research aims to guide policymakers, heritage authorities, and industry stakeholders in their efforts to leverage emerging technologies to unlock new dimensions of visitor engagement and sustainable site management.

CASE DESCRIPTION: EGYPTIAN'S HERITAGE SITES

The study exploring AI's impact on enhancing the tourist experience at Egypt's heritage sites is critically important because it bridges the gap between technological progress and cultural preservation in a region rich with historical significance. Iconic sites like the Great Pyramids and the Sphinx are not only pivotal to Egypt's tourism sector but also vital to global cultural heritage. Balancing the influx of visitors with the need to protect these ancient landmarks poses considerable challenges. AI technologies, such as AR, virtual reality (VR), and sophisticated data analytics, present innovative solutions that can significantly improve the visitor experience. They offer interactive, immersive, and tailored tours that bring historical narratives to life, provide in-depth educational content, and forge a stronger connection between tourists and the sites. Additionally, AI can enhance visitor management, boost operational efficiency, and aid conservation efforts by monitoring site conditions and controlling visitor flow. This study will yield valuable strategies for integrating AI in ways that enhance both the quality of the visitor experience and the sustainable management of Egypt's cultural heritage, ensuring that technological advancements contribute positively to the preservation and educational impact of these historical treasures.

Heritage sites of Egypt mirror a mixture of diverse cultures starting as early as the pyramids at the Giza Plateau to modern times monuments. This mixture of cultures is obvious in the architecture, art and practices maintained at these sites (Tyldesley, 2023). The colossal pyramids at Giza and Saqqara reflect the mystery of architecture and engineering of ancient Egypt. The step pyramid of Djoser at Saqqara exemplifies the early stages of the construction of pyramids. The pyramids of Giza, the Great Pyramid in particular, represent the height of innovation in Egyptian architecture (Lehner, 1997). Religious beliefs and practices of ancient Egypt were evident in its temples. The Karnak temple serves as an open-air museum. The architectural styles included in the Karnak temples extend from the Twelfth Dynasty throughout the Graeco-Roman times. The splendor of the Karnak temple with its Great Hypostyle Hall and Sacred Lake, highlights the devotion to the deity Amun-Re and the political integration of religion (Barguet, 1962; Golvin & Goyon, 1987). Also in Luxor, the prominent Opet festival was celebrated every year. The ritual procession included the carrying of a statue of the Theban traid, Amun-Re, Mut and Khonsu, from Karnak temple to Luxor temple and aimed at reinforcing the divine status of the king who was recognised as the god's "beloved son" (Abdel Raziq, 1974; Abdel Raziq, 1987).

For nearly five hundred years, the kings of the New Kingdom were interred in the Valley of the Kings. With at least 63 tombs excavated there, these richly decorated tombs give the visitor an excellent opportunity to explore the beliefs in the afterlife as envisaged by the ancient Egyptians. Among the prominent tombs in the Valley of the Kings are the tombs of Thutmose III, in whose tombs the first complete version of the earliest afterlife book in the New Kingdom, the Amduat (Book of what is in the Netherworld) was attested. Also significant is the marvelous tomb of Tutankhamun (Reeves & Wilkinson, 1996). The Valley of the Queens housed the burials of the Queens of the New Kingdom as well as noble women. Valley of the Queens was known as "Place of the Beauty". In this valley, the tomb of Nefertari is a real masterpiece. The various scenes depicted in her tomb are impressive and the colors are vivid to this day. The queen is represented playing the Senet game. Other scenes show her in the presence of various deities including Ptah, Neith, Serqet, Atum and Osiris (McDonald, 1996).

The builders and artisans who build and decorated the tombs of the kings and the queens of the New Kingdom settled in a neighboring village now known as Deir el Medina. The significance of the site comes from two reasons. Firstly, Deir el-Medina is a main source of our knowledge oof ancient Egypt's jurisdiction, economy, practices of administration, and daily life. Secondly, the site gives a glimpse on the life of a working category in ancient Egypt about which mainly royalty is known. We now know that about 70 families of the workers and the craftsmen at the Valley of the Kings have lived in Deir el-Medina. The tombs of these craftsmen and artisans are still preserved. These include the tombs of Amenemhat (TT340), Inerkhau (TT359 and TT 299), Nakhtamun (TT 335), Neferhotep and Nebnefer (TT 6), Neferhotep (216), Pashedu (TT 3), Ramose, and Sennedjem (TT 1). These tombs are beautifully decorated and the scenes in them show aspects from the afterlife as well as the daily life of the deceased (Davies, 1999).

Ramesses II commissioned the two giant rock-cut temples of Abu Simbel, which were relocated from their original site to save them from the rising water of Lake Nasser, which stood as signals of the Egyptian power and influence over Nubia. The temples are features, among many other things, by solar alignment which takes places twice a year (on 22nd February and 22nd October). These dates, despite lack of evidence, are perhaps the king's birthday and his coronation (Hawass, 2000; UNESCO World Heritage).

With the introduction of the Greeks, the tradition of dedicating temples to Egyptian deities continued. Among the distinguished temples of the Graeco-Roman Period are the temples of Edfu, the temple of Dendera, the temple Esna and the Philae temple. The later was dedicate to goddess Isis and combines Ptolemaic and Egyptian religious and architectural styles (Cauville & Mohamed Aly, 2013).

Following the introduction of Christianity to Egypt, the monks built monasteries in the heart of the desert. Halfway between Cairo and Alexandria, there are four remarkable Coptic monasteries: Anba Beshoy, El Baramous, El Suryian and Anba Makar. The Monastery of El Suryian was founded in the Sixth Century. There are three main churches in the monastery. The first is that of the Virgin Mary which dates to 645 AD and can be reached through a courtyard. That courtyard adjoins another larger courtyard with a garden whose south side is bordered by El Adhra "The Virgin" church. To the west of the church is the old refectory with a kitchen. This was where the monks, living in isolation during the week, met on Sunday and spent the night praying. Another church is that of Saint John which is a small single-ailed chapel (Khs-Burmester, 1954).

The Islamic Period witnessed the introduction of novel structures that were not known in earlier periods like the sabils. Sabils (water dispensaries) are buildings that were used for providing drinking water for pedestrians as well as animals. Sabils existed almost everywhere in Old Islamic Cairo and their number reached 300 sabils. Among the well-known sabils of Cairo are those of Qait Bey, AbdulRahman Katukhda and Mohammed Ali Pasha (Al-Husseiny (1988).

AI AND HERITAGE SITES

AI is increasingly transforming the tourism and hospitality industries by revolutionizing business operations and enhancing the overall customer experience. AI-powered solutions enable hotels, airlines, and travel organizations to streamline operations, personalize services, and gain insights into consumer behavior. The use of chatbots, predictive analytics, and intelligent recommendation systems has changed how travelers plan, book, and interact with service providers (Buhalis et al., 2019; Milton, 2024). By automating tasks, optimizing resource allocation, and providing personalized recommendations, AI helps these businesses improve efficiency, reduce costs, and deliver exceptional service. As technology evolves, AI's role in tourism and hospitality is expected to grow, driving innovation, and enhancing the travel experience for both businesses and consumers (Limna, 2023; Bulchand-Gidumal, 2022).

AI's application in the management and preservation of heritage sites has become increasingly important. AI-powered technologies address various challenges, from digitizing and cataloging historical artifacts to enhancing visitor experiences. Using computer vision, natural language processing, and predictive analytics, AI systems assist in identifying, classifying, and conserving cultural heritage objects. Additionally, AI-driven virtual and augmented reality experiences immerse visitors in the history and context of these sites, making the past come alive in engaging and educational ways. AI-powered chatbots and intelligent navigation systems improve wayfinding and provide personalized information to visitors, enhancing their overall engagement and understanding. As AI continues to evolve, its integration with heritage management promises new opportunities for preserving, interpreting, and accessing our shared cultural legacies (Farahat, 2023).

The integration of AI technologies in heritage sites has revolutionized preservation, management, and visitor engagement by enabling precise monitoring of structural health and environmental conditions for effective maintenance, using advanced data analysis to predict risks and deterioration, and employing tools like 3D modeling for detailed restoration insights. This approach not only safeguards the physical integrity of heritage sites but also enhances the understanding and appreciation of their cultural value (Nag & Mishra, 2024; Rueda-Esteban, 2019). AI-driven virtual tours, augmented reality experiences, and interactive exhibits further transform visitor engagement by making these sites more accessible and educational globally. However, challenges such as data privacy, ethical considerations, and significant investment in technology and expertise must be addressed to sustainably integrate AI in heritage site management, ensuring these cultural treasures are preserved for future generations (Farahat, 2023; Farahat et al., 2023).

The integration of AI in heritage sites has revolutionized the preservation, management, and visitor experience of these cultural treasures. AI technologies enable precise monitoring of structural health and environmental conditions, facilitating timely maintenance and effective conservation efforts. Advanced data analysis allows AI to predict potential risks and deterioration, ensuring proactive measures are taken to protect these invaluable sites. Additionally, AI-driven tools such as 3D modeling and digital reconstruction provide detailed insights into the historical and architectural significance of heritage sites, aiding in their restoration and documentation (Trček, 2022; Sofi et al., 2022; Bourgeois et al., 2024).

There are many heritage sites that are already using advanced technologies. A prominent example is the Egyptian Museum in Cairo, which has adopted a range of cutting-edge technologies to both protect its priceless artifacts and enhance visitor engagement. Known for housing some of the most significant artifacts from ancient Egyptian civilization, the museum has implemented digital preservation methods to safeguard its delicate pieces. For example, 3D scanning is used to produce detailed digital replicas of artifacts, ensuring that even if the originals suffer damage over time, their precise details are preserved. This approach is crucial for preserving ancient sculptures, mummies, and fragile relics that are vulnerable to environmental wear. These digital records not only serve as a safeguard for preservation but also provide researchers worldwide with virtual access to the artifacts, eliminating the need for physical handling or transport.

In addition to preservation, the Egyptian Museum has integrated VR and AR to enhance the educational experience for visitors. Through AR, guests can use their smartphones or tablets to interact with exhibits in innovative ways, such as viewing reconstructions of ancient temples or tombs as they might have appeared millennia ago. For instance, visitors can use AR to see how artifacts from the Tutankhamun collection were originally arranged in the tomb, deepening their understanding of the collection's historical and cultural context. VR experiences also allow visitors to take virtual tours of ancient Egyptian sites, such as the Pyramids of Giza or the Valley of the Kings, providing a dynamic, immersive experience that static displays cannot match. Moreover, the museum utilizes AI-driven tools to analyze and interpret its extensive collection. AI helps catalog and cross-reference artifacts, streamlining research and facilitating the identification of connections between different historical pieces. For example, AI algorithms can compare artifacts with extensive databases to determine materials or origins, supporting studies on ancient Egyptian trade and craftsmanship. AI also aids in deciphering hieroglyphs, enriching the historical narrative presented to visitors (Farahat, 2023).

AI AND TOURIST EXPERIENCE IN HERITAGE SITES

Pre-Visit

Visit Planning and Trip Personalization

AI-powered chatbots and virtual assistants are transforming the trip planning process for tourists visiting heritage sites. These intelligent systems leverage machine learning algorithms to analyze users' interests, budgets, and schedules, providing personalized recommendations for relevant heritage sites, exhibits, and activities. By examining a tourist's browsing history, social media activity, and other data, AI curates tailored itineraries that enhance the visitor's experience (Farahat et al., 2022). In addition to personalized recommendations, AI optimizes the overall trip planning experience. Intelligent planning tools create efficient itineraries by considering factors such as opening hours, crowd levels, and transportation options. Some systems even use real-time data on queue times to provide dynamic updates, ensuring visitors can maximize their time at the heritage site (Guo et al., 2024; Yu et al., 2018). Personalization stands as a central aspect of AI incorporation during the pre-visit phase. AI-driven booking platforms enable tourists to effortlessly purchase tickets, make reservations, and coordinate their entire trip from a single, user-friendly platform. Leveraging machine learning, these platforms analyze user preferences and behaviors, offering tailored package deals and intelligent suggestions to enrich the overall trip experience. Moreover, advanced translation and natural language processing technologies empower heritage sites to furnish pre-visit information, booking services, and trip planning support in multiple languages. This ensures a more accessible and intuitive planning process for international tourists, eliminating language barriers and enhancing the overall accessibility of the heritage site experience (Naramski, 2020; Farahat, 2023).

Providing Tourists with Customized Itineraries

AI has revolutionized the pre-visit phase of the tourist experience at heritage sites through the provision of personalized itineraries. AI-powered platforms leverage extensive datasets to analyze individual preferences, past behaviors, and interests, enabling them to craft customized travel plans tailored to each tourist's specific requirements. This capability ensures that visitors receive recommendations aligned with their interests, whether they are passionate about history, art, or adventure (Al-Romeedy, 2024b). A primary advantage of AI in this context is its capacity to streamline the planning process. Tourists can input their preferences and constraints, such as budget, time availability, and specific interests, into AI-driven applications.

Subsequently, the AI processes this data to compose an itinerary that optimizes the visitor's experience. For example, it may suggest optimal times to visit popular sites to avoid crowds, recommend nearby attractions or dining establishments, and even highlight special events or exhibitions tailored to the tourist's interests (Alhosani & Alhashmi, 2024; Shrestha et al., 2024; Pisoni et al., 2021). Furthermore, AI can provide virtual previews of recommended itineraries using AR and VR technologies, allowing tourists to take virtual tours of heritage sites and gain insights into what they can expect during their visit. This immersive experience not only aids in informed decision-making but also generates excitement and anticipation for the upcoming trip. Additionally, AI-driven chatbots and virtual assistants are accessible to assist tourists with any inquiries they may have during the planning process. These tools deliver real-time information and assistance, ensuring that visitors have all the necessary details to finalize their itineraries confidently. Whether it's historical context, practical travel advice, or logistical information such as opening hours and ticket prices, AI ensures that tourists are well-equipped before embarking on their journey (Farheen et al., 2024; Farahat, 2023).

Immersive Virtual Experiences

In addition to its role in personalized trip planning and itinerary suggestions, AI is reshaping the pre-visit stage by enabling more immersive virtual experiences for tourists. Leveraging technologies such as VR, AR, and mixed reality (MR), heritage sites can now offer potential visitors a richer preview of their forthcoming on-site visit. These AI-driven virtual experiences enable tourists to virtually explore historical landmarks, navigate detailed 3D renderings of ancient structures, and engage with digital representations of artifacts and exhibits. Through the integration of computer vision, natural language processing, and other AI functionalities, these virtual tours can be highly interactive, responding to users' movements, gaze, and voice commands to create a truly immersive encounter (Fan et al., 2022; Al-Romeedy, 2024c). Innovatively, some heritage sites are employing AI to craft personalized, narrative-driven virtual experiences that guide users through thematic journeys. For instance, a virtual expedition of an ancient temple might feature AI-generated characters sharing anecdotes and insights about the site's historical and cultural significance, rendering the encounter more captivating and informative (Reinhard, 2019; Mohamed et al., 2022). These immersive virtual pre-visit encounters not only evoke excitement and anticipation for the actual on-site visit but also assist tourists in better planning their itinerary and pinpointing specific exhibits or attractions they wish to prioritize during their visit. By facilitating a deeper level of exploration and acquaintance even before visiting the heritage site physically, AI is fundamentally transforming how tourists prepare for and engage with these significant cultural landmarks (Aliyah et al., 2023; Pillai & Sivathanu, 2020).

Real-Time Availability Updates

AI has notably enhanced the pre-visit phase of the tourist journey at heritage sites through the provision of real-time availability updates. These updates ensure that tourists are equipped with the latest information regarding site conditions, availability, and events, enabling them to plan their visits more effectively and circumvent potential inconveniences (Sia et al., 2023; Benckendorff et al., 2019). AI systems can actively monitor and disseminate real-time data concerning heritage sites. For instance, AI-driven platforms can deliver immediate updates on ticket availability, operating hours, and any alterations in access due to maintenance or special events. This up-to-the-minute information aids tourists in avoiding disappointment and scheduling their visits during periods of optimal accessibility and reduced crowding (Mishra et al., 2024; Al-Romeedy, 2024a).

Additionally, AI can seamlessly integrate with various booking platforms and reservation systems to provide timely updates on availability. Tourists can receive notifications regarding the optimal times to visit, ensuring they can secure their preferred slots effortlessly. This feature is particularly valuable for popular heritage sites facing high visitor demand, aiding in the effective management and distribution of tourist flow (Periasamy & Dinesh, 2024; Legrand et al., 2022). Moreover, AI enhances the pre-visit experience by offering real-time insights into visitor capacity and crowd levels. By analyzing data from diverse sources such as sensors and cameras installed at the sites, AI can furnish accurate estimates of current and anticipated visitor numbers. Tourists can leverage this information to select less congested times for their visits, enhancing their overall experience by avoiding lengthy queues and overcrowded areas. Furthermore, AI-powered chatbots and virtual assistants are on hand to furnish immediate responses to any queries tourists may have concerning real-time availability. These tools can address inquiries about specific site particulars, upcoming events, or last-minute alterations, ensuring that visitors are well-informed and can adapt their plans accordingly (Farahat, 2023).

Personalized Recommendations

AI has notably improved the pre-visit phase of the tourist experience at heritage sites by delivering personalized recommendations tailored to individual interests and preferences. This customized approach ensures that each visitor's journey is uniquely crafted to suit their preferences, resulting in a more immersive and gratifying experience (Nag & Mishra, 2024; Alabau-Montoya & Ruiz-Molina, 2020). AI possesses the capability to analyze extensive datasets to comprehend a tourist's preferences thoroughly. By examining past behaviors, search history, and demographic details, AI systems can generate tailored suggestions for heritage sites, attractions, and activities that resonate with each visitor's specific interests. For instance, history enthusiasts might receive recommendations for sites steeped in historical significance, while art aficionados could be directed to venues celebrated for their artistic heritage (Kırtıl & Aşkun, 2021; Yang et al., 2024). Moreover, AI-powered platforms continuously adjust these recommendations in real-time based on tourists' evolving preferences, ensuring ongoing relevance and engagement throughout the planning phase. Visitors receive meticulously crafted itineraries featuring must-visit attractions, hidden gems, and bespoke events tailored to their interests, thereby enhancing their overall satisfaction and experience (Farheen et al., 2024; Song & He, 2023). Another notable benefit of AI-driven personalization lies in its capacity to augment tourists' decision-making process. By furnishing detailed descriptions, reviews, and multimedia content for each suggested site, AI assists travelers in making well-informed choices regarding their itinerary composition. This comprehensive information empowers tourists to prioritize their preferences effectively, maximizing their visit's enjoyment and value. Additionally, AI seamlessly integrates with various travel planning tools and services, offering a cohesive, end-to-end personalized journey. For instance, AI recommends nearby accommodations, dining options, and transportation services that align with the visitor's preferences and budget, streamlining the planning process and ensuring every aspect of the trip caters to the tourist's requirements (Singh & Bhadani, 2020; Chaudhari & Thakkar, 2020).

On-Site Experience

AI-Driven Audio Guides

AI has revolutionized the on-site experience for heritage site tourists with AI-driven audio guides, offering personalized and immersive exploration. Unlike traditional guides, AI versions tailor content to individual preferences, interests, and location within the site, providing dynamic and context-sensitive information. For instance, if a tourist shows interest in architectural details, the guide offers deeper insights into construction techniques. This customization enhances engagement and relevance. Additionally, AI guides offer real-time updates, adjusting narrative pace and content as visitors move through the site, ensuring timely and contextually appropriate information. Interactive elements like quizzes further enrich the experience, fostering engagement and learning (Balling et al., 2021; Kowalczyk-Anioł, 2023). Another notable benefit of AI-driven audio guides lies in their capacity to accommodate multiple languages and accessibility requirements. These guides can seamlessly switch between languages, catering to the diverse needs of international visitors. Additionally, they can incorporate features tailored to individuals with disabilities, such as visual aids for the hearing impaired or simplified language for those with cognitive impairments. This inclusiveness ensures that a wider audience can fully engage with and appreciate the offerings of the heritage site. Moreover, AI-driven audio guides have the capability to integrate with various digital tools and services to enhance the on-site experience. For instance, they can interface with augmented reality (AR) applications to provide visual overlays that complement the audio narration, thereby offering a more immersive and interactive experience. Additionally, they can connect to social media platforms, enabling visitors to share their experiences and insights in real time (Farahat, 2023).

Translation Services

AI has significantly enhanced the on-site experience at heritage sites by employing advanced translation services, thereby rendering these locations more accessible and enjoyable for international visitors. Powered by AI, translation tools can promptly convert written and spoken content into various languages, effectively dismantling language barriers and ensuring that non-native speakers can fully participate in the site's exhibits and information (Pisoni et al., 2021; Karakas, 2023). AI-driven translation services offer real-time and precise translations of signage, informational plaques, and exhibit descriptions. Visitors can utilize their smartphones or dedicated devices to scan text and receive immediate translations in their chosen language. This functionality empowers tourists to grasp the historical and cultural context of the exhibits without necessitating pre-arranged translations or guidebooks. Consequently, visitors can explore the site at their own pace and acquire a more profound understanding of its significance (Marr, 2019; Al-Romeedy, 2024b, c). AI-powered tools provide real-time audio translation services in addition to text translations, enabling visitors to understand spoken content during guided tours, presentations, and interactive displays in their native language. By utilizing earpieces connected to AI translation apps, tourists can receive live translations of tour guides or recorded audio guides, ensuring they don't miss important information due to language barriers. This feature enhances the inclusivity and accessibility of heritage sites, catering to a global audience (Chowdhary, 2020). Furthermore, AI translation extends to interactive kiosks and digital displays within heritage sites, automatically adjusting content based on the user's preferred language. This personalized experience not only enhances understanding but also fosters a more engaging and interactive exploration of the site (Farahat, 2023; Karayılanoğlu & Arabacıoğlu, 2020). Additionally, AI translation technology facilitates multilingual communication between staff and visitors at heritage sites. Equipped with AI translation apps, heritage site staff can efficiently assist international tourists, overcoming language barriers in interactions. Whether addressing inquiries, giving directions, or sharing additional information about exhibits, staff can communicate more seamlessly, thus enriching the visitor experience. This personalized engagement fosters a sense of welcome and appreciation among visitors, thereby leaving a positive impression of the heritage site (Al-Romeedy, 2024c).

Immersive Storytelling

In the domain of heritage tourism, the incorporation of AI technologies is fundamentally transforming the on-site experience for tourists by introducing immersive storytelling techniques. AI-powered tools are redefining how narratives are presented, providing visitors with captivating and interactive methods to engage with the history and cultural significance of heritage sites. Through immersive storytelling, tourists are transported into the past, experiencing historical events with vivid detail and gaining a profound insight into the site's heritage (Jia et al., 2023; Hutson & Hutson, 2024). A notable aspect of AI-driven immersive storytelling is its capacity to craft dynamic and personalized narratives customized to the interests and preferences of each visitor. By analyzing real-time visitor data and interactions, AI algorithms can adjust storytelling experiences in real-time, delivering content that resonates with individual visitors. Whether through augmented reality (AR) headsets, audio guides, or interactive exhibits, tourists can explore heritage sites at their own pace, uncovering hidden stories and insights along the journey (Farahat, 2023). Furthermore, AI technologies elevate the authenticity of storytelling encounters by integrating diverse multimedia components like 3D reconstructions, archival footage, and augmented reality overlays. These immersive features transport tourists across various historical epochs, enabling them to envision the site's evolution and its historical importance. Through the seamless fusion of digital and tangible elements, AI-driven storytelling crafts a multisensory journey that sparks curiosity and nurtures emotional bonds with the heritage site (Paulauskas et al., 2023; Hutson & Hutson, 2024).

Optimizing Crowd Management

The integration of AI technologies is significantly improving crowd management during on-site experiences in the heritage tourism sector (Nag & Mishra, 2024). Heritage sites frequently attract large volumes of visitors, posing challenges in ensuring a seamless and enjoyable visit for all while safeguarding the site's integrity and safety (Singh et al., 2024). AI-powered crowd management systems offer innovative solutions to these challenges by harnessing data analytics, predictive modeling, and real-time monitoring to optimize visitor flow and enhance overall satisfaction (Suthar et al., 2023; Chiwaridzo & Chiwaridzo, 2024). One primary application of AI in crowd management involves analyzing visitor behavior and movement patterns to pinpoint congestion areas and potential bottlenecks. Through the deployment of sensors, cameras, and other IoT devices, heritage sites gather data on visitor traffic, queue lengths, and dwell times, providing valuable insights into crowd dynamics and interactions within the site. AI algorithms then process this information to forecast future crowd movements and efficiently allocate resources to high-demand areas like ticket counters, entrances, or popular attractions (Mohamed et al., 2022; Orama et al., 2022). Additionally, AI-driven crowd management systems empower heritage sites to deploy dynamic pricing and ticketing tactics that respond to real-time demand and capacity limitations. Through dynamically altering ticket prices or entry schedules based on fluctuating visitor volumes, sites can encourage visits during off-peak hours, alleviate congestion during peak periods, and optimize revenue generation. These flexible pricing strategies not only enhance visitor experiences by minimizing wait times and overcrowding but also allow heritage sites to enhance operational efficiency and sustainability (Farheen et al., 2024; Farahat et al., 2022).

Improving Accessibility

As heritage sites aim for greater inclusivity and accessibility, AI-driven technologies are playing a crucial role in enhancing the on-site experience for visitors with diverse needs and abilities. By incorporating intelligent systems that cater to various accessibility requirements, these cultural establishments are striving to ensure that all tourists can fully engage with and appreciate the profound history and cultural significance of the sites (Pisoni et al., 2021; Farahat et al., 2022). One significant way AI enhances accessibility is by integrating voice-controlled navigation and audio description services. These intelligent systems utilize natural language processing and text-to-speech functionalities to grant visitors with visual or mobility impairments seamless access to information and navigation of the site via voice commands. This enables them to explore exhibits, access multimedia content, and even communicate with on-site staff without relying on traditional physical interfaces (Khang et al., 2023). Moreover, AI-driven captioning and translation services are being incorporated into the on-site experience, allowing visitors with hearing impairments or those speaking different languages to fully understand interpretive signage, audio guides, and interactive exhibits. By offering real-time, contextually appropriate captions and translations, these sophisticated systems help dismantle barriers and promote a more inclusive and immersive experience for everyone. Additionally, some heritage sites are exploring the utilization of AI-powered assistive technologies, such as robotic mobility aids or augmented reality overlays, to assist visitors with physical disabilities in navigating the often challenging terrain and environments of historic sites. These intelligent systems can offer guidance, assistance, and even virtual enhancements to the physical space, ensuring accessibility and appreciation of the site's cultural treasures for all (Farahat, 2023; Al-Romeedy, 2024b, c).

Safety and Security of Heritage Sites

As heritage sites witness a steady rise in visitor numbers, ensuring the safety and security of both tourists and cultural assets has become paramount. Fortunately, AI-driven systems are playing a pivotal role in enhancing on-site safety and security measures seamlessly and discreetly. One significant contribution of AI in this regard is through sophisticated video analytics and surveillance systems. By leveraging computer vision algorithms and deep learning models, these intelligent systems can autonomously detect and monitor suspicious activities, recognize potential threats, and promptly alert security personnel in real-time. This proactive approach enables heritage site operators to swiftly respond to incidents and preemptively address risks, thereby maintaining a safe and secure environment for all visitors (Zreik, 2024; Jaafar & Pierre, 2023; Muhammad et al., 2021). In addition to threat detection, AI-driven systems can also assist in refining crowd control strategies and emergency response protocols. Through the analysis of visitor movement patterns and the utilization of predictive analytics, these intelligent systems can anticipate congestion points or bottlenecks, allowing staff to implement crowd management measures more efficiently. Moreover, in emergency situations, these systems can rapidly identify the safest evacuation routes and offer real-time guidance to visitors, thereby improving the overall safety and responsiveness of the site (Bayashot, 2024; Padovano et al., 2024).

AI'S LIMITATIONS: ACKNOWLEDGING THE CHALLENGES

While AI brings numerous benefits to various sectors, especially in customer relations, it's crucial to acknowledge its limitations to maintain a balanced perspective. As AI technology evolves and becomes more integrated into everyday life and business practices, several notable concerns emerge that warrant careful consideration. These include data privacy issues, algorithmic bias, and the risk of over-reliance on technology.

A major limitation of AI lies in its dependency on extensive data to function effectively. AI systems, particularly those used in customer relations, rely heavily on customer data to deliver personalized experiences, recommendations, and support. This reliance raises significant privacy concerns as the collection, storage, and analysis of personal data can lead to discomfort among customers if the purposes and methods of data collection are not transparent. For instance, AI tools often access sensitive information like purchasing habits, location data, and interaction histories. Without adequate data protection measures, there is a risk of unauthorized access, breaches, or misuse. Although regulations like the General Data Protection Regulation (GDPR) in Europe address these concerns, discrepancies in regional and industry-specific standards mean that the risk of misuse persists. As customers become increasingly aware of and concerned about data privacy, businesses must carefully balance leveraging AI for enhanced customer experiences with ensuring rigorous data handling practices (Al-Romeedy, 2024, 2024a, b; Farahat, 2023).

Algorithmic bias is another significant limitation of AI, where unintended biases in training data can skew AI system outputs. AI systems, especially those utilizing machine learning, learn from historical data, and any inherent biases in this data can lead to biased predictions and decisions. This can result in unfair treatment or reinforcement of existing societal inequalities. For example, biased AI chatbots might offer unequal service based on demographic factors like gender or race. Such biases can also affect decision-making in hiring, credit scoring, and personalized marketing. To mitigate this, companies must ensure that training data is representative and free from biases, and they should continuously monitor and audit AI systems to correct any biased behaviors (Gaafar, 2020).

The risk of over-reliance on technology is another crucial limitation. As AI systems advance, there is a danger that businesses and individuals may overly depend on these technologies, potentially diminishing human judgment and oversight. Over-reliance can lead to a loss of human skills, reduced critical thinking, and difficulties in managing complex or nuanced situations that AI may not handle well. For example, while AI can efficiently address routine customer inquiries, it may struggle with more complex or emotionally charged issues, where human empathy and problem-solving are crucial. Additionally, over-reliance can result in lack of accountability, especially if AI systems make biased or incorrect decisions. Determining responsibility for such decisions can be challenging, which may erode customer trust. Furthermore, businesses heavily reliant on AI may face operational disruptions if the technology fails or produces errors, especially if human staff are unprepared to take over (Farahat, 2023).

CONCLUSION AND IMPLICATIONS

The chapter highlights the significant potential of AI in elevating the tourist experience at Egypt's heritage sites, fostering deeper appreciation, comprehension, and preservation of the cultural riches from this ancient civilization. With the ongoing evolution of AI technologies, Egypt is well-positioned to harness innovation and ingenuity, paving the way for sustainable tourism growth and cultural conservation. Egyptian policymakers should establish comprehensive regulatory frameworks that foster the adoption of AI technologies at heritage sites while prioritizing data privacy and ethical considerations. These frameworks must ensure that heritage organizations handle visitor and operational data responsibly, adhering to global privacy standards like the GDPR, while also considering the cultural and ethical implications of using AI in heritage management. In addition, clear guidelines should be created for AI deployment to ensure that technology is used to enhance, not distort, the historical and cultural narratives of Egypt's heritage.

To encourage investment in AI, policymakers should provide financial incentives such as grants, subsidies, or tax breaks specifically for heritage sites looking to integrate AI-driven technologies. By offering dedicated funding, the government can support the development of the necessary digital infrastructure, including data collection, storage systems, and AI-based tools for managing and analyzing site-specific information. Furthermore, creating public-private partnerships and incentivizing industry stakeholders to invest in AI solutions tailored to heritage sites will help accelerate the adoption of these technologies. Integrating AI-driven heritage management into Egypt's broader tourism and environmental strategies will promote a more sustainable approach, ensuring that AI supports both economic growth and conservation efforts.

As well, heritage authorities in Egypt should prioritize the integration of AI-powered data analytics into their management practices, allowing for more informed decision-making processes. This will require significant investment in digital infrastructure, such as sensors, data collection systems, and AI platforms that can process large volumes of heritage data. These technologies will provide real-time insights into visitor behavior, site conditions, and conservation needs, helping authorities optimize both the visitor experience and site preservation. In addition to technology investments, heritage authorities must focus on upskilling their workforce by providing training in AI tools and data interpretation to ensure staff can effectively leverage these systems.in addition, interdisciplinary collaboration will be critical for success. Authorities should establish teams that include heritage specialists, AI technologists, and tourism experts to develop comprehensive, data-driven strategies that address the unique challenges faced by each site. These teams can balance the goals of tourism, conservation, and sustainability by using AI to analyze data and predict the impact of tourism on heritage sites. By harnessing the power of AI, heritage authorities will be able to create more sustainable and visitor-friendly strategies while preserving the cultural and historical integrity of Egypt's heritage sites.

Moreover, industry stakeholders, such as technology companies, tourism operators, and consulting firms, have a crucial role in enhancing the use of AI at Egypt's heritage sites. These stakeholders should collaborate directly with heritage institutions to co-develop AI-powered solutions that address specific challenges, such as managing visitor flows, enhancing security, and ensuring the conservation of artifacts. By partnering with heritage authorities, industry stakeholders can tailor AI applications to the unique needs of each site, ensuring that the technology is both practical and effective. In addition, industry players should provide training and ongoing technical support to heritage staff, helping them maximize the value of AI systems. This includes offering workshops and hands-on guidance to ensure smooth integration of AI into daily operations. Beyond direct collaboration with heritage sites, industry stakeholders should work closely with policymakers and academic institutions to drive innovation in AI applications tailored to heritage management. This collaboration will help create industry-wide standards and best practices for the use of AI in cultural preservation, ensuring that the deployment of AI technologies is sustainable, ethical, and aligned with long-term heritage conservation goals.

Future Research Directions

Future research on "AI's Role in Enhancing the Tourist Experience at Egypt's Heritage Sites" should concentrate on several critical areas to enhance understanding and optimize the benefits of AI in cultural heritage tourism. Initially, longitudinal studies are essential to assess the long-term effects of AI technologies on visitor satisfaction and engagement. This research should monitor how AI-driven tools, such as virtual reality (VR), augmented reality (AR), and personalized recommendations, impact tourists' experiences and their perceptions of heritage sites over time. Furthermore, evaluating the effectiveness of various AI applications in improving educational content and interactive experiences can provide valuable insights into refining these technologies to meet diverse visitor needs. It is also important to investigate how cultural and contextual factors influence the efficacy of AI technologies, as understanding how different demographics and cultural backgrounds interact with AI-driven experiences can help tailor solutions to specific audiences. Additionally, addressing the ethical implications and privacy concerns related to AI in tourism is crucial to ensure that data collection and usage comply with rigorous standards of transparency and security. Comparative studies that assess AI-enhanced experiences against traditional methods can offer benchmarks for best practices and identify areas for improvement.

REFERENCES

Abdel Raziq, M. (1974). The dedicatory and building texts of Ramesses II in Luxor temple. *The Journal of Egyptian Archaeology*, 60(1), 142–160. DOI: 10.1177/030751337406000116

Abdel Raziq, M. (1986). *Das Sanktuar Amenophis III im Luxor-Tempel, Studies in Egyptian Culture No. 3*. Peeters.

Al-Husseiny, M. (1988). *The Ottoman Sabils in Cairo 1517-1798*. Medbouli Press. (in Arabic)

Al-Romeedy, B. (2024a). Breaking chains, building futures: Blockchain's impact on sustainable tourism. In *Promoting responsible tourism with digital platforms*. IGI Global. DOI: 10.4018/979-8-3693-3286-3.ch006

Al-Romeedy, B. (2024b). Web of wonders: Sustainable digital marketing strategies for unforgettable African tourism destinations. In *Promoting responsible tourism with digital platforms*. IGI Global. DOI: 10.4018/979-8-3693-3286-3.ch010

Al-Romeedy, B. (2024c). AI and HRM in tourism and hospitality in Egypt: Inevitability, impact and future. In *HRM, artificial intelligence and the future of work: Critical insights from the global South*. Palgrave Macmillan. DOI: 10.1007/978-3-031-62369-1_13

Alabau-Montoya, J., & Ruiz-Molina, M. E. (2020). Enhancing visitor experience with war heritage tourism through information and communication technologies: Evidence from Spanish Civil War museums and sites. *Journal of Heritage Tourism*, 15(5), 500–510. DOI: 10.1080/1743873X.2019.1692853

Alhosani, K., & Alhashmi, S. M. (2024). Opportunities, challenges, and benefits of AI innovation in government services: A review. *Discover Artificial Intelligence*, 4(1), 1–19. DOI: 10.1007/s44163-024-00111-w

Aliyah, L., Lukita, C., Pangilinan, G., Chakim, M., & Saputra, D. (2023). Examining the impact of artificial intelligence and internet of things on smart tourism destinations: A comprehensive study. *APTISI Transactions on Technopreneurship*, 5(2sp), 135–145. DOI: 10.34306/att.v5i2sp.332

Balling, L. W., Townend, O., Mølgaard, L. L., Jespersen, C. B., & Switalski, W. (2021). AI-driven insights from AI-driven data. *Health Review*, 28(01), 27–29. DOI: 10.1108/HR-01-2021-0020

Barguet, P. (1962). *Le Temple d'Amon-Re à Karnak: Essai d'exégèse*. Cairo.

Bayashot, Z. A. (2024). The contribution of AI-powered mobile apps to smart city ecosystems. *Journal of Software Engineering and Applications*, 17(3), 143–154. DOI: 10.4236/jsea.2024.173008

Benckendorff, P. J., Xiang, Z., & Sheldon, P. J. (2019). *Tourism information technology*. CABI. DOI: 10.1079/9781786393432.0000

Bibri, S. E., Krogstie, J., Kaboli, A., & Alahi, A. (2024). Smarter eco-cities and their leading-edge artificial intelligence of things solutions for environmental sustainability: A comprehensive systematic review. *Environmental Science and Ecotechnology*, 19, 100330. DOI: 10.1016/j.ese.2023.100330 PMID: 38021367

Bourgeois, I., Ascensão, G., Ferreira, V., & Rodrigues, H. (2024). Methodology for the application of 3D technologies for the conservation and recovery of built heritage elements. *International Journal of Architectural Heritage*, 1–12. Advance online publication. DOI: 10.1080/15583058.2024.2341327

Buhalis, D., Harwood, T., Bogicevic, V., Viglia, G., Beldona, S., & Hofacker, C. (2019). Technological disruptions in services: Lessons from tourism and hospitality. *Journal of Service Management*, 30(4), 484–506. DOI: 10.1108/JOSM-12-2018-0398

Bulchand-Gidumal, J. (2022). Impact of artificial intelligence in travel, tourism, and hospitality. In *Handbook of e-Tourism* (pp. 1943–1962). Springer International Publishing., DOI: 10.1007/978-3-030-48652-5_110

Cameron, F. R. (2021). *The future of digital data, heritage and curation: In a more-than-human world*. Routledge. DOI: 10.4324/9781003149606

Cauville, S., & Mohamed Aly, I. (2013). *Philæ. Itinéraire du visiteur*. Peeters, Leuven, Paris, Walpole.

Centorrino, P., Corbetta, A., Cristiani, E., & Onofri, E. (2021). Managing crowded museums: Visitors flow measurement, analysis, modeling, and optimization. *Journal of Computational Science*, 53, 101357. DOI: 10.1016/j.jocs.2021.101357

Chashyn, D., Khurudzhi, Y., & Daukšys, M. (2024). Directions for the formation of city intelligent models using artificial intelligence for the post-war reconstruction of historical buildings. *Budownictwo i architektura*, 23(1), 73-86. https://doi.org/ DOI: 10.35784/bud-arch.570

Chaudhari, K., & Thakkar, A. (2020). A comprehensive survey on travel recommender systems. *Archives of Computational Methods in Engineering*, 27(5), 1545–1571. DOI: 10.1007/s11831-019-09363-7

Chhabra, D. (2010). *Sustainable marketing of cultural and heritage tourism.* Routledge. DOI: 10.4324/9780203855416

Chisom, O. N., Biu, P. W., Umoh, A. A., Obaedo, B. O., Adegbite, A. O., & Abatan, A. (2024). Reviewing the role of AI in environmental monitoring and conservation: A data-driven revolution for our planet. *World Journal of Advanced Research and Reviews*, 21(1), 161–171. DOI: 10.30574/wjarr.2024.21.1.2720

Chiwaridzo, O. T., & Chiwaridzo, S. (2024). From crisis to prosperity: Leveraging robots, artificial intelligence, and service automation for sustainable tourism in Zimbabwe. *Business Strategy & Development*, 7(2), e380. DOI: 10.1002/bsd2.380

Chowdhary, K. R. (2020). Fundamentals of artificial intelligence. In *Artificial Intelligence: Principles and Applications* (pp. 603-649). Springer. DOI: 10.1007/978-81-322-3972-7

Davies, B. (1999). *Who's who at Deir el-Medina: A prosopographic study of the royal workmen's community.* Nederlands Instituut.

Fan, X., Jiang, X., & Deng, N. (2022). Immersive technology: A meta-analysis of augmented/virtual reality applications and their impact on tourism experience. *Tourism Management*, 91, 104534. DOI: 10.1016/j.tourman.2022.104534

Farahat, E. (2023). Applications of artificial intelligence as a marketing tool and their impact on the competitiveness of the Egyptian tourist destination (Doctoral dissertation, Minia University).

Farahat, E., Mohamed, M., & Al-Romeedy, B. (2022). Artificial intelligence applications and their impact on the competitiveness of the Egyptian tourist destination. *Research Journal of the Faculty of Tourism and Hotels. Mansoura University*, 11(2), 57–93.

Farheen, N. S., Badiger, C. S., Kishore, L., Dheeraj, V., & Rajendran, S. R. (2024). A future look at artificial intelligence in the world of tourism. In *Marketing and big data analytics in tourism and events* (pp. 1–16). IGI Global., DOI: 10.4018/979-8-3693-3310-5.ch001

Fritze, R. H. (2021). *Egyptomania: A history of fascination, obsession and fantasy.* Reaktion Books.

Golvin, A. J., & Goyon, J. (1987). *Les bâtisseurs de Karnak.* CNRS.

Guo, J., He, J., & Wu, X. (2024). Shopping trip recommendations: A novel deep learning–enhanced global planning approach. *Decision Support Systems*, 182, 114238. Advance online publication. DOI: 10.1016/j.dss.2024.114238

Hawass, Z. (2000). *The mysteries of Abu Simbel*. The American University in Cairo Press.

Hutson, J., & Hutson, P. (2024). Immersive technologies. In *Inclusive smart museums: Engaging neurodiverse audiences and enhancing cultural heritage accessibility* (pp. 77–96). Routledge., DOI: 10.1007/978-3-031-43615-4_5

Khalil, E. A., Khedher, R. A., & Al-Romeedy, B. (2023). Leveraging machine learning in smart city tourism: A strategic approach. In *Artificial Intelligence in Sustainable Development: A Smart Tourism Perspective* (pp. 56–76). IGI Global., DOI: 10.4018/978-1-7998-8563-7.ch003

Klein, M. (2021). *Data protection in cultural heritage institutions: A comparative perspective*. Routledge.

Mahnken, J. (2024). Digitalization in heritage tourism: Challenges and opportunities for Egyptian tourism in the digital age. In *Sustainable tourism in heritage sites: Managing environmental challenges and promoting cultural preservation* (pp. 45–60). IGI Global., DOI: 10.4018/978-1-7998-6893-7.ch003

Majumdar, A., & Kumar, R. (2024). The future of digitalization in heritage tourism: Impacts on cultural preservation and sustainable development. In *Smart and sustainable tourism: Emerging concepts and technologies* (pp. 100–120). IGI Global., DOI: 10.4018/978-1-7998-8022-9.ch006

Mekhlif, M. (2023). Utilizing AI technology for promoting sustainable tourism in Egypt. *International Journal of Culture, Tourism and Hospitality Research*, 17(1), 45–59. DOI: 10.1108/IJCTHR-01-2022-0025

Mekhlif, M., & Al-Romeedy, B. (2023). Leveraging AI and machine learning for enhancing customer experience in Egypt's tourism sector. *Journal of Tourism and Services*, 14(1), 10–25. DOI: 10.2139/ssrn.4319181

Mohamed, M., & El-Bakry, H. (2023). Virtual reality in tourism: A potential game changer in promoting cultural heritage sites. *Tourism (Zagreb)*, 71(1), 93–108. DOI: 10.1016/j.tour.2022.03.004

Mohamed, M. I., & Ameer, A. (2024). Future of artificial intelligence in the tourism industry: A study of the trends and opportunities in the Middle East. *Middle East Journal of Business*, 19(1), 45–58. DOI: 10.5742/MEJB.2024.85296

Mohamed, M. I., & Lamsal, R. B. (2024). AI applications in smart tourism: A systematic review and research agenda. *Tourism Management Perspectives*, 47, 100850. DOI: 10.1016/j.tmp.2023.100850

Murray, J., & Pinder, D. (2024). Artificial intelligence and sustainable tourism: Opportunities and challenges in Africa. *African Journal of Hospitality, Tourism and Leisure*, 13(1), 10–30. DOI: 10.46222/ajhtl.19770720-66

Nader, Y. (2023). Role of AI in enhancing the travel experience: The case of Egypt. *Journal of Travel Research*, 62(2), 134–150. DOI: 10.1177/00472875211051310

Nawaz, N., & Ali, M. (2023). Unleashing the potential of AI in tourism management: A comparative analysis of developed and developing countries. *Tourism Review*. Advance online publication. DOI: 10.1108/TR-06-2021-0168

Odeh, M. (2023). AI in tourism: A comprehensive analysis of its impact on sustainable development in Egypt. *Tourism and Hospitality Research*, 23(1), 40–54. DOI: 10.1177/14673584211061773

Osman, A. R., Nasha, E. H., & Al-Khouri, A. (2023). The role of artificial intelligence in enhancing tourist experience: A case study of Egypt. *Journal of Destination Marketing & Management*, 24, 100722. DOI: 10.1016/j.jdmm.2023.100722

Parker, E. (2024). Digital marketing in tourism: New directions and challenges in the era of artificial intelligence. In *Innovations in digital marketing: A global perspective* (pp. 1–15). IGI Global., DOI: 10.4018/978-1-7998-7674-7.ch001

Petrov, P. V., & Kovalchuk, N. I. (2023). The role of machine learning and big data in promoting cultural heritage: Opportunities and challenges for the tourism industry. *Journal of Tourism Research*, 31(1), 30–45. DOI: 10.1016/j.jtr.2022.07.008

Pons, J., & Munoz, A. (2024). Smart tourism and AI: Future directions and implications for heritage management. *International Journal of Tourism Research*. Advance online publication. DOI: 10.1002/jtr.2570

Poot, T., & Huijbregts, H. (2023). Enhancing the visitor experience in cultural heritage: A model of smart technologies in tourism. *International Journal of Culture, Tourism and Hospitality Research*, 17(2), 198–215. DOI: 10.1108/IJCTHR-01-2023-0004

Raev, G. (2023). The future of tourism in Egypt: Trends and opportunities in AI. *International Journal of Tourism Research*, 25(3), 407–420. DOI: 10.1002/jtr.2638

Sakson, A. (2024). *Digital technologies in cultural heritage: The future of tourism*. Springer.

Samson, R. (2023). *Augmented reality in the travel industry: A guide to best practices*. Routledge.

Savic, D. (2023). Exploring the integration of AI in enhancing user experiences in tourism: A case study from Egypt. *Tourism Management Perspectives*, 51, 124–136. DOI: 10.1016/j.tmp.2024.100862

Shah, P., & Rahman, M. (2024). The impact of artificial intelligence on the hospitality industry: Current trends and future perspectives. *International Journal of Hospitality Management*, 40, 14–28. DOI: 10.1016/j.ijhm.2023.104172

Sidani, S. (2024). Implementing AI and big data analytics in tourism: A strategic approach for sustainable development. *Journal of Business Research*, 144, 1–15. DOI: 10.1016/j.jbusres.2022.06.019

Stevens, R., & McMurray, D. (2023). AI and the future of smart tourism: Opportunities and challenges in Africa. *Tourism and Hospitality Research*, 23(2), 117–134. DOI: 10.1177/14673584211061773

Tam, Y. S., & Wong, C. W. Y. (2023). Implementing smart technologies in heritage tourism: A study of Chinese tourist attractions. *Journal of Tourism and Cultural Change*, 22(1), 64–79. DOI: 10.1080/14766825.2022.2151538

Wang, H. (2024). *Digital transformation in tourism: Opportunities for smart cities*. IGI Global.

Wang, J., & Chen, L. (2023). The impact of AI on the hospitality and tourism industries: Current trends and future directions. *Journal of Business Research*, 146, 454–467. DOI: 10.1016/j.jbusres.2022.06.019

Zayed, R. A. (2024). Role of artificial intelligence in transforming the Egyptian tourism landscape: A perspective on future opportunities. *International Journal of Culture, Tourism and Hospitality Research*, 18(1), 1–15. DOI: 10.1108/IJCTHR-10-2022-0238

Zhao, Y., & Zhang, H. (2023). Smart tourism: A new direction for tourism development. *International Journal of Tourism Research*, 25(1), 67–84. DOI: 10.1002/jtr.2619

Zhou, H. (2024). Exploring the role of AI in promoting cultural tourism: Insights from case studies. *Journal of Heritage Tourism*. Advance online publication. DOI: 10.1080/1743873X.2024.2341325

KEY TERMS AND DEFINITIONS

Artificial Intelligence: The creation of machines that mimic human cognitive functions, allowing them to perform tasks such as problem-solving, learning, and decision-making.

Augmented Reality: A technology that enhances the real world by adding virtual elements, such as images or sounds, through devices like smartphones or AR glasses.

Heritage Sites: Places of historical, cultural, or natural importance that are preserved due to their value to human history.

Tourist Engagement: The degree to which travelers actively interact with and participate in the offerings of a destination.

Tourist Experience: The overall perception and activities a visitor goes through during their travels.

Tourist Satisfaction: A traveler's level of happiness with their trip, based on how well it met their expectations.

Virtual Reality: A digitally created three-dimensional environment that users can explore and interact with, giving the feeling of a real-world experience.

Chapter 13
Travel the World From the Comfort of Your Own Home:
Exploring Factors Related to Virtual Place Applications' Visitor Satisfaction

Ece Özer Çizer
 https://orcid.org/0000-0002-8597-2073
Yıldız Technical University, Turkey

Şirin Gizem Köse
 https://orcid.org/0000-0003-4075-7166
MEF University, Turkey

Arzu Karaman Akgül
 https://orcid.org/0000-0002-4606-6756
Yıldız Technical University, Turkey

ABSTRACT

Virtual place applications (VPA) have increased their popularity especially with the interest of innovative people. VPAs provide the opportunity to visit anywhere in the world without leaving home. In addition, the electronic world of mouth encourages people to use VPA. However, there is still a question of whether the virtual visitors will want to visit these places later, and how the price cost of the physical visit will affect this intention. In the light of these, data were collected online from the participants by questionnaire method and analyzed with structural equation model. The results of the analysis show that the relationships between entertainment, edu-

DOI: 10.4018/979-8-3693-7021-6.ch013

cation, innovation, and e-WOM with customer satisfaction and visitor satisfaction with travel intention were significant and positive. Furthermore, the study presents the moderating role of price cost in the relationship between visitor satisfaction and travel intention.

INTRODUCTION

As digitalization continues to proliferate, everything is getting virtual. In line with the development in technology, music, games, books, and more all took their place in a virtual environment. The Covid-19 pandemic has also accelerated the virtualization process (Shore et al., 2020). Jobs, education, shopping, and even travel have become virtual. As the coronavirus pandemic has brought tourism, travel and accommodation to a halt around the world, it has led companies to create new experiences for tourists by quickly adopting virtual experiences. With virtual experiences, tourists can perform touristic activities and see new places without leaving their homes. Although time has passed since the coronavirus, the use of virtual experiences in tourism continues. There are now more options available to consumers than just physically going somewhere. Virtual tourism experiences create a completely new type of tourism and open new horizons in customer experience (Wei et al., 2023). Virtual tourism can be defined as a type of tourism where visitors learn about tourist destinations in a virtual setting without having to travel physically (Kim & Hall, 2019). Virtual tourism enhances an actual journey. With virtual tourism, people can go to touristic places, view museum exhibits, even go on virtual walks without leaving house (Bilińska et al., 2023).

The arrival of new technologies such as virtual reality has transformed the experiences (Flavián et al., 2019). Verma et al.'s study (2022) indicates that the way various virtual tourism components such as smartphones, augmented reality, virtual reality, big data, artificial intelligence is changing the virtual tourism landscape. The experiences improved and altered via technology is called extended reality experiences. Virtual and real environments are blended with the help of technological advancements. Virtual reality (VR), mixed reality (MR) and augmented reality (AR) are all tools of experiences transmitted through technology (Orr et al., 2021). The advent of virtual tourism has made it possible for people to travel and explore new locations, giving people access to experiences and opportunities they might not have had in the past. They also increase well-being of people, which is very important (Zhang & Hacikara, 2023). Virtual tourism also decreases perceived risk of tourism consumers associated with physical tourism (Özdemir-Uçgun & Şahin, 2024).

Lockdown, social distance restrictions, and travel barriers caused by the Covid-19 pandemic have led people to seek alternatives. People who could not leave their homes started to spend more time on the Internet (Hawdon et al., 2020). People who stayed inside have been educated in virtual classes worked from home and shopped over the Internet (de Oliveira Dias et al., 2020). They also used the internet to travel and see new places (Jarratt, 2021). A recent study revealed that social distancing practices have decreased in-person tours while increased the intention to use virtual reality touristic activities (Itani & Hollebeek, 2021).

The developers who realized this need responded by virtualizing the spaces. In this way, places have moved to virtual reality applications. The demand for virtual spaces such as virtual museums was increased (Audunson et al., 2020; Carvajal et al., 2020; Parker & Saker, 2020). People who want to have fun and learn to see new places have increasingly started to use virtual reality applications. These applications provided easy-to-reach virtual spaces for those who want to see museums, holiday destinations, foreign countries, and national recreation areas. For example, a person who could not leave their home due to the Covid-19 pandemic had the opportunity to visit a famous museum in another country while at home with virtual reality applications.

Virtual reality (VR) is defined as human-computer interface that simulates the real environment by moving it into a virtual environment. Participants can act as they wish in this virtual world as long as allowed by the developer (Zheng et al., 1998). A person using virtual reality is immersed in an entirely simulated world that greatly obscures their real-world surroundings. Usually, additional tools are needed to be fully immersed in the virtual environment (Orr vd., 2021). According to Guttentag (2010), three-dimensional environments are called virtual environments. In this study, 3D environments are considered virtual environment applications (VEAs), and the inputs and outputs related to tourism VEAs are examined. In VEAs, visitors can navigate and interact with the VEAs using a mouse, keyboard, controller, or touch screen (Guttentag, 2010). Google's Street View is the one of examples VEAs. Google's Street View lets visitors tour the famous places from home can and they can discover wonderful artworks from various eras.

Digital technologies have improved tourism experience from the bottom to the top and tourism and travel industries have become innovative and smart industries (Pencarelli, 2020). Various artificial intelligence technologies such as virtual reality have also changed the traditional way people travel. As such, virtual reality applications are also frequently used in tourism industry (Li & Chen, 2019; Gibson & O'Rawe, 2018; Tussyadiah et al., 2017; Guttentag, 2010). The studies in the literature show that virtual reality applications with entertainment and educational content in tourism marketing increase the satisfaction of the applications by attracting the attention of the users (Lee, 2020; Han et al, 2019; Southall et al, 2019; Huang et al;

2016; Pallud & Straub 2014). These applications are frequently used by innovative individuals who are most open to innovations and technology and like to try new things (Chung, 2015). In addition, these individuals tend to share their level of satisfaction with the educational and entertaining experiences offered by virtual reality applications with others by using electronic word of mouth communication e-WOM (González-Rodríguez et al., 2020; Ruben et al, 2017; López & Sicilia, 2014). Also, the satisfaction levels of visitors with virtual reality applications affect their intention to visit places in real life (Kim et al, 2020; Lee et al., 2020; Chung et al., 2015).

While anyone with internet access can easily access virtual space applications, it costs more to visit physically. At this point, the perceived price cost of visiting physically is a crucial construct to explain intention. In this study, unlike the studies on virtual reality applications in tourism marketing, the moderator role of price cost in the relationship between visitor satisfaction and travel intention will be examined in addition to other relationships between variables.

To analyze and answer to issues related to VR, this study attempts (1) to examine visitors' VPAs satisfaction as an educational platform, (2) to analyze visitors' VPAs satisfaction as an entertainment platform (3) to assess the effect of visitors' innovativeness level on VPAs satisfaction, (4) to explore if there is a relationship between visitors' VPAs satisfaction and visitors' e-WOM, (5) to test the relationship between VPA satisfaction and travel intention and, (6) to investigate the moderating role of price cost in the relationship between VPA satisfaction and travel intention.

LITERATURE REVIEW

Education and Entertainment Experience

Experience economics underlines how economies should shift towards a service-oriented approach (Pine & Gilmore, 1998). Experience economy attracted great attention in various fields including tourism. The focus was on the fact that tourism not only offers products and services but also satisfies the experience needs of travelers. The importance of experience in tourism stems from the expectation that the process of consuming services or products of tourists would turn into a process they would value and then be remembered by them (Lee et al., 2020). Pine and Gilmore (1998, 1999) categorized customer experience into two concepts: absorption and immersion. Absorbing experiences means living the experience from a distance. In contrast, immersion refers to completely joining in the experience (Song et al., 2015; Hosany & Witham, 2010). Extended Reality (XR) is an umbrella term that encompasses various immersive technologies, including Virtual Reality (VR), Augmented Reality (AR), and Mixed Reality (MR). These technologies blend the physical and digital worlds in different ways, creating various types of immersive experiences. Virtual travel experience (VTE) is defined as an immersive experience in which guests and hosts cooperate to engage in a location, activity, or destination made possible by synchronous technology (Wei et al., 2023). The search for pleasure and learning are two broad motivations to consume cultural and art products (Hume & Mills, 2011; Sürme & Atılgan, 2020) therefore this study includes education and entertainment experience.

Educational Aspects of Virtual Tourism

The future of travel is considered as virtual tourism, which transforms the traveler experience at a reasonable cost. Virtual reality modifies how travelers view travel destinations and change the experience landscape (Verma et al., 2022). The educational aspect of virtual reality was investigated by various studies in the literature. Virtual museums have proved their usefulness in education, and they are increasingly becoming attractive (Barbieri et al, 2017). Many studies focused on the use of virtual reality, especially in the field of education (Ibañez-Etxeberria et al., 2020; Deale 2013; Hsu 2012; Singh & Lee, 2009). One of the main purposes of using VPAs is visitors' desire to increase their understanding and ability through educational experience at the chosen destinations. VPAs allow the visitor to look up useful content while viewing the art and therefore helps the learning process (Aiello, et al., 2019). This has led to the formulation of following hypothesis.

H1: There is a significant and positive relationship between education experience and VPAs' visitor satisfaction.

Entertainment Aspects of Virtual Tourism

On the other hand, entertainment refers to the act of entertaining or amusing people (Hwang & Lee, 2019). In the simplest form, entertainment is an activity that generates enjoyment and pleasure (Benny, 2015). Entertainment was described as a mixture of tourists' absorption and passive participation by Pine and Gilmore (1998). The widespread use of virtual reality (VR) in entertainment and the general public's familiarity with it set the stage for VR's eventual inclusion into the tourism industry. This means creating a new type of tourism that is solely dependent on virtual reality technology that has the power to transform traditional ideas about travel. Virtual tourism creates a new triadic realm that consists of the tourist, the virtual destination, and the physical destination (Polishchuk et al., 2023). Entertainment is seen as a passive attitude since it refers to simply watching without direct involvement in activities (Oh et al., 2007). For example, visitors can visit the earth's most coveted destinations on personal devices with National Geographic's 360-degree videos without any active participation, they can visit art galleries, explore inside of spaceship or watch The Philadelphia Orchestra from the front side by using Google Arts & Culture. In this study, the concept of entertainment is used to express the enjoyment felt while using VPAs.

Studies point out that VPAs can educate and give pleasure to the visitor, and they can increase satisfaction through these experiences (Mahdzar et al., 2020; San-Martín et al., 2015; Petrick et al., 2001). Bae et al. (2020) point out that perceived immersion and enjoyment of mixed reality applications leads to satisfaction. This has led to the formulation of following hypothesis.

H2: There is a significant and positive relationship between entertainment and VPAs' visitor satisfaction.

Innovativeness and Electronic Word of Mouth

Innovativeness refers to how the individual is a pioneer in technology and the degree of adaptation to innovations (Mahat et al., 2012). Another definition of innovativeness is the level of willingness to accept new technologies (Agarwal & Prasad 1998). Furthermore, innovation is one of the constructs that represent a person's technology readiness (Parasuraman, 2000). Being innovative and interactive are key elements of 3D interaction interfaces (Sylaiou et al., 2010), therefore, innovative people tend to use those technologies more. A positive point of view towards acceptance of technologies leads to satisfaction (Khan et al., 2019).

One of the fundamental concepts related to technology and consumer relationship is the electronic word of mount (e-WOM) which is the electronic form of WOM. WOM is the interpersonal communication between customers, which helps them to decrease uncertainty about products and/or services (Zinko et al., 2021). For this purpose, consumers share their information and opinions about a particular product, brand, or service with other people (Hawkins et al., 2004; Anastasiei et al., 2021). With the increasing usage of the internet, consumers often use the internet to search for information about products. As a result of the information-seeking and sharing process, e-WOM has emerged (Litvin et al., 2008). The definition of eWOM was developed based on the traditional WOM concept. Accordingly, e-WOM refers to the communication that takes place on the internet about the usage or characteristics of certain goods and services by consumers (Jeong & Jang, 2011). Customer satisfaction or dissatisfaction determine e-WOM's direction (Duarte et al., 2018; Setiawan et al., 2014; Yoo et al., 2013). A satisfied visitor of a virtual tour is expected to recommend the tour to others. Therefore, the following hypotheses are formed.

H3: There is a significant and positive relationship between innovativeness and VPAs' visitor satisfaction.

H4: There is a significant and positive relationship between VPAs' visitor satisfaction and electronic word of the mount.

Visitor Satisfaction and Travel Intention

In the tourism context, satisfaction is defined as the tourist's feeling or enjoyment when the post-travel experience is better than expected (Altunel & Erkurt, 2015). Visitor satisfaction is one of the key elements of successful destination marketing (Yoon & Uysal, 2005). As satisfaction is an important construct in tourism studies; a lot of studies measured visitor satisfaction variable (Kim, 2018; Genç, 2018; Huo & Miller, 2007).

Research has proven that positive experiences and visitor satisfaction affect behavioral intentions such as visiting places in the future. Studies in the literature reveal the effects of experiences on behavioral intentions especially in tourism and museums (He & Luo, 2020; Kim et al., 2019; Jung et al., 2016; Chung et al., 2015; Chang et al., 2015; Pallud & Straub, 2014). Technological improvements in museums lead to customer satisfaction (Trunfio, 2020; Bellini et al., 2018). In this study, it is expected that visitors who are satisfied with VPAs will want to visit those places in real life and will recommend VPAs to other people. In light of the literature, the following hypothesis was proposed.

H5: There is a significant and positive relationship between VPAs' visitor satisfaction and travel intention.

Perceived Price Cost

Perceived price cost refers to the consumer's evaluation of costs associated with a product or service relative to the value they believe they will receive (Zeithaml, 1988). Travel intention and visitor satisfaction are greatly impacted by perceived pricing cost in virtual tourism because it influences users' assessments of the value of their experiences in relation to their costs. The literature considers price cost as an obstacle to travel intention since a high level of perceived price cost is likely to decrease visitors' willingness to travel (Ahn & Kwon, 2020; Chi et al., 2020; Stevens 1992). While places can be visited for free using VPAs, physical travel is costly (Erdem et al., 2006). In addition, people who are satisfied with VPAs may not want to visit if they perceive the price cost of the physical visit as high. So, price cost may affect the relationship between satisfaction and travel intention. Therefore, the following hypothesis is proposed to test the moderating role of price cost.

H6: Price cost moderates the relationship between VPAs' visitor satisfaction and travel intention.

Based on the research hypotheses, a research model is formed. Figure 1 illustrates the proposed model of the study.

Figure 1. Research model

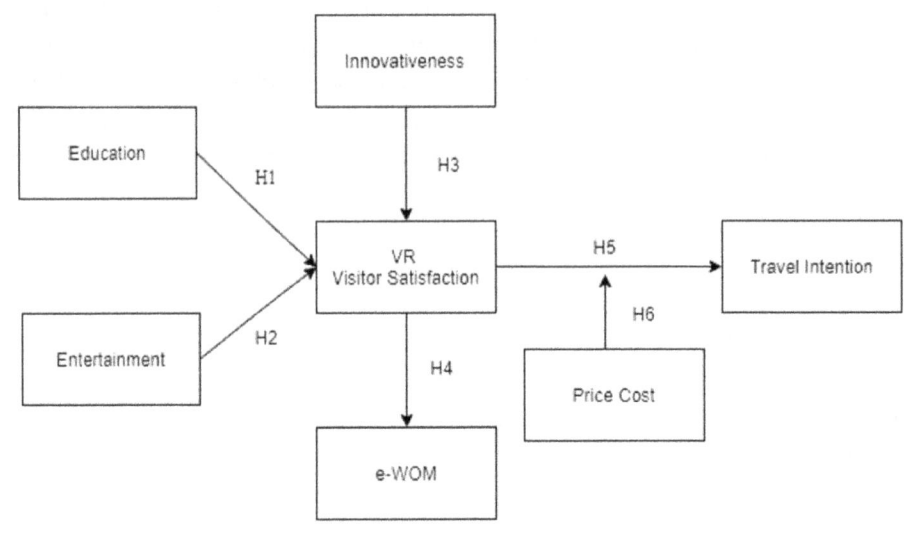

(Author's own creation)

METHODOLOGY

Survey Design

The data of the study was collected via structured questionnaires from a sample of representative people in the online environment. The questionnaire includes four parts. The aim and scope of the study were given in the first part of the questionnaire. The questionnaire's second part includes 28 items of research measures that utilized a five-point Likert scale. Measures used in the questionnaire were developed based on previous literature. The sources of the questionnaire are given in Table 1. The scales used in the study were adapted from measurement tools that have been proven to be reliable and valid in previous literature. However, certain adaptations were made to the scales considering the subject and target audience of the study. These adaptations were carried out in order to make the scales suitable for the context of the study. The original versions of the scales may contain expressions and concepts that do not exactly match the subject of the study. Therefore, changes were made to the expressions in the study to make these scales more meaningful and suitable for the context. In particular, the terminology and conceptual explanations were rearranged to appeal to the target audience of the study, the Turkish participants. In the process of translating into Turkish, the semantic integrity of the scales was preserved by taking into account linguistic and cultural differences, while ensuring that they were understandable for the participants. These changes were necessary to increase the validity and reliability of the research findings. Direct application of scales commonly used in the literature could lead to erroneous interpretations due to cultural and linguistic differences. Therefore, these adaptations made to the scales are of critical importance in order to obtain results that are suitable for the purpose of the study and the understanding of the participants. Demographic questions were asked in the third part. The general questions about virtual environment apps were asked in the final part of the questionnaire.

Table 1. Scales

Scale	Source
E-WOM	Jeong & Jang (2011)
Customer satisfaction	Han & Ryu (2012)
Education & Entertainment	Lee et al. (2020)
Visit intention	Lee et al. (2020)
Innovativeness	Chung et al. (2015)
Perceived price cost	Ahn & Kwon (2020)

Source: Author's own creation

Data Collection and Demographic Characteristics

The research population of this study is users of virtual environment applications. The convenience sampling method is chosen as the sample selection method. The main reason for choosing the convenience sampling method is that this method provides efficiency in terms of time and resources during the research process. More complex methods such as random sampling in academic research can cause serious burdens in terms of both money and time, especially in studies targeting a large population (Valerio et al., 2016). In this study, it was thought that working with quickly accessible participant groups would speed up the data access process and allow the research to be conducted more effectively. Convenience sampling helps simplify the data collection process and provides a general idea of the findings in the early stages of the research (Hossan et al., 2023). In addition, the limited resources available and the necessity to complete the research in a certain time period were also effective in choosing this method. However, this method has some limitations in terms of representing the population, and these limitations require caution regarding the generalizability of the results. 392 participants living in Turkey answered the questionnaires. However, 7 questionnaires were excluded since they were incomplete. 385 questionnaires were included in the analyses. As shown in Table 2, the data consisted of 184 females (47.8%) and 201 males (52.2%). Although the gender ratio is relatively balanced, the proportion of male participants is slightly higher. The majority of the participants (36.1%) are between the ages of 18-25. This shows that young adults predominantly participated in the study. Participants between the ages of 26-33 also constitute a significant proportion (31.7%). There is a 20.5% participation between the ages of 34-41. The rate of participants over the age of 42 is lower (6.8% - 4.9%). According to this information, it can be said that the participation of middle-aged and older individuals in the study is less than that of younger age groups. The majority of the participants have a bachelor's degree (29.9%) or a master's degree (27.3%). This shows that the participants' level of education is generally high. The rate of doctoral graduates is also significant at 15.3%. In other words, there are those who have advanced academic education among the participants in the study. On the other hand, there are 7.5% of the participants with high school education or less, which makes up a smaller portion of the participants. As a result, the participants in the study are largely young adults and individuals with a higher level of education. The gender distribution is balanced, but the young and educated participant profile is striking. This shows that the profile of users of virtual environment applications consists of young adults with a higher level of education.

Table 2. Demographic information

Variables	Characteristics	Frequency (n = 385)	Percentage (%)
Gender	Female	184	47,8
	Male	201	52,2
Age	18–25 years old	139	36,1
	26–33 years old	122	31,7
	34–41 years old	79	20,5
	42–47 years old	26	6,8
	More than 48 years old	19	4,9

continued on following page

Table 2. Continued

Variables	Characteristics	Frequency (n = 385)	Percentage (%)
Education	High school or less	29	7,5
	Associate degree	77	20
	Bachelor's degree	115	29,9
	Master's degree	105	27,3
	Doctoral degree	59	15,3

Source: Author's own creation

Measurement Model

The data were analyzed by SPSS 21 and AMOS 23. First exploratory factor analysis, reliability, and validity analyses were conducted, and then confirmatory factor analysis was conducted. Thus, scales were verified, and the research model was tested before path analyses. Table 3 shows factor loadings, reliability, and convergent validity results. According to Table 3, all of the factor loadings ranged from 0.837 to 0.983 exceeded 0.70 determined as the threshold value. All constructs' average variance extracted (AVE) values ranged from 0.63 to 0.94, exceeding the criteria of 0.5, and composite reliability (CR) for all constructs ranged from 0.87 to 0.98, exceeding the criteria of 0.7, suggesting satisfactory convergent validity (Hair et al., 2010). In addition, Cronbach's alpha (α) values ranged from 0.87 to 0.98 suggesting internal consistency (Nunnally, 1978). According to confirmatory factor analysis results, model fit indices are CFI:0,982; CMIN/df:1,744; SRMR:0,031; GFI:0,905; AGFI:0,882; RMSEA: 0,043. These results indicate that the model showed a good fit for the data (Hair et al., 2010).

Table 3. Convergent validity results

Items	Factor Loadings		Cronbach α		CR		AVE	
Education	KMO:	0,80	Bartlett's:	754,53	df:	6,00	Sig.:	0,00
EDU4	0,861		0,87		0,87		0,63	
EDU3	0,859							
EDU1	0,839							
EDU2	0,837							
Entertainment	KMO:	0,87	Bartlett's:	2074,97	df:	6,00	Sig.:	0,00

continued on following page

Table 3. Continued

Items	Factor Loadings		Cronbach α		CR		AVE	
ENT1	0,972		0,97		0,97		0,88	
ENT3	0,968							
ENT4	0,946							
ENT2	0,933							
Satisfaction	KMO:	0,78	Bartlett's:	1398,61	df:	3,00	Sig.:	0,00
S1	0,971		0,96		0,97		0,90	
S3	0,968							
S2	0,963							
Innovativeness	KMO:	0,90	Bartlett's:	1701,54	df:	10,00	Sig.:	0,00
INN4	0,939		0,94		0,94		0,75	
INN2	0,916							
INN5	0,893							
INN3	0,879							
INN1	0,848							
Electronic Word of Mouth	KMO:	0,93	Bartlett's:	3610,81	df:	15,00	Sig.:	0,00
EWOM4	0,973		0,98		0,98		0,88	
EWOM2	0,964							
EWOM1	0,947							
EWOM5	0,945							
EWOM3	0,939							
EWOM6	0,931							
Visit Intention	KMO:	0,79	Bartlett's:	1774,00	df:	3,00	Sig.:	0,00
VI2	0,983		0,98		0,98		0,94	
VI3	0,979							
VI1	0,979							
Price	KMO:	0,78	Bartlett's:	1257,31	df:	3,00	Sig.:	0,00
PRI2	0,965		0,95		0,96		0,88	
PRI3	0,961							
PRI1	0,955							

Source: Author's own creation

Table 4 demonstrates the square roots of the AVE values for all constructs diagonally. These are greater than the corresponding construct correlations. In this way, discriminant validity was assessed (Fornell & Larcker, 1981). Table 4 also shows descriptive statistics. All constructs' mean values were 2.449–3.980; standard deviation values were 0.806–1.180. Skewness and kurtosis values of all variables ranged between −1,5 and +1,5. Thus, normality was achieved (Tabachnick & Fidell, 2013).

Table 4. Discriminant validity results

Factor	Mean	SD	Skew.	Kurt.	1	2	3	4	5	6	7
EDU	3,479	0,854	-0,373	-0,222	**0,793**						
ENT	3,980	0,806	-0,289	-0,698	0,111	**0,940**					
SAT	3,685	0,845	-0,768	0,993	0,254	0,313	**0,951**				
INN	3,560	0,886	-0,258	-0,492	0,107	0,170	0,561	**0,869**			
EWOM	3,795	1,070	-1,151	0,726	0,092	-0,103	0,164	0,023	**0,940**		
VI	3,705	0,980	-0,430	-0,878	0,117	0,226	0,187	0,187	-0,090	**0,970**	
PRI	2,449	1,180	0,622	-0,820	-0,104	-0,084	-0,284	-0,188	0,157	-0,622	**0,939**

Source: Author's own creation

RESULTS

Structural Model and Hypothesis Testing

Figure 2 shows the hypotheses testing results.

Figure 2. Hypotheses testing results

(Author's own creation)
Note: ***p < .001; **p < .01; *p < .05

Table 5 shows the structural model fit indices were shown. According to the table, the results indicated a good fit to the data (Hair, 2010). All the paths were significant (p < 0.05) and positive. Thus, H1, H2, H3, H4, and H5 hypotheses are supported. Figure 2 shows the hypotheses testing results.

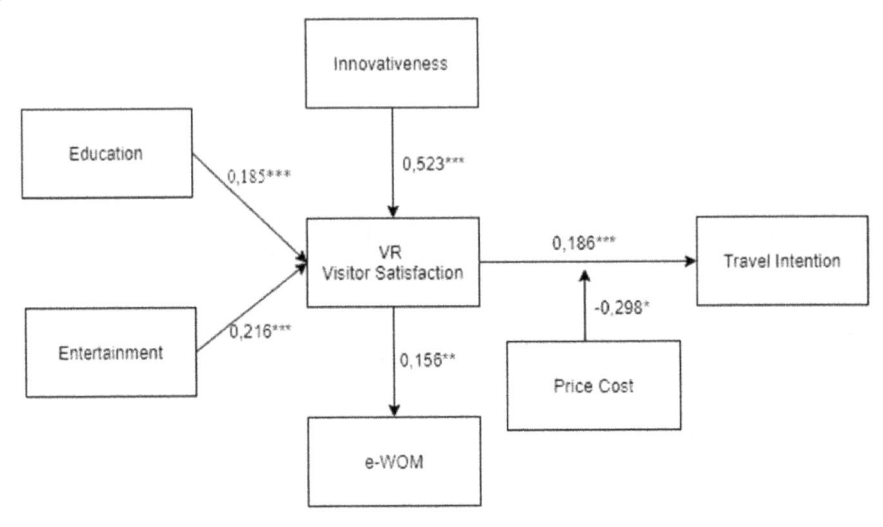

Table 5. Path results

Hypo.	Path		Std. β	Std. Error	C.R.	P	Result
H1	EDU	SAT	0,185	0,049	3,979	0,000	Supported
H2	ENT	SAT	0,216	0,045	4,978	0,000	Supported
H3	INN	SAT	0,523	0,047	10,79	0,000	Supported
H4	SAT	WOM	0,156	0,065	3,007	0,003	Supported
H5	SAT	VI	0,186	0,06	3,596	0,000	Supported

Model Fit Indices: CFI:0,983; CMIN/df:1,744; SRMR:0,078; GFI:0,911; AGFI:0,892 ; RMSEA: 0,044
Source: Author's own creation

Moderation Analysis

The moderating effect of the perceived price (PRI) is examined in the relationship between satisfaction and visit intention. First, the interaction term was created by multiplying the averages of satisfaction and perceived price, and then it was tested in the path between the interaction term and visit intention. According to Table 6, the perceived price was a moderator (β = -0,298; p = 0,045) in the relationship between satisfaction and visit intention. Therefore, Hypothesis 6 was supported.

Table 6. Moderating effect of perceived price cost

Hypo.	Path		Std. β	Std. Error	C.R.	P	Result
H6	int_PRI	VI	-0,298	0,034	-2,005	0,045	Supported

int_PRI: Interaction Term
Source: Author's own creation

Figure 3 shows the values of attitude and purchase intention at varying levels of perceived price with a 95% confidence interval.

Figure 3. Moderating effect of perceived price cost

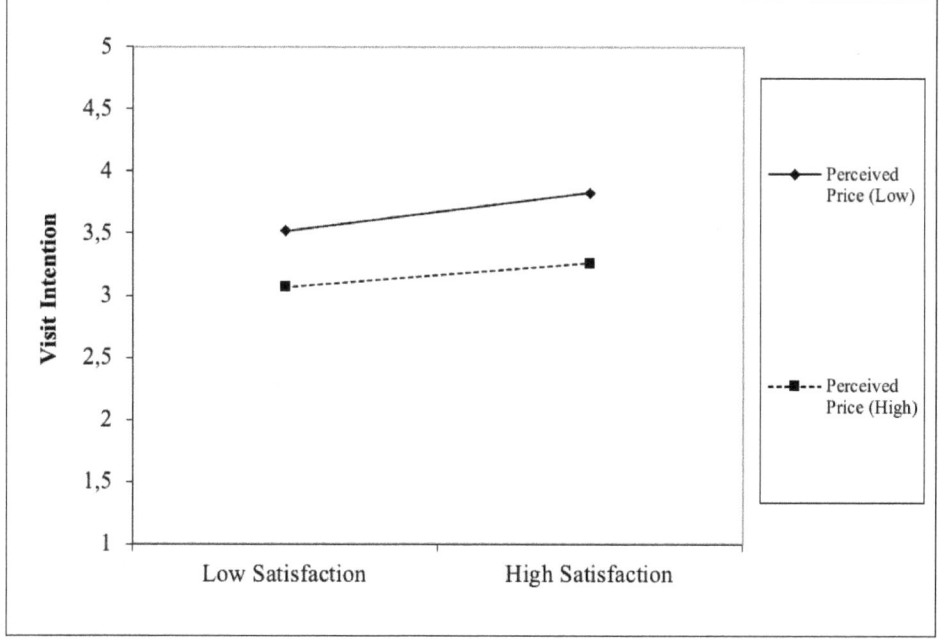

(Author's own creation)

DISCUSSION AND IMPLICATIONS

Theoretical Implications

VPAs present a great opportunity to be able to see the world, all from the comfort of your own home. In line with the technological advancements and the trends, this study explores antecedents of VPAs satisfaction, and factors affected by VPAs satisfaction were studied. In this respect, this study aims to examine the roles of education, entertainment, satisfaction, innovativeness, e-WOM, price cost, and travel intention in the context of VPAs. The antecedents of VPAs satisfaction and factors affected by VPAs satisfaction are presented in the study. The results will provide an understanding of how to increase VPAs' satisfaction and travel intention.

Some studies focused on the importance of experience creation of museums in the literature (Lee et al., 2020; Wu, 2020; Beck & Egger et al., 2018; Wagler & Hanus, 2018; Sylaiou et al., 2017). However, the potential of virtual reality and augmented reality for travel is still not extensively explored. There are very few empirical studies in the literature on this subject (Chung et al., 2015). To fill this void, this study aims to investigate factors related to virtual place applications' visitors' satisfaction and travel intention. Furthermore, this research is different from previous studies since it includes all virtual places such as museums, holiday places, and operas. The study also extends the literature by underlining the importance of price cost by adding the construct as a moderator variable.

Firstly, this study proves that education, entertainment, and innovativeness are the antecedents of visitor satisfaction of VPAs. Innovativeness has the highest effect on visitor satisfaction of VPAs (β:0,523). Pham et al. (2020) also showed that innovativeness is the strongest predictor of satisfaction among technology readiness components. Entertainment (β:0,216) and education experience provided by VPAs (β:0,185) also affect visitor satisfaction of VPAs. These results are supported by research in the literature which suggested that the dimension of absorption of the experience affects satisfaction (Aşan et al., 2020; Radder, & Han, 2015). Another finding of the study shows that visitor satisfaction of VPAs affects e-WOM (β:0,156). This finding is also congruent with previous studies (Alrwashdeh et al., 2020; Duarte et al., 2018). In addition, the study found that visitor satisfaction of VPAs influences travel intention (β:0,186) as also proven by He & Luo (2020) and Kim et al. (2019). The study also presented the moderator role of price cost in the relationship between visitor satisfaction of VPAs and travel intention (β:-0,298). This finding highlights the fact that when the price cost is higher, the intention to travel is lower. This result is similar to the results of the studies in the literature (Ahn & Kwon, 2020; Chi et al., 2020).

Practical Implications

Managing a sustainable business in an environment that is sensitive to external conditions is arduous and therefore requires constant monitoring of trends. In line with customer trends, tourism businesses have taken steps towards the digitalization of touristic activities. This study intends to provide some suggestions for the tourism industry to pave the way for the successful integration of digitalization into tourism operations. The findings revealed that the most important determinant of visitor satisfaction is innovativeness. Innovative users are open to innovations; they like to try new things. At this point, it is vital to produce innovative solutions for innovative users. VPA is an attractive tool for innovative users since it is one of the most innovative methods in this digital era. Also, innovative customers are a valuable segment for virtual place applications. Providing personal experiences, enhancing social interaction and sensory features could be innovative suggestions to target this segment. VPA developers can significantly enhance the user experience, making virtual place applications more engaging, personalized, and immersive by creatively integrating VPAs with other developing technologies.

On the other hand, high visitor satisfaction positively affects visitors' intention to travel, and satisfied visitors are more likely to visit the places physically. The findings accentuate the need to virtualize the places by creating VPAs as the virtualization leads to more visits in real life. The mediating role of perceived price cost is also important. When users find virtual experiences worthwhile compared to the cost, they are more likely to continue using the service and might even be encouraged to visit the physical destinations featured. Thus, effectively managing perceived price cost can drive both user satisfaction and increased engagement with virtual and real-world tourism.

The results of the study also show that the education and entertainment experience provided by VPAS are positively related to VPAs visitors' satisfaction, underlining the importance of creating enjoyable, educational content to satisfy visitors. Findings also point out the creating of holistic experience including both emotional and educational dimensions; however, the entertainment content of VPAs should be prioritized since it contributes more to the satisfaction of users. Other recent studies also found that enjoyment is the most effective variable to explain satisfaction with the virtual touristic place (Yang et al. 2021, Han et al., 2021). Therefore, the virtual place applications should include features that increase the level of entertainment and amusement.

Another finding highlights that VPAs visitors' satisfaction affects e-WOM; indicating that visitors who have a high satisfaction level tend to create positive e-WOM. Vice versa, a low level of satisfaction causes negative e-WOM. Therefore, VPAs' developers should consider and carefully monitor the satisfaction level of

VPAs' visitors. Otherwise, negative information could be spread to possible users by current users who have low satisfaction. Furthermore, the managers of touristic places are encouraged to offer a reasonable price to increase the likelihood of visit of the satisfied customers. By attracting more visitors, the tourism industry may recover from the wounds of the pandemic crisis.

Limitations and Future Research Directions

Despite the study's significant contributions, it also has some limitations. The data of the study is limited only to the participants in Turkey. Considering that every country is at a different level of digitalization, it would be fruitful to collect data from other countries and compare the results. In addition, in order to improve the methodology in future studies, it can be suggested to expand the sampling method and select a more representative population. Although convenience sampling provides advantages in terms of time and resources, choosing more representative methods such as random sampling to make broader generalizations will increase the reliability of the results of the study. Another point that should be mentioned is, a more comprehensive sample can be created to include different demographic groups and socioeconomic levels. In addition, data collection methods can be supported by various survey techniques or mixed methodologies to analyze the findings of the study in more depth. As a result, by using a broader and more representative sample in future studies, the generalizability of the findings of the study can be increased and the effects of these findings on different populations can be examined more comprehensively. Furthermore, in this study, the aim is to present an integrative perspective on virtual place applications. Future studies may focus on a specific type of VPA. This study focused on understanding customers' perspectives; research can be conducted to understand the issue from the companies' viewpoints.

REFERENCES

Agarwal, R., & Prasad, J. (1998). A conceptual and operational definition of personal innovativeness in the domain of information technology. *Information Systems Research*, 9(2), 204–215. DOI: 10.1287/isre.9.2.204

Ahn, J., & Kwon, J. (2020). Green hotel brands in Malaysia: Perceived value, cost, anticipated emotion, and revisit intention. *Current Issues in Tourism*, 23(12), 1559–1574. DOI: 10.1080/13683500.2019.1646715

Aiello, D., Fai, S., & Santagati, C. (2019). Virtual museums as a means for promotion and enhancement of cultural heritage. *The International Archives of the Photogrammetry, Remote Sensing and Spatial Information Sciences*, XLII-2(W11), 17–24. DOI: 10.5194/isprs-archives-XLII-2-W9-17-2019

Alrwashdeh, M., Jahmani, A., Ibrahim, B., & Aljuhmani, H. Y. (2020). Data to model the effects of perceived telecommunication service quality and value on the degree of user satisfaction and e-WOM among telecommunications users in North Cyprus. *Data in Brief*, 28, 104981. DOI: 10.1016/j.dib.2019.104981 PMID: 31890816

Altunel, M. C., & Erkurt, B. (2015). Cultural tourism in Istanbul: The mediation effect of tourist experience and satisfaction on the relationship between involvement and recommendation intention. *Journal of Destination Marketing & Management*, 4(4), 213–221. DOI: 10.1016/j.jdmm.2015.06.003

Anastasiei, B., Dospinescu, N., & Dospinescu, O. (2021). Understanding the adoption of incentivized word-of-mouth in the online environment. *Journal of Theoretical and Applied Electronic Commerce Research*, 16(4), 992–1007. DOI: 10.3390/jtaer16040056

Aşan, K., Kaptangil, K., & Kınay, A. G. (2020). Mediating role of perceived festival value in the relationship between experiences and satisfaction. *International Journal of Event and Festival Management*, 11(3), 329–343. DOI: 10.1108/IJEFM-07-2019-0049

Audunson, R., Andresen, H., Fagerlid, C., Henningsen, E., Hobohm, H. C., Jochumsen, H., & Larsen, H. (2020). Introduction–Physical places and virtual spaces: Libraries, archives and museums in a digital age. In *Libraries, archives and museums as democratic spaces in a digital age* (pp. 1–22). De Gruyter Saur., DOI: 10.1515/9783110636628-001

Bae, S., Jung, T. H., Moorhouse, N., Suh, M., & Kwon, O. (2020). The influence of mixed reality on satisfaction and brand loyalty in cultural heritage attractions: A brand equity perspective. *Sustainability (Basel)*, 12(7), 2956. DOI: 10.3390/su12072956

Barbieri, L., Bruno, F., & Muzzupappa, M. (2017). Virtual museum system evaluation through user studies. *Journal of Cultural Heritage*, 26, 101–108. DOI: 10.1016/j.culher.2017.02.005

Beck, J., & Egger, R. (2018). Emotionalise me: Self-reporting and arousal measurements in virtual tourism environments. In *Information and communication technologies in tourism 2018* (pp. 3–15). Springer., DOI: 10.1007/978-3-319-72923-7_1

Bellini, N., Bergamasco, M., Brehonnet, R., Carrozzino, M., & Lagier, J. (2018). Virtual cultural experiences: The drivers of satisfaction. *Symphonya.Emerging Issues in Management*, 2(2), 52–65. DOI: 10.4468/2018.2.5bellini.bergamasco.brehonnet.carozzino.lagier

Benny, L. K. W. (2015). Entertainment studies–A perspective. *American International Journal of Research in Humanities. Arts and Social Sciences*, 10, 7–11. DOI: 10.9790/7388-100000701011

Bilińska, K., Pabian, B., Pabian, A., & Reformat, B. (2023). Development trends and potential in the field of virtual tourism after the COVID-19 pandemic: Generation Z example. *Sustainability (Basel)*, 15(3), 1889. DOI: 10.3390/su15031889

Carvajal, D. A. L., Morita, M. M., & Bilmes, G. M. (2020). Virtual museums: Captured reality and 3D modeling. *Journal of Cultural Heritage*, 45, 234–239. DOI: 10.1016/j.culher.2020.04.013

Chang, S. H., & Lin, R. (2015). Building a total customer experience model: Applications for the travel experiences in Taiwan's creative life industry. *Journal of Travel & Tourism Marketing*, 32(4), 438–453. DOI: 10.1080/10548408.2014.908158

Chi, H. K., Huang, K. C., & Nguyen, H. M. (2020). Elements of destination brand equity and destination familiarity regarding travel intention. *Journal of Retailing and Consumer Services*, 52, 101728. DOI: 10.1016/j.jretconser.2018.12.012

Chung, N., Han, H., & Joun, Y. (2015). Tourists' intention to visit a destination: The role of augmented reality (AR) application for a heritage site. *Computers in Human Behavior*, 50, 588–599. DOI: 10.1016/j.chb.2015.02.068

de Oliveira Dias, M., Lopes, R. D. O. A., & Teles, A. C. (2020). Will virtual replace classroom teaching? Lessons from virtual classes via Zoom in the times of COVID-19. *Journal of Advances in Education and Philosophy*, 4(05), 208–213. DOI: 10.36348/jaep.2020.v04i05.004

Deale, C. S. (2013). Incorporating Second Life into online hospitality and tourism education: A case study. *Journal of Hospitality, Leisure, Sport and Tourism Education*, 13, 154–160. DOI: 10.1016/j.jhlste.2013.09.002

Duarte, P., Silva, S. C., & Ferreira, M. B. (2018). How convenient is it? Delivering online shopping convenience to enhance customer satisfaction and encourage e-WOM. *Journal of Retailing and Consumer Services*, 44, 161–169. DOI: 10.1016/j.jretconser.2018.06.007

Erdem, T., Swait, J., & Valenzuela, A. (2006). Brands as signals: A cross-country validation study. *Journal of Marketing*, 70(1), 34–49. DOI: 10.1509/jmkg.70.1.034.qxd

Fidell, S., Tabachnick, B., Mestre, V., & Fidell, L. (2013). Aircraft noise-induced awakenings are more reasonably predicted from relative than from absolute sound exposure levels. *The Journal of the Acoustical Society of America*, 134(5), 3645–3653. DOI: 10.1121/1.4823838 PMID: 24180775

Flavián, C., Ibáñez-Sánchez, S., & Orús, C. (2019). The impact of virtual, augmented and mixed reality technologies on the customer experience. *Journal of Business Research*, 100, 547–560. DOI: 10.1016/j.jbusres.2018.10.050

Fornell, C., & Larcker, D. F. (1981). Evaluating structural equation models with unobservable variables and measurement error. *JMR, Journal of Marketing Research*, 18(1), 39–50. DOI: 10.1177/002224378101800104

Genç, R. (2018). The impact of augmented reality (AR) technology on tourist satisfaction. In *Augmented reality and virtual reality* (pp. 109–116). Springer. DOI: 10.1007/978-3-319-64027-3_9

Gibson, A., & O'Rawe, M. (2018). Virtual reality as a travel promotional tool: Insights from a consumer travel fair. In *Augmented reality and virtual reality* (pp. 93–107). Springer., DOI: 10.1007/978-3-319-64027-3_7

González-Rodríguez, M. R., Díaz-Fernández, M. C., & Pino-Mejías, M. Á. (2020). The impact of virtual reality technology on tourists' experience: A textual data analysis. *Soft Computing*, 24(18), 1–14. DOI: 10.1007/s00500-020-04883-y

Guttentag, D. A. (2010). Virtual reality: Applications and implications for tourism. *Tourism Management*, 31(5), 637–651. DOI: 10.1016/j.tourman.2009.07.003

Hair, J. F., Celsi, M., Ortinau, D. J., & Bush, R. P. (2010). *Essentials of marketing research* (Vol. 2). McGraw-Hill/Irwin.

Han, D. I. D., Weber, J., Bastiaansen, M., Mitas, O., & Lub, X. (2019). Virtual and augmented reality technologies to enhance the visitor experience in cultural tourism. In *Augmented reality and virtual reality* (pp. 113–128). Springer., DOI: 10.1007/978-3-030-06246-0_9

Han, H., & Ryu, K. (2012). Key factors driving customers' word-of-mouth intentions in full-service restaurants: The moderating role of switching costs. *Cornell Hospitality Quarterly*, 53(2), 96–109. DOI: 10.1177/1938965511433599

Han, S., Yoon, J. H., & Kwon, J. (2021). Impact of experiential value of augmented reality: The context of heritage tourism. *Sustainability (Basel)*, 13(8), 4147. DOI: 10.3390/su13084147

Hawdon, J., Parti, K., & Dearden, T. E. (2020). Cybercrime in America amid COVID-19: The initial results from a natural experiment. *American Journal of Criminal Justice*, 45(4), 546–562. DOI: 10.1007/s12103-020-09534-4 PMID: 32837157

He, X., & Luo, J. M. (2020). Relationship among travel motivation, satisfaction, and revisit intention of skiers: A case study on the tourists of Urumqi Silk Road Ski Resort. *Administrative Sciences*, 10(3), 56. DOI: 10.3390/admsci10030056

Hosany, S., & Witham, M. (2010). Dimensions of cruisers' experiences, satisfaction, and intention to recommend. *Journal of Travel Research*, 49(3), 351–364. DOI: 10.1177/0047287509346859

Hossan, D., Dato'Mansor, Z., & Jaharuddin, N. S. (2023). Research population and sampling in quantitative study. [IJBT]. *International Journal of Business and Technopreneurship*, 13(3), 209–222. DOI: 10.58915/ijbt.v13i3.263

Hsu, L. (2012). Web 3D simulation-based application in tourism education: A case study with Second Life. *Journal of Hospitality, Leisure, Sport and Tourism Education*, 11(2), 113–124. DOI: 10.1016/j.jhlste.2012.02.013

Huang, Y. C., Backman, K. F., Backman, S. J., & Chang, L. L. (2016). Exploring the implications of virtual reality technology in tourism marketing: An integrated research framework. *International Journal of Tourism Research*, 18(2), 116–128. DOI: 10.1002/jtr.2038

Hume, M., & Mills, M. (2011). Building the sustainable iMuseum: Is the virtual museum leaving our museums virtually empty? *International Journal of Nonprofit and Voluntary Sector Marketing*, 16(3), 275–289. DOI: 10.1002/nvsm.425

Huo, Y., & Miller, D. (2007). Satisfaction measurement of small tourism sector (museum): Samoa. *Asia Pacific Journal of Tourism Research*, 12(2), 103–117. DOI: 10.1080/10941660701243331

Hwang, J., & Lee, J. (2019). A strategy for enhancing senior tourists' well-being perception: Focusing on the experience economy. *Journal of Travel & Tourism Marketing*, 36(3), 314–329. DOI: 10.1080/10548408.2018.1541776

Ibañez-Etxeberria, A., Gómez-Carrasco, C. J., Fontal, O., & García-Ceballos, S. (2020). Virtual environments and augmented reality applied to heritage education: An evaluative study. *Applied Sciences (Basel, Switzerland)*, 10(7), 2352. DOI: 10.3390/app10072352

Itani, O. S., & Hollebeek, L. D. (2021). Light at the end of the tunnel: Visitors' virtual reality (versus in-person) attraction site tour-related behavioral intentions during and post-COVID-19. *Tourism Management*, 84, 104290. DOI: 10.1016/j.tourman.2021.104290 PMID: 36530603

Jarratt, D. (2021). An exploration of webcam-travel: Connecting to place and nature through webcams during the COVID-19 lockdown of 2020. *Tourism and Hospitality Research*, 21(2), 156–168. DOI: 10.1177/1467358420963370

Jeong, E., & Jang, S. S. (2011). Restaurant experiences triggering positive electronic word-of-mouth (eWOM) motivations. *International Journal of Hospitality Management*, 30(2), 356–366. DOI: 10.1016/j.ijhm.2010.08.005

Jung, T., tom Dieck, M. C., Lee, H., & Chung, N. (2016). Effects of virtual reality and augmented reality on visitor experiences in museum. In Inversini, A., & Schegg, R. (Eds.), *Information and communication technologies in tourism 2016* (pp. 621–635). Springer., DOI: 10.1007/978-3-319-28231-2_45

Khan, A., Masrek, M. N., & Mahmood, K. (2019). The relationship of personal innovativeness, quality of digital resources and generic usability with users' satisfaction. *Digital Library Perspectives*, 35(3), 178–194. DOI: 10.1108/DLP-12-2017-0046

Kim, J. H. (2018). The impact of memorable tourism experiences on loyalty behaviors: The mediating effects of destination image and satisfaction. *Journal of Travel Research*, 57(7), 856–870. DOI: 10.1177/0047287517721369

Kim, J. Y., Chung, N., & Ahn, K. M. (2019). The impact of mobile tour information services on destination travel intention. *Information Development*, 35(1), 107–120. DOI: 10.1177/0266666917730437

Kim, M. J., & Hall, C. M. (2019). A hedonic motivation model in virtual reality tourism: Comparing visitors and non-visitors. *International Journal of Information Management*, 46, 236–249. DOI: 10.1016/j.ijinfomgt.2018.11.016

Kim, M. J., Lee, C. K., & Jung, T. (2020). Exploring consumer behavior in virtual reality tourism using an extended stimulus-organism-response model. *Journal of Travel Research*, 59(1), 69–89. DOI: 10.1177/0047287518818915

Lee, H., Jung, T. H., tom Dieck, M. C., & Chung, N. (2020). Experiencing immersive virtual reality in museums. *Information & Management*, 57(5), 103229. DOI: 10.1016/j.im.2019.103229

Li, T., & Chen, Y. (2019). Will virtual reality be a double-edged sword? Exploring the moderation effects of the expected enjoyment of a destination on travel intention. *Journal of Destination Marketing & Management*, 12, 15–26. DOI: 10.1016/j.jdmm.2019.02.003

López, M., & Sicilia, M. (2014). Determinants of E-WOM influence: The role of consumers' internet experience. *Journal of Theoretical and Applied Electronic Commerce Research*, 9(1), 28–43. DOI: 10.4067/S0718-18762014000100004

Mahat, J., Ayub, A. F. M., Luan, S., & Wong, . (2012). An assessment of students' mobile self-efficacy, readiness and personal innovativeness towards mobile learning in higher education in Malaysia. *Procedia: Social and Behavioral Sciences*, 64, 284–290. DOI: 10.1016/j.sbspro.2012.11.033

Mahdzar, M., Saiful Raznan, A. M., Ahmad Jasmin, N., & Abdul Aziz, N. A. (2020). Exploring relationships between experience economy and satisfaction of visitors in rural tourism destination. *Journal of International Business. Economics and Entrepreneurship*, 5(1), 69–75. DOI: 10.24191/jibe.v5i1.14277

Nunnally, J. C. (1978). An overview of psychological measurement. In McReynolds, P. (Ed.), *Clinical diagnosis of mental disorders* (pp. 97–146). Springer. DOI: 10.1007/978-1-4684-2490-4_4

Oh, H., Fiore, A. M., & Jeoung, M. (2007). Measuring experience economy concepts: Tourism applications. *Journal of Travel Research*, 46(2), 119–132. DOI: 10.1177/0047287507304039

Orr, M., Poitras, E., & Butcher, K. (2021). Informal learning with extended reality environments: Current trends in museums, heritage and tourism. In Geroimenko, V. (Ed.), *Augmented reality in tourism, museums and heritage: A new technology to inform and entertain* (pp. 67–90). Springer., DOI: 10.1007/978-3-030-70198-7_1

Özdemir Uçgun, G., & Şahin, S. Z. (2024). How does Metaverse affect the tourism industry? Current practices and future forecasts. *Current Issues in Tourism*, 27(17), 2742–2756. DOI: 10.1080/13683500.2023.2238111

Pallud, J., & Straub, D. W. (2014). Effective website design for experience-influenced environments: The case of high culture museums. *Information & Management*, 51(3), 359–373. DOI: 10.1016/j.im.2014.02.010

Papista, E., & Krystallis, A. (2013). Investigating the types of value and cost of green brands: Proposition of a conceptual framework. *Journal of Business Ethics*, 115(1), 75–92. DOI: 10.1007/s10551-012-1367-6

Parasuraman, A. (2000). Technology Readiness Index (TRI): A multiple-item scale to measure readiness to embrace new technologies. *Journal of Service Research*, 2(4), 307–320. DOI: 10.1177/109467050024001

Parker, E., & Saker, M. (2020). Art museums and the incorporation of virtual reality: Examining the impact of VR on spatial and social norms. *Convergence (London)*, 26(5–6), 1159–1173. DOI: 10.1177/1354856519897251

Pencarelli, T. (2020). The digital revolution in the travel and tourism industry. *Information Technology & Tourism*, 22(3), 455–476. DOI: 10.1007/s40558-019-00160-3

Petrick, J. F., Morais, D. D., & Norman, W. C. (2001). An examination of the determinants of entertainment vacationers' intentions to revisit. *Journal of Travel Research*, 40(1), 41–48. DOI: 10.1177/004728750104000106

Pham, L., Williamson, S., Lane, P., Limbu, Y., Nguyen, P. T. H., & Coomer, T. (2020). Technology readiness and purchase intention: Role of perceived value and online satisfaction in the context of luxury hotels. *International Journal of Management and Decision Making*, 19(1), 91–117. DOI: 10.1504/IJMDM.2020.104208

Pine, B. J., & Gilmore, J. H. (1998). The experience economy. *Harvard Business Review*, 76(6), 18–23. PMID: 10181589

Pine, B. J., Pine, J., & Gilmore, J. H. (1999). *The experience economy: Work is theatre & every business a stage*. Harvard Business Press.

Polishchuk, E., Bujdosó, Z., El Archi, Y., Benbba, B., Zhu, K., & Dávid, L. D. (2023). The theoretical background of virtual reality and its implications for the tourism industry. *Sustainability (Basel)*, 15(13), 10534. DOI: 10.3390/su151310534

Radder, L., & Han, X. (2015). An examination of the museum experience based on Pine and Gilmore's experience economy realms. *Journal of Applied Business Research*, 31(2), 455–470. DOI: 10.19030/jabr.v31i2.9129

Rizky, R. M., Kusdi, R., & Yusri, A. (2017). The impact of e-WOM on destination image, attitude toward destination and travel intention. *Russian Journal of Agricultural and Socio-Economic Sciences*, 61(1), 26–32. DOI: 10.18551/rjoas.2017-01.04

San-Martín, S., Prodanova, J., & Jiménez, N. (2015). The impact of age in the generation of satisfaction and WOM in mobile shopping. *Journal of Retailing and Consumer Services*, 23, 1–8. DOI: 10.1016/j.jretconser.2014.11.001

Schmitt, B. (2010). Experience marketing: Concepts, frameworks and consumer insights. *Foundations and Trends in Marketing*, 5(2), 55–112. DOI: 10.1561/1700000027

Setiawan, P. Y., Troena, E. A., & Armanu, N. (2014). The effect of e-WOM on destination image, satisfaction and loyalty. *International Journal of Business and Management Invention*, 3(1), 22–29.

Shore, J. H., Schneck, C. D., & Mishkind, M. C. (2020). Telepsychiatry and the coronavirus disease 2019 pandemic—Current and future outcomes of the rapid virtualization of psychiatric care. *JAMA Psychiatry*, 77(12), 1211–1212. DOI: 10.1001/jamapsychiatry.2020.1643 PMID: 32391861

Singh, N., & Lee, M. J. (2009). Exploring perceptions toward education in 3-D virtual environments: An introduction to "Second Life.". *Journal of Teaching in Travel & Tourism*, 8(4), 315–327. DOI: 10.1080/15313220903047896

Song, H. J., Lee, C. K., Park, J. A., Hwang, Y. H., & Reisinger, Y. (2015). The influence of tourist experience on perceived value and satisfaction with temple stays: The experience economy theory. *Journal of Travel & Tourism Marketing*, 32(4), 401–415. DOI: 10.1080/10548408.2014.898606

Southall, H., Marmion, M., & Davies, A. (2019). Adapting Jake Knapp's design sprint approach for AR/VR applications in digital heritage. In Jung, T., & tom Dieck, M. C. (Eds.), *Augmented reality and virtual reality* (pp. 59–70). Springer., DOI: 10.1007/978-3-030-06246-0_5

Stevens, B. F. (1992). Price value perceptions of travelers. *Journal of Travel Research*, 31(2), 44–48. DOI: 10.1177/004728759203100208

Sürme, M., & Atılgan, E. (2020). Sanal müzede sanal tur yapan bireylerin memnuniyet düzeylerini belirlemeye yönelik bir araştırma. *Türk Turizm Araştırmaları Dergisi*, 4(3), 1794–1805. DOI: 10.26677/TR1010.2020.451

Sylaiou, S., Mania, K., Karoulis, A., & White, M. (2010). Exploring the relationship between presence and enjoyment in a virtual museum. *International Journal of Human-Computer Studies*, 68(5), 243–253. DOI: 10.1016/j.ijhcs.2009.11.002

Sylaiou, S., Mania, K., Paliokas, I., Pujol-Tost, L., Killintzis, V., & Liarokapis, F. (2017). Exploring the educational impact of diverse technologies in online virtual museums. *International Journal of Arts and Technology*, 10(1), 58–84. DOI: 10.1504/IJART.2017.083907

Trunfio, M., & Campana, S. (2020). A visitors' experience model for mixed reality in the museum. *Current Issues in Tourism*, 23(9), 1053–1058. DOI: 10.1080/13683500.2019.1586847

Tussyadiah, I. P., Wang, D., & Jia, C. H. (2017). Virtual reality and attitudes toward tourism destinations. In Schegg, R., & Stangl, B. (Eds.), *Information and communication technologies in tourism 2017* (pp. 229–239). Springer., DOI: 10.1007/978-3-319-51168-9_17

Valerio, M. A., Rodriguez, N., Winkler, P., Lopez, J., Dennison, M., Liang, Y., & Turner, B. J. (2016). Comparing two sampling methods to engage hard-to-reach communities in research priority setting. *BMC Medical Research Methodology*, 16(1), 1–11. DOI: 10.1186/s12874-016-0242-z PMID: 27793191

Verma, S., Warrier, L., Bolia, B., & Mehta, S. (2022). Past, present, and future of virtual tourism: A literature review. *International Journal of Information Management Data Insights*, 2(2), 100085. DOI: 10.1016/j.jjimei.2022.100085

Wagler, A., & Hanus, M. D. (2018). Comparing virtual reality tourism to real-life experience: Effects of presence and engagement on attitude and enjoyment. *Communication Research Reports*, 35(5), 456–464. DOI: 10.1080/08824096.2018.1525350

Wei, W., Baker, M. A., & Onder, I. (2023). All without leaving home: Building a conceptual model of virtual tourism experiences. *International Journal of Contemporary Hospitality Management*, 35(4), 1284–1303. DOI: 10.1108/IJCHM-12-2021-1560

Wu, W. (2020). Analysis of digital tourism, virtual tourism and wisdom tourism. In Xu, Z., & Kaya, M. N. (Eds.), *The International Conference on Cyber Security Intelligence and Analytics* (pp. 18–25). Springer. DOI: 10.1007/978-3-030-43309-3_3

Yang, T., Lai, I. K. W., Fan, Z. B., & Mo, Q. M. (2021). The impact of a 360° virtual tour on the reduction of psychological stress caused by COVID-19. *Technology in Society*, 64, 101514. DOI: 10.1016/j.techsoc.2020.101514 PMID: 33424061

Yoo, C. W., Sanders, G. L., & Moon, J. (2013). Exploring the effect of e-WOM participation on e-loyalty in e-commerce. *Decision Support Systems*, 55(3), 669–678. DOI: 10.1016/j.dss.2013.02.001

Zeithaml, V. A. (1988). Consumer perceptions of price, quality, and value: A means-end model and synthesis of evidence. *Journal of Marketing*, 52(3), 2–22. DOI: 10.1177/002224298805200302

Zhang, T., & Hacikara, A. (2023). Virtual tourism and consumer wellbeing: A critical review, practices, and new perspectives. In Uysal, M., & Perdue, R. R. (Eds.), *Handbook of tourism and quality-of-life research II* (pp. 545–557). Springer., DOI: 10.1007/978-3-031-31513-8_37

Zheng, J. M., Chan, K. W., & Gibson, I. (1998). Virtual reality. *IEEE Potentials*, 17(2), 20–23. DOI: 10.1109/45.666641

Zinko, R., Patrick, A., Furner, C. P., Gaines, S., Kim, M. D., Negri, M., & Villarreal, C. (2021). Responding to negative electronic word of mouth to improve purchase intention. *Journal of Theoretical and Applied Electronic Commerce Research*, 16(6), 1945–1959. DOI: 10.3390/jtaer16060109

KEY TERMS AND DEFINITIONS

Destination Marketing: The process of marketing destinations in order to influence visitors, strengthen the image of the locations and leverage economic growth.

Digital Marketing: The process of marketing products or services utilizing internet, online platforms, and electronic media.

Innovativeness: A personal characteristic that reflects a person's inclination to implement or accept new ideas or approaches.

Tourism Marketing: The practice of marketing destinations or experiences to prospective travelers and visitors.

Virtual Place Application: A digital platform that either simulates real word locations or completely fictional settings.

Virtual Reality: A stimulated experience that utilizes computer technology in order to make a three-dimensional, engaging environment that looks like real word or looks different than real word.

Chapter 14
Medical Tourism in India:
A Study to Identify the Growth Factors and Scope for Medical Tourism in India

Eliza Sharma
https://orcid.org/0000-0002-2713-301X
Symbiosis International University, India

ABSTRACT

The study aims to identify factors driving medical tourism in India and assess its scope from the perspective of foreign tourists. Data were collected from 150 foreign tourists seeking medical treatment in hospitals across New Delhi, Mumbai, and Bangalore using a questionnaire. The study highlighted total ten factors which attract the foreign tourists to see India as medical tourism destination. These factors are mainly healthcare infrastructure, healthcare professionals, quality of healthcare services, cost of medical services, transportation connectivity, documentation processes, Government support for medical tourism promotion, Technological innovations, medical insurance and tie ups for medical services and local or regional factors. The cost of medical services was identified as a major factor, while government support, healthcare infrastructure, and other factors need improvement. The study suggests that India's potential as a medical tourism destination can be enhanced by improving the healthcare, transportation, hospitality, infrastructure and governmental support.

DOI: 10.4018/979-8-3693-7021-6.ch014

INTRODUCTION

Medical tourism has emerged as one of the highest growth prospective areas, which is getting attention across the globe. All the countries are focusing on medical services to attract the foreign tourists to increase their foreign exchange reserves. Under the concept of medical tourism, nations are focusing on developing and providing world-class healthcare services to the customers from different countries at competitive rates to develop their country as a destination for medical tourism (Kumar, 2009). It's a new revolution in the area of healthcare sector, which is gaining popularity across the globe and has also impacted a large population of the world (George, 2010). Epidauria is known as first medical tourism destination in the history, which was traveled by people of Greek for specific diseases and this has actually given the birth to the concept of medical tourism (Kumar, 2009). While India is well known for the Unani and Ayurveda treatment for the medical purpose and people used to travel India for the purpose of getting these treatments. In world medical history, there are various signs of medical tourism, as people of Greek, Britain and other countries used to travel to other countries during summer season to take bath in holy water for curing their diseases. Nile River of the Egypt has always remained a major source of attraction for the pilgrims who travelled for the medical purpose all through the Egypt. The concept of Spa was prevalent even in the 18th century and river water was used for medical therapies. People used to travel to other places for getting mineral water useful for the skin diseases, and other medical treatment. But, travelling for medical purpose was difficult and time consuming in old age, due to lack of connectivity (George, 2010). In 21st century, travelling has become easy and much more time saving. All the countries across the globe are connected to each other, travelers can easily move from one country to another. Hence, medical tourism has become more popular and affordable too. One can travel to other country for any medical treatment and to get the medicines which is not available in their home country (Jadhav, 2014). India being the origin country of Ayurveda, Yoga, and Shalay Chikitsa, has gained lot of attention by the foreign tourists for getting medical treatment through Yoga, or Ayurveda. People believe in treatment of their diseases through Ayurveda or Yoga, as these techniques have no side effects and can cure the diseases from root level (Jyothis, 2009). The factors like the advancements in technology, growing cult of consumerism, awareness among people and ability of people to travel abroad and promotion of healthy living have made transcontinental medical transformations and consultations a crystal-clear reality across the globe (World Health Organization, 2008). The emergence of corporate health care and growth in the private sector during 1980s and 1990s had been the important part of the conscious policy adopted by the government for the promotion of these spheres in the medical industry (Ernst & Young, 2007). India is a home of herbs and natural remedies, Ayurveda professionals, yoga instructors, and many wellness centers which provide this kind of medical treatment (Singh, 2014). But to make it popular among the foreign tourists and making India a destination for medical tourism requires huge efforts to be done by the government, healthcare sector and the tourism department of the country (Ernst & Young, 2007).

Current study is based on the measuring the scope of the medical tourism in India in the modern era of technology and advancement. The structure of the research can be described as; researcher has identified total ten factors based on the review of literature which helps in promotion of medical tourism. Consequent to review section, research gaps followed with the objectives of the study have been discussed. The section of results and discussion gives a detailed picture of what exactly are the opinions of the foreign tourists towards the medical tourism in India. The conclusion section concludes the whole research followed by the limitations and future scope of the study.

LITERATURE REVIEW

Researchers have done various studies on medical tourism, issues or challenges in medical tourism, growth or future prospects of the medical tourism and the factors which help the medical tourism development in a country. Based on the review of literature, the following factors have been identified by the researcher which are actually responsible for the medical tourism in any country. These factors have been studied in Indian context in the current study.

Healthcare Infrastructure

Healthcare infrastructure is one of the important factors which promotes medical tourism in the country. It includes the number of hospitals in the country, variety of healthcare services provided by the hospitals, multispecialty hospitals, number of beds facility in the hospitals, variety of medical equipment, tools availability, space and capacity of the hospitals and the affiliation of the hospitals by the medical council of India (Uniyal et al., 2014). While many studies highlight the importance of healthcare infrastructure (Uniyal et al., 2014), this study focuses on the perceived gaps between infrastructure and patient satisfaction. World class infrastructure of the healthcare sector attracts the foreign tourists to choose India as a destination for medical tourism. In India, majority of the big hospitals are multispecialty hospitals and in terms of infrastructure these hospitals are comparable to the foreign hospitals in the other countries.

Healthcare Professionals

The people who provide healthcare services play an important role in the medical tourism. Healthcare professionals should be experts in their area, they should have skills for providing medical treatment to the patients, and the behavior of the healthcare professionals is of utmost importance to the patients (Ajmeri, 2012). The license of the healthcare professionals should be verified and should meet the basic qualification for medical practices. In India, there are strict rules for selection of the medical professionals by the hospitals management based on the certain parameter (Tiwari, 2012). As the success of any hospital depends completely on the healthcare professionals. Due to the highly qualified and skilled healthcare professionals in Indian healthcare sector, there are huge scope for India to become a popular destination for medical tourism.

Cost of Medical Services

Cost of medical services is an important parameter or factor which attracts the medical tourists from all over world to India. The cost of medical services differs in countries, due to the difference in the quality of the medical services, remuneration or fees of medical professionals, cost of medical equipment and cost of the healthcare infrastructure etc (Soloman, 2011). Indian currency is cheaper than Gulf, European, US, and other Asian countries, which attracts the foreign tourists from other countries to India for getting medical treatment at lower cost. Same medical process or surgery if they avail in their own country, cost them higher and if they avail the medical service in India, it cost them lower (Sharma et al., 2012). Hence, cost of medical services is the major factor which Indian healthcare sector can use to attract the foreign tourists and can help in promotion of medical tourism.

Quality of Healthcare Services

Healthcare services are of utmost importance to mankind. Quality of healthcare services get affected by many factors such as; physical ambience of the hospitals, hygiene in the hospitals, spacing, cafeteria, nutritious food to patients, cleanliness in the hospitals, behavior of doctors, staff and nurses with the patients, latest medical equipment, speediness of the staff in handling medical processes, knowledge and skills of nurses, availability of the medical equipment or tools, presence of the doctors in emergency ward, ambulance services of the hospital etc. (Reddy & Imrana, 2010). All these parameters are looked upon by the patients while availing medical treatment from any hospital (Pritchard & Howard, 1997). Medical tourism promotion depends heavily on all these factors, how patients from foreign countries perceive the quality of healthcare services of the Indian hospitals.

Government Support for Medical Tourism Promotion

Government support is very much important for the promotion of medical tourism in India. Government provides subsidies to the hospitals, authorize licenses to the hospitals and healthcare professionals, and also provide support to build world-class infrastructure and facilities by healthcare sector (Petrick, 1999). Further, the marketing and promotion of the healthcare sector for the purpose of medical tourism is taken care by tourism department of central and state government in collaboration (Chacko, 2006). Hence, the medical tourism in India can be a success only with the support of government and the collective working of the private and public sector in India (Mukherjee & Mookerji, 2004). Where public sector will help in authorizing the processes, and fix standards for the quality while private sector will invest funds and take care of the execution of the operations.

Documentation Processes

Documentation processes related to medical tourism mainly divided into two categories, one is related to the medical treatment, and another is related to the documentation required by the foreign patients to enter into the country (Mal, 2010). It mainly includes the visa, and immigration process of the country, and the time period of the visa approval as medical treatment mainly requires long term visa and multiple entry visa for foreign patients as they may need to come for checkup, several times both before and after final medical treatment/operation/surgery (Kelley, 2013). Hence, the documentation process should be easy so that foreigners can come to India for medical treatment without much trouble. Secondly the documentation processes at the end of the hospital staff should also be easy to understand and fill up by the foreign nationals having different language and culture (Ajmeri, 2012).

Technological Innovations

Use of latest and advanced technology in healthcare sector ensures the high quality of healthcare services and development or growth in healthcare sector (Dawn & Pal, 2011). For the purpose of the medical tourism, it is required that healthcare sector make use of latest technology, should have all the facilities for conducting experiments to develop new and better solution for the medical treatment (Jain, 2006). Technological innovations in healthcare sector, can help any nation in attracting the foreign tourists for medical purpose (Bookman & Bookman, 2007). Medical tourism is based on the technology and innovations only, hence government should fund the medical projects which are involve in discovering or developing new or innovative kind of medical services or processes (Chacko, 2006).

Medical Insurance and Tie Ups for Medical Services

Medical insurance is the first factor which is looked upon by the patients. Healthcare sectors which have facilities for the medical insurance and have tie up with the insurance companies for the medical services at cheaper cost, or where insurance companies bear the cost of the medical services (Jawahar, 2007). This helps the patients in saving of money on their medical treatment. For developing medical tourism, healthcare sector should focus on collaborating with insurance companies to benefit the foreign patients (Dawn & Pal, 2011). Hospitals should have the facility to accommodate the medical insurance policies of foreign insurance companies too, as all the foreign tourists who will be coming to India will have their medical insurance done by foreign insurance companies only. This can help in attracting the foreign tourists to India for medical treatment.

Local or Regional Factors

Local or regional factors include the political conditions of the host country, cultural factors, language, weather or climatic conditions, theft or robbery conditions, safety, basic facilities, and the most important is the friendly relation between the countries (Goodrich & Goodrich, 1987). These are the major factors which plays an important role in medical tourism. Foreign tourists think about all these factors while selection of the country for getting medical treatment (Chacko, 2006). Tourism agencies should work on these factors for the development of India as a tourist's destination for medical purpose.

Transportation Connectivity

Transportation is the basic and fundamental factor for development of medical tourism. There should be connectivity of the countries to other countries across nation, either through airways, or waterways (Bookman & Bookman, 2007, Goyal & Kumar, 2010). Foreign tourists should not face problem due to the lack of connectivity with the country. Number of flights for the specific routes, quality of airlines services, number of ships or cruises for the waterway connectivity with other countries, and the cost of the airlines or water transportation should be affordable to attract the foreign tourists (Durrani, 2016).

RESEARCH METHODOLOGY

There are very studies which have considered all the factors in one study, to measure the scope of medical tourism in India. Further, medical tourism has been studied from the point of view of either the general tourist who visit the country for the purpose of leisure, or entertainment. But specifically, the responses of the foreign tourists getting medical treatment in the Indian hospitals have not been considered by the researchers. The study will focus on bridging the gaps from previous research. Current study will reflect what foreign tourists think about India as a medical tourism destination based on their actual experiences with Indian healthcare sector.

The increasing popularity of medical tourism has positioned India as a key destination for international patients seeking affordable and high-quality healthcare services. This study aims to analyze the various factors contributing to the growth of medical tourism in India and to understand how these factors influence the perception of foreign tourists. By examining both the opportunities and challenges within this sector, the research seeks to provide insights into the industry's potential from the perspective of foreign tourists. The specific objectives of the study are as follows:

- to study the factors responsible for the growth of the medical tourism in India
- to measure the scope of medical tourism in India from foreign tourists' point of view
- to measure the impact of demographic characteristics of the foreign tourists on their perception towards the scope of medical tourism in India

Current study is exploratory in nature, and researcher has explored the various factors which makes India a medical tourism destination. Further, the researcher makes use of primary data collected with the help of questionnaire to record the opinions of the foreign tourists availing healthcare services in Indian hospitals towards the scope of medical tourism in India. The perceptions of the foreign tourists have been measured using five-point scale where one is very bad and five is very good. Researcher has taken a sample of 150 foreign tourists visiting Indian hospitals from three major cities of India namely Delhi/NCR, Mumbai, and Bangalore. These cities were chosen due to their established medical facilities and their significant role in India's medical tourism industry. The list of hospitals visited by the researcher for data collection has been annexed in the research paper as Annexure 1. Researchers have identified a list of factors which are responsible for the medical tourism through review of literature and the same list was used to get the responses of the foreign tourists. Descriptive analysis, one-way Anova, t-test was used for the purpose of data analysis. The following hypothesis have been formulated and tested during current study:

Null Hypothesis: Foreign tourists perceive huge scope in India to be developed as medical tourism destination.

Null Hypothesis: The demographic characteristics of foreign tourists do not have an impact on their perceptions towards the scope of medical tourism in India.

RESULTS AND DISCUSSIONS

This section includes the analysis related to the primary data collected from the 150 foreign tourists from three major cities of India namely Delhi/NCR, Mumbai, and Bangalore. SPSS software and MS Excel have been used for the analysis purpose.

Objective 1: To Study the Factors Responsible for the Growth of the Medical Tourism in India

The first objective was to study the factors responsible for the growth of the medical tourism in India. Following are a list of ten factors which have been identified using review of literature. The detailed descriptive analysis of the data has been shown in Table 1.

Table 1. Descriptive analysis

Factors of medical tourism	N	Mean	Std. Deviation	Variance	Skewness	
	Statistic	Statistic	Statistic	Statistic	Statistic	Std. Error
Healthcare Infrastructure	150	2.9933	1.01991	1.040	-.025	.198
Healthcare Professionals	150	3.0333	1.00613	1.012	.053	.198
Cost of Medical services	150	3.6600	1.16337	1.353	-.939	.198
Quality of healthcare services	150	2.9800	1.08973	1.188	.198	.198
Government support for medical tourism promotion	150	2.9533	1.08891	1.186	-.001	.198
Documentation processes	150	2.1733	1.37449	1.889	.987	.198
Technological innovations	150	2.3533	1.30120	1.693	.929	.198
Medical insurance and tie ups for medical services	150	2.3800	1.22978	1.512	.929	.198
Local or regional factors	150	2.3933	1.26860	1.609	.843	.198
Transportation connectivity	150	2.6733	1.17865	1.389	.686	.198

Source: Author's own creation

Researcher has identified total ten factors which lead to growth of the medical tourism in India, and these factors makes India attractive to the foreigners for getting any kind of medical treatment. The mean value of the 'Cost of Medical services' factor is 3.66, which shows that foreign tourists prefer India for healthcare services due to the low cost of the medical services in India. While the factor which contribute least to the medical tourism is 'Documentation processes' with a mean value of 2.17. Further, the skewness of all ten factors was found between -1 to 1, which signifies that the data is normal and not suffering from skewness.

Objective 2: To Measure the Scope of Medical Tourism in India from Foreign Tourists' Point of View

Second objective of the study was to measure the scope of the medical tourism in India from foreign tourists' point of view. Researcher has used one sample t-test to measure the difference in the opinions of the foreign tourists towards the scope of the medical tourism.

Table 2. Results of T-test

Factors of medical tourism	t-value	df	p-value	Mean difference
Healthcare Infrastructure	35.945	149	.000	2.99333
Healthcare Professionals	36.924	149	.000	3.03333
Cost of Medical services	38.531	149	.000	3.66000
Quality of healthcare services	33.492	149	.000	2.98000
Government support for medical tourism promotion	33.217	149	.000	2.95333
Documentation processes	19.366	149	.000	2.17333
Technological innovations	22.151	149	.000	2.35333
Medical insurance and tie ups for medical services	23.703	149	.000	2.38000
Local or regional factors	23.106	149	.000	2.39333
Transportation connectivity	27.779	149	.000	2.67333

Source: Author's own creation

The value of t-test was found significant at one percent level of significance for all the ten factors which are responsible for the medical tourism in India. It showed that the opinions of the foreign tourists were different for the scope of the medical tourism in India. It can be stated that foreign tourists perceive huge scope in India to be developed as medical tourism destination. Further, the frequency distribution showed that the 47.3 percent of the foreign tourists perceive the transportation connectivity to the medical tourists from foreign countries, as bad, while 11.3 percent of the foreign tourists perceive the transportation connectivity in India as very good. 46.7 percent of the foreign tourists perceive the local or regional factors as bad, while 10.0 percent of the foreign tourists perceived the local or regional factors as very good. 49.3 percent of the foreign tourists perceived the medical insurance and tie ups for medical services as bad, while 10.0 percent of the foreign tourists perceived it as very good. 45.3 percent of foreign tourists perceive technological innovations as good, while 12.0 percent of the foreign tourists perceived technological innovations factor as very bad.

Figure 1. Scope of medical tourism

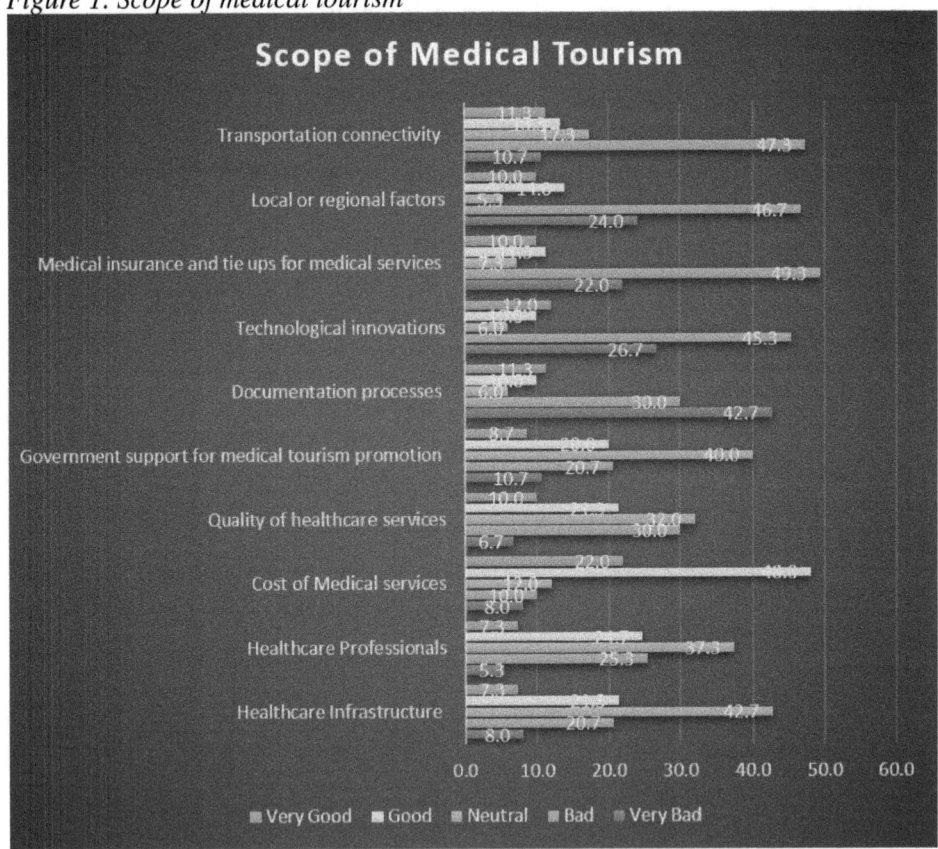

(Author's own creation)

Hence, based on the four major factors, namely transportation, connectivity, local or regional factors, technological innovations and medical insurance and tie ups for medical services; the scope of medical tourism is less in India. Foreign tourists do not perceive these factors as in good status. 42.7 percent of foreign tourists perceived the documentation processes factor as very bad while 11.3 percent of the foreign tourists perceived this factor as very good. Majority of foreign tourists perceived government support for medical tourism promotion, healthcare professionals and healthcare infrastructure factors as in average state, neither good nor bad. Hence, the government may work on these factors to promote medical tourism in the country. The cost of medical services is the only factor which is perceived as good by the foreign tourists. Hence, from foreign tourists' point of view, medical tourism in India can be promoted based on the cost of medical services, while government support for medical tourism promotion, healthcare professionals and healthcare infrastructure factors can be worked upon to promote medical tourism. Transportation connectivity, local or regional factors, technological innovations and medical insurance and tie ups for medical services are the four major factors should be improved and need utmost attention for promotion of medical tourism in India. Cost of the medical services are cheaper in India, as the currency value is cheaper for India when compared to currency value of other countries. Same services cost higher to the foreign tourists in their domestic country than India. Hence, they prefer India for the medical services.

Objective 3: To Measure the Impact of Demographic Characteristics of the Foreign Tourists on Their Perception Towards the Scope of Medical Tourism in India

Total number of foreign tourists surveyed in the study were 150, out of which 34.7 percent of the foreign tourists were from an age group of 45 to 65 years, while the foreign tourists above 65 years of age group were only 32.0 percent. Only 11.3 percent of the foreign tourists were less than 25 years of age group. Out of 150 foreign tourists, 95.3 percent foreign tourists who were getting medical treatment from the hospitals were male patients and only 4.7 percent of foreign tourists were female. 47.3 percent of the foreign tourists were the residents of Asian countries other than India, 24.7 percent of the foreign tourists were from Gulf countries, and 17.3 percent were from African countries. While only 10.7 percent of the foreign tourists were from European countries. Out of 150 foreign tourists selected in the study, were in equal proportion from three major cities of India namely; Delhi/NCR, Mumbai and Bangalore. Majority of the foreign tourists were getting treatment for organ replacement, 22.7 percent of the foreign tourists were getting cancer or tumor treatment, 20.7 percent of the foreign tourists have come for heart surgery, 16.7 percent of the foreign tourists were getting skin treatment from Indian hospitals, while only 4.7 percent of the foreign tourists for Physiotherapy/yoga/wellness/Ayurveda treatment in India. Out of 150 foreign tourists were visiting the Indian hospitals two or three times in their life, while 45.3 percent of the foreign tourists were visiting India for first time for the purpose of medical treatment. While only 2.7 percent of the foreign tourists have visited India for more than three times in their life for more than three times.

Table 3. Age group and scope of medical tourism

	N	Mean	Std. Deviation	Std. Error	Minimum	Maximum
Less than 25 years	17	2.7765	.91483	.22188	1.80	4.90
25 to 45 years	33	2.8758	1.05949	.18443	1.60	4.80
45 to 65 years	52	2.7019	1.01759	.14111	1.40	5.00
Above 65 years	48	2.7354	.91802	.13250	1.30	5.00
Total	150	2.7593	.97754	.07982	1.30	5.00

f-value = 0.224, p-value = 0.880, Welch test value = 0.196 (Sig. = 0.899)
Source: Author's own creation

The foreign tourists from age group of 25 to 45 years have an opinion that there is a huge scope for the medical tourism in India, as majority of the factors which are responsible for the medical tourism promotion were found to be good by these foreign tourists. While the foreign tourists from age group of 45 to 65 years found the scope of medical tourism not much but low based on the current status of the various factors which helps in promotion of medical tourism in India. Overall, if we look at the mean values of the scope of medical tourism for all the age groups, there is not much difference in the opinions of the foreign tourists from different age groups. Further, the results of Anova test also made it clear that the difference in the mean values of the various age groups is insignificant. The value of Welch test conducted to check the robustness was also found to be insignificant and the independent groups can be considered to have equal variance.

Table 4. Post hoc analysis

(I) Age	(J) Age	Mean Difference (I-J)	Std. Error	Sig.
Less than 25 years	25 to 45 years	-.09929	.29414	.736
	45 to 65 years	.07455	.27527	.787
	Above 65 years	.04105	.27808	.883
25 to 45 years	Less than 25 years	.09929	.29414	.736
	45 to 65 years	.17383	.21928	.429
	Above 65 years	.14034	.22280	.530

(I) Age	(J) Age	Mean Difference (I-J)	Std. Error	Sig.
45 to 65 years	Less than 25 years	-.07455	.27527	.787
	25 to 45 years	-.17383	.21928	.429
	Above 65 years	-.03349	.19721	.865
Above 65 years	Less than 25 years	-.04105	.27808	.883
	25 to 45 years	-.14034	.22280	.530
	45 to 65 years	.03349	.19721	.865

Source: Author's own creation

Post hoc analysis results showed that none of the two groups have significantly different mean values and all the differences in the various age groups for the variable 'scope of medical tourism was found to be insignificant for each of age group. Hence, it is evident that age has no impact on the perception of the foreign tourists towards the scope of the medical tourism in India. The mean value of all the groups were found to be above 2 which indicates that the scope of medical tourism in India is on an average, not too high not too low but of average in nature. There are few factors on which Indian healthcare sectors are performing well to attract the foreign tourists and there are various factors on which there is a clear cut need to give attention by the policy makers.

Table 5. Gender and scope of medical tourism

	N	Mean	Std. Deviation	Std. Error	Minimum	Maximum
Male	143	2.7203	.94097	.07869	1.30	5.00
Female	7	3.5571	1.41287	.53401	1.40	4.80
Total	150	2.7593	.97754	.07982	1.30	5.00

f-value = 5.023, p-value = 0.027, Welch test value = 2.404 (Sig. = 0.170)
Source: Author's own creation

Female foreign tourists have perceived the higher scope of medical tourism in India in comparison to male foreign tourists. The mean value for female foreign tourists was 3.55 which is above average and indicates that the female foreign tourists have perceived the factors responsible for the medical tourism in India as in good condition and they have an opinion that Indian can be developed as medical tourism destination if focused upon by the government and the healthcare sector. While mean value for the male foreign tourists was 2.72, which is close to 3 and signifies that male foreign tourist have perceived the scope of medical tourism in India only average, and the factors responsible for the growth of medical tourism in India could not attract much to them. The f-value was 5.023, which is significant and showed that gender makes a difference in the opinions of the foreign tourists towards the scope of the medical tourism in India. The value of Welch test conducted to check the robustness was also found to be insignificant and the independent groups can be considered to have equal variance.

Table 6. Country and scope of medical tourism

	N	Mean	Std. Deviation	Std. Error	Minimum	Maximum
Gulf countries	37	2.6703	1.04506	.17181	1.40	5.00
Asian countries	71	2.6155	.82369	.09775	1.40	5.00
African Countries	26	3.1500	1.04700	.20533	1.60	4.90
European Countries	16	2.9688	1.20373	.30093	1.30	4.70
Total	150	2.7593	.97754	.07982	1.30	5.00

f-value = 2.303, p-value = 0.080, Welch test value = 2.039 (Sig. = 0.121)
Source: Author's own creation

Foreign tourists from African countries have perceived the higher scope of medical tourism in India in comparison to foreign tourists from other countries. The mean value for foreign tourists from African countries was 3.15 which is above average and indicates that the foreign tourists from African countries have perceived the factors responsible for the medical tourism in India as in good condition and they have an opinion that Indian can be developed as medical tourism destination if focused upon by the government and the healthcare sector. While mean value for the foreign tourists from Asian countries was 2.61, which is close to 3 and signifies that foreign tourist from Asian countries have perceived the scope of medical tourism in India only average, and the factors responsible for the growth of medical tourism in India could not attract much to them. The f-value was 2.303, which is insignificant and showed that country to whom foreign tourists belong to, does not make a difference in the opinions of the foreign tourists towards the scope of the medical tourism in India. The value of Welch test conducted to check the robustness was also found to be insignificant and the independent groups can be considered to have equal variance.

Table 7. Post hoc analysis

(I) Country belongs to	(J) Country belongs to	Mean Difference (I-J)	Std. Error	Sig.
Gulf countries	Asian countries	.05478	.19566	.780
	African Countries	-.47973	.24694	.054
	European Countries	-.29848	.28873	.303

continued on following page

Table 7. Continued

(I) Country belongs to	(J) Country belongs to	Mean Difference (I-J)	Std. Error	Sig.
Asian countries	Gulf countries	-.05478	.19566	.780
	African Countries	-.53451*	.22120	.017
	European Countries	-.35326	.26704	.188
African Countries	Gulf countries	.47973	.24694	.054
	Asian countries	.53451*	.22120	.017
	European Countries	.18125	.30661	.555
European Countries	Gulf countries	.29848	.28873	.303
	Asian countries	.35326	.26704	.188
	African Countries	-.18125	.30661	.555

Source: Author's own creation

The mean value for the variable 'scope of medical tourism' was found to be significantly different among two groups, mainly foreign tourists from gulf countries and African Countries. It signifies that foreign tourist from gulf countries and African Countries have experienced different quality of medical treatment, healthcare services and they have perceived the factors promoting growth of medical tourism differently. Similarly, mean value for the variable 'scope of medical tourism' was found to be significantly different among two groups mainly; foreign tourists from Asian countries and African Countries. It signifies that foreign tourist from Asian countries and African Countries have experienced different quality of medical treatment, healthcare services and they have perceived the factors promoting growth of medical tourism differently. While for rest of the other countries, no significant difference was found in the opinions of the foreign tourists towards the scope of medical tourism in India. Overall, country do not have a significant impact on the opinions of the foreign tourists towards the scope of medical tourism in India.

Table 8. City and scope of medical tourism

	N	Mean	Std. Deviation	Std. Error	Minimum	Maximum
New Delhi	50	3.7460	1.08801	.15387	1.30	5.00
Mumbai	50	2.2560	.35350	.04999	1.60	3.10
Bangalore	50	2.2760	.32674	.04621	1.50	3.10
Total	150	2.7593	.97754	.07982	1.30	5.00

f-value = 77.384, p-value = 0.000, Welch test value = 43.784 (Sig. = 0.000)
Source: Author's own creation

Foreign tourists getting medical treatment in the hospitals of New Delhi, have perceived the higher scope of medical tourism in India in comparison to foreign tourists from other two cities, namely Mumbai and Bangalore. The mean value for foreign tourists from New Delhi was 3.74 which is above average and indicates that the foreign tourists from New Delhi have perceived the factors responsible for the medical tourism in India as in good condition and they have an opinion that Indian can be developed as medical tourism destination if focused upon by the government and the healthcare sector. While mean value for the foreign tourists from Mumbai and Bangalore was 2.25 and 2.27 respectively, which is slightly above 2 and signifies that foreign tourist from Mumbai and Bangalore have perceived the scope of medical tourism in India as poor, and the factors responsible for the growth of medical tourism in India could not attract much to them. The f-value was 77.384, which is significant and showed that city from where the foreign tourists were getting medical treatment, makes a difference in the opinions of the foreign tourists towards the scope of the medical tourism in India. The value of the Welch test conducted to check the robustness was also found to be significant and the independent groups can be considered to have unequal variance.

Table 9. Post hoc analysis

(I) City of medical treatment	(J) City of medical treatment	Mean Difference (I-J)	Std. Error	Sig.
New Delhi	Mumbai	1.49000*	.13738	.000
	Bangalore	1.47000*	.13738	.000
Mumbai	New Delhi	-1.49000*	.13738	.000
	Bangalore	-.02000	.13738	.884
Bangalore	New Delhi	-1.47000*	.13738	.000
	Mumbai	.02000	.13738	.884

Source: Author's own creation

The mean value for the variable 'scope of medical tourism' was found to be significantly different among two groups, foreign tourists from New Delhi and Mumbai. It signifies that foreign tourists getting treatment in New Delhi and Mumbai have experienced different quality of medical treatment, healthcare services and they have perceived the factors promoting growth of medical tourism differently. Similarly, the mean value for the variable 'scope of medical tourism' was found to be significantly different among two groups, foreign tourists from New Delhi and Bangalore. It signifies that foreign tourists getting treatment in New Delhi and Bangalore have experienced different quality of medical treatment, healthcare services and they have perceived the factors promoting growth of medical tourism differently. While for

Mumbai and Bangalore, no significant difference was found in the opinions of the foreign tourists towards the scope of medical tourism in India. Overall, city plays an important role in forming the perceptions of the foreign tourists towards scope of medical tourism in India. New Delhi has been perceived as the higher scope for developing as medical tourism destination in India than Mumbai or Bangalore.

Table 10. Kind of medical treatment and scope of medical tourism

Kind of medical treatment	N	Mean	Std. Deviation	Std. Error	Minimum	Maximum
Heart surgery	31	2.7839	1.06336	.19098	1.40	5.00
Organ replacement	53	2.6887	.90355	.12411	1.40	5.00
Cancer or Tumors	34	2.8971	1.05299	.18059	1.60	4.80
Skin Treatment	25	2.8320	1.02214	.20443	1.50	4.80
Physiotherapy/yoga/wellness/ Ayurveda treatment	7	2.2571	.50285	.19006	1.30	2.70
Total	150	2.7593	.97754	.07982	1.30	5.00

f-value = 0.734, p-value = 0.570, Welch test value = 1.720 (Sig. = 0.165)
Source: Author's own creation

Foreign tourists availing medical treatment for Cancer or Tumors, have perceived the higher scope of medical tourism in India in comparison to other foreign tourists. The mean value for foreign tourists availing medical treatment for Cancer or Tumors, was 2.89; which is above average and indicates that the foreign tourists availing medical treatment for Cancer or Tumors, have perceived the factors responsible for the medical tourism in India as in good condition and they have an opinion that Indian can be developed as medical tourism destination if focused upon by the government and the healthcare sector. While mean value for the foreign tourists availing Physiotherapy/yoga/wellness/Ayurveda treatment, was 2.25, which is less than average and signifies that foreign tourist availing Physiotherapy/yoga/wellness/Ayurveda treatment, have perceived the scope of medical tourism in India poor, and the factors responsible for the growth of medical tourism in India could not attract much to them. The f-value was 0.734, which is insignificant and showed that Kind of medical treatment do not affect the opinions of the foreign tourists towards the scope of the medical tourism in India. The value of Welch test conducted to check the robustness was also found to be insignificant and the independent groups can be considered to have equal variance. Hence, India can be developed as a medical tourism destination especially for cancer and tumors' patients from foreign countries as cancer and tumor patients have perceived high quality of the medical services in India.

Table 11. Post hoc analysis

(I) Kind of medical treatment	(J) Kind of medical treatment	Mean Difference (I-J)	Std. Error	Sig.
Heart surgery	Organ replacement	.09519	.22183	.668
	Cancer or Tumors	-.11319	.24363	.643
	Skin Treatment	-.04813	.26371	.855
	Physiotherapy/yoga/wellness/ Ayurveda treatment	.52673	.41054	.202
Organ replacement	Heart surgery	-.09519	.22183	.668
	Cancer or Tumors	-.20838	.21556	.335
	Skin Treatment	-.14332	.23803	.548
	Physiotherapy/yoga/wellness/ Ayurveda treatment	.43154	.39453	.276
Cancer or Tumors	Heart surgery	.11319	.24363	.643
	Organ replacement	.20838	.21556	.335
	Skin Treatment	.06506	.25847	.802
	Physiotherapy/yoga/wellness/ Ayurveda treatment	.63992	.40719	.118
Skin Treatment	Heart surgery	.04813	.26371	.855
	Organ replacement	.14332	.23803	.548
	Cancer or Tumors	-.06506	.25847	.802
	Physiotherapy/yoga/wellness/ Ayurveda treatment	.57486	.41951	.173
Physiotherapy/yoga/wellness/ Ayurveda treatment	Heart surgery	-.52673	.41054	.202
	Organ replacement	-.43154	.39453	.276
	Cancer or Tumors	-.63992	.40719	.118
	Skin Treatment	-.57486	.41951	.173

Source: Author's own creation

Post hoc analysis results showed that none of the two groups have significantly different mean values and all the differences in the various groups of foreign tourists availing different kind of medical treatment, for the variable 'scope of medical tourism was found to be insignificant for each of the group. Hence, it is evident that kind of medical treatment has no impact on the perception of the foreign tourists towards the scope of the medical tourism in India. The mean value of all the groups were found to be above 2 and close to 3, which indicates that the scope of medical tourism in India is on an average, not too high not too low but of average in nature. Foreign tourists have same opinions towards the scope of medical tourism in India, irrespective of the kind of medical treatment they are availing in the Indian hospitals.

Table 12. Number of times visiting India for medical purpose and scope of medical tourism

Number of times visiting India for medical purpose	N	Mean	Std. Deviation	Std. Error	Minimum	Maximum
First time Visitor	68	3.1353	1.14901	.13934	1.40	5.00
Visited two three times	78	2.4615	.68400	.07745	1.30	5.00
More than three times	4	2.1750	.05000	.02500	2.10	2.20
Total	150	2.7593	.97754	.07982	1.30	5.00

f-value = 10.565, p-value = 0.000, Welch test value = 27.787 (Sig. = 0.000)
Source: Author's own creation

Foreign tourists visiting India for the first time, have perceived the higher scope of medical tourism in India in comparison to other foreign tourists. The mean value for first time visitors was 3.13 which is above average and indicates that the foreign tourists visiting India for the first time, have perceived the factors responsible for the medical tourism in India as in good condition and they have an opinion that Indian can be developed as medical tourism destination if focused upon by the government and the healthcare sector. While mean value for the foreign tourists visiting India for two or three times or more than three times, was 2.46 and 2.17 respectively, which is close to 3 and signifies that these foreign tourists have perceived the scope of medical tourism in India only average, and the factors responsible for the growth of medical tourism in India could not attract much to them. The f-value was 10.565, which is significant and showed that Number of visits to India for medical purpose, makes a difference in the opinions of the foreign tourists towards the scope of the medical tourism in India. The value of Welch test conducted to check the robustness was also found to be significant and the independent groups can be considered to have unequal variance.

Table 13. Post hoc analysis

(I) Number of times visiting India for medical purpose	(J) Number of times visiting India for medical purpose	Mean Difference (I-J)	Std. Error	Sig.
First time Visitor	Visited two three times	.67376*	.15268	.000
	More than three times	.96029*	.47346	.044
Visited two three times	First time Visitor	-.67376*	.15268	.000
	More than three times	.28654	.47177	.545
More than three times	First time Visitor	-.96029*	.47346	.044
	Visited two three times	-.28654	.47177	.545

Source: Author's own creation

The mean value for the variable 'scope of medical tourism' was found to be significantly different among two groups mainly; foreign tourists visiting India for the first time and those who have visited India for two three times for medical treatment. Similarly, the mean value for the variable 'scope of medical tourism' was found to be significantly different among two groups mainly; foreign tourists visiting India for the first time and those who have visited India for more than three times for medical treatment. It signifies that foreign tourist getting treatment in in India for the first time and those who have visited India two three times, or more than three times; have experienced different quality of medical treatment, healthcare services and they have perceived the factors promoting growth of medical tourism differently. While for foreign tourists visited India for two three times and more than three times, no significant difference was found in the opinions of the foreign tourists towards the scope of medical tourism in India. Overall, the number of visits by foreign tourists to India for getting medical treatment is an important factor in forming the perceptions of the foreign tourists towards scope of medical tourism in India. First time visitors have perceived huge scope for the medical tourism in India than other foreign tourists.

CONCLUSION AND SUGGESTIONS

The scope of medical tourism in India from foreign tourists is average only. The only factor which attracts foreign tourists to India for medical treatment is the difference in the cost of medical treatment and that too due to difference in currency value. Other than this no other factor was perceived as in good or very good state in India which can help in medical tourism promotion. Study put more light on this area, and it was noted that New Delhi has high quality of healthcare services, and the other factors which promote medical tourism in India. Hence, Delhi government along with central government should take steps for improving healthcare infrastructure in New Delhi. One more interesting findings of the study is that Cancer and Tumor related healthcare services can be targeted to attract foreign tourists as the foreign tourists availing treatment for cancer and Tumor have perceived huge scope for medical tourism in India. In order to promote the medical tourism in India, government need to work on the following factors: World class infrastructure facilities in healthcare to attract the tourists from all over the world. Budget allocation for the cutting-edge medical equipment, and health care services. International accreditation to both the hospitals and the healthcare workers is important to ensure the medical facilities are at par with international standards. Quality is one of the important and foremost criteria for the success of any healthcare system. Hence, the government should work on maintaining the quality standards of the hospitals to promote the medical tourism in the country. Cost comes after quality, if the quality services are provided at reasonable cost, tourist can be automatically attracted for getting healthcare services in India, which can boost the medical tourism in India. Government plays a vital role in ensuring the cost effectiveness of the medical services by hospitals. The government can put in place clear guidelines for the hospitals for the maximum charges for the medical services that can be charged, and by ensuring ethical practices of the hospitals. Branding and marketing campaigns can also give a boost to medical tourism in the country. National tourism policy should include the medical tourism as an agenda and tourism policy can be used as a tool for promotion and branding of the same. Government needs to work on establishing the medical tourism brand at national level, by participating in international forums, expos, and medical conferences. Digital marketing is the best tool to be used to reach international tourists. A dedicated helpline for international tourists, and a website which can only be available for medical tourists, displaying all the information about the hospitals, healthcare facilities, details of healthcare workers along with their achievements, and success stories.

Tourist visa is another important domain to focus upon by the government while promoting medical tourism. Simpler the visa processes higher will be the chances for tourists' inflow in the country. Most of cases the medical tourists are already in stress when they start looking for other country for medical services, if the visa formalities will be complex, it will increase their stress level more. Hence, for medical tourists the visa processes can be simple and quick, so that the chances of losing the tourists because of visa process can be minimized. Issue and extension processes of medical visa should be simple and less time consuming to promote medical tourism. Collaborations or partnerships are the key for promoting medical tourism, especially with the international insurance agencies, or already established brands in the market. Most of the foreign tourists go for medical insurance for availing medical services due to the cost factor. Hence, collaborating with foreign insurance agencies can bring more business to the healthcare sector. Partnership with the foreign travel companies providing all-inclusive services related to healthcare can boost the medical tourism sector. Government can also provide incentives to hospitals and healthcare workers to boost their morale for promoting quality services and improving their infrastructure.

Training programs are a must for the healthcare workers to update their knowledge, and to improve the healthcare service quality. Training programs to handle the international patients and soft skills to communicate with them should be utmost priority to improve customer experiences. Customers' feedback can also be used to make changes or develop strategies for the medical tourism in the country. Patient experience throughout the journey from arrival to departure for availing medical tourism affects their decision to avail the medical services from same country in future. Medical tourism can also be promoted through Ayurvedic and yoga, the ancient system of healthcare. Wellness packages can be promoted for treatments, under these traditional Indian therapies. While a thorough follow-up and post-treatment care could add more value to these healthcare services.

Limitations and Future Research

The study has geographical limitations and limited sample size. The study can be explored to other cities of India who have world class facilities in healthcare sector such as Ahmedabad, Kolkata, Hyderabad and Chandigarh. The sample size of the study can also be included for a depth understanding. The inputs of the healthcare professionals should also be included to know about the factors which are responsible for the growth of medical tourism in India. In future, studies can be conducted to measure the perceptions of the healthcare professionals and parties involved in medical tourism promotion in India.

REFERENCES

Ajmeri, S. R. (2012). Medical tourism: A healthier future for India. *Arth Prabandh: A Journal of Economics and Management*, 1(5), 11-18.

Bookman, M. Z., & Bookman, K. R. (2007). Medical tourism in developing countries. *University of Toronto Medical Journal*, 74(3), 1–20. http://utmj.org/ojs/index.php/UTMJ/article/viewFile/373/355

Chacko, P. (2006). Medical tourism in India: Issues and challenges. In *Health tourism: An introduction* (p. 123). ICFAI University Press.

Dawn, S. K., & Pal, S. (2011). Medical tourism in India: Issues, opportunities, and designing strategies for growth and development. *International Journal of Multidisciplinary Research*, 1(13), 185–202.

Durrani, H. (2016). Healthcare and healthcare systems: Inspiring progress and future prospects. *Journal of Healthcare Management*, 61(5), 1–10. https://www.ncbi.nlm.nih.gov/pmc/articles/PMC5344175/ PMID: 28293581

Ernst & Young. (2007). Diagnosing India's health care survey. *Business World*, 25(5), 56.

George, B. P. (2010). Medical tourism: An analysis with special reference to India. *Journal of Hospitality Application and Research*, 2(4), 1–15.

Goodrich, G., & Goodrich, J. (1987). Healthcare tourism: An exploratory study. *Tourism Management*, 8(3), 217–222. DOI: 10.1016/0261-5177(87)90053-7

Goyal, S. L., & Kumar, R. (2010). *Medical tourism and hospital services*. University Press.

Jadhav, S., Yeravdekar, R., & Kulkarni, M. (2014). Cross-border healthcare access in South Asian countries: Learning for sustainable healthcare tourism in India. *International Conference on India and Development Partnerships in Asia and Africa: Towards a New Paradigm (IRC-2013)*, 157, 109-117. DOI: 10.1016/j.sbspro.2014.11.014

Jain, N. (2006). Health tourism in India. *EzineArticles*. http://EzineArticles.com/?expert=Nakuljain/

Jawahar, S. K. (2007). Health care services in India. *ICU Management and Practice*, 6(4), 1–5.

Jyothis, T. (2009). *An evaluation of the potentials of health tourism with special reference to Kerala* (Master's thesis, University of Calicut, India).

Kelley, E. (2013). Medical tourism. WHO Patient Safety Programme. https://www.who.int/patientsafety/medicaltourism/en/

Mal, J. (2010). Globalization of healthcare: Case studies of medical tourism in multi-specialty hospitals in India (Doctoral dissertation, Manchester Business School).

Mukherjee, W., & Mookerji, M. (2004). Hospitals busy tying up with hospitality Inc. *The Economic Times*, 6.

Petrick, J. F. (1999). *An examination of the relationships between golf travelers' satisfaction, perceived value and loyalty and their intentions to revisit* (Doctoral dissertation, Clemson University).

Pritchard, M. P., & Howard, D. R. (1997). The loyal traveler: Examining a typology of service patronage. *Journal of Travel Research*, 35(4), 2–10. DOI: 10.1177/004728759703500401

Reddy, S., & Qadeer, I. (2010). Medical tourism in India: Progress and predicament. *Economic and Political Weekly*, XLV(20), 1–7.

World Report. (2010). Medical tourism in India, but at what cost? *World Report*, 1-2.

Sharma, A., Sharma, A., & Tiwari, S. (2012). Medical tourism: Building the India brand abroad: An analytical study of potential of medical tourism in Gurgaon. *International Journal of Business and Management Invention*, 1(12), 1–6.

Singh, L. (2014). An evaluation of medical tourism in India. *African Journal of Hospitality, Tourism and Leisure*, 3(1), 1–11.

Soloman, H. (2011). Affective journeys: The emotional structuring of medical tourism in India. *Anthropology & Medicine*, 18(1), 105–118. DOI: 10.1080/13648470.2010.525878 PMID: 21563006

Tiwari, V. (2012). Healthcare scenario in India. https://www.slideshare.net/mobile/vikasba123/healthcare-scenario-in-india/

Uniyal, M., Dhodi, R. K., Dhodi, R., & Sharma, S. (2014). SWOT analysis of the Indian medical tourism industry. *Tourism (Zagreb)*, 3(2), 1–2.

World Health Organization. (2008). *World report on health*.

World Health Organization. (2011). *World report on health*.

World Health Organization. (2011). *World report on health*.

KEY TERMS AND DEFINITIONS

Cost of Medical Services: The price patients pay for medical procedures, treatments, or surgeries. Lower costs in countries like India are a major draw for international patients seeking affordable care.

Documentation Process: The necessary paperwork for medical tourists, including visas, medical records, and insurance documentation. Simplifying these processes can improve the medical tourism experience.

Government Support: Involves policies, subsidies, and initiatives from the government aimed at promoting the country as a medical tourism hub. This can include streamlined visa processes and investment in healthcare facilities.

Healthcare Infrastructure: The physical and organizational systems that support medical care, such as hospitals, clinics, medical equipment, and healthcare facilities.

Healthcare Professionals: Doctors, nurses, and other medical staff who provide treatment and care to patients. Their expertise and reputation are key factors in attracting medical tourists.

Medical Insurance: Insurance coverage for medical procedures, which can include international health insurance that covers treatment abroad. Partnerships between hospitals and insurers are crucial in medical tourism.

Medical Tourism: The practice of traveling to another country for medical treatment, often to access more affordable or higher-quality healthcare than is available in the patient's home country.

Quality of Healthcare Services: Refers to the standard of medical care, including cleanliness, technology, and patient satisfaction. High-quality care is a critical factor in a country's appeal as a medical tourism destination.

Technology Innovations: Advances in medical technology that enhance the quality of treatment, from state-of-the-art surgical equipment to diagnostic tools, making a destination more attractive for foreign patients.

Transportation Connectivity: The ease of travel to and from the medical tourism destination, including the availability of flights, airports, and other modes of transport, which can influence a country's appeal for medical tourists.

Compilation of References

Aarabe, M., Khizzou, N. B., Alla, L., & Benjelloun, A. (2024a). Marketing Applications of Emerging Technologies : A Systematic Literature Review. In *AI and Data Engineering Solutions for Effective Marketing* (p. 23-47). IGI Global. DOI: 10.4018/979-8-3693-3172-9.ch002

Aarabe, M., Khizzou, N. B., Alla, L., & Benjelloun, A. (2024b). Smart Tourism Experience and Responsible Travelers' Behavior : A Systematic Literature Review. In *Promoting Responsible Tourism With Digital Platforms* (p. 128-147). IGI Global. DOI: 10.4018/979-8-3693-3286-3.ch008

Abdel Raziq, M. (1974). The dedicatory and building texts of Ramesses II in Luxor temple. *The Journal of Egyptian Archaeology*, 60(1), 142–160. DOI: 10.1177/030751337406000116

Abdel Raziq, M. (1986). *Das Sanktuar Amenophis III im Luxor-Tempel, Studies in Egyptian Culture No. 3*. Peeters.

Abdelhaq, L. (2024). Economic resilience in tourism: Forecasting financial survival in Moroccan SME hotels. *Zenodo*. https://doi.org/DOI: 10.5281/ZENODO.11110423

Abdunurova, A. A., Razakova, D. I., & Davletova, M. T. (2022). Global portrait of a modern tourist: Travel trends in marketing. *Bulletin of 'Turan'. University*, 1(1), 166–173. DOI: 10.46914/1562-2959-2022-1-1-166-173

Abhijeet, D., & Noul, D. (2024). Safety at the core: IoT, knowledge management, and sustainable development. https://doi.org/DOI: 10.13140/RG.2.2.33544.64007

Aburub, F. (2023). Applying augmented reality in tourism: Analyzing relevance as it concerns consumer satisfaction and purchase intention. In Shishkov, B. (Ed.), *Business modeling and software design* (Vol. 483, pp. 278–288). Springer Nature Switzerland., DOI: 10.1007/978-3-031-36757-1_19

Abushenkova, M. V. (2022). The impact of COVID-19 on the tourism and hotel business in the Kursk region. *Proceedings of the Southwest State University. Series: Economics. Sociology.Management*, 12(1), 106–114. DOI: 10.21869/2223-1552-2022-12-1-106-114

Adanma, U. M., & Ogunbiyi, E. O.Uwaga Monica AdanmaEmmanuel Olurotimi Ogunbiyi. (2024). Artificial intelligence in environmental conservation: Evaluating cyber risks and opportunities for sustainable practices. *Computer Science & IT Research Journal*, 5(5), 1178–1209. DOI: 10.51594/csitrj.v5i5.1156

Advertising Standards Authority [ASA]. (2024). *Advertising codes: The UK advertising codes lay down rules for advertisers, agencies and media owners to follow.* ASA. Retrieved September 20, 2024, from https://www.asa.org.uk/codes-and-rulings/advertising-codes.html

Adwan, A. A., & Altrjman, G. (2024). The role of social media marketing and marketing management in promoting and developing brand sustainability strategy. *International Journal of Data and Network Science*, 8(1), 439–452. DOI: 10.5267/j.ijdns.2023.9.011

Agarwal, R., & Prasad, J. (1998). A conceptual and operational definition of personal innovativeness in the domain of information technology. *Information Systems Research*, 9(2), 204–215. DOI: 10.1287/isre.9.2.204

Ahmad, N., Ahmad, A., & Siddique, I. (2023). Responsible tourism and hospitality: The intersection of altruistic values, human emotions, and corporate social responsibility. *Administrative Sciences*, 13(4), 105. DOI: 10.3390/admsci13040105

Ahmad, S. Y., & Idris, N. Q. A. P.Siti Yuliandi AhmadNur Qasdina Asyura Pg Idris. (2024). Tourist preferences, the use of social media, and travel behaviours among youth in Malaysia. *Journal of Advanced Study in Business and Management Studies*, 35(1), 44–54. DOI: 10.37934/arbms.35.1.4454

Ahn, J., & Kwon, J. (2020). Green hotel brands in Malaysia: Perceived value, cost, anticipated emotion, and revisit intention. *Current Issues in Tourism*, 23(12), 1559–1574. DOI: 10.1080/13683500.2019.1646715

Aho, S. K. (2001). Towards a general theory of touristic experiences: Modelling experience process in tourism. *Tourism Review*, 56(1), 33–37. DOI: 10.1108/eb058368

Aiello, D., Fai, S., & Santagati, C. (2019). Virtual museums as a means for promotion and enhancement of cultural heritage. *The International Archives of the Photogrammetry, Remote Sensing and Spatial Information Sciences*, XLII-2(W11), 17–24. DOI: 10.5194/isprs-archives-XLII-2-W9-17-2019

Airbnb. (2018). Ageless travel: The growing popularity of Airbnb for the over 60s. Airbnb Newsroom. https://news.airbnb.com/ageless-travel-the-growing-popularity-of-airbnb-for-the-over-60s/

Airbnb. (2022). Shareholder letter Q4 2021. Airbnb. https://s26.q4cdn.com/656283129/files/doc_financials/2021/q4/Airbnb_Q4-2021-Shareholder-Letter_Final.pdf

Ajmeri, S. R. (2012). Medical tourism: A healthier future for India. *Arth Prabandh: A Journal of Economics and Management*, 1(5), 11-18.

Akel, G., & Noyan, E. (2024). Exploring the criteria for a green and smart hotel: Insights from hotel managers' perspectives. *Journal of Hospitality and Tourism Insights*. https://doi.org/DOI: 10.1108/JHTI-08-2023-0555

Akter Poli, T., Hasan Sawon, Md. M., Nasir Mia, Md., Ali, W., Rahman, M., Hossain, R., & Mani, L. (2024). Tourism and climate change: Mitigation and adaptation strategies in a hospitality industry in Bangladesh. *Tourism and Climate Change: Mitigation and Adaptation Strategies in a Hospitality Industry in Bangladesh*. https://doi.org/DOI: 10.53555/kuey.v30i5.3798

Akter, M. S. (2024). Harnessing technology for environmental sustainability: Utilizing AI to tackle global ecological challenges. [JAIGS]. *Journal of Artificial Intelligence General Science*, 2(1), 61–70.

Al Karim, R., & Hassan, A. (2021). Investment barriers and opportunities in the tourism and hospitality industry of Bangladesh. In Hassan, A. (Ed.), *Tourism in Bangladesh: Investment and development perspectives* (pp. 417–431). Springer Nature Singapore., DOI: 10.1007/978-981-16-1858-1_25

Alabau-Montoya, J., & Ruiz-Molina, M. E. (2020). Enhancing visitor experience with war heritage tourism through information and communication technologies: Evidence from Spanish Civil War museums and sites. *Journal of Heritage Tourism*, 15(5), 500–510. DOI: 10.1080/1743873X.2019.1692853

Alam, M. N., Ogiemwonyi, O., Hago, I. E., Azizan, N. A., Hashim, F., & Hossain, M. S. (2023). Understanding consumer environmental ethics and the willingness to use green products. *SAGE Open*, 13(1), 215824402211497. DOI: 10.1177/21582440221149727

Alasadi, E. A., & Baiz, C. R. (2023). Generative AI in education and research: Opportunities, concerns, and solutions. *Journal of Chemical Education*, 100(8), 2965–2971. DOI: 10.1021/acs.jchemed.3c00323

Al-Azab, M. R., & Zaki, H. S. (2023). Towards sustainable development: Antecedents of green entrepreneurship intention among tourism and hospitality students in Egypt. *Journal of Hospitality and Tourism Insights.* https://doi.org/DOI: 10.1108/JHTI-03-2023-0146

Albarq, A. N. (2024). Mobile services sector in Saudi Arabia: A systematic literature review of the effective strategies for enhancing customer satisfaction. *International Journal of Data and Network Science*, 8(1), 585–596. DOI: 10.5267/j.ijdns.2023.8.026

Alhosani, K., & Alhashmi, S. M. (2024). Opportunities, challenges, and benefits of AI innovation in government services: A review. *Discover Artificial Intelligence*, 4(1), 1–19. DOI: 10.1007/s44163-024-00111-w

Al-Husseiny, M. (1988). *The Ottoman Sabils in Cairo 1517-1798.* Medbouli Press. (in Arabic)

Aliyah, L., Lukita, C., Pangilinan, G., Chakim, M., & Saputra, D. (2023). Examining the impact of artificial intelligence and internet of things on smart tourism destinations : A comprehensive study. *Aptisi Transactions on Technopreneurship*, 5(2sp), 135–145. DOI: 10.34306/att.v5i2sp.332

Alla, L., Bentalha, B., & Elyoussfi, A. (2023). Intelligence territoriale et positionnement stratégique des regions au Maroc : Le cas de la région de Fès Meknes en perspective. *Le concept de l'intéligence en sciences juridiques, économiques et sociales*, 215-237.

Almobaideen, W., Allan, M., & Saadeh, M. (2016). Smart archaeological tourism : Contention, convenience and accessibility in the context of cloud-centric IoT. *Mediterranean Archaeology & Archaeometry. International Journal*, 16(1), 227–227.

Aloisi, A., & De Stefano, V. (2022). *Your boss is an algorithm: Artificial intelligence, platform work, and labour.* Bloomsbury Publishing. DOI: 10.5040/9781509953219

Aloni, E. (2016). Pluralizing the "sharing" economy. *Washington Law Review (Seattle, Wash.)*, 91(4), 1397–1459. https://digitalcommons.law.uw.edu/wlr/vol91/iss4/2/

Al-Romeedy, B. (2024a). Breaking chains, building futures - Blockchain's impact on sustainable tourism. In *Promoting responsible tourism with digital platforms.* IGI Global. DOI: 10.4018/979-8-3693-3286-3.ch006

Al-Romeedy, B. (2024b). AI and HRM in tourism and hospitality in Egypt: Inevitability, impact, and future. In *HRM, artificial intelligence, and the future of work: Critical insights from the Global South.* Palgrave Macmillan. DOI: 10.1007/978-3-031-62369-1_13

Al-Romeedy, B. (2024c). Sky high sustainability – Shaping the future of green aviation through innovation. In *Sustainability in travel and tourism* (pp. 44–53). Bharti Publications.

Alrwashdeh, M., Jahmani, A., Ibrahim, B., & Aljuhmani, H. Y. (2020). Data to model the effects of perceived telecommunication service quality and value on the degree of user satisfaction and e-WOM among telecommunications users in North Cyprus. *Data in Brief*, 28, 104981. DOI: 10.1016/j.dib.2019.104981 PMID: 31890816

Altunel, M. C., & Erkurt, B. (2015). Cultural tourism in Istanbul: The mediation effect of tourist experience and satisfaction on the relationship between involvement and recommendation intention. *Journal of Destination Marketing & Management*, 4(4), 213–221. DOI: 10.1016/j.jdmm.2015.06.003

Alves, P., Martins, H., Saraiva, P., Carneiro, J., Novais, P., & Marreiros, G. (2022). Group Recommender Systems for Tourism : How does Personality predicts Preferences for Attractions, Travel Motivations, Preferences and Concerns? DOI: 10.21203/rs.3.rs-1762820/v1

Alves, P., Martins, H., Saraiva, P., Carneiro, J., Novais, P., & Marreiros, G. (2023). Group recommender systems for tourism : How does personality predict preferences for attractions, travel motivations, preferences and concerns? *User Modeling and User-Adapted Interaction*, 33(5), 1141–1210. DOI: 10.1007/s11257-023-09361-2 PMID: 37359944

Amanor, W. K., Adanu, E. K., Adams, C. A., & Adi, S. B. (2024). Assessing road users' preference for various travel demand management strategies for adoption in Accra, Ghana. *Preprints*. https://doi.org/DOI: 10.20944/preprints202405.1325.v1

Amjad, A., Kordel, P., & Fernandes, G. (2023). The systematic review in the field of management sciences. *Zeszyty Naukowe. Organizacja i Zarządzanie/Politechnika Śląska*. https://yadda.icm.edu.pl/baztech/element/bwmeta1.element.baztech-12a05f97-6339-4215-a0a7-cb6e0963c108

Anastasiei, B., Dospinescu, N., & Dospinescu, O. (2021). Understanding the adoption of incentivized word-of-mouth in the online environment. *Journal of Theoretical and Applied Electronic Commerce Research*, 16(4), 992–1007. DOI: 10.3390/jtaer16040056

Anaya, G. J., & Lehto, X. (2020). Traveler-facing technology in the tourism experience : A historical perspective. *Journal of Travel & Tourism Marketing*, 37(3), 317–331. DOI: 10.1080/10548408.2020.1757561

Angelov, V., Petkov, E., Shipkovenski, G., & Kalushkov, T. (2020, June). Modern virtual reality headsets. In *2020 International Congress on Human-Computer Interaction, Optimization and Robotic Applications (HORA)* (pp. 1-5). IEEE.

An, S., Suh, J., & Eck, T. (2019). Examining structural relationships among service quality, perceived value, satisfaction and revisit intention for Airbnb guests. *International Journal of Tourism Sciences*, 19(3), 145–165. DOI: 10.1080/15980634.2019.1663980

Antonio, N., Almeida, A. D., & Nunes, L. (2019). Hotel booking demand datasets. *Data in Brief*, 22, 41–49. DOI: 10.1016/j.dib.2018.11.126 PMID: 30581903

Antoniou, A. (2024). When likes go rogue: Advertising standards and the malpractice of unruly social media influencers. *Journal of Media Law*, 1-44.

Antunes, A. C. (2021). The role of social media influencers on the consumer decision-making process. In Antunes, A. C. (Ed.), *Handbook of research on promoting brands with social media influencers* (pp. 138–154)., DOI: 10.4018/978-1-7998-4718-2.ch008

Archer, C., Wolf, K., & Nalloor, J. (2021). Capitalising on chaos: Exploring the impact and future of social media influencer engagement during the early stages of a global pandemic. *Media International Australia, Incorporating Culture & Policy*, 178(1), 106–113. DOI: 10.1177/1329878X20958157

Arslan, H. M., Khan, I., Latif, M. I., Komal, B., & Chen, S. (2022). Understanding the dynamics of natural resources rents, environmental sustainability, and sustainable economic growth: New insights from China. *Environmental Science and Pollution Research International*, 29(39), 58746–58761. DOI: 10.1007/s11356-022-19952-y PMID: 35368236

ASA. (2021a, February 3). Beauty and cosmetics: The use of production techniques. Retrieved July 15, 2024, from https://www.asa.org.uk/advice-online/cosmetics-the-use-of-production-techniques.html

ASA. (2021b, February 11). The (mis)use of social media beauty filters when advertising cosmetic products. Retrieved July 15, 2024, from https://www.asa.org.uk/news/the-mis-use-of-social-media-beauty-filters-when-advertising-cosmetic-products.html

ASA. (2022). Non-compliant social media influencers. Retrieved September 20, 2024, from https://www.asa.org.uk/codes-and-rulings/non-compliant-social-media-influencers.html

ASA. (2024a, July 29). Remit: Country of origin. Retrieved September 20, 2024, from https://www.asa.org.uk/advice-online/remit-country-of-origin.html

ASA. (2024b). Rulings. Retrieved September 20, 2024, from https://www.asa.org.uk/codes-and-rulings/rulings.html?topic=4DF9FA97-F0A0-4B57-A8E73F8D695F073E,E5C6E825-2A0C-43EF-92C89820C76B6726&issue=B62E671E-81D6-42FD-8BDA1611D194B1D3,9EDD13C6-91FE-4698-A7517E0C28EB1729,&media_channel=2FED54B5-5B19-40BC-B75BD73F29665855&date_period=past_year

Aşan, K., Kaptangil, K., & Kınay, A. G. (2020). Mediating role of perceived festival value in the relationship between experiences and satisfaction. *International Journal of Event and Festival Management*, 11(3), 329–343. DOI: 10.1108/IJEFM-07-2019-0049

Ashok, C. (2023). Enhancing customer experience in e-commerce through AI-powered personalization: A case study. *Tuijin Jishu/Journal of Propulsion Technology, 43*(4), 516–524. https://doi.org/DOI: 10.52783/tjjpt.v43.i4.6018

Assenza, P., & Lewis, M. S. (2019). Can Chipotle compete by delivering "food with integrity"? *The CASE Journal*, 15(4), 233–252. DOI: 10.1108/TCJ-08-2018-0092

Asshofi, I. U. A., & Pranata, P. S. J. (2021). Strategi peningkatan occupancy rate dan average room rate pada masa pandemi COVID-19 di hotel Noormans Semarang. *LITE: Jurnal Bahasa, Sastra, dan Budaya*, 16(2), 234–249. https://doi.org/DOI: 10.33633/lite.v16i2.4412

Audunson, R., Andresen, H., Fagerlid, C., Henningsen, E., Hobohm, H. C., Jochumsen, H., & Larsen, H. (2020). Introduction–Physical places and virtual spaces: Libraries, archives and museums in a digital age. In *Libraries, archives and museums as democratic spaces in a digital age* (pp. 1–22). De Gruyter Saur., DOI: 10.1515/9783110636628-001

Ayutthaya, D. H. N., & Koomsap, P. (2018). Embedding Memorable Experience to Customer Journey. In Moon, I., Lee, G. M., Park, J., Kiritsis, D., & VonCieminski, G. (Eds.), *Advances in Production Management Systems: Production Management for Data-driven, Intelligent, Collaborative, and Sustainable Manufacturing, APMS 2018* (Vol. 535, pp. 222–229). Springer-Verlag Berlin., DOI: 10.1007/978-3-319-99704-9_27

Badruddoza Talukder, M., Kumar, S., Misra, L. I., & Firoj Kabir, . (2024). Determining the role of eco-tourism service quality, tourist satisfaction, and destination loyalty: A case study of Kuakata beach. *Acta Scientiarum Polonorum. Administratio Locorum*, 23(1), 133–151. DOI: 10.31648/aspal.9275

Bae, S., Jung, T. H., Moorhouse, N., Suh, M., & Kwon, O. (2020). The influence of mixed reality on satisfaction and brand loyalty in cultural heritage attractions: A brand equity perspective. *Sustainability (Basel)*, 12(7), 2956. DOI: 10.3390/su12072956

Bagriya, S., Khandewal, S., Mohammd, S., Sharma, S., & Mahala, V. (2024). Microcontroller based voice control home automation system. *International Journal for Research in Applied Science and Engineering Technology*, 12(4), 2918–2923. DOI: 10.22214/ijraset.2024.60163

Bakar, N. A., Rosbi, S., & Uzaki, K. (2022). Impact of coronavirus disease (COVID-19) towards hotel tourism industry. *International Journal of Advanced Engineering Study and Science*, 9(3), 043–050. https://doi.org/DOI: 10.22161/ijaers.93.6

Baker, J., Nam, K., & Dutt, C. S. (2023). A user experience perspective on heritage tourism in the metaverse: Empirical evidence and design dilemmas for VR. *Information Technology & Tourism*, 25(3), 265–306. DOI: 10.1007/s40558-023-00256-x

Balling, L. W., Townend, O., Mølgaard, L. L., Jespersen, C. B., & Switalski, W. (2021). AI-driven insights from AI-driven data. *Health Review*, 28(01), 27–29. DOI: 10.1108/HR-01-2021-0020

Bano, N., & Siddiqui, S. (2024). Consumers' intention towards the use of smart technologies in tourism and hospitality (T&H) industry : A deeper insight into the integration of TAM, TPB and trust. *Journal of Hospitality and Tourism Insights*, 7(3), 1412–1434. DOI: 10.1108/JHTI-06-2022-0267

Baratta, A., Cimino, A., Longo, F., Solina, V., & Verteramo, S. (2023). The impact of ESG practices in industry with a focus on carbon emissions: Insights and future perspectives. *Sustainability (Basel)*, 15(8), 6685. DOI: 10.3390/su15086685

Barbieri, L., Bruno, F., & Muzzupappa, M. (2017). Virtual museum system evaluation through user studies. *Journal of Cultural Heritage*, 26, 101–108. DOI: 10.1016/j.culher.2017.02.005

Bardin, L. (2016). *Análise de conteúdo*. Edições.

Barguet, P. (1962). *Le Temple d'Amon-Re à Karnak: Essai d'exégèse*. Cairo.

Bastrygina, T., Lim, W. M., Jopp, R., & Weissmann, M. A. (2024). Unraveling the power of social media influencers: Qualitative insights into the role of Instagram influencers in the hospitality and tourism industry. *Journal of Hospitality and Tourism Management*, 58, 214–243. DOI: 10.1016/j.jhtm.2024.01.007

Batlles-de la Fuente, A., & Abad-Segura, E. (2023). Exploring research on the management of business ethics. *Cuadernos de Gestión*, 23(1), 11–21. DOI: 10.5295/cdg.221694ea

Bault, N., & Rusconi, E. (2020). The art of influencing consumer choices: A reflection on recent advances in decision neuroscience. *Frontiers in Psychology*, 10, 3009. Advance online publication. DOI: 10.3389/fpsyg.2019.03009 PMID: 32038387

Bayashot, Z. A. (2024). The contribution of AI-powered mobile apps to smart city ecosystems. *Journal of Software Engineering and Applications*, 17(3), 143–154. DOI: 10.4236/jsea.2024.173008

Beck, J., & Egger, R. (2018). Emotionalise me: Self-reporting and arousal measurements in virtual tourism environments. In *Information and communication technologies in tourism 2018* (pp. 3–15). Springer., DOI: 10.1007/978-3-319-72923-7_1

Belghachi, M. (2023). A review on explainable artificial intelligence methods, applications, and challenges. [IJEEI]. *Indonesian Journal of Electrical Engineering and Informatics*, 11(4), 1007–1024. DOI: 10.52549/ijeei.v11i4.5151

Belgibayeva, Z. Z., Nadyrov, S. M., Zhanguttina, G. O., Belgibayev, A. K., & Belgibayev, A. A. (2020). Tourist flows of kazakhstan: Statistics, geography, trends. *Научный Журнал. Вестник НАН РК*, (6), 232–239.

Bellini, N., Bergamasco, M., Brehonnet, R., Carrozzino, M., & Lagier, J. (2018). Virtual cultural experiences: The drivers of satisfaction. *Symphonya.Emerging Issues in Management*, 2(2), 52–65. DOI: 10.4468/2018.2.5bellini.bergamasco.brehonnet.carozzino.lagier

Benbba, B., Ismaili, F. E. A., & Archi, Y. E. (2022). Smart tourism destination et développement durable : Quels apports à l'expérience touristique? *Alternatives Managériales Economiques,* 4(0), Article 0. DOI: 10.48374/IMIST.PRSM/ame-v1i0.36926

Benckendorff, P. J., Xiang, Z., & Sheldon, P. J. (2019). *Tourism information technology*. CABI. DOI: 10.1079/9781786393432.0000

Benny, L. K. W. (2015). Entertainment studies–A perspective. *American International Journal of Research in Humanities. Arts and Social Sciences*, 10, 7–11. DOI: 10.9790/7388-100000701011

Benrimoh, D., Chheda, F. D., & Margolese, H. C. (2022). The best predictor of the future—The metaverse, mental health, and lessons learned from current technologies. *JMIR Mental Health*, 9(10), e40410. DOI: 10.2196/40410 PMID: 36306155

Bharadiya, J. P. (2023). Machine learning and AI in business intelligence: Trends and opportunities. [IJC]. *International Journal of Computer*, 48(1), 123–134.

Bhatia, A., Roy, B., & Kumar, A. (2022). A review of tourism sustainability in the era of COVID-19. *Journal of Statistics and Management Systems*, 22(8), 1871–1888. DOI: 10.1080/09720510.2021.1995196

Bibri, S. E., Krogstie, J., Kaboli, A., & Alahi, A. (2024). Smarter eco-cities and their leading-edge artificial intelligence of things solutions for environmental sustainability: A comprehensive systematic review. *Environmental Science and Ecotechnology*, 19, 100330. DOI: 10.1016/j.ese.2023.100330 PMID: 38021367

Bielan, O., Humeniuk, V., Kaziuka, N., Semyrga, L., & Hryvnak, B. (2023). Financial and legal regulation of hotel and tourism business. *Economic Analysis*, 33(4), 8–16. DOI: 10.35774/econa2023.04.008

Bie, X. (2023). Countermeasures of hotel industry for tourism crisis management under the influence of epidemic situation. *International Journal of Education and Humanities*, 11(2), 249–252. DOI: 10.54097/ijeh.v11i2.13845

Bigné, E., Andreu, L., & Oltra, E. (2017). DMOs promote hotel occupancy in tourist destinations: An abstract. In Rossi, P. (Ed.), *Marketing at the confluence between entertainment and analytics* (pp. 999–1000). Springer International Publishing., DOI: 10.1007/978-3-319-47331-4_198

Bilińska, K., Pabian, B., Pabian, A., & Reformat, B. (2023). Development trends and potential in the field of virtual tourism after the COVID-19 pandemic: Generation Z example. *Sustainability (Basel)*, 15(3), 1889. DOI: 10.3390/su15031889

Blanco-Cerradelo, L., Diéguez-Castrillón, M. I., Fraiz-Brea, J. A., & Gueimonde-Canto, A. (2022). Protected areas and tourism resources: Toward sustainable management. *Land (Basel)*, 11(11), 2059. DOI: 10.3390/land11112059

Bleher, H., & Braun, M. (2022). Diffused responsibility: Attributions of responsibility in the use of AI-driven clinical decision support systems. *AI and Ethics*, 2(4), 747–761. DOI: 10.1007/s43681-022-00135-x PMID: 35098247

Bookman, M. Z., & Bookman, K. R. (2007). Medical tourism in developing countries. *University of Toronto Medical Journal*, 74(3), 1–20. http://utmj.org/ojs/index.php/UTMJ/article/viewFile/373/355

Borges, C. (2009). *Globalização e turismo: Análise de seus impactos no Estado do Ceará na década 1992/2002*. Gráfica e Editora Nacional.

Borovcanin, D., Cuk, I., Lesjak, M., & Juvan, E. (2020). The importance of sport event on hotel performance for restarting tourism after COVID-19. *Societies (Basel, Switzerland)*, 10(4), 90. DOI: 10.3390/soc10040090

Boudri, R., Bentalha, B., & Benjelloun, O. (2024). Phygital Marketing and the Pain of Paying : An Amazon Go Netnographic Case Study. In *AI and Data Engineering Solutions for Effective Marketing* (p. 348-363). IGI Global. https://www.igi-global.com/chapter/phygital-marketing-and-the-pain-of-paying/350762

Bouhtati, N., Alla, L., & Bentalha, B. (2023). Marketing Big Data Analytics and Customer Relationship Management : A Fuzzy Approach. In *Integrating Intelligence and Sustainability in Supply Chains* (p. 75-86). IGI Global. https://www.igi-global.com/chapter/marketing-big-data-analytics-and-customer-relationship-management/331980

Bouhtati, N., Alla, L., & Ed-Daakouri, I. (2024). Smart Data Analysis and Prediction of Responsible Customer Behaviour in Tourism : An Exploratory Review of the Literature. *Promoting Responsible Tourism With Digital Platforms*, 189-212.

Bourgeois, I., Ascensão, G., Ferreira, V., & Rodrigues, H. (2024). Methodology for the application of 3D technologies for the conservation and recovery of built heritage elements. *International Journal of Architectural Heritage*, 1–12. Advance online publication. DOI: 10.1080/15583058.2024.2341327

Boza, P., & Evgeniou, T. (2021). Artificial intelligence to support the integration of variable renewable energy sources to the power system. *Applied Energy*, 290, 116754. DOI: 10.1016/j.apenergy.2021.116754

Branke, J. (2012). *Evolutionary optimization in dynamic environments*. Springer.

Brickson, L., Zhang, L., Vollrath, F., Douglas-Hamilton, I., & Titus, A. J. (2023). Elephants and algorithms: A review of the current and future role of AI in elephant monitoring. *Journal of the Royal Society, Interface*, 20(208), 20230367. DOI: 10.1098/rsif.2023.0367 PMID: 37963556

Bridges, J., & Vásquez, C. (2016). If nearly all Airbnb reviews are positive, does that make them meaningless? *Current Issues in Tourism*, 21(18), 2065–2083. DOI: 10.1080/13683500.2016.1267113

Bryman, A. (2016). *Social Research Methods*. Oxford University Press.

Buhalis, D. (2020). Technology in tourism—from information communication technologies to eTourism and smart tourism towards ambient intelligence tourism: A perspective article. *Tourism Review*, 75(1), 267–272. DOI: 10.1108/TR-06-2019-0258

Buhalis, D., Harwood, T., Bogicevic, V., Viglia, G., Beldona, S., & Hofacker, C. (2019). Technological disruptions in services: Lessons from tourism and hospitality. *Journal of Service Management*, 30(4), 484–506. DOI: 10.1108/JOSM-12-2018-0398

Buhalis, D., & Law, R. (2008). Progress in information technology and tourism management : 20 years on and 10 years after the Internet—The state of eTourism research. *Tourism Management*, 29(4), 609–623. DOI: 10.1016/j.tourman.2008.01.005

Bulchand-Gidumal, J. (2022). Impact of artificial intelligence in travel, tourism, and hospitality. In *Handbook of e-Tourism* (pp. 1943–1962). Springer International Publishing., DOI: 10.1007/978-3-030-48652-5_110

Burns, K. S. (2021). The history of social media influencers. In *Research perspectives on social media influencers and brand communication* (pp. 1–22). IGI Global.

Busuioc, M. (2021). Accountable artificial intelligence: Holding algorithms to account. *Public Administration Review*, 81(5), 825–836. DOI: 10.1111/puar.13293 PMID: 34690372

Byeon, H., Kumar, P., Manu, M., Maaliw, R. R., Singh, P. P., & Maranan, R. (2023). Editable blockchain for secure IoT transactions. In *2023 Second International Conference on Smart Technologies for Smart Nation (SmartTechCon)* (pp. 255–263). https://doi.org/DOI: 10.1109/SmartTechCon57526.2023.10391293

Calisto, M. de L., & Sarkar, S. (2024). A systematic review of virtual reality in tourism and hospitality : The known and the paths to follow. *International Journal of Hospitality Management*, 116, 103623. DOI: 10.1016/j.ijhm.2023.103623

Calza, F., Trunfio, M., Pasquinelli, C., Sorrentino, A., Campana, S., & Rossi, S. (2022). *Technology-driven innovation. Exploiting ICTs tools for digital engagement, smart experiences, and sustainability in tourism destinations*. SLIOB. Enzo Albano Edizioni Naples. https://www.disaq.uniparthenope.it/wp-content/uploads/2022/02/Technology-driven-innovation-Exploiting-ICTs-tools-for-digital-engagement-smart-experiences-and-sustainability-in-tourism-destinations.pdf

Cameron, F. R. (2021). *The future of digital data, heritage and curation: In a more-than-human world*. Routledge. DOI: 10.4324/9781003149606

Camprubí, R., Guia, J., & Comas, J. (2013). The new role of tourists in destination image formation. *Current Issues in Tourism*, 16(2), 203–209. DOI: 10.1080/13683500.2012.733358

Cannas, R. (2012). An overview of tourism seasonality: Key concepts and policy. *AlmaTourism*, 3(5), 40–58.

Carey, R., Ross, D., & Seitzman, N. (2017). The (ongoing) trouble with travel distribution: Customer experience. McKinsey & Company. https://www.mckinsey.com/industries/travel-transport-and-logistics/our-insights/the-ongoing-trouble-with-travel-distribution-customer-experience

Carneiro, T., Picoto, W. N., & Pinto, I. (2023). Big data analytics and firm performance in the hotel sector. *Tourism and Hospitality*, 4(2), 244–256. DOI: 10.3390/tourhosp4020015

Carpenter, S. M., & Niedenthal, P. M. (2018). Emotional processes in risky and multiattribute health decisions. *Psychology & Health*, 33(1), 58–76. DOI: 10.1080/08870446.2017.1314478 PMID: 28452564

Carvajal, D. A. L., Morita, M. M., & Bilmes, G. M. (2020). Virtual museums: Captured reality and 3D modeling. *Journal of Cultural Heritage*, 45, 234–239. DOI: 10.1016/j.culher.2020.04.013

Casebourne, I. (2024). Left to their own devices: An exploration of context in seamless work-related mobile learning. *British Journal of Educational Technology*, 55(4), 1772–1789. Advance online publication. DOI: 10.1111/bjet.13410

Casquero-Vera, J. A., Pérez-Ramírez, D., Lyamani, H., Rejano, F., Casans, A., Titos, G., Olmo, F. J., Dada, L., Hakala, S., Hussein, T., Lehtipalo, K., Paasonen, P., Hyvärinen, A., Pérez, N., Querol, X., Rodríguez, S., Kalivitis, N., González, Y., Alghamdi, M. A., & Alados-Arboledas, L. (2023). Impact of desert dust on new particle formation events and the cloud condensation nuclei budget in dust-influenced areas. *Atmospheric Chemistry and Physics*, 23(24), 15795–15814. DOI: 10.5194/acp-23-15795-2023

Castro, J., Pérez, J., & Alomoto, L. (2019). Imagen del destino desde la perspectiva del turista. *Turismo e Sociedade*, 26, 45–66. DOI: 10.18601/01207555.n26.02

Cauville, S., & Mohamed Aly, I. (2013). *Philæ. Itinéraire du visiteur.* Peeters, Leuven, Paris, Walpole.

Cavusoglu, F., & Avcikurt, C. (2021). *The Relationship between Personal Traits, Travel Motivation, Perceived Value and Behavioural Intention of Tourists Participating in Adventure Activities.* DOI: 10.5281/ZENODO.5831677

Çeltek, E. (2023). Analysis of smart technologies used in smart hotels. *Journal of Business Research - Turk*, 15.https://doi.org/DOI: 10.20491/isarder.2023.1754

Centorrino, P., Corbetta, A., Cristiani, E., & Onofri, E. (2021). Managing crowded museums: Visitors flow measurement, analysis, modeling, and optimization. *Journal of Computational Science*, 53, 101357. DOI: 10.1016/j.jocs.2021.101357

Cetin, G., & Bilgihan, A. (2016). Components of cultural tourists' experiences in destinations. *Current Issues in Tourism*, 19(2), 137–154. DOI: 10.1080/13683500.2014.994595

Chacko, P. (2006). Medical tourism in India: Issues and challenges. In *Health tourism: An introduction* (p. 123). ICFAI University Press.

Chagas, M. M. D., Marques Júnior, S., & Silva, V. H. D. (2016). *Imagens de destinos turísticos: Conceitos, modelos e casos*. https://memoria.ifrn.edu.br/handle/1044/961

Chagas, M. M. das. (2009). Formação da Imagem de Destinos Turísticos: Uma discussão dos principais modelos internacionais. *Caderno Virtual de Turismo, 9*(1), Article 1. https://www.ivt.coppe.ufrj.br/caderno/article/view/333

Chagas, M. M. das. (2008). IMAGEM DE DESTINOS TURÍSTICOS: Uma discussão teórica da literatura especializada. *Turismo: Visão e Ação*, 10(3), 3. Advance online publication. DOI: 10.14210/rtva.v10n3.p435-455

Chan, M. M. Wa, Dickson, & Chiu. (2022). Alert-driven customer relationship management in online travel agencies: Event-condition-actions rules and key performance indicators. In *Building a brand image through electronic customer relationship management* (pp. 286–303). IGI Global.

Chang, S. H., & Lin, R. (2015). Building a total customer experience model: Applications for the travel experiences in Taiwan's creative life industry. *Journal of Travel & Tourism Marketing*, 32(4), 438–453. DOI: 10.1080/10548408.2014.908158

Chashyn, D., Khurudzhi, Y., & Daukšys, M. (2024). Directions for the formation of city intelligent models using artificial intelligence for the post-war reconstruction of historical buildings. *Budownictwo i architektura, 23*(1), 73-86. https://doi.org/ DOI: 10.35784/bud-arch.570

Chaudhari, K., & Thakkar, A. (2020). A comprehensive survey on travel recommender systems. *Archives of Computational Methods in Engineering*, 27(5), 1545–1571. DOI: 10.1007/s11831-019-09363-7

Chen, G. (2022). Tourism Management Strategies under the Intelligent Tourism IoT Service Platform. *Computational Intelligence and Neuroscience*, 7750098, 1–11. Advance online publication. DOI: 10.1155/2022/7750098 PMID: 35463292

Cheng, M., & Foley, C. (2019). Algorithmic management: The case of Airbnb. *International Journal of Hospitality Management*, 83, 33–36. DOI: 10.1016/j.ijhm.2019.04.009

Cheng, W., Tian, R., & Chiu, D. K. W. (2024). Travel vlogs influencing tourist decisions: Information preferences and gender differences. *Aslib Journal of Information Management*, 76(1), 86–103. DOI: 10.1108/AJIM-05-2022-0261

Chen, M.-H. (2011). The response of hotel performance to international tourism development and crisis events. *International Journal of Hospitality Management*, 30(1), 200–212. DOI: 10.1016/j.ijhm.2010.06.005 PMID: 32287854

Chen, X. H., Tee, K., Elnahass, M., & Ahmed, R. (2023). Assessing the environmental impacts of renewable energy sources: A case study on air pollution and carbon emissions in China. *Journal of Environmental Management*, 345, 118525. DOI: 10.1016/j.jenvman.2023.118525 PMID: 37421726

Chen, Y., Qin, Z., & Yin, X. (2023). The impact of the opening policy of the COVID-19 on catering, tourism and hotel industries. *Advances in Economics. Management and Political Sciences*, 45(1), 256–262. DOI: 10.54254/2754-1169/45/20230295

Chen, Y., Wang, X., Le, B., & Wang, L. (2024). Why people use augmented reality in heritage museums : A socio-technical perspective. *Heritage Science*, 12(1), 108. DOI: 10.1186/s40494-024-01217-1

Chenyambuga, D. N., & Mneney, C. E. (2022). The impact of COVID-19 pandemic on the EAC tourism and hospitality industry. *African Journal of Accounting and Social Science Studies*, 4(1), 73–92. DOI: 10.4314/ajasss.v4i1.4

Chen, Z., & Fu, S. (2023). Research on the Evaluation of the Effect of Tourism Revitalization of Intangible Cultural Heritage in China in the Context of New Media. *Applied Mathematics and Nonlinear Sciences*, 9(1), 20230518. DOI: 10.2478/amns.2023.2.00518

Cheong, F. K. W., Dickson, K. W., Chiu, S. C., & Cheung, P. C. K., & Hung. (2007). Developing a distributed e-monitoring system for enterprise website and web services: An experience report with free libraries and tools. *IEEE International Conference on Web Services (ICWS 2007)*. https://doi.org/DOI: 10.1109/ICWS.2007.77

Chhabra, D. (2010). *Sustainable marketing of cultural and heritage tourism*. Routledge. DOI: 10.4324/9780203855416

Chi, H. K., Huang, K. C., & Nguyen, H. M. (2020). Elements of destination brand equity and destination familiarity regarding travel intention. *Journal of Retailing and Consumer Services*, 52, 101728. DOI: 10.1016/j.jretconser.2018.12.012

Chihwai, P. (2024). COVID-19 impact and recovery on tourism in Africa: An introduction and background. In Chihwai, P. (Ed.), *COVID-19 impact on tourism performance in Africa* (pp. 3–12). Springer Nature Singapore., DOI: 10.1007/978-981-97-1931-0_1

Chinazzi, M., Davis, J. T., Ajelli, M., Gioannini, C., Litvinova, M., Merler, S., & Piontti, A. P. Y. (2020). The effect of travel restrictions on the spread of the 2019 novel coronavirus (COVID-19) outbreak. *Science*, 368(6489), 395–400. DOI: 10.1126/science.aba9757 PMID: 32144116

Chinonye, E. U., Ofodile, O. C., Okoye, C. C., & Akinrinola, O. (2024). Sustainable smart cities: The role of fintech in promoting environmental sustainability. *Engineering Science & Technology Journal*, 5(3), 821–835. DOI: 10.51594/estj.v5i3.906

Chisom, O. N., Biu, P. W., Umoh, A. A., Obaedo, B. O., Adegbite, A. O., & Abatan, A. (2024). Reviewing the role of AI in environmental monitoring and conservation: A data-driven revolution for our planet. *World Journal of Advanced Research and Reviews*, 21(1), 161–171. DOI: 10.30574/wjarr.2024.21.1.2720

Chiu, D. K. W., Cheung, S. C., Kafeza, E., & Leung, H.-F. (2003). A three-tier view-based methodology for m-services adaptation. *IEEE Transactions on Systems, Man, and Cybernetics. Part A, Systems and Humans*, 33(6), 725–741. DOI: 10.1109/TSMCA.2003.819489

Chiu, D. K. W., Cheung, S. C., & Leung, H.-F. (2005). A multi-agent infrastructure for mobile workforce management in a service-oriented enterprise. *Proceedings of the 38th Annual Hawaii International Conference on System Sciences*. https://doi.org/DOI: 10.1109/HICSS.2005.28

Chiu, D. K. W., Kok, D., Lee, A. K. C., & Cheung, S. C. (2005). Integrating legacy sites into web services with WebXcript. *International Journal of Cooperative Information Systems*, 14(01), 25–44. DOI: 10.1142/S0218843005001006

Chiu, D. K. W., Lee, O. K. F., Leung, E. W. K., Au, M. C. W., & Wong, H.-F. (2005). A multi-modal agent-based mobile route advisory system for public transport network. *Proceedings of the 38th Annual Hawaii International Conference on System Sciences*. https://doi.org/DOI: 10.1109/HICSS.2005.30

Chiwaridzo, O. T., & Chiwaridzo, S. (2024). From crisis to prosperity: Leveraging robots, artificial intelligence, and service automation for sustainable tourism in Zimbabwe. *Business Strategy & Development*, 7(2), e380. DOI: 10.1002/bsd2.380

Choi, S. J., & Pritchard, A. C. (2003). Behavioral economics and the SEC. *Stanford Law Review*, 56(1), 1–73. DOI: 10.2307/1229705

Chowdhary, K. R. (2020). Fundamentals of artificial intelligence. In *Artificial Intelligence: Principles and Applications* (pp. 603-649). Springer. DOI: 10.1007/978-81-322-3972-7

Christidis, P., Christodoulou, A., Navajas-Cawood, E., & Ciuffo, B. (2021). The post-pandemic recovery of transport activity: Emerging mobility patterns and repercussions on future evolution. *Sustainability (Basel)*, 13(11), 6359. DOI: 10.3390/su13116359

Christofi, M., Vrontis, D., Shams, R., Belyaeva, Z., & Czinkota, M. R. (2022). Sustained competitive advantage for sustainable hospitality and tourism development: A stakeholder causal scope analysis. *Journal of Hospitality & Tourism Research (Washington, D.C.)*, 46(5), 823–825. DOI: 10.1177/10963480221091976

Chung, N., Han, H., & Joun, Y. (2015). Tourists' intention to visit a destination: The role of augmented reality (AR) application for a heritage site. *Computers in Human Behavior*, 50, 588–599. DOI: 10.1016/j.chb.2015.02.068

Chyniak, V., & Salyuk, M. (2022). Trends in the functioning of the tourism sector in crisis conditions on the example of hotel enterprises of the Transcarpathian region, Ukraine. *Economics & Education*, 7(4), 20–26. DOI: 10.30525/2500-946X/2022-4-3

Clarke, P., & Newcomer, E. (2020). Airbnb's future depends on a post-pandemic travel boom. *The Irish Times*. https://www.irishtimes.com/life-and-style/travel/airbnb-s-future-depends-on-a-post-pandemic-travel-boom-1.4238881

Claudio-Quiroga, G., De Villanueva, C. F., & Gil-Alana, L. A. (2024). Tourism and COVID-19 in three European cities: Change in persistence. *Cogent Social Sciences*, 10(1), 2358159. DOI: 10.1080/23311886.2024.2358159

Coeckelbergh, M. (2020). *AI ethics*. MIT Press. DOI: 10.7551/mitpress/12549.001.0001

Coffin, J., & Egan-Wyer, C. (2022). The ethical consumption cap and mean market morality. *Marketing Theory*, 22(1), 105–123. DOI: 10.1177/14705931211058772

Coghlan, S., & Parker, C. (2023). Harm to nonhuman animals from AI: A systematic account and framework. *Philosophy & Technology*, 36(2), 25. Advance online publication. DOI: 10.1007/s13347-023-00627-6

Collins, C., & Hall, J. C. (2022). Presidential inauguration tourism and hotel occupancy: Evidence from the Obama and Trump inaugurals. *Tourism Economics*, 28(1), 83–88. DOI: 10.1177/1354816620956821

Committee of Advertising Practice [CAP]. (2023). Updated guidance for influencer marketing. ASA. Retrieved September 20, 2024, from https://www.asa.org.uk/news/updated-guidance-for-influencer-marketing.html

Competition & Markets Authority [CMA]. (2022, November 3). Guidance: Hidden ads: Being clear with your audience. Gov.UK. Retrieved September 20, 2024, from https://www.gov.uk/government/publications/social-media-endorsements-guide-for-influencers/social-media-endorsements-being-transparent-with-your-followers

Cooper, C., Fletche, J., Fyall, A., Gilbert, D., & Wanhill, S. (2007). *Turismo: Principios e prática* (3rd ed.). Bookman.

Creswell, J. W., & Creswell, J. D. (2017). *Research Design: Qualitative, Quantitative, and Mixed Methods Approaches*. SAGE Publications.

Croes, R., Ridderstaat, J., Bak, M., & Zientara, P. (2021). Tourism specialization, economic growth, human development and transition economies: The case of Poland. *Tourism Management*, 82, 104181. DOI: 10.1016/j.tourman.2020.104181

Csizmadia, N. (2020). Hubs in the Network: Hub Cities. *World Scientific Book Chapters*, 301–307.

Cuomo, M. T., Tortora, D., Foroudi, P., Giordano, A., Festa, G., & Metallo, G. (2021). Digital transformation and tourist experience co-design : Big social data for planning cultural tourism. *Technological Forecasting and Social Change*, 162, 120345. DOI: 10.1016/j.techfore.2020.120345

da Costa Mendes, J., Oom do Valle, P., Guerreiro, M. M., & Silva, J. A. (2010). The tourist experience : Exploring the relationship between tourist satisfaction and destination loyalty. *Tourism: An International Interdisciplinary Journal*, 58(2), 111–126.

da Silva Castro, T., & Pereira, A. Q. (2019). Produção dos territórios turísticos no Ceará. *Ateliê Geográfico*, 13(2), 51–72. DOI: 10.5216/ag.v13i2.58288

da Silva, E. A. M., Sobrinho, F. L. A., & Fortes, J. A. A. S. (2015). A importância geoestratégica do Aeroporto Internacional de Brasília no desenvolvimento do turismo regional. *Caderno Virtual de Turismo*, 15(3), 3. https://www.ivt.coppe.ufrj.br/caderno/article/view/1220

Dagustani, D., Kartini, D., Oesman, Y. M., & Kaltum, U. (2018). Destination Image of Tourist : Effect of Travel Motivation and Memorable Tourism Experience. *ETIKONOMI*, 17(2), 307–318. DOI: 10.15408/etk.v17i2.7211

Danthinne, E. S., Giorgianni, F. E., Ando, K., & Rodgers, R. F. (2022). Real beauty: Effects of a body-positive video on body image and capacity to mitigate exposure to social media images. *British Journal of Health Psychology*, 27(2), 320–337. DOI: 10.1111/bjhp.12547 PMID: 34278653

Das, I. R., Islam, A. S., & Talukder, M. B. (2024). Customer satisfaction in hospitality marketing from a technological perspective. In Talukder, M., Kumar, S., & Tyagi, P. (Eds.), *Impact of AI and tech-driven solutions in hospitality and tourism* (pp. 383–407). IGI Global., DOI: 10.4018/979-8-3693-6755-1.ch019

Dauvergne, P. (2020). *AI in the wild: Sustainability in the age of artificial intelligence*. MIT Press. DOI: 10.7551/mitpress/12350.001.0001

Dauvergne, P. (2022). Is artificial intelligence greening global supply chains? Exposing the political economy of environmental costs. *Review of International Political Economy*, 29(3), 696–718. DOI: 10.1080/09692290.2020.1814381

Davies, B. (1999). *Who's who at Deir el-Medina: A prosopographic study of the royal workmen's community*. Nederlands Instituut.

Davis, F. D. (1989). Technology acceptance model : TAM. *Al-Suqri, MN, Al-Aufi, AS. Information Seeking Behavior and Technology Adoption*, 205, 219.

Davis, O. (2023). The new normal: Navigating legal challenges in the world of influencer marketing & how ADR can help. *Pepperdine Dispute Resolution Law Journal*, 23, 70.

Dawn, S. K., & Pal, S. (2011). Medical tourism in India: Issues, opportunities, and designing strategies for growth and development. *International Journal of Multidisciplinary Research*, 1(13), 185–202.

De Brito, C. (2021). Almosafer study reveals Saudi's top post-pandemic travel trends. https://connectingtravel.com/news/almosafer-study-reveals-saudis-top-post-pandemic-travel-trends

De Bruyne, N. (2023). Building a caring network of formal and informal help (offline and online) in a super-diverse neighbourhood. *International Journal of Integrated Care*, 23(S1), 542. DOI: 10.5334/ijic.ICIC23200

de Lenne, O., Vandenbosch, L., Smits, T., & Eggermont, S. (2021). Framing real beauty: A framing approach to the effects of beauty advertisements on body image and advertising effectiveness. *Body Image*, 37, 255–268. DOI: 10.1016/j.bodyim.2021.03.003 PMID: 33773395

De Luna, M. C. E., Santiago, R. R. L., & Villaceran, I. N.Mary Christine E. De LunaRachelyn Ruth L. SantiagoIrvin N. Villaceran. (2024). Preferences and travel motivations of pink tourists among Filipinos. *Journal of Tourism and Hospitality Studies*, 2(1), 25–29. DOI: 10.32996/jths.2024.2.1.4

de Moura, I. R., dos Santos Silva, F. J., Costa, L. H. G., Neto, E. D., & Viana, H. R. G. (2021). Airport pavement evaluation systems for maintenance strategies development: A systematic literature review. *International Journal of Pavement Research and Technology*, 14(6), 676–687. DOI: 10.1007/s42947-020-0255-1

de Oliveira Dias, M., Lopes, R. D. O. A., & Teles, A. C. (2020). Will virtual replace classroom teaching? Lessons from virtual classes via Zoom in the times of COVID-19. *Journal of Advances in Education and Philosophy*, 4(05), 208–213. DOI: 10.36348/jaep.2020.v04i05.004

de Ruyter, K., Keeling, D. I., Plangger, K., Montecchi, M., Scott, M. L., & Dahl, D. W. (2022). Reimagining marketing strategy: Driving the debate on grand challenges. *Journal of the Academy of Marketing Science*, 50(1), 13–21. DOI: 10.1007/s11747-021-00806-x PMID: 34426711

De Veirman, M., De Jans, S., Van den Abeele, E., & Hudders, L. (2020). Unraveling the power of social media influencers: A qualitative study on teenage influencers as commercial content creators on social media. In *The regulation of social media influencers* (pp. 126–166). Edward Elgar Publishing. DOI: 10.4337/9781788978286.00015

Deale, C. S. (2013). Incorporating Second Life into online hospitality and tourism education: A case study. *Journal of Hospitality, Leisure, Sport and Tourism Education*, 13, 154–160. DOI: 10.1016/j.jhlste.2013.09.002

Deb, S. K., Kuri, B. C., & Nafi, S. M. (2024). Application of knowledge management in tourism and hospitality industry: A sustainable approach. In Valeri, M. (Ed.), *Knowledge management and knowledge sharing* (pp. 99–116). Springer Nature Switzerland., DOI: 10.1007/978-3-031-37868-3_7

Deepthi, S. S., & Shariff, Dr. S. J. (2024). Role of hotel industry in tourism development. *Educational Administration: Theory and Practice*. https://doi.org/DOI: 10.53555/kuey.v30i5.4347

Delgado Quintana, E. M. (2022). Role of motivational theories in the study of consumer behavior. *Revista Científica Sinapsis*, 2(21). Advance online publication. DOI: 10.37117/s.v2i21.662

Deliana, D. (2023). Contribution of tourism objects in Banyumas Kota Lama to the hotel occupancy. *Jurnal Manajemen Perhotelan dan Pariwisata*, 6(2), 493–504. https://doi.org/DOI: 10.23887/jmpp.v6i2.64829

Demjanovičová, M., & Varmus, M. (2021). Changing the perception of business values in the perspective of environmental sustainability. *Sustainability (Basel)*, 13(9), 5226. DOI: 10.3390/su13095226

Dencheva, V. (2024, February 6). Influencer marketing market size worldwide from 2016 to 2024. *Statista*. Retrieved September 20, 2024, from https://www.statista.com/statistics/1092819/global-influencer-market-size/

Dias, D., & Coriolano, L. N. (2022). A Metrópole Fortaleza-Ce Turistificada. *Caderno de Geografia*, 32(69), 575. DOI: 10.5752/P.2318-2962.2022v32n69p575

Dias, R., & Cassar, M. (2004). *Fundamentos do marketing turístico*. Pearson Universidades.

Dichter, A., Cheryl, S. H., Lim, D.-Y., & Lin. (2016). Cracking the world's biggest business-travel market. *McKinsey & Company*. https://www.mckinsey.com/industries/travel-transport-and-logistics/our-insights/cracking-the-worlds-biggest-business-travel-market

Ding, M., & Xu, Y. (2021). Real-Time Wireless Sensor Network-Assisted Smart Tourism Environment Suitability Assessment for Tourism IoT. *Journal of Sensors*, 2021(1), 8123014. DOI: 10.1155/2021/8123014

Diógenes, L. G. G., do Nascimento, A. P., de Oliveira, R. M. A., de Oliveira, G., & da Silva, F. J. A. (2020). *Achados recentes sobre a qualidade da água do rio cocó em um trecho urbano da cidade de Fortaleza–Ceará*. https://repositorio.ufc.br/handle/riufc/59213

Djafarova, E., & Foots, S. (2022). Exploring ethical consumption of generation Z: Theory of planned behaviour. *Young Consumers*, 23(3), 413–431. DOI: 10.1108/YC-10-2021-1405

Domazet, E., Rahmani, D., & Mechkaroska, D. (2023). Blockchain empowering Web 3.0: Decentralized trust and secure transactions for the future Internet. In *2023 31st Telecommunications Forum (TELFOR)* (pp. 1–4). https://doi.org/DOI: 10.1109/TELFOR59449.2023.10372778

Duarte, P., Silva, S. C., & Ferreira, M. B. (2018). How convenient is it? Delivering online shopping convenience to enhance customer satisfaction and encourage e-WOM. *Journal of Retailing and Consumer Services*, 44, 161–169. DOI: 10.1016/j.jretconser.2018.06.007

Dube, K., Nhamo, G., & Chikodzi, D. (2021). COVID-19 cripples global restaurant and hospitality industry. *Current Issues in Tourism*, 24(11), 1487–1490. DOI: 10.1080/13683500.2020.1773416

Duboust, O. (2023, June 5). France has approved a law that targets influencers. What does it mean for social media stars? *Euronews*. Retrieved July 15, 2024, from https://www.euronews.com/next/2023/06/05/france-has-approved-a-law-that-targets-influencers-what-does-it-mean-for-social-media-star

Dudnyk, I., Borysiuk, O., & Saichuk, V. (2023). GEOGRAPHICAL INTERPRETATION OF THE TOURIST PROCESS. *Ekonomichna Ta Sotsialna Geografiya*, 42–52. DOI: 10.17721/2413-7154/2023.89.42-52

Duflot, R., Avon, C., Roche, P., & Bergès, L. (2018). Combining habitat suitability models and spatial graphs for more effective landscape conservation planning: An applied methodological framework and a species case study. *Journal for Nature Conservation*, 46, 38–47. DOI: 10.1016/j.jnc.2018.08.005

Durrani, H. (2016). Healthcare and healthcare systems: Inspiring progress and future prospects. *Journal of Healthcare Management*, 61(5), 1–10. https://www.ncbi.nlm.nih.gov/pmc/articles/PMC5344175/ PMID: 28293581

Dwivedi, Y. K., Hughes, L., Wang, Y., Alalwan, A. A., Ahn, S. J. G., Balakrishnan, J., & Wirtz, J. (2023).

Dyikanov, K., & Maksüdünov, A. (2024). Bibliometric Exploration of Tourism Destination Competitiveness Studies: A Comprehensive Overview. [JAVStudies]. *Journal of Academic Value Studies*, 10(1), 1. Advance online publication. DOI: 10.29228/javs.73403

Dzingirai, M., Chirodzero, T. C., & Moyo, T. (2024). Impact of COVID-19 on the tourism and hospitality industry: A case study of hotels in Mutare urban, Zimbabwe. *Journal of Hospitality, Leisure, Sport and Tourism Education*, 43, 100384. DOI: 10.1016/j.jhlste.2023.100384

Edelman, B. G., & Luca, M. (2014). Digital discrimination: The case of Airbnb. SSRN *Electronic Journal*. https://doi.org/DOI: 10.2139/ssrn.2377353

Efthymiou, L. (2018). Worker body-art in upper-market hotels: Neither accepted, nor prohibited. *International Journal of Hospitality Management*, 74, 99–108. DOI: 10.1016/j.ijhm.2018.02.012

Ekinci, Y., & Hosany, S. (2006). Destination Personality : An Application of Brand Personality to Tourism Destinations. *Journal of Travel Research*, 45(2), 127–139. DOI: 10.1177/0047287506291603

El Archi, Y., & Benbba, B. (2023). The Applications of Technology Acceptance Models in Tourism and Hospitality Research : A Systematic Literature Review. *Journal of Environmental Management and Tourism*, 14(2), 379. DOI: 10.14505/jemt.v14.2(66).08

EL JAOUHARI, S., & Lhoussaine, A. (2022). L'approche territoriale et la gestion de l'impact de la pandémie de Covid-19 : Cas des collectivités territoriales. *Alternatives Managériales Economiques*, 4(1), 245–265.

Erdem, A., & Şeker, F. (2022). Tourist experience and digital transformation. In *Handbook of research on digital communications, Internet of Things, and the future of cultural tourism* (pp. 103–120). IGI Global., https://www.igi-global.com/chapter/tourist-experience-and-digital-transformation/295499 DOI: 10.4018/978-1-7998-8528-3.ch006

Erdem, T., Swait, J., & Valenzuela, A. (2006). Brands as signals: A cross-country validation study. *Journal of Marketing*, 70(1), 34–49. DOI: 10.1509/jmkg.70.1.034.qxd

Ernst & Young. (2007). Diagnosing India's health care survey. *Business World*, 25(5), 56.

Esipova, S. A., & Gokova, O. V. (2020). Marketing tools as a way to promote tourism destination. *International Conference on Economics, Management and Technologies 2020 (ICEMT 2020)*, 602–605. https://www.atlantis-press.com/proceedings/icemt-20/125940056

Expedia Group. (2018). Expedia group acquires Pillow and ApartmentJet to enhance its alternative accommodations marketplace for residents, owners and managers in urban markets. *Expedia Group*. https://www.prnewswire.com/news-releases/expedia-group-acquires-pillow-and-apartmentjet-to-enhance-its-alternative-accommodations-marketplace-for-residents-owners-and-managers-in-urban-markets-300737677.html

Expedia Group. (2020). Expedia group reports fourth quarter and full year 2019 results. https://www.sec.gov/Archives/edgar/data/1324424/000132442420000006/earningsrelease-q42019.htm

Expedia. (2022). 2021 Annual Report. *Expedia*. https://s27.q4cdn.com/708721433/files/doc_financials/2021/ar/Expedia-Group-2021-Annual-Report.pdf

Fang, Z., & Savkin, A. V. (2024). Strategies for optimized UAV surveillance in various tasks and scenarios: A review. *Drones (Basel)*, 8(5), 193. DOI: 10.3390/drones8050193

Fan, X., Jiang, X., & Deng, N. (2022). Immersive technology: A meta-analysis of augmented/virtual reality applications and their impact on tourism experience. *Tourism Management*, 91, 104534. DOI: 10.1016/j.tourman.2022.104534

Farahat, E. (2023). Applications of artificial intelligence as a marketing tool and their impact on the competitiveness of the Egyptian tourist destination (Doctoral dissertation, Minia University).

Farahat, E., Mohamed, M., & Al-Romeedy, B. (2022). Artificial intelligence applications and their impact on the competitiveness of the Egyptian tourist destination. *Research Journal of the Faculty of Tourism and Hotels. Mansoura University*, 11(2), 57–93.

Farheen, N. S., Badiger, C. S., Kishore, L., Dheeraj, V., & Rajendran, S. R. (2024). A future look at artificial intelligence in the world of tourism. In *Marketing and big data analytics in tourism and events* (pp. 1–16). IGI Global., DOI: 10.4018/979-8-3693-3310-5.ch001

Fedeli, G., & Cheng, M. (2023). Influencer marketing and tourism: Another threat to integrity for the industry? *Tourism Analysis*, 28(2), 323–328. DOI: 10.3727/108354222X16510114086370

Federal Trade Commission. (2019). Disclosures 101 for social media influencers. Retrieved July 15, 2024, from https://www.ftc.gov/business-guidance/resources/disclosures-101-social-media-influencers

Fei, G., Xiong, K., Fei, G., Zhang, H., & Zhang, S. (2023). The conservation and tourism development of World Natural Heritage sites: The current situation and future prospects of research. *Journal for Nature Conservation*, 72, 126347. DOI: 10.1016/j.jnc.2023.126347

Femenia-Serra, F., Perles-Ribes, J. F., & Ivars-Baidal, J. A. (2019). Smart destinations and tech-savvy millennial tourists : Hype versus reality. *Tourism Review*, 74(1), 63–81. DOI: 10.1108/TR-02-2018-0018

Feng, Y., Chen, H., & He, L. (2019). Consumer responses to femvertising: A data-mining case of Dove's "Campaign for Real Beauty" on YouTube. *Journal of Advertising*, 48(3), 292–301. DOI: 10.1080/00913367.2019.1602858

Fernandes, L. M. M., Soares, J. R. R., & Coriolano, L. N. M. T. (2020). Governança na política de regionalização do turismo no Estado do Ceará/Brasil. *RPER*, 55(55), 95–108. DOI: 10.59072/rper.vi55.15

Fidell, S., Tabachnick, B., Mestre, V., & Fidell, L. (2013). Aircraft noise-induced awakenings are more reasonably predicted from relative than from absolute sound exposure levels. *The Journal of the Acoustical Society of America*, 134(5), 3645–3653. DOI: 10.1121/1.4823838 PMID: 24180775

Financial Times. (2020). Microsoft throws weight behind open data movement. *Financial Times*. https://www.ft.com/content/661b16ff-f86c-4dad-a557-2e231501bf58

Flavián, C., Ibáñez-Sánchez, S., & Orús, C. (2019). The impact of virtual, augmented and mixed reality technologies on the customer experience. *Journal of Business Research*, 100, 547–560. DOI: 10.1016/j.jbusres.2018.10.050

Font, X. (1997). Managing the tourist destination's image. *Journal of Vacation Marketing*, 3(2), 123–131. DOI: 10.1177/135676679700300203

Fornell, C., & Larcker, D. F. (1981). Evaluating structural equation models with unobservable variables and measurement error. *JMR, Journal of Marketing Research*, 18(1), 39–50. DOI: 10.1177/002224378101800104

Fritze, R. H. (2021). *Egyptomania: A history of fascination, obsession and fantasy*. Reaktion Books.

Fritzsche, D. J. (1987). Marketing/business ethics. *Business & Professional Ethics Journal*, 6(4), 65–79. DOI: 10.5840/bpej19876432

G, S., Chakraborty, D., Polisetty, A., Khorana, S., & Buhalis, D. (2023). Use of metaverse in socializing: Application of the big five personality traits framework. *Psychology & Marketing, 40*(10), 2132–2150. https://doi.org/DOI: 10.1002/mar.21863

Gaafar, H. (2020). Artificial intelligence in Egyptian tourism companies: Implementation and perception. *Journal of Association of Arab Universities for Tourism and Hospitality*, 18(1), 66–78. DOI: 10.21608/jaauth.2020.31704.1028

Gade, S., Chatterjee, U., & Mukhopadhyay, D. (2022). PAKAMAC: A PUF-based keyless automotive entry system with mutual authentication. *Journal of Hardware and Systems Security*, 6(3–4), 67–78. DOI: 10.1007/s41635-022-00126-8

Gahlawat, I. N., & Lakra, P. (2020). Global climate change and its effects. *Integrated Journal of Social Sciences*, 7(1), 14–23.

Galaz, V., Centeno, M. A., Callahan, P. W., Causevic, A., Patterson, T., Brass, I., & Levy, K. (2021). Artificial intelligence, systemic risks, and sustainability. *Technology in Society*, 67, 101741. DOI: 10.1016/j.techsoc.2021.101741

García-Milon, A., Juaneda-Ayensa, E., Olarte-Pascual, C., & Pelegrín-Borondo, J. (2020). Towards the smart tourism destination : Key factors in information source use on the tourist shopping journey. *Tourism Management Perspectives*, 36, 100730. DOI: 10.1016/j.tmp.2020.100730 PMID: 32834961

Garner, B. A. (2024). *Black's law dictionary* (12th ed.).

Gartner, W. C. (1994). Image formation process. *Journal of Travel & Tourism Marketing*, 2(2-3), 191–216. DOI: 10.1300/J073v02n02_12

Gautam, P. (2021). The effects and challenges of COVID-19 in the hospitality and tourism sector in India. *Journal of Tourism and Hospitality Education*, 11, 43–63. DOI: 10.3126/jthe.v11i0.38242

Genç, R. (2018). The impact of augmented reality (AR) technology on tourist satisfaction. In *Augmented reality and virtual reality* (pp. 109–116). Springer. DOI: 10.1007/978-3-319-64027-3_9

George, B. P. (2010). Medical tourism: An analysis with special reference to India. *Journal of Hospitality Application and Research*, 2(4), 1–15.

Gibson, A., & O'Rawe, M. (2018). Virtual reality as a travel promotional tool: Insights from a consumer travel fair. In *Augmented reality and virtual reality* (pp. 93–107). Springer., DOI: 10.1007/978-3-319-64027-3_7

Godovykh, M., Baker, C., & Fyall, A. (2022). VR in tourism : A new call for virtual tourism experience amid and after the COVID-19 pandemic. *Tourism and Hospitality*, 3(1), 265–275. DOI: 10.3390/tourhosp3010018

Go, H., & Kang, M. (2023). Metaverse tourism for sustainable tourism development: Tourism agenda 2030. *Tourism Review*, 78(2), 381–394. DOI: 10.1108/TR-02-2022-0102

Golvin, A. J., & Goyon, J. (1987). *Les bâtisseurs de Karnak*. CNRS.

Gómez, J. V. (2022). Enhancing mammal conservation in multi-functional landscapes using artificial intelligence, joint species distribution modeling, and ecological experimentation (Doctoral dissertation, University of Minnesota).

Gonçalves, T. E., Lima, F. E. S., & de Araújo, E. F. (2021). Turismo e transporte aéreo: O HUB KLM/AIRFRANCE no aeroporto internacional de Fortaleza. *Geografia Ensino & Pesquisa*, •••, e06–e06. DOI: 10.5902/2236499445343

Gonzalez, L. F., Montes, G. A., Puig, E., Johnson, S., Mengersen, K., & Gaston, K. J. (2016). Unmanned aerial vehicles (UAVs) and artificial intelligence revolutionizing wildlife monitoring and conservation. *Sensors (Basel)*, 16(1), 97. DOI: 10.3390/s16010097 PMID: 26784196

González-Rodríguez, M. R., Díaz-Fernández, M. C., Bilgihan, A., Okumus, F., & Shi, F. (2022). The impact of eWOM source credibility on destination visit intention and online involvement : A case of Chinese tourists. *Journal of Hospitality and Tourism Technology*, 13(5), 855–874. DOI: 10.1108/JHTT-11-2021-0321

González-Rodríguez, M. R., Díaz-Fernández, M. C., & Pino-Mejías, M. Á. (2020). The impact of virtual reality technology on tourists' experience: A textual data analysis. *Soft Computing*, 24(18), 1–14. DOI: 10.1007/s00500-020-04883-y

Goodrich, G., & Goodrich, J. (1987). Healthcare tourism: An exploratory study. *Tourism Management*, 8(3), 217–222. DOI: 10.1016/0261-5177(87)90053-7

Goodship, P. (2019). Influencer marketing: What you need to know. Competition and Markets Authority. Retrieved July 15, 2024, from https://competitionandmarkets.blog.gov.uk/2019/04/30/influencer-marketing-what-you-need-to-know/

Goo, J., Huang, C. D., Yoo, C. W., & Koo, C. (2022). Smart Tourism Technologies' Ambidexterity : Balancing Tourist's Worries and Novelty Seeking for Travel Satisfaction. *Information Systems Frontiers*, 24(6), 2139–2158. DOI: 10.1007/s10796-021-10233-6 PMID: 35103046

Gössling, S., Hall, C. M., & Scott, D. (2021). Tourism and climate change: Impacts, adaptation, and mitigation. In Hall, C. M., & Page, S. J. (Eds.), *The Routledge handbook of tourism and sustainability* (pp. 368–381). Routledge., DOI: 10.4324/9780203072332-37

Gov.UK. (2022). Regulatory roles in tackling hidden advertising. Retrieved September 20, 2024, from https://assets.publishing.service.gov.uk/media/63626ba6d3bf7f04f3a5479c/221020_CMA_ASA_Ofcom_-_Regulatory_Landscape.pdf

Governo do Brasil. (2024). *Mais de 8 milhões de passageiros movimentaram os principais aeroportos em maio*. Secretaria de Comunicação Social. https://www.gov.br/secom/pt-br/assuntos/noticias/2024/07/mais-de-8-milhoes-de-passageiros-movimentaram-os-principais-aeroportos-em-maio

Governo do Estado do Ceará. (2017). *Turismo*. Governo do Estado do Ceará. https://www.ceara.gov.br/turismo

Governo do Estado do Ceará. (2024, June 25). *Pelo segundo mês seguido, Ceará foi o estado que mais recebeu turistas internacionais das regiões Norte e Nordeste.* Governo do Estado do Ceará. https://www.ceara.gov.br/2024/06/25/pelo-segundo-mes-seguido-ceara-foi-o-estado-que-mais-recebeu-turistas-internacionais-das-regioes-norte-e-nordeste/

Goyal, S. L., & Kumar, R. (2010). *Medical tourism and hospital services.* University Press.

Gretzel, U. (2017). Influencer marketing in travel and tourism. In Sigala, M., & Gretzel, U. (Eds.), *Advances in social media for travel, tourism and hospitality* (pp. 147–156). Routledge. DOI: 10.4324/9781315565736-13

Guan, W., Zhang, H., & Leung, V. C. (2021). Customized slicing for 6G: Enforcing artificial intelligence on resource management. *IEEE Network*, 35(5), 264–271. DOI: 10.1109/MNET.011.2000644

Guerrieri, V., Lorenzoni, G., Straub, L., & Werning, I. (2020). Macroeconomic implications of COVID-19: Can negative supply shocks cause demand shortages? *National Bureau of Economic Research.* https://www.nber.org/papers/w26918

Gultek, M., & Heroux, L. (2019). Marketing strategies of alternative revenue sources for full-service hotels in the United States and Canada: A comparative revenue management approach. *Journal of Tourism and Hospitality Management*, 7(2), 1–9. DOI: 10.15640/jthm.v7n2a1

Guo, J., He, J., & Wu, X. (2024). Shopping trip recommendations: A novel deep learning–enhanced global planning approach. *Decision Support Systems*, 182, 114238. Advance online publication. DOI: 10.1016/j.dss.2024.114238

Guo, W., Lv, C., Guo, M., Zhao, Q., Yin, X., & Zhang, L. (2023). Innovative applications of artificial intelligence in zoonotic disease management. *Science in One Health*, 2, 100045. DOI: 10.1016/j.soh.2023.100045 PMID: 39077042

Gupta, R., Nair, K., Mishra, M., Ibrahim, B., & Bhardwaj, S. (2024). Adoption and impacts of generative artificial intelligence: Theoretical underpinnings and research agenda. *International Journal of Information Management Data Insights*, 4(1), 100232. DOI: 10.1016/j.jjimei.2024.100232

Gupta, V. (2019). The influencing role of social media in the consumer's hotel decision-making process. *Worldwide Hospitality and Tourism Themes*, 11(4), 378–391. DOI: 10.1108/WHATT-04-2019-0019

Guridno, E., & Guridno, A. (2020). COVID-19 impact: Indonesia tourism in new normal era. [IJMH]. *International Journal of Management and Humanities*, 4(11), 31–34. DOI: 10.35940/ijmh.K1049.0741120

Guttentag, D. A. (2010). Virtual reality: Applications and implications for tourism. *Tourism Management*, 31(5), 637–651. DOI: 10.1016/j.tourman.2009.07.003

Guttentag, D., Griffin, T., & Lee, S. H. (2018). The future is now: How virtual reality and augmented reality are transforming tourism. In *The Sage Handbook of Tourism Management* (pp. 443–462). Sage. DOI: 10.4135/9781526461490.n30

Hagenbuch, D. J., & Mgrdichian, L. M. (2020). Mindful marketing: A strategy-based, branded approach for encouraging ethical marketing. *Marketing Education Review*, 30(1), 15–28. DOI: 10.1080/10528008.2019.1686993

Hair, J. F., Celsi, M., Ortinau, D. J., & Bush, R. P. (2010). *Essentials of marketing research* (Vol. 2). McGraw-Hill/Irwin.

Handler, I., & Tan, C. S. L. (2022). Impact of Japanese travelers' psychographics on domestic travel intention during the COVID-19 pandemic. *Journal of Vacation Marketing*. Advance online publication. DOI: 10.1177/13567667221122108

Han, H., Hsu, L. T. J., & Lee, J. S. (2009). Empirical investigation of the roles of attitudes toward green behaviors, overall image, gender, and age in hotel customers' eco-friendly decision-making process. *International Journal of Hospitality Management*, 28(4), 519–528. DOI: 10.1016/j.ijhm.2009.02.004

Han, H., & Ryu, K. (2012). Key factors driving customers' word-of-mouth intentions in full-service restaurants: The moderating role of switching costs. *Cornell Hospitality Quarterly*, 53(2), 96–109. DOI: 10.1177/1938965511433599

Han, S., Yoon, J. H., & Kwon, J. (2021). Impact of experiential value of augmented reality: The context of heritage tourism. *Sustainability (Basel)*, 13(8), 4147. DOI: 10.3390/su13084147

Hapsari, R. A. (2018). Psychological factors affecting memorable tourism experiences. *Request PDF – ResearchGate*.https://www.researchgate.net/publication/332807375_Psychological_factors_affecting_memorable_tourism_experiences

Hassanien, A. E., Torky, M., Goda, E., Snasel, V., & Gaber, T. (2021). Proof of space transactions: A novel blockchain protocol for secure authentication of satellite transactions. https://doi.org/DOI: 10.21203/rs.3.rs-820584/v1

Hawass, Z. (2000). *The mysteries of Abu Simbel*. The American University in Cairo Press.

Hawdon, J., Parti, K., & Dearden, T. E. (2020). Cybercrime in America amid COVID-19: The initial results from a natural experiment. *American Journal of Criminal Justice*, 45(4), 546–562. DOI: 10.1007/s12103-020-09534-4 PMID: 32837157

Hayes, A. (2019, October 18). The age of the influencer - How it all began! *LinkedIn*. Retrieved September 20, 2024, from https://www.linkedin.com/pulse/age-influencer-how-all-began-amelia-neate

Heilig, T., & Scheer, I. (2023). *Decision intelligence: Transform your team and organization with AI-driven decision-making*. John Wiley & Sons.

Helms, M. M., & Nixon, J. (2010). Exploring SWOT analysis - Where are we now? *Journal of Strategy and Management*, 3(3), 215–251. DOI: 10.1108/17554251011064837

Hemker, S., Herrando, C., & Constantinides, E. (2021a). The transformation of data marketing: How an ethical lens on consumer data collection shapes the future of marketing. *Sustainability (Basel)*, 13(20), 11208. DOI: 10.3390/su132011208

Herrero Crespo, A., San Martín Gutiérrez, H., & García de los Salmones, M. del M. (2017). *Explaining the adoption of social networks sites for sharing user-generated content : A revision of the UTAUT2*. https://repositorio.unican.es/xmlui/handle/10902/12845

Hew, K., Foon, B., Huang, K. W. S., Chu, D., & Chiu, D. K. W. (2016). Engaging Asian students through game mechanics: Findings from two experiment studies. *Computers & Education*, 92, 221–236. DOI: 10.1016/j.compedu.2015.10.010

He, X., & Luo, J. M. (2020). Relationship among travel motivation, satisfaction, and revisit intention of skiers: A case study on the tourists of Urumqi Silk Road Ski Resort. *Administrative Sciences*, 10(3), 56. DOI: 10.3390/admsci10030056

Hien, H. N., & Trang, P. H. (2024). Decoding smart tech's influence on tourist experience quality. *Asian Journal of Business Research Volume,* 14(1). https://ajbr.co.nz/ajbr/ajbr240167.pdf

Higgins, M. (2019, March 25). Frye festival aftermath: New rules for influencers? *UC Law Review*. Retrieved July 15, 2024, from https://uclawreview.org/2019/03/25/fyre-festival-aftermath-new-rules-for-influencers/

Himeur, Y., Rimal, B., Tiwary, A., & Amira, A. (2022). Using artificial intelligence and data fusion for environmental monitoring: A review and future perspectives. *Information Fusion*, 86, 44–75. DOI: 10.1016/j.inffus.2022.06.003

Hmioui, A., Alla, L., & Bentalha, B. (2017). *Piloting territorial tourism in Morocco Proposal for a tourism index for the destination Fez [Pilotage de la touristicité territoriale au Maroc Proposition d'un indice de touriscticité pour la destination Fès]*. https://ideas.repec.org/p/hal/journl/hal-02334913.html

Hoang, H., & Trang, P. H. (2023). Navigating the Rise of Smart Tourism : Implications of Technology and Data for Sustainable Industry Growth. *Brawijaya Journal of Social Science*, 3(1), 1. Advance online publication. DOI: 10.21776/ub.bjss.2023.003.01.1

Hoffman, S. K. (2020). Online exhibitions during the COVID-19 pandemic. *Museum Worlds*, 8(1), 210–215. DOI: 10.3167/armw.2020.080115

Hong, D., Chiu, D. K. W., Shen, V. Y., Cheung, S. C., & Kafeza, E. (2007). Ubiquitous enterprise service adaptations based on contextual user behavior. *Information Systems Frontiers*, 9(4), 343–358. DOI: 10.1007/s10796-007-9039-2

Horng, J. S., Hsu, H., & Tsai, C. Y. (2018). An assessment model of corporate social responsibility practice in the tourism industry. *Journal of Sustainable Tourism*, 26(7), 1085–1104. DOI: 10.1080/09669582.2017.1388384

Hosany, S., & Witham, M. (2010). Dimensions of cruisers' experiences, satisfaction, and intention to recommend. *Journal of Travel Research*, 49(3), 351–364. DOI: 10.1177/0047287509346859

Hospitalitynet. (2021). Trip.com group and WTTC publish 'Trending in Travel' report uncovering current and upcoming consumer trends. *Hospitalitynet*. https://www.hospitalitynet.org/news/4107747.html

Hossan, D., Dato'Mansor, Z., & Jaharuddin, N. S. (2023). Research population and sampling in quantitative study. [IJBT]. *International Journal of Business and Technopreneurship*, 13(3), 209–222. DOI: 10.58915/ijbt.v13i3.263

Hsu, L. (2012). Web 3D simulation-based application in tourism education: A case study with Second Life. *Journal of Hospitality, Leisure, Sport and Tourism Education*, 11(2), 113–124. DOI: 10.1016/j.jhlste.2012.02.013

Huang, C. D., Goo, J., Nam, K., & Yoo, C. W. (2017). Smart tourism technologies in travel planning : The role of exploration and exploitation. *Information & Management*, 54(6), 757–770. DOI: 10.1016/j.im.2016.11.010

Huang, X., Xiang, Y., Bertino, E., Zhou, J., & Xu, L. (2014). Robust multi-factor authentication for fragile communications. *IEEE Transactions on Dependable and Secure Computing*, 11(6), 568–581. DOI: 10.1109/TDSC.2013.2297110

Huang, Y. C., Backman, K. F., Backman, S. J., & Chang, L. L. (2016). Exploring the implications of virtual reality technology in tourism marketing: An integrated research framework. *International Journal of Tourism Research*, 18(2), 116–128. DOI: 10.1002/jtr.2038

Huang, Y.-C. (2023). Integrated concepts of the UTAUT and TPB in virtual reality behavioral intention. *Journal of Retailing and Consumer Services*, 70, 103127. DOI: 10.1016/j.jretconser.2022.103127

Hughes-Noehrer, L. (2023). Artificial intelligence, museum environments, and their constituents: A cross-disciplinary study using recommender systems to explore digital collections (Doctoral dissertation, New York University).

Hu, J., Xiong, L., Lv, X., & Pu, B. (2021). Sustainable rural tourism: Linking residents' environmentally responsible behavior to tourists' green consumption. *Asia Pacific Journal of Tourism Research*, 26(8), 879–893. DOI: 10.1080/10941665.2021.1925316

Hultman, M., Skarmeas, D., Oghazi, P., & Beheshti, H. M. (2015). Achieving tourist loyalty through destination personality, satisfaction, and identification. *Journal of Business Research*, 68(11), 2227–2231. DOI: 10.1016/j.jbusres.2015.06.002

Hume, M., & Mills, M. (2011). Building the sustainable iMuseum: Is the virtual museum leaving our museums virtually empty? *International Journal of Nonprofit and Voluntary Sector Marketing*, 16(3), 275–289. DOI: 10.1002/nvsm.425

Hung, N. T., & Hang, V. T. T. (2020). A studying on factors affecting decision to use smart tourism applications using extended TAM. *WSEAS Transactions on Business and Economics*, 17, 288–299. DOI: 10.37394/23207.2020.17.30

Huo, Y., & Miller, D. (2007). Satisfaction measurement of small tourism sector (museum): Samoa. *Asia Pacific Journal of Tourism Research*, 12(2), 103–117. DOI: 10.1080/10941660701243331

Hutson, J., & Hutson, P. (2024). Immersive technologies. In *Inclusive smart museums: Engaging neurodiverse audiences and enhancing cultural heritage accessibility* (pp. 77–96). Routledge., DOI: 10.1007/978-3-031-43615-4_5

Hwang, J., & Lee, J. (2019). A strategy for enhancing senior tourists' well-being perception: Focusing on the experience economy. *Journal of Travel & Tourism Marketing*, 36(3), 314–329. DOI: 10.1080/10548408.2018.1541776

Ibañez-Etxeberria, A., Gómez-Carrasco, C. J., Fontal, O., & García-Ceballos, S. (2020). Virtual environments and augmented reality applied to heritage education: An evaluative study. *Applied Sciences (Basel, Switzerland)*, 10(7), 2352. DOI: 10.3390/app10072352

Ilieva, G., Yankova, T., Ruseva, M., Dzhabarova, Y., Klisarova-Belcheva, S., & Bratkov, M. (2024). Social media influencers: Customer attitudes and impact on purchase behaviour. *Information (Basel)*, 15(6), 359. DOI: 10.3390/info15060359

India's hospitality sector reviving article (2022). Retrieved from https://www.aninews.in/news/national/general-news/indias-hospitality-sector-reviving-steadily-post-covid-1920221018102232/

Ingram, H., & Grieve, D. (2013). Exploring the nature and effects of perception and image in hospitality and tourism. *Worldwide Hospitality and Tourism Themes*, 5(1), 7–13. DOI: 10.1108/17554211311292402

Ingrassia, M., Bellia, C., Giurdanella, C., Columba, P., & Chironi, S. (2022). Digital influencers, food and tourism: A new model of open innovation for businesses in the Ho. Re. Ca. sector. *Journal of Open Innovation*, 8(1), 50. DOI: 10.3390/joitmc8010050

Iqbal, Z., & Wajid, S. (2024). Guardians of the IoT realm: A comparative analysis of cryptographic security solutions for bolstering IoT device networks. *Lahore Garrison University Research Journal of Computer Science and Information Technology*, 8(1). Advance online publication. DOI: 10.54692/lgurjcsit.2024.081484

Islam, G. (2020). Psychology and business ethics: A multi-level research agenda. *Journal of Business Ethics*, 165(1), 1–13. DOI: 10.1007/s10551-019-04107-w

Itani, O. S., & Hollebeek, L. D. (2021). Light at the end of the tunnel: Visitors' virtual reality (versus in-person) attraction site tour-related behavioral intentions during and post-COVID-19. *Tourism Management*, 84, 104290. DOI: 10.1016/j.tourman.2021.104290 PMID: 36530603

Ivanov, S., & Webster, C. (Eds.). (2020). *Robots, Artificial Intelligence, and Service Automation in Travel, Tourism, and Hospitality*. Emerald Publishing.

Iyengar, R., Van den Bulte, C., & Valente, T. W. (2011). Opinion leadership and social contagion in new product diffusion. *Marketing Science*, 30(2), 195–212. DOI: 10.1287/mksc.1100.0566

Jabeen, F., Al Zaidi, S., & Al Dhaheri, M. H. (2022). Automation and artificial intelligence in hospitality and tourism. *Tourism Review*, 77(4), 1043–1061. DOI: 10.1108/TR-09-2019-0360

Jadhav, S., Yeravdekar, R., & Kulkarni, M. (2014). Cross-border healthcare access in South Asian countries: Learning for sustainable healthcare tourism in India. *International Conference on India and Development Partnerships in Asia and Africa: Towards a New Paradigm (IRC-2013)*, 157, 109-117. DOI: 10.1016/j.sbspro.2014.11.014

Jaime, F. J., Muñoz, A., Rodríguez-Gómez, F., & Jerez-Calero, A. (2023). Strengthening privacy and data security in biomedical microelectromechanical systems by IoT communication security and protection in smart healthcare. *Sensors (Basel)*, 23(21), 8944. DOI: 10.3390/s23218944 PMID: 37960646

Jain, N. (2006). Health tourism in India. *EzineArticles*. http://EzineArticles.com/?expert=Nakuljain/

Jani, D. (2014). Big five personality factors and travel curiosity : Are they related? *Anatolia*, 25(3), 444–456. DOI: 10.1080/13032917.2014.909366

Jani, D., Jang, J.-H., & Hwang, Y.-H. (2014). Big Five Factors of Personality and Tourists' Internet Search Behavior. *Asia Pacific Journal of Tourism Research*, 19(5), 600–615. DOI: 10.1080/10941665.2013.773922

Jarratt, D. (2021). An exploration of webcam-travel: Connecting to place and nature through webcams during the COVID-19 lockdown of 2020. *Tourism and Hospitality Research*, 21(2), 156–168. DOI: 10.1177/1467358420963370

Javed, M., Tučková, Z., & Jibril, A. B. (2020). The role of social media on tourists' behavior : An empirical analysis of millennials from the Czech Republic. *Sustainability (Basel)*, 12(18), 7735. DOI: 10.3390/su12187735

Jawahar, S. K. (2007). Health care services in India. *ICU Management and Practice*, 6(4), 1–5.

Jenkins, O. (2003). Photography and travel brochures: The circle of representation. *Tourism Geographies*, 5(3), 305–328. DOI: 10.1080/14616680309715

Jeong, E., & Jang, S. S. (2011). Restaurant experiences triggering positive electronic word-of-mouth (eWOM) motivations. *International Journal of Hospitality Management*, 30(2), 356–366. DOI: 10.1016/j.ijhm.2010.08.005

Jeon, H., Ok, C. M., & Choi, J. (2018). Destination marketing organization website visitors' flow experience : An application of Plog's model of personality. *Journal of Travel & Tourism Marketing*, 35(4), 397–409. DOI: 10.1080/10548408.2017.1358234

Jiang, Y. (2022). OTA platforms online travel in the post-epidemic era: Case study of Trip.com group. *Highlights in Business, Economics and Management, 2*, 322-326. https://drpress.org/ojs/index.php/HBEM/article/view/2381

Jiang, X., & Hao, P. (2024). Hub Airport End-Around Taxiway Construction Planning Development: A Review. *Applied Sciences (Basel, Switzerland)*, 14(8), 8. Advance online publication. DOI: 10.3390/app14083500

Johnson, C. K., Gutzwiller, R. S., Gervais, J., & Ferguson-Walter, K. J. (2021). Decision-making biases and cyber attackers. In *2021 36th IEEE/ACM International Conference on Automated Software Engineering Workshops (ASEW)* (pp. 140–144). https://doi.org/DOI: 10.1109/ASEW52652.2021.00038

Joshi, Y., Lim, W. M., Jagani, K., & Kumar, S. (2023). Social media influencer marketing: Foundations, trends, and ways forward. *Electronic Commerce Research*, •••, 1–55. DOI: 10.1007/s10660-023-09719-z

Jovanović, T., Božić, S., Bodroža, B., & Stankov, U. (2019). Influence of users' psychosocial traits on Facebook travel–related behavior patterns. *Journal of Vacation Marketing*, 25(2), 252–263. DOI: 10.1177/1356766718771420

Jung, T., tom Dieck, M. C., Lee, H., & Chung, N. (2016). Effects of virtual reality and augmented reality on visitor experiences in museum. In Inversini, A., & Schegg, R. (Eds.), *Information and communication technologies in tourism 2016* (pp. 621–635). Springer., DOI: 10.1007/978-3-319-28231-2_45

Junqueiro, Â., Correia, R., Carvalho, A., & Cunha, C. R. (2022). Smart Technologies in Tourist Destination Marketing : A Literature Review. In T. Guarda, F. Portela, & M. F. Augusto (Éds.), *Advanced Research in Technologies, Information, Innovation and Sustainability* (Vol. 1676, p. 283-293). Springer Nature Switzerland. DOI: 10.1007/978-3-031-20316-9_22

Jyothis, T. (2009). *An evaluation of the potentials of health tourism with special reference to Kerala* (Master's thesis, University of Calicut, India).

Kabus, J. (2015). Marketing in tourism. *AD ALTA International Interdisciplinary Research Journal, 5*, 34–37.

Kafeza, E., Chiu, D. K. W., Cheung, S. C., & Kafeza, M. (2004). Alerts in mobile healthcare applications: Requirements and pilot study. *IEEE Transactions on Information Technology in Biomedicine*, 8(2), 173–181. DOI: 10.1109/TITB.2004.828888 PMID: 15217262

Kahane, S. (2022). The impact of artificial intelligence on job displacement: Evidence from recent developments. *Economics of Innovation and New Technology*, 31(1), 76–93.

Kapferer, J.-N., & Valette-Florence, P. (2021). Which consumers believe luxury must be expensive and why? A cross-cultural comparison of motivations. *Journal of Business Research*, 132, 301–313. DOI: 10.1016/j.jbusres.2021.04.003

Kariru, A. N. (2023). Contemporary trends and issues in the hospitality and tourism industry. *International Journal of Study and Innovation in Social Science*, 7(4), 970–986. DOI: 10.47772/IJRISS.2023.7481

Kashiwagi, K., Yokoyama, H., & Furukawa, Y. (2023). Machine learning and decision support for wildlife conservation. *Conservation Biology*, 37(2). Advance online publication. DOI: 10.1111/cobi.13870

Kasim, H., Abdurachman, E., Furinto, A., & Kosasih, W. (2019). Social network for the choice of tourist destination : Attitude and behavioral intention. *Management Science Letters*, 9(13), 2415–2420. DOI: 10.5267/j.msl.2019.7.014

Katuk, N., Wan Abdullah, W. A. N., Sugiharto, T., & Ahmad, I. (2023). Smart technology: Ecosystem, impacts, challenges, and the path forward. *Information System and Smart City*, 1(1). Advance online publication. DOI: 10.59400/issc.v1i1.63

Katz, E., & Lazarsfeld, P. F. (2006). *Personal influence: The part played by people in the flow of mass communications* (1st ed.).

Kazandzhieva, V., & Filipova, H. (2019). Customer attitudes toward robots in travel, tourism, and hospitality: A conceptual framework. In S. Ivanov & C. Webster (Eds.), *Robots, Artificial Intelligence, and Service Automation in Travel, Tourism and Hospitality* (pp. 79-92). Emerald Publishing. DOI: 10.1108/978-1-78756-687-320191004

Kelley, E. (2013). Medical tourism. WHO Patient Safety Programme. https://www.who.int/patientsafety/medicaltourism/en/

Kemp, A. (2023, April 9). 'We applaud this movement of transparency': Marketers react to French influencer law. *The Drum*. Retrieved July 15, 2024, from https://www.thedrum.com/news/2023/06/05/we-applaud-movement-transparency-marketers-react-french-influencer-law

Kh, N., Komilova, N., Usmonov, M., Safarova, N., Matchanova, A., & Murtazaeva, G. (2021). *Tourist Destination as an Object of Research of Social and Economic Geography*. 2058–2067.

Khaled, G., & Alena, F. (2021). Industry 4.0 and human resource management in the hotel business. *Human Progress*, 7(2), 1–10.

Khalil, E. A., Khedher, R. A., & Al-Romeedy, B. (2023). Leveraging machine learning in smart city tourism: A strategic approach. In *Artificial Intelligence in Sustainable Development: A Smart Tourism Perspective* (pp. 56–76). IGI Global., DOI: 10.4018/978-1-7998-8563-7.ch003

Khan, A., Masrek, M. N., & Mahmood, K. (2019). The relationship of personal innovativeness, quality of digital resources and generic usability with users' satisfaction. *Digital Library Perspectives*, 35(3), 178–194. DOI: 10.1108/DLP-12-2017-0046

Khan, N., Hassan, A. U., Fahad, S., & Naushad, M. (2020). Factors affecting the tourism industry and its impacts on the global economy. *SSRN*. DOI: 10.2139/ssrn.3559353

Kilipiri, E., Papaioannou, E., & Kotzaivazoglou, I. (2023). Social media and influencer marketing for promoting sustainable tourism destinations: The Instagram case. *Sustainability (Basel)*, 15(8), 6374. DOI: 10.3390/su15086374

Kim, Y., Yeon, S., & Kim, J. (2012). A review of memorable experiences and their implications for tourism experiences. *Management and Marketing Science*. https://journals.openedition.org/tourisme/5053

Kim, H., & Stepchenkova, S. (2017). Understanding destination personality through visitors' experience : A cross-cultural perspective. *Journal of Destination Marketing & Management*, 6(4), 416–425. DOI: 10.1016/j.jdmm.2016.06.010

Kim, H., Yilmaz, S., & Choe, Y. (2019). Traveling to your match? Assessing the predictive potential of Plog's travel personality in destination marketing. *Journal of Travel & Tourism Marketing*, 36(9), 1025–1036. DOI: 10.1080/10548408.2019.1683485

Kim, J. H. (2018). The impact of memorable tourism experiences on loyalty behaviors: The mediating effects of destination image and satisfaction. *Journal of Travel Research*, 57(7), 856–870. DOI: 10.1177/0047287517721369

Kim, J. Y., Chung, N., & Ahn, K. M. (2019). The impact of mobile tour information services on destination travel intention. *Information Development*, 35(1), 107–120. DOI: 10.1177/0266666917730437

Kim, M. J., & Hall, C. M. (2019). A hedonic motivation model in virtual reality tourism: Comparing visitors and non-visitors. *International Journal of Information Management*, 46, 236–249. DOI: 10.1016/j.ijinfomgt.2018.11.016

Kim, M. J., Lee, C. K., & Jung, T. (2020). Exploring consumer behavior in virtual reality tourism using an extended stimulus-organism-response model. *Journal of Travel Research*, 59(1), 69–89. DOI: 10.1177/0047287518818915

Kim, S. H., & Chen, J. S. (2020). Pengaruh memorable tourist experience terhadap storytelling behavior (The influence of memorable tourist experiences on storytelling behaviour). *E-Journal UNDIP*, 24(2), 1–10.

Kim, Y., Ritchie, B. W., & McCormick, J. (2012). A review of memorable experiences and their implications for tourism experiences in management and marketing science. *Tourism Management*, 33(6), 1443–1456. DOI: 10.1016/j.tourman.2012.02.007

Kinsella, E. (2022). *Artificial intelligence and environmental governance: An interdisciplinary approach*. Routledge.

Klein, M. (2021). *Data protection in cultural heritage institutions: A comparative perspective*. Routledge.

Koerten, K., & Abbink, D. (2023). Selecting robots to take over tasks in hospitality settings: Joining two research fields. In Marques, J., & Marques, R. P. (Eds.), *Digital transformation of the hotel industry* (pp. 65–86). Springer International Publishing., DOI: 10.1007/978-3-031-31682-1_4

Köhler, W. (2015). *The task of Gestalt psychology*. Princeton University Press. DOI: 10.1515/9781400868964

Kotler, P., Keller, K. L., Brady, M., Goodman, M., & Hansen, T. (2016). *Marketing management* (3rd ed.). Pearson Higher Ed.

Kouroupi, N., & Metaxas, T. (2023). Can the Metaverse and its associated digital tools and technologies provide an opportunity for destinations to address the vulnerability of overtourism? *Tourism and Hospitality*, 4(2), 355–373. DOI: 10.3390/tourhosp4020022

Kowalska-Napora, E. (2018). The hub- and- spoke: Central Airport Project. *AUTOBUSY – Technika, Eksploatacja. Systemy Transportowe*, 19(12), 12. Advance online publication. DOI: 10.24136/atest.2018.557

Krauss, J., Tonn, A., & Peters, M. (2023). Ethical implications of artificial intelligence in wildlife conservation: Balancing benefits and harms. *Journal of Environmental Ethics*, 30(3), 195–212.

Krivokuća, M. (2020). Social responsibility in the application of integrated marketing communication. *Serbian Journal of Engineering Management*, 5(2), 33–41. DOI: 10.5937/SJEM2002033K

Kukulska-Kozieł, A., Noszczyk, T., Gorzelany, J., & Młocek, W. (2024). Greenery in times of crisis: Accessibility, residents' travel preferences and the impact of travel time. *Land Use Policy*, 141, 107130. DOI: 10.1016/j.landusepol.2024.107130

Kumar, A., Tripathi, S., Bansal, A., Tiwari, V., & Kumar, A. (2023). Artificial intelligence in smart tourism: A systematic review and future research agenda. *Tourism Management Perspectives*, 45, 270–290.

Kumar, S., Talukder, M. B., & Kaiser, F. (2024). Artificial intelligence in business: Negative social impacts. In Dadwal, S., Goyal, S., Kumar, P., & Verma, R. (Eds.), (pp. 81–97). Advances in human resources management and organizational development. IGI Global., DOI: 10.4018/979-8-3693-0724-3.ch005

Kumar, S., Talukder, M. B., & Pego, A. (Eds.). (2024). *Utilizing smart technology and AI in hybrid tourism and hospitality*. IGI Global., DOI: 10.4018/979-8-3693-1978-9

Ladwein, R., & Sánchez Romero, A. M. (2021). The role of trust in the relationship between consumers, producers and retailers of organic food: A sector-based approach. *Journal of Retailing and Consumer Services*, 60, 102508. Advance online publication. DOI: 10.1016/j.jretconser.2021.102508

Lamba., ... (2023). HVS India hospitality industry overview 2023. Retrieved from https://www.hvs.com/article/9918-hvs-india-hospitality-industry-overview-2023#:~:text=Inbound%20tourism%20displayed%20promising%20signs,highs%20last%20experienced%20in%202019

Lau, L. C., Wong, Y. Y., & Tham, S. Y. (2023). AI-enabled wildlife conservation: A systematic review of applications, challenges, and future directions. *Conservation Biology*, 37(1). Advance online publication. DOI: 10.1111/cobi.13824

Lee, L. H., Braud, T., Zhou, P., Wang, L., Xu, D., Lin, Z., . . . Hui, P. (2021). All one needs to know about the metaverse: A complete survey on technological singularity, virtual ecosystem, and research agenda. *arXiv preprint arXiv:2110.05352*.

Lee, H., Jung, T. H., tom Dieck, M. C., & Chung, N. (2020). Experiencing immersive virtual reality in museums. *Information & Management*, 57(5), 103229. DOI: 10.1016/j.im.2019.103229

Lee, K.-Y., & Park, S.-H. (2021). Does face consciousness affect tourist behaviour at festival events? A Korean perspective. *Sustainability (Basel)*, 13(20), 11558. DOI: 10.3390/su132011558

Lee, S., Pan, B., & Park, S. (2019). RevPAR vs. GOPPAR: Property-and firm-level analysis. *Annals of Tourism Research*, 76, 180–190. DOI: 10.1016/j.annals.2019.04.006

Leiras, A., & Eusébio, C. (2024). Perceived image of accessible tourism destinations : A data mining analysis of Google Maps reviews. *Current Issues in Tourism*, 27(16), 2584–2602. DOI: 10.1080/13683500.2023.2230338

Leong, M. W. A., Kocak, E., Bai, J., & Okumus, F. (2024). Macau hotel industry's response to global shocks. *Tourism Economics*, 30(7), 1914–1921. Advance online publication. DOI: 10.1177/13548166241234096

Leung, W. K., Chang, M. K., Cheung, M. L., & Shi, S. (2023). VR tourism experiences and tourist behavior intention in COVID-19 : An experience economy and mood management perspective. *Information Technology & People*, 36(3), 1095–1125. DOI: 10.1108/ITP-06-2021-0423

Leung, X. Y., Bai, B., & Stahura, K. A. (2015). The marketing effectiveness of social media in the hotel industry: A comparison of Facebook and Twitter. *Journal of Hospitality & Tourism Research (Washington, D.C.)*, 39(2), 147–169. DOI: 10.1177/1096348012471381

Liang, H.-W., Chu, Y.-C., & Han, T.-H. (2023). Fortifying health care intellectual property transactions with blockchain. *Journal of Medical Internet Research*, 25, e44578. DOI: 10.2196/44578 PMID: 37594787

Liberato, D., Costa, E., Barradas, I., Liberato, P., & Ribeiro, J. (2024). Events' tourism and hospitality marketing. In Carvalho, J. V., Abreu, A., Liberato, D., & Rebolledo, J. A. D. (Eds.), *Advances in tourism, technology and systems* (Vol. 384, pp. 483–493). Springer Nature Singapore., DOI: 10.1007/978-981-99-9758-9_38

Li, H., Chen, Y., Sun, L., & Wu, G. (2022). AI for environmental management: Current status and future prospects. *Environmental Science & Technology*, 56(10), 6345–6365.

Li, H., Wang, D., Jiang, W., & Yang, C. (2024). The impact of AI on eco-friendly practices in tourism: Evidence from China. *Sustainability*, 16(1), 289.

Lima, L., Iamanaka, L., & Okano, M. (2019). A proposta de valor de um Hub aeroportuário: Uma análise sob a lente teórica dos modelos de negócios. *Research. Social Development*, 9(3), e13932314. Advance online publication. DOI: 10.33448/rsd-v9i3.2314

Lim, W. M., Mohamed Jasim, K., & Das, M. (2024). Augmented and virtual reality in hotels: Impact on tourist satisfaction and intention to stay and return. *International Journal of Hospitality Management*, 116, 103631. DOI: 10.1016/j.ijhm.2023.103631

Lin, Y.-X., Su, C.-H., & Chen, M.-H. (2024). Undrstanding the contribution of domestic tourism to hotel industry. *Tourism Analysis*, 29(3), 367–383. Advance online publication. DOI: 10.3727/108354224X17065682130471

Li, T., & Chen, Y. (2019). Will virtual reality be a double-edged sword? Exploring the moderation effects of the expected enjoyment of a destination on travel intention. *Journal of Destination Marketing & Management*, 12, 15–26. DOI: 10.1016/j.jdmm.2019.02.003

Liu, J., & Jia, F. (2021). Construction of a nonlinear model of tourism economy forecast based on wireless sensor network from the perspective of digital economy. *Wireless Communications and Mobile Computing*, 2021(1), 1–14. DOI: 10.1155/2021/8576534

Liu, S. (2020). Thinking about the legal attribute of live broadcast for goods promotion. *Research on China Market Regulation*, 5, 21–23.

Liu, S., Chen, L., Yu, H., Zhang, Y., & Yu, Y. (2022). The use of AI technology for wildlife conservation: A review. *Environmental Research Letters*, 17(8), 083010.

Liu, X., Nicolau, J. L., Law, R., & Li, C. (2023). Applying image recognition techniques to visual information mining in hospitality and tourism. *International Journal of Contemporary Hospitality Management*, 35(6), 2005–2016. DOI: 10.1108/IJCHM-03-2022-0362

Liu, Y., & Li, N. (2021). The legal regulation of the false promotion of the live broadcast e-commerce. *Intellectual Property*, 5, 68–82.

Li, W., & Leung, R. (2023). Data-driven conservation: How artificial intelligence can transform wildlife monitoring. *The Journal of Wildlife Management*, 87(2), 129–139.

Li, X., Kim, J. S., & Lee, T. J. (2021). Collaboration for community-based cultural sustainability in island tourism development: A case in Korea. *Sustainability (Basel)*, 13(13), 7306. DOI: 10.3390/su13137306

Li, Y., Gunasekeran, D. V., RaviChandran, N., Tan, T. F., Ong, J. C. L., Thirunavukarasu, A. J., Polascik, B. W., Habash, R., Khaderi, K., & Ting, D. S. W. (2024). The next generation of the healthcare ecosystem in the metaverse. *Biomedical Journal*, 47(3), 100679. DOI: 10.1016/j.bj.2023.100679 PMID: 38048990

López, M., & Sicilia, M. (2014). Determinants of E-WOM influence: The role of consumers' internet experience. *Journal of Theoretical and Applied Electronic Commerce Research*, 9(1), 28–43. DOI: 10.4067/S0718-18762014000100004

Lukanova, G., & Ilieva, G. (2019). Robots, artificial intelligence and service automation in hotels. In *Travel, Tourism, and Hospitality* (pp. 157-183). Emerald Publishing. DOI: 10.1108/978-1-78756-687-320191009

Luo, J., Joybari, M. M., Ma, Y., Liu, J., & Lai, K. (2024). Assessment of renewable power generation applied in homestay hotels: Energy and cost-benefit considering dynamic occupancy rates and reservation prices. *Journal of Building Engineering*, 87, 109074. DOI: 10.1016/j.jobe.2024.109074

Lvov, A., & Komppula, R. (2023). The essence of the hotel room in the hotel business – The hotel managers' perspective. *European Journal of Tourism Research*, 36, 3609. DOI: 10.54055/ejtr.v36i.3158

Ma, J., Scott, N., & Wu, Y. (2023). Tourism destination advertising: Effect of storytelling and sensory stimuli on arousal and memorability. *Tourism Review*, ahead-of-print. https://doi.org/DOI: 10.1108/TR-07-2022-0319

Ma, H. (2021). Research on the advertising regulation of influencer marketing in the era of social networks. [Philosophy and Social Science]. *Journal of Southwest University (Natural Science Edition)*, 23(1), 32–40.

Maharana, P., & Mahesh, M. (2024). Digital transformation in hospitality: Current trends and future prospects. In P. Jena & B. Singh (Eds.), *Trends in hospitality management: The role of AI and robotics* (pp. 1–20). Springer International Publishing. https://doi.org/DOI: 10.1007/978-3-031-12940-1_1

Mahat, J., Ayub, A. F. M., Luan, S., & Wong, . (2012). An assessment of students' mobile self-efficacy, readiness and personal innovativeness towards mobile learning in higher education in Malaysia. *Procedia: Social and Behavioral Sciences*, 64, 284–290. DOI: 10.1016/j.sbspro.2012.11.033

Mahdzar, M., Saiful Raznan, A. M., Ahmad Jasmin, N., & Abdul Aziz, N. A. (2020). Exploring relationships between experience economy and satisfaction of visitors in rural tourism destination. *Journal of International Business. Economics and Entrepreneurship*, 5(1), 69–75. DOI: 10.24191/jibe.v5i1.14277

Mahnken, J. (2024). Digitalization in heritage tourism: Challenges and opportunities for Egyptian tourism in the digital age. In *Sustainable tourism in heritage sites: Managing environmental challenges and promoting cultural preservation* (pp. 45–60). IGI Global., DOI: 10.4018/978-1-7998-6893-7.ch003

Majumdar, A., & Kumar, R. (2024). The future of digitalization in heritage tourism: Impacts on cultural preservation and sustainable development. In *Smart and sustainable tourism: Emerging concepts and technologies* (pp. 100–120). IGI Global., DOI: 10.4018/978-1-7998-8022-9.ch006

Mal, J. (2010). Globalization of healthcare: Case studies of medical tourism in multi-specialty hospitals in India (Doctoral dissertation, Manchester Business School).

Malaysia, T. (2023, March 17). Tourism Malaysia - Air Asia collaboration brings Taiwanese influencers and bloggers to promote Malaysia. *Tourism Malaysia*. Retrieved October 1, 2023, from https://www.tourism.gov.my/media/view/tourism-malaysia-air-asia-collaboration-brings-taiwanese-influencers-and-bloggers-to-promote-malaysia

Mali, S. (2022). Artificial intelligence for biodiversity conservation: Opportunities and challenges. *Journal of Environmental Management*, 312, 114840.

Malti, T., Peplak, J., & Acland, E. (2020). Emotional experiences in moral contexts. In Jensen, L. A. (Ed.), *The Oxford handbook of moral development* (pp. 243–263). Oxford University Press., DOI: 10.1093/oxfordhb/9780190676049.013.14

Manda, V. K., Sagi, S., & Yadav, A. (2024). Blockchain in advertising and marketing: Revolutionizing the industry through transparency and trust. In *New trends in marketing and consumer science* (pp. 89–112). IGI Global., DOI: 10.4018/979-8-3693-2754-8.ch005

Mansouri, R., Amari, M., & El-Haibi, A. (2023). Integrating AI with sustainable practices in tourism: A systematic literature review. *Journal of Tourism Management*, 89, 104387.

Manzoor, A., & Khan, M. A. (2023). AI-powered tourism management: An examination of applications and implications. *Tourism Management Perspectives*, 45, 1030–1041.

Mariani, M. M., Hashemi, N., & Wirtz, J. (2023). Artificial intelligence empowered conversational agents : A systematic literature review and research agenda. *Journal of Business Research*, 161, 113838. DOI: 10.1016/j.jbusres.2023.113838

Market data forecast report. (n.d.). Retrieved from https://www.marketdataforecast.com/market-reports/big-data-market

Martinho, A., Herber, N., Kroesen, M., & Chorus, C. (2021). Ethical issues in focus by the autonomous vehicles industry. *Transport Reviews*, 41(5), 556–577. DOI: 10.1080/01441647.2020.1862355

Martinz, J., Anjos, S., & Sohn, A. (2022). Determinantes da competitividade em destinos turísticos: Um estudo sobre a cidade de Fortaleza. *Revista de Turismo Contemporâneo*, 10(2). Advance online publication. DOI: 10.21680/2357-8211.2022v10n2ID23926

Mateo, S. (2020). Procédure pour conduire avec succès une revue de littérature selon la méthode PRISMA. *Kinésithérapie, la Revue*, 20(226), 29–37. DOI: 10.1016/j.kine.2020.05.019

Mathews, S., & Nair, S. R. (2020). Ethical consumerism and effectiveness from a cause-related marketing (CRM) perspective. In Mathews, S., & Nair, S. R. (Eds.), *Handbook of research on marketing and promoting brands with cause-related marketing* (pp. 186–210)., DOI: 10.4018/978-1-5225-8270-0.ch008

Matsuura, T., & Saito, H. (2022). The COVID-19 pandemic and domestic travel subsidies. *Annals of Tourism Research*, 92, 103326. DOI: 10.1016/j.annals.2021.103326 PMID: 34815608

Matviienko, N., & Matviienko, V. (2020). State and prospects of international tourism development in Japan. *Bulletin of Taras Shevchenko National University of Kyiv.Geography (Sheffield, England)*, 76–77(76-77), 64–69. DOI: 10.17721/1728-2721.2020.76-77.9

Mazilescu, V. (2019). Tourism and travel can effectively benefit from technologies associated with Industry 4.0. *XXth International Conference "Risk in Contemporary Economy*. https://scholar.archive.org/work/7yqickbjhrchvp7jygzgy4kxai/access/wayback/http://www.rce.feaa.ugal.ro/images/stories/RCE2019/Mazilescu.pdf

Mcdougall, P. B. R. (2020). Digital tools. *Psychology and Marketing*, 40(4), 750–776. DOI: 10.1002/mar.21767

McGauley, J. (2019). These are the top companies to work for right now, according to LinkedIn. *Thrillist*. https://www.thrillist.com/news/nation/top-companies-to-work-for-2019-linkedin-ranking

Mehdizadeh, M. (2024). The ramifications of emerging mobility modes on active travel. *Journal of Transport & Health*, 37, 101839. DOI: 10.1016/j.jth.2024.101839

Mehra, A. (2024). A comparative analysis of smart and traditional hotels: The impact on guest experiences. *Tourism Review*. Advance online publication. DOI: 10.1108/TR-05-2023-0238

Mehta, P. (2022). Artificial intelligence and wildlife conservation: A review of techniques and applications. *Ecological Informatics*, 68, 101686.

Mekhlif, M. (2023). Utilizing AI technology for promoting sustainable tourism in Egypt. *International Journal of Culture, Tourism and Hospitality Research*, 17(1), 45–59. DOI: 10.1108/IJCTHR-01-2022-0025

Mekhlif, M., & Al-Romeedy, B. (2023). Leveraging AI and machine learning for enhancing customer experience in Egypt's tourism sector. *Journal of Tourism and Services*, 14(1), 10–25. DOI: 10.2139/ssrn.4319181

Merriam-Webster Online Dictionary. (n.d.). Influencer. In https://www.merriam-webster.com/dictionary/influencer

Mezzofiore, G. (2019, May 4). Beach club owner rips into freeloading Instagram 'influencers'. *CNN Travel*. Retrieved July 15, 2024, from https://edition.cnn.com/travel/article/instagram-influencers-beach-club-philippines-intl-scli/index.html

Milton, T.Dr.T. Milton. (2024). Artificial intelligence transforming hotel gastronomy: An in-depth review of AI-driven innovations in menu design, food preparation, and customer interaction, with a focus on sustainability and future trends in the hospitality industry. *International Journal for Multidimensional Research Perspectives*, 2(3), 47–61. DOI: 10.61877/ijmrp.v2i3.126

Mindset, T. (2024). Hot tips from Webinar 2: Influencer marketing during and post. *COVID*, 19, •••. Retrieved July 15, 2024, from https://www.travelmindset.com/hot-tips-from-webinar-2-influencer-marketing-during-and-post-covid-19/

Ministério do Turismo. (2015). *Plano Nacional de Turismo*. https://www.gov.br/turismo/pt-br/assuntos/assuntos-categoria/plano-nacional-de-turismo

Ministério do Turismo. (2018). *Ceará vive novo boom na economia do turismo*. https://www.gov.br/turismo/pt-br/assuntos/noticias/ceara-vive-novo-boom-na-economia-do-turismo

Ministério do Turismo. (2020). *Estudo da Demanda Turística Internacional—Brasil 2019*. Ministério do Turismo. https://www.gov.br/turismo/pt-br/acesso-a-informacao/acoes-e-programas/observatorio/demanda-turistica/demanda-turistica-internacional-1/demanda-turistica-internacional

Mishra, V., & Das, R. (2023). Blockchain-based smart contracts for tourism industry: A secure and transparent approach. *Tourism Review*, 78(4), 1013–1026. DOI: 10.1108/TR-07-2022-0269

Miyawaki, A., Tabuchi, T., Tomata, Y., & Tsugawa, Y. (2021). Association between participation in the government subsidy programme for domestic travel and symptoms indicative of COVID-19 infection in Japan: Cross-sectional study. *BMJ Open*, 11(4), 49069. DOI: 10.1136/bmjopen-2021-049069 PMID: 33849861

Moges, Y. E., Lajoie, J., & Giebelhausen, M. D. (2023). Effect of digital payment on customer satisfaction in hotel industry: A study in Ethiopia. *Journal of Tourism and Services*, 14(26), 117–136. DOI: 10.29036/jots.v14i26.1771

Mohamad, N., Tan, V., & Tan, P. P. (2022). Travel experience on social media : The impact towards tourist destination choice. [SMRJ]. *Social and Management Research Journal*, 19(2), 21–52. DOI: 10.24191/smrj.v19i2.19253

Mohamed, M. I., & Ameer, A. (2024). Future of artificial intelligence in the tourism industry: A study of the trends and opportunities in the Middle East. *Middle East Journal of Business*, 19(1), 45–58. DOI: 10.5742/MEJB.2024.85296

Mohamed, M. I., & Lamsal, R. B. (2024). AI applications in smart tourism: A systematic review and research agenda. *Tourism Management Perspectives*, 47, 100850. DOI: 10.1016/j.tmp.2023.100850

Mohamed, M., & El-Bakry, H. (2023). Virtual reality in tourism: A potential game changer in promoting cultural heritage sites. *Tourism (Zagreb)*, 71(1), 93–108. DOI: 10.1016/j.tour.2022.03.004

Mohammad, A., Jones, E., Dawood, A. A., & Sayed, H. A. (2012). The impact of the Egyptian political events during 2011 on hotel occupancy in Cairo. *Journal of Tourism Study & Hospitality*, 1(3). Advance online publication. DOI: 10.4172/2324-8807.1000102

Mohammad, B. T., Mushfika, H., & Iva, R. D. (2024). Opportunities of tourism and hospitality education in Bangladesh: Career perspectives. *I-Manager's. Journal of Management*, 18(3), 21. DOI: 10.26634/jmgt.18.3.20385

Mohammed, A. A. (2023). The role of AI in promoting sustainable tourism in Egypt. *Journal of Sustainable Tourism*, 31(1), 19–36.

Moher, D., Liberati, A., Tetzlaff, J., & Altman, D. G.The PRISMA Group. (2009). Preferred Reporting Items for Systematic Reviews and Meta-Analyses : The PRISMA Statement. *PLoS Medicine*, 6(7), e1000097. DOI: 10.1371/journal.pmed.1000097 PMID: 19621072

Morales, J., Cornide-Reyes, H., Rossel, P. O., Sáez, P., & Silva-Aravena, F. (2023, July). Virtual reality, augmented reality, and the metaverse: Customer experience approach and user experience evaluation methods. In *International Conference on Human-Computer Interaction* (pp. 554-566). Cham: Springer Nature. DOI: 10.1007/978-3-031-35915-6_40

Mordor Intelligence. (2023). *Artificial Intelligence in hospitality market - growth, trends, COVID-19 impact, and forecasts (2024-2029)*. https://www.mordorintelligence.com/industry-reports/artificial-intelligence-in-hospitality-market

Mpinganjira, M., & Maduku, D. K. (2019). Ethics of mobile behavioral advertising: Antecedents and outcomes of perceived ethical value of advertised brands. *Journal of Business Research*, 95, 464–478. DOI: 10.1016/j.jbusres.2018.07.037

Mrsic, L., Surla, G., & Balkovic, M. (2020). Technology-Driven Smart Support System for Tourist Destination Management Organizations. In A. Khanna, D. Gupta, S. Bhattacharyya, V. Snasel, J. Platos, & A. E. Hassanien (Éds.), *International Conference on Innovative Computing and Communications* (Vol. 1087, p. 65-76). Springer Singapore. DOI: 10.1007/978-981-15-1286-5_7

Mukherjee, W., & Mookerji, M. (2004). Hospitals busy tying up with hospitality Inc. *The Economic Times*, 6.

Murray, J., & Pinder, D. (2024). Artificial intelligence and sustainable tourism: Opportunities and challenges in Africa. *African Journal of Hospitality, Tourism and Leisure*, 13(1), 10–30. DOI: 10.46222/ajhtl.19770720-66

Murray, K., Chen, C., Kuo, T. C., Chen, Y., & Hu, C. (2023). Blockchain and tourism: A systematic literature review and future research agenda. *Tourism Management Perspectives*, 52, 107–121. DOI: 10.1016/j.tmp.2022.06.013

Nabi, S., Khan, M., & Khan, S. (2023). Security and privacy in smart home environments: A review of contemporary trends and future directions. *Journal of Network and Computer Applications*, 239, 103723. DOI: 10.1016/j.jnca.2023.103723

Nader, Y. (2023). Role of AI in enhancing the travel experience: The case of Egypt. *Journal of Travel Research*, 62(2), 134–150. DOI: 10.1177/00472875211051310

Nasiche, N. (2024). The role of wellness tourism in the growth of the hospitality industry. *Journal of Modern Hospitality*, 3(1), 53–64. DOI: 10.47941/jmh.1954

Naumov, M., & Naumova, E. (2023). AI technologies and their potential in wildlife management. *Ecology and Evolution*, 13(6), e9935.

Nawaz, N., & Ali, M. (2023). Unleashing the potential of AI in tourism management: A comparative analysis of developed and developing countries. *Tourism Review*. Advance online publication. DOI: 10.1108/TR-06-2021-0168

Nechoud, L., Ghidouche, F., & Seraphin, H. (2021). The influence of eWOM credibility on visit intention : An integrative moderated mediation model. *Journal of Tourism* [JTHSM]. *Heritage & Services Marketing*, 7(1), 54–63.

Nedic, A., & Ozdaglar, A. (2009). Distributed subgradient methods for multi-agent optimization. *IEEE Transactions on Automatic Control*, 54(1), 48–61. DOI: 10.1109/TAC.2008.2009515

Neuhofer, B., Buhalis, D., & Ladkin, A. (2014). A Typology of Technology-Enhanced Tourism Experiences. *International Journal of Tourism Research*, 16(4), 340–350. DOI: 10.1002/jtr.1958

Ng, D. T. K. (2022). What is the metaverse? Definitions, technologies, and the community of inquiry. *Australasian Journal of Educational Technology*, 38(4), 190–205. DOI: 10.14742/ajet.7945

Nightingale, E. (2023). The future of the hotel industry: Smart technologies and their implications. *Journal of Hospitality and Tourism Management*, 49, 50–60. DOI: 10.1016/j.jhtm.2023.09.002

Ni, J., Chiu, D. K. W., & Ho, K. K. W. (2022). Information search behavior among Chinese self-drive tourists in the smartphone era. *Information Discovery and Delivery*, 50(3), 285–296. DOI: 10.1108/IDD-05-2020-0054

Nill, A. (2022). Socially responsible marketing: A moving target in need of a normative-ethical doctrine. *Journal of Macromarketing*, 42(4), 583–589. DOI: 10.1177/02761467221099815

Noguerra, C. P.Jr. (2023). Ethical and legal challenges in information system development and implementation. *International Journal of Advanced Research in Science. Tongxin Jishu*, •••, 852–858. DOI: 10.48175/IJARSCT-12383

Nouhaila, B. K., Aarabe, M., & Alla, L. (2024). The Impact of Digitalisation on the Customer Experience in Medical Tourism : A Systematic Review. In *Impact of AI and Tech-Driven Solutions in Hospitality and Tourism* (pp. 408–428). IGI Global., DOI: 10.4018/979-8-3693-6755-1.ch020

Ntem, E., & Cheng, C. (2022). The impact of AI on wildlife conservation: A systematic review. *Biodiversity and Conservation*, 31(5), 1333–1351.

Nunnally, J. C. (1978). An overview of psychological measurement. In McReynolds, P. (Ed.), *Clinical diagnosis of mental disorders* (pp. 97–146). Springer. DOI: 10.1007/978-1-4684-2490-4_4

O'Connor, P. (2020). Data privacy and the travel sector. In *Handbook of e-Tourism* (pp. 1-14).

O'Neil, C. (2016). *Weapons of math destruction: How big data increases inequality and threatens democracy*. Crown Publishing.

Obersteiner, G., Gollnow, S., & Eriksson, M. (2021). Carbon footprint reduction potential of waste management strategies in tourism. *Environmental Development*, 39, 100617. DOI: 10.1016/j.envdev.2021.100617 PMID: 34513580

Odeh, M. (2023). AI in tourism: A comprehensive analysis of its impact on sustainable development in Egypt. *Tourism and Hospitality Research*, 23(1), 40–54. DOI: 10.1177/14673584211061773

Ofcom. (2021, July 12). Video-sharing platform guidance: Guidance for providers on advertising harms and measures. Retrieved September 20, 2024, from https://www.ofcom.org.uk/siteassets/resources/documents/consultations/category-1-10-weeks/219750-proposals-for-the-regulation-of-advertising-on-video-sharing-platforms-/associated-documents/vsp-guidance-harms-and-measures.pdf?v=327263

Ohe, Y. (2022). Rural tourism under the new normal: New potentials from a Japanese perspective. *WIT Transactions on Ecology and the Environment*, 256, 51–62. DOI: 10.2495/ST220051

Oh, H., Fiore, A. M., & Jeoung, M. (2007). Measuring experience economy concepts: Tourism applications. *Journal of Travel Research*, 46(2), 119–132. DOI: 10.1177/0047287507304039

Oh, H., Kim, Y., & Morrison, A. M. (2007). The roles of emotions in current consumption experiences and future consumption intentions. *Journal of Business Research*, 60(9), 462–469. DOI: 10.1016/j.jbusres.2007.01.014

Oliha, J. S., Biu, P. W., & Obi, O. C.Johnson Sunday OlihaPreye Winston BiuOgagua Chimezie Obi. (2024). Securing the smart city: A review of cybersecurity challenges and strategies. *Engineering Science & Technology Journal*, 5(2), 496–506. DOI: 10.51594/estj.v5i2.827

Oliveira, T., Araujo, B., & Tam, C. (2020). Why do people share their travel experiences on social media? *Tourism Management*, 78, 104041. DOI: 10.1016/j.tourman.2019.104041 PMID: 32322615

Olorunsola, V. O. (2020). *Green practices: The experiences of guests in eco-centric hotels in the UK* (Master's thesis, Eastern Mediterranean University).

Om, S. (2023). The role of artificial intelligence in the hospitality industry. In P. Jena & B. Singh (Eds.), *Artificial Intelligence and the Future of Tourism and Hospitality* (pp. 37–57). Springer International Publishing. https://doi.org/DOI: 10.1007/978-3-031-37614-3_3

Oncioiu, I., & Priescu, I. (2022). The Use of Virtual Reality in Tourism Destinations as a Tool to Develop Tourist Behavior Perspective. *Sustainability (Basel)*, 14(7), 4191. DOI: 10.3390/su14074191

Ordóñez, M. D., Gómez, A., Ruiz, M., Ortells, J. M., Niemi-Hugaerts, H., Juiz, C., Jara, A., & Butler, T. A. (2022). IoT technologies and applications in tourism and travel industries. In *Internet of Things–The call of the edge* (pp. 341–360). River publishers., https://www.taylorfrancis.com/chapters/oa-edit/10.1201/9781003338611-8/iot-technologies-applications-tourism-travel-industries-dolores-ord%C3%B3%C3%B1ez-andrea-g%C3%B3mez-maurici-ruiz-juan-manuel-ortells-hanna-niemi-hugaerts-carlos-juiz-antonio-jara-tayrne-alexandra-butler DOI: 10.1201/9781003338611-8

Oropeza, S. A., Chinchilla, E. R., & Ordoñez, L. M. (2022). Artificial intelligence and sustainable urban development: A systematic literature review. *Sustainable Cities and Society*, 83, 103886.

Orr, M., Poitras, E., & Butcher, K. (2021). Informal learning with extended reality environments: Current trends in museums, heritage and tourism. In Geroimenko, V. (Ed.), *Augmented reality in tourism, museums and heritage: A new technology to inform and entertain* (pp. 67–90). Springer., DOI: 10.1007/978-3-030-70198-7_1

Osman, A. R., Nasha, E. H., & Al-Khouri, A. (2023). The role of artificial intelligence in enhancing tourist experience: A case study of Egypt. *Journal of Destination Marketing & Management*, 24, 100722. DOI: 10.1016/j.jdmm.2023.100722

Ospital, P., Masson, D., Beler, C., & Legardeur, J. (2023). Toward product transparency: Communicating traceability information to consumers. *International Journal of Fashion Design, Technology and Education*, 16(2), 186–197. DOI: 10.1080/17543266.2022.2142677

Ostrowska-Tryzno, A., & Pawlikowska-Piechotka, A. (2022). Tourism, the hotel industry at the time of the COVID-19 pandemic. *Sport i Turystyka. Środkowoeuropejskie Czasopismo Naukowe*, 5(2), 139–152. https://doi.org/DOI: 10.16926/sit.2022.02.08

Otoo, F. E., Kim, S., Agrusa, J., & Lema, J. (2021). Classification of senior tourists according to personality traits. *Asia Pacific Journal of Tourism Research*, 26(5), 539–556. DOI: 10.1080/10941665.2021.1876118

Özdemir Uçgun, G., & Şahin, S. Z. (2024). How does Metaverse affect the tourism industry? Current practices and future forecasts. *Current Issues in Tourism*, 27(17), 2742–2756. DOI: 10.1080/13683500.2023.2238111

Page, M. J., McKenzie, J. E., Bossuyt, P. M., Boutron, I., Hoffmann, T. C., Mulrow, C. D., Shamseer, L., Tetzlaff, J. M., Akl, E. A., & Brennan, S. E. (2021). The PRISMA 2020 statement : An updated guideline for reporting systematic reviews. *BMJ (Clinical Research Ed.)*, 372, •••. https://www.bmj.com/content/372/bmj.n71.short PMID: 33782057

Page, S. J., & Connell, J. (2020). Tourism and entrepreneurship. In *Tourism* (pp. 262–279). Routledge., https://www.taylorfrancis.com/chapters/edit/10.4324/9781003005520-15/tourism-entrepreneurship-stephen-page-joanne-connell DOI: 10.4324/9781003005520-15

Pai, C.-K., Liu, Y., Kang, S., & Dai, A. (2020). The Role of Perceived Smart Tourism Technology Experience for Tourist Satisfaction, Happiness and Revisit Intention. *Sustainability (Basel)*, 12(16), 16. Advance online publication. DOI: 10.3390/su12166592

Painter, M., Hibbert, S., & Cooper, T. (2019). The development of responsible and sustainable business practice: Value, mind-sets, business models. *Journal of Business Ethics*, 157(4), 885–891. DOI: 10.1007/s10551-018-3958-3

Palhares, G. L. (2002). *Transportes Turísticos*.

Pallud, J., & Straub, D. W. (2014). Effective website design for experience-influenced environments: The case of high culture museums. *Information & Management*, 51(3), 359–373. DOI: 10.1016/j.im.2014.02.010

Palumbo, F. (2015). Developing a new service for the digital traveler satisfaction : The Smart Tourist App. *The International Journal of Digital Accounting Research*, 15, •••. https://core.ac.uk/download/pdf/60666233.pdf. DOI: 10.4192/1577-8517-15_2

Papista, E., & Krystallis, A. (2013). Investigating the types of value and cost of green brands: Proposition of a conceptual framework. *Journal of Business Ethics*, 115(1), 75–92. DOI: 10.1007/s10551-012-1367-6

Parasuraman, A. (2000). Technology Readiness Index (TRI): A multiple-item scale to measure readiness to embrace new technologies. *Journal of Service Research*, 2(4), 307–320. DOI: 10.1177/109467050024001

Parker, E. (2024). Digital marketing in tourism: New directions and challenges in the era of artificial intelligence. In *Innovations in digital marketing: A global perspective* (pp. 1–15). IGI Global., DOI: 10.4018/978-1-7998-7674-7.ch001

Parker, E., & Saker, M. (2020). Art museums and the incorporation of virtual reality: Examining the impact of VR on spatial and social norms. *Convergence (London)*, 26(5–6), 1159–1173. DOI: 10.1177/1354856519897251

Pasaco-González, B. S., Campón-Cerro, A. M., Moreno-Lobato, A., & Sánchez-Vargas, E. (2023). The Role of Demographics and Previous Experience in Tourists' Experiential Perceptions. *Sustainability (Basel)*, 15(4), 3768. DOI: 10.3390/su15043768

Patton, M. Q. (2014). *Qualitative research & evaluation methods: Integrating theory and practice.* Sage publications. https://www.google.com/books?hl=pt-PT&lr=&id=ovAkBQAAQBAJ&oi=fnd&pg=PP1&dq=Patton,+M.+Q.+(2015).+Qualitative+Research+%26+Evaluation+Methods.+SAGE+Publications.&ots=ZSY-6svBH2&sig=DMS3wgSBqe4wAF2g2J2m-lcIoSU

Pawlik, L., Wroblewska, A., Kaczmarek, A., & Kaczmarek, P. (2024). Digital transformation and consumer behavior in the hospitality industry: Implications for managers. *Journal of Business Research*, 171, 353–362. DOI: 10.1016/j.jbusres.2023.12.045

Pencarelli, T. (2020). The digital revolution in the travel and tourism industry. *Information Technology & Tourism*, 22(3), 455–476. DOI: 10.1007/s40558-019-00160-3

Peters, G., Rauschenbach, T., & Rojas, R. (2022). AI-based approaches to biodiversity monitoring: Recent advances and future directions. *Frontiers in Ecology and the Environment*, 20(8), 490–499.

Petrick, J. F. (1999). *An examination of the relationships between golf travelers' satisfaction, perceived value and loyalty and their intentions to revisit* (Doctoral dissertation, Clemson University).

Petrick, J. F., Morais, D. D., & Norman, W. C. (2001). An examination of the determinants of entertainment vacationers' intentions to revisit. *Journal of Travel Research*, 40(1), 41–48. DOI: 10.1177/004728750104000106

Petrov, P. V., & Kovalchuk, N. I. (2023). The role of machine learning and big data in promoting cultural heritage: Opportunities and challenges for the tourism industry. *Journal of Tourism Research*, 31(1), 30–45. DOI: 10.1016/j.jtr.2022.07.008

Pettersen-Sobczyk, M. (2023). Social media influencer marketing in the promotion of tourist destinations. *Tourism Management*, 42, 31–45.

Pham, L., Williamson, S., Lane, P., Limbu, Y., Nguyen, P. T. H., & Coomer, T. (2020). Technology readiness and purchase intention: Role of perceived value and online satisfaction in the context of luxury hotels. *International Journal of Management and Decision Making*, 19(1), 91–117. DOI: 10.1504/IJMDM.2020.104208

Piga, C., & Melis, G. (2021). Identifying and measuring the impact of cultural events on hotels' performance. *International Journal of Contemporary Hospitality Management*, 33(4), 1194–1209. DOI: 10.1108/IJCHM-07-2020-0749

Pillai, R., & Sivathanu, B. (2020). Adoption of AI-based chatbots for hospitality and tourism. *International Journal of Contemporary Hospitality Management*, 32(10), 3199–3226. DOI: 10.1108/IJCHM-04-2020-0259

Pine, B. J., & Gilmore, J. H. (1998). The experience economy. *Harvard Business Review*, 76(6), 18–23. PMID: 10181589

Pine, B. J., Pine, J., & Gilmore, J. H. (1999). *The experience economy: Work is theatre & every business a stage*. Harvard Business Press.

Pittman, M., Oeldorf-Hirsch, A., & Brannan, A. (2022). Green advertising on social media: Brand authenticity mediates the effect of different appeals on purchase intent and digital engagement. *Journal of Current Issues and Research in Advertising*, 43(1), 106–121. DOI: 10.1080/10641734.2021.1964655

Pöhler, L., & Teuteberg, F. (2023). Suitability-and utilization-based cost–benefit analysis: A techno-economic feasibility study of virtual reality for workplace and process design. *Information Systems and e-Business Management*, •••, 1–41. DOI: 10.1007/s10257-023-00622-0

Polat, E., Çelik, F., Ibrahim, B., & Gursoy, D. (2024). Past, present, and future scene of influencer marketing in hospitality and tourism management. *Journal of Travel & Tourism Marketing*, 41(3), 322–343. DOI: 10.1080/10548408.2024.2317741

Polishchuk, E., Bujdosó, Z., El Archi, Y., Benbba, B., Zhu, K., & Dávid, L. D. (2023). The theoretical background of virtual reality and its implications for the tourism industry. *Sustainability (Basel)*, 15(13), 10534. DOI: 10.3390/su151310534

Pons, J., & Munoz, A. (2024). Smart tourism and AI: Future directions and implications for heritage management. *International Journal of Tourism Research*. Advance online publication. DOI: 10.1002/jtr.2570

Poot, T., & Huijbregts, H. (2023). Enhancing the visitor experience in cultural heritage: A model of smart technologies in tourism. *International Journal of Culture, Tourism and Hospitality Research*, 17(2), 198–215. DOI: 10.1108/IJCTHR-01-2023-0004

Pop, R.-A., Săplăcan, Z., Dabija, D.-C., & Alt, M.-A. (2022). The impact of social media influencers on travel decisions: The role of trust in consumer decision journey. *Current Issues in Tourism*, 25(5), 823–843. DOI: 10.1080/13683500.2021.1895729

Popșa, R. E. (2024). Exploring the Generation Z travel trends and behavior. *Studies in Business and Economics*, 19(1), 189–189. DOI: 10.2478/sbe-2024-0010

Pradhan, M. K., Oh, J., & Lee, H. (2018). Understanding travelers' behavior for sustainable smart tourism : A technology readiness perspective. *Sustainability (Basel)*, 10(11), 4259. DOI: 10.3390/su10114259

Prelipcean, M., Acatrinei, C., Gradinescu, I., & Cânda, A. (2023). The impact of blockchain technology on marketing through social media. *Journal of Emerging Trends in Marketing and Management*, 1, 46–54.

Pritchard, M. P., & Howard, D. R. (1997). The loyal traveler: Examining a typology of service patronage. *Journal of Travel Research*, 35(4), 2–10. DOI: 10.1177/004728759703500401

Pugh, M., & Robinson, R. (2024). The impact of mobile payment systems on hotel guest experiences: Evidence from the UK hospitality sector. *Tourism Management Perspectives*, 51, 145–153. DOI: 10.1016/j.tmp.2024.03.004

Qiu, B. (2020). The legal liabilities in advertising endorsements and influencer marketing. *Research on China Market Regulation*, 5, 26–29.

Quesnel, D., & Riecke, B. E. (2018). Are You Awed Yet? How Virtual Reality Gives Us Awe and Goose Bumps. *Frontiers in Psychology*, 9, 2158. DOI: 10.3389/fpsyg.2018.02158 PMID: 30473673

Rabahy, W. A. (2020). Análise e perspectivas do turismo no Brasil. *Revista Brasileira de Pesquisa em Turismo*, 14(1), 1–13. Advance online publication. DOI: 10.7784/rbtur.v14i1.1903

Rachmad, Y. E. (2024). *The future of influencer marketing: Evolution of consumer behavior in the digital world. PT*. Sonpedia Publishing Indonesia.

Radder, L., & Han, X. (2015). An examination of the museum experience based on Pine and Gilmore's experience economy realms. *Journal of Applied Business Research*, 31(2), 455–470. DOI: 10.19030/jabr.v31i2.9129

Raev, G. (2023). The future of tourism in Egypt: Trends and opportunities in AI. *International Journal of Tourism Research*, 25(3), 407–420. DOI: 10.1002/jtr.2638

Ragas, M. W., & Roberts, M. S. (2009). Communicating corporate social responsibility and brand sincerity: A case study of Chipotle Mexican Grill's "Food with Integrity" program. *International Journal of Strategic Communication*, 3(4), 264–280. DOI: 10.1080/15531180903218697

Rahimizhian, S., Ozturen, A., & Ilkan, M. (2020). Emerging realm of 360-degree technology to promote tourism destination. *Technology in Society*, 63, 101411. DOI: 10.1016/j.techsoc.2020.101411

Ramli, A. (2024). China shines as Malaysians' top holiday destination. *Travel Weekly Asia*. Retrieved May 31, 2024, from https://www.travelweekly-asia.com/Travel-News/Trade-Shows-and-Events/China-shines-as-Malaysians-top-holiday-destination

Ratna, S., Saide, S., Putri, A. M., Indrajit, R. E., & Muwardi, D. (2024). Digital transformation in tourism and hospitality industry: A literature review of blockchain, financial technology, and knowledge management. *EuroMed Journal of Business*, 19(1), 84–112. DOI: 10.1108/EMJB-04-2023-0118

Raun, J., Shoval, N., & Tiru, M. (2020). Gateways for intra-national tourism flows: Measured using two types of tracking technologies. *International Journal of Tourism Cities*, 6(2), 261–278. DOI: 10.1108/IJTC-08-2019-0123

Reddy, S., & Qadeer, I. (2010). Medical tourism in India: Progress and predicament. *Economic and Political Weekly*, XLV(20), 1–7.

Reyes, F. A., Ahrens, D., & Amiri, A. (2023). The role of AI in sustainable tourism practices: A global perspective. *Tourism Management*, 98, 104572.

Rios, M. V., Levino, N. de A., & Finger, A. B. (2021). Atividades características da cadeia do turismo: Uma revisão sistemática da literatura. *Revista Turismo em Análise*, 32(2), 2. Advance online publication. DOI: 10.11606/issn.1984-4867.v32i2p344-366

Ritchie, J. R. B., & Crouch, G. I. (2000). The competitive destination: A sustainable perspective. *Tourism Management*, 21(1), 1–7. DOI: 10.1016/S0261-5177(99)00080-1

Rivera-López, F. B. (2023). Analysis of the impact of the COVID-19 pandemic on hotel occupancy in the main tourist destinations in Mexico. *Revista de Desarrollo Económico*, 1–7. https://doi.org/DOI: 10.35429/JED.2023.30.10.1.7

Rizky, R. M., Kusdi, R., & Yusri, A. (2017). The impact of e-WOM on destination image, attitude toward destination and travel intention. *Russian Journal of Agricultural and Socio-Economic Sciences*, 61(1), 26–32. DOI: 10.18551/rjoas.2017-01.04

Rockström, J., Steffen, W., Noone, K., Persson, A., Chapin, F. S.III, Lambin, E. F., Lenton, T. M., Scheffer, M., Folke, C., Schellnhuber, H. J., Nykvist, B., de Wit, C. A., Hughes, T., van der Leeuw, S., Rodhe, H., Sörlin, S., Snyder, P. K., Costanza, R., Svedin, U., & Foley, J. A. (2009). A safe operating space for humanity. *Nature*, 461(7263), 472–475. DOI: 10.1038/461472a PMID: 19779433

Roopchund, R. (2020). Mauritius as a Smart Tourism Destination : Technology for Enhancing Tourism Experience. In Pati, B., Panigrahi, C. R., Buyya, R., & Li, K.-C. (Eds.), *Advanced Computing and Intelligent Engineering* (Vol. 1089, pp. 519–535). Springer Singapore., DOI: 10.1007/978-981-15-1483-8_44

Rovolis, G., & Habibipour, A. (2024). When participatory design meets data-driven decision making: A literature review and the way forward. *Management Science Letters*, 14(2), 107–126. DOI: 10.5267/j.msl.2023.9.002

Roy, B. K., & Pagaldiviti, S. R. (2023). Advancements in arena technology : Enhancing customer experience and employee adaptation in the tourism and hospitality industry. *Smart Tourism*, 4(1), 2330. DOI: 10.54517/st.v4i2.2330

Rusli, M., Spector, D., Macmillan, E. M., & Rusli, A. (2014). TPG-led group closes $450 million investment in Airbnb. *The Wall Street Journal*.

Sagayama, H., Shizuma, K., Toguchi, M., Mizuhara, H., Machida, Y., Yamada, Y., Ebine, N., Higaki, Y., & Tanaka, H. (2018). Effect of the health tourism weight loss programme on body composition and health outcomes in healthy and excess-weight adults. *British Journal of Nutrition*, 119(10), 1133–1141. DOI: 10.1017/S0007114518000582 PMID: 29759101

Sainaghi, R., Abrate, G., & Mauri, A. (2021). Price and RevPAR determinants of Airbnb listings: Convergent and divergent evidence. *International Journal of Hospitality Management*, 92, 102709. DOI: 10.1016/j.ijhm.2020.102709

Sakawa, H., & Watanabel, N. (2022). Impact of the COVID-19 outbreak on stock market returns: Evidence from Japanese-listed tourism firms. *Applied Economics*, 54(46), 5373–5377. DOI: 10.1080/00036846.2022.2044996

Sakson, A. (2024). *Digital technologies in cultural heritage: The future of tourism*. Springer.

Samson, R. (2023). *Augmented reality in the travel industry: A guide to best practices*. Routledge.

San-Martín, S., Prodanova, J., & Jiménez, N. (2015). The impact of age in the generation of satisfaction and WOM in mobile shopping. *Journal of Retailing and Consumer Services*, 23, 1–8. DOI: 10.1016/j.jretconser.2014.11.001

Santos, C., & Costa, D. (2022). Turismo no Brasil: Estratégias e contribuições para economia brasileira. *E-Acadêmica*, 3(3), e5433350. DOI: 10.52076/eacad-v3i3.350

Santos, J. R., Gonçalves, R. F., & Gonçalves, M. C. (2023). Consumer perceptions of sustainability in hotels: A study in Portugal. *Sustainability*, 15(2), 928. DOI: 10.3390/su15020928

Santos, J., & Freitas, A. (2022). The impact of the metaverse on tourism and hospitality: A new era of digital experiences. *Journal of Tourism and Hospitality Management*, 10(2), 45–56. DOI: 10.20868/jthm.2022.10.2.45

Sari, Y. K. (2024). Gone or go on? The existence of hybrid events as urban tourism strategy. *Tourisma: Jurnal Pariwisata*, 5(2), 172. DOI: 10.22146/gamajts.v5i2.95005

Saunders, H. D. (1992). The Khazzoom-Brookes postulate and neoclassical growth. *The Energy Journal (Cambridge, Mass.)*, 13(4), 131–179. DOI: 10.5547/ISSN0195-6574-EJ-Vol13-No4-7

Savic, D. (2023). Exploring the integration of AI in enhancing user experiences in tourism: A case study from Egypt. *Tourism Management Perspectives*, 51, 124–136. DOI: 10.1016/j.tmp.2024.100862

Scelza, R. (2023). Smart cities: A technological approach to urban challenges. *Technological Forecasting and Social Change*, 189, 123284. DOI: 10.1016/j.techfore.2023.123284

Schiaffino, S., & Amandi, A. (2009). Building an expert travel agent as a software agent. *Expert Systems with Applications*, 36(2), 1291–1299. DOI: 10.1016/j.eswa.2007.11.032

Schmitt, B. (2010). Experience marketing: Concepts, frameworks and consumer insights. *Foundations and Trends in Marketing*, 5(2), 55–112. DOI: 10.1561/1700000027

Schöbel, S. M., & Leimeister, J. M. (2023). Metaverse platform ecosystems. *Electronic Markets*, 33(1), 12–25. DOI: 10.1007/s12525-023-00623-w

Schouten, A. P., Janssen, L., & Verspaget, M. (2021). Celebrity vs. influencer endorsements in advertising: The role of identification, credibility, and product-endorser fit. In Geuens, M., De Pelsmacker, P., & Van den Bergh, K. (Eds.), *Leveraged marketing communications* (pp. 208–231). Routledge. DOI: 10.4324/9781003155249-12

Schuman, S. J., & Rojas, R. (2023). Machine learning and big data for wildlife conservation: Current trends and future directions. *The Journal of Wildlife Management*, 87(5), 847–860.

Schwartz, S. H. (2012). An Overview of the Schwartz Theory of Basic Values. *Online Readings in Psychology and Culture*, 2(1). Advance online publication. DOI: 10.9707/2307-0919.1116

Schwepker, C. H. Jr. (2019). Strengthening customer value development and ethical intent in the salesforce: The influence of ethical values person–organization fit and trust in manager. *Journal of Business Ethics*, 159(3), 913–925. DOI: 10.1007/s10551-018-3851-0

Scott, N., & Jun, G. G. J., & Ma JianYu, M. J. (Éds.). (2017). *Visitor experience design*. CABI. DOI: 10.1079/9781786391896.0000

Seddighi, H. R., & Theocharous, A. L. (2002). A model of tourism destination choice: A theoretical and empirical analysis. *Tourism Management*, 23(5), 475–487. DOI: 10.1016/S0261-5177(02)00012-2

Sen, A., & Sinha, A. P. (2011). IT alignment strategies for customer relationship management. *Decision Support Systems*, 51(3), 609–619. DOI: 10.1016/j.dss.2010.12.014

Sendhil, R., C R, B., Yadav, S., G, G., Ragupathy, R., A, P., & Ramasundaram, P. (2024). Consumer perception and preference toward plant-based meat alternatives – Bibliometric trends and policy implications. *Food and Humanity*, 2, 100229. DOI: 10.1016/j.foohum.2024.100229

Sertkan, M., Neidhardt, J., & Werthner, H. (2018). What is the "Personality" of a tourism destination? *Information Technology & Tourism*, 21(1), 105–133. DOI: 10.1007/s40558-018-0135-6

Setiawan, P. Y., Troena, E. A., & Armanu, N. (2014). The effect of e-WOM on destination image, satisfaction and loyalty. *International Journal of Business and Management Invention*, 3(1), 22–29.

SETUR. (2017). *Evolução recente do turismo no Ceará 2006/16*. https://www.setur.ce.gov.br/wp-content/uploads/sites/59/2016/11/evolucao-turismo-2006-2016-artigo.pdf

Seyfang, G., & Haxeltine, A. (2022). *Green growth and sustainable prosperity: Disentangling the contradictions*. Cambridge University Press.

Sgoura, A., Kontis, A. P., & Stergiou, D. (2024). Views and motivations of members of dance groups during their participation in traditional dance tourist events. In Kavoura, A., Borges-Tiago, T., & Tiago, F. (Eds.), *Strategic Innovative Marketing and Tourism* (pp. 441–447). Springer Nature Switzerland., DOI: 10.1007/978-3-031-51038-0_48

Shah, P., & Rahman, M. (2024). The impact of artificial intelligence on the hospitality industry: Current trends and future perspectives. *International Journal of Hospitality Management*, 40, 14–28. DOI: 10.1016/j.ijhm.2023.104172

Sharma, A., Sharma, A., & Tiwari, S. (2012). Medical tourism: Building the India brand abroad: An analytical study of potential of medical tourism in Gurgaon. *International Journal of Business and Management Invention*, 1(12), 1–6.

Shin, K., Lee, Y., & Lee, H. (2024). AI for wildlife protection: A survey of current applications and future trends. *Wildlife Biology*, 2024(1), 1–13.

Shore, J. H., Schneck, C. D., & Mishkind, M. C. (2020). Telepsychiatry and the coronavirus disease 2019 pandemic—Current and future outcomes of the rapid virtualization of psychiatric care. *JAMA Psychiatry*, 77(12), 1211–1212. DOI: 10.1001/jamapsychiatry.2020.1643 PMID: 32391861

Sianturi, C. M., Pasaribu, V. A. R., Pasaribu, R. M., & Simanjuntak, J. (2022). The impact of social media marketing on purchase intention. *SULTANIST: Jurnal Manajemen dan Keuangan*, 10(1), 60–68. https://doi.org/DOI: 10.37403/sultanist.v10i1.425

Sicilia, M., & López, M. (2023). What do we know about influencers on social media? Toward a new conceptualization and classification of influencers. In *The Palgrave handbook of interactive marketing* (pp. 593–622). Springer., DOI: 10.1007/978-3-031-14961-0_26

Sidani, S. (2024). Implementing AI and big data analytics in tourism: A strategic approach for sustainable development. *Journal of Business Research*, 144, 1–15. DOI: 10.1016/j.jbusres.2022.06.019

Silva, J. S. de S. e. (2009). *A visão holística do turismo e a sua modelação* [doctoralThesis, Universidade de Aveiro]. https://ria.ua.pt/handle/10773/1853

Singh, J. J., Iglesias, O., & Batista-Foguet, J. M. (2012). Does having an ethical brand matter? The influence of consumer perceived ethicality on trust, affect, and loyalty. *Journal of Business Ethics*, 111(4), 541–549. DOI: 10.1007/s10551-012-1216-7

Singh, L. (2014). An evaluation of medical tourism in India. *African Journal of Hospitality, Tourism and Leisure*, 3(1), 1–11.

Singh, N., & Lee, M. J. (2009). Exploring perceptions toward education in 3-D virtual environments: An introduction to "Second Life.". *Journal of Teaching in Travel & Tourism*, 8(4), 315–327. DOI: 10.1080/15313220903047896

Siqueira, M. C. (2008). *Critérios para preparação de aeroportos para operar como hub*. DOI: 10.26512/2008.06.TCC.1606

Soloman, H. (2011). Affective journeys: The emotional structuring of medical tourism in India. *Anthropology & Medicine*, 18(1), 105–118. DOI: 10.1080/13648470.2010.525878 PMID: 21563006

Solomon, M. R. (2020). *Consumer behaviour: Buying, having and being* (13th ed.). Pearson.

Somany, N. (2023). Greenwashing in business: Examining the impact of deceptive environmental claims on consumer behavior and corporate accountability. *International Journal of Social Science and Economic Research*, 08(04), 908–920. DOI: 10.46609/IJSSER.2023.v08i04.024

Song, H. J., Lee, C. K., Park, J. A., Hwang, Y. H., & Reisinger, Y. (2015). The influence of tourist experience on perceived value and satisfaction with temple stays: The experience economy theory. *Journal of Travel & Tourism Marketing*, 32(4), 401–415. DOI: 10.1080/10548408.2014.898606

Song, Y. (2020). Business model and legal regulation of live broadcast for goods promotion. *Research on China Market Regulation*, 8, 9–16.

Soutelido, A. L. D. (2006). *Desmistificando o sistema Hub-and-Spoke*. https://docplayer.com.br/5502890-Desmistificando-sistema-hub-and-spoke.html

Statista. (2021). Social media & user-generated content. Retrieved from https://www.statista.com/statistics/278414/number-of-worldwide-social-network-users/

Statista. (2024). Total travel and tourism spending worldwide from 2019 to 2023, by type. https://www.statista.com/statistics/298060/contribution-of-travel-and-tourism-to-the-global-economy-by-type-of-spending/

Steils, N., Martin, A., & Toti, J.-F. (2022). Managing the transparency paradox of social-media influencer disclosures. *Journal of Advertising Research*, 62(2), 148–166. DOI: 10.2501/JAR-2022-008

Steitz, C., & Hall, J. (2020). The impact of conventions on hotel demand: Evidence from Indianapolis using daily hotel occupancy data. *Journal of Risk and Financial Management*, 13(10), 229. DOI: 10.3390/jrfm13100229

Stevens, B. F. (1992). Price value perceptions of travelers. *Journal of Travel Research*, 31(2), 44–48. DOI: 10.1177/004728759203100208

Sthapit, S., & Coudounaris, C. (2017). Memorable tourism experiences and critical outcomes among nature-based visitors: A fuzzy-set qualitative comparative analysis approach. *Journal of Sustainable Tourism*, 25(11), 1729–1748. DOI: 10.1080/09669582.2016.1251986

Stoldt, R., Wellman, M., Ekdale, B., & Tully, M. (2019). Professionalizing and profiting: The rise of intermediaries in the social media influencer industry. *Social Media + Society*, 5(1), 2056305119832587. Advance online publication. DOI: 10.1177/2056305119832587

Suardana, W., Baharuddin, A., & Suni, M. (2021). The effect of room price on occupancy at Kenari Hotel. *Jurnal Ad'ministrare*, 8(2), 409. DOI: 10.26858/ja.v8i1.24534

Subawa, N. S., Yanti, N. K. W., Mimaki, C. A., Utami, M. S. M., & Prabarini, N. S. D. (2024). Exploring tourist behavior towards Bali wellness tourism visits. *International Journal of Innovation and Scientific Research*, 11(4), 705–730. DOI: 10.51244/IJRSI.2024.1104051

Sun, J., Sarfraz, M., Khawaja, K. F., Ozturk, I., & Raza, M. A. (2022). The perils of the pandemic for the tourism and hospitality industries: Envisaging the combined effect of COVID-19 fear and job insecurity on employees' job performance in Pakistan. *Psychology Research and Behavior Management*, 15, 1325–1346. DOI: 10.2147/PRBM.S365972 PMID: 35642192

Sun, M., Tian, Y., Zhang, Y., Nadeem, M., & Xu, C. (2021). Environmental Impact and External Costs Associated with Hub-and-Spoke Network in Air Transport. *Sustainability (Basel)*, 13(2), 2. Advance online publication. DOI: 10.3390/su13020465

Sürme, M., & Atılgan, E. (2020). Sanal müzede sanal tur yapan bireylerin memnuniyet düzeylerini belirlemeye yönelik bir araştırma. *Türk Turizm Araştırmaları Dergisi*, 4(3), 1794–1805. DOI: 10.26677/TR1010.2020.451

Sustacha, I., Baños-Pino, J. F., & Del Valle, E. (2023). The role of technology in enhancing the tourism experience in smart destinations: A meta-analysis. *Journal of Destination Marketing & Management*, 30, 100817. DOI: 10.1016/j.jdmm.2023.100817

Sweeney, J., Payne, A., Frow, P., & Liu, D. (2020). Customer advocacy: A distinctive form of word of mouth. *Journal of Service Research*, 23(2), 139–155. DOI: 10.1177/1094670519900541

Sylaiou, S., Mania, K., Karoulis, A., & White, M. (2010). Exploring the relationship between presence and enjoyment in a virtual museum. *International Journal of Human-Computer Studies*, 68(5), 243–253. DOI: 10.1016/j.ijhcs.2009.11.002

Sylaiou, S., Mania, K., Paliokas, I., Pujol-Tost, L., Killintzis, V., & Liarokapis, F. (2017). Exploring the educational impact of diverse technologies in online virtual museums. *International Journal of Arts and Technology*, 10(1), 58–84. DOI: 10.1504/IJART.2017.083907

Talukder, M. B., Kumar, S., Kaiser, F., & Mia, Md. N. (2024). Pilgrimage creative tourism: A gateway to sustainable development goals in Bangladesh. In M. Hamdan, M. Anshari, N. Ahmad, & E. Ali (Eds.), *Advances in public policy and administration* (pp. 285–300). IGI Global. https://doi.org/DOI: 10.4018/979-8-3693-1742-6.ch016

Talukder, M. B. (2020). The future of culinary tourism: An emerging dimension for the tourism industry of Bangladesh. *I-Manager's. Journal of Management*, 15(1), 27. DOI: 10.26634/jmgt.15.1.17181

Talukder, M. B. (2021). An assessment of the roles of the social network in the development of the tourism industry in Bangladesh. *International Journal of Business, Law, and Education*, 2(3), 85–93. DOI: 10.56442/ijble.v2i3.21

Talukder, M. B. (2024). Implementing artificial intelligence and virtual experiences in hospitality. In Manohar, S., Mittal, A., Raju, S., & Nair, A. J. (Eds.), *Advances in hospitality, tourism, and the services industry* (pp. 145–160). IGI Global., DOI: 10.4018/979-8-3693-2019-8.ch009

Talukder, M. B., Kumar, S., & Das, I. R. (2024). Perspectives of digital marketing for the restaurant industry. In Erol, G., & Kuyucu, M. (Eds.), (pp. 118–134). Advances in media, entertainment, and the arts. IGI Global., DOI: 10.4018/979-8-3693-0855-4.ch009

Talukder, M. B., Kumar, S., Sood, K., & Grima, S. (2023). Information technology, food service quality and restaurant revisit intention. *International Journal of Sustainable Development and Planning*, 18(1), 295–303. DOI: 10.18280/ijsdp.180131

Talukder, M. B., & Muhsina, K. (2024). Prospect of smart tourism destination in Bangladesh. In Correia, R., Martins, M., & Fontes, R. (Eds.), *AI innovations for travel and tourism* (pp. 163–179). IGI Global., DOI: 10.4018/979-8-3693-2137-9.ch009

Tam, Y. S., & Wong, C. W. Y. (2023). Implementing smart technologies in heritage tourism: A study of Chinese tourist attractions. *Journal of Tourism and Cultural Change*, 22(1), 64–79. DOI: 10.1080/14766825.2022.2151538

Tang, R. (2023). Can digital economy improve tourism economic resilience? Evidence from China. *Tourism Economics*. Advance online publication. DOI: 10.1177/13548166231206241

Tanveer, M., Ahmad, A.-R., Mahmood, H., & Haq, I. U. (2021a). Role of ethical marketing in driving consumer brand relationships and brand loyalty: A sustainable marketing approach. *Sustainability (Basel)*, 13(12), 6839. DOI: 10.3390/su13126839

Tan, W.-K. (2020). Destination selection : Influence of tourists' personality on perceived travel constraints. *Journal of Vacation Marketing*, 26(4), 442–456. DOI: 10.1177/1356766720942556

Tan, W.-K., & Tang, C.-Y. (2013). Does personality predict tourism information search and feedback behaviour? *Current Issues in Tourism*, 16(4), 388–406. DOI: 10.1080/13683500.2013.766155

Tapanainen, T., Dao, T. K., & Nguyen, T. T. H. (2021). Impacts of online word-of-mouth and personalities on intention to choose a destination. *Computers in Human Behavior*, 116, 106656. DOI: 10.1016/j.chb.2020.106656

Tchamyou, V. S., & Niyonzima, M. (2023). Artificial intelligence and environmental sustainability in Africa: Opportunities and challenges. *African Journal of Science, Technology, Innovation and Development*, 15(3), 255–268.

Tešin, A., Kovačić, S., & Obradović, S. (2023). The experience I will remember : The role of tourist personality, motivation, and destination personality. *Journal of Vacation Marketing*, 13567667231164768. Advance online publication. DOI: 10.1177/13567667231164768

The Star. (2024a, June 8). Fan Bingbing's appointment as tourism ambassador to draw international tourists, says Melaka CM. Retrieved July 15, 2024, from https://www.thestar.com.my/news/nation/2024/06/08/fan-bingbing039s-appointment-as-tourism-ambassador-to-draw-international-tourists-says-melaka-cm

The Star. (2024b, April 2). Tourism Malaysia eyes five million Chinese tourists. Retrieved May 31, 2024, from https://www.thestar.com.my/news/nation/2024/04/02/tourism-malaysia-eyes-five-million-chinese-tourists

The White Moose Café. (2018, January 16). *Facebook post*. https://www.facebook.com/WhiteMooseCafe/

Thusoo, A., Shao, Z., Anthony, S., Borthakur, D., Jain, N., Sarma, J. S., & Liu, H. (2010). Data warehousing and analytics infrastructure at Facebook. *Proceedings of the 2010 ACM SIGMOD International Conference on Management of Data*. https://doi.org/DOI: 10.1145/1807167.1807278

Timón, D. (2023). El Concepto de destino turístico: Una aproximación geográfico-territorial. *Revista de Estudios Turísticos*, 45–68. DOI: 10.61520/et.1602004.936

Tiwari, V. (2012). Healthcare scenario in India. https://www.slideshare.net/mobile/vikasba123/healthcare-scenario-in-india/

Tiwari, P., & Sharma, A. (2024). Examining the influence of smart technologies on consumer decision-making in the hospitality sector. *Journal of Retailing and Consumer Services*, 72, 102143. DOI: 10.1016/j.jretconser.2023.102143

Tleuberdinova, A., Kulik, X., Pratt, S., & Kulik, V. B. (2022). Exploring the Resource Potential for the Development of Ecological Tourism in Rural Areas: The Case of Kazakhstan. *Tourism Review International*, 26(4), 321–336. Advance online publication. DOI: 10.3727/154427222X16716277765989

Tobon, S., & García-Madariaga, J. (2021). The influence of opinion leaders' eWOM on online consumer decisions: A study on social influence. *Journal of Theoretical and Applied Electronic Commerce Research*, 16(4), 748–767. DOI: 10.3390/jtaer16040043

Top cities where Airbnb is legal or illegal. (2019). *Investopedia*. https://www.investopedia.com/articles/investing/083115/top-cities-where-airbnb-legal-or-illegal.asp

Topsakal, Y., Icoz, O., & Icoz, O. (2022). *Digital Transformation and Tourist Experiences*., DOI: 10.4018/978-1-7998-8528-3.ch002

Torabi, Z.-A., Rezvani, M. R., Hall, C. M., & Allam, Z. (2023). On the post-pandemic travel boom: How capacity building and smart tourism technologies in rural areas can help - Evidence from Iran. *Technological Forecasting and Social Change*, 193, 122633. DOI: 10.1016/j.techfore.2023.122633 PMID: 37223653

Tran, L. T. T. (2024). Metaverse-driven sustainable tourism: A horizon 2050 paper. *Tourism Review*, ahead-of-print. https://doi.org/DOI: 10.1108/TR-12-2023-0857

Trentesaux, D., & Caillaud, E. (2020). Ethical stakes of Industry 4.0. *IFAC-PapersOnLine*, 53(2), 17002–17007. DOI: 10.1016/j.ifacol.2020.12.1486

Triana, N. (2022). The need for sustainability and CSR in undergraduate business education. *Journal of Undergraduate Research (Gainesville, Fla.)*, 24. Advance online publication. DOI: 10.32473/ufjur.24.130792

Trunfio, M., & Campana, S. (2020). A visitors' experience model for mixed reality in the museum. *Current Issues in Tourism*, 23(9), 1053–1058. DOI: 10.1080/13683500.2019.1586847

Tsypko, V., Andrusenko, S., Podpisnov, V., & Podpisnov, D. (2024). The potential of the global automotive industry as a tourist attraction. *E3S Web of Conferences*, 508, 08026. https://doi.org/DOI: 10.1051/e3sconf/202450808026

Tung, P. C., & Ritchie, B. W. (2011). Measuring memorable tourism experiences. *Journal of Travel Research*, 50(3), 300–312. DOI: 10.1177/0047287510385460

Tung, V., & Au, N. (2018). Exploring customer experiences with robotics in hospitality. *International Journal of Contemporary Hospitality Management*, 30(7), 2680–2697. DOI: 10.1108/IJCHM-06-2017-0322

Tussyadiah, I. (2013). Expectation of Travel Experiences with Wearable Computing Devices. In Xiang, Z., & Tussyadiah, I. (Eds.), *Information and Communication Technologies in Tourism 2014* (pp. 539–552). Springer International Publishing., DOI: 10.1007/978-3-319-03973-2_39

Tussyadiah, I. P., Wang, D., & Jia, C. H. (2017). Virtual reality and attitudes toward tourism destinations. In Schegg, R., & Stangl, B. (Eds.), *Information and communication technologies in tourism 2017* (pp. 229–239). Springer., DOI: 10.1007/978-3-319-51168-9_17

Uhodnikova, O., Sokolenko, A., Ryabev, A., Abramov, V., Pokolodna, M., Kravtsova, S., Shevchenko, V., & Miroshnichenko, Yu. (2022). Innovative approaches to the management of effective communications in tourism and the hotel and restaurant industry. *Municipal Economy of Cities*, 7(174), 9–13. DOI: 10.33042/2522-1809-2022-7-174-9-13

United Nations World Tourism Organization. (2020). *Global code of ethics for tourism*. Retrieved from https://www.unwto.org/global-code-of-ethics-for-tourism

Uniyal, M., Dhodi, R. K., Dhodi, R., & Sharma, S. (2014). SWOT analysis of the Indian medical tourism industry. *Tourism (Zagreb)*, 3(2), 1–2.

Valerio, M. A., Rodriguez, N., Winkler, P., Lopez, J., Dennison, M., Liang, Y., & Turner, B. J. (2016). Comparing two sampling methods to engage hard-to-reach communities in research priority setting. *BMC Medical Research Methodology*, 16(1), 1–11. DOI: 10.1186/s12874-016-0242-z PMID: 27793191

Vallespin, G., & Zubeldia, J. M. (2023). Impact of COVID-19 on the perception of security in hotels: A perspective from customers. *International Journal of Hospitality Management*, 106, 102257. DOI: 10.1016/j.ijhm.2022.102257

Valverde, M. D., & Echeverri, D. (2024). The role of AI in achieving the UN sustainable development goals: A systematic review. *Sustainability Science*, 19, 51–67.

Vancia, A. P. P., & Băltescu, C. A. (2022). Travel trends during the COVID-19 pandemic: A view of online travel agencies. *Proceedings of the International Conference on Business Excellence, 16*(1), 906-917. https://doi.org/DOI: 10.2478/picbe-2022-0085

Vasan, P., & Khemka, K. (2024). Artificial intelligence for sustainable tourism: Opportunities and challenges. *Sustainable Tourism*, 32(2), 277–290.

Verma, S., Warrier, L., Bolia, B., & Mehta, S. (2022). Past, present, and future of virtual tourism: A literature review. *International Journal of Information Management Data Insights*, 2(2), 100085. DOI: 10.1016/j.jjimei.2022.100085

Vermeulen, I. E., & Seegers, D. (2009). Tried and tested: The impact of online hotel reviews on consumer consideration. *Tourism Management*, 30(1), 123–127. DOI: 10.1016/j.tourman.2008.04.008

Vesin, B., Ivanović, M., Klašnja-Milićević, A., & Budimac, Z. (2012). Protus 2.0: Ontology-based semantic recommendation in programming tutoring system. *Expert Systems with Applications*, 39(15), 12229–12246. DOI: 10.1016/j.eswa.2012.04.052

Vidgen, R., Hindle, G., & Randolph, I. (2020). Exploring the ethical implications of business analytics with a business ethics canvas. *European Journal of Operational Research*, 281(3), 491–501. DOI: 10.1016/j.ejor.2019.04.036

Vidrago, B. (2015). *Aeroportos*. Seminário Aeroespacial II -Técnico Lisboa. https://id.tecnico.ulisboa.pt/cas/login?service=https:%2F%2Ffenix.tecnico.ulisboa.pt%2Fapi%2Fcas-client%2Flogin%2FaHR0cHM6Ly9mZW5peC50ZWNuaWNvLnVsaXNib2EucHQvZG93bmxvYWRGaWxlLzU2MzU2ODQyODcyNzk2MC9HcnVwbyUyMDA0LnBkZg==

Volo, S. (2013). Conceptualizing experience : A tourist based approach. In *Marketing of tourism experiences* (pp. 19–34). Routledge., https://www.taylorfrancis.com/chapters/edit/10.4324/9781315875293-6/conceptualizing-experience-tourist-based-approach-serena-volo

Vrondou, O. P. (2023). Olympic Games and mega events legacy planning as a tourism initiation strategy: Developments and implications. In Katsoni, V. (Ed.), *Tourism, travel, and hospitality in a smart and sustainable world* (pp. 265–282). Springer Nature Switzerland., DOI: 10.1007/978-3-031-29426-6_17

Wagler, A., & Hanus, M. D. (2018). Comparing virtual reality tourism to real-life experience: Effects of presence and engagement on attitude and enjoyment. *Communication Research Reports*, 35(5), 456–464. DOI: 10.1080/08824096.2018.1525350

Wang, H. (2024). *Digital transformation in tourism: Opportunities for smart cities*. IGI Global.

Wang, J., Tao, J., & Chu, M. (2020). Behind the label: Chinese consumers' trust in food certification and the effect of perceived quality on purchase intention. *Food Control*, 108, 106825. DOI: 10.1016/j.foodcont.2019.106825

Wang, S. Y., Lin, J. F., & Huang, Y. C. (2023). Examining the impact of AI on sustainability practices in tourism: An integrated framework. *Tourism Management Perspectives*, 47, 195–207.

Wang, T. (2021). The definition of legal status and responsibilities of influencers in live broadcast for goods promotion. *Foreign Economic Relations and Trade*, 7, 86–88.

Wang, T., Li, H., & Zhang, J. (2024). Artificial intelligence and biodiversity: How AI can contribute to species conservation. *Journal of Environmental Management*, 310, 114948.

Wang, Y., So, K. K. F., & Sparks, B. A. (2016). Technology Readiness and Customer Satisfaction with Travel Technologies : A Cross-Country Investigation. *Journal of Travel Research*, 56(5), 563–577. DOI: 10.1177/0047287516657891

Wang, Z., & Zhan, H. (2022). AI in wildlife conservation: An overview of applications and challenges. *Biodiversity and Conservation*, 31(8), 2139–2160.

Weihrich, H. (1982). The TOWS matrix: A tool for situational analysis. *Long Range Planning*, 15(2), 54–66. DOI: 10.1016/0024-6301(82)90120-0

Wei, W., Baker, M. A., & Onder, I. (2023). All without leaving home: Building a conceptual model of virtual tourism experiences. *International Journal of Contemporary Hospitality Management*, 35(4), 1284–1303. DOI: 10.1108/IJCHM-12-2021-1560

Wohlin, C. (2014). Guidelines for snowballing in systematic literature studies and a replication in software engineering. *Proceedings of the 18th International Conference on Evaluation and Assessment in Software Engineering*, 1-10. DOI: 10.1145/2601248.2601268

World Health Organization. (2008). *World report on health.*

World Report. (2010). Medical tourism in India, but at what cost? *World Report*, 1-2.

World Travel & Tourism Council. (2023). The impact of terrorism on global tourism. Retrieved from https://www.wttc.org/research/policy-research/impact-of-terrorism-on-tourism

Wu, W. (2020). Analysis of digital tourism, virtual tourism and wisdom tourism. In Xu, Z., & Kaya, M. N. (Eds.), *The International Conference on Cyber Security Intelligence and Analytics* (pp. 18–25). Springer. DOI: 10.1007/978-3-030-43309-3_3

Xie, C., Bagozzi, R. P., & Grønhaug, K. (2019). The impact of corporate social responsibility on consumer brand advocacy: The role of moral emotions, attitudes, and individual differences. *Journal of Business Research*, 95, 514–530. DOI: 10.1016/j.jbusres.2018.07.043

Xu, S., Liu, J., Li, S., Yang, S., & Li, F. (2023). Exploring and visualizing study progress and emerging trends of event prediction: A survey. *Applied Sciences (Basel, Switzerland)*, 13(24), 13346. DOI: 10.3390/app132413346

Yagasaki, N. (2021). Impact of COVID-19 on the Japanese travel market and the travel market of overseas visitors to Japan, and subsequent recovery. *IATSS Research*, 45(4), 451–458. DOI: 10.1016/j.iatssr.2021.11.008

Yan, L., Alagas, E. N., Jambulingam, M., & Wang, L. (2024). Destination brand identity as a mediator between accessibility and tourist perception: Promoting Bama Yao as potential wellness tourist destination in China. *Turyzm/Tourism*, 109–120. https://doi.org/DOI: 10.18778/0867-5856.34.1.10

Yang, L., Ni, S. T., Wang, Y., Yu, A., Lee, J. A., & Hui, P. (2024). Interoperability of the metaverse: A digital ecosystem perspective review. *arXiv preprint arXiv:2403.05205*. DOI: 10.2139/ssrn.4929167

Yang, T., Lai, I. K. W., Fan, Z. B., & Mo, Q. M. (2021). The impact of a 360° virtual tour on the reduction of psychological stress caused by COVID-19. *Technology in Society*, 64, 101514. DOI: 10.1016/j.techsoc.2020.101514 PMID: 33424061

Yao, M. (2023). The impact of the COVID-19 on the mood of hotel employee. In X. Li, C. Yuan, & J. Kent (Eds.), *Proceedings of the 6th International Conference on Economic Management and Green Development* (pp. 1217–1224). Springer Nature Singapore. https://doi.org/DOI: 10.1007/978-981-19-7826-5_116

Yasintha, P. N., Ginting, R. T., & Wirantari, I. D. A. P. (2022). The potential of virtual methods as a means of ecotourism education in the era of Society 5.0. In M. A. S. Megafury Apriandhini (Chair), *Proceedings of the 4th OSC* (p. 304).

YiFei, L., & Othman, M. K. YiFei. (2024). Investigating the behavioural intentions of museum visitors towards VR : A systematic literature review. *Computers in Human Behavior*, 155, 108167. DOI: 10.1016/j.chb.2024.108167

Yilmaz, M., O'Farrell, E., & Clarke, P. (2023). Examining the training and education potential of the metaverse: Results from an empirical study of next generation SAFe training. *Journal of Software (Malden, MA)*, 35(9), e2531. DOI: 10.1002/smr.2531

Yoo, C. W., Sanders, G. L., & Moon, J. (2013). Exploring the effect of e-WOM participation on e-loyalty in e-commerce. *Decision Support Systems*, 55(3), 669–678. DOI: 10.1016/j.dss.2013.02.001

Yuwantiningrum, S. E. (2023). The influence of the Covid-19 pandemic and government policy on hotel room occupancy rates. *Jurnal Ilmiah Pariwisata Kesatuan*, 4(2), 61–70. DOI: 10.37641/jipkes.v4i2.2060

Zainordin, N. A. F., Syed Jaafar, S. M. R., & Md Khairi, N. D. (2021). Publication trend on travel preferences of senior tourists from 2000 to 2020. *Journal of Tourism. Hospitality and Environment Management*, 6(26), 172–185. DOI: 10.35631/JTHEM.626015

Zayed, R. A. (2024). Role of artificial intelligence in transforming the Egyptian tourism landscape: A perspective on future opportunities. *International Journal of Culture, Tourism and Hospitality Research*, 18(1), 1–15. DOI: 10.1108/IJCTHR-10-2022-0238

Zeithaml, V. A. (1988). Consumer perceptions of price, quality, and value: A means-end model and synthesis of evidence. *Journal of Marketing*, 52(3), 2–22. DOI: 10.1177/002224298805200302

Zeno, J. (2022). Information in consumer contracts: Reforming consumer protection law in Malaysia. *Asian Journal of Comparative Law*, 17(2), 242–267. DOI: 10.1017/asjcl.2022.18

Zgodavová, Z., Rozenberg, R., & Szabo, S. (2018). Analysis of Point-to-Point versus Hub-and-Spoke airline networks. *2018 XIII International Scientific Conference - New Trends in Aviation Development (NTAD)*, 158–163. DOI: 10.1109/NTAD.2018.8551733

Zhang, H. (2024). The evolving role of technology in hospitality: A critical review. *International Journal of Hospitality Management*, 112, 102262. DOI: 10.1016/j.ijhm.2022.102262

Zhang, J. (2021). Impacts of the emissions policies on tourism: An important but neglected aspect of sustainable tourism. *Journal of Hospitality and Tourism Management*, 47, 453–461. DOI: 10.1016/j.jhtm.2021.02.006

Zhang, L., Liu, Q., & Wei, Y. (2023). AI-driven environmental monitoring: Innovations and applications. *Sensors (Basel)*, 23(5), 2845. PMID: 36905051

Zhang, T. (2020). Analysis of the multiple legal status of digital influencers in goods promotion. *Research on China Market Regulation*, 5, 12–15.

Zhang, T., & Hacikara, A. (2023). Virtual tourism and consumer wellbeing: A critical review, practices, and new perspectives. In Uysal, M., & Perdue, R. R. (Eds.), *Handbook of tourism and quality-of-life research II* (pp. 545–557). Springer., DOI: 10.1007/978-3-031-31513-8_37

Zhang, X., & Yue, W. T. (2020). Integration of on-premises and cloud-based software: The product bundling perspective. *Journal of the Association for Information Systems*, 21, 1507–1551. Advance online publication. DOI: 10.17705/1jais.00645

Zhang, Y., Zong, R., Kou, Z., Shang, L., & Wang, D. (2021). Collablearn: An uncertainty-aware crowd-AI collaboration system for cultural heritage damage assessment. *IEEE Transactions on Computational Social Systems*, 9(5), 1515–1529. DOI: 10.1109/TCSS.2021.3109143

Zhang, Z. (2023). Digital operational strategies in the post-pandemic era for travel companies: A case study of Ctrip. *Highlights in Business. Economics and Management*, 23, 521–525. DOI: 10.54097/h0w3ar97

Zhao, Y., & Zhang, H. (2023). Smart tourism: A new direction for tourism development. *International Journal of Tourism Research*, 25(1), 67–84. DOI: 10.1002/jtr.2619

Zheng, J. M., Chan, K. W., & Gibson, I. (1998). Virtual reality. *IEEE Potentials*, 17(2), 20–23. DOI: 10.1109/45.666641

Zhou, H. (2024). Exploring the role of AI in promoting cultural tourism: Insights from case studies. *Journal of Heritage Tourism*. Advance online publication. DOI: 10.1080/1743873X.2024.2341325

Zhu, C., Fong, L. H. N., Liu, C. Y. N., & Song, H. (2023). When social media meets destination marketing: The mediating role of attachment to social media influencer. *Journal of Hospitality and Tourism Technology*, 14(4), 643–657. DOI: 10.1108/JHTT-04-2022-0119

Zhu, X., & Zhang, Q. (2023). Understanding the role of AI in promoting green technology: A framework for research. *Technology Analysis and Strategic Management*, 35(2), 233–247.

Zinko, R., Patrick, A., Furner, C. P., Gaines, S., Kim, M. D., Negri, M., & Villarreal, C. (2021). Responding to negative electronic word of mouth to improve purchase intention. *Journal of Theoretical and Applied Electronic Commerce Research*, 16(6), 1945–1959. DOI: 10.3390/jtaer16060109

Zuo, C., Lin, Z., & Zhang, Y. (2019). Why does your data leak? Uncovering the data leakage in cloud from mobile apps. *2019 IEEE Symposium on Security and Privacy (SP)*. https://doi.org/DOI: 10.1109/SP.2019.00009

About the Contributors

Maria Amélia Carvalho (Ph.D.) is an invited adjunct professor at the Business School of Polytechnic of Porto. She has published papers in the Journal of Marketing Theory and Practice, the International Journal of Tourism Cities, the Tourism Recreation Research Journal, and the Journal of Hospitality and Tourism Insights, among others. She is also a member of CEOS PP, a research Centre of Porto Accounting and Business School of Polytechnic of Porto.

Maria Antónia Rodrigues (Ph.D.) is a senior lecturer at the Business School of Polytechnic of Porto. She is a Director of BA in Marketing. She has published several papers in Journal of Strategic Marketing, Journal of Services Marketing, Managing Service Quality (the Journal of Service Theory and Practice), European Journal of Applied Business and Management, International Journal of Engineering and Industrial Management, International Journal of Marketing, Communication and New Media, among others. She has published an IGI book. She is a member of CEOS PP, a research Centre of Porto Accounting and Business School of Polytechnic of Porto. She has business experience in services companies.

Joaquim Pratas has a PhD in Business and Management Studies (with a specialization in Marketing and Strategy) from Faculdade de Economia do Porto - University of Porto. Currently, he is an Adjunct Professor at Instituto Superior de Contabilidade e Administração - Instituto Politécnico do Porto (ISCAP - IPP), and invited lecturer in Porto Business School - University of Porto. He is a researcher at Centro de Estudos Organizacionais e Sociais do Politécnico do Porto (CEOS. PP), and at Governance, Competitiveness and Public Policy (GOVCOPP) unit research from Universidade de Aveiro. His main interests involve Retail, Marketing, Management, Sales and Tourism, and has published academic papers and book chapters in these topics

***

Mourad Aarabe is a PhD student at the National School of Business and Management of Fez, Sidi Mohamed de Ben Abdellah University. His research focuses on tourism, marketing, digital marketing, and management.

Lhoussaine Alla, professor in management sciences at the National School of Applied Sciences, researcher at the LAREMEF laboratory, Sidi Mohamed Ben Abdellah University, Fez, Morocco. Prof. Lhoussaine Alla has invested more in scientific research in various themes inherent in marketing, finance, entrepreneurship, tourism, logistics. He is also editor of the journal "Management et Alternatives Economiques - AME" (https://revues.imist.ma/index.php/AME). Prof. Lhoussaine Alla has accumulated as many educational and scientific experiences, which he constantly mobilizes to catalyze a large team of researchers and experts in analysis, reflexivity and application of innovative and intelligent solutions from Data Engineering and AI in various management dimensions. Prof. Lhoussaine Alla is a co-editor of collective works published by IGI Global: Integrating Intelligence and Sustainability in Supply Chains; Applying Qualitative Research Methods to Science and Management; Using Technology to Manage Territories.

Nouhaila Ben Khizzou is a PhD student at the National School of Business and Management of Fez, Sidi Mohamed de Ben Abdellah University.

Oindrila Chakraborty is a gold medalist in her MBA programme from University of Calcutta. She has 15 years of teaching experience in management education. She has completed her PhD from University of Calcutta and has several publications to furnish in National and International Journals of high repute.

Dickson K.W. Chiu received the B.Sc. (Hons.) degree in Computer Studies from the University of Hong Kong in 1987. He received the M.Sc. (1994) and Ph.D. (2000) degrees in Computer Science from the Hong Kong University of Science and Technology (HKUST). He started his own computer consultant company while studying part-time. He has also taught at several universities in Hong Kong. His teaching and research interest is in Library & Information Management, Service Computing, and E-learning with a cross-disciplinary approach involving library and information management, e-learning, e-business, service sciences, and databases. The results have been widely published in nearly 400 international publications (most of them have been indexed by SCI/-E, SSCI, and EI, such as top journals MIS Quarterly, Computer & Education, Government Information Quarterly, Decision Support Systems, Information Sciences, Knowledge-Based Systems, Expert Systems with Application, Information Systems Frontiers, IEEE Transactions, including many taught master and undergraduate project results and around 20 edited books. He received a best paper award at the 37th Hawaii International Conference on System

Sciences in 2004. He is an Editor (-in-chief) of Library Hi Tech, a prestigious journal (SSCI IF=3.4), and a Senior Editor of the Journal of Organizational Computing and Electronic Commerce (SCIE IF=2.9). He is the Editor-in-chief Emeritus of the International Journal on Systems and Service-Oriented Engineering (founding) and the International Journal of Organizational and Collective Intelligence, and serves on the editorial boards of several international journals. He co-founded several international workshops and co-edited many journal special issues. He also served as a program committee member for over 300 international conferences and workshops. Dr. Chiu is a Senior Member of both the ACM and the IEEE and a life member of the Hong Kong Computer Society. According to Google Scholar, he has over 9,600 citations, h-index=51, i-10 index=205, and ranked worldwide 1st in "LIS," "m-learning," and "e-services." He received nearly 1,000 citations in 2022 and 2,600 in 2023.

Kevin K.W. Ho is the Professor of Management Information Systems at the MBA International Business Program, Graduate School of Business Sciences, University of Tsukuba. Kevin's research interests include electronic service, information systems strategy, social media, fake news and misinformation, and sustainability management. He is the Editor-in-Chief of Journal of Organizational Computing and E-Commerce and the Co-Editor(-in-Chief) of Library Hi Tech and Journal of Organizational Computing and E-Commerce. His research has been published in Behaviour & Information Technology, Communications of the Association for Information Systems, Computers in Human Behavior, Decision Support Systems, Government Information Quarterly, Health Policy, Information Systems Frontiers, Internet Research, Information & Management, IT Professional, Journal of Computer Information Systems, Journal of Organizational Computing and Electronic Commerce, Journal of Retailing and Consumer Services, Library Hi Tech, and Online Information Review, among others.

Mushfika Hoque, a distinguished figure in the field of tourism and hospitality management, serves as an esteemed lecturer in the department of Tourism and Hospitality Management at Daffodil Institute of IT. With a wealth of academic expertise and a passion for cultivating the next generation of industry leaders, Mushfika Hoque's career has been defined by her commitment to merging theoretical knowledge with practical applications. Her groundbreaking research on sustainable tourism and experiential hospitality has earned her recognition in academic circles and her engaging teaching style has left an indelible mark on countless students. A trailblazer in her field, Mushfika continues to inspire and shape the future of tourism and hospitality education through her innovative approach and dedication to excellence.

Ruchi Kakkar is currently working as an Assistant Professor in Mittal School of Business, Lovely Professional University. She has completed her MFC and MBA from Punjabi University, Patiala and is currently pursuing her Ph.D. from Lovely Professional University in Management domain.

Musfiqur Rahoman Khan is an accomplished author and Teaching Assistant at the Department of Tourism and Hospitality Management at Daffodil Institute of IT (DIIT), Dhaka, Bangladesh. He holds a Bachelor's degree in Business Administration (BBA), majoring in Tourism and Hospitality Management, from the same institute. With a strongo academic background and a passion for exploring the intersection of travel and culture, Musfiq's diverse areas of interest include Adventure tourism, Cultural tourism, and Wildlife tourism. Through his teaching and writing, he strives to inspire others to discover the richness and diversity of the world through travel.

Şirin Gizem Köse completed Business Administration in English undergraduate program at Marmara University, Production Management and Marketing master's program at Galatasaray University, Business Administration/ Marketing PhD program at Yıldız Technical University. She worked as a research assistant at Yıldız Technical University Business Administration, production management and marketing department between 2014-2021. She works at MEF University Business Administration department as an assistant professor of marketing. Her academic research areas are sustainability, food marketing, and consumer behavior.

Titu Miah is a lecturer and researcher in the field of economics at the International University of Business Agriculture and Technology, Bangladesh with a strong academic background in Master of Arts in Economics from Jahangirnagar University and a Bachelor of Arts in Economics from IUBAT. He was awarded various academic excellence awards during his studies, including Prof. Dr. Muttalib scholarships. He worked as a Teaching Assistant for three years, a Research Assistant for one year, and an Administrative Officer for eight years. His diverse areas of interest include microeconomics, macroeconomics, public policy and finance.

Zaila Oliveira has a PhD in Management and Business – Specialization in Marketing and Strategy from the University of Porto, Portugal. She teaches at the University of Maia-ISMAI and at the Instituto Superior de Contabilidade e Administração do Porto – ISCAP. Member of CEOS.PP. Researcher in the area of marketing, consumer behavior and sustainability, with published articles, some of them SCOPUS.

Md. Zubair Rahman is a Lecturer in the Department of English and Modern Language, IUBAT. He has accomplished his BA in English and MA in Literatures in English and Cultural Studies from Jahangirnagar University, Savar, Dhaka. Before joining IUBAT, he had taught at State University of Bangladesh for a year. Md. Zubair Rahman is passionate to teach and talk about Language, Literature, and Culture. His areas of interest include cultural exchanges in literature, romantic poetry, gothic literature, comparative literature, and the power dynamics in culture. He is also open towards any interdisciplinary field of works where he can contribute his ideas and insights. Apart from being a full-time teacher, Md. Zubair Rahman is a poet and lyricist of impulse with a few songs available on different online platforms.

Manpreet Kaur Riyat is a dedicated and innovative PhD scholar at Lovely Professional University (LPU). With a strong academic background in marketing, including an MBA, she has developed a keen interest in the cutting-edge fields of gamification, the metaverse, consumer engagement, and education technology. Her research aims to bridge the gap between traditional marketing approaches and the rapidly evolving digital landscape. Manpreet's gamification work focuses on using game-like elements to motivate and engage users in a variety of contexts, from marketing campaigns to educational settings. Her exploration of the metaverse delves into how virtual and augmented reality can transform consumer experiences and create new opportunities for brands.

Bassam Samir Al-Romeedy is a motivated Associate Professor at the faculty of tourism and hotels, University of Sadat City - Egypt, and an Accredited external auditor at the National Authority for Quality Assurance of Education and Accreditation – Egypt. I also work as a market research consultant and statistical analyst. Dr. Al-Romeedy has published in premier peer-reviewed journals including Tourism Review, Journal of Human Resources in Hospitality & Tourism, International Journal of Tourism and Hospitality Management, Corporate Social Responsibility and Environmental Management, and others.

Eliza Sharma, currently working with Symbiosis International University, Bengaluru. She has worked with the Indian Institute of Management, Ahmadabad (India), as a Research Assistant for a Government of India project to develop the Integrity Index for Public sector organizations. She holds a Ph.D. in Management and Finance from 'Jaypee Institute of Information Technology, Noida. Her research work was on "Performance of Indian Commercial Banks and Its Relationship with Human Aspects in Banking". She has 14 years of work experience in academics and research. She has published 50 plus research papers in national and international journals and conference proceedings.

Mohammad Badruddoza Talukder is an Associate Professor, College of Tourism and Hospitality Management, IUBAT - International University of Business Agriculture and Technology, Dhaka-1230, Bangladesh. He holds PhD in Hotel Management from Lovely Professional University, India. He has been teaching various courses in the Department of Tourism and Hospitality at various universities in Bangladesh since 2008. His research areas include tourism management, hotel management, hospitality management, food & beverage management, and accommodation management, where he has published research papers in well-known journals in Bangladesh and abroad. Mr. Talukder is one of the executive members of the Tourism Educators Association of Bangladesh. He has led training and consulting for a wide range of hospitality organizations in Bangladesh. He just became an honorary facilitator at the Bangladesh Tourism Board's Bangabandhu international tourism and hospitality training institution.

Sara Teixeira has a PhD in Communication from the University of Vigo - Spain. Sara performs teaching functions in higher education at ISCAP. She worked in the area of digital marketing and e-learning in Portugal. She is a researcher at CEOS. PP - Center for Organizational and Social Studies at the Polytechnic of Porto.

Index

A

Advertising Law 93, 104, 105, 106, 110, 118
AI-enabled Nature Conservation 211, 231
Artificial Intelligence 8, 21, 27, 37, 58, 177, 181, 189, 190, 191, 206, 207, 215, 225, 226, 227, 228, 229, 230, 231, 268, 275, 289, 295, 298, 302, 305, 309, 316, 319, 320, 321, 325, 326, 344, 345, 346, 347, 348, 349, 350, 352, 353
Augmented Reality 95, 130, 133, 137, 140, 178, 179, 180, 181, 182, 183, 205, 207, 209, 216, 243, 251, 253, 254, 268, 272, 275, 276, 287, 291, 298, 309, 312, 317, 318, 326, 327, 331, 337, 338, 339, 343, 348, 350, 352, 354, 366, 370, 371, 372, 373, 374, 376
Automated Systems 220, 301, 322, 323
Aviation 61, 63, 67, 68, 71, 72, 78, 85, 175, 225
Awareness 4, 5, 89, 102, 113, 116, 117, 118, 136, 160, 161, 163, 164, 165, 191, 198, 200, 244, 245, 260, 261, 380

B

Brand 15, 28, 35, 53, 89, 91, 92, 95, 101, 113, 114, 121, 128, 129, 132, 134, 136, 137, 138, 139, 140, 151, 154, 155, 156, 157, 158, 159, 160, 161, 162, 163, 164, 165, 167, 170, 171, 184, 192, 193, 194, 234, 238, 292, 356, 369, 370, 399, 402
Brazil 61, 62, 63, 65, 67, 73, 74, 77, 78, 86, 238

C

Challenges 2, 4, 17, 19, 20, 52, 87, 90, 93, 101, 102, 103, 112, 114, 116, 117, 118, 121, 133, 134, 140, 151, 152, 153, 156, 157, 162, 168, 170, 173, 174, 177, 178, 192, 195, 198, 205, 210, 211, 212, 213, 218, 219, 220, 221, 222, 223, 225, 226, 229, 230, 245, 254, 256, 259, 265, 266, 270, 271, 275, 276, 303, 304, 306, 307, 308, 309, 312, 313, 319, 321, 325, 326, 327, 328, 331, 338, 340, 342, 343, 344, 347, 348, 349, 381, 385, 401
China 28, 35, 52, 85, 87, 92, 93, 95, 104, 108, 111, 112, 114, 115, 116, 118, 119, 123, 124, 125, 126, 204, 229, 291
Consumer Behavior 2, 90, 93, 124, 126, 128, 135, 136, 137, 139, 143, 144, 152, 154, 155, 162, 163, 165, 168, 171, 268, 271, 321, 330, 373
Consumer Law 93
Consumer Psychology 165
Cost of Medical Services 379, 382, 386, 387, 389, 403
COVID-19 1, 2, 3, 5, 7, 9, 11, 12, 20, 21, 22, 23, 24, 26, 28, 31, 32, 33, 35, 36, 43, 51, 52, 53, 54, 55, 56, 57, 89, 123, 174, 176, 178, 205, 208, 292, 294, 321, 322, 352, 353, 370, 372, 373, 377
Crisis Management 23, 29
Cuisine 15, 74, 90, 94, 234, 266
Culture 8, 12, 15, 16, 51, 120, 128, 131, 132, 134, 136, 143, 145, 147, 164, 165, 183, 188, 189, 191, 237, 239, 240, 241, 242, 249, 251, 253, 254, 255, 256, 257, 258, 259, 260, 261, 262, 264, 265, 297, 326, 344, 347, 348, 349, 356, 374, 383

D

Data Analytics 20, 182, 249, 290, 301, 302, 306, 307, 311, 315, 316, 317, 318, 322, 328, 338, 342, 346, 349
Data Security 197, 201, 213, 275, 301, 302, 316, 319, 322
Decision Making 139, 170, 375
Destination 4, 5, 15, 16, 17, 19, 20, 21, 22, 28, 61, 62, 63, 64, 65, 66, 67, 69, 71, 72, 73, 76, 77, 78, 79, 80, 82, 83, 86, 90, 91, 92, 95, 124, 125, 128, 129,

131, 132, 133, 134, 135, 136, 137, 138, 139, 140, 144, 147, 149, 150, 207, 227, 234, 236, 238, 239, 243, 245, 249, 250, 251, 256, 258, 260, 262, 263, 264, 265, 266, 267, 268, 269, 270, 271, 272, 274, 276, 277, 279, 280, 282, 283, 285, 286, 287, 288, 290, 291, 292, 293, 294, 295, 297, 299, 311, 346, 348, 350, 355, 357, 369, 370, 373, 374, 375, 376, 378, 379, 380, 381, 382, 384, 385, 386, 387, 391, 392, 394, 395, 397, 403

Destination Marketing 20, 125, 132, 138, 147, 274, 277, 280, 294, 297, 348, 357, 369, 374, 378

Digital Marketing 27, 103, 112, 344, 348, 378, 399

Digital Transformation 26, 291, 292, 297, 319, 320, 321, 349

E

Egypt 211, 225, 229, 325, 326, 328, 329, 330, 341, 342, 343, 344, 347, 348, 349, 380

Emotional Resonance 160, 162, 163, 172

Ethical Consumption 151, 152, 161, 163, 164, 165, 167, 168, 172

Ethical Marketing 151, 152, 153, 154, 155, 156, 157, 158, 159, 160, 161, 162, 163, 164, 165, 166, 168, 171, 172

Ethical Values 153, 154, 155, 156, 157, 160, 162, 163, 164, 170

Expectation 153, 256, 259, 260, 298, 354

Experiences 4, 6, 7, 8, 15, 16, 19, 20, 27, 34, 35, 38, 39, 43, 44, 64, 71, 86, 89, 90, 92, 94, 95, 96, 101, 106, 115, 118, 129, 130, 131, 132, 133, 134, 135, 136, 137, 138, 139, 140, 143, 145, 147, 148, 150, 155, 159, 163, 169, 177, 179, 180, 181, 182, 183, 184, 187, 189, 190, 191, 192, 193, 194, 195, 196, 197, 198, 200, 202, 207, 208, 211, 212, 214, 216, 217, 222, 233, 234, 235, 236, 237, 238, 239, 240, 241, 242, 243, 244, 245, 248, 249, 250, 251, 252, 253, 254, 255, 256, 257, 260, 261, 262, 263, 264, 265, 268, 269, 271, 272, 273, 274, 275, 276, 277, 282, 283, 284, 285, 286, 287, 288, 291, 294, 295, 297, 298, 301, 302, 303, 305, 306, 309, 310, 311, 312, 315, 316, 317, 320, 321, 322, 323, 326, 327, 331, 332, 334, 337, 338, 339, 340, 341, 343, 349, 352, 354, 355, 356, 357, 367, 369, 370, 372, 373, 377, 378, 385, 399

G

Global Event 11, 15
Guest Experience 180, 301, 302, 308, 309, 310, 311, 312, 314, 315, 316, 317, 322

H

Healthcare Infrastructure 379, 381, 382, 386, 387, 389, 398, 403

Healthcare Professionals 379, 382, 383, 386, 387, 389, 400, 403

Heart-Share 262

Heritage Sites 214, 227, 259, 325, 326, 327, 328, 330, 331, 332, 333, 334, 335, 336, 337, 338, 339, 340, 341, 342, 343, 347, 350

Hospitality 1, 2, 3, 4, 11, 12, 14, 15, 16, 20, 21, 22, 23, 24, 25, 26, 27, 28, 29, 37, 53, 89, 92, 93, 120, 124, 125, 127, 128, 129, 130, 134, 135, 136, 137, 139, 140, 141, 142, 145, 146, 147, 148, 149, 150, 167, 173, 174, 175, 176, 177, 178, 180, 181, 182, 183, 184, 185, 187, 189, 190, 192, 193, 194, 195, 197, 199, 202, 204, 205, 206, 207, 208, 209, 211, 212, 225, 227, 233, 240, 241, 280, 290, 291, 292, 295, 297, 302, 303, 304, 305, 306, 308, 309, 310, 311, 313, 315, 316, 317, 318, 319, 320, 321, 322, 323, 330, 331, 344, 345, 347, 348, 349, 370, 372, 373, 377, 379, 401, 402

Hospitality Industry 3, 14, 22, 23, 24, 26, 29, 127, 128, 137, 139, 140, 141, 147, 174, 175, 177, 180, 182, 185, 187, 190,

194, 202, 205, 206, 233, 297, 302, 303, 304, 308, 309, 310, 311, 313, 316, 317, 320, 321, 322, 323, 349

Hub-and-Spoke 67, 68, 69, 70, 71, 84, 85, 86

I

Immersive Experience 179, 180, 210, 254, 282, 332, 334, 339, 355

India 35, 127, 151, 173, 177, 205, 206, 233, 239, 241, 242, 244, 245, 248, 251, 252, 253, 254, 256, 257, 258, 259, 260, 261, 265, 266, 379, 380, 381, 382, 383, 384, 385, 386, 387, 388, 389, 390, 391, 392, 393, 394, 395, 396, 397, 398, 399, 400, 401, 402, 403

Innovativeness 354, 356, 359, 362, 366, 367, 369, 373, 374, 378

Integration 8, 16, 35, 37, 45, 51, 130, 140, 147, 180, 193, 198, 199, 202, 209, 211, 212, 214, 215, 216, 217, 218, 222, 226, 243, 249, 250, 253, 254, 256, 268, 271, 272, 275, 286, 290, 301, 302, 326, 327, 329, 331, 334, 338, 342, 343, 349, 367

L

Local 2, 5, 6, 8, 10, 13, 15, 16, 18, 19, 20, 29, 52, 62, 63, 65, 66, 70, 72, 74, 89, 90, 93, 94, 98, 113, 119, 129, 139, 143, 145, 147, 164, 177, 182, 188, 189, 195, 197, 209, 212, 214, 220, 221, 222, 223, 231, 234, 237, 239, 241, 242, 243, 244, 249, 250, 251, 252, 253, 254, 255, 256, 257, 258, 259, 260, 261, 262, 264, 265, 266, 270, 271, 275, 309, 311, 312, 315, 379, 384, 386, 387, 388, 389

M

Malaysia 22, 87, 92, 93, 95, 97, 101, 103, 104, 111, 112, 114, 115, 116, 118, 119, 123, 125, 126, 369, 374

Management Information System 31, 35, 58, 59

Marketing 13, 15, 20, 22, 23, 24, 25, 27, 55, 64, 77, 82, 87, 88, 89, 90, 91, 92, 93, 94, 95, 97, 100, 101, 102, 103, 104, 110, 111, 112, 113, 114, 115, 116, 117, 118, 119, 121, 122, 123, 124, 125, 126, 127, 128, 129, 130, 131, 132, 133, 134, 135, 136, 137, 138, 139, 140, 141, 145, 146, 147, 149, 151, 152, 153, 154, 155, 156, 157, 158, 159, 160, 161, 162, 163, 164, 165, 166, 167, 168, 169, 170, 171, 172, 177, 182, 183, 184, 195, 198, 200, 205, 206, 207, 227, 235, 238, 240, 256, 258, 263, 270, 271, 274, 277, 280, 284, 285, 289, 290, 294, 295, 297, 298, 311, 312, 319, 322, 341, 344, 346, 348, 353, 354, 357, 369, 370, 371, 372, 374, 376, 377, 378, 383, 399

Medical Tourism 295, 379, 380, 381, 382, 383, 384, 385, 386, 387, 388, 389, 390, 391, 392, 393, 394, 395, 396, 397, 398, 399, 400, 401, 402, 403

Memories 129, 139, 234, 235, 236, 237, 238, 242, 243, 249, 260, 262, 265, 304, 310

N

Nature Reverse 231

O

Occupancy Rate 22, 76, 174, 175

P

Perception 4, 5, 18, 26, 28, 72, 79, 96, 137, 141, 142, 149, 159, 163, 168, 182, 227, 256, 258, 269, 271, 282, 283, 284, 285, 287, 299, 322, 350, 372, 385, 389, 391, 396

Q

Quality of Healthcare Services 379, 382, 383, 386, 387, 398, 403

S

Services Marketing 295
Smart Hotel Technologies 301, 308, 323
Smart Tourism 28, 33, 57, 204, 229, 268, 272, 275, 276, 289, 290, 292, 293, 296, 297, 299, 344, 347, 348, 349
Social Media Influencers Marketing 87
Stakeholders 1, 2, 20, 47, 52, 71, 87, 90, 93, 112, 114, 115, 116, 117, 147, 162, 197, 198, 202, 210, 212, 213, 220, 223, 268, 325, 327, 328, 342, 343
Sustainability 6, 8, 17, 18, 21, 25, 53, 54, 84, 123, 159, 160, 162, 165, 167, 168, 171, 172, 173, 174, 177, 185, 186, 187, 188, 189, 190, 191, 192, 195, 202, 204, 207, 210, 212, 214, 215, 216, 217, 219, 221, 223, 225, 226, 227, 229, 230, 231, 233, 240, 244, 245, 250, 256, 257, 259, 260, 266, 268, 276, 280, 290, 291, 294, 296, 299, 301, 302, 303, 307, 308, 315, 316, 318, 320, 321, 323, 339, 342, 345, 369, 370, 372, 375
Sustainable Tourism 4, 8, 17, 20, 21, 123, 173, 188, 190, 191, 205, 208, 209, 214, 215, 225, 228, 229, 230, 231, 257, 259, 264, 270, 271, 326, 342, 344, 346, 347, 348

T

Technological Innovation 20, 201, 241
Tourism 1, 2, 3, 4, 5, 6, 7, 8, 9, 10, 11, 12, 13, 14, 15, 16, 17, 18, 19, 20, 21, 22, 23, 24, 25, 26, 27, 28, 29, 33, 34, 51, 52, 53, 56, 57, 61, 62, 63, 64, 65, 66, 67, 68, 71, 72, 73, 74, 75, 76, 77, 78, 79, 80, 82, 83, 84, 85, 86, 87, 89, 90, 91, 92, 93, 94, 95, 96, 97, 98, 101, 103, 104, 106, 107, 109, 110, 111, 112, 114, 115, 116, 118, 119, 120, 121, 122, 123, 124, 125, 127, 128, 129, 130, 131, 132, 133, 134, 135, 136, 137, 138, 140, 141, 145, 146, 148, 149, 150, 167, 173, 174, 175, 176, 177, 178, 180, 181, 182, 184, 185, 187, 188, 189, 190, 191, 192, 193, 194, 195, 197, 198, 199, 201, 202, 204, 205, 206, 207, 208, 209, 211, 212, 213, 214, 215, 225, 227, 228, 229, 230, 231, 233, 234, 235, 236, 238, 239, 240, 241, 244, 245, 248, 250, 251, 252, 253, 254, 255, 256, 257, 258, 259, 260, 261, 262, 263, 264, 265, 266, 268, 269, 270, 271, 272, 273, 274, 275, 276, 277, 280, 282, 284, 285, 286, 287, 289, 290, 291, 292, 293, 294, 295, 296, 297, 298, 299, 318, 319, 320, 321, 322, 325, 326, 328, 330, 331, 338, 342, 343, 344, 345, 346, 347, 348, 349, 352, 353, 354, 355, 357, 367, 368, 369, 370, 371, 372, 373, 374, 375, 376, 377, 378, 379, 380, 381, 382, 383, 384, 385, 386, 387, 388, 389, 390, 391, 392, 393, 394, 395, 396, 397, 398, 399, 400, 401, 402, 403
Tourism Development 23, 24, 25, 61, 63, 65, 80, 204, 205, 207, 227, 270, 349, 381
Tourism Industry 2, 4, 7, 9, 10, 15, 18, 23, 25, 27, 51, 52, 62, 87, 89, 90, 91, 92, 93, 94, 95, 96, 97, 101, 103, 104, 109, 111, 112, 114, 115, 118, 119, 120, 135, 137, 146, 174, 175, 176, 177, 181, 189, 206, 212, 228, 233, 234, 245, 248, 254, 257, 262, 268, 269, 274, 275, 285, 287, 299, 320, 347, 348, 353, 355, 367, 368, 374, 375, 385, 402
Tourism Marketing 64, 101, 111, 115, 124, 128, 129, 130, 131, 132, 133, 134, 136, 137, 149, 280, 284, 285, 290, 294, 353, 354, 370, 372, 376, 378
Tourism Patterns 3, 9, 10, 11, 12, 13
Tourist 1, 2, 3, 4, 7, 8, 9, 12, 15, 18, 19, 20, 21, 22, 23, 25, 26, 27, 28, 29, 37, 50, 53, 58, 59, 61, 62, 63, 64, 65, 66,

72, 73, 74, 75, 76, 77, 78, 79, 80, 81, 82, 83, 95, 96, 97, 106, 107, 116, 119, 124, 128, 132, 136, 149, 177, 178, 180, 183, 184, 187, 188, 190, 191, 196, 197, 202, 203, 212, 227, 234, 235, 236, 238, 243, 249, 251, 252, 255, 256, 257, 258, 259, 263, 264, 265, 266, 268, 269, 270, 271, 272, 273, 279, 282, 283, 284, 285, 287, 291, 292, 293, 294, 295, 296, 297, 298, 299, 320, 325, 327, 328, 333, 334, 335, 336, 341, 343, 346, 348, 349, 350, 352, 355, 357, 369, 371, 376, 384, 385, 391, 392, 393, 394, 395, 398, 399

Tourist Engagement 350

Tourist Experience 65, 188, 190, 263, 282, 291, 292, 293, 299, 325, 327, 328, 333, 335, 341, 343, 348, 350, 369, 376

Tourist Satisfaction 22, 235, 255, 270, 271, 282, 284, 287, 291, 296, 320, 350, 371

Travel 1, 2, 3, 4, 5, 6, 7, 8, 9, 10, 11, 12, 13, 14, 16, 17, 19, 20, 21, 22, 24, 25, 26, 28, 29, 31, 32, 33, 34, 35, 36, 37, 38, 42, 43, 44, 52, 53, 54, 55, 56, 57, 58, 59, 62, 65, 66, 67, 74, 75, 77, 89, 90, 91, 92, 93, 96, 97, 109, 112, 115, 116, 118, 123, 124, 129, 130, 131, 132, 133, 134, 135, 136, 137, 138, 140, 143, 147, 148, 149, 173, 174, 175, 176, 177, 178, 180, 181, 182, 183, 187, 188, 189, 190, 191, 192, 193, 194, 195, 196, 197, 198, 199, 200, 202, 203, 206, 207, 209, 214, 225, 233, 234, 235, 236, 243, 244, 245, 249, 250, 251, 252, 254, 257, 264, 266, 267, 268, 269, 270, 271, 272, 273, 274, 275, 276, 279, 280, 281, 282, 283, 284, 285, 286, 287, 288, 289, 290, 291, 292, 293, 294, 295, 296, 297, 298, 308, 310, 322, 330, 331, 333, 334, 336, 345, 348, 351, 352, 353, 354, 355, 357, 366, 367, 370, 371, 372, 373, 374, 375, 376, 380, 399, 402, 403

Travel Restrictions 3, 5, 7, 9, 12, 29, 33, 52, 54

U

User Engagement 200, 202

V

Virtual Environment 179, 187, 193, 200, 352, 353, 359, 360

Virtual Place Application 378

Virtual Reality 8, 21, 130, 133, 137, 140, 177, 178, 179, 181, 182, 183, 194, 195, 204, 205, 207, 208, 209, 244, 253, 254, 268, 271, 272, 274, 275, 282, 284, 285, 287, 291, 293, 296, 299, 309, 317, 320, 328, 343, 346, 347, 350, 352, 353, 354, 355, 366, 371, 372, 373, 374, 375, 376, 377, 378

Visual Image 127, 138, 139, 141, 145, 146, 147

W

Workshop 237, 241, 254